KAPLAN® BAR REVIEW

MBE® SUBJECTS OUTLINE MATERIALS 2024–2025

COURSE COMPANION

Special thanks to: Brian Carlidge, Adam Feren, Esq., Elizabeth Horowitz, Esq., Adam Maze, Esq., Shalom Sands, Esq., Amit Schlesinger, Esq., Ryan Williams, Esq., Lauren Yost, Esq., Jacob Zampier

Published by Kaplan North America, LLC.
1515 W. Cypress Creek Road
Fort Lauderdale, FL 33309

Printed in the United States of America

10 9 8 7 6 5 4 3 2 1

ISBN: 978-1-5062-9398-1

MASTER TABLE OF CONTENTS

CIVIL PROCEDURE

I. Jurisdiction and Venue ... 4
II. Law Applied by Federal Courts ... 27
III. Pretrial Procedures ... 31
IV. Jury Trials ... 65
V. Motions ... 69
VI. Verdicts and Judgments ... 76
VII. Appealability and Review ... 80

CONSTITUTIONAL LAW

I. The Nature of Judicial Review ... 86
II. Separation of Powers ... 97
III. The Relation of the Nation and the States in the Federal System ... 110
IV. Type of Action Governed by the Constitution ... 117
V. Due Process and the Incorporation of Portions of the Bill of Rights ... 120
VI. Equal Protection of the Laws ... 134
VII. Privileges and Immunities Clauses ... 142
VIII. Retroactive Legislation ... 144
IX. First Amendment Freedoms ... 146

CONTRACTS

I. Sources of Contract Law ... 176
II. Contract Formation: Offer and Acceptance ... 180
III. Consideration and Promissory Estoppel ... 200
IV. Statute of Frauds ... 209
V. Gap-Fillers, Interpretation, and the Parol Evidence Rule ... 225
VI. Performance, Modification, and Excuse ... 239
VII. Defenses ... 264
VIII. Remedies ... 282
IX. Third-Party Beneficiaries ... 301
X. Assignment of Rights and Delegation of Duties ... 306

CRIMINAL LAW

I. General Principles 316
II. Homicide 323
III. Other Crimes Against the Person 337
IV. Crimes Against Property 344
V. Inchoate Crimes 362
VI. Parties to Crime and Accomplice Liability 369
VII. Defenses 372

CRIMINAL PROCEDURE

I. Introduction to Criminal Procedure 386
II. The Fourth Amendment 391
III. Statements and Confessions 417
IV. Identifications 427
V. Pretrial Procedures: Chronology from Arrest to Trial 429
VI. Pretrial Rights 434
VII. Double Jeopardy 436
VIII. Guarantees of a Fair Trial 440
IX. Post-Trial Stage 449
X. Rights of Prisoners, Juveniles, and Aliens 454
XI. Miscellaneous Procedural Considerations 456

EVIDENCE

I. General Provisions 462
II. Judicial Notice 466
III. Presumptions 467
IV. Relevancy and Its Limits 469
V. Privileges 479
VI. Witnesses 490
VII. Opinions and Expert Testimony 498
VIII. Hearsay 501
IX. Authentication and Identification 520
X. Contents of Writings, Recordings, and Photographs 525

REAL PROPERTY

I. Ownership of Real Property 532
II. Rights in Land 571
III. Contracts 589
IV. Mortgages/Security Devices 597
V. Titles 608

TORTS

I. Intentional Torts 630
II. Negligence 647
III. Strict Liability 684
IV. Products Liability 687
V. Nuisance 698
VI. Defamation 704
VII. Invasion of Privacy 713
VIII. Wrongful Institution of Legal Proceedings 716
IX. Economic Torts 719
X. Miscellaneous Tort Concepts 725

KAPLAN BAR REVIEW

Civil Procedure

TABLE OF CONTENTS

I. JURISDICTION AND VENUE

Federal Subject-Matter Jurisdiction....4
Territorial Jurisdiction....13
Personal Jurisdiction....14
Service of Process and Notice....21
Venue, Transfer, and *Forum non Conveniens*....23

II. LAW APPLIED BY FEDERAL COURTS

State Law in Federal Court....27
Federal Common Law....28

III. PRETRIAL PROCEDURES

Pleadings....31
Rule 11....35
Provisional Relief....36
Joinder of Claims and Parties....38
Pretrial Conferences and Orders....47
Discovery....49
Adjudication without a Trial....62

IV. JURY TRIALS

Right to Jury Trial....65
Demand for a Jury Trial....65
Jury Selection....66
Jury Instructions....67

V. MOTIONS

General Rules....69
Pre-Trial Motions....69
Post-Trial Motions....72

VI. VERDICTS AND JUDGMENTS

Jury Verdicts....76
Judicial Findings and Conclusions....77
Effect of Verdicts—Claim and Issue Preclusion....78

VII. APPEALABILITY AND REVIEW

Availability of Interlocutory Review....80
Final Judgment Rule....81
Scope of Review for Judge and Jury....81

I. JURISDICTION AND VENUE

A. Federal Subject-Matter Jurisdiction

1. Federal Question Jurisdiction

a. Federal district courts have original jurisdiction over all civil actions "arising under the Constitution, laws, and treaties of the United States" [28 U.S.C. § 1331]. A case arises under federal law if the federal question appears on a fair reading of a well-pleaded complaint.

b. The Constitution or federal statutes may create a right of action. In that case, federal courts have jurisdiction to hear those suits.

c. A defendant's use of federal law as the basis for her defense will not, by itself, create federal question jurisdiction. Under the **well pleaded complaint rule**, to create federal question jurisdiction, the federal question must arise within the plaintiff's affirmative claim—regardless of any defense the defendant might raise.

   EXAMPLE: The Mottleys entered into a contract to provide copper ore to the Louisville & Nashville Railroad in exchange for free passes. Later on, Congress passed a law banning free passes to railroads, and the Mottleys' passes were revoked. They sued in federal court for conversion of the copper ore and an injunction against continuing the contract and asserted, as a basis for federal jurisdiction, that the defendant would argue in the federal law in its defense. The Supreme Court held that asserting an anticipated defense grounded in federal law is insufficient to establish federal-question jurisdiction [Louisville & Nashville Railroad Company v. Mottley, 211 U.S. 149 (1908)].

d. A violation of a federal statute does not create a federal cause of action unless the statute also provides a remedy for the violation.

e. A state question that involves a question of federal law may be sufficient to create federal question jurisdiction. The mere presence of federal law in a claim is insufficient to create jurisdiction. The federal law must have a substantial impact on the state law issue.

   EXAMPLE: Federal question jurisdiction was found to arise in a landowner's state law claim to quiet title against someone who had purchased the land at auction, because embedded in that claim was an argument that the Internal Revenue Service had given him inadequate notice of the sale [Grable & Sons Metal Products, Inc. v. Darue Engineering & Mfg., 545 U.S. 308 (2005)].

   EXAMPLE: Federal question jurisdiction did not arise in a legal malpractice claim in which the plaintiff alleged that his attorney did not raise a defense under federal patent law. The disputed issue of federal law was not substantial in any relevant sense [Gunn v. Minton, 568 U.S. 251 (2013)].

f. Federal courts have original jurisdiction over admiralty or maritime cases.

(1) Admiralty jurisdiction requires that a case have a "maritime nexus." A maritime nexus requires that the incident giving rise to the case had a "potentially disruptive effect on maritime commerce," and the general character of the activity giving rise to the incident shows a "substantial relationship to traditional maritime activity" [Jerome B. Grubart, Inc. v. Great Lakes Dredge & Dock Co., 513 U.S. 527 (1995)].

(2) Plaintiffs may pursue maritime claims as common-law claims in state courts; however, remedies that are specific to admiralty courts will not be available [28 U.S.C. § 1333].

g. Federal courts have subject-matter jurisdiction to review the state court conviction of a prisoner through a writ of *habeas corpus,* challenging the confinement of the prisoner on federal constitutional grounds [28 U.S.C. § 2254(a)].

(1) A petition for a writ of *habeas corpus* is a civil cause of action brought against the jailor or custodian of a person currently under confinement.

(2) A writ of *habeas corpus* is not an appeal, and it does not continue the criminal case against the prisoner in any manner. The writ does not make a determination of the prisoner's guilt or innocence.

(3) A petition for a writ of *habeas corpus* may be based only on the following grounds:

(a) violation of the Due Process Clause of the Fifth and Fourteenth Amendments;

(b) violation of the prohibition of compelled self-incrimination of the Fifth and Fourteenth Amendments;

(c) violation of the protection against double jeopardy of the Fifth and Fourteenth Amendments; or

(d) violation of the right not to be subject to cruel and unusual punishment under the Eighth Amendment.

(4) *Habeas corpus* relief is only available when the state court's determination was contrary to, or involved an unreasonable application of, clearly established federal law as determined by the Supreme Court of the United States.

(5) In order to seek a writ of *habeas corpus* from a federal court, the prisoner must have exhausted all remedies available at the state level, including all state appellate review.

(6) A petition for a writ of *habeas corpus* must be brought within one year of the final judgment of custody [28 U.S.C. § 2244(d)].

(a) A prisoner may not file successive petitions for *habeas corpus* relief without the approval of the U.S. Court of Appeals.

2. **Diversity Jurisdiction**

a. Federal district courts have original jurisdiction over matters involving litigants who are citizens of different states, U.S. citizens and citizens of a foreign country, or a foreign state and a U.S. citizen, if the amount in controversy is more than $75,000 [28 U.S.C. § 1332].

b. The amount in controversy between the litigants must exceed $75,000, exclusive of the costs and expenses associated with the litigation.

(1) If the suit is based on a contract or statute that allows a winning party to collect attorney's fees, the amount in controversy includes the likely amount of those fees.

(2) A suit in which the amount in controversy is *exactly* $75,000 does not meet the diversity jurisdiction requirement.

(3) An action based on diversity will be dismissed if it appears "to a legal certainty" that the plaintiff's claim does not exceed $75,000. The burden falls on the defendant to prove that the amount in controversy is not more than $75,000.

(4) There is a split of authority among the circuits regarding how the amount in controversy is determined.

(a) Under the majority rule, which is the rule followed in most circuits, the amount in controversy is determined according to the amount sought by the plaintiff. This is referred to as the "plaintiff's viewpoint" rule.

(b) Under the minority rule, known as the "either viewpoint rule," the amount in controversy is not necessarily the amount sought or recovered, but it is the value of the consequences which may result from the litigation.

(5) A plaintiff may meet the amount in controversy requirement by combining or aggregating the total claims against the defendant. Claims against multiple defendants may not be aggregated to meet the threshold unless the claims are common and undivided.

(a) Multiple plaintiffs cannot aggregate their claims for purposes of 28 U.S.C. § 1332. The U.S. Supreme Court 5-4 decision in Exxon Mobil Corp. v. Allapattah Services, Inc., 545 U.S. 546 (2005), held that a federal court has supplemental jurisdiction over claims of other plaintiffs who do not meet the jurisdictional amount for a diversity action, when at least one plaintiff in the action does satisfy the jurisdictional amount. So we need at least one plaintiff with a claim over $75,000.

(6) If the suit seeks an injunction, the amount in controversy is either the injunction's worth to the plaintiff, or the cost of the injunction to the defendant [JTH Tax, Inc. v. Frashier, 624 F.3d 635 (4th Cir. 2010)].

c. Diversity jurisdiction requires complete diversity, meaning a dispute that involves citizens of different states. There will be no diversity jurisdiction if any plaintiff and any defendant share citizenship of the same state.

(1) Diversity must be met only at the time the suit is filed. If a defendant moves to the same state as the plaintiff after the suit has been commenced, diversity will not be destroyed. However, if a complaint is amended to add or dismiss a party, this can affect jurisdiction.

(2) A party is considered to be a citizen of her state of domicile. Domicile is not the same as residence. **Domicile** requires a physical presence in the state and the intent to remain in that state indefinitely.

(a) The intent to remain in the new state includes the intent to abandon the former domicile permanently or indefinitely. If a person moves to a new residence but intends to return to his previous residence at a later date and stay there permanently or indefinitely, he does not demonstrate an intent to remain in the new state sufficient to establish a new domicile.

EXAMPLE: A and B, a married couple, live in Alabama. They are registered to vote there, have a car registered there, and own a home in that state. A and B are domiciled in Alabama. If A were to take a long-term work assignment in Texas, but she intended to move back to her home in Alabama with B, she would not be domiciled in Texas.

(b) The intent to remain in the new state cannot be conditioned upon the happening of a future event or be contingent on the permanency of employment.

EXAMPLE: John, a resident of Maine, moves to Vermont in the hopes of finding a new career. John signs a one-year lease on an apartment while looking for a job. If he finds a new job, John plans to sell his old home in Maine and buy a new one in Vermont. At this time, John does not demonstrate an intent to remain in Vermont indefinitely because his staying there is only conditioned on his finding employment.

(c) A "floating" intention to return to a former home at some indefinite future time will not defeat the establishment of a new domicile, provided that the person has actually moved to a new state and intends to remain there indefinitely.

EXAMPLE: Greg lived in a house that he owned in Colorado, in the same city where he was born and raised. Because of a new job opportunity, Greg sold his home and moved to Utah, where he purchased a new house. However, Greg hoped that one day in the future, he would move back to his home town and raise a family there. Greg will be considered a citizen of Utah. Because Greg has the intent to remain in Utah indefinitely, his "floating" intention to return home at some indefinite time in the future will not prevent his establishing Utah as his present state of domicile.

(d) The purpose of the change in domicile is irrelevant. While the person's motivation may impact a determination of whether she intends to remain in the new state indefinitely, as long as the person demonstrates the intent to remain in the new state indefinitely, her reason for moving does not matter, even if she was motivated by self-interest. For example, courts have found that people changed their domicile despite the fact that their reason for moving was motivated by:

1) defeating or creating federal diversity jurisdiction [Bank One, Texas, N.A. v. Montle, 964 F.2d 48 (1st Cir. 1992); Williamson v. Osenton, 232 U.S. 619 (1914)];
2) taking advantage of the new state's divorce laws [Wicker v. Wicker, 269 S.W.2d 311 (Ark. 1954)];
3) taking advantage of another jurisdiction's in-state tuition rates [Eastman v. University of Michigan, 30 F.3d 670 (6th Cir. 1994)]; or
4) having a will proved and probated in another jurisdiction [In re Newcomb's Estate, 84 N.E. 950 (N.Y. 1908)].

(3) **Alien** refers to an individual who is a citizen of a foreign country. For diversity purposes, if an alien is admitted to permanent residence in the United States (i.e., that person has a green card), he is a citizen of the state in which he is domiciled. Therefore, diversity is improper if a permanent resident alien is a resident of the same state of the citizen whom he is suing or is being sued by. In such a situation, there is no diversity jurisdiction.

(a) Similarly, there is no diversity jurisdiction over a lawsuit involving an alien on one side, and an alien and a citizen on the other side.

(4) A corporation is a citizen of both the state or foreign country of its incorporation and the state or foreign country where it has its principal place of business. A corporation may only have one principal place of business. The principal place of business is the state in which the corporation has its "nerve center," or the place from which the corporation's high-level officers direct, control, and coordinate the corporation's activities [Hertz Corp. v. Friend, 559 U.S. 77 (2010)].

EXAMPLE: ABC Corporation is incorporated in Delaware, but has its principal place of business in New York. If ABC brought suit against a competitor, XYZ, which has its principal place of business in New Jersey, but which is also incorporated in Delaware, there would be no diversity jurisdiction.

(5) The citizenship of an unincorporated association, such as a partnership or limited liability company, is the citizenship of all of the members of the association. For purposes of class actions, however, an unincorporated association is a citizen of the state under whose laws the association is organized, and the state in which it has its principal place of business.

d. There is an exception to the complete diversity requirement for class actions. In class actions where the class contains over 100 persons and the amount in controversy exceeds $5,000,000, diversity need only be "minimal," meaning that federal jurisdiction exists if any single member of the class is diverse from any single defendant.

e. There are two situations when a federal court will decline jurisdiction even where the requirements for diversity jurisdiction are met, because they are traditionally viewed as being matters for state courts to decide.

(1) Under the probate exception, federal courts will typically not exercise jurisdiction over probate matters, such as the validity of a will and the administration of an estate.

(2) Federal courts will also decline jurisdiction in family law matters, such as divorce, child custody, and child support proceedings. This is known as the family law exception.

3. **Supplemental Jurisdiction**

a. **Supplemental jurisdiction** allows a federal district court to hear claims over which it would not ordinarily have jurisdiction (e.g., state law claims that do not involve diversity jurisdiction) [28 U.S.C. § 1367]. Supplemental jurisdiction permits a claim falling outside of federal question jurisdiction or diversity jurisdiction to "piggyback" on a claim that does fall within one of those jurisdictions.

b. To exercise supplemental jurisdiction over an additional claim, there must be a claim over which a court has original jurisdiction [Id.]. In other words, supplemental jurisdiction is only available over a claim if the claim arises out of the same transaction or occurrence as a claim over which the court would have federal question or diversity jurisdiction.

(1) Claims arise out of the same transaction or occurrence if they arise out of a common nucleus of operative fact.

(2) In determining whether claims against multiple defendants arise out of the same transaction or occurrence or series of transactions/occurrences, courts often ask whether the plaintiff's claims against the defendants are logically related. Where there is a logical relationship between the claims and it would serve judicial economy to hear the (related) claims together, the test is met.

EXAMPLE: C was injured when he was wrongfully arrested by a police officer. The federal courts have jurisdiction to hear his claim for violation of his federal constitutional rights [42 U.S.C. § 1983]. The federal courts have supplemental jurisdiction to hear his state law claim against the arresting officer for battery arising out of the same incident.

c. Supplemental jurisdiction may include claims that involve the joinder or intervention of additional parties, even if there would not otherwise be federal jurisdiction over those parties.

(1) In a diversity case, supplemental jurisdiction may be exercised over the claims of a party other than the plaintiff if the only reason the other party's claims do not qualify for diversity jurisdiction is the failure to meet the amount-in-controversy requirement.

EXAMPLE: A nine-year-old child seriously injures her hand on a can of fish sold by a corporation incorporated and having its principal place of business in another state. The child's injuries meet the amount-in-controversy requirement. The child's mother also has a state-law claim against the corporation, but the amount of her claim does not meet the amount-in-controversy requirement. The federal court may exercise supplemental jurisdiction to hear the mother's claim along with the child's claim.

(2) In a diversity case, a court may not exercise supplemental jurisdiction over a claim by a plaintiff proposed to be joined under Rule 19 (compulsory joinder), or a claim by a plaintiff seeking to intervene under Rule 24, when exercising supplemental jurisdiction would destroy complete diversity of the parties [28 U.S.C. § 1367(b)].

(3) Moreover, in a diversity case a court may not exercise supplemental jurisdiction over claims by plaintiffs against persons made party to the suit under Rule 14 (impleader), 19, 20 (permissive joinder), or 24.

(4) If non-diverse parties are joined to a case, and there is no supplemental jurisdiction to hear their claims, the court may dismiss only the claims of the non-diverse parties.

d. Even if the additional claim arises out of the same transaction or occurrence and the plaintiff is not trying to circumvent diversity jurisdiction, the court may (but is not required to) decline to exercise supplemental jurisdiction in the following situations:

(1) the state law claim raises a novel or complex issue of state law;

(2) the state law claim "substantially predominates" over the claim over which the district court has jurisdiction;

(3) the court has dismissed all the claims over which it had jurisdiction; or

(4) in "exceptional circumstances," there are other "compelling reasons" to decline jurisdiction.

4. **Concurrent Jurisdiction**

a. A federal court has concurrent jurisdiction over a particular case if the case could also have been brought in state court.

b. When a court has concurrent jurisdiction to hear a case, both state and federal laws or policies may apply, resulting in a conflict of laws.

5. **Removal**

a. A case that was originally brought in state court may be removed to federal court if the plaintiff could have brought the case in federal court [28 U.S.C. § 1441]. The defendant in such a situation has a right to remove or shift that case from state court to federal court.

(1) Note that removal is only an option for defendants; plaintiffs cannot remove a suit to federal court after having chosen state court.

b. If removal is based on diversity, all of the defendants must be diverse from the plaintiff. Removal on the basis of diversity will not be granted if any of the defendants is a citizen of the forum state.

(1) Under the **fraudulent joinder rule**, the right to removal will not be defeated if a defendant was fraudulently joined for the purpose of defeating diversity jurisdiction and preventing removal to federal court [Marshall v. Manville Sales Corp., 6 F.3d 229 (4th Cir. 1993)].

(a) A party who claims fraudulent joinder has the burden of proving:

1) that there is no possibility the plaintiff would be able to establish a cause of action in state court against the in-state defendant; or

2) that there was outright fraud in the plaintiff's pleading of jurisdictional facts.

(2) The fraudulent joinder rule applies to defendants named in the original complaint, as well as to those joined as parties any time prior to removal [Mayes v. Rapoport, 198 F.3d 457 (4th Cir. 1999)]. In other words, if the removal is based on diversity, diversity is needed both at the time the original claim is filed and at the time when the notice of removal is filed.

c. The defendant has the right to remove when the plaintiff is suing the defendant in a jurisdiction that is not the defendant's home state. However, if the plaintiff is suing the defendant in state court located in that defendant's home state, there is no risk of being "homered." Therefore, that defendant cannot remove [28 U.S.C. § 1441(b)(2)].

d. If a plaintiff's suit is based on federal law, the defendant may have the case removed without a showing of diversity.

e. Removal is allowed only when at least one of the plaintiff's claims would fall within the subject-matter jurisdiction of the federal courts.

EXAMPLE: A files suit in her home state court against B, a citizen of another state. A's suit claims several violations of her home state's unfair trade practice laws. Her suit also alleges breach of contract, with a claim of $80,000 in damages. B may have the suit removed to federal court, and the federal court will hear her unfair trade practice claims.

EXAMPLE: C, a New York resident, files suit against D, also a New York resident, in a New York state court. C's complaint seeks $80,000 in damages. Two weeks later D gets a new job and moves to Florida, establishing residency and an intent to permanently live there. D may not have the suit removed to federal court because diversity must exist both at the time of filing and the time of removal.

f. If the basis for removal is federal question jurisdiction, and appended to the federal question claim is a state claim not within the original or supplemental jurisdiction of the district court or a claim that has been made non-removable by statute (i.e., a diversity claim against a defendant from the forum state or a claim as to which the defendant did not join in or agree to the removable notice), the entire case is removed to federal court [28 U.S.C. § 1441(c)].

(1) Once in federal court, the federal district court judge must sever those non-removable pieces and remand them back to state court.

g. **Multiple Defendants**

(1) In a case involving multiple defendants, all defendants who have been properly joined and served in the case must

consent to or join in removal for removal to be proper [28 U.S.C. § 1446(b)].

(2) Absent that unanimity, removal is improper.

h. **Procedure**

(1) In order to remove a case, a defendant must file a notice in the federal district court in the district in which the action is currently pending.

(a) The defendant must include with the notice a copy of all pleadings served on the defendant.

(b) The defendant must notify all adverse parties.

(c) The defendant must file a copy of the notice with the state court, after which the state court must proceed no further, unless and until the case is remanded.

(2) The federal court will consider whether removal is proper. If removal is not proper, the court will remand the action to state court.

i. **Timing**

(1) Notice must be filed within 30 days of service of the initial pleading. If a case is not removable when the initial pleading is filed, and the complaint is amended in a way that now makes the case removable, a notice of removal must be made within 30 days of service of the amended pleading.

(a) Each defendant receives a 30-day period to decide whether to remove to federal court. This is important with respect to later-joined defendants.

EXAMPLE: In the original lawsuit, the plaintiff is suing two defendants. Those two defendants have 30 days to decide whether or not to remove. If they do not remove and the plaintiff later joins a third defendant, that new defendant has 30 days to decide whether or not to remove. If that defendant decides to remove, the first two defendants who originally said they did not want to remove can join in the new request for notice of removal and the entire case will be deemed timely removed to federal court [28 U.S.C. § 1446(b)(2)(B), (C)].

(2) A case removable on the basis of diversity jurisdiction may not be removed more than one year after the commencement of the action (i.e., when the action was filed not served) [28 U.S.C. § 1446].

(a) However, if the plaintiff acted in bad faith so as to prevent the defendant from removing, that one-year time period can be relaxed.

j. The venue of a removed case is the district court where the state court is located.

k. Removal is allowed only for state court cases. Agency or administrative proceedings cannot be removed to federal court.

l. If a plaintiff believes that a case was improperly removed to federal court, he may bring a motion to remand the case to state court.

EXAMPLE: A consumer from State A brings a $100,000 products liability action in state court against the manufacturer of a product that injured her and the retailer from whom she bought the product. The manufacturer is a corporation that is a citizen of State B, while the retailer is incorporated in State C but has its headquarters in State A. The manufacturer and retailer have the case removed to federal court, based on diversity of citizenship and the amount in controversy. The consumer may bring a motion to remand to state court, on the grounds that retailer is not a diverse defendant.

(1) A motion to remand on the basis of any defect other than lack of subject-matter jurisdiction must be made within 30 days after the filing of the removal notice [28 U.S.C. § 1447(c)].

(a) Objections to subject-matter jurisdiction can never be waived and therefore a motion to remand based on lack of subject-matter jurisdiction is not subject to any time limit. If at any time before the final judgment a court lacks subject-matter jurisdiction, the case must be remanded [Id.].

(2) The defendant has the burden of showing that the removal was proper.

6. **Dismissal**

a. The court must dismiss an action if it determines that it does not have subject-matter jurisdiction over the case [Fed. R. Civ. P. 12(h)(3)].

b. Lack of subject-matter jurisdiction may not be waived by the parties.

7. **Lawsuit Based on Invalid Law**

a. A lawsuit cannot be filed based on an invalid law. If an action has been removed to federal court and the court determines that this is the case, it must either be dismissed or remanded back to state court for an amended complaint.

b. The federal court cannot consider any pleading subsequent to the removal petition. If the action is remanded and an amended complaint is filed, the defendants can file to remove the case to federal court a second time.

B. Territorial Jurisdiction

1. **Territorial jurisdiction** is the authority of a court to bind a party to the action. There are three essential ways to establish territorial personal jurisdiction:

a. a federal court has territorial jurisdiction over the state in which that federal district is located;

b. a federal statute that creates a cause of action may provide that federal courts have nationwide jurisdiction; or

c. the "100 mile bulge" rule states that a federal court may exercise jurisdiction over a defendant outside the state in which the court is located if the defendant is joined under Rule 14 or 19 and is served within a judicial district of the United States not more than 100 miles from where the summons was issued [Fed. R. Civ. P. 4(k)].

(1) In order for jurisdiction to be proper under this rule, the defendant must have the type of minimum contacts with the "bulge" that would support personal jurisdiction for a court in the "bulge."

C. **Personal Jurisdiction**

1. **Personal jurisdiction** refers to a court's authority over a defendant. Personal jurisdiction must be established separately for each defendant. There are three types of personal jurisdiction:
   a. *in personam* jurisdiction over the parties;
   b. *in rem* jurisdiction over the property that is the subject of the action; and
   c. *quasi in rem* jurisdiction over property that is attached to satisfy the judgment in an action.
2. ***In personam* jurisdiction** is jurisdiction over the parties to a lawsuit. The defendant typically is physically present in the forum state, or has some significant contacts with the state. To determine whether a federal court has personal jurisdiction over a particular party, the personal jurisdiction law of the state in which the federal court sits must be satisfied and the exercise of personal jurisdiction must comply with the United States Constitution.
   a. **State Long-Arm Statute**
      (1) For a federal court to have personal jurisdiction over a defendant, the state court in which the federal court sits must be able to exercise personal jurisdiction over that defendant.
         (a) If the state court could not assert personal jurisdiction, then the federal court may not assert personal jurisdiction either.
      (2) A state court may exercise personal jurisdiction over an out-of-state defendant if authorized by the state's long-arm statute. Long-arm statutes place limitations on the state's ability to establish personal jurisdiction by setting out the types of contacts that will support jurisdiction. Typically, the types of contacts that establish personal jurisdiction include the following:
         (a) the defendant transacts business within the state;
         (b) the defendant contracts to supply goods and services anywhere within the state; or
         (c) the defendant owns, uses, or possesses any real property within the state.
   b. **Constitutional Considerations**
      (1) Just because state law permits personal jurisdiction over a particular party does not mean that the federal court may automatically assert it. The federal court must also determine whether the state law is constitutional under the Due Process Clause of the Fourteenth Amendment.

NOTE Many states authorize personal jurisdiction to the full extent of the Fourteenth Amendment. If a state does that, all you need to do is determine whether personal jurisdiction over a particular defendant is permissible under the Constitution. If it is, then both state law and constitutional law are satisfied.

(2) A state law will be constitutional if it authorizes personal jurisdiction in one of five following circumstances:
   (a) residency;
   (b) consent;
   (c) service;
   (d) minimum contacts; or
   (e) substantial business.

(3) **Residency**
   (a) If the defendant is domiciled in the forum state, personal jurisdiction over the defendant is constitutional. A person is domiciled in a jurisdiction if she:
      1) resides in that jurisdiction; and
      2) has expressed her intent to remain in that jurisdiction indefinitely.

(4) **Consent**
   (a) If the defendant consents to the federal court's personal jurisdiction over him, personal jurisdiction is constitutional.
      1) A person may expressly consent to personal jurisdiction by agreement with the other party. For example, parties to a contract often put a choice-of-forum clause in their contracts that specifies the forum in which any lawsuit arising from the contract must be litigated. If a defendant signs a contract with a choice of forum clause, she has consented to the power of the court specified in the clause.

         EXAMPLE: A man obtains a line of credit from the bank. The credit agreement provides that all disputes relating to the agreement will be heard by the federal district court in Delaware. The man has consented to personal jurisdiction in Delaware.

      2) A state may provide by law that a non-resident has consented to personal jurisdiction in that state if the non-resident engages in a particular activity that the state has a substantial interest in regulating, such as driving on public roads.

         EXAMPLE: A non-resident who drives a car in another state has given his implied consent to personal jurisdiction in that state, for suits arising out of his operation of a car in the state.

      3) A party can also consent to federal jurisdiction by waiving her objection to personal jurisdiction. If a defendant appears in court without making a motion to dismiss for lack of personal jurisdiction, or does not include lack

of personal jurisdiction in a responsive pleading, the defense is waived [Fed. R. Civ. P. 12(h)(1)]. The defendant must object to personal jurisdiction in its initial filing or appearance before the court. A defendant does not waive objections to lack of personal jurisdiction by making an appearance before the court to contest jurisdiction.

(5) **Service**

(a) If a defendant is physically present in the jurisdiction, and is served with process while present, the court's exercise of personal jurisdiction over the defendant is constitutional.

1) It does not matter that the defendant's presence in the jurisdiction is temporary, or that it is unrelated to the lawsuit.

2) The defendant's presence must be voluntary; the plaintiff cannot have coaxed the defendant into the state under false pretenses. Moreover, personal jurisdiction would not be constitutional if the defendant is in the forum state to participate in a legal proceeding.

EXAMPLE: A businessman is a resident of Missouri. While driving to Louisiana on a business trip, he stops for lunch at a restaurant in Arkansas. A process server sees him in the restaurant, and serves him with a summons and complaint for an action in federal district court in Arkansas. The court has jurisdiction over the businessman, based on service.

EXAMPLE: A singer, a resident of Maryland, receives a telephone call telling her that she has won a prize in a raffle. In order to pick up that prize, she is told that she must go to the raffle sponsor's headquarters in Virginia. When the singer gets to the address she is given, she learns that there is no raffle prize. Instead, she is served with a summons and complaint. The court in Virginia does not have jurisdiction over the singer based on service.

(6) **Minimum Contacts**

(a) For jurisdiction to be constitutional under a "minimum contacts" analysis, three conditions must be satisfied:

1) the defendant must have established a minimum contact with the forum state;

2) the claim against the defendant must be related to that contact; and

a) A lawsuit is related to a defendant's contacts if the contacts played a role in causing the lawsuit.

3) the exercise of jurisdiction must not offend traditional notions of fair play and substantial justice.

(b) A defendant has minimum contacts with a particular state if he causes harm in the state, does business in the state, or has an interest in real property in the state. Importantly, the defendant does not have to be in the state to cause the harm, do the business, or have a property interest, but his contact with the state has to be purposefully established.

(c) Therefore, for a plaintiff to establish a minimum contact, the defendant must "purposefully avail" itself to the privilege of conducting activities within the forum state [World-Wide Volkswagen Corp. v. Woodson, 444 U.S. 286 (1980)].

1) If a defendant purposefully availed herself of the protections and benefits of the forum state, sufficient minimum contacts for personal jurisdiction will exist. Purposeful availment involves actions that are directed towards a particular state. A defendant who purposely involves herself in transactions within the state receives the benefits and privileges of that state's laws, so it is fair that she be exposed to the jurisdiction of that forum state as well.

2) By purposefully availing itself, a party is deemed to have reasonably foreseen the possibility of being haled into court in that state to defend an action.

3) Merely placing a product into the stream of commerce is not enough to establish purposeful availment; the defendant must also have had additional contacts with the forum state [Asahi Metal Industry Co. v. Superior Court, 480 U.S. 102 (1987)].

(d) If a defendant has minimum contacts with the forum state, the defendant bears the burden of proving that it would be fundamentally unfair for him to litigate in that state in order to avoid the court's personal jurisdiction [Burger King v. Rudzewicz, 471 U.S. 462 (1985)].

(e) Courts consider the following five factors when determining whether it is fair to require the defendant to litigate in the forum state [World-Wide Volkswagen Corp. v. Woodson, 444 U.S. 286 (1980)]:

1) the burden on the defendant;
2) the interests of the forum state;
3) the plaintiff's interests in obtaining relief;
4) the interstate judicial system's interest in efficiency; and
5) shared policy interests of the states.

(f) Generally, the burden on the defendant drives the analysis and must be quite substantial for a court to reject personal jurisdiction on the basis of fairness.

EXAMPLE: D, a resident of North Carolina, was driving through Rhode Island on her way to Boston when she struck P with her car. In a subsequent suit in Rhode Island, D is subject to personal jurisdiction because she caused harm in the state, the lawsuit arises from those contacts, and Rhode Island has an interest in protecting its citizens from negligent drivers and maintaining order on its roads.

EXAMPLE: P heard from a friend that D, a company in Nebraska, makes great custom tailgates for pickup trucks. P, a resident of Kansas, called D and asked to order one. D does all its business in Nebraska but agreed to make P a tailgate and send it to him. P received the tailgate but couldn't install it because it was designed incorrectly. P can sue D in Kansas because it did business in the state, the lawsuit arose from that activity, and Kansas has an interest in protecting its citizens from breaches of contract.

EXAMPLE: P, a citizen of Texas, was driving in Connecticut when she got into a car accident with D. D is a Connecticut citizen, but spends six weeks each summer in Texas with his grandmother (and has been doing so for the past 10 years). P cannot sue D in Texas because his contacts with the state did not give rise to the lawsuit. (P could, however, wait until D comes back into the state next summer and have him served then.)

EXAMPLE: Motor MFG manufactured an electric motor in Michigan and sold it to Golf Cart Co. in Ohio, which then installed it in a golf cart. P, a resident of Georgia, purchased the cart over the phone, and Golf Car Co. then shipped it from Ohio to P at home. P was later injured when the cart's electric motor caught fire and he wants to bring suit in Georgia. Golf Cart Co. will be subject to personal jurisdiction in Georgia because it transacted business in the state or caused harm in the state, the suit arises from those acts, and fair play concerns are not implicated. In contrast, Motor MFG will not be subject to personal jurisdiction in Georgia because it did not purposefully establish any contacts with the state that gave rise to P's suit. Even if Motor MFG had sent other motors to the state in the past, personal jurisdiction is not permissible because those contacts did not give rise to P's claim.

(7) **Substantial Business**

(a) A federal court can constitutionally assert personal jurisdiction over a defendant if it is doing "substantial business" in a particular state. The Supreme Court has made clear that "substantial business" is a very high bar to clear. There is no easy definition for "substantial business" but recent opinions by the Supreme Court instruct that the business activity in a particular state must be so significant that the company is "essentially at home" in that state.

(b) A corporation would probably not be considered "essentially at home" and thus subject to general jurisdiction in a state in which it is not incorporated nor has its principal place of business [Daimler AG v. Bauman, 571 U.S. 117 (2014)].

1) Note that the principal place of business does not need to be a permanent one; it can be temporary. This is also a means by which a state may have general jurisdiction over a foreign corporation, which is one organized in a foreign country and which ordinarily has its principal place of business in a foreign country.

2) In Perkins v. Benguet Consol. Mining Co. [342 U.S. 437 (1952)], the Supreme Court held that it was not a violation of due process for a foreign corporation to be subject to general jurisdiction in a state where the corporation had temporarily relocated its principal place of business, even where the cause of action did not arise from the corporation's actions within that state. This holding was reaffirmed by the Supreme Court in Daimler AG v. Bauman [571 U.S. 117 (2014)], because the state had become the corporation's principal, if temporary, place of business.

(c) As a corollary to this, the Court has suggested that a company cannot be "essentially at home" in more than a couple of states.

EXAMPLE: P was vacationing in Utah when she slipped and fell in a convenience store. After returning home to Arizona, P desired to bring suit against the convenience store chain in Arizona. The convenience store chain operates 131 stores in the state, roughly 8% of its total operations. The convenience store chain is not subject to personal jurisdiction in Arizona because its business, whether substantial or not, is not the sort that renders it "essentially at home" because if that were so, it would be essentially at home in all 50 states.

(d) The Supreme Court has recently limited the scope of specific personal jurisdiction in this area as well. In order for a court to exercise specific jurisdiction over a claim, there must be a connection between the forum and the underlying controversy—in essence, an activity or an occurrence—that takes place in the forum state [Goodyear Dunlop Tires Operations, S.A. v. Brown, 564 U.S. 915 (2011)].

1) When there is no such connection, specific jurisdiction is lacking regardless of the extent of a defendant's unconnected activities in the forum state [Bristol-Myers Squibb Co. v. Superior Court of California, 582 U.S. 255 (2017)].

2) Even regularly occurring sales of a product in a state do not justify the exercise of jurisdiction over a claim unrelated to those sales [Goodyear Dunlop Tires Operations, S.A. v. Brown, 564 U.S. 915 (2011)].

3. ***In rem* jurisdiction** is based on the interests of a particular piece of property or thing located within the forum state.

EXAMPLE: The courts of a state have *in rem* jurisdiction to hear an action to quiet title to a parcel of real estate in the state.

a. A federal court may exercise *in rem* jurisdiction when:
   (1) there is real or personal property of value located within the state where the federal district is located;
   (2) the court seizes the item; and
      (a) A court's *in rem* jurisdiction cannot begin until the court has effective control of the asset.
   (3) the owner of the property received proper notice of the proceeding.

b. A defendant who is no longer domiciled in the forum state may be subject to *in rem* jurisdiction if:
   (1) the cause of action is of a domestic nature; and
   (2) the forum state was the place of matrimonial domicile, the defendant abandoned the plaintiff in the forum state, or an agreement or settlement for support was entered into in the forum state.

4. A federal court has ***quasi in rem*** **jurisdiction** in actions in which the attachment of real or personal property is part of the relief requested. The federal court located in the state in which that property is situated has *quasi in rem* jurisdiction over the property being attached.

   a. The following elements are required for *quasi in rem* jurisdiction:
      (1) there is real or personal property of value located within the state or territorial limits of the federal court;
      (2) the defendant owns the property;
      (3) the property is being attached or seized; and
      (4) the defendant has been provided proper notice of the proceedings.

   b. The court may not exercise *quasi in rem* jurisdiction unless there are minimum contacts with the forum state or territory [Shaffer v. Heitner, 433 U.S. 186 (1977)].
      (1) If the dispute concerns the parties' rights in the property itself, the presence of the property in the state will provide sufficient minimum contacts.
      (2) The minimum contacts requirements for *quasi in rem* jurisdiction are similar to those for *in personam* jurisdiction.
      (3) The minimum contacts requirements make *quasi in rem* jurisdiction a rarely used gap filler. It is used only when the constitutional requirements (minimum contacts, and a finding that the exercise of jurisdiction does not offend traditional notions of fair play and substantial justice) are satisfied, but *in personam* jurisdiction is unavailable because the long-arm statute does not authorize jurisdiction.

5. **Judgment Entered without Personal Jurisdiction**

   a. If the court entered a judgment against a defendant over whom it did not have constitutional personal jurisdiction, that judgment is void and not entitled to Full Faith and Credit by another court.

b. However, a judgment has preclusive effect on future litigation if the defendant in the first case had the opportunity to challenge personal jurisdiction and either:
   (1) waived the personal jurisdiction challenge; or
   (2) made the personal jurisdiction challenge and lost.

D. Service of Process and Notice

1. **Commencement of an Action**
   a. A civil action in federal court is commenced by filing the complaint with the court.
   b. After the complaint is filed, the plaintiff presents a summons to the clerk for signature and seal. If the summons meets the requirements for format of a summons, the clerk certifies it and issues it to the plaintiff for service on the defendant.
   c. A summons is a court document that informs the defendant that the complaint has actually been filed and that he must respond to it, or else be held in default. The process served to compel the attendance of witnesses is a subpoena [Fed. R. Civ. P. 45].
   d. The formal requirements for a summons are set out in Rule 4, which requires a summons:
      (1) be signed by the clerk;
      (2) identify the court and the parties;
      (3) be directed to the defendant;
      (4) state the name and address of either the plaintiff's attorney or the plaintiff itself, if unrepresented;
      (5) notify the defendant of:
         (a) the time period within which it must appear or file an answer; and
         (b) the potential for a default judgment if the defendant fails to appear within the time specified; and
      (6) contain the seal of the court.
2. **Service of Process**
   a. The plaintiff is charged with service of process.
   b. A summons must be served with a copy of the complaint. Unless both the complaint and summons are served on the defendant at the same time, process has not been completed.
      (1) The plaintiff is responsible for any insufficiency of either the service of process or the process itself.
   c. Service of process must occur within 90 days of filing of the complaint [Fed. R. Civ. P. 3, 4(m)].
      (1) If the plaintiff does not timely serve the defendant with process, the court must dismiss the suit without prejudice unless the plaintiff can show good cause why service was not timely.

d. Service may be effected by any person who is:
   (1) at least 18 years of age; and
   (2) not a party to the suit.

e. **How Process is Served**
   (1) Process can be served on the defendant (whether a natural person or corporation, partnership, or association) by following the manner prescribed by the state court in the state where the federal suit has been filed or the state court in the state where the defendant will be served [Fed. R. Civ. P. 4(e)(1)].
   (2) If the defendant is a natural person, process can also be served by doing any of the following [Fed. R. Civ. P. 4(e)(2)]:
      (a) personally delivering the process to the defendant himself, wherever he maybe;
      (b) leaving process at the defendant's usual place of abode with a person of suitable age and discretion who resides there; or
      (c) serving the defendant's registered agent.
   (3) If the defendant is a corporation, partnership, or association, process can also be served by delivering a copy of the summons and the complaint to [Fed. R. Civ. P. 4(h)]:
      (a) an officer;
      (b) a managing agent or general agent; or
      (c) any other agent authorized by appointment or by law to receive service of process. Note that if the agent is one authorized by law and the law requires service by mail, process must be served by personal delivery to the agent and by mail.

f. **Waiver of Service**
   (1) A defendant may also waive service of process, upon request of the plaintiff. A waiver allows the plaintiff to save the costs of service.
   (2) Waiver of service is not a waiver of any objections the defendant may have regarding the court's subject-matter or personal jurisdiction over the suit or as to the venue of the suit.
   (3) A request for waiver of service of process must:
      (a) be in writing and addressed to the individual defendant;
         1) If the defendant is a corporation, partnership, or association, the request is addressed to an officer, manager, or authorized agent.
      (b) be sent via first-class mail or other reliable means;
      (c) be accompanied by a copy of the complaint;
      (d) identify the court where the complaint was filed;
      (e) inform the defendant of the consequences of waiving and not waiving service;
      (f) state the date on which the request was sent;
      (g) allow the defendant a reasonable time to return the waiver, which is considered to be:

1) at least 30 days after the request was sent; or
2) at least 60 days after the request was sent for defendants located outside any judicial district of the United States; and

(h) provide the defendant with an extra copy of the request, as well as prepaid postage or other means of compliance in writing.

(4) Upon request of the plaintiff, a defendant has a duty to waive service unless the defendant is:
(a) a minor or incompetent person;
(b) the United States or an agency of the United States; or
(c) a state, local, or foreign government.

(5) A defendant who agrees to waive service need not answer the complaint until 60 days after the waiver request. If the complaint was sent to the defendant outside of any U.S. judicial district, the defendant does not need to answer until 90 days after the waiver request.

(6) If a defendant located in the United States fails without good cause to sign and return a waiver requested by a plaintiff located within the United States, the court may impose on the defendant:
(a) expenses incurred in making service; and
(b) reasonable expenses, including attorney's fees, of any motion required to collect service expenses.

(7) Sanctions will not be imposed if the defendant had good cause for failure to waive.
(a) "Good cause" does not include a belief that the complaint is unfounded, or that the action was filed in the wrong court.
(b) Failure to receive the waiver request would constitute good cause.

g. If a plaintiff fails to effect service according to the rules, the case should be dismissed for insufficiency of service of process.
(1) A defendant may raise objections to service of process in a motion to dismiss [Fed. R. Civ. P. 12(b)].
(2) Failure to raise the objection to insufficiency of service of process in a pre-answer motion or in the answer waives the defendant's right to object.
(3) A court will dismiss an action for insufficient service of process even if the defendant received actual notice of the action by some means other than service of process.

E. Venue, Transfer, and *Forum non Conveniens*

1. Venue

a. While subject matter jurisdiction dictates whether a suit can be brought in the federal court system, and personal jurisdiction informs the plaintiff what state the suit can be brought in, **venue** dictates the region within a particular state (known as a judicial district) where a suit can occur.

b. The venue of an action is the federal court in which the action is filed.

c. In any action venue is proper in [28 U.S.C. § 1391]:

  (1) the district in which any defendant resides, if all of the defendants reside in the same state;

    EXAMPLE: Plaintiff, a resident of Minnesota, brings a diversity action against Defendant A, a resident of Madison, Wisconsin (located in the Western District of Wisconsin), and Defendant B, a resident of Milwaukee (located in the Eastern District of Wisconsin). Venue is appropriate in either the Eastern or Western District.

  (2) the district in which a substantial part of the events or omissions giving rise to the claim occurred or the district in which a substantial part of the property that is the subject of the action is located; or

    EXAMPLE: Plaintiff sues Defendant, a recording artist, for copyright infringement for recording one of Plaintiff's songs without permission. The song was recorded at a studio in Nashville. Venue is proper in the Middle District of Tennessee, the district in which Nashville is located.

  (3) the district in which any defendant would be subject to personal jurisdiction, if there is no other district in which the action could be brought.

d. Venue is also considered proper where a party either consents to the venue, consents to personal jurisdiction in the venue, or waives her objection by failing to raise it.

e. The court may raise the issue of improper venue *sua sponte*.

f. For purposes of venue, a defendant's place of residence is determined according to the following rules [28 U.S.C. § 1391(c)]:

  (1) **Residence of Natural Persons**

    (a) Natural persons are deemed to reside where they are domiciled.

    (b) This applies to aliens who are admitted to permanent residence in the United States. They are considered to reside, for venue purposes, where they are domiciled.

  (2) **Residence of Entities**

    (a) If the entity is a plaintiff, venue is proper where that plaintiff maintains its principal place of business.

    (b) If the entity is a defendant, venue is proper where that defendant is subject to personal jurisdiction.

    (c) If a corporation resides in a state that has multiple districts, venue is proper in the district that would have had personal jurisdiction over that corporation had that district been its own state.

  (3) **Non-Resident Aliens**

    (a) Venue over non-resident aliens is proper in any judicial district.

    (b) In multi-defendant cases, we disregard non-resident aliens when computing venue.

2. **Transfer of Venue**

   a. If an action was brought in a particular venue, a federal court still may transfer the action to any other district in which it might have been brought, "for the convenience of parties and witnesses, in the interest of justice" [28 U.S.C. § 1404(a)]. The court does not dismiss the action so that the plaintiff may refile, but instead transfers the action to the more appropriate judicial district.

      (1) Courts usually give substantial deference to the plaintiff's choice of forum. The defendant bears the burden of proving that an adequate alternative forum exists, and that the plaintiff's choice of forum is significantly inappropriate.

      (2) The burden is on the party making a motion to transfer to show that:

         (a) the convenience of the parties and witnesses, the ease of access to proof, calendar congestion, and other factors favor transfer; and

         (b) the court to which the action will be transferred has personal and subject-matter jurisdiction over the suit.

      (3) When an action filed in a proper venue is transferred to a different court, the substantive law applied should be the same law that would have been applied by the transferor court.

      <u>EXAMPLE</u>: Plaintiff, a resident of Oregon, brings a diversity action for wrongful termination of employment against Defendant, a corporation incorporated in Delaware but located in Washington, in U.S. District Court in Delaware. Defendant's only physical location is in Washington, and it has no assets or physical presence in Delaware. All of the records relating to Plaintiff's employment and termination are in Washington, and all of the witnesses who might be called to testify are in either Washington or Oregon. The court may transfer Plaintiff's action under Rule 1404.

   b. If a case is brought in an improper venue, a federal court "shall dismiss, or if it be in the interest of justice, transfer such case to any district...in which it could have been brought" [28 U.S.C. § 1406(a)].

      (1) Transfers due to improper venue are appropriate only if the action could originally have been brought in the transferee court.

      (2) In an action transferred under § 1406, the action never "belonged" in the transferor court. The transferee court will therefore apply its own conflict of laws principles to determine the applicable substantive law.

3. ***Forum non Conveniens***

   a. The doctrine of *forum non conveniens* allows a court to decline to exercise its jurisdiction and dismiss an action if the court where the action was brought would be a seriously inconvenient forum and an adequate alternative forum exists in a foreign country or different jurisdiction.

(1) A federal court does not have the power to transfer a case to a foreign country, so the case will be dismissed. The plaintiff may then file his action in the alternative forum.

(a) If the federal court grants the *forum non conveniens* motion in favor of another federal district court, the initial court can transfer the case to the "more convenient" district court. This difference is because federal courts do not have the power to transfer a case to a foreign court, but do have the ability to transfer a case to another federal court.

(2) Courts may give substantial weight to the possibility of any change in substantive law as a result of bringing suit in the foreign forum if the remedy is so clearly inadequate or unsatisfactory as to be no remedy at all.

(3) Any deference given to the plaintiff's forum carries less weight when the plaintiff is from a foreign country.

b. Once the court has determined that an adequate alternative forum exists, it will weigh the public and private interests to determine whether to dismiss an action under the doctrine of *forum non conveniens.*

(1) Public interests include the interests in:

(a) resolving disputes locally and not burdening local courts with distant disputes;

(b) avoiding application of foreign law, if the case will require applying the law of another jurisdiction; and

(c) avoiding the imposition of jury duty for a case that would not have a substantial impact on the potential jurors' community.

(2) Private interests include:

(a) ease of access to evidence;

(b) cost of witness attendance at trial;

(c) availability of compulsory process; and

(d) any other factors that might lessen the time and expense of trial.

II. LAW APPLIED BY FEDERAL COURTS

A. State Law in Federal Court

1. **Rules of Decision Act**
   a. The Rules of Decision Act states that applicable provisions of the federal Constitution, treaties, and constitutional statutes enacted by Congress always take precedence over state law [28 U.S.C. § 1652].
   b. The federal courts apply federal law when considering issues involving:
      (1) the U.S. Constitution; and
      (2) constitutional federal statutes.
2. **The Erie Doctrine**
   a. The Erie doctrine states that a federal court that hears a state law claim in a case based on diversity or supplemental jurisdiction must apply the substantive law of the state in which the court sits [Erie R.R. Co. v. Tompkins, 304 U.S. 64 (1938)].
      (1) Under Erie, state law applies if it is a law that deals with the substantive rights of state citizens. Federal courts use federal, not state, procedural rules.
   b. The Erie doctrine applies only where the following are both present:
      (1) the court has subject-matter jurisdiction over a case, based on diversity or supplemental jurisdiction; and
      (2) the state law that would apply conflicts with the federal rule, statute, doctrine, or procedure at issue.
   c. If a valid federal statute or constitutional provision is on point, the federal court must apply the relevant provision; it is irrelevant whether the provision is substantive or procedural.
      (1) The federal rule will not apply if the federal rule abridges, modifies, or enlarges a substantive right.
      (2) If there is a valid federal rule promulgated under the Rules Enabling Act dealing with an issue, that rule is applied [28 U.S.C. § 2071, *et seq.*].
   d. If there is no valid federal statutory or constitutional law on point, the federal court will follow its ordinary practices unless doing so would lead to either a preference for one court system over another (forum shopping) or fundamental unfairness.

NOTE This part of the Erie analysis (when there is no valid federal statute or constitution provision on point) is really the substantive versus procedure law distinction. If this inquiry instructs the court to apply state law, the state law is called "substantive" regardless of its true nature. If this inquiry instructs the court to stick with ordinary federal practice, that practical is called "procedural," regardless of its true nature.

   e. Although the rules discussed above are the steps to apply in an Erie analysis, there is general agreement that certain substantive state laws should be applied in federal diversity cases.

(1) Federal courts in a diversity action will apply the statute of limitations of the state in which the court sits.

(2) Federal courts in a diversity action will apply the choice-of-law rules of the state in which the court is located.

f. On the other hand, the Supreme Court has held that the right to a jury trial in federal courts is to be determined as a matter of federal law. The court held that "[i]n diversity cases, the substantive dimension of the claim asserted finds its source in state law, but the characterization of that state-created claim as legal or equitable for purposes of whether a right to jury trial is indicated must be made by recourse to federal law" [Simler v. Conner, 372 U.S. 221 (1963)]. The reason for this was to ensure that the right to a jury trial, as guaranteed by the Seventh Amendment, was exercised uniformly.

3. **Uncertain State Law**

a. If the federal court is uncertain about the state law to be followed, or if the law is unclear or unsettled, the court may:

(1) abstain from hearing the state law claim;

(2) if state law allows, certify the question to the state courts and obtain a ruling on the issue; or

(3) try to predict how the state courts would rule on the issue, using all available and relevant resources.

b. Federal circuit courts of appeal do not give deference to district courts' interpretations of unsettled state law, but review those decisions *de novo.*

B. Federal Common Law

1. **In General**

a. Under the Erie doctrine, there is no general federal common law. Courts apply the laws of the states in which they are located.

b. Federal common law now exists to interpret congressional intent, or the meaning of statutes.

(1) Congress has made broad rules, with unclear or indefinite standards, for courts to interpret.

EXAMPLE: Federal law provides that the "fair use" of copyright-protected material is not infringement; however, the statute does not define "fair use" [17 U.S.C. § 107]. The courts have thus been left to develop the parameters of the fair use defense.

(2) Congressional action will take precedence over common law rules.

EXAMPLE: The Clean Air Act gives the Environmental Protection Agency authority to regulate greenhouse gases. The statutory grant of authority precludes federal common law nuisance claims against producers of those gases [American Elec. Power Co. v. Connecticut, 564 U.S. 410 (2011)].

2. **Federal or Constitutional Interests**
   a. Federal courts may make federal common law when [Clearfield Trust Co. v. U.S., 318 U.S. 360 (1943)]:
      (1) federal or constitutional interests are at stake;
      (2) Congress has inadequately addressed the situation concerned; and
      (3) the application of individual state laws in various jurisdictions would create unacceptable levels of diversity or uncertainty.
   b. Federal common law rules are adopted when Congress has given courts the power to make common law rules, or when Congress has been silent on a question involving federal law.

      EXAMPLE: Punitive damages are available in federal maritime cases when the owner of a vessel fails to pay maintenance and cure to an injured seaman. The damages are available as a matter of federal common law, because Congress has not acted to prohibit such damages [Atlantic Sounding Co. v. Townsend, 557 U.S. 404 (2009)].
   c. Generally, federal common law is confined to the following fields of law:
      (1) maritime law;
      (2) foreign relations;
      (3) commercial rights and liabilities of the federal government; and
      (4) property rights and liabilities of the federal government.

ERIE DOCTRINE

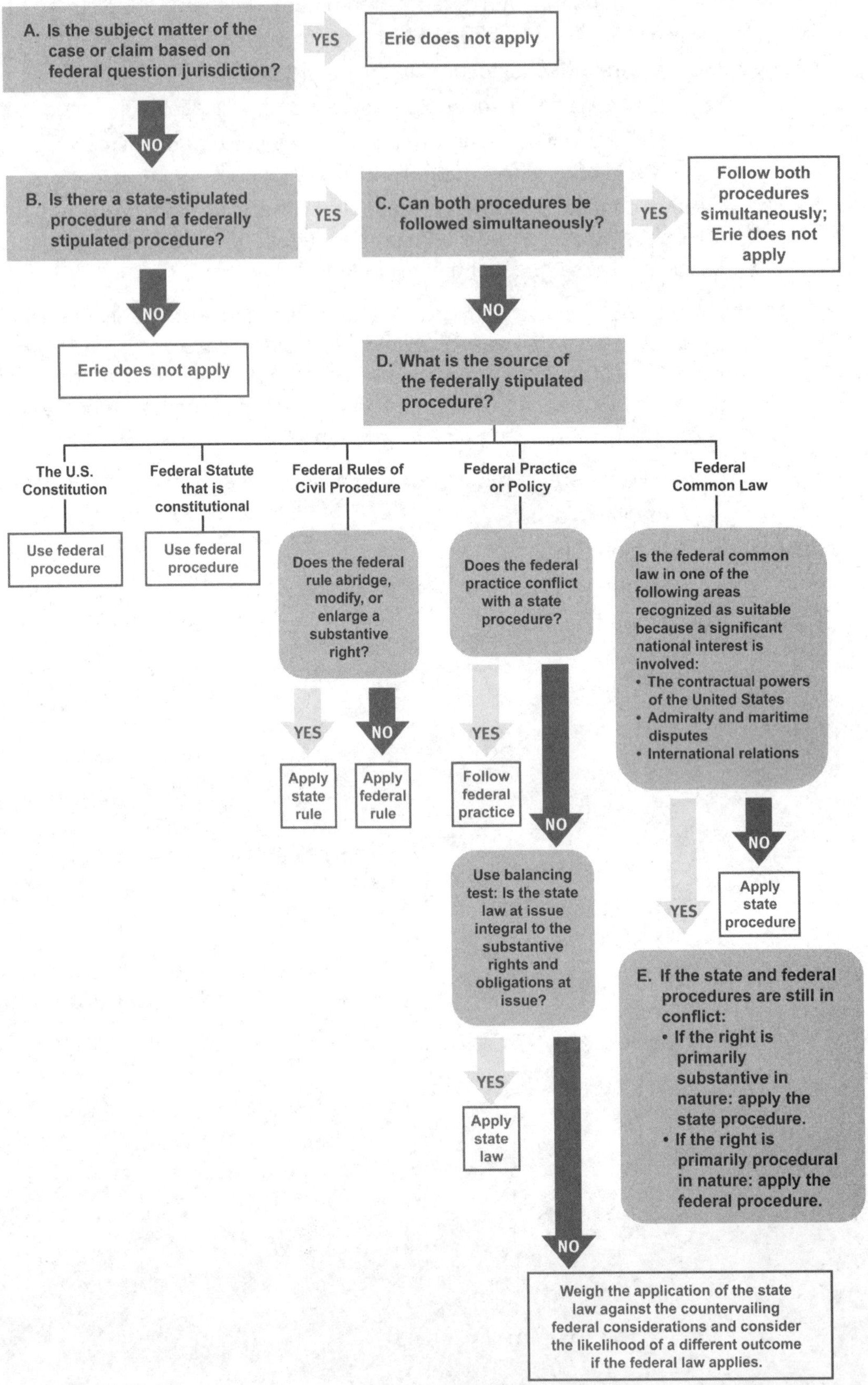

III. PRETRIAL PROCEDURES

A. Pleadings

1. Types of Pleadings

a. The following types of pleadings are allowed under the Federal Rules of Civil Procedure:

(1) complaints;

(2) answers to complaints;

(3) answers to counterclaims;

(4) answers to cross-claims;

(5) third-party complaints;

(6) answers to third-party complaints; and

(7) replies to answers, if ordered by the court.

2. Rules of Pleading

a. To initiate a lawsuit, the first step is filing a complaint.

b. A pleading that states a claim for relief (including a complaint), must contain [Fed. R. Civ. P. 8]:

(1) a short and plain statement of the grounds for the court's jurisdiction;

(2) a short and plain statement of the claim showing that the pleader is entitled to relief; and

(a) The "short and plain statement of the claim" must include "sufficient factual matter" to state a plausible claim that is more than a "sheer possibility that a defendant has acted unlawfully" [Bell Atlantic Corp. v. Twombly, 550 U.S. 544 (2007); Ashcroft v. Iqbal, 556 U.S. 662 (2009)].

(3) a demand for the relief sought.

c. A pleading may make inconsistent claims or defenses. The court will allow inconsistent pleadings to be determined by the trier of facts.

EXAMPLE: A sues B, claiming that B's dog bit him. B's answer denies that A was bitten. The answer also claims that A was bit because he provoked the dog.

d. A party may set out two or more statements of a claim or defense alternatively or hypothetically, either in a single count or defense or in separate ones.

EXAMPLE: C is hit by a car driven by D. C sues D, alleging that D negligently hit C. C also alleges that D intentionally hit her with his car.

e. Generally, pleadings in federal court are to be liberally construed.

(1) Courts are directed to ignore technical defects in pleadings, if no substantial right of the parties is prejudiced.

(2) Note that the Twombly and Iqbal cases referenced *supra* set out heightened standards for the allegations in pleadings that may affect how pleadings are construed.

f. Parties must plead claims or defenses in a simple, direct, and concise manner.
   (1) No technical pleading forms are necessary.
   (2) Although parties should use general terms and omit evidentiary material, a pleading must contain "sufficient factual matter" to set out a plausible claim for relief.

g. Some cases involve special matters that must be pleaded with particularity [Fed. R. Civ. P. 9]. Those special matters are:
   (1) capacity or authority to sue, if required to show the court has jurisdiction;
   (2) fraud, mistake, or condition of the mind;
   (3) conditions precedent, but only when denying that the condition has occurred;
   (4) time and place, when testing the sufficiency of a pleading; and
   (5) special damages.

   EXAMPLE: A sues B for injuries sustained in a traffic accident. A alleges that B's negligence caused her to incur medical bills, and to lose wages because she was unable to work. A must plead with specificity the amount of lost wages and the amount of her medical bills.

3. **Responsive Pleading**

a. An **answer** is a pleading in which the responding party admits or denies the opposing party's allegations and lists any defenses he might have.
   (1) The responding party must admit those allegations, or parts of allegations, that are true, and deny the others [Fed. R. Civ. P. 8(b)].
   (2) A general denial is appropriate only when the responding party intends in good faith to deny all the allegations in the pleading.
   (3) If the defendant fails to deny an allegation, it is deemed admitted.

b. A party must plead certain affirmative defenses in its answer or reply to a counterclaim.
   (1) An **affirmative defense** is a defense that relies on factual issues not presented in the complaint. It does not necessarily deny the allegations of the complaint, but pleads additional facts.
   (2) Affirmative defenses that must be pleaded in a responsive pleading include:
      (a) accord and satisfaction;
      (b) arbitration and award;
      (c) assumption of risk;
      (d) contributory negligence;
      (e) duress;
      (f) estoppel;
      (g) failure of consideration;
      (h) fraud;
      (i) illegality;
      (j) injury by fellow servant;

(k) laches;
(l) licenses;
(m) payment;
(n) release;
(o) *res judicata*;
(p) Statute of Frauds;
(q) statute of limitations; and
(r) waiver.

(3) Affirmative defenses that raise objections based on jurisdiction or procedural matters may be raised either in a responsive pleading, or in a pre-answer motion.

(a) If an objection will be raised by a motion, rather than in a responsive pleading, the motion must be made before a responsive pleading is made [Fed. R. Civ. P. 12(b)]. These motions are therefore known as pre-answer motions.

1) A motion to dismiss, a motion for a more definite statement, and a motion to strike are all pre-answer motions that must be made before a responsive pleading is made.

(b) Objections that may be raised either by a pre-answer motion to dismiss or responsive pleading are the following:

1) lack of subject-matter jurisdiction;
2) lack of personal jurisdiction;
3) improper venue;
4) insufficient process;
5) insufficient service of process;
6) failure to state a claim upon which relief can be granted; and
7) failure to join a party under Rule 19.

(4) A motion under this rule may be joined with any other motion allowed by this rule. However, except as provided in Rule 12(h)(2) or (3), a party that makes a motion under this rule must not make another motion under this rule raising a defense or objection that was available to the party but omitted from its earlier motion [Fed. R. Civ. P. 12(g)].

(5) Failure to raise an objection in an answer or pre-answer motion to dismiss constitutes a waiver of these defenses with the exception of objections to subject-matter jurisdiction, failure to state a claim upon which relief can be granted, and failure to join a party [Fed. R. Civ. P. 12(h)(1)].

(6) A motion to dismiss for failure to state a claim upon which relief can be granted, failure to join a necessary party, or failure to state a legal defense to a claim may be raised [Fed. R. Civ. P. 12(g)(2)]:

(a) in any pleading allowed or ordered under Rule 7(a);
(b) by a motion under Rule 12(c); or
(c) at trial.

(7) If the court determines at any time that it lacks subject-matter jurisdiction, the court must dismiss the action [Fed. R. Civ. P. 12(h)(3)].

c. **Timing of Responsive Pleading**

(1) An answer (or pre-answer motion) must be filed:

(a) within 21 days of service of process; or

NOTE The 21-day period does not include the date of service, but does include weekends and holidays. If the 21st day is on a weekend or a holiday, the answer must be filed on the next business day.

(b) if service was waived, within 60 days after the request for a waiver was sent, or within 90 days after it was sent to the defendant outside any judicial district of the United States.

(2) If the defendant responds to plaintiff's complaint by filing a pre-answer motion that is denied, the defendant must then file an answer within 14 days of the denial.

4. **Amended and Supplemental Pleadings**

a. A party may amend a pleading once as a matter of course if the amendment is filed [Fed. R. Civ. P. 15]:

(1) within 21 days of service of the original pleading; or

(2) if the pleading requires a response, within 21 days after service of a responsive pleading or 21 days after service of a motion to dismiss, a motion for a more definite statement, or a motion to strike, whichever is earlier.

b. In situations in which a party is not entitled to amend as a matter of course, a pleading may be amended with the written consent of the opposing party, or with the leave of the court.

(1) Leave to amend must be freely given when justice requires. In deciding whether to grant a request to amend, the court will consider:

(a) the reason for the delay in raising the matter to be raised by the amendment; and

(b) the prejudice to the opposing party caused by the delay.

c. If a party objects at trial to evidence as not being within the scope of the issues raised in the pleadings, the court may permit the pleadings to be amended to conform to the evidence.

d. A response to an amended pleading is required if the original pleading required a response.

e. **Doctrine of Relation Back**

(1) Under the **doctrine of relation back**, the court will treat an amendment to a pleading as though it had been filed with the original pleading.

(2) An amendment to a pleading that adds a new claim will be considered filed on the date in which the original complaint was filed as long as the amendment asserts a claim or defense that

arose out of the same conduct, transaction, or occurrence as the original claim [Fed. R. Civ. P. 15(c)].

(3) An amendment to a pleading that adds a new party will be considered filed on the date in which the original complaint was filed as long as [Id.]:

(a) the amendment asserts a claim or defense that arose out of the same conduct, transaction, or occurrence as the original claim;

(b) the party to be added by the amendment received notice of the original action within 90 days of service of the claim such that it will not be prejudiced in defending on the merits; and

(c) the party to be added knew, or should have known, that the original action would have been asserted against it, but for a mistake concerning the proper party's identity.

B. Rule 11

1. Every pleading, written motion, and other paper filed with the court must be signed by at least one attorney of record in the attorney's name, or by a party personally, if the party is not represented by an attorney [Fed. R. Civ. P. 11].
   a. The signed document must state the signer's address, e-mail address, and telephone number.
   b. The court must strike an unsigned paper unless the omission is promptly corrected after it is called to the attorney's or party's attention.
   c. Rule 11 does not apply to discovery matter, whether it is a discovery request, response, motion or any other matter, although other rules may be applied to abusive discovery.
2. The attorney or unrepresented party who presents to the court a pleading, written motion, or other document certifies that to the best of the person's knowledge, information, and belief, formed after an inquiry reasonable under the circumstances that:
   a. the document is not being presented for any improper purpose, such as to harass, cause unnecessary delay, or needlessly increase the cost of litigation;
   b. the claims, defenses, and other legal contentions are warranted by existing law or by a nonfrivolous argument for extending, modifying, or reversing existing law or for establishing new law;
   c. the factual contentions have evidentiary support or will likely have evidentiary support after a reasonable opportunity for further investigation or discovery; and
   d. the denials of factual contentions are either warranted on the evidence or are reasonably based on belief or a lack of information.

   EXAMPLE: A brings a lawsuit against B for false light invasion of privacy. A's state has never recognized a cause of action for false light, but A argues that, under existing precedent, the courts of the state would likely recognize such an action. A has not violated Rule 11, even if his action is ultimately unsuccessful.

3. If the court finds that any of the above representations are untrue, it has discretion to impose sanctions on the party or the party's attorney. Sanctions are ordered after notice to the offending party and an opportunity to be heard.

   EXAMPLE: C brings a lawsuit against D for employment discrimination, claiming that C's application for employment was denied. C never applied for a job with D. The court may order sanctions against C.

   a. A party may not file a motion for sanctions without first serving the motion upon the opposing party and providing the opposing party with 21 days to withdraw or correct the offending pleading, written motion, or other paper (this is known as the **safe harbor rule**).
   b. A court may *sua sponte* issue an order to show cause why conduct described in the order does not violate Rule 11.
   c. The nature of the sanction must be limited to "what suffices to deter repetition of the conduct or comparable conduct by others."
   d. An order imposing sanctions must describe the sanctioned conduct and explain the basis for the sanctions.

C. Provisional Relief

1. Purpose

a. Provisional relief is available to maintain the status quo and prevent irreparable damage or wasting of assets during litigation or pending arbitration.
b. Provisional relief consists of two remedies:
   (1) temporary restraining orders (TROs); and
   (2) preliminary injunctions.
c. Both are extraordinary remedies as they are issued prior to a decision on the merits and provide immediate or quick but short-term injunctive relief.
   (1) The temporary restraining order is used in an emergency situation, when the injunction must issue before any hearing, and lasts only a few days, generally long enough for the parties to seek a preliminary injunction.
   (2) The preliminary injunction, if granted, will last until a decision on the merits, however long that may take.

2. Standard for Granting

a. A party seeking either a temporary restraining order or a preliminary injunction must first establish [Forsyth County v. United States Army Corps of Eng'rs, 633 F.3d 1032]:
   (1) a substantial likelihood of success on the merits;
   (2) irreparable harm will be suffered unless the remedy sought is issued;
   (3) the harm to the plaintiff if the temporary restraining order or preliminary injunction is denied is greater than the harm to the defendant if the remedy is granted; and
   (4) the provisional remedy, if granted, will not be adverse to the public interest.

b. A court may issue a temporary restraining order or a preliminary injunction only if the moving party gives security sufficient to cover the costs and damages sustained by any party who is wrongfully enjoined or restrained [Fed. R. Civ. P. 65(c)].

3. **Notice**

a. **Temporary Restraining Order**

(1) A court may issue a temporary restraining order without written or oral notice to the adverse party [Fed. R. Civ. P. 65(b)(1)].

(a) If a temporary restraining order is issued without notice, a motion for a preliminary injunction must be set for hearing at the earliest possible time, taking precedence over all other matters [Fed. R. Civ. P. 65(b)(3)].

(b) If the party who obtained the temporary restraining order does not proceed with the motion for a preliminary injunction, the restraining order must be dissolved.

(2) Temporary restraining orders will issue without notice only if:

(a) specific facts in an affidavit or verified complaint clearly show that immediate and irreparable injury, loss, or damage will result to the movant before the adverse party can be heard in opposition; and

(b) the movant's attorney certifies in writing any efforts made to give notice and the reasons why notice should not be required.

(3) Every temporary restraining order issued without notice must [Fed. R. Civ. P. 65(b)(2)]:

(a) state the date and hour it was issued;

(b) describe the injury and state why it is irreparable;

(c) state why the order was issued without notice; and

(d) be promptly filed in the clerk's office and entered in the record.

(4) A temporary restraining order issued without notice expires at the time set by the court.

(a) The time for expiration must not exceed 14 days after entry.

(b) The court may, for good cause, extend the duration for a like period or the adverse party may consent to a longer extension. The reasons for an extension must be entered in the record.

b. **Preliminary Injunction**

(1) A preliminary injunction may only be issued by a court on notice to the adverse party [Fed. R. Civ. P. 65(a)(1)].

(2) Before or after beginning a hearing on a motion for a preliminary injunction, the court may advance the trial on the merits and consolidate it with the hearing on the injunction.

(a) The court must preserve any party's right to a jury trial.

(b) Whether or not consolidation is ordered, any evidence entered on the motion for a preliminary injunction that would be admissible at trial becomes part of the trial record. This evidence need not be repeated at trial.

4. **Content and Scope of Relief**
    a. Every order granting a preliminary injunction or temporary restraining order must [Fed. R. Civ. P. 65(d)(1)]:
        (1) state the reasons why it was issued;
        (2) state its terms specifically; and
        (3) describe in reasonable detail the act or acts restrained or required. The description may not be a reference to the complaint or other document.
    b. The order will only bind the following parties after actual notice is received, whether by personal service or otherwise [Fed. R. Civ. P. 65(d)(2)]:
        (1) the parties;
        (2) the parties' officers, servants, agents, employees, and attorneys; and
        (3) any persons who are in active concert or participation with anyone described above otherwise.

D. Joinder of Claims and Parties

1. **Multiple Claims by Single Claimant against Single Defendant**
    a. A party may join as many claims in a single action as the party has against an opposing party [Fed. R. Civ. P. 18].
    b. There is no requirement that all of the claims in a complaint be related. The goal of joining all claims in one action is to achieve a complete resolution of all disputes between the parties.
        (1) For convenience, to avoid prejudice, or to expedite and economize, the court may order a separate trial of one or more separate issues, claims, cross-claims, counterclaims, or third-party claims. When ordering a separate trial, the court must preserve any federal right to a jury trial [Fed. R. Civ. P. 42(b)].
        (2) Federal joinder of claims is usually permissive, but it is compelled when the failure to join could result in splitting a cause of action. The doctrine of claim preclusion prevents relitigation of a claim.
        (3) Rule 18 addresses pleadings only. It cannot expand the jurisdiction of a federal court, if there is not jurisdiction over the claim otherwise. If supplemental jurisdiction is needed, then the parties must still show that their additional claims "are so related to claims in the action within such original jurisdiction that they form part of the same case or controversy" [28 U.S. Code § 1367(a)].

2. **Counterclaims**
    a. A **counterclaim** may be brought by any party against any other opposing party and can be compulsory or permissive.
        (1) A **compulsory counterclaim** is one that arises out of the same transaction or occurrence as the original claim in the lawsuit.

EXAMPLE: Plaintiff brings a breach of contract action against Defendant, for failure to pay for construction work done by Plaintiff. Defendant's claim that the work was done negligently, and caused Defendant to sustain personal injuries, is a compulsory counterclaim.

(a) A failure to raise a compulsory counterclaim waives the right to assert the claim in any future action.

(b) The federal court has supplemental jurisdiction over a compulsory counterclaim even in the absence of an independent basis for federal jurisdiction [28 U.S.C. § 1367(a)].

(2) A **permissive counterclaim** is any claim that a party has against an opposing party that does not arise out of the same transaction or occurrence that is the subject matter of the opposing party's claim.

EXAMPLE: Plaintiff sues Defendant for breach of contract for failure to paint Plaintiff's house. Defendant's personal injury claim against Plaintiff that arose out of a later traffic accident is a permissive counterclaim.

(a) A party is not required to assert a permissive counterclaim.

(b) Federal courts do not have supplemental jurisdiction over permissive counterclaims, because they do not arise out of the same transaction or occurrence as the original claim. There must be an independent ground for federal jurisdiction before the federal court will hear a permissive counterclaim.

3. **Cross-Claims**

a. A **cross-claim** is a claim filed by a party against a co-party (not opposing party). Cross-claims may be brought by any party against any co-party. In order for the court to have jurisdiction, the cross-claim must either have an independent basis for jurisdiction (either federal-question or diversity) or arise out of the same transaction or occurrence as the original claim or a counterclaim.

EXAMPLE: A sues B and C for failure to complete a construction project as promised. B claims that C breached a contract with B to perform certain work on the project. B may bring a cross-claim against C.

(1) A cross-claim may include a claim that the party against whom it is asserted is or may be liable for all or part of the claim asserted in the action against the cross-claimant.

EXAMPLE: A sues B, a surgeon, and C, an anesthesiologist, for medical malpractice. C may bring a cross-claim against B, based on C's claim that the damages sustained by A were entirely B's fault.

(2) The federal court has supplemental jurisdiction over a cross-claim even in the absence of an independent basis for federal jurisdiction, because the cross-claim arises out of the same transaction or occurrence as the original claim [28 U.S.C. § 1367(a)].

4. **Impleader Claims**

a. After a defendant to an action has served her answer, that defendant may proceed against a non-party who may be liable for all or part of the plaintiff's claim against the defendant [Fed. R. Civ. P. 14].

b. Impleader thus allows a defending party to shift all or part of the liability owed to the plaintiff to a new party who is or may be liable for it.

EXAMPLE: A sues B for injuries she sustained when B hit her while driving his car. B claims that he hit A because the steering mechanism on his car was damaged when C, a mechanic, did faulty repair work. B may proceed against C.

c. The two most important impleader claims are contribution and indemnity claims.

(1) A **contribution claim** is a claim against a joint tortfeasor that shifts part of the defendant's liability to a new party.

(2) An **indemnity claim** is a claim that shifts all of the defendant's liability to a new party (e.g., an insurance claim).

d. The defendant must file a third-party summons and complaint with the court where the original action is pending. The defendant becomes the third-party plaintiff.

(1) Service on the non-party makes that party the third-party defendant.

(2) A defendant may file a third-party complaint any time within 14 days of filing her answer. After that, third-party complaints may be filed only with leave of court.

(3) When the defendant brings in a third-party, the plaintiff may amend his original complaint to assert claims against the third-party defendant.

e. A plaintiff may file a third-party complaint to bring in a third-party defendant if a counterclaim has been asserted against the plaintiff and there is a basis for the plaintiff to argue that a third party is liable for all or part of the liability pursuant to the counterclaim.

f. Third-party defendants have the same rights as any other party to the action. These rights include the right to:

(1) service of process;

(2) file an answer to the third-party complaint (the answer may include any defenses that the third-party plaintiff asserted in her answer to the original complaint);

(3) assert counterclaims or cross-claims;

(4) implead additional non-parties by third-party complaint; and

(5) appeal orders or final judgment in the action.

g. The court may dismiss a third-party complaint without prejudice, or order a separate trial of the third-party claim or any separate issue within it, if it finds that the controversy between a third-party plaintiff and third-party defendant would unduly delay the determination of the original action or prejudice a substantial right of one of the parties.

5. **Permissive Joinder of Parties**

a. Permissive joinder allows multiple plaintiffs to join together in a single action and allows multiple defendants to be sued in a single action.

b. Multiple persons may be joined together as plaintiffs or defendants in one action if [Fed. R. Civ. P. 20]:

(1) the joined parties claim relief (if plaintiffs) or face liability (if defendants) that arises out of the same transaction or occurrence; and

(2) any question of law or fact is common to the joined parties.

EXAMPLE: A and B are injured while they are passengers on an airplane that makes a bad landing. They may join their claims in the same action.

6. **Compulsory Joinder of Parties**

a. A person who is subject to service of process and whose joinder will not deprive the court of subject-matter jurisdiction must be joined as a necessary party if [Fed. R. Civ. P. 19]:

(1) in that party's absence, the court cannot grant complete relief among existing parties; or

(2) the party claims an interest relating to the subject of the action, and an adjudication without the party may:

(a) as a practical matter, impair or impede that party's ability to protect his interests; or

(b) leave an existing party subject to a substantial risk of incurring double, multiple, or otherwise inconsistent obligations.

EXAMPLE: P leased a valuable painting to D. P believed the lease term was 3 years, and D believed it was 4. After possessing the painting for 2.5 years, D leased the painting to X for 1 year. When the 3-year mark arrived, P brought suit to reclaim the painting. X is a necessary party because it has an interest in the subject matter of the litigation (the painting), because D could be subject to duplicative liability (D could end up being liable to both P and X) and because the court cannot order the painting returned unless the person with the painting (X) is within the jurisdiction of the court.

EXAMPLE: A is injured while a passenger on a train owned and operated by B. She was injured when another train, owned and operated by C, collided with the train she was riding on. A sued B. B argues that C is a necessary party and must be joined. This argument will fail. As a rule, joint tortfeasors are not necessary parties. There is no mandatory joinder in this situation.

b. If a person who is required to be joined cannot be joined for jurisdictional reasons, the court must determine whether, in equity and good conscience, the action should proceed among the existing parties or be dismissed. The factors for the court to consider include:

(1) the extent to which a judgment rendered in the person's absence might prejudice that person or the existing parties;

(2) the extent to which any prejudice could be lessened or avoided by:

(a) protective provisions in the judgment;

(b) shaping the relief; or

(c) other measures;

(3) whether a judgment rendered in the person's absence would be adequate; and

(4) whether the plaintiff would have an adequate remedy if the action were dismissed for nonjoinder.

7. **Interpleader**

a. **Interpleader** is used where a plaintiff has some holding that would expose the plaintiff to multiple liability from adverse claims. The stakeholding party, or "stakeholder," can commence an action for interpleader to resolve liability where there are two or more adverse claimants. Interpleader is only applicable where multiple claims demand the same thing or obligation—usually, a piece of property, prize, or, most commonly, the proceeds of an insurance policy.

b. Interpleader is either rule interpleader, authorized by the Federal Rules of Civil Procedure, or statutory interpleader.

EXAMPLE: B dies leaving a life insurance policy, the proceeds of which are claimed by his wife, ex-wife, and two children. The insurance company is the stakeholder. As a neutral third party, it may bring an action in court to determine the rights of each claimant.

c. Rule interpleader is authorized by Fed. R. Civ. P. 22.

(1) **Rule interpleader** may be initiated pursuant to Rule 22 by any person who may be exposed to multiple liability.

(2) In an interpleader under Rule 22, the stakeholder may initiate the claim or invoke the rule interpleader by his own initiative. The stakeholder may also initiate interpleader by counter-claiming or cross-claiming against a claimant in an action that has already commenced against the stakeholder.

(3) Rule interpleader has no effect on jurisdictional or venue requirements. Subject-matter jurisdiction must still be established through diversity jurisdiction, federal question jurisdiction, or supplemental jurisdiction.

d. Statutory interpleader is authorized by 28 U.S.C. § 1335.

(1) **Statutory interpleader** allows a person holding property which may be claimed, or is claimed by two or more adverse claimants, to interplead all possible claimants.

(2) Once a statutory interpleader suit is commenced, the court may restrain all of the claimants from commencing any related action or continuing any other action that has already begun.

(3) Statutory interpleader has the following advantages over rule interpleader:

(a) nationwide service of process is available for statutory interpleader, but not for rule interpleader;

(b) the federal court has diversity jurisdiction as long as there is minimal diversity between the adverse claimants and an amount in controversy over $500; and

EXAMPLE: When A died, she left $1,000 in an account with Bank. The money in the account is claimed by D, her surviving husband, and E, her daughter. D is a citizen of the same state as Bank, but E lives in a different state. The federal court has diversity jurisdiction to hear a statutory interpleader action brought by Bank.

(c) venue is established where any one of the adverse claimants resides.

8. **Intervention**

a. Intervention allows a non-party to assert a right or interest in an ongoing action. If the non-party can meet the test for intervention as a matter of right, then the court must allow the party to intervene. A non-party may also be allowed to intervene by permission of the court.

EXAMPLE: A conservation group may seek leave to intervene in an action against a developer.

b. The purpose of intervention is to enable a person outside an action to enter the suit to present an interest, a claim, or a defense relevant to the issues presented by the existing parties.

(1) Intervention can contribute to judicial economy and protect a non-party from having its interest adversely affected by the litigation conducted without that person's participation.

(2) Intervention can also delay or complicate the litigation by involving parties that the plaintiff chose not to join in the first instance.

c. In order to intervene in an action, a non-party's request for intervention must be timely. The factors the court may consider in deciding whether the application was timely are:

(1) the length of time the non-party knew or should have known about its interest in the case before making the application;

(2) the extent of prejudice that the existing parties may suffer as a result of the delay; and

(3) the likelihood and gravity of the prejudice the non-party may suffer if the application is denied.

d. Upon a finding by the court that a non-party's application was timely, the non-party must be allowed to intervene in an action if [Fed. R. Civ. P. 24]:

(1) a federal statute confers an absolute right of the party to intervene; or

(2) a non-party is asserting a protectable interest relating to the property or transaction involved in the lawsuit, and:

(a) the non-party is so situated that disposing of the action may as a practical matter impair or impede its ability to protect its interest; and

(b) the non-party's interests are not adequately represented by existing parties.

EXAMPLE: The United States may seek to intervene as a matter of right in a discrimination action by students against a board of education where plaintiffs request only monetary damages and do not represent the government's interest in enforcing anti-discrimination laws.

e. If a non-party may not intervene in an action as a matter of right, the court may permit intervention if:

(1) a federal statute allows a conditional right to intervention; or

(2) the non-party has a claim or defense that shares a common question of law or fact with the primary action.

f. The trial court has discretion to grant permissive leave to intervene. In making its determination, the court will consider:

(1) the complexity of the existing action and the complexity of the applicant's claim or defense;

(2) the length of time the primary action has been pending; and

(3) how much the existing parties will be delayed or prejudiced by the addition of the applicant's claim or defense.

9. **Class Actions**

a. A class action may be maintained by a party if the court finds that each of the following requirements have been met [Fed. R. Civ. P. 23]:

(1) numerosity;

(a) The numerosity requirement is met if the number of members of the class is so numerous that separate joinder of each member is impracticable.

(b) No particular number is needed, nor is the number of potential class members determinative of whether the court will allow an action to proceed as a class action.

(2) commonality;

(a) The commonality requirement is met if there are questions of law or fact common to the class.

(b) Rule 23 does not require that all questions of law and fact be common, nor that the common questions predominate. Instead, the party who seeks class certification must show that the class members have suffered the same injury [Wal-Mart Stores, Inc. v. Dukes, 564 U.S. 338 (2011)]. Specifically, there must be a common contention that is capable of a class-wide resolution in one stroke [Id.]. Simply showing common facts or a common accusational type will not be enough to satisfy the commonality requirement.

(3) typicality; and
   (a) The typicality requirement is met if the claims or defenses of the representative party are typical of those raised by each member of the class.
   (b) To meet this requirement, the representative's interest in prosecuting his own case must simultaneously tend to advance the interests of the absent class members. This means that the plaintiff's claim cannot be so different from the claims of potential class members that those class members' claims will not be advanced by the plaintiff's proof of his own individual claim.

(4) adequacy of representation.
   (a) The adequacy of representation requirement is met if the representative party can fairly and adequately protect and represent the interests of each member of the class.
   (b) The representative party must have standing to bring her claim.

b. In addition to the four requirements in Rule 23, courts will allow an action to be maintained as a class action only if at least one of the following is true:
   (1) the prosecution of separate actions would create a risk of:
      (a) inconsistent or varying judgments for individual class members that would establish incompatible standards of conduct for the party opposing the class; or
      (b) judgments for individual members of the class that would substantially impede or impair the ability of other members to protect their interests;
   (2) the party opposing the class has acted or refused to act on grounds that are generally applicable to the class as a whole; or
   (3) the court finds that common questions predominate over individual questions, and class representation is superior to other methods for adjudicating the controversy. Factors used to determine common questions include:
      (a) pending individual litigation;
      (b) the interests of class members in individually controlling litigation of claims or defenses;
      (c) the desirability of concentrating litigation in the forum; and
      (d) the difficulties of managing the class action.

c. Federal rules for class certification apply to all class actions in federal court, including those based on diversity. State laws on class certification are superseded [Shady Grove Orthopedic Associates v. Allstate Insurance Co., 559 U.S. 393 (2010)].

d. A motion to certify a class action must be made "at an early practicable time" after the suit is commenced [Fed. R. Civ. P. 23(c)]. Local rules may provide a specific deadline for a class certification motion.
   (1) The order permitting a class action must describe the class.

(2) When appropriate, the court may limit the class to those members who do not request exclusion from the class within the specified time after the notice.

EXAMPLE: A class certification order certifies a class of all persons who bought a computer with a certain operating system who do not inform the court that they do not wish to be a part of the action within 90 days of the class certification order.

e. An action may be brought or maintained as a class action with respect to any particular issue, or a class may be divided into subclasses with each subclass treated as a class.

f. The court may direct appropriate notice to class members.

(1) For classes certified as a result of common questions of law or fact, notice is required and must include:

(a) the nature of the action;

(b) the definition of the certified class;

(c) the class claims, issues, or defenses;

(d) the ability of a class member to make an appearance;

(e) the ability of a class member to request exclusion from the class; and

(f) the binding effect of a judgment on all members of the class.

EXAMPLE: Notice to potential class members in an action against the seller of computer operating systems must inform members that if they do not opt out of the class, they will be bound by the judgment in the class action, even if they did not file an individual appearance.

(2) Where a class action is brought primarily for injunctive or declaratory relief, notice need not be given to the class unless the court finds it necessary in order to protect the class.

g. In every case, the court must have personal jurisdiction over every defendant and each of the plaintiffs named in the action.

(1) The federal court is not required to have personal jurisdiction over absent members of the plaintiff class as long as they receive adequate notice of the pendency of the action and are afforded the opportunity to opt out of the class [Phillips Petroleum Co. v. Shutts, 472 U.S. 797 (1985)].

(2) It is unclear whether the court must have personal jurisdiction over the absent members of the plaintiff classes where there is no notice and/or opportunity to opt out of the class.

h. Class actions based on diversity jurisdiction are governed by the Class Action Fairness Act (CAFA) passed in 2005, which has transformed the doctrine in cases founded on diversity jurisdiction.

(1) Prior to CAFA, diversity jurisdiction required complete diversity between all of the named representative plaintiffs and all of the defendants.

(2) CAFA expands federal subject-matter jurisdiction to include classes where:

(a) the class has more than 100 persons;

(b) at least one member of the class is diverse from at least one defendant; and

(c) the total amount in controversy exceeds $5 million.

(3) CAFA's broad grant of subject-matter jurisdiction excludes local controversies, certain civil rights cases, and other categories of cases.

i. Class actions may not be dismissed or compromised without court approval. In evaluating a settlement proposal, a court must consider whether it is fair, reasonable, and in the best interests of the individuals affected by it [Fed. R. Civ. P. 23(e)].

j. A court that certifies a class action must appoint class counsel to represent the class [Fed. R. Civ. P. 23(g)]. The court may deny certification if suitable counsel is not found.

k. Counsel for the successful representative parties typically will be awarded an appropriate fee. If a fee may not be awarded pursuant to an applicable fee-shifting provision, the court may award fees out of the common fund created by the recovery from the defendant.

l. A court of appeals may permit an appeal from an order granting or denying class action certification if the petition for appeal is filed within 14 days after the order is entered [Fed. R. Civ. P. 23(f)].

E. Pretrial Conferences and Orders

1. Discovery Planning Conference

a. Rule 26(f) requires the parties to meet and have a discovery planning conference as soon as practicable, but at least 21 days before a scheduling order is to be held or is due under Rule 16(b) [Fed. R. Civ. P. 26(f)].

b. In the discovery conference, the parties must [Id.]:

(1) discuss the nature and basis of their claims and defenses and the possibilities of timely settling or resolving the case;

(2) make or arrange for the mandatory disclosures required by Rule 26(a)(1);

(3) discuss any issues about preserving discoverable information; and

(4) develop a proposed discovery plan.

c. A written report outlining the proposed discovery plan must then be submitted to the court within 14 days after the discovery conference.

2. Pretrial Conferences

a. After a Rule 26(f) conference has been held, the court may order the attorneys and any unrepresented parties to appear for one or more pretrial conferences for such purposes as [Fed. R. Civ. P. 16(a)]:

(1) expediting disposition of the action;

(2) establishing early and continuing control so that the case will not be protracted because of lack of management;

(3) discouraging wasteful pretrial activities;

(4) improving the quality of the trial through more thorough preparation; and

(5) facilitating settlement.

b. Except in categories of actions exempted by local rule, the district judge—or a magistrate judge when authorized by local rule—must issue a scheduling order that limits the time to join other parties, amend the pleadings, complete discovery, and file motions. A schedule may be modified only for good cause and with the judge's consent [Fed. R. Civ. P. 16(b)].

c. The scheduling order must be issued within the earlier of [Id.]:

(1) 90 days after any defendant has been served with the complaint; or

(2) 60 days after any defendant has appeared.

d. At any pretrial conference, the court may consider and take appropriate action on the following matters [Fed. R. Civ. P. 16(c)]:

(1) formulating and simplifying the issues, and eliminating frivolous claims or defenses;

(2) amending the pleadings if necessary or desirable;

(3) obtaining admissions and stipulations about facts and documents to avoid unnecessary proof, and ruling in advance on the admissibility of evidence;

(4) avoiding unnecessary proof and cumulative evidence, and limiting the use of testimony under the Federal Rules of Evidence;

(5) determining the appropriateness and timing of summary adjudication;

(6) controlling and scheduling discovery;

(7) identifying witnesses and documents, scheduling the filing and exchange of any pretrial briefs, and setting dates for further conferences and for trial;

(8) referring matters to a magistrate judge or a master;

(9) settling the case and using special procedures to assist in resolving the dispute when authorized by statute or local rule;

(10) determining the form and content of the pretrial order;

(11) disposing of pending motions;

(12) adopting special procedures for managing potentially difficult or protracted actions that may involve complex issues, multiple parties, difficult legal questions, or unusual proof problems;

(13) ordering a separate trial of a claim, counterclaim, cross-claim, third-party claim, or particular issue;

(14) ordering the presentation of evidence;

(15) establishing a reasonable limit on the time allowed to present evidence; and

(16) facilitating in other ways the just, speedy, and inexpensive disposition of the action.

e. After any pretrial conference, the court should issue an order reciting the action taken, which controls the course of the action unless the court modifies it [Fed. R. Civ. P. 16(d)].

f. The court may hold a final pretrial conference to formulate a trial plan, including a plan to facilitate the admission of evidence. The conference must be held as close to the start of trial as is reasonable, and must be attended by at least one attorney who will conduct the trial for each party and by any unrepresented party. The court may modify the order issued after a final pretrial conference only to prevent manifest injustice [Fed. R. Civ. P. 16(e)].

g. On motion or on its own, the court may issue sanctions if a party or its attorney:

(1) fails to appear at a scheduling or other pretrial conference;

(2) is substantially unprepared to participate—or does not participate in good faith—in the conference; or

(3) fails to obey a scheduling or other pretrial order.

(a) Instead of, or in addition to, any other sanction, the court must order the party, its attorney, or both to pay the reasonable expenses—including attorney's fees—incurred because of any noncompliance with this rule, unless the noncompliance was substantially justified or other circumstances make an award of expenses unjust [Fed. R. Civ. P. 16(f)].

F. Discovery

1. Overview

a. The primary purpose of the pleading stage is to provide notice to the parties; thus, the facts may not be stated in detail in the pleadings.

b. The facts surrounding a cause of action come to light during discovery.

c. The primary function of the discovery process is to provide litigants with an opportunity to obtain and review all of the pertinent evidence prior to trial.

d. There are mandatory disclosure obligations as well as specific discovery devices that are designed to elicit information within the permissible scope of discovery.

e. In general, discovery is initiated by the parties. A court will become involved only when there is a discovery dispute that cannot be resolved by the parties.

2. Mandatory Disclosures

a. Initial Disclosures

(1) With limited exceptions, parties are required to disclose some information as a matter of course upon the commencement of the litigation, without waiting for a discovery request. Mandatory disclosure is required by both parties for the following information [Fed. R. Civ. P. 26(a)(1)]:

(a) the name (and if known, address and telephone number) of individuals likely to have discoverable information, along with the subject of that information, that the disclosing party may use to support its claims or defenses (unless the use would be solely for impeachment);

EXAMPLE: A plaintiff must disclose to the defendant the names of all witnesses to an accident that is the subject of the plaintiff's action that the plaintiff may use to support his claim.

(b) a copy or description of all documents, electronically stored information, and tangible things that the disclosing party has in its possession, custody, or control and may use to support its claims or defenses (unless the use would be solely for impeachment);

(c) a computation of damages claimed by the disclosing party, together with supporting materials; and

(d) insurance agreements under which an insurance company may be liable to satisfy all or part of a possible judgment.

(2) The initial mandatory disclosures must be made within 14 days after the Rule 26 discovery conference. A party must make these disclosures based upon the information then reasonably available.

b. **Expert Disclosures**

(1) A party must also disclose the identity of any witness that may testify at trial [Fed. R. Civ. P. 26(a)(2)(A)].

(2) If the witness is retained or specially employed to provide expert testimony in the case, or one whose duties as the party's employee regularly involve giving expert testimony, the disclosure must be accompanied by the expert's final written report. The report must contain [Fed. R. Civ. P. 26(a)(2)(B]:

(a) all opinions, including the basis and reasons for them, that the witness will testify to;

(b) all facts and data considered by the witness in forming the opinions;

(c) any exhibits that will be used;

(d) the witness's qualifications, including a list of all publications authored in the previous 10 years;

(e) a list of all cases during the previous 4 years in which witness testified as an expert; and

(f) a statement of the compensation to be paid for the study and testimony in the case.

(3) If the witness does not need to provide a written report, the disclosure must state [Fed. R. Civ. P. 26(a)(2)(C]:

(a) the subject matter on which the witness will testify; and

(b) a summary of the facts and opinions that the witness will testify to.

(4) Unless provided otherwise by court order, these disclosures must be made [Fed. R. Civ. P. 26(a)(2)(D]:

(a) at least 90 days before trial; or

(b) if the evidence is intended solely to contradict or rebut evidence on the same subject matter identified by another party through the mandatory witness disclosure, within 30 days after the party's disclosure.

c. **Pretrial Disclosures**

(1) In addition to the mandatory disclosures discussed above, at least 30 days before trial each party must provide to the other parties and promptly file the following information about evidence that it may present at trial [Fed. R. Civ. P. 26(a)(3)(A)]:

(a) the name (and if not previously provided the contact information) for each witness the party expects to present and those it may call if needed;

(b) a list of witnesses whose testimony will be presented through a deposition; and

(c) a list of documents or physical evidence the party expects to present and may present if need be.

d. **Supplementation**

(1) A party must supplement a discovery response with any information that would have been subject to the mandatory disclosure requirement [Fed. R. Civ. P. 26(e)].

(2) Failure to comply may lead to the exclusion of that evidence at trial [Fed. R. Civ. P. 37(c)(1)].

EXAMPLE: Using the above example, the plaintiff must supplement its witness list if the plaintiff learns of any additional witnesses after it first discloses the list to the defendant.

3. **Scope of Discovery**

a. In general, a party is entitled to demand the discovery of any matter that is [Fed. R. Civ. P. 26(b)]:

(1) nonprivileged;

(2) relevant to any party's claim or defense; and

(3) proportional to the needs of the case.

b. The factors to consider when determining whether a matter is proportional to the needs of the case include the importance of the issues at stake in the action, the amount in controversy, the parties' relative access to relevant information, the parties' resources, the importance of the matter sought in resolving the issues, and whether the burden or expense of the proposed discovery outweighs its likely benefit [Id.].

c. Information is relevant if it is likely to make any fact in dispute more or less likely to be true, regardless of whether the information would be admissible at trial. Information within this scope of discovery need not be admissible into evidence in order to be discoverable [Fed. R. Civ. P. 26(b)(1)].

EXAMPLE: Plaintiff may question Defendant about a document even if that document would not be admissible into evidence, as long as the question is relevant.

d. If the requested information can be obtained from another source that is more convenient, less burdensome, or less expensive, a party may be required to obtain it from the other source. A request for electronically stored information could be particularly vulnerable to this criticism.

e. **Privilege**

(1) Privileged matter is not discoverable.

(2) A privilege may arise under the laws of evidence or constitutional principles. The most frequently invoked privilege is the attorney-client privilege, which precludes the discovery of confidential communications between an attorney and her client for the purposes of obtaining or rendering legal advice.

EXAMPLE: Defendant may object to Plaintiff's request for attorney invoices as being privileged.

(3) Many states also recognize some combination of the following privileges:

(a) priest-penitent;

(b) doctor-patient;

(c) psychotherapist-patient; and

(d) spousal.

f. **Work-Product**

(1) A party may not discover documents and tangible objects prepared in anticipation of litigation or for trial by or for another party or its representative, including an attorney, consultant, surety, indemnitor, insurer, or agent [Fed. R. Civ. P. 26(b)(3)(A)]. This is known as an attorney's **work-product**.

(2) However, such materials are still discoverable if [Id.]:

(a) they are otherwise discoverable under Rule 26(b)(1); and

(b) the party shows both substantial need for the material to prepare its case and it cannot, without undue hardship, obtain their substantial equivalent elsewhere.

(3) If the court orders the materials discoverable, the court must protect from disclosure the attorney's mental impressions, conclusions, opinions, or legal theories, which always remain privileged [Fed. R. Civ. P. 26(b)(3)(B)].

g. **Experts**

(1) A party may depose any person who has been identified as an expert who is expected to testify at trial, but only to a limited extent because communications between an attorney and his expert are considered work-product.

(2) Besides the information contained in the mandatory expert report (discussed above) a party can also obtain communications relating to [Fed. R. Civ. P. 26(b)(4)(C)]:

(a) compensation for the expert's study or testimony;
(b) any facts or data provided by the attorney to the expert that the expert considered in forming her opinion; and
(c) any assumption the attorney provided and the expert relied on in forming her opinion.

(3) Expert reports that are prepared in draft (i.e., non-finalized) are also considered work-product.

(4) A party may not, by interrogatories or deposition, obtain facts known or opinions held by an expert retained in anticipation of litigation or to prepare for trial, but who is not expected to be called to testify at trial, unless the party shows exceptional circumstances under which it is impracticable to obtain the facts or opinions by any other means, or in the case of an expert who conducts a Rule 35 examination [Fed. R. Civ. P. 26(b)(4)(D)].

4. **Objections**

a. Parties who receive discovery requests that are beyond the scope of discovery (or are otherwise allegedly defective) can either object to the requests or request a protective order.

b. In the event of an objection, the party requesting discovery has at least two options:

(1) abandon or reframe the discovery request; or
(2) bring the dispute to the attention of the court by filing a motion to compel.

c. If the responding party requests a protective order, the party thereby brings the discovery dispute to the attention of the court.

5. **Discovery Devices**

a. **Depositions**

(1) Depositions permit the direct questioning of a party or witness under oath. They are typically conducted orally, and every word that is spoken is recorded verbatim and transcribed.

(2) A party may, by oral questions, depose any person, including a party, without leave of court except as provided in Rule 30(a)(2). The deponent's attendance may be compelled by subpoena under Rule 45 [Fed. R. Civ. P. 30(a)(1)].

(3) A party must obtain leave of court, and the court must grant leave to the extent consistent with Rule 26(b)(1) and (2) [Fed. R. Civ. P. 30(a)(2)]:

(a) if the parties have not stipulated to the deposition and:

1) the deposition would result in more than 10 depositions being taken under this rule or Rule 31 by the plaintiffs, or by the defendants, or by the third-party defendants;
2) the deponent has already been deposed in the case; or
3) the party seeks to take the deposition before the time specified in Rule 26(d), unless the party certifies in

the notice, with supporting facts, that the deponent is expected to leave the United States and be unavailable for examination in this country after that time; or

(b) if the deponent is confined in prison.

(4) The witness (called the deponent) is given an opportunity to review the transcript and make technical corrections [Fed. R. Civ. P. 30(e)].

(5) **Scheduling**

(a) A deposition may be scheduled on reasonable notice in writing. If the deponent is a party, the deposition is scheduled by a notice of deposition served on all counsel.

(b) The party requesting the deposition may ask the witness to bring documents to the deposition.

(c) If the deponent is a non-party, the party requesting the deposition must also provide for the attendance of the witness, usually by serving a subpoena.

(d) A deposition may not be used against a party at trial if the party received less than 14 days' notice of the deposition and promptly moved for a protective order that it not be taken, and the motion was still pending when the deposition was taken.

(6) Depositions of corporations are permitted. The corporation must designate one or more persons whose answers bind the corporation and who must have completed a reasonably diligent investigation prior to testifying.

EXAMPLE: A corporation could designate its financial officer to testify at a deposition concerning the corporation's financial statements.

(7) A party may take only 10 depositions in an action as a matter of right. The primary advantages of depositions vis-à-vis other discovery techniques include engaging in a spontaneous dialogue with the witness and assessing the demeanor and credibility of potential trial witnesses. The most significant disadvantage is the expense.

(8) **Use of Depositions in Court Proceedings**

(a) **In General**

1) In general, at a hearing or trial, all or part of a deposition may be used against a party on these conditions [Fed. R. Civ. P. 32(a)(1)]:

a) the party was present or represented at the taking of the deposition or had reasonable notice of it;

b) it is used to the extent it would be admissible under the Federal Rules of Evidence if the deponent were present and testifying; and

c) the use is allowed by Rule 32(a)(2) through (8).

2) Any party may use a deposition to contradict or impeach the testimony given by the deponent as a witness, or

for any other purpose allowed by the Federal Rules of Evidence [Fed. R. Civ. P. 32(a)(2)].

3) An adverse party may use for any purpose the deposition of a party or anyone who, when deposed, was the party's officer, director, managing agent, or designee [Fed. R. Civ. P. 32(a)(3)].
4) A party may use for any purpose the deposition of a witness, whether or not a party, if the court finds [Fed. R. Civ. P. 32(a)(4)]:
    a) that the witness is dead;
    b) that the witness is more than 100 miles from the place of hearing or trial or is outside the United States, unless it appears that the witness's absence was procured by the party offering the deposition;
    c) that the witness cannot attend or testify because of age, illness, infirmity, or imprisonment;
    d) that the party offering the deposition could not procure the witness's attendance by subpoena; or
    e) on motion and notice, that exceptional circumstances make it desirable—in the interest of justice and with due regard to the importance of live testimony in open court—to permit the deposition to be used.
5) A deposition must not be used against a party who, having received less than 14 days' notice of the deposition, promptly moved for a protective order under Rule 26(c)(1)(B) requesting that it not be taken or be taken at a different time or place—and this motion was still pending when the deposition was taken [Fed. R. Civ. P. 32(a)(5)(A)].
6) A deposition taken without leave of court under the unavailability provision of Rule 30(a)(2)(A)(iii) must not be used against a party who shows that, when served with the notice, it could not, despite diligent efforts, obtain an attorney to represent it at the deposition [Fed. R. Civ. P. 32(a)(5)(B)].
7) If a party offers in evidence only part of a deposition, an adverse party may require the offeror to introduce other parts that in fairness should be considered with the part introduced, and any party may itself introduce any other parts [Fed. R. Civ. P. 32(a)(6)].
8) Substituting a party under Rule 25 does not affect the right to use a deposition previously taken [Fed. R. Civ. P. 32(a)(7)].
9) A deposition lawfully taken and, if required, filed in any federal- or state-court action may be used in a later

action involving the same subject matter between the same parties, or their representatives or successors in interest, to the same extent as if taken in the later action, and may also be used as allowed by the Federal Rules of Evidence [Fed. R. Civ. P. 32(a)(8)].

(b) **Form of Presentation**

1) Unless the court orders otherwise, a party must provide a transcript of any deposition testimony the party offers, but may provide the court with the testimony in nontranscript form as well. On any party's request, deposition testimony offered in a jury trial for any purpose other than impeachment must be presented in nontranscript form, if available, unless the court for good cause orders otherwise [Fed. R. Civ. P. 32(c)].

(c) **Objections to Admissibility**

1) Subject to Rules 28(b) and 32(d)(3), an objection may be made at a hearing or trial to the admission of any deposition testimony that would be inadmissible if the witness were present and testifying [Fed. R. Civ. P. 32(b)].

(d) **Waivers of Objections**

1) An objection to an error or irregularity in a deposition notice is waived unless promptly served in writing on the party giving the notice [Fed. R. Civ. P. 32(d)(1)].

2) An objection based on disqualification of the officer before whom a deposition is to be taken is waived if not made [Fed. R. Civ. P. 32(d)(2)]:

   a) before the deposition begins; or

   b) promptly after the basis for disqualification becomes known or, with reasonable diligence, could have been known.

3) An objection to a deponent's competence—or to the competence, relevance, or materiality of testimony—is not waived by a failure to make the objection before or during the deposition, unless the ground for it might have been corrected at that time [Fed. R. Civ. P. 32(d)(3)(A)].

4) An objection to an error or irregularity at an oral examination is waived if [Fed. R. Civ. P. 32(d)(3)(B)]:

   a) it relates to the manner of taking the deposition, the form of a question or answer, the oath or affirmation, a party's conduct, or other matters that might have been corrected at that time; and

   b) it is not timely made during the deposition.

5) An objection to the form of a written question under Rule 31 is waived if not served in writing on the party submitting

the question within the time for serving responsive questions or, if the question is a recross-question, within seven days after being served with it [Fed. R. Civ. P. 32(d)(3)(C)].

6) An objection to how the officer transcribed the testimony—or prepared, signed, certified, sealed, endorsed, sent, or otherwise dealt with the deposition—is waived unless a motion to suppress is made promptly after the error or irregularity becomes known or, with reasonable diligence, could have been known [Fed. R. Civ. P. 32(d)(4)].

b. **Interrogatories**

(1) Interrogatories are written questions that must be answered by another party in writing under oath [Fed. R. Civ. P. 33].

EXAMPLE: The defendant serves interrogatories upon the plaintiff regarding information related to the time and place of a particular accident.

(2) Interrogatories may only be served on parties to an action.

(3) Each party may submit up to 25 questions on any other party.

(4) Interrogatories must be answered in writing, under oath, within 30 days after service of the interrogatories.

c. **Document Requests**

(1) A party may serve on any other party a request within the scope of Rule 26(b) [Fed. R. Civ. P. 34(a)]:

(a) to produce and permit the requesting party or its representative to inspect, copy, test, or sample the following items in the responding party's possession, custody, or control:

1) any designated documents or electronically stored information—including writings, drawings, graphs, charts, photographs, sound recordings, images, and other data or data compilations—stored in any medium from which information can be obtained either directly or, if necessary, after translation by the responding party into a reasonably usable form; or

2) any designated tangible things; or

(b) to permit entry onto designated land or other property possessed or controlled by the responding party, so that the requesting party may inspect, measure, survey, photograph, test, or sample the property or any designated object or operation on it.

(2) More than 21 days after the summons and complaint are served on a party, a request under Rule 34 may be delivered [Fed. R. Civ. P. 26(d)(2)]:

(a) to that party by any other party; and

(b) by that party to any plaintiff or to any other party that has been served.

(3) The request [Fed. R. Civ. P. 34(b)(1)]:

(a) must describe with reasonable particularity each item or category of items to be inspected;

(b) must specify a reasonable time, place, and manner for the inspection and for performing the related acts; and

(c) may specify the form or forms in which electronically stored information is to be produced.

(4) The party to whom the request is directed must respond in writing within 30 days after being served or—if the request was delivered under Rule 26(d)(2)—within 30 days after the parties' first Rule 26(f) conference. A shorter or longer time may be stipulated to under Rule 29 or be ordered by the court [Fed. R. Civ. P. 34(b)(2)(A)].

(5) For each item or category, the response must either state that inspection and related activities will be permitted as requested or state with specificity the grounds for objecting to the request, including the reasons [Fed. R. Civ. P. 34(b)(2)(B)].

(a) The responding party may state that it will produce copies of documents or of electronically stored information instead of permitting inspection. The production must then be completed no later than the time for inspection specified in the request or another reasonable time specified in the response.

(6) An objection must state whether any responsive materials are being withheld on the basis of that objection. An objection to part of a request must specify the part and permit inspection of the rest [Fed. R. Civ. P. 34(B)(2)(C)].

(7) The response may state an objection to a requested form for producing electronically stored information. If the responding party objects to a requested form—or if no form was specified in the request—the party must state the form or forms it intends to use [Fed. R. Civ. P. 34(B)(2)(D)].

(8) Unless otherwise stipulated or ordered by the court, these procedures apply to producing documents or electronically stored information [Fed. R. Civ. P. 34(b)(2)(E)]:

(a) a party must produce documents as they are kept in the usual course of business or must organize and label them to correspond to the categories in the request;

(b) if a request does not specify a form for producing electronically stored information, a party must produce it in a form or forms in which it is ordinarily maintained or in a reasonably usable form or forms; and

(c) a party need not produce the same electronically stored information in more than one form.

(9) As provided in Rule 45, a nonparty may be compelled to produce documents and tangible things or to permit an inspection [Fed. R. Civ. P. 34(c)].

EXAMPLE: A plaintiff may request minutes of the defendant's corporate board meetings for the previous five years.

d. **Requests for Admissions**

(1) A party may submit to any other party a request for admission of any matter within the scope of discovery [Fed. R. Civ. P. 36].

(2) Requests for admissions are typically "question and answer" statements that are used by either party to further explore specific contentions. Any request that is admitted is deemed established for all purposes in the litigation.

EXAMPLE: During a wrongful death lawsuit resulting from a car crash, the plaintiff may ask the defendant to admit that he was driving the Toyota involved in the crash. If the defendant makes the admission, the plaintiff will not have to prove that issue at trial.

(3) A party served with a request for admission has 30 days to respond.

e. **Physical and Mental Examinations**

(1) When a party's condition is in controversy, a physical or mental examination of the person may be requested [Fed. R. Civ. P. 35].

(2) Physical and mental examinations are the only discovery tools for which advance court approval is required. The court requires a showing of "good cause" for the examination.

EXAMPLE: If the plaintiff is claiming emotional distress, the defendant may request that the plaintiff submit to a psychological exam.

6. **E-discovery**

a. Electronic discovery (or e-discovery) refers to discovery regarding the exchange of electronically stored information, or ESI. The e-discovery process generally involves the following steps.

(1) Electronically stored data (and their custodians) are identified by counsel as potentially relevant for further analysis and review.

(2) ESI identified as potentially relevant is placed on a legal hold to ensure that the data cannot be destroyed.

(3) The data is transferred from a company to its legal counsel, who will determine relevance.

(4) Files are prepared to be loaded into a document review platform.

(5) Documents are reviewed for responsiveness to discovery requests and for privilege.

(6) Documents are turned over to opposing counsel, based on agreed-upon specifications.

b. **Procedure**

(1) A response in writing is required within 30 days after being served or, if the request was delivered under Rule 26(d)(2), within 30 days after the parties' first Rule 26(f) conference [Fed. R. Civ. P. 37(b)(2)].

(2) Instead of permitting inspection of documents or ESI, the responding party can produce copies of the documents or the ESI. The production of the copies of ESI must take place within the same timeframe as the requested inspection or another reasonable time specified in the response [Fed. R. Civ. P. 37(b)(2)(B)]. ESI does not have to be reproduced in the form requested. If a party objects to the requested form of producing ESI, or if the form is specified in the request, the response must state the form the party intends to use [Fed. R. Civ. P. 37(b)(C)].

(3) Unless otherwise stipulated or ordered by the court, these procedures apply to producing documents or ESI [Fed. R. Civ. P. 37(b)(E)]:

(a) a party must produce documents as they are kept in the usual course of business or must organize and label them to correspond to the categories in the request;

(b) if a request does not specify a form for producing ESI, a party must produce it in a form in which it is ordinarily maintained or in a reasonably usable form; and

(c) a party need not produce the same ESI in more than one form.

c. **Sanctions**

(1) If ESI that should have been preserved in the anticipation or conduct of litigation is lost because a party failed to take reasonable steps to preserve it, and it cannot be restored or replaced through additional discovery, the court [Fed. R. Civ. P. 37(e)]:

(a) upon finding prejudice to another party from loss of the information, may order measures no greater than necessary to cure the prejudice; or

(b) if the courts finds that the party acted with the intent to deprive another party of the information's use in the litigation, the court can:

1) presume that the lost information was unfavorable to the party;

2) instruct the jury that it may or must presume the information was unfavorable to the party; or

3) dismiss the action or enter a default judgment.

7. **Discovery Sanctions**

a. **Motion to Compel**

(1) On notice to other parties and all affected persons, a party may move for an order compelling disclosure or discovery. The motion must include a certification that the movant has in good faith conferred or attempted to confer with the person or party failing to make disclosure or discovery in an effort to obtain it without court action [Fed. R. Civ. P. 37(a)].

(2) A motion for an order to a party must be made in the court where the action is pending. A motion for an order to a non-party must be made in the court where the discovery is or will be taken.

b. **Failure to Comply with Court Order**

(1) If the court where the discovery is taken orders a deponent to be sworn or to answer a question and the deponent fails to obey, the failure may be treated as contempt of court [Fed. R. Civ. P. 37(b)].

(2) If a party or a party's officer, director, or managing agent, or a designated witness, fails to obey an order to provide or permit discovery, the court where the action is pending may issue further just orders, including the following:

(a) declaring that the facts sought are established in favor of the requesting party;

(b) prohibiting the disobedient party from supporting or opposing designated claims or defenses, or from introducing designated matters in evidence;

(c) striking pleadings in whole or in part;

(d) staying further proceedings until the order is obeyed;

(e) dismissing the action or proceeding in whole or in part;

(f) rendering a default judgment against the disobedient party; or

(g) treating as contempt of court the failure to obey any order except an order to submit to a physical or mental examination.

(3) If a party fails to provide required information or identify a witness, the party is not allowed to use that information or witness to supply evidence on a motion, at a hearing, or at a trial, unless the failure was substantially justified or is harmless [Fed. R. Civ. P. 37(c)].

(4) If a party fails to make an admission, and if the requesting party later proves a document to be genuine or the matter true, the requesting party may move that the party who failed to admit, pay the reasonable expenses, including attorney's fees, incurred in making that proof [Id.].

c. **Additional Sanctions**

(1) The court where the action is pending may, on motion, order sanctions if [Fed. R. Civ. P. 37(d)]:

(a) a party or a party's officer, director, or managing agent fails, after being served with proper notice, to appear for that person's deposition; or

(b) a party, after being properly served with interrogatories or a request for inspection, fails to serve its answers, objections, or written response.

(2) Instead of, or in addition to, the sanctions listed above, the court must require the party failing to act, the attorney advising that party, or both, to pay the reasonable expenses, including attorney's fees, caused by the failure, unless the failure was substantially justified or other circumstances make an award of expenses unjust [Id.].

(3) If a party or its attorney fails to participate in good faith in developing and submitting a proposed discovery plan, the court may, after giving an opportunity to be heard, require that party or attorney

to pay to any other party the reasonable expenses, including attorney's fees, caused by the failure [Fed. R. Civ. P. 37(f)].

G. Adjudication without a Trial

1. Most cases do not result in a full trial. Possible methods of resolving disputes without a trial include:
    a. voluntary dismissal;
    b. involuntary dismissal;
    c. default judgments;
    d. settlements; and
    e. pretrial motions (discussed *infra*).
2. **Voluntary Dismissal**
    a. A plaintiff may voluntarily dismiss an action by filing a notice of dismissal at any time prior to service of defendant's answer or motion for summary judgment [Fed. R. Civ. P. 41(a)].
    b. Before or after a responsive pleading, a plaintiff may voluntarily dismiss an action by filing a stipulation signed by all parties.
    c. If the plaintiff cannot obtain another party's agreement to the dismissal, the plaintiff may make a motion for voluntary dismissal. Such a motion rests within the broad discretion of the trial court. The court will likely grant the motion unless the opponent will suffer prejudice.
    d. The filing of the notice of dismissal automatically terminates the case without prejudice. If the plaintiff has already voluntarily dismissed the action once before, the notice of dismissal operates as an adjudication upon the merits.
3. **Involuntary Dismissals**
    a. **Dismissal for Failure to State a Claim**
        (1) Pleadings must contain "a short and plain statement of the claim showing that the pleader is entitled to relief" [Fed. R. Civ. P. 8(a)(2)]. If this requirement is not met, the party against whom the claim is alleged may move to dismiss for failure to state a claim for which relief can be granted [Fed. R. Civ. P. 12(b)(6)].

        EXAMPLE: Defendant may move to dismiss for failure to state a claim on the ground that the complaint fails to allege that Defendant is responsible for Plaintiff's injuries.

        (2) When an action is dismissed based on failure to state a claim, the dismissal is with prejudice unless the court states otherwise in its order [Fed. R. Civ. P. 41(b)].

        (3) A court would dismiss the claim without prejudice (or with leave to amend) in circumstances where the pleading defect can and should be rectified.
    b. **Dismissal for Failure to Prosecute**
        (1) If a plaintiff fails to prosecute or to comply with the Federal Rules or a court order, a defendant may move to dismiss. A dismissal

for failure to prosecute is a dismissal with prejudice, unless the dismissal order states otherwise [Fed. R. Civ. P. 41(b)].

EXAMPLE: Plaintiff brings a lawsuit against defendant. Eighteen months later, plaintiff has not engaged in any discovery, and has not made any efforts to move the case forward. Defendant may bring a motion to dismiss for failure to prosecute.

4. **Default Judgment**
   a. Default judgments involve two steps:
      (1) the entry of default; and
      (2) the entry of the default judgment.
   b. An **entry of default** must be entered on behalf of a party against whom a judgment for affirmative relief is sought when the party has failed to plead or otherwise defend the claim and that failure is shown by affidavit or otherwise [Fed. R. Civ. P. 55(a)].
   c. Only after an entry of default has been entered may a default judgment be entered.
   d. A **default judgment** can be entered by the clerk or the court.
      (1) If the plaintiff's claim is for a sum certain, upon the plaintiff's request and with an affidavit showing the amount due, the clerk must enter judgment for that amount and costs against a defendant who has been defaulted for not appearing [Fed. R. Civ. P. 55(b)].

NOTE A clerk cannot enter default judgments against minors or incompetent persons.

      (2) In all other cases, the party must apply to the court for a default judgment to be entered.
      (3) If the party against whom a default judgment is sought has appeared personally or by a representative, that party or representative must be served with written notice of the application for default judgment at least seven days before the hearing [Id.].
      (4) The court may conduct hearings or make referrals when, to enter or effectuate judgment, it needs to [Id.]:
         (a) conduct an accounting;
         (b) determine the amount of damages;
         (c) establish the truth of any allegation by evidence; or
         (d) investigate any other matter.
   e. The court may set aside an entry of default for good cause. If the clerk or court entered a default judgment, the court may set it aside in accordance with a Rule 60(b) post-trial motion.
5. **Settlements**
   a. Settlements may be achieved through counsel and the parties themselves, or through alternative dispute resolution (ADR) methods such as arbitration or mediation.

b. A settlement conference is appropriate at any time. It may be held with a pretrial or discovery conference, or separately.

c. Settlement conferences are not mandatory under the Federal Rules.

d. A judge may, on her own or at a party's request, refer a settlement conference to another judge or magistrate.

e. **Offer of Judgment**

(1) At least 14 days before the date set for trial, a party defending against a claim may serve on an opposing party an offer to allow judgment on specified terms, with the costs then accrued [Fed. R. Civ. P. 68(a)]. If, within 14 days after being served, the opposing party serves written notice accepting the offer, either party may then file the offer and notice of acceptance, plus proof of service. The clerk must then enter judgment.

(2) An unaccepted offer is considered withdrawn, but it does not preclude a later offer. Evidence of an unaccepted offer is not admissible except in a proceeding to determine costs [Fed. R. Civ. P. 68(b)].

(3) When one party's liability to another has been determined but the extent of liability remains to be determined by further proceedings, the party held liable may make an offer of judgment. It must be served within a reasonable time—but at least 14 days—before the date set for a hearing to determine the extent of liability [Fed. R. Civ. P. 68(c)].

(4) If the judgment that the offeree finally obtains is not more favorable than the unaccepted offer, the offeree must pay the costs incurred after the offer was made [Fed. R. Civ. P. 68(d)].

IV. JURY TRIALS

A. Right to Jury Trial

1. The right to a jury trial in a civil action can be conferred by statute and is guaranteed by the Seventh Amendment to the U.S. Constitution.
2. Equitable actions are not triable by a jury as a matter of right. In determining whether a right to a jury trial exists, the court will consider:
   a. whether the claim more closely resembles actions in law or in equity; and
   b. whether the remedy sought is legal or equitable in nature (i.e. monetary relief or injunctive relief).

NOTE If both legal and equitable relief are sought in an action, the right to a jury exists for any issue of fact underlying a damages claim, even if the resolution of that issue may also support injunctive relief.

B. Demand for a Jury Trial

1. If the right to a jury trial exists in an action, any party can exercise the right by filing with the court and serving on the other parties a written demand for a jury trial.
2. The demand for a jury trial must be made within 14 days after the service of the last pleading directed to the triable issue.
3. If the demand for a jury trial is not timely filed and served, the right to a trial by jury is waived [Fed. R. Civ. P. 38].
   a. Issues on which a jury trial is not properly demanded are to be tried by the court. However, the court may, on motion, order a jury trial on any issue for which a jury might have been demanded [Fed. R. Civ. P. 39(b)].
   b. In an action not triable of right by a jury, the court, on motion or on its own [Fed. R. Civ. P. 39(c)]:
      (1) may try any issue with an advisory jury; or
      (2) may, with the parties' consent, try any issue by a jury whose verdict has the same effect as if a jury trial had been a matter of right, unless the action is against the United States and a federal statute provides for a nonjury trial.
4. **Removal**
   a. If a party has expressly demanded a jury trial in accordance with state law prior to the case being removed to federal court, the demand need not be renewed after removal.
   b. If the state law did not require express demand, a party need not make such demand unless the court orders the parties to do so. The court may so order on its own, or must so order at a party's request [Fed. R. Civ. P. 81(c)(3)(A)].
   c. Failure to make a demand when ordered will constitute waiver [Id.].

d. If all necessary pleadings have been served at the time of removal, a party entitled to a jury trial under Rule 38 must be given one if the party serves a demand within 14 days after [Fed. R. Civ. P. 81(c)(3)(B)]:

(1) filing a notice of removal; or

(2) being served with a notice of removal filed by another party.

C. Jury Selection

1. A federal jury can be composed of six to twelve members. Each juror must participate in the verdict unless excused [Fed. R. Civ. P. 48(a)].
2. The federal jury is selected by the *voir dire* process [Fed. R. Civ. P. 47]. The court may conduct the examination or permit the attorneys to question directly the prospective jurors.
3. The purpose of the *voir dire* is to explore germane factors that might expose a basis for challenge, whether for cause or peremptory.
4. Attorneys may ask the court to excuse any juror for cause. There are three categories of challenges for cause:

a. general disqualification—a person may lose the right to sit on any jury because of a felony conviction or some other inherent disqualification;

b. implied bias—potential jurors may be removed if the attorney believes a bias may exist; and

EXAMPLE: A juror who has a relationship with the parties or their attorneys could be removed due to an implied bias.

c. actual bias—jurors may be removed for cause if they indicate during *voir dire* that they would use predetermined beliefs or principles to decide the case instead of deciding the case based upon the facts.

5. **Peremptory Challenges**

a. In federal court, each party may exercise three peremptory challenges to excuse jurors without having to state the reason before the court.

b. Peremptory challenges may not be used to exclude jurors on the basis of race, ethnicity, or gender.

c. Peremptory challenges may be objected to by the opposing party only where the exclusion gives rise to an inference of racial, ethnic, or gender discrimination. If objected to, the excluding party must provide a nondiscriminatory explanation for the strikes or else rescind its strike of each juror involved.

(1) The exclusion of prospective jurors based on race, ethnicity, or gender violates the Equal Protection Clause. A Batson challenge can remedy this situation. In a Batson challenge, based on race, nationality, gender, religion, or some other cognizable group [Batson v. Kentucky, 476 U.S. 79 (1986)]:

(a) the party opposing the peremptory challenge must establish a "prima facie case" of discrimination;

(b) the proponent of the strike must offer a neutral explanation for choosing to strike the juror; and

(c) the court will decide whether the party raising the Batson challenge has proved purposeful discrimination [Purkett v. Elem, 514 U.S. 765, 767 (1995)].

(2) The party making the Batson challenge has the burden of persuasion. Equal protection applies to civil and criminal trials equally [Edmonson v. Leesville Concrete Company, 500 U.S. 614 (1991)].

D. Jury Instructions

1. Requests

a. At the close of the evidence or at any earlier reasonable time that the court orders, a party may file and furnish to every other party written requests for the jury instructions it wants the court to give [Fed. R. Civ. P. 51(a)].

b. After the close of the evidence, a party may [Id.]:

(1) file requests for instructions on issues that could not reasonably have been anticipated by an earlier time that the court set for requests; and

(2) with the court's permission, file untimely requests for instructions on any issue.

2. Instructions

a. The court [Fed. R. Civ. P. 51(b)]:

(1) must inform the parties of its proposed instructions and proposed action on the requests before instructing the jury and before final jury arguments;

(2) must give the parties an opportunity to object on the record and out of the jury's hearing before the instructions and arguments are delivered; and

(3) may instruct the jury at any time before the jury is discharged.

3. Objections

a. A party who objects to an instruction or the failure to give an instruction must do so on the record, stating distinctly the matter objected to and the grounds for the objection.

b. An objection is timely if [Fed. R. Civ. P. 51(c)]:

(1) a party objects on the record and out of the jury's hearing before the instructions and arguments are delivered; or

(2) a party was not informed of an instruction or action on a request before that opportunity to object, and the party objects promptly after learning that the instruction or request will be, or has been, given or refused.

c. The timing requirements for objecting to jury deliberations are strict, and the key thing is that the objection has to be made before, and not after, the jury begins its deliberations. Once the jury begins deliberating, it is too late to object.

4. **Assigning Error**
    a. A party may assign as error [Fed. R. Civ. P. 51(d)]:
        (1) an error in an instruction actually given, if that party properly objected; or
        (2) a failure to give an instruction, if that party properly requested it and—unless the court rejected the request in a definitive ruling on the record—also properly objected.
5. A court may consider a plain error in the instructions that has not been preserved as required by the Federal Rules if the error affects substantial rights [Id.].

V. MOTIONS

A. General Rules

1. Requirements Regarding Form

a. Any applications to the court for an order shall be made by motion.

b. A motion must:

(1) be in writing, unless made during a hearing or trial; and

(2) state with particularity the grounds for the request and a request for relief.

c. All rules governing matters of form in pleadings also apply to motions.

2. Other Requirements

a. Local court rules may set out specific requirements for motion practice, such as the papers to be filed, and the timing for making a motion.

b. The court may issue standing orders in a particular case regarding the timing of motions.

B. Pre-Trial Motions

1. Motion to Dismiss

a. A motion to dismiss is a motion filed by a defending party seeking the dismissal of a claim filed against him.

b. A motion to dismiss may be made on any of the following grounds [Fed. R. Civ. P. 12(b)]:

(1) lack of subject-matter jurisdiction;

(2) lack of personal jurisdiction;

(3) improper venue;

(4) insufficient process;

(5) insufficient service of process;

(6) failure to state a claim upon which relief can be granted; and

(7) failure to join a party under Rule 19.

c. A motion to dismiss based on lack of personal jurisdiction, improper venue, insufficient process, or insufficient service of process must be made in the defending party's first response to the court—either a pre-answer motion to dismiss or an answer.

(1) If the defending party makes a motion to dismiss and one of the aforementioned defenses is not included, that defense is waived and cannot later be included in the answer.

(2) If no pre-answer motion to dismiss is made, the defense must be in the defending party's answer, or else it is waived.

d. A motion to dismiss based on failure to state a claim upon which relief can be granted or failure to join a necessary party can be raised at any time before the trial ends, or else it is waived.

e. Lack of subject-matter jurisdiction is never waived, it can be raised at any time, even on appeal.

f. **Rule 12(b)(6) Dismissal**

(1) A court will dismiss a complaint for failure to state a claim upon which relief can be granted if the complaint:

(a) fails to state a cognizable claim;

(b) provides insufficient facts; or

(c) contains an allegation that negates one or more elements of the cause of action.

(2) Dismissal of a complaint under Rule 12(b)(6) is with prejudice unless the court states otherwise.

(3) If there is a defect in the pleading that the court deems rectifiable, the court may:

(a) dismiss the complaint without prejudice; or

(b) grant the plaintiff leave to amend the complaint.

2. **Motion for Judgment on the Pleadings**

a. After the pleadings are closed—but early enough not to delay trial—a party may move for judgment on the pleadings [Fed. R. Civ. P. 12(c)].

b. If, on a motion under Rule 12(b)(6) or 12(c), matters outside the pleadings are presented to and not excluded by the court, the motion must be treated as one for summary judgment under Rule 56. All parties must be given a reasonable opportunity to present all the material that is pertinent to the motion [Fed. R. Civ. P. 12(d)].

3. **Motion for a More Definite Statement**

a. A party may move for a more definite statement of a pleading to which a responsive pleading is allowed but which is so vague or ambiguous that the party cannot reasonably prepare a response [Fed. R. Civ. P. 12(e)].

b. The motion must be made before filing a responsive pleading and must point out the defects complained of and the details desired.

c. If the court orders a more definite statement and the order is not obeyed within 14 days after notice of the order or within the time the court sets, the court may strike the pleading or issue any other appropriate order.

4. **Motion to Strike**

a. The court may strike from a pleading an insufficient defense or any redundant, immaterial, impertinent, or scandalous matter. The court may act [Fed. R. Civ. P. 12(f)]:

(1) on its own; or

(2) on motion made by a party either before responding to the pleading or, if a response is not allowed, within 21 days after being served with the pleading.

5. **Summary Judgment Motions**

a. A motion for summary judgment is a motion challenging a claim or defense on the merits. Summary judgments are intended to pierce the pleadings to determine if there is credible evidence to factually support a party's claim.

b. Summary judgment will be granted if the moving party "shows that there is no genuine dispute as to any material fact and the movant is entitled to judgment as a matter of law" [Fed. R. Civ. P. 56].

c. Any party may move for summary judgment as to any individual issue that has been joined, or as to the cause of action as a whole.

d. The parties may move with or without supporting affidavits for summary judgment.

e. Unless a local rule or court order provides otherwise:

 (1) a party may move for summary judgment at any time before 30 days after the close of discovery;

 (2) a party opposing a motion for summary judgment must file a response within 21 days after the motion is served or a responsive pleading is due, whichever is later; and

 (3) a reply may be filed within 14 days after the response is served.

f. When a party moves for summary judgment, the court must first consider whether the moving party has shown—based on her arguments alone—that the non-moving party lacks sufficient facts and/or law to prevail on the claim or defense in question. The moving party can make this argument by either:

 (1) pointing out holes in the opposing party's claims or defenses; or

 (2) adducing new evidence demonstrating that the claim or defense cannot be true.

g. If the moving party can establish that the non-moving party lacks sufficient facts or law to prevail on the claim or defense in question, the court then turns to the non-moving party to defeat the motion.

 (1) To survive summary judgment, the non-moving party must adduce evidence sufficient for a reasonable jury to find in his favor on a claim or defense.

 (2) The non-moving party may not rely on allegations in the complaint to defeat a motion for summary judgment.

h. Although both plaintiffs and defendants can move for summary judgment, defendants do so far more often because it is harder for a plaintiff to prevail. For a plaintiff to prevail on her own motion for summary judgment, she must produce evidence in support of every element of her claim and the defendant must not respond with evidence of any element of the claim.

i. The evidence presented at a summary judgment motion will be viewed in the light most favorable to the non-moving party to determine whether the movant is entitled to prevail as a matter of law.

 (1) A party may offer affidavits and/or evidence obtained during discovery.

 (2) A party may not rely on evidence that will be inadmissible at trial to satisfy the production burden. If the evidence is in an inadmissible form at the summary judgment stage, but will be in an admissible form at trial, then the production burden is satisfied.

EXAMPLE: The inadmissibility of an affidavit that contains hearsay would be remedied by a hearsay exception of presentation of the witness who made the statement.

(3) Plaintiffs may not rely on evidence that no rational fact finder would believe or would find sufficient to establish the element.

EXAMPLE: If the only expert testimony offered by the plaintiff is "implausible," a court will enter summary judgment on behalf of the defendant [Matsushita v. Zenith, 475 U.S. 574 (1986)].

j. **Powers of the District Judge**

(1) The judge may grant or deny summary judgment in favor of or against the person asking for it.

(2) After giving notice to all parties and a reasonable time to respond, the judge can also [Fed. R. Civ. P. 56(f)]:

(a) grant summary judgment even when nobody asks for it (a *sua sponte* grant of summary judgment is proper);

(b) grant summary judgment on grounds that neither party has asked for—i.e., for completely different reasons than the moving party was seeking for summary judgment; or

(c) grant summary judgment not just for the moving party, but against the moving party and in favor of the non-moving party.

(3) Judges may grant partial summary judgment.

(4) Judges are required to state on the record the grounds for granting or denying summary judgment.

(5) Judges do not have to canvas the entire record hunting for a genuine issue of material fact. Instead, the trial judge can limit his review on a motion for summary judgment to only those portions of the record cited by the parties.

C. Post-Trial Motions

1. Judgment as a Matter of Law

a. A motion for judgment as a matter of law (JMOL) was formerly known as a motion for a directed verdict.

b. The defendant or the plaintiff may move for JMOL after the other party closes her case. If the motion is granted, the motion results in judgment for the moving party [Fed. R. Civ. P. 50(a)].

c. A JMOL will be granted if the court finds that a reasonable jury would not have a legally sufficient evidentiary basis to find for the non-moving party on the issue at hand [Id.].

EXAMPLE: In an action for copyright infringement, the plaintiff fails to show that he is the owner of the copyright in question. The defendant's motion for JMOL should be granted.

d. The analysis for JMOL motions is identical to that on a summary judgment motion.

(1) A summary judgment motion is based on evidence that a party may introduce at trial, while the JMOL motion is based on evidence actually introduced at trial.

(2) The evidence will be viewed in the light most favorable to the non-moving party to determine whether the movant is entitled to prevail as a matter of law.

(3) A JMOL must specify the judgment sought and the law and facts that entitle the moving party to the judgment [Id.].

e. Motions for JMOL are typically made at the close of the non-moving party's case, but may be made at any time after all of the non-moving party's evidence has been submitted but before the case is submitted to the jury.

f. Most attorneys will make a motion for JMOL as a matter of course, in order to preserve the right to renew the motion at the conclusion of the trial.

2. **Renewed Motion for Judgment as a Matter of Law**

a. A renewed motion for judgment as a matter of law was formerly known as a motion for judgment notwithstanding the verdict (JNOV, or judgment *non obstante veredicto*).

b. Within 28 days after the entry of judgment (or discharge of the jury if the motion addresses a jury issue not decided by verdict), a party who has timely moved for JMOL may serve a motion to set aside the verdict and any judgment entered on the verdict [Fed. R. Civ. P. 50(b)].

NOTE A party that did not timely move for a JMOL during trial cannot move for a renewed JMOL.

c. A renewed motion for JMOL requires analysis identical to the JMOL motion.

(1) Even after the jury has rendered a verdict, if a judge finds that no reasonable jury could interpret the evidence presented as supporting the verdict, a judge may grant to the party against whom the judgment was rendered JMOL.

d. In ruling on a renewed motion for JMOL, the court may [Id.]:

(1) allow judgment on the verdict to stand, if the jury returned a verdict;

(2) order a new trial; or

(3) direct the entry of judgment as a matter of law.

e. When making a renewed motion for JMOL, the moving party may also move jointly or in the alternative for a new trial under Rule 59.

(1) If the court grants the renewed motion for JMOL, it must also issue a conditional ruling on any motion for a new trial [Id.].

3. **Motion for a New Trial**

a. A new trial may be granted to all or any of the parties on all or some of the issues litigated at trial [Fed. R. Civ. P. 59].

b. A motion for a new trial must be filed within 28 days of the entry of judgment.

c. A motion for a new trial is generally made as a form of alternative relief to a renewed JMOL motion.

d. A motion for a new trial is generally appropriate in the following instances:

(1) in order to avoid an inevitable appeal and reversal if the trial judge has committed reversible error;

(2) when a jury verdict is so excessive as to demonstrate that the jury has misunderstood its duty or has acted with extreme prejudice;

(3) if evidence of jury misconduct exists, and Fed. R. Evid. 606(b) limits judicial inquiry to external influences on the deliberation process; or

(4) when the verdict is against the clear weight of the evidence.

e. On a motion for a new trial, the court is not required to view the evidence in a light most favorable to the verdict and may grant the new trial, even though there was enough evidence to prevent JMOL or renewed JMOL.

f. The court may also consider a new trial conditioned on certain circumstances.

EXAMPLE: If the jury verdict awarded an improper or excessive amount of damages, the court may grant a new trial on the issue of damages alone. Liability would not be relitigated.

4. **Remittitur and Additur**

a. A motion for remittitur asks the judge to reduce the award of damages that are excessive. Federal courts will routinely grant motions for remittitur.

b. The converse of a remittitur is an additur, or an increase in the award of damages. Additur is unconstitutional in federal court.

5. **Motion for Relief from a Judgment or Order**

a. The court may correct a clerical mistake or a mistake arising from oversight or omission whenever one is found in a judgment, order, or other part of the record.

(1) The court may do so on motion of a party or on its own, with or without notice [Fed. R. Civ. P. 60(a)].

(2) If an appeal has been docketed with the appellate court and is pending, however, the mistake may be corrected only with the appellate court's leave [Id.].

b. On motion and on just terms, the court may grant a motion for relief from judgment for the following reasons [Fed. R. Civ. P. 60(b)(1)–(6)]:

(1) mistake, inadvertence, surprise, or excusable neglect;

(2) newly discovered evidence that, with reasonable diligence, could not have been discovered in time to move for a new trial under Rule 59(b);

(3) fraud, misrepresentation, or misconduct by an opposing party;

(4) the judgment is void;

(a) A judgment is void where it is "so affected by a fundamental infirmity that the infirmity may be raised even after the judgment becomes final" [United States Aid Funds, Inc. v. Espinosa, 559 U.S. 260 (2010)].

(b) Rule 60(b)(4) applies only in the rare instance when a judgment is premised either on a certain type of jurisdictional error or on a violation of due process that deprived a party of notice or the opportunity to be heard. This standard does not include erroneous judgments or situations where a legal error has occurred.

(5) the judgment has been satisfied, released, or discharged, it is based on an earlier judgment that has been reversed or vacated, or applying it prospectively is no longer equitable; or

(6) any other reason that justifies relief.

c. A motion under Rule 60(b) must be made within a reasonable time. If the motion is being made for any of the first three reasons listed above (mistake, new evidence, or fraud), the motion must be made no more than a year after entry of the judgment, order, or the date of the proceeding.

d. A motion for relief from judgment does not affect the finality of the judgment, nor does it suspend its operation [Fed. R. Civ. P. 60(c)].

e. Rule 60 does not limit a court's power to entertain an independent action to relieve a party from a judgment, order, or proceeding, grant relief to a defendant who was not personally notified of the action, or set aside a judgment due to fraud on the court [Fed. R. Civ. P. 60(d)].

VI. VERDICTS AND JUDGMENTS

A. Jury Verdicts

1. In General

a. Unless the parties stipulate otherwise, a jury verdict must be unanimous and must be returned by a jury of at least six members [Fed. R. Civ. P. 48(b)].

b. After a verdict is returned but before the jury is discharged, the court must on a party's request, or may on its own, poll the jurors individually. If the poll reveals a lack of unanimity or lack of assent by the number of jurors that the parties stipulated to, the court may direct the jury to deliberate further or may order a new trial [Fed. R. Civ. P. 48(c)].

2. General Verdicts

a. The court may direct the jury to return a general verdict, which simply states which party should win, the plaintiff or defendant, without addressing specific findings on each issue of fact.

3. Special Verdicts

a. The court may require a jury to return only a special verdict in the form of a special written finding on each issue of fact. The court may do so by [Fed. R. Civ. P. 49(a)(1)]:

(1) submitting written questions susceptible of a categorical or other brief answer;

(2) submitting written forms of the special findings that might properly be made under the pleadings and evidence; or

(3) using any other method that the court considers appropriate.

b. The court must give the instructions and explanations necessary to enable the jury to make its findings on each submitted issue [Fed. R. Civ. P. 49(a)(2)].

c. A party waives the right to a jury trial on any issue of fact raised by the pleadings or evidence but not submitted to the jury unless, before the jury retires, the party demands its submission to the jury. If the party does not demand submission, the court may make a finding on the issue. If the court makes no finding, it is considered to have made a finding consistent with its judgment on the special verdict [Fed. R. Civ. P. 49(a)(3)].

4. General Verdict with Answers to Written Questions

a. The court may submit to the jury forms for a general verdict, together with written questions on one or more issues of fact that the jury must decide. The court must give the instructions and explanations necessary to enable the jury to render a general verdict and answer the questions in writing, and must direct the jury to do both [Fed. R. Civ. P. 49(b)(1)].

b. When the general verdict and the answers are consistent, the court must approve, for entry under Rule 58, an appropriate judgment on the verdict and answers [Fed. R. Civ. P. 49(b)(2)].

c. When the answers are consistent with each other but one or more is inconsistent with the general verdict, the court may [Fed. R. Civ. P. 49(b)(3)]:
   (1) approve for entry an appropriate judgment according to the answers, notwithstanding the general verdict;
   (2) direct the jury to further consider its answers and verdict; or
   (3) order a new trial.

d. When the answers are inconsistent with each other and one or more is also inconsistent with the general verdict, judgment must not be entered; instead, the court must direct the jury to further consider its answers and verdict, or must order a new trial [Fed. R. Civ. P. 49(b)(4)].

B. Judicial Findings and Conclusions

1. In an action tried on the facts without a jury or with an advisory jury, the court must find the facts specially, and state its conclusions of law separately. The findings and conclusions may be stated on the record after the close of the evidence or may appear in an opinion or a memorandum of decision filed by the court. Judgment must be entered under Rule 58 [Fed. R. Civ. P. 52(a)(1)].
2. In granting or refusing an interlocutory injunction, the court must similarly state the findings and conclusions that support its action [Fed. R. Civ. P. 52(a)(2)].
3. The court is not required to state findings or conclusions when ruling on a motion to dismiss or for summary judgment or, unless these rules provide otherwise, on any other motion [Fed. R. Civ. P. 52(a)(3)].
4. A master's findings, to the extent adopted by the court, must be considered the court's findings [Fed. R. Civ. P. 52(a)(4)].
5. A party may later question the sufficiency of the evidence supporting the findings, whether or not the party requested findings, objected to them, moved to amend them, or moved for partial findings [Fed. R. Civ. P. 52(a)(5)].
6. Findings of fact, whether based on oral or other evidence, must not be set aside unless clearly erroneous, and the reviewing court must give due regard to the trial court's opportunity to judge the witnesses' credibility [Fed. R. Civ. P. 52(a)(6)].
7. On a party's motion filed no later than 28 days after the entry of judgment, the court may amend its findings—or make additional findings—and may amend the judgment accordingly. The motion may accompany a motion for a new trial [Fed. R. Civ. P. 52(b)(1)].
8. If a party has been fully heard on an issue during a nonjury trial and the court finds against the party on that issue, the court may enter judgment against the party on a claim or defense that, under the controlling law, can be maintained or defeated only with a favorable finding on that issue. The court may, however, decline to render any judgment until the close of the evidence. A judgment on partial findings must be supported by findings of fact and conclusions of law [Fed. R. Civ. P. 52(c)].

C. Effect of Verdicts—Claim and Issue Preclusion

1. Claim Preclusion

a. Claim preclusion (also known as *res judicata*) and issue preclusion (also known as collateral estoppel) are judicial doctrines intended to promote the policy of judicial economy and the finality of litigation. The general rule created by these doctrines is that once a case has reached a final judgment, then that case, and related claims and issues, have been decided or settled permanently and are not eligible for relitigation.

b. The doctrine of **claim preclusion** prevents relitigation of a claim:

(1) between the same parties and those who are in privity with them;

(2) arising out of the same transaction or occurrence underlying the prior suit; and

(3) that was determined on the merits by a court with proper subject-matter and personal jurisdiction.

EXAMPLE: During trial, the jury determines that the defendant was not liable for the plaintiff's injuries arising out of a car accident. The plaintiff may not file a subsequent action against the same defendant seeking property damages resulting from the same car accident.

c. A judgment is not on the merits if it is a dismissal for lack of personal jurisdiction, subject-matter jurisdiction, or venue. A dismissal with prejudice is considered a dismissal on the merits.

d. Claim preclusion operates as an affirmative defense that is waived if not properly asserted. It can also be asserted as a basis for a summary judgment motion.

e. Claim preclusion also prevents relitigation of claims that could have been brought in the earlier action, if they arise from the same transaction or occurrence.

2. Issue Preclusion

a. **Issue preclusion** prevents relitigation of issues that were fully and fairly litigated, and were necessarily decided in a proceeding that reached a final judgment on the merits.

b. An issue is narrower than a claim. The litigation of a single claim may involve the determination of several different issues.

c. For litigation of a particular factual issue to be precluded, four elements must be met:

(1) the issue must have been litigated and determined in the prior suit;

(2) the issue must have been essential to the judgment;

(3) the prior suit must have ended in a valid final judgment on the merits; and

(4) the party against whom preclusion is asserted must have had a full and fair opportunity and incentive to litigate the issue in the first suit.

EXAMPLE: During a trial against John, a jury determines that the light was red when Adam crossed the street. In a subsequent action against Mark arising from the same occurrence, Adam cannot relitigate the issue of whether the light was red or green.

d. **Parties**

(1) Issue preclusion may not be used against someone who was not a party to the previous action.

(2) Although the party invoking the doctrine need not have been a party to the previous action, it would be a violation of due process to bind a non-party (or someone not in privity with a party) since that person had not yet had her day in court.

e. **Offensive Use**

(1) Issue preclusion may be used offensively by one who was not a party to the first action against one who was a party in the earlier suit.

(2) Courts are a bit reluctant to permit offensive use of issue preclusion and will base their determination on the following:

(a) whether the plaintiff in the second suit could have easily joined in the first action;

(b) whether there are procedural opportunities available to the defendant in the second suit that were unavailable in the earlier action; and

(c) whether the defendant had incentive to litigate the issue in the first action.

EXAMPLE: If the defendant was forced to defend in an inconvenient forum or was unable to engage in meaningful discovery, it may be unfair to deny the defendant the opportunity to relitigate the issue.

(3) **Use of Criminal Convictions in Civil Proceedings**

(a) If a defendant has been convicted of a crime that has an element common to an issue in a subsequent civil proceeding, the conviction may have issue preclusive effect in the civil case, provided that the issue was fully and fairly litigated and was necessarily decided.

(b) An acquittal is not likely to have issue preclusive effect in a subsequent action, as the burden of proof is more modest in a civil case.

3. **Courts Sitting in Diversity**

a. The Supreme Court has held that the preclusive effect of a judgment of a federal court sitting in diversity should be determined by the preclusion rules that would be applied by the state courts in the state in which the federal diversity court sits. However, the question of the effect of a federal judgment remains a question of federal law, and state rules can be ignored "in situations in which the state law is incompatible with federal interests" [Semtek Int'l Inc. v. Lockheed Martin Corp., 531 U.S. 497 (2001)].

b. This may be relevant where a state continues to apply the doctrine of mutuality, or does not allow for offensive use by a nonparty.

VII. APPEALABILITY AND REVIEW

A. Availability of Interlocutory Review

1. **Interlocutory orders** are orders either asserting provisional relief or made upon motion or application during the trial, but which are not final adjudications on the merits. Interlocutory orders may not be reviewed before final judgment with limited exceptions.

   EXAMPLE: An order requiring a party to produce documents claimed to be protected by privilege is an interlocutory order.

2. **Collateral Order Doctrine**
   a. Appellate review is authorized for an interlocutory order rendered by a trial judge that:
      (1) conclusively determines the disputed question;
      (2) resolves an important issue completely separate from the merits of the action; and
      (3) is effectively unreviewable on appeal from a final judgment.

      EXAMPLE: An order determining that a party is immune from certain claims would be reviewable under the collateral order doctrine.

3. **Injunctive Relief**
   a. Congress has given to the federal courts subject-matter jurisdiction over appeals from an interlocutory order of the trial court that grants, denies, continues, modifies, or dissolves an injunction [28 U.S.C. § 1292(a)(1)].
   b. Interlocutory orders for injunctive relief are not appealable if a similar suit is pending in state court.

4. **Certification of Interlocutory Orders**
   a. Federal trial courts may certify an order for appeal when [28 U.S.C. § 1292(b)]:
      (1) the order involves a controlling question of law as to which a substantial ground for difference of opinion exists; and
      (2) an immediate appeal from the order may materially advance the termination of the litigation.
   b. Following the written certification, the party seeking appeal must apply to the federal court of appeals, which has discretion to grant or deny the application.

5. Federal courts of appeals have the power to issue extraordinary writs [28 U.S.C. § 1651].

6. **Multi-Claim or Multi-Party Judgments**
   a. When a final decision has been made on at least one of the claims in a multi-claim or multi-party case, the trial judge may direct the entry of a final judgment as to that claim by a finding on the record that there is no reason to delay judgment on that claim until the entire case is resolved [Fed. R. Civ. P. 54(b)].

b. Any party affected by the judgment may appeal the judgment while the rest of the action remains pending.

B. Final Judgment Rule

1. Congress has given to the federal courts subject-matter jurisdiction over appeals from all final decisions of the federal district trial courts [28 U.S.C. § 1291].
2. The basic principle in the federal system is that only final judgments may be taken to the appellate courts. This rule is modified by a few other principles, which when available, provide the appellant with an avenue for interlocutory appeal even though the underlying action has not gone to final judgment. Appellate courts will apply different standards of review depending on the subject matter of the appeal.
3. A final judgment is generally defined as one that disposes of all issues as to all of the parties, it disposes of the entire case.

   EXAMPLE: A judgment on behalf of the plaintiff in an action for medical malpractice is a final judgment.

C. Scope of Review for Judge and Jury

1. Although an appellant may want an appeals court to review all errors alleged to have occurred at the trial court level, there are restrictions on what is reviewable:
   a. with few exceptions, courts will not review errors that are not on the record of the trial court proceeding; and

      EXAMPLE: If the appellant did not raise or object to an error at a time when the trial court had the opportunity to correct it, the issue is not preserved and is, thus, unreviewable.

   b. errors that do not affect substantial rights will be labeled harmless and may be unreviewable.
2. Errors will receive different levels of scrutiny upon appellate review depending on the category of error.
   a. Conclusions of law will typically be reviewed *de novo. De novo* review means the appellate court will conduct a non-deferential review and address the legal issue as if it has never been addressed in the case.
   b. Factual findings may be disturbed only if clearly erroneous.
   c. Other discretionary determinations by the judge will be affirmed absent some indication that the judge abused his discretion.

KAPLAN BAR REVIEW

Constitutional Law

TABLE OF CONTENTS

I. THE NATURE OF JUDICIAL REVIEW

Organization of the Courts in the Federal System 86
The United States Supreme Court 94

II. SEPARATION OF POWERS

The Powers of Congress 97
Executive Power 104
Interbranch Checks upon the Exercise of Federal Power 108

III. THE RELATION OF THE NATION AND THE STATES IN THE FEDERAL SYSTEM

Nature and Scope of Federal and State Powers 110
Intergovernmental Immunities 110
Authority Reserved for the States 112
Reserved State Power in Taxation 114

IV. TYPE OF ACTION GOVERNED BY THE CONSTITUTION

State Action versus Private Action 117
National Power to Override State Authority 119

V. DUE PROCESS AND THE INCORPORATION OF PORTIONS OF THE BILL OF RIGHTS

Incorporation of the Bill of Rights 120
Procedural Due Process 122
Substantive Due Process 127
Takings Clause 132

VI. EQUAL PROTECTION OF THE LAWS

Constitutional Basis 134
Standards of Review 134
Proving Discrimination 135
Suspect Classifications 136

VII. PRIVILEGES AND IMMUNITIES CLAUSES

Privileges or Immunities under the Fourteenth Amendment 142
Privileges and Immunities under Article IV, Section 2 142

VIII. RETROACTIVE LEGISLATION

The Contract Clause 144
Ex Post Facto Laws 144
Bills of Attainder 145

IX. FIRST AMENDMENT FREEDOMS

Freedom of Religion and Separation of Church and State 146
Freedom of Expression 152

I. THE NATURE OF JUDICIAL REVIEW

A. Organization of the Courts in the Federal System

1. Federal Court System

a. **Source of Federal Judicial Power**

(1) Article III, Section 1 provides that the "judicial power of the United States shall be vested in one Supreme Court and in such inferior Courts as the Congress may from time to time ordain and establish."

b. **Scope of Federal Judicial Power**

(1) Article III, Section 2 limits the jurisdiction of the federal courts to:

(a) cases, in law and equity, arising under the U.S. Constitution, federal laws, and treaties;

(b) cases affecting ambassadors, public ministers, and consuls;

(c) cases of admiralty and maritime jurisdiction;

(d) controversies to which the United States shall be a party;

(e) controversies between two or more states;

(f) cases between a state and citizens of another state; and

(g) cases between citizens of different states (diversity of citizenship cases).

c. The Eleventh Amendment prohibits the citizens of one state from suing their own state or another state in federal court on federal claims for money damages or an injunction, without the state's consent.

(1) The states also have sovereign immunity from suits by citizens for damages in their own state courts, unless sovereign immunity has been waived [Alden v. Maine, 527 U.S. 706 (1999)].

(2) The Eleventh Amendment recognizes the states and their governmental immunity.

(3) It applies not only to diversity suits but to federal question cases as well.

(4) The concept of **governmental immunity**, or **sovereign immunity**, means that the government may not be sued without its consent. However, subdivisions of a state (e.g., cities, towns, and counties) do not have immunity from suit under the Eleventh Amendment [Lincoln County v. Luning, 133 U.S. 529 (1890)].

(5) Despite Congress's enumerated powers under Article I, Section 8, the Eleventh Amendment nonetheless prohibits federal court adjudication of claims by private parties against a state.

EXAMPLE: Congress could not use Article I to circumvent the limitations placed on federal jurisdiction and, therefore, could not allow a Native American tribe to sue a state in federal court [Seminole Tribe of Florida v. Florida, 517 U.S. 44 (1996)].

(a) However, pursuant to its enforcement powers under the post-Civil War amendments (Thirteenth, Fourteenth, and Fifteenth), Congress can authorize private suits by individuals to compensate for state violations of those amendments [Fitzpatrick v. Bitzer, 427 U.S. 445 (1979)].

(6) Exceptions to the application of the Eleventh Amendment include:

(a) suits against state officials for abusing their power in enforcing an unconstitutional state statute [Ex parte Young, 209 U.S. 123 (1908)];

(b) federal suits brought by one state against another state, or suits brought by the federal government against a state; and

(c) most suits for injunctions brought against state officials—e.g., a private citizen may sue to enjoin a state official from acting in violation of the plaintiff's federal constitutional rights.

(7) A state may consent to suit in federal court if it clearly waives its Eleventh Amendment immunity and does so expressly and unequivocally (or by voluntarily invoking a federal court's jurisdiction). A state will not be held to have impliedly or constructively waived its immunity simply because Congress provides that a state will be subject to private suit if it engages in certain federally regulated conduct (such as infringing a federally granted patent) and the state voluntarily elects to engage in that conduct [College Savings Bank v. Florida Prepaid Postsecondary Education Expense Board, 527 U.S. 666 (1999)].

(8) Generally, Congress may abrogate a state's immunity where:

(a) the act asserts that it is abrogating the state's immunity; and

(b) Congress enacts the act under a grant of power that may abrogate the state's immunity.

EXAMPLE: State workers alleging age discrimination under the federal Age Discrimination in Employment Act may not sue their employers (i.e., the state) using the federal statute as a cause of action, because Congress lacks the power to override the state's Eleventh Amendment immunity from federal lawsuits in the absence of a pattern of unconstitutional action by the states violative of the Fourteenth Amendment [Kimel v. Board of Regents, 528 U.S. 62 (2000)].

(9) Complete preclusion of all jurisdiction may occur in certain instances.

EXAMPLE: Probation officers owed money under federal law cannot sue for it in either federal or state court.

EXAMPLE: States can infringe patents or copyrights and thus violate federal law, but cannot be sued in either federal or state court by private parties.

(a) Remember, however, that state officials can be sued for injunctive relief, but injured private plaintiffs have no damage remedy against state governments.

2. **Limitations on Jurisdiction of Federal Courts**

a. **Case or Controversy**

(1) Article III, Section 2 limits the jurisdiction of federal courts to "cases" and "controversies." A **case** or **controversy** is a real and substantial dispute that touches the legal relations of parties having adverse interests and that can be resolved by a judicial decree of a conclusive character [Aetna Life Insurance Co. v. Haworth, 300 U.S. 227 (1937)].

(a) The Supreme Court will not give advisory opinions to either the president or Congress concerning the constitutionality of proposed action or legislation.

NOTE State courts may be allowed to render advisory opinions.

(b) The prohibition against advisory opinions does not preclude federal courts from granting declaratory judgments. A **declaratory judgment** is a decision in which the court is requested to determine the legality of proposed conduct without awarding damages or injunctive relief. However, the plaintiff must meet the case or controversy tests, as well as the "RAMPS" requirements explained below.

Federal Court Jurisdiction RAMPS Up
Ripeness, **A**bstention & Adequate State Grounds, **M**ootness, **P**olitical Questions, **S**tanding

b. **Mootness**

(1) If a controversy or matter has already been resolved, then the case will be dismissed as **moot**. An actual case or controversy must exist at all stages of the litigation [Liner v. Jafco, Inc., 375 U.S. 301 (1964)].

(a) Although the principal issue in a lawsuit has been resolved, if a party still has an interest in resolving collateral (or lesser) matters, the case will not be dismissed.

EXAMPLE: A case about wrongful termination is not moot even though the plaintiff had his employment restored if issues of back pay remain [Powell v. McCormick, 395 U.S. 486 (1969)].

(b) The case will not be dismissed for mootness if the injury is "capable of repetition, yet evading review," meaning that it is a practical impossibility for there to be adjudication or appellate review before the claims of the plaintiff, or other individuals who are members of the class, become moot.

EXAMPLE: A pregnant woman's suit challenging the constitutionality of a state abortion statute was held not to be moot even though she was no longer pregnant at the time the case reached the Supreme Court. Pregnancy is "capable of repetition, yet evading review," for the plaintiff and for members of the class she represents [Roe v. Wade, 410 U.S. 113 (1973)].

(2) There is a long-recognized exception to mootness known as the **voluntary cessation doctrine**. Under this doctrine, a defendant's voluntary cessation of a challenged practice does not deprive a federal court of its power to determine the legality of that practice [Friends of the Earth, Inc. v. Laidlaw Envtl. Servs., Inc., 528 U.S. 167 (2000)]. Otherwise, dismissing a case as moot would leave the defendant "free to return to his old ways."

(3) Instead, a court will apply a stringent standard to determine whether a case has become moot due to the defendant's behavior. A case will be considered moot in this situation if subsequent events make it "absolutely clear that the allegedly wrongful behavior could not reasonably be expected to recur" [Id.].

(a) The burden of persuasion that the challenged conduct cannot reasonably be expected to begin again lies with the party asserting mootness.

(b) One factor that the Supreme Court has used to determine whether voluntary cessation should render a claim moot or if the activity is likely to start up again is whether or not the defendant has defended its actions [Parents Involved in Cmty. Schs. v. Seattle Sch. Dist. No. 1, 551 U.S. 701 (2007)].

c. **Ripeness**

(1) Whereas mootness bars consideration of claims after they have been resolved, **ripeness** bars consideration of claims before they have fully developed.

(a) Generally, a court may not review or grant a declaratory judgment of a state law before it is enforced or when there is no real threat the statute will ever be enforced [Poe v. Ullman, 367 U.S. 497 (1961)].

EXAMPLE: The Supreme Court dismissed a claim against the Army's data-gathering activities because there was no showing that the Army's surveillance system resulted in any specific present harm or threat of future harm to the complainants [Laird v. Tatum, 408 U.S. 1 (1972)].

EXAMPLE: The Supreme Court refused to grant equitable relief because there was no evidence that the pattern of allegedly unconstitutional racial discrimination in the bail and sentencing practices in the Cairo, Illinois court system threatened the plaintiffs, who were not in imminent danger of being prosecuted [O'Shea v. Littleton, 414 U.S. 488 (1974)].

EXAMPLE: The Supreme Court did rule on the constitutionality of a statute prohibiting the teaching of evolution in public schools even though the statute had not been enforced [Epperson v. Arkansas, 393 U.S. 97 (1968)].

(b) However, if the plaintiff can show, before enforcement of the law, that the law presents a specific or present harm or a threat of specific future and imminent harm, the court may grant a declaratory judgment [Abbott Laboratories v. Gardner, 387 U.S. 136 (1967)].

d. **Abstention**

(1) The federal court may **abstain**, or refuse to hear a particular case, when there are undecided issues of state law presented. The abstention doctrine permits the state court to resolve issues of state law, thereby making a decision of the constitutional issue unnecessary. Thus, proper deference is paid to the state court system and harmonious federal-state relations are furthered [Railroad Commission v. Pullman, 312 U.S. 496 (1941)].

(a) The federal court may abstain if the meaning of a state law or regulation is unclear. In this situation, the state court might interpret the statute so as to avoid the constitutional issue [Harris County Commissioners Court v. Moore, 420 U.S. 77 (1975)].

(b) Where state criminal proceedings are pending, the federal court will abstain in a suit seeking an injunction against the state prosecution, absent a showing of bad-faith harassment on the part of the state prosecutors [Younger v. Harris, 401 U.S. 37 (1971)]. This principle has been extended to cases:

1) where state civil proceedings had commenced (seeking an injunction against operation of a state public nuisance statute used to close a pornography movie house) [Huffman v. Pursue, Ltd., 420 U.S. 592 (1975)]; and

2) where civil contempt hearings had begun [Judice v. Vail, 430 U.S. 327 (1977)].

(2) There are two areas where federal courts traditionally decline to hear cases.

(a) Under the probate exception to federal court jurisdiction, federal courts always decline to probate estates, viewing these as traditionally belonging to the state courts.

(b) Federal courts generally do not hear family law claims (i.e., divorce, child custody, or child support matters), as these belong to states. This is known as the family law exception.

e. **Standing**

(1) Article III requires a person litigating a constitutional question to show:

(a) injury-in-fact;

1) The plaintiff must show a direct and personal injury, actual or imminent, caused by the action that she is challenging. Where the plaintiff has not suffered any personal injury or harm, she does not have standing [Sierra Club v. Morton, 405 U.S. 727 (1972)].

2) A concrete injury is required, even in the context of a statutory violation. The fact that damages would be available because of the violation is not enough. The plaintiff must suffer "an invasion of a legally protected interest" that is "concrete" as well as "particularized" [Spokeo, Inc. v. Robins, 578 U.S. 330 (2016)].

a) To be concrete, the injury must be *de facto*, or actually exist.

b) To be particularized, the injury must be affecting the plaintiff in a personal and individual way.

3) Monetary harm is not required for injury-in-fact; a plaintiff may suffer an "intangible" injury sufficient for standing. However, the Supreme Court made it clear that a plaintiff does not satisfy the injury-in-fact requirement for standing merely because a statute granted the plaintiff a statutory right and the defendant allegedly violated that statute [Id.].

(b) causation (the injury was caused by the challenged action); and

1) The injury must be caused by the violation of a duty affecting the plaintiff's rights arising under the constitution or federal law [Simon v. Eastern Kentucky Welfare Rights Organization, 426 U.S. 26 (1976)].

(c) redressability.

1) The plaintiff must show that he will benefit from the remedy sought in the litigation.

EXAMPLE: Environmentalists sued the government because they did not receive notice when the government sold burnt timber after a particular forest fire. After settling the suit, the environmentalists brought a second suit, asking the court to require the government to give notice before conducting any future timber-salvage activities. Held: The environmentalists had standing in the first action because they suffered the concrete harm of being excluded from the sale of particular burnt timber. However, they lacked standing in the second action, because there was no new imminent harm caused by the government's general policy of not giving notice before timber-salvage activities [Summers v. Earth Island Institute, 555 U.S. 488 (2009)].

(2) **Specialized Problems of Standing**

(a) As a general rule, federal taxpayers do not have standing to challenge allegedly unconstitutional federal expenditures on the grounds that their injury is comparatively minute and indeterminable, and their interest is too remote [Massachusetts v. Mellon, 262 U.S. 447 (1923)].

EXCEPTION: In 1968, the Supreme Court held that a federal taxpayer had standing to challenge federal expenditures to aid parochial schools where the taxpayer was challenging the expenditure of money by Congress under its taxing and spending power and the expenditure allegedly violated the Establishment Clause [Flast v. Cohen, 392 U.S. 83 (1968)].

NOTE: The Flast v. Cohen principle has not been extended to other areas of government activity.

EXAMPLE: Taxpayers did not have standing to challenge a transfer of valuable real estate, under the Property Clause, to a Christian college from a local government [Valley Forge Christian College v. Americans United for Separation of Church and State, 454 U.S. 464 (1982)].

EXAMPLE: Citizens did not have standing to challenge a senator's or representative's service in the Armed Forces Reserve as violating Article I, Section 6, prohibiting a member of Congress from "holding any office under the United States" [Schlesinger v. Reservists Committee to Stop the War, 418 U.S. 208 (1974)].

(b) Under the traditional view, a litigant lacks standing to assert the rights of third parties not before the court [Tileston v. Ullman, 318 U.S. 44 (1943)].

1) The Supreme Court has permitted a party to raise the constitutional rights of a third party where she herself has suffered injury and:

a) a special relationship exists between the claimant and third party because of the connection between the interests of the claimant and the constitutional rights of the third person; and

EXAMPLE: The Supreme Court acknowledged the right of a physician to raise the rights of his patients in challenging an abortion ruling because of the close relationship between the doctor and his patient, and also because the patient was unable to bring suit on her own behalf [Singleton v. Wulff, 429 U.S. 106 (1976)].

EXAMPLE: A vendor of beer had standing to assert the rights of males under the age of 21 in a challenge to a law prohibiting the sale of beer to them [Craig v. Boren, 429 U.S. 190 (1976)].

EXAMPLE: A seller of contraceptives had standing to assert the rights of potential purchasers against a law prohibiting the sale of such devices [Carey v. Population Services International, 431 U.S. 678 (1977)].

b) the third party is unable or finds it difficult to bring suit on his own behalf.

2) An association has standing to assert the claims of its members, even if the association has not suffered any injury itself, if [Hunt v. Washington Apple Advertising Commission, 432 U.S. 333 (1977)]:

a) the members would otherwise have standing to sue in their own right;

b) the interest asserted is germane to the association's purpose; and

c) neither the claim asserted nor the relief requested would require participation by the individual members in the lawsuit.

f. **Political Questions**

(1) Federal courts cannot hear cases involving political questions. A **political question** is a matter assigned to another branch by the Constitution or incapable of a judicial answer. The Supreme Court set forth the following relevant factors to consider to determine if the political question doctrine applies [Baker v. Carr, 369 U.S. 186 (1962)]:

(a) whether there is a textually demonstrable constitutional commitment of the issue to a coordinate political department;

(b) a lack of judicially discoverable and manageable standards for resolving it;

(c) the impossibility of deciding without an initial policy determination of a kind clearly for nonjudicial discretion;

(d) the impossibility of a court's undertaking independent resolution without expressing lack of respect due coordinate branches of government;

(e) an unusual need for unquestioning adherence to a political decision already made; and

(f) the potential for embarrassment from multifarious pronouncements by various departments on one question.

(2) There are two principal factors related to the political question doctrine. First, considerations (a), (d), (e), and (f) enumerated above are rooted in the separation of powers. On the other hand, considerations (b) and (c) recognize the limitations of the judiciary in resolving certain types of controversies.

EXAMPLE: The ability of a grand jury to subpoena documents in the possession of the president against a claim of executive privilege does not present a political question apart from a claim based on national security [United States v. Nixon, 418 U.S. 683 (1974)].

(3) Other areas of political questions include decisions in regard to:
   (a) the impeachment process;
   (b) the amendment ratification process;
   (c) the president's power to unilaterally terminate a treaty;
   (d) foreign affairs; and
   (e) Guaranty Clause issues under Article IV.

NOTE A claim that a state has redrawn its electoral districts in a racially discriminatory manner is not a political question. However, a claim that a state has redrawn electoral districts to benefit one political party is a political question and, therefore, is nonjusticiable. The Supreme Court has ruled that there are manageable judicial standards for deciding claims of race discrimination, but that there are no such standards for deciding when a political party has been unfairly advantaged when electoral districts are redrawn.

B. The United States Supreme Court

1. Jurisdiction of the Supreme Court

a. Under Article III, Section 2, the Supreme Court has original jurisdiction "in all cases affecting ambassadors, other public ministers and consuls and those in which a state shall be a party." Congress may neither enlarge nor restrict the Supreme Court's original jurisdiction [Marbury v. Madison, 5 U.S. 137 (1803)].

b. Article III, Section 2 further provides that "in all other cases before mentioned, the Supreme Court shall have appellate jurisdiction, both as to law and fact, with such exceptions, and under such regulations as the Congress shall make." The Supreme Court has the power to:
   (1) hold acts of the other branches of the federal government (the executive branch and Congress) unconstitutional [Marbury v. Madison, 5 U.S. 137 (1803)];
   (2) hold state statutes unconstitutional [Fletcher v. Peck, 10 U.S. 87 (1810)];
   (3) review state court decisions to ensure that the states act in conformity with the U.S. Constitution and federal statutes [Martin v. Hunter's Lessee, 14 U.S. 304 (1816)]; and
   (4) decide other state law questions.
      (a) In cases of diversity jurisdiction:
         1) the Supreme Court will defer to an existing state court interpretation of state law;
         2) the Supreme Court will interpret a state law which has not already been interpreted by the state court based on the Supreme Court's prediction of how the state court will interpret the statute; and

3) the Supreme Court will abstain from a decision if the state court's interpretation of unsettled state law could end the dispute and the Supreme Court cannot predict how the state court will rule.

c. Under federal law, there are two methods for invoking Supreme Court appellate jurisdiction [28 U.S.C. § 1257]:

(1) by appeal (where jurisdiction is mandatory); and

(a) In 1988, an act of Congress reduced obligatory review on appeal to decisions of three-judge federal district courts.

(2) by writ of *certiorari* (discretionary review where four or more justices vote to hear the case).

(a) Since the two categories of decisions that were subject to obligatory review on appeal have been eliminated, practically all decisions from state supreme courts and federal courts are now reviewable by a writ of *certiorari*, except decisions made purely on state law.

(b) Grounds for *certiorari* include:

1) cases involving conflicts between different federal courts of appeal;

2) cases involving conflicts between the highest courts of two states;

3) cases involving conflicts between the highest state court and a federal court of appeals; or

4) cases from state courts or U.S. courts of appeal involving important, yet unresolved, issues.

d. **Adequate and Independent State Grounds**

(1) Although a state court decision may involve a federal question, if the state court judgment can be supported on an adequate and independent state ground, the Supreme Court will not take jurisdiction. To do so would be tantamount to rendering an "advisory opinion" [Herb v. Pitcairn, 324 U.S. 117 (1945)].

(a) Unlike other doctrines of judicial review, which apply to the entire federal judiciary, adequate state grounds apply only to the Supreme Court.

(2) Where a state court clearly states that a state law violates other state law or a provision of the state constitution, that decision will be an adequate and independent state ground (regardless of whether the opinion also decides that the state law violates a federal law as well).

(a) Where a state court holds that a state law violates both the state and federal constitutions, the doctrine of adequate state grounds will apply.

(3) Where a state court's decision is based upon a federal interpretation of a similar federal law, adequate and independent state grounds will not apply. The Supreme Court may review in this situation.

(4) Where it is unclear whether the state court made its decision based upon state or federal interpretations of statutes, the Supreme Court may take the case, although it also has the power in that situation to dismiss or remand the case for clarification from the state court.

(a) The independence prong focuses on whether it is "apparent from the four corners" of the opinion that the state court judgment was settled based on a state court interpretation of state law precedent or the state's constitution. If not, the Supreme Court may [Michigan v. Long, 463 U.S. 1032 (1983)]:

1) obtain clarification from the state court; or

2) presume that the state court decision was rooted—at least in part—in federal law, and review the case.

II. SEPARATION OF POWERS

A. The Powers of Congress

1. Legislative Power

a. Legislative power is primarily the power to make laws, but incidental to that power is the right to conduct investigations and hearings, consider matters upon which legislation may be enacted, and do all other things "necessary and proper" to the enactment of legislation [U.S. Const. art. I, § 1].

(1) Congress has enumerated powers to collect taxes and spend money for the general welfare, to borrow money on the credit of the United States, to regulate commerce with foreign nations and among the several states, to declare war, and to raise and support the army, navy, and militia [U.S. Const. art. I, § 8].

(2) The Necessary and Proper Clause gives Congress the implied power "to make all Laws which shall be necessary and proper for carrying into Execution the foregoing Powers, and all other Powers vested by this Constitution in the Government of the United States, or any Department or Officer thereof" [U.S. Const. art. I, § 8].

(3) The Enabling Clauses of the Thirteenth, Fourteenth, and Fifteenth Amendments give Congress the power to enforce those amendments by "appropriate legislation."

2. Commerce Power

a. Despite the broad language used by the Supreme Court in Gibbons v. Ogden [22 U.S. 1 (1824)], subsequent cases used various criteria to restrict the power of Congress to regulate "commerce which concerns more states than one." Today, Congress can regulate:

(1) channels of interstate commerce (i.e., highways, waterways, and air traffic);

(2) instrumentalities of interstate commerce (i.e., cars, trucks, ships, and airplanes); and

(3) activities that "substantially affect" interstate commerce.

(a) Under the **affectation doctrine**, Congress now has the power to regulate any economic activity, whether carried on in one state or many, that has a substantial effect (whether directly or indirectly) upon interstate commerce.

1) This doctrine was first formulated in National Labor Relations Board v. Jones and Laughlin Steel Co. [301 U.S. 1 (1937)], which upheld the constitutionality of the Wagner Act in requiring collective bargaining in all industries "affecting" interstate commerce.

(b) The affectation doctrine was expanded upon by the **cumulative effect doctrine**, in which the Supreme Court held that the federal commerce power permitted regulation of the amount of wheat a farmer could grow on his own land, for his own consumption, because his activity, together with that of other growers of wheat for their own consumption, had a substantial cumulative effect upon interstate commerce [Wickard v. Filburn, 317 U.S. 111 (1942)].

(c) Congress's plenary commerce power is not without limits. In United States v. Lopez [514 U.S. 549 (1995)], for the first time in more than half a century, the Supreme Court struck down a federal law that made it a crime for any individual knowingly to possess a firearm in a school zone. Since gun possession near schools is neither itself an "economic" activity nor an activity that "substantially" affects interstate commerce, and since no "jurisdictional element" connecting particular gun possession to interstate commerce was expressed in the language of the statute, the Supreme Court held that Congress was acting beyond the limits of the Commerce Clause.

NOTE To validly exercise its Commerce Clause power under the "substantial effects" test, Congress must now show: (1) that the regulated activity is "economic" in nature; and (2) that the regulated activity (when taken cumulatively throughout the nation) has a substantial effect on interstate commerce.

(d) The Commerce Clause has been used as the vehicle to uphold laws aimed at barring racial discrimination in activities connected with interstate commerce.

EXAMPLE: Congress may prohibit racial discrimination in private restaurants if a substantial portion of the food consumed traveled in interstate commerce [Katzenbach v. McClung, 379 U.S. 294 (1964)].

EXAMPLE: The Court has upheld provisions of the Civil Rights Act of 1964 barring discrimination in places of public accommodation (e.g., as applied to a motel) as "affecting" interstate commerce [Heart of Atlanta Motel v. United States, 379 U.S. 241 (1964)].

(e) The Supreme Court has upheld, under the commerce power, a federal law prohibiting extortionate credit transactions (i.e., loan sharking) on the grounds that such transactions provide a major source of revenue for organized crime, and that organized crime, in turn, has an adverse effect upon interstate commerce [Perez v. United States, 402 U.S. 146 (1971)].

(f) The Tenth Amendment, which provides that powers not delegated to the federal government are reserved to the states, or to the people, serves as a very weak limitation on the federal commerce power today. Generally applicable federal laws that regulate the states (state businesses and/or employees) do not violate the Tenth Amendment [Garcia v. San Antonio Metropolitan Transit Authority, 469 U.S. 528 (1985)].

NOTE The Tenth Amendment does prevent Congress from interfering with a state's lawmaking processes. Congress may not commandeer the legislative processes of the states by directly compelling them to enact and enforce a federal regulatory program.

EXAMPLE: The Supreme Court has held invalid as violating the Tenth Amendment a federal law that required the state of New York to pass legislation to arrange for the disposal of radioactive waste generated within its borders [New York v. United States, 505 U.S. 144 (1992)].

NOTE The Tenth Amendment also prevents Congress from commandeering state executive officials. That is, Congress may not order state officials to act as administrators of federal programs.

EXAMPLE: The Supreme Court held unconstitutional the federal Brady Handgun Violence Protection Act, because it commandeered state and local law enforcement officers for performance of various acts required by federal legislation [Printz v. United States, 521 U.S. 898 (1997)].

3. **Taxing Power**

   a. Congress has the power to lay and collect taxes, duties, imposts, and excises to pay the debts and provide for the common defense and general welfare [U.S. Const. art. I, § 8].

EXAM TIP A congressional act purporting to be a "tax" should be upheld as a valid exercise of the taxing power provided that it does, in fact, raise revenue (the **objective test**) or that it was intended to raise revenue (the **subjective test**).

NOTE The Sixteenth Amendment gives Congress the power to collect taxes on incomes derived from any source.

   b. Congress has used its taxing power as a necessary and proper means of achieving a regulatory effect. Generally, as long as Congress has the power to regulate the activity taxed, the tax can then be used as a regulating device rather than for revenue-raising purposes.

   EXAMPLE: The Supreme Court sustained a tax on coal producers who violated a fair competition law, even though it was clearly designed to be a penalty rather than revenue-raising [Sunshine Anthracite Coal Co. v. Adkins, 310 U.S. 381 (1940)].

      (1) Even when Congress does not have power to regulate the activity taxed, the tax will nevertheless be upheld if its "dominant intent" is revenue-raising. Thus, even though the tax may have a substantial regulatory effect, if the tax in fact raises revenue, it will be valid.

EXAMPLE: The Supreme Court upheld as revenue-raising a discriminatory tax on colored oleomargarine, even though Congress did not have the power to regulate its production directly [McCray v. United States, 195 U.S. 27 (1904)].

(2) As a general rule, the modern judicial trend is to uphold any tax as valid if it is, in fact, a revenue-raising measure.

EXAMPLE: Although a tax on bookmaking activities had a regulatory effect, it was upheld as producing revenue (albeit negligible in amount) [United States v. Kahriger, 345 U.S. 22 (1953)].

EXAMPLE: The taxing power was held by the Supreme Court to justify a penalty on individuals who opt not to purchase health insurance [National Federation of Independent Business v. Sebelius, 567 U.S. 519 (2012)].

4. **Spending Power**

a. Congress has the power to lay and collect taxes "to pay the Debts and provide for the common Defense and General Welfare of the United States" [U.S. Const. art. I, § 8, cl. 1].

(1) The Supreme Court has construed the General Welfare Clause as a limitation on Congress's taxing and spending powers and not as an independent source of congressional power. In other words, Congress's power to tax and spend must be exercised for the "general welfare" of the United States [United States v. Butler, 297 U.S. 1 (1936)].

EXAMPLE: The Federal Election Campaign Act, which limited the amount a candidate could spend if she accepted money from the federal government, is a valid exercise of the power to spend for the "general welfare." The Supreme Court sustained the power of Congress to finance elections because this would reduce the harmful effect of candidates' reliance on large private contributions [Buckley v. Valeo, 424 U.S. 1 (1976)]. However, the power is not unlimited. Threatening the states with complete loss of Federal Medicaid funding if the states refused to comply with the expansion of the program was held unconstitutional [National Federation of Independent Business v. Sebelius, 567 U.S. 519 (2012)].

(2) By exercising its spending power, Congress can require states to comply with specified conditions in order to qualify for federal funds.

EXAMPLE: Congress conditioned further grants of highway funds upon the resignation of a state highway administrator who was also the state Democratic Party chairman [Oklahoma v. Civil Service Commission, 330 U.S. 127 (1947)].

(3) The Supreme Court held that Congress may place a condition on the receipt of federal funds by a state if [South Dakota v. Dole, 483 U.S. 203 (1987)]:

(a) the spending serves the general welfare;
(b) the condition is unambiguous;
(c) the condition relates to the federal program;
(d) the state is not required to undertake unconstitutional action; and
(e) the amount in question is not so great as to be considered coercive to the state's acceptance.

EXAMPLE: The Supreme Court rejected South Dakota's Tenth and Twenty-First Amendment arguments and upheld Congress's withholding of federal highway funds from states permitting the purchasing of alcoholic beverages by individuals under age 21.

5. **War and Defense Powers**
   a. Congress may [U.S. Const. art. I, § 8]:
      (1) declare war;
      (2) raise and support armies;
      (3) provide and maintain a navy; and
      (4) organize, arm, discipline, and call forth a militia.
   b. The war power confers upon Congress a very broad authority to initiate whatever measures it deems necessary to provide for the national defense, in peacetime as well as in wartime.
      (1) Thus, the military draft and selective service systems have repeatedly been upheld [United States v. O'Brien, 391 U.S. 367 (1968)].
      (2) Similarly, the power of Congress to initiate wage, price, and rent control of the civilian economy during wartime has been sustained [Yakus v. United States, 321 U.S. 414 (1944)].
   c. The exclusion of civilians from certain restricted areas during wartime has been approved [Korematsu v. United States, 323 U.S. 214 (1944)]. Congress has the power to establish military courts and tribunals. Since military courts are not Article III courts, the accused in court-martial proceedings is not entitled to the same procedural safeguards set forth in the Bill of Rights (e.g., the right to jury trial or grand jury indictment). Rather, an accused is safeguarded by the procedures provided in the Uniform Code of Military Justice [U.S. Const. art. I, § 8, cl. 14].
      (1) Military courts have jurisdiction over offenses committed by service members on a military post or in an area under military control. Jurisdiction is determined by the status of the individual as an armed service member, not the connection between service and the offense [Solorio v. United States, 483 U.S. 435 (1987)].
      (2) Military courts also have jurisdiction over current members of the armed forces, even while on a pass or on leave, for nonservice matters.
      (3) As long as civilian courts are available, military courts are denied jurisdiction over civilians and their dependents unless Congress has affirmatively granted such jurisdiction.

EXAMPLE: The Supreme Court held that, absent military exigency, the president may not try alleged terrorists in special military courts if Congress has enacted a statute denying the president that authority. Congress, however, may affirmatively grant that authority to the president [Hamdan v. Rumsfeld, 548 U.S. 557 (2006)].

(4) Although civilian courts have no general power of review over court-martial proceedings, there can be a limited examination of the regularity of such proceedings by a civilian court [Burns v. Wilson, 339 U.S. 103 (1950)].

6. **Investigatory Power**

a. Although Congress does not have any express constitutional power to investigate, the Necessary and Proper Clause permits Congress to conduct investigations incident to its legislative power [McGrain v. Daugherty, 273 U.S. 135 (1927)].

(1) Congress's investigatory power is broad, and it may extend to any matter within a "legitimate legislative sphere."

(2) If a witness fails to appear after being summoned before a congressional committee or fails to answer a question posed by such a committee, Congress may either:

(a) cite the witness for contempt; or

(b) refer the matter to the U.S. attorney general for prosecution.

(3) Generally, a witness can raise as a defense:

(a) the privilege against self-incrimination;

(b) lack of due process safeguards; or

(c) interference with the First Amendment rights to privacy and freedom of association.

EXAMPLE: The Supreme Court upheld the refusal of a member of the NAACP to release membership lists to a legislative committee because there was not a sufficient nexus between the investigation and the records sought [Gibson v. Florida Legislative Committee, 372 U.S. 539 (1963)].

7. **Property Power**

a. Congress has the power "to dispose of and make all needful Rules and Regulations respecting the Territory or other Property belonging to the United States" [U.S. Const. art. IV, § 3].

8. **Power of Eminent Domain**

a. Although the Constitution does not expressly give Congress the power of eminent domain, the power to take property is "implied in aid of the other powers granted to the federal government" [Kohl v. United States, 91 U.S. 367 (1876)].

b. This power is limited, however. The Fifth Amendment provides, in part, that private property shall not be taken for public use without just compensation.

EXAM TIP Be sure to consider and include an analysis under the Takings Clause.

9. **Admiralty and Maritime Power**
   a. The Supreme Court has determined that the Necessary and Proper Clause gives Congress complete and plenary power to fix and determine the maritime laws throughout the country [Southern Pacific Co. v. Jensen, 244 U.S. 205 (1917)].
10. **Bankruptcy Power**
   a. Congress has the power "to establish uniform Laws on the subject of Bankruptcies throughout the United States" [U.S. Const. art. I, § 8, cl. 4].
11. **Postal Power**
   a. Congress may establish post offices and post roads [U.S. Const. art. I, § 8, cl. 7].

NOTE The post office has now been moved out of the Cabinet and is a self-operating entity within the government.

12. **Copyright and Patent Power**
   a. Congress may "promote the Progress of Science and useful Arts, by securing for limited Times to Authors and Inventors the exclusive Right to their respective Writings and Discoveries" [U.S. Const. art. I, § 8, cl. 8].
13. **Speech and Debate Clause**
   a. "The Senators and Representatives...for any Speech or Debate in either House...shall not be questioned in any other Place" [U.S. Const. art. I, § 6, cl. 1].
   b. The Speech and Debate Clause protects legislators and their aides against criminal or civil proceedings for "legislative acts" [United States v. Johnson, 383 U.S. 169 (1966); Gravel v. United States, 408 U.S. 606 (1972)]. Members of Congress, however, can be liable based on defamation for issuing press releases or newsletters that injure reputation [U.S. Const. art. I, § 6, cl. 1].
      (1) The clause insulates members of Congress for "acts that occur in the regular course of the legislative process," but does not bar prosecution for taking a bribe to influence legislation [United States v. Brewster, 408 U.S. 501 (1972)].
      (2) The Speech and Debate Clause forbids the courts from enjoining members of Congress or their aides from issuing subpoenas or conducting their inquiry [Eastland v. United States Servicemen's Fund, 421 U.S. 491 (1975)].
14. **Civil War Amendments**
   a. Congress has the power to enforce:
      (1) the Thirteenth Amendment, banning slavery;
      (2) the Fourteenth Amendment, prohibiting the states from violating protections regarding due process, equal protection, and privileges and immunities; and

(3) the Fifteenth Amendment, prohibiting the states from discriminating in voting rights.

b. To validly enforce the Fourteenth or Fifteenth Amendment, Congress must show that:

(1) state governments have engaged in widespread violations of the amendment; and

(2) the legislative remedy is "congruent with and proportional to" the violations.

c. Congress may enforce the Thirteenth Amendment ban on slavery even when the state governments have not violated the amendment. However, Congress may enforce the Fourteenth and Fifteenth Amendments only when state governments have widely violated those Amendments.

B. Executive Power

1. Chief Executive

a. "The Executive Power shall be vested in a President of the United States." This provision confers broad authority in the president to execute the laws of the United States. There are few enumerated powers expressly granted to the president under Article II. Many of the president's domestic and foreign powers are implied. The Supreme Court has held that the president has no power to make laws, but has the power to execute them [U.S. Const. art. II, § 1].

(1) **Appointment Power**

(a) Article II gives the president the power, "with the Advice and Consent of the Senate," to nominate and appoint all "Ambassadors, other public Ministers and Consuls, Judges of the Supreme Court, and all other Officers of the United States, whose appointments are not herein otherwise provided for" [U.S. Const. art. II, § 2].

NOTE The presidential appointment power should be construed as a limitation on the congressional appointment power. Although Congress can appoint officials to its legislative committees, it cannot appoint members to any agency or commission with administrative powers.

EXAMPLE: An attempt to vest the power to appoint members of the Federal Elections Commission in the speaker of the House of Representatives was held unconstitutional [Buckley v. Valeo, 424 U.S. 1 (1976)].

(b) The president, therefore, has the exclusive power to nominate high-level officials such as cabinet members, ambassadors, and heads of agencies. The Senate, however, has the power to confirm or reject the president's nominees for such high-level appointments.

(c) Congress can delegate the appointment of "inferior" officers (including special prosecutors) to:
1) the president;
2) the judiciary; or
3) heads of departments.

(2) **Removal Power**

(a) Although the U.S. Constitution is silent with respect to removal power, it is generally agreed that the president may remove any executive appointee (e.g., an ambassador or cabinet member) without cause.

(b) However, the president must have cause (i.e., good reasons) to remove executive officers having fixed terms and officers performing judicial or *quasi*-judicial functions (e.g., a member of the Federal Trade Commission).

(c) Congress has no power to summarily remove an executive officer [Bowsher v. Synar, 478 U.S. 714 (1986)].

(d) Federal judges cannot be removed by either Congress or the president during "good behavior"; formal impeachment proceedings are required for removal.

(3) **Veto Power**

(a) Once Congress has passed legislation and presented it to the president, the president has 10 days in which to act upon it. Unless he vetoes it within the 10-day period, the proposed legislation will become law [U.S. Const. art. I, § 7].

(b) The president can **pocket veto** a bill passed within 10 days of the end of the congressional term by not signing it.

(c) Congress has the power to override a veto by a two-thirds vote of both the Senate and House of Representatives [U.S. Const. art. I, § 7].

(d) A **line-item veto**, which gives the president the power to cancel particular provisions of new federal legislation, has been held unconstitutional as a grant of power to the president to amend a statute. Amendments are valid only when Congress enacts a new statute followed by a presidential signature [Clinton v. City of New York, 524 U.S. 417 (1998)].

(4) **Congressional Legislation and Presidential Power**

(a) The president may exercise only those powers expressly or impliedly granted by the Constitution or an act of Congress. Moreover, if Congress validly exercises one of its powers and overrides the president, then Congress prevails over the president.

EXAMPLE: The president may not validly use his power as commander-in-chief to seize a factory in order to prevent a strike during wartime if Congress opposes such action [Youngstown Sheet and Tube Co. v. Sawyer, 343 U.S. 579 (1952)].

(b) Congress can enact legislation that delegates rulemaking power to an executive or administrative agency in some designated subject area (such as securities law, labor law, environmental law, and so on), creating a huge exception to the general rule that the executive branch may not make law.

(c) The Supreme Court has found that Congress has the power to delegate the authority to make rules having the power of law to the executive branch as long as Congress provides an intelligible principle to guide the executive branch [J.W. Hampton, Jr., & Co. v. United States, 276 U.S. 394 (1928)].

(5) **Pardon Power**

(a) The president may "grant reprieves and pardons for offenses against the United States, except in cases of impeachment" [U.S. Const. art. II, § 2].

(6) **Executive Privilege**

(a) The president has an absolute privilege to refuse to disclose information relating to military, diplomatic, or sensitive national security secrets.

(b) Other confidential communications between the president and his advisors are presumptively privileged [United States v. Nixon, 418 U.S. 683 (1974)]. The presumption is overcome when confidential communications are subpoenaed as evidence in a criminal trial.

(7) **Obligation to Report**

(a) The president "shall from time to time give to the Congress Information of the State of the Union, and recommend to their Consideration such Measures as he shall judge necessary and expedient." This obligation has evolved into the annual "State of the Union" address given by the president [U.S. Const. art. II, § 3].

(8) **Faithful Execution**

(a) The Constitution requires that the president "take Care that the Laws be faithfully executed" [U.S. Const. art. II, § 3]. This has been referred to as the Take Care Clause, Faithful Execution Clause, and Faithfully Executed Clause.

(b) This clause has been interpreted as placing a duty on the president and executive branch to enforce the laws of the United States, even where the president may disagree with the purpose of that law. It does not imply a power to forbid a law's execution [Kendall v. United States, 37 U.S. 524 (1838)].

(c) However, while the exact scope of this has never been defined, courts have construed the provision as vesting the executive branch "with substantial discretion in choosing when and how to prosecute cases" [United States v. Bolden, 353 F.3d 870 (10th Cir. 2003)].

2. **Commander-in-Chief**

a. "The President shall be the Commander in Chief of the Army and Navy of the United States, and of the militia of the several States when called into the actual service of the United States by Congress" [U.S. Const. art. II, § 2].

(1) **Military Powers**

(a) The president has the power to deploy military forces without a formal declaration of war in response to an attack upon the United States (as determined by the Prize Cases) [Brig Amy Warwick, 67 U.S. 635 (1863)].

(b) He additionally has the power to seize private property during wartime unless Congress denies him that power [United States v. Pewee Coal Co., 341 U.S. 114 (1951)].

(c) However, the president does not have the power to declare war.

(2) **Unsettled Areas**

(a) Clearly, the president may commit troops to repel a sudden attack on the United States. However, certain issues remain unclear, such as:

1) whether the president may commit forces without congressional approval to aid a U.S. ally under attack (although provisions in certain defense treaties would authorize such intervention); and

2) whether the president may order a preemptive strike in anticipation of an enemy attack.

3. **International Affairs**

a. **Treaty Power**

(1) The president has the power to make treaties with foreign nations "by and with the Advice and Consent of the Senate" [U.S. Const. art. II, § 2, cl. 2]. Treaties require consent of two-thirds of the Senate before they can be enacted.

(a) A treaty is **self-executing** when it takes effect without the necessity of any further action by Congress beyond consent or ratification [Missouri v. Holland, 252 U.S. 416 (1920)].

(b) A treaty is not self-executing when it requires Congress (or state legislatures) to pass legislation to implement its provisions—i.e., requiring a change in either federal or state law which would enable fulfillment of treaty obligations.

(2) In accordance with the Supremacy Clause, treaties are "the supreme Law of the land; and the Judges of every State shall

be bound thereby, any Thing in the Constitution of Laws of any State to the Contrary notwithstanding" [U.S. Const. art. VI, cl. 2].

(a) Self-executing treaties are considered the supreme law of the land, whereas treaties which are not self-executing become part of the supreme law of the land, and thus supersede existing federal and state statutes, only when further legislative action is taken by Congress.

NOTE Treaties take precedence over any conflicting state law regardless of whether a treaty precedes or follows the enactment of the state law [Nielsen v. Johnson, 279 U.S. 47 (1929)]. However, when a treaty and federal statute conflict on the issue in question, time determines the controlling authority—the last-in-time will prevail.

b. **Executive Agreements**

(1) The president has the power to enter into executive agreements and compacts with foreign nations. Such agreements are valid and prevail over inconsistent state law [United States v. Belmont, 301 U.S. 324 (1937)].

(2) Executive agreements are the sole responsibility of the president, and need not be ratified by Congress.

(3) Executive agreements do not prevail over federal statutes.

TREATIES AND EXECUTIVE AGREEMENTS: PRECEDENCE CHART

	U.S. Constitution	Federal Law	State Law
Treaties	Constitution prevails.	Last-in-time prevails.	Treaty prevails.
Executive Agreements	Constitution prevails.	Conflicting federal statute prevails.	Executive agreement prevails.

C. Interbranch Checks upon the Exercise of Federal Power

1. Congressional Limits on the Executive

a. **Foreign Affairs**

(1) If Congress is acting within its constitutional powers, Congress may block the president from acting.

b. **Impeachment Power**

(1) "The President, Vice President, and all civil Officers of the United States shall be removed from Office on Impeachment for, and Conviction of, Treason, Bribery or other high Crimes and Misdemeanors" [U.S. Const. art. II, § 4].

(a) The House of Representatives has the sole power to impeach.

(b) The Senate has the sole power to try impeachments. A two-thirds vote in the Senate is required for conviction.

c. **Legislative Veto**

(1) A legislative veto occurs when Congress enacts a law containing a provision that Congress can change the law without a new Congressional vote or presidential signature.

(2) The Supreme Court has held that a legislative veto violated the constitutional requirements of bicameralism and presentment to the president [Immigration & Naturalization Service v. Chadha, 462 U.S. 919 (1983)].

d. **Investigative Power**

(1) As indicated earlier, under the Necessary and Proper Clause, Congress has the implied power to conduct investigations concerning all matters over which Congress has jurisdiction.

e. **Delegation to Executive**

(1) On numerous occasions Congress has delegated to the executive branch the authority to make rules having the power of law (through rulemaking by such agencies, such as the Department of Health, Education, and Welfare; the Environmental Protection Agency; and the Nuclear Regulatory Commission).

f. **Appropriations Power**

(1) Where Congress by legislative act explicitly directs the president to spend appropriated money, the president has no power to impound (i.e., refuse to spend or delay spending) the authorized funds.

2. **Presidential Limits on Congress**

a. Every act of Congress must be approved and signed by the president before it can become law, or, being disapproved, must be passed by a two-thirds vote of each House [U.S. Const. art. I, § 7].

3. **Judicial Limits on Congress and the President**

a. The federal judiciary is the ultimate arbiter of cases whose disposition depends upon construction of the Constitution, an act of Congress, or a federal treaty [U.S. Const. art. III, § 2].

PYRAMID OF POWER IN U.S. LAW

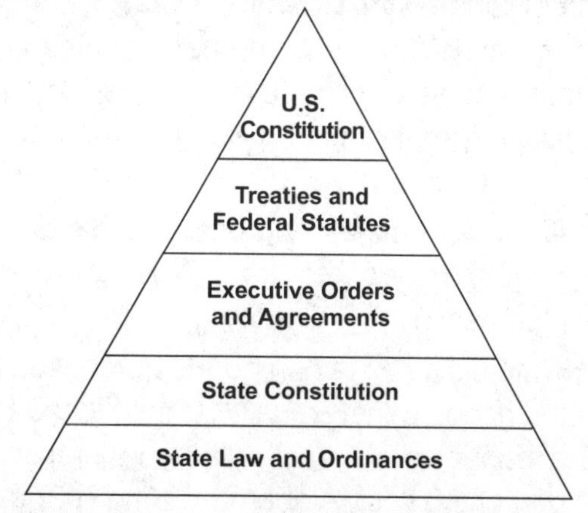

III. THE RELATION OF THE NATION AND THE STATES IN THE FEDERAL SYSTEM

A. Nature and Scope of Federal and State Powers

1. The fundamental principle of federalism is the co-existence of the national government and the state governments.
2. The Tenth Amendment provides that "[t]he powers not delegated to the United States by the Constitution, nor prohibited by it to the States, are reserved to the States respectively, or to the people."
3. While each state has a general police power, there is no federal police power. The federal government must legislate through one of its enumerated powers, whereas the states may regulate any health, safety, welfare, moral, or aesthetic interest through their respective police powers.
4. The U.S. Constitution limits the state's police powers by:
   a. reserving certain enumerated powers exclusively for the federal government;
   b. restricting both the federal and state governments from acting in violation of constitutional provisions; and
   c. providing under the Supremacy Clause that if Congress enacts legislation with the intention of preempting state law, the congressional regulation will control.

B. Intergovernmental Immunities

1. **Immunity of the Federal Government**
   a. The federal government and its agencies are immune from suits by private individuals except where they allow themselves to be sued (e.g., the Federal Tort Claims Act).

      EXAMPLE: The U.S. Postal Service is part of the federal government rather than a separate antitrust "person" under the Sherman Act, and therefore is not subject to antitrust liability [U.S. Postal Service v. Flamingo Industries (USA) Ltd., 540 U.S. 736 (2004)].

   b. **Taxation of the Federal Government by a State**
      (1) In accordance with McCulloch v. Maryland [17 U.S. 316 (1819)], the federal government and its agencies are immune from state taxation and state regulation. States may nevertheless collect a nondiscriminatory tax on persons who deal or contract with the federal government.
         (a) A nondiscriminatory gross-receipts tax applied to a contractor performing work for the federal government has been upheld [James v. Dravo Contracting Co., 302 U.S. 134 (1937)].
         (b) A state's sales tax on goods purchased by a contractor, even if the goods will eventually be sold to the United States, is valid. In a "cost-plus" contract with the federal government, the tax will be part of the cost [Alabama v. King & Boozer, 314 U.S. 1 (1941)].

1) However, such a sales tax is invalid if it falls upon the federal government itself.

(c) A state property tax is valid when applied upon a building owned by the United States but used by a contractor [Detroit v. Murray Corp., 355 U.S. 489 (1959)]. Likewise, a building owned by a contractor doing work for the United States will be subject to a property tax.

(d) A state income tax applied to employees of the United States domiciled within that state is valid [Graves v. O'Keefe, 306 U.S. 466 (1939)].

c. As a general rule, the Supremacy Clause impliedly prevents the states from regulating the activities of agents or instrumentalities of the federal government if the regulation will interfere with the government's ability to carry out its federal functions [Johnson v. Maryland, 254 U.S. 51 (1920)].

(1) Congress has the power "to dispose of and make all needful rules and regulations respecting the territory or other property belonging to the United States." Thus, federal lands (e.g., military bases, Indian reservations, FBI offices, etc.) are subject to the authority of the federal government, except to the extent that Congress has ceded jurisdiction to the state [U.S. Const. art. IV, § 3, cl. 2].

EXAMPLE: States cannot require a federal contractor to obtain a state license to construct facilities at an Air Force base located within the state [Miller Inc. v. Arkansas, 352 U.S. 187 (1956)].

2. **Immunity of State Governments**

a. The federal government, or one of its agencies or instrumentalities, may sue a state without its consent. In this case, the Supreme Court has original, but not exclusive, jurisdiction.

b. A state may be sued by a sister state without its consent. In this case, the Supreme Court has original and exclusive jurisdiction.

c. As a general rule, the Eleventh Amendment prohibits citizens of one state from suing another state in federal court. This rule has been extended to prohibit suits by a citizen of a state against his own state. However, some exceptions do exist to this rule. In particular [Ex parte Young, 209 U.S. 123 (1908)]:

(1) a state may be sued if it consents to the suit; and

(2) a state officer may be sued for injunctive relief on the theory that her allegedly unlawful conduct was beyond the scope of her authority.

d. Congress is generally limited to the powers granted to it by the Constitution and, as explained above, is prohibited by the Tenth Amendment from "commandeering" state governments. The Supreme Court has attempted to limit Congress' use of the Commerce Clause to regulate integral operations in areas of traditional government functions [National League of Cities v. Usery, 426 U.S. 833 (1976)].

(1) However, Usery was overruled in 1985 by a decision in which the Supreme Court found that drawing immunity boundaries around "traditional government functions" was unworkable and "inconsistent with established principles of federalism" [Garcia v. San Antonio Metro. Transit Auth., 469 U.S. 528 (1985)].

e. A state now enjoys immunity from federal taxation if the tax is applied to either:
   (1) unique state activities; or
   (2) essential governmental functions.

NOTE Where a state engages in a proprietary business (i.e., one similar in nature to a business operated by a private individual), then the state may be taxed to the same extent as the private citizen.

C. Authority Reserved for the States

1. The Tenth Amendment

a. The Tenth Amendment provides that the "powers not delegated to the United States by the Constitution, nor prohibited by it to the States, are reserved to the States respectively, or to the people."

EXAM TIP The Tenth Amendment is frequently a "red herring" wrong answer choice except when the facts show the federal government "commanding" the states.

b. The Constitution specifically prohibits any state from [U.S. Const. art. I, § 10]:
   (1) making treaties with other nations;
   (2) coining money;
   (3) passing a bill of attainder;
   (4) enacting an *ex post facto* law;
   (5) impairing the obligation of contracts;
   (6) laying any duty on imports or exports, except where necessary for executing its inspection laws;
   (7) engaging in war; or
   (8) maintaining a peacetime army.

c. The Tenth Amendment prohibits the federal government from using an enumerated power to force a state legislature to pass a law or a state executive official to administer a federal program. This is known as the **anti-commandeering doctrine**.

2. The Dormant Commerce Clause

a. The Commerce Clause gives Congress the power to regulate interstate commerce. Where Congress has not enacted legislation, the states are free to regulate local transactions affecting interstate commerce, subject to certain limitations. These limitations are generally known as the **dormant Commerce Clause**, or the **negative implications doctrine**.

b. If a state law discriminates on its face between in-state and out-of-state economic actors, the state must show that:
   (1) the regulation serves a compelling state interest; and
   (2) the regulation is narrowly tailored to serve that interest.

c. If a state law merely incidentally burdens interstate commerce, the court will apply a balancing test and the law will be upheld unless the burden imposed on interstate commerce clearly outweighs the local benefits [Pike v. Bruce Church, Inc., 397 U.S. 137, 142 (1970)].

d. There are some exceptions to the dormant Commerce Clause which should be noted:
   (1) Congress may affirmatively authorize states to legislate in areas that would violate the dormant Commerce clause; and
   (2) when states act as market participants, they may discriminate between in-state and out-of-state businesses.

e. Traditionally, it is within the state's police power to enact legislation for the protection of the health, safety, and welfare of its citizens.

   EXAMPLE: A Detroit smoke-abatement ordinance that affected ships traveling in interstate commerce was upheld as a valid health measure [Huron Portland Cement Co. v. City of Detroit, 362 U.S. 440 (1960)].

   (1) The Privileges and Immunities Clause under Article IV, Section 2 prohibits states from enacting legislation that discriminates against out-of-state residents. No state or municipality may deny citizens of other states any rights that it affords its own citizens without substantial justification. This applies only to individuals, not aliens or corporations. The dormant Commerce Clause is applicable to aliens, businesses and corporations, as well as individuals, as it deals with laws affecting interstate commerce.

f. If a state regulation furthers no ostensible benefit and imposes a substantial burden on interstate commerce, it will likely be held unconstitutional.

   EXAMPLE: An Illinois statute requiring all trucks to be equipped with a new type of contour mudguards (instead of the flat mudguards permitted in all other states) was declared unconstitutional because it placed an undue burden on interstate carriers [Bibb v. Navajo Freight Lines, Inc., 359 U.S. 520 (1959)].

   EXAMPLE: A state law limiting the length of trucks traveling on state highways or trains rolling through the state is unconstitutional because the regulation unduly burdened interstate commerce, and the state failed to demonstrate any significant safety benefit [Raymond Motor Transportation, Inc. v. Rice, 434 U.S. 429 (1978)].

g. Generally, public health measures (e.g., quarantine and inspection laws) are upheld so long as they do not discriminate against or unduly burden interstate commerce [Hannibal & St. Joseph Railroad v. Husen, 95 U.S. 465 (1877)].

D. Reserved State Power in Taxation

1. As a general rule, state taxation of interstate commerce is permissible as long as the tax does not discriminate against or unduly burden interstate commerce. In determining the validity of a state tax affecting interstate commerce, the court will generally consider the following four factors [Complete Auto Transit, Inc. v. Brady, 430 U.S. 274 (1977)]:
   a. there must be a substantial nexus between the activity taxed and the taxing state;
      (1) In other words, the taxpayer must have "sufficient contacts" or presence within the taxing state.
      (2) "Substantial nexus" is more than "minimum contacts" under the Due Process Clause.

NOTE A regular operation within a state, despite owning no property, is enough to show "substantial nexus"—for example, an airline operating regularly scheduled flights from a rented station [Braniff Airways, Inc. v. Neb. Bd. of Equalization, 347 U.S. 590 (1954)].

   b. the tax must be fairly apportioned;
      (1) The taxpayer has the burden of proving unfair apportionment.

      EXAMPLE: The Supreme Court invalidated an apportionment based upon track mileage within the state, as compared with total track mileage, which resulted in a disproportionate tax because the railroad had an unusually large amount of track in the taxing state [Norfolk & Western Railway v. Missouri Tax Commission, 390 U.S. 317 (1968)].

   c. the tax must not discriminate against interstate commerce; and
      (1) A tax favoring local commerce over interstate commerce will be invalidated under the Commerce Clause unless it is authorized by Congress [Prudential Insurance Co. v. Benjamin, 328 U.S. 408 (1946)].
      (2) Article IV, Section 2 (the Privileges and Immunities Clause) prohibits state taxes that discriminate against nonresidents [Austin v. New Hampshire, 420 U.S. 656 (1975)].
   d. the tax must be fairly related to the services provided by the taxing state.

THE STATE TAX ON INTERSTATE COMMERCE IS VALID IF...

- It is not preempted by federal law.
- It does not discriminate against interstate commerce.
- It has a substantial nexus.
- There is a fair apportionment and relationship.

2. **Various Types of State Taxes**
   a. States are not permitted to levy an *ad valorem* tax on "goods" that happen to be in the taxing state on the tax day if those goods are still in the course of transit [Standard Oil Co. v. Peck, 342 U.S. 382 (1952)]. However, the validity of such *ad valorem* property taxes as applied to "instrumentalities of commerce" (e.g., airplanes or railroad cars) depends upon:
      (1) whether there is a taxable *situs* (or nexus) within the state; and
      (2) whether the tax is fairly apportioned to the amount of time the equipment is in the state.
   b. A **sales tax** is a tax upon the transfer of title of goods consummated within the state.
      (1) If the sale is consummated within the state (even though the buyer takes the goods outside the state), a sales tax is valid. If, however, the sale is made to a buyer outside the state (i.e., if the seller delivers the goods to an out-of-state buyer), then the sales tax is invalid.
   c. On the other hand, a **use tax** is a tax upon the use of goods within the state that were purchased outside the state.
      (1) The ability of a state to collect a use tax usually depends upon whether the interstate seller, who receives goods from outside the state, has a sufficient nexus within the taxing state.
         (a) Where the seller maintains offices within the taxing state (or even sends salespeople into the state as employees or independent contractors), there is a sufficient nexus even though the use tax was imposed on interstate mail-order sales [National Geographic Society v. California Board of Equalization, 430 U.S. 551 (1977)].
         (b) In contrast, if no sales office is maintained in the state and all selling is done by mail, there is not a sufficient nexus with the taxing state to justify the collection of a use tax [National Bellas Hess, Inc. v. Department of Revenue, 386 U.S. 753 (1967)].
   d. **Doing-business taxes** (variously referred to as "privilege," "occupation," "franchise," "license," "gross receipts," or "net income" taxes) can be measured by either a flat annual fee or a graduated rate based in proportion on the amount of revenue derived from the taxing state. As a general rule, such taxes must "relate to the benefits" conferred by the taxing state upon the interstate business.

      EXAMPLE: A fee applied to airport users was held constitutional because it bore a reasonable relationship to use of the facilities by the passengers [Evansville-Vanderburgh Airport Authority v. Delta Airlines, Inc., 405 U.S. 707 (1972)].

e. **Net income taxes** may be applied by the state upon a company engaging in interstate commerce or on a nonresident engaged in business in the taxing state. A net income tax is valid only as long as the tax is fairly apportioned, has a significant nexus, and is nondiscriminatory [Northwestern States Portland Cement Co. v. Minnesota, 358 U.S. 450 (1959)].

f. A **flat license fee** is generally unconstitutional. This is a fee levied by the state upon drummers, or solicitors who solicit local orders and then fill them out-of-state and ship them through interstate commerce [Nippert v. Richmond, 327 U.S. 416 (1946)].

g. A **license tax** on a peddler, or itinerant salesperson, is valid when a state levies it upon a seller who actually sells and delivers the product within the state. A license is valid as nondiscriminatory only as long as the tax is fairly apportioned with an equal application to local salespeople.

IV. TYPE OF ACTION GOVERNED BY THE CONSTITUTION

A. State Action versus Private Action

1. In order to show a constitutional violation either by the state or federal governments, the plaintiff must first show that there is governmental action. Constitutional rights can be violated only by governmental actors, not by private actors. This is called the **state action requirement**. In this context, **state action** is a term of art referring to governmental action either by the federal or state governments.
2. **Fourteenth and Fifteenth Amendments**
   a. The Fourteenth Amendment says, "No State shall make or enforce any law which shall abridge the privileges or immunities of citizens of the United States; nor shall any State deprive any person of life, liberty or property without due process of the law; nor deny to any person within its jurisdiction the equal protection of the laws."
   b. The Fifteenth Amendment prohibits the state and federal governments from denying the right to vote based on race.
   c. The Fourteenth and Fifteenth Amendments therefore prohibit governmental conduct, and not private conduct which infringes upon protected individual rights.
3. **Federal Violation of Constitutional Rights**
   a. Private actors cannot violate the Bill of Rights and other constitutional amendments that constrain the federal government. Those constitutional amendments only bind the federal government; private actors are not bound by them.
4. **Exceptions**
   a. There are two exceptions to the rule that constitutional rights can be violated only by governmental action. State action can be found in the actions of private actors under:
      (1) the **public function theory**, where a private entity is carrying on activities traditionally and exclusively performed by the government; or
      (2) the **significant state involvement, endorsement, or encouragement theory**, where the government and private entity are so closely related that the action by the private party fairly can be treated as action by the government.
5. **Examples of State Action**
   a. **Where the Private Activity Performs an Exclusive Public Function**
      (1) In Marsh v. Alabama [326 U.S. 501 (1946)], a private company owned an entire town. A member of the Jehovah's Witnesses was arrested and convicted of violating a state trespass law that made it a crime "to enter or remain on the premises of another." The Supreme Court reversed the trespass conviction because the town's streets, although privately owned, were the functional equivalent of city streets. The Supreme Court held that the

company's actions were in violation of the First and Fourteenth Amendments because neither a state nor a private owner can totally ban the expression of free speech.

NOTE The Supreme Court has ruled that the "company town" rationale did not apply to a privately owned shopping center [Hudgens v. National Labor Relations Board, 424 U.S. 507 (1976)].

(2) In Smith v. Allwright [321 U.S. 649 (1944)], the Supreme Court held that because holding an election is a public function, a political party could not racially discriminate against Black people by excluding them from voting in a primary election.

b. Where there is "significant state involvement" in private discrimination, the constitutional right of equal protection may be applicable.

EXAMPLE: A restaurant owner, whose business was located in a building owned by the city, was prohibited from discriminating against racial minorities. The Court found that there was a "symbiotic relationship" between the city and the restaurant [Burton v. Wilmington Parking Authority, 365 U.S. 715 (1961)].

EXAMPLE: State court enforcement of restrictive covenants prohibiting the sale of property to Black people was held to involve sufficient state involvement so as to constitute state action [Shelley v. Kraemer, 334 U.S. 1 (1948)].

EXAMPLE: However, state action was not found in granting a liquor license to a private club that racially discriminated against Black people [Moose Lodge No. 107 v. Irvis, 407 U.S. 163 (1972)].

EXAMPLE: More recently, the Supreme Court found state action because of the "entwinement" between a state and a private organization that regulated interscholastic athletic competitions among public and private secondary schools [Brentwood Academy v. Tennessee Secondary School Athletic Association, 531 U.S. 288 (2001)].

(1) 42 U.S.C. § 1983 provides citizens with the opportunity to seek redress against those who are acting under the authority of a state or local government, and denying citizens their federal constitutional and statutory rights.

6. **Thirteenth Amendment**

a. The Thirteenth Amendment prohibits slavery and involuntary servitude. The amendment has been interpreted as providing Congress with the power to pass legislation prohibiting badges and incidents of slavery, and thus can be used to proscribe purely private acts of forced labor without the requirement of state action. The Peonage Abolition Act of 1867 was designed to help enforce the Thirteenth Amendment and abolished "the voluntary or involuntary service or labor of any persons... in liquidation of any debt or obligation."

b. The Thirteenth Amendment to the United States Constitution applies to both state action and private action. It prohibits slavery and involuntary servitude, except as punishment for crime.

(1) The phrase "involuntary servitude" can mean being compelled to work by the use of force, the threat of force, or the threat of legal coercion.

(2) The United States Supreme Court has held that the nation's military draft does not violate the Thirteenth Amendment, but that laws regarding peonage (involuntary service to work off a debt) do violate this provision.

(3) The Second Circuit has ruled that community service required to graduate from high school does not violate the Thirteenth Amendment.

B. National Power to Override State Authority

1. Supremacy Clause

a. The Supremacy Clause provides that the Constitution, treaties, and laws of the United States are "the supreme Law of the Land." In general, a federal law will supersede any state law with which it is in direct conflict. Furthermore, Congress can preempt any state law in an area in which the exercise of federal power is constitutional [U.S. Const. art. VI, cl. 2].

(1) Where Congress does not intend to occupy a field completely, and state laws are not otherwise preempted, the states may enact similar legislation.

EXAMPLE: A state statute prohibiting racial discrimination was held valid even though there was a substantially identical federal law [Colorado Anti-Discrimination Commission v. Continental Air Lines, Inc., 372 U.S. 714 (1963)].

(2) Greater state protection is also permitted. Where Congress has legislated to establish minimum standards (such as in the areas of health and safety requirements pertaining to food and drugs or the regulation of roads and highways), then the states are free to enact more stringent standards than those mandated by federal law.

EXAMPLE: A municipal smoke-abatement statute was held valid even though it imposed stricter standards than the federal regulation [Huron Portland Cement Co. v. City of Detroit, 362 U.S. 440 (1960)].

V. DUE PROCESS AND THE INCORPORATION OF PORTIONS OF THE BILL OF RIGHTS

A. Incorporation of the Bill of Rights

1. As originally enacted, the Bill of Rights (the first 10 amendments to the U.S. Constitution) was applicable only to the federal government, not to the states. In 1868, the Fourteenth Amendment was adopted, which provided: "No State shall make or enforce any law which shall abridge the privileges or immunities of citizens of the United States; nor shall any State deprive any person of life, liberty, or property, without due process of law; nor deny to any person within its jurisdiction the equal protection of the laws."
2. **Fourteenth Amendment Privileges or Immunities Clause**
   a. A few years after the Fourteenth Amendment was adopted, the Supreme Court held that the fundamental rights set forth in the Bill of Rights were not privileges and immunities of national citizenship [Slaughter-House Cases, 83 U.S. 36 (1873)].
   b. In 1999, the Supreme Court held that under the Fourteenth Amendment Privileges or Immunities Clause (along with the fundamental right to travel), new residents could challenge a state's denial of full unemployment benefits until a specified waiting period had been satisfied.
   c. The Court struck down a California law that limited the payment of welfare benefits for first-year residents to the amount they would have received from their former state. The law violated the right to travel freely from state to state, which the Court said is protected by the Fourteenth Amendment Privileges or Immunities Clause as a right of national citizenship [Saenz v. Roe, 526 U.S. 489 (1999)].
3. **Fourteenth Amendment Due Process Clause**
   a. Although the Supreme Court rejected the argument that the Due Process Clause incorporated all of the Bill of Rights, under the **doctrine of selective incorporation**, the following specific provisions are now applicable to the states [Adamson v. California [332 U.S. 46 (1947)]:
      (1) the First Amendment freedom of speech and freedom of press, the right to assemble and petition the government for a redress of grievances, the right to free exercise of religion, and the prohibition against the establishment of religion;
      (2) the Fourth Amendment provisions guaranteeing the right to be free from unreasonable searches and seizures [Ker v. California, 374 U.S. 23 (1963)];
      (3) the Fifth Amendment protection against double jeopardy [Benton v. Maryland, 395 U.S. 784 (1969)], privilege against self-incrimination [Malloy v. Hogan, 378 U.S. 1 (1964)], and requirement of just compensation when private property is taken for public use;
      (4) the Sixth Amendment rights guaranteeing the accused in criminal prosecutions a speedy and public trial [Klopfer v. North Carolina,

386 U.S. 213 (1967)], the right to confront and cross-examine witnesses [Pointer v. Texas, 380 U.S. 400 (1965)], the right to counsel [Gideon v. Wainwright, 372 U.S. 335 (1963)], and the right to a jury trial in criminal cases [Duncan v. Louisiana, 391 U.S. 145 (1968)];

(5) the Eighth Amendment prohibitions against cruel and unusual punishments, excessive bails, and most recently, excessive fines [Timbs v. Indiana, 139 S. Ct. 682 (2019)]; and

(6) the Second Amendment right to keep and bear arms applies to state and local governments, in addition to applying to the District of Columbia.

EXAMPLE: A Chicago law banning possession of handguns by almost all private citizens was found to be invalid. In *dictum*, however, the Court said that many traditional state gun regulations will still be upheld [McDonald v. City of Chicago, 561 U.S. 742 (2010)].

b. The Supreme Court has also held that the Due Process Clause does not permit a state to infringe on the fundamental right of parents to make childrearing decisions, and that parents can make decisions concerning the care, custody, and control of their children [Troxel v. Granville, 530 U.S. 57 (2000)].

c. Major rights not incorporated include:

(1) the Fifth Amendment right to a grand jury in criminal cases; and

(2) the Seventh Amendment right to a jury trial in civil cases.

THE BILL OF RIGHTS STOPS HERE!	
The Fourteenth Amendment extends the Bill of Rights to the states EXCEPT:	
NO RIGHT TO	• Prevent quartering soldiers in your home (Third). • Grand jury indictment (Fifth). • Civil jury trial (Seventh).

d. **Scope of the Due Process Clause**

(1) The Due Process and Equal Protection Clauses of the Fourteenth Amendment protect the rights of "persons," and not merely "citizens."

(2) A corporation is considered a "person" for purposes of due process and equal protection. Note, however, that a corporation is not entitled to the privilege against self-incrimination.

(3) Aliens are considered "persons" for purposes of due process and equal protection.

B. Procedural Due Process

1. Both the Fifth and Fourteenth Amendments protect against the deprivation of life, liberty, or property without the due process of the law. Where there is a deprivation of one's "life," "liberty," or "property" interests, the individual is entitled to fundamentally fair procedural safeguards (e.g., some form of notice and a meaningful hearing within a reasonable time).

2. **Deprivation of Liberty**
   a. Acts that invade a liberty interest include:
      (1) freedom from bodily restraints;
         (a) A state must grant a parolee an evidentiary hearing before it revokes parole or probation [Morrissey v. Brewer, 408 U.S. 471 (1972)].
      (2) physical punishment; and
         (a) Corporal punishment of pupils in a public school is valid, although a liberty interest exists [Ingraham v. Wright, 430 U.S. 651 (1977)].
      (3) commitment to a mental institution.
         (a) An adversary hearing must be provided to adults before they are committed to a mental institution against their will. Minor children have a liberty interest in not being confined unnecessarily for medical treatment. In the case of minor children, a screening by a neutral fact-finder is required [Parham v. J.R., 442 U.S. 584 (1979)].
   b. Acts that do not invade a liberty interest include:
      (1) injury to reputation; and
         (a) Injury to one's reputation in the absence of a related harm to a more tangible interest (such as an employment opportunity) is not a deprivation of a liberty interest [Paul v. Davis, 424 U.S. 693 (1976)].
      (2) forced administration of medicine.
         (a) The federal government may administer antipsychotic drugs against a defendant's will in order to render him competent to stand trial, as long as the treatment is medically appropriate, does not cause substantial side effects, and is necessary to significantly further important governmental trial-related interests [Sell v. United States, 539 U.S. 166 (2003)].

3. **Property Interests**
   a. **Public Education**
      (1) There is a constitutionally protected property interest in the statutory entitlement to continued attendance at a public school [Goss v. Lopez, 419 U.S. 565 (1975)].
      (2) On the other hand, no prior evidentiary hearing is required when a student is dismissed for academic reasons [Board of Curators of University of Missouri v. Horowitz, 435 U.S. 78 (1978)].

b. **Continued Welfare Benefits**

(1) A property interest is created by a statutory entitlement to continued welfare benefits [Goldberg v. Kelly, 397 U.S. 254 (1970)].

c. **Retention of Driver's License**

(1) A state may not revoke a driver's license without a hearing [Bell v. Burson, 402 U.S. 535 (1971)].

(2) However, the Supreme Court has held a statute revoking a driver's license without a pre-termination hearing to be constitutional where [Dixon v. Love, 431 U.S. 105 (1977)]:

(a) the statute contained special provisions for hardship cases or holders of commercial licenses;

(b) the risk of erroneous deprivation was not great; and

(c) the regulation promoted the public interests in administrative efficiency, highway and traffic safety, and the prompt removal of a safety hazard.

d. **Public Employment**

(1) There is a property interest in a person keeping her job if the employment is under a tenure system or there is a clear understanding, either express or implied, that the employee can be terminated only for "cause" [Perry v. Sindermann, 408 U.S. 593 (1972)].

(2) However, the Supreme Court has held that there was no property interest where a police officer held his position "at the will of" the public employer [Bishop v. Wood, 426 U.S. 341 (1976)].

(3) Furthermore, there is no property interest when a state refuses to renew a fixed-term contract [Board of Regents v. Roth, 408 U.S. 564 (1972)].

e. **Prejudgment Garnishment**

(1) Prejudgment attachment or garnishment of wages, without notice or hearing, violates procedural due process [Sniadach v. Family Finance Corp., 395 U.S. 337 (1969)].

(2) A due process property interest does not arise when an individual is first applying for employment. However, if the person has already been getting employment benefits, she has a property interest in continuing the receipt of those benefits.

f. **Forfeiture of Property**

(1) Due process is satisfied where the government sends a certified letter to prison to notify an inmate that property seized will be forfeited, because such an action is "reasonably calculated, under the circumstances, to apprise interested parties of the pendency of the action and afford them an opportunity to present their objections." Actual notice is not required; constructive notice will suffice [Dusenbery v. United States, 534 U.S. 161 (2002)].

g. **Business Licensing**

(1) The First Amendment and due process require that a licensing scheme for adult businesses provide applicants with "prompt judicial determination" of their claim that the government unconstitutionally denied a license, as opposed to mere prompt access to judicial review [City of Littleton v. Z.J. Gifts D-4, L.L.C., 541 U.S. 774 (2004)].

NOTE As with any other constitutional right, procedural due process is not required where there is no "state action" [Flagg Brothers v. Brooks, 436 U.S. 149 (1978)].

4. **Life Interests**

a. Capital punishment is clearly a deprivation of a life interest, and rigorous due process protections are applicable. When life interests have been claimed in other contexts, such as in right-to-die situations, the Supreme Court has addressed it under other provisions of the Constitution.

5. **Type of Process Required**

a. Once it is determined that there is a sufficient deprivation of life, liberty, or property, the next step is to decide what process is required. In order to determine what procedural safeguards are necessary, the Supreme Court set forth the following factors to look at [Mathews v. Eldridge, 424 U.S. 319 (1976)]:

(1) the private interest that will be affected by the official action;

(2) the risk of an erroneous deprivation of this interest through the procedures used, and the probable value of additional or substitute procedures; and

(3) the government's interest in streamlined procedures, including the function involved and the fiscal and administrative burdens that the additional or substitute procedural requirements would entail.

EXAMPLE: The Supreme Court held that a full hearing was not required for the dismissal of a medical student from a state medical school for academic deficiency because the decision was an evaluative one, made by faculty officers and outside practitioners [Bd. of Curators of Univ. of Missouri v. Horowitz, 435 U.S. 78 (1979)].

EXAMPLE: The Supreme Court held that it was not necessary for a public school to give a student a hearing before imposing corporal punishment [Ingraham v. Wright, 430 U.S. 651 (1997)].

EXAMPLE: The Supreme Court ruled that a temporary suspension of a driver's license without a hearing, where the driver refused to take a breathalyzer test, was valid, because he had a right to an immediate hearing following the suspension [Mackey v. Montrym, 443 U.S. 1 (1979)].

b. Due process requires a judge to recuse himself when the judge has a pecuniary interest in the case, such that an average judge would "possibly be tempted" to render an "imbalanced or untrue" judgment.

EXAMPLE: If one party to a case had a "significant and disproportionate influence" in getting the judge elected, then due process requires that the judge recuse herself. Such a disproportionate influence exists when, for example, an appellant contributed more than 50% of all campaign contributions to the appellate judge's election campaign [Caperton v. A. T. Massey Coal Co., 556 U.S. 868 (2009)].

6. **Irrebuttable Presumptions**
   a. In recent cases, the Supreme Court has held that irrebuttable presumptions violate procedural due process.
   b. **Civil Proceedings**
      (1) The Supreme Court held that a statutory presumption that a pregnant schoolteacher was physically incapable of performing her duties was unconstitutional [Cleveland Board of Education v. LaFleur, 414 U.S. 632 (1974)].
      (2) A state law requiring children of unwed fathers to become wards of the court was invalidated because its statutory effect was to create a conclusive presumption that unwed fathers were unfit parents [Stanley v. Illinois, 405 U.S. 645 (1972)].
   c. **Criminal Cases**
      (1) A statutory presumption that possession of marijuana was conclusive proof that the drug had been imported was invalidated, because marijuana is frequently grown in the United States as well as abroad [Leary v. United States, 395 U.S. 6 (1969)].

CONSTITUTIONAL LAW ANALYSIS TIPS	
when you see this...	**...remember this**
Thirteenth Amendment	• Best answer when private individuals, who do not qualify as state actors, discriminate.
Fourteenth Amendment	• All the elements of the Constitution incorporated into the amendment are, hence, protected by it. • Frequently best answer when First Amendment right of free speech or freedom of religion is not offered as a choice.
Commerce Clause	• Grants Congress the power to enact legislation that affects interstate commerce. • Important source of congressional power over civil rights. • Does not empower Congress to push states into acting.
Contract Clause	• Can be an issue where the state revokes a contract to which it is a party.
Dormant Commerce Clause	• Legal doctrine inferred from Commerce Clause. • Prohibits a state from passing legislation that improperly burdens or discriminates against interstate commerce.

CONSTITUTIONAL LAW ANALYSIS TIPS	
when you see this...	**...remember this**
Due Process Clause	• Best choice for an unconstitutional argument when: 1. state acts; or 2. state does not grant a hearing or invades privacy rights.
Equal Protection Clause	• Best option when state action interferes with a fundamental interest (e.g., right to vote or travel, or classifications by race, alienage, or sex).
General Welfare Power or Spending Power	• Congress's power to spend treasury funds, but not to regulate activity. • Best answer when voluntary cooperation by party with federal government is the ONLY way to reach result.
Police Power	• Can be the answer only when state action versus federal action.
Privileges and Immunities Clauses	• Article IV's Privileges and Immunities Clause bars states from discriminating against nonresident citizens on fundamental matters, unless the regulation in question specifically targets a problem arising from such nonresident's behavior. • The Privileges or Immunities Clause of the Fourteenth Amendment is almost never a correct answer.
Supremacy Clause	• Not a congressional power. • Not a good choice unless there is a congressional statute or provision conflicting with a state activity.
Taxing Power	• Allowed for regulatory purposes if there is a revenue-raising function. • Best answer if Commerce Clause isn't available.

EXAM TIP When answering a question involving the various arguments that can be used to attack the constitutionality of a statute regulating economic activity, you should still consider the argument that it violates substantive due process, especially if the statute operates in an arbitrary and unreasonable manner and there is no legitimate reason for the legislature to pass the statute.

WHEN SHOULD THE SUPREME COURT AVOID A CONSTITUTIONAL DECISION?
1. When there is no issue in controversy—no adversarial conflict between the parties. 2. When the complainant cannot show injury by the statute in question. 3. When the issue isn't ripe and the Supreme Court doesn't feel the issue has arisen yet. 4. When the decision requires a ruling broader than the facts of the case. 5. When the complaint can be resolved in a nonconstitutional manner (e.g., by a statute). 6. When the Court can determine a statutory construction that avoids constitutional analysis. 7. When the complainant benefited from the statute it now argues is unconstitutional.

C. Substantive Due Process

1. Economic Regulation

a. While the doctrine of substantive due process was originally used to protect the rights of property and contract and to invalidate legislation that regulated economic activity, this approach was abandoned by the Supreme Court in the 1930s.

b. Since then, such an economic regulation will be upheld if it is rationally related to a legitimate government interest.

2. Fundamental Rights

a. The substantive due process doctrine is now used to evaluate governmental regulations that affect fundamental rights of personhood, rather than rights of property. Strict scrutiny review, or other forms of heightened scrutiny, apply to laws that burden the exercise of fundamental rights, including the right to vote, the right to travel, the right to privacy, First Amendment rights, family rights, and other rights referred to as fundamental rights.

b. The following are some of the categories that fall under the penumbra of privacy rights.

c. **Contraceptives**

(1) The Supreme Court invalidated a state law prohibiting the use of contraceptive devices, thus recognizing a right of marital privacy [Griswold v. Connecticut, 381 U.S. 479 (1965)].

(2) The Supreme Court later expanded the Griswold decision and held that the right to use contraceptives belonged to single as well as married persons [Eisenstadt v. Baird, 405 U.S. 438 (1972)].

(3) In Carey v. Population Services International [431 U.S. 678 (1977)], the Supreme Court invalidated a state law that prohibited the sale of contraceptives to minors except through a licensed pharmacist.

(4) But in 2014, the Court held that corporations cannot be required to pay for contraception coverage for their female workers (the first time that the court has recognized a for-profit corporation's claim of religious belief) [Burwell v. Hobby Lobby, 573 U.S. 682 (2014)].

d. **Marriage**

(1) The right to marry is deemed fundamental. Any substantial interference with that right must be necessary to further a compelling interest [Zablocki v. Redhail, 434 U.S. 374 (1978)].

(2) In June 2015, the United States Supreme Court announced that governmental bans on same-sex marriage are unconstitutional under the U.S. Constitution. Specifically, the Court held that such bans violate the substantive due process doctrine and the fundamental right to marriage. This ruling impacts every state with a statutory or constitutional ban on same-sex marriage. All states must now recognize the same-sex marriages legally performed in other states, assuming that such marriages are otherwise in accord with the laws of the state where the marriage occurred.

Most significantly, all states must now allow same-sex couples to get married and accord such couples the same rights and obligations otherwise accorded people who marry [Obergefell v. Hodges, 576 U.S. 644 (2015)].

e. **Abortion**

(1) The Supreme Court has ruled that no fundamental right to abortion exists under the Constitution. Specifically, no privacy right extends to abortion as it does to marriage or birth control [Dobbs v. Jackson Women's Health Org., 142 S. Ct. 2228 (2022)]. Instead, the right to abortion was left for states to decide.

(2) **Protests**

(a) The Supreme Court reversed a Massachusetts law which made it a crime to stand on a public road or sidewalk within thirty-five feet of a reproductive health care facility, allowing protests, counseling, and other speech and rejecting the concept of "buffer zones" around these clinics [McCullen v. Coakley, 573 U.S. 464 (2014)].

f. **Family Relations**

(1) A fundamental right exists for related persons to live together. A zoning ordinance prohibiting members of an extended family from living in a single household has been subjected to heightened scrutiny and held unconstitutional [Moore v. City of East Cleveland, 431 U.S. 494 (1977)].

NOTE This fundamental right does not apply to unrelated persons [Belle Terre v. Boraas, 416 U.S. 1 (1974)].

(2) The Supreme Court has held that the Due Process Clause does not permit a state to infringe on the fundamental right of parents to make childrearing decisions, and that parents can make decisions concerning the care, custody, and control of their children [Troxel v. Granville, 530 U.S. 57 (2000)]. Parents have the substantive due process right to make fundamental decisions affecting the lives of their children.

(a) This includes a parent's protected liberty interest concerning the control of visitation with their children by others, including grandparents [Id.].

(3) Before a state can involuntarily terminate a parent's rights in their children, due process requires that the state support its allegations by at least clear and convincing evidence [Santosky v. Kramer, 455 U.S. 745 (1982)].

g. **Sexual Orientation**

(1) In Lawrence v. Texas [539 U.S. 558 (2003)], the Supreme Court applied a stringent form of rational basis scrutiny and held that a statute making it a crime for a person to engage "in deviate sexual intercourse with another individual of the same sex" furthered no legitimate state interest.

(2) In 2013, it was held unconstitutional to restrict U.S. federal interpretation of "marriage" and "spouse" to apply only to heterosexual unions, giving same-sex couples the rights of married couples in terms of tax benefits, health care, retirement, and other areas of federal regulation [United States v. Windsor, 570 U.S. 744 (2013)].

(3) As of 2015, the fundamental right to marry is guaranteed to same-sex couples [Obergefell v. Hodges, 576 U.S. 644 (2015)].

(4) In 2020, the Supreme Court ruled that, with regard to employment discrimination under Title VII, discrimination "on the basis of sex" includes discrimination based on sexual orientation and gender identity [Bostock v. Clayton Cty., 140 S. Ct. 1731 (2020)]. This means sexual orientation discrimination would be subject to intermediate scrutiny.

(a) While the decision in Bostock was limited to interpreting the language of Title VII, lower courts have since applied the same logic to other areas, including Title IX (education) and the Affordable Care Act (healthcare).

h. **Private Education**

(1) Parents have a right to privately educate their children outside the public school system [Pierce v. Society of Sisters, 268 U.S. 510 (1925)].

i. **Obscene Material**

(1) The right to possess obscene material in the privacy of one's home is protected [Stanley v. Georgia, 394 U.S. 557 (1969)].

(2) However, the government can severely restrict the sale, purchase, receipt, transport, and distribution of obscene materials, both in stores and through the mail. Furthermore, the state can criminalize even the private possession of child pornography [Osborne v. Ohio, 495 U.S. 103 (1990)].

j. **Right to Die**

(1) The right of a terminally ill or comatose person to choose to die is not presently a fundamental right.

(2) Nevertheless, a person has a well-established due process "liberty" interest in not being forced to undergo unwanted medical procedures, such as life-support [Cruzan v. Missouri Department of Health, 497 U.S. 261 (1990)].

(3) However, the state has a countervailing interest in preserving life. A terminally ill patient has no right to assisted suicide [Washington v. Glucksberg, 521 U.S. 702 (1997)].

k. **Right to Travel**

(1) The Privileges and Immunities Clause of Article IV, Section 2, the Privileges or Immunities Clause of the Fourteenth Amendment, and the Commerce Clause mutually enforce the right of every citizen to travel freely from state to state [Griffin v. Breckenridge, 403 U.S. 88 (1971)].

(2) Durational residency requirements for dispensing government benefits are subject to strict scrutiny.

EXAMPLE: A one-year waiting period before receiving welfare benefits or state-subsidized medical care is invalid.

EXAMPLE: Reasonable residency requirements are valid for obtaining a divorce as well as for obtaining reduced tuition at state universities.

(3) The right to international travel is not absolute and may be subject to reasonable restrictions, and Congress may authorize the president to restrict travel to certain countries or danger areas [Zemel v. Rusk, 381 U.S. 1 (1965)].

EXAM TIP The Privileges or Immunities Clause of the Fourteenth Amendment has frequently been a wrong answer on the bar exam. Almost all the privileges and immunities are protected by the Commerce Clause, Due Process Clause, or Equal Protection Clause. However, the Privileges or Immunities Clause is not entirely dead: In Saenz v. Roe [526 U.S. 489 (1999)], the Supreme Court ruled that it was an alternative to an Equal Protection Clause protection with regard to the right to travel.

I. **Right to Vote**

(1) The fundamental right of U.S. citizens over age 18 to vote extends to all federal, state, and local elections, as well as to primaries. Strict scrutiny review is used to adjudicate restrictions on the right to vote.

(2) However, government regulations of ballot-access by candidates–based upon age, duration of residency, or payment of filing fees–require only minimum rational basis scrutiny.

(a) In addition, voter registration requirements and regulation of the time, place, and manner of casting ballots are valid so long as they do not impose an "undue burden" on the right to vote.

(3) A rule of "one-person, one-vote" is generally followed. Whenever the government attempts to establish a new apportionment or redistricting scheme, fairly exact mathematical equality between districts is required so as not to dilute the fundamental right to vote.

(4) There must be equality in the distribution of the right to vote.

EXAMPLE: Imposition of a poll tax as a prerequisite to vote violates equal protection and is unconstitutional [Harper v. Virginia Board of Elections, 383 U.S. 663 (1966)].

EXAMPLE: Limiting voting for school board elections to parents of schoolchildren and/or property owners is unconstitutional [Kramer v. Union Free School District, 345 U.S. 662 (1969)].

EXCEPTION: Voting can be limited to landowners for a special purpose "water-storage district" (which cannot enact laws or perform government functions) [Ball v. James, 451 U.S. 355 (1981)].

(5) In 2013, the Court effectively struck down the portions of the Voting Rights Act of 1965 that required certain states and local governments to obtain federal pre-clearance before changing their voting laws or practices, enabling states to implement new voter identification laws, eliminate same-day registration, and other measures that affect voting rights [Shelby County v. Holder, 570 U.S. 529 (2013)].

m. **Medical Records**

(1) There is some right to privacy recognized for medical records, but "informational privacy is not a fundamental right" and the privacy interest must be balanced against the public interest in disclosure. A law requiring physicians to report certain prescriptions to the state for storage in a database has been held constitutional [Whalen v. Roe, 429 U.S. 589 (1977)].

(2) In 1977, the Supreme Court seemed to hold:

(a) that there is an implied zone of privacy into which medical records would fall; but

(b) a patient ID requirement was a reasonable exercise of the state's broad police powers, and no Fourteenth Amendment Due Process violation occurred.

(3) The Court recognized two privacy interests: "the individual interest in avoiding disclosure of personal matters" and "the interest in independence in making certain kinds of important decisions" [Whalen v. Roe, 429 U.S. 589 (1977)].

(4) However, Whalen v. Roe provided little guidance for lower courts dealing with medical privacy issues. Regarding the first of the Court's dual privacy interests, "the individual interest in avoiding disclosure of personal matters," Whalen left unclear what constituted a violation of the right, and failed to establish what type of constitutional treatment the courts were to use when assessing it. The Court's second privacy interest in "independence in making certain kinds of important decisions," had been fleshed out by other Supreme Court decisions, but there was no clear legal precedent for a privacy interest in nondisclosure of personal matters [Id.].

(5) The courts of appeals have split over whether Whalen v. Roe created a constitutional right to confidentiality. Most courts of appeals have affirmed the existence of the right; two courts of appeals have practically denied it.

(6) In addition, the constitutional treatments used to assess the right contrast greatly among all the courts of appeals. In some circuits, the federal courts hold that the needs of the government always supersede the patient's implied right of privacy. In other circuits, the federal court

apply a balancing test. While the factors of the balancing tests differ between circuits, the main factors used to determine whether an intrusion into an individual's privacy is justified center around [United States v. Westinghouse Electric Corp., 638 F.2d 570 (3rd Cir. 1980)]:

(a) the type of record requested;

(b) the information it does or might contain;

(c) the potential for harm in any subsequent nonconsensual disclosure;

(d) the injury from disclosure to the relationship in which the record was generated;

(e) the adequacy of safeguards to prevent unauthorized disclosure;

(f) the degree of need for access; and

(g) whether there is an express statutory mandate, articulated public policy, or other recognizable public interest militating toward access.

D. Takings Clause

1. The Fifth Amendment provides that private property shall not be taken for public use without just compensation. This prohibition also applies to the states through the Due Process Clause of the Fourteenth Amendment.
2. In Agins v. City of Tiburon [447 U.S. 255 (1980)], the Supreme Court held that a taking of property occurs if a regulation of private property "does not substantially advance legitimate state interests."
    a. Agins was overruled in Lingle v. Chevron U.S.A., Inc. [544 U.S. 528 (2005)], in which the Supreme Court held that the extent to which a regulation advances a legitimate state interest is not a relevant factor in determining if a taking has occurred.
3. Property can be taken by a variety of means, including:
    a. direct government appropriation;
        (1) Where the state validly regulates for health, safety, or welfare purposes under its police power, the government action merely amounts to a regulation, and payment of just compensation is not required. However, a taking does occur where there is an actual appropriation of one's property [Loretto v. Teleprompter Manhattan CATV Corp., 455 U.S. 904 (1982)].
    b. a regulatory taking;
        (1) Any permanent, physical invasion, no matter how minor, will constitute a taking.
        (2) A land-use regulation is a taking if it denies an owner all reasonable, economically beneficial uses of her land. This is otherwise known as an inverse condemnation.
        (3) To analyze regulations that merely decrease economic value, the court may use a balancing test to determine if there is a taking. The court must balance [Pennsylvania Coal Co. v. Mahon, 260

U.S. 393 (1922); Penn Central Transportation Co. v. New York, 438 U.S. 104 (1978)]:

(a) the economic impact of the regulation on the claimant;

(b) the extent to which the regulation has interfered with distinct investment-backed expectations; and

(c) the character or nature of the governmental action.

(4) The duration of the restriction is also a factor to be considered, but the Supreme Court has hesitated to make it an explicit factor in order to avoid setting specific rules in terms of what is or is not a sufficient duration [Tahoe-Sierra Preservation Council, Inc. v. Tahoe Regional Planning Agency, 535 U.S. 302 (2002)].

EXAMPLE: A state zoning law was passed after the owner purchased the property, and was held to constitute a taking because the law precluded the owner from erecting any permanent structure on his land [Lucas v. South Carolina Coastal Council, 505 U.S. 1003 (1992)].

c. temporary restrictions; or

(1) When considering whether a taking has occurred, a court will look at both the dimensions of a property interest (metes and bounds) and the term of years.

EXAMPLE: A temporary restriction causing a diminution in value (such as a 32-month moratorium on development in an area) is not a taking of the parcel as a whole because the property will recover value when the prohibition is lifted, and thus the regulation will not "permanently deprive" the owner of "all economically beneficial uses" of his land [Tahoe-Sierra Preservation Council, Inc. v. Tahoe Regional Planning Agency, 535 U.S. 302 (2002)].

d. conditional permits.

(1) The government can place a condition on the grant of a permit for land development if [Nollan v. California Coastal Commission, 483 U.S. 825 (1987); Dolan v. City of Tigard, 512 U.S. 374 (1994)]:

(a) there is a logical nexus between the condition and the governmental purposes; and

(b) there is rough proportionality between the impact on the proposed development and the governmental objectives served by the condition.

4. The Supreme Court has interpreted the "public use" language of the Takings Clause to mean "public purpose," and held that a city has the power to take private property and transfer it to a private developer because of the public benefits of the proposed development [Kelo v. City of New London, 545 U.S. 469 (2005)].

VI. EQUAL PROTECTION OF THE LAWS

A. Constitutional Basis

1. The Fourteenth Amendment provides that no state shall "deny to any person within its jurisdiction the equal protection of the laws." The Supreme Court has ruled that equal protection also applies to the federal government under the Due Process Clause of the Fifth Amendment.
2. The guarantee of substantive due process assures that a law will be fair and reasonable, not arbitrary; equal protection review is triggered where persons similarly situated are treated differently.
   a. Substantive due process review applies where a law affects the rights of all persons with respect to a specific activity (e.g., a state law prohibits the sale of birth control devices except by prescription).
   b. Equal protection review applies where a law affects the rights of some persons with respect to a specific activity (e.g., a state law prohibits the sale of birth control devices to unmarried persons except by prescription).

B. Standards of Review

1. Under the **strict scrutiny standard**, the burden of persuasion is on the government to prove that the measure being challenged is necessary to further a compelling interest.
   a. The word **necessary** means that there is no less restrictive alternative means available. There must be a very close "fit" between the means and the end.
   b. The government usually fails to prove its burden under strict scrutiny, so an equal protection challenge to a law is generally successful (i.e., the law is presumptively invalid).
   c. Strict scrutiny review applies to government action that uses suspect classifications—race, alienage, and national origin.
2. Under the **intermediate scrutiny standard**, the burden of persuasion is placed on the government to prove that the measure being challenged is substantially related to the achievement of an important governmental interest.
   a. The key term, **substantially related**, means that an exceedingly persuasive justification must be shown. Intermediate scrutiny is much closer to strict scrutiny than it is to rational basis.
   b. Intermediate scrutiny applies to government action using *quasi*-suspect classifications—gender and illegitimacy.
3. Under the **rational basis standard** of review, the burden of persuasion is on the plaintiff to show that the measure being challenged serves no legitimate government interest or is not rationally related to any legitimate interest.
   a. **Rational relationship** is a minimal requirement which means that the law cannot be arbitrary or unreasonable.

b. Practically any police power regulation which furthers a health, safety, or welfare purpose will be found "legitimate." For this reason, laws scrutinized under rational basis are almost always upheld. From the plaintiff's standpoint, an equal protection challenge under rational basis is generally unsuccessful.

c. Rational basis review applies to all classifications not falling under strict or intermediate scrutiny, such as classifications based on age, poverty, wealth, disability, and need for necessities of life (food, shelter, clothing, medical care).

THE THREE STANDARDS OF SCRUTINY		
Rational Basis	**Intermediate Scrutiny**	**Strict Scrutiny**
The plaintiff must prove **no legitimate** governmental interest.	The government must prove its classification is substantially related to an **important** government interest.	The government must prove its classification is **necessary** to achieve a **compelling** government interest.

C. Proving Discrimination

1. A claim of discrimination under the Equal Protection Clause places upon the challenger the initial burden to show that the government acted with discriminatory intent (purposeful discrimination). Absent an initial showing of purposeful discrimination, there can be no violation of the Equal Protection Clause. Discriminatory intent may be shown facially, as applied, or where a discriminatory motive exists.

   a. **Facial discrimination** arises where a law, by its very language, creates distinctions between classes of persons (e.g., "only white, male U.S. citizens may apply for positions with the state police department").

   b. Where a law that appears neutral on its face but in its application has a disproportionate effect on a particular class of persons, strict or intermediate scrutiny will apply only if the court finds a discriminatory purpose exists.

   EXAMPLE: The fact that black applicants scored lower than white applicants on a police qualifying test did not *per se* prove a discriminatory purpose in hiring practices, so strict scrutiny review was not triggered and no equal protection violation was found [Washington v. Davis, 426 U.S. 229 (1976)].

   c. A facially neutral law can be applied in a discriminatory manner. Where the challenger can show a discriminatory purpose, the law will be invalidated.

   EXAMPLE: Where a law prohibited the operation of laundries in wooden buildings, most of which were owned by Chinese individuals, and government officials granted discretionary exemptions to white-owned laundries, the Supreme Court found that purposeful discrimination in the application of the law violated equal protection [Yick Wo v. Hopkins, 118 U.S. 356 (1886)].

D. Suspect Classifications

1. Strict Scrutiny

a. Strict scrutiny applies to classifications based on race, alienage, and national origin. Such laws will be presumptively invalid absent a showing by the state that the measure is necessary to achieve a compelling state interest.

(1) A state law prohibiting interracial marriages was held unconstitutional [Loving v. Virginia, 388 U.S. 1 (1967)]. Similarly, a state law prohibiting interracial cohabitation was held invalid [McLaughlin v. Florida, 379 U.S. 184 (1964)].

(2) Deliberate *de jure* segregation violates equal protection [Brown v. Board of Education, 347 U.S. 483 (1954); Plessy v. Ferguson, 163 U.S. 537 (1896)].

(a) Various plans to hinder desegregation have been deemed unconstitutional, including the closing of all public schools [Griffin v. County School Board of Prince Edward County, 377 U.S. 218 (1964)].

(b) The Supreme Court has held that public aid to private, segregated schools—such as tuition grants and the exclusive use of public facilities—was unconstitutional [Norwood v. Harrison, 413 U.S. 455 (1973)].

(c) School boards have an affirmative duty to eliminate the intentional racial segregation of schools.

1) Court-ordered busing is constitutional where it is implemented to remedy past discrimination in a particular school system, rather than to attract nonminority students from outside districts to achieve integration. Court-ordered busing is a temporary measure that must be terminated once the vestiges of past discrimination have been eliminated [Board of Education v. Dowell, 498 U.S. 237 (1991)].

(3) Where it can be shown that race was the "predominant factor" in defining the borders of new election districts (rather than contiguity, compactness, or community interest), then such a plan will be subject to strict scrutiny [Miller v. Johnson, 515 U.S. 900 (1995)].

b. The Court will generally apply strict scrutiny when a state law discriminates against aliens.

EXAMPLE: A state law prohibiting aliens from owning land was invalidated [Oyama v. California, 332 U.S. 633 (1948)].

EXAMPLE: A state law denying commercial-fishing licenses to resident aliens who were ineligible for citizenship was held invalid [Takahashi v. Fish & Game Commission, 334 U.S. 410 (1948)].

EXAMPLE: The Supreme Court invalidated a state law that excluded financial assistance for higher education to aliens who were eligible for U.S. citizenship as not furthering any "compelling state interest" [Nyquist v. Mauclet, 432 U.S. 1 (1977)].

(1) States may discriminate against aliens in activities where participation in the functioning of government is involved.

(a) A New York statute requiring state police officers to be citizens was held valid, under what is called the "**government function test**" [Foley v. Connelie, 435 U.S. 291 (1978)].

(b) Aliens also may be denied positions as public school teachers because they influence students' views toward government and the political process [Ambach v. Norwick, 441 U.S. 68 (1979)].

(2) The Supreme Court has not held undocumented aliens to be a suspect class; the rational basis analysis will apply.

(a) However, in Plyler v. Doe [457 U.S. 202 (1982)], the Court determined that undocumented immigrant children have a right to free public elementary and secondary education. The Court used a stringent version of the rational basis scrutiny test and held that the discrimination against the children "can hardly be considered rational unless it furthers some substantial goal of the state."

NOTE Federal laws that discriminate against aliens are not subject to the strict scrutiny test because Congress has broad plenary power to regulate immigration.

2. **Intermediate Scrutiny**

a. Distinctions drawn between legitimate and illegitimate children are subject to an intermediate, or "*quasi*-suspect," standard [Mathews v. Lucas, 427 U.S. 495 (1976)]. As a result, it is now close to the "almost suspect" standard used for gender discrimination [Mills v. Habluetzel, 456 U.S. 91 (1982)].

(1) Classifications must be "substantially related to an important state interest" [Id.].

(2) Classifications that favor legitimate children and disfavor illegitimate children are generally struck down because the overriding government interest in this area is not to punish the offspring of an illicit relationship.

EXAMPLE: In Levy v. Louisiana [391 U.S. 68 (1968)], the Supreme Court struck down a state law that permitted legitimate children, but not illegitimate children, to maintain a wrongful death action.

EXAMPLE: Similarly, the Supreme Court invalidated a state law that excluded illegitimate children from sharing equally with other children in worker's compensation death benefits [Weber v. Aetna Casualty and Surety Co., 406 U.S. 164 (1972)].

EXAMPLE: Likewise, illegitimate children are entitled to welfare benefits [New Jersey Welfare Rights Organization v. Cahill, 411 U.S. 619 (1973)].

b. As with federal laws that discriminate against aliens, the Supreme Court has been more lenient in applying an intermediate standard of scrutiny to illegitimacy under federal law than under state law. The Supreme Court upheld a federal law granting immigration preferences to legitimate children as within Congress's plenary power to regulate immigration [Fiallo v. Bell, 430 U.S. 787 (1977)].

(1) In 2012, the Court permitted to stand a law that required officers to verify the immigration status of anyone they stopped, detained, or arrested who they reasonably suspected was in the country illegally [Arizona v. United States, 567 U.S. 387 (2012)].

c. Classifications based on gender are "*quasi*-suspect" and violate the Equal Protection Clause unless they "serve important governmental objectives and [are] substantially related to achievement of those objectives" [Craig v. Boren, 429 U.S. 190 (1976)]. In Craig, an Oklahoma statute permitted the sale of beer to females who were 18 years of age or older, but prohibited the sale of beer to males under 21 years of age. The statute was held unconstitutional because it was not substantially related to any important government objectives. (Where separate treatment of men and women is found to be proper, a state may offer different, but equivalent, facilities to each gender.)

(1) Intermediate review applies whether the classification is **invidious** (intended to harm) or **benign** (intended to help or to remedy past discrimination). Intentional, or purposeful, discrimination is required to trigger middle-tier scrutiny; discriminatory effect alone is insufficient.

(2) Statutes that reinforce archaic, gender-based stereotypes will almost certainly be struck down.

EXAMPLE: The Supreme Court required a state to show an "exceedingly persuasive justification" for its gender discrimination in admissions to the Virginia Military Institute. This language reflects the rigorous nature of the Craig v. Boren intermediate-level test [United States v. Virginia, 518 U.S. 515 (1996)].

(3) In recent decisions, the Court has held unconstitutional, under equal protection, all laws discriminating against women.

EXAMPLE: A state law giving preference to men over equally qualified women to be administrators of decedents' estates was held unconstitutional [Reed v. Reed, 404 U.S. 71 (1971)].

EXAMPLE: Discrimination in military benefits to servicewomen was held invalid [Frontiero v. Richardson, 411 U.S. 677 (1973)].

(4) Similarly, the Supreme Court has held unconstitutional under an equal protection analysis laws discriminating against men [Craig v. Boren, 429 U.S. 190 (1976)].

EXAMPLE: The Court struck down a law authorizing alimony payments upon divorce to women but not to men [Orr v. Orr, 440 U.S. 268 (1979)].

EXAMPLE: A New York law that permitted an unwed mother, but not an unwed father, to block the adoption of their child was held to be invalid [Caban v. Mohammed, 441 U.S. 380 (1979)].

EXAMPLE: The Supreme Court held that the exclusion of males from a state nursing school violated a male applicant's right to equal protection [Mississippi University for Women v. Hogan, 458 U.S. 718 (1982)].

EXAM TIP In some cases, laws discriminating against men have been upheld when they are "substantially related to the achievement of an important government interest."

EXAMPLE: Statutory rape laws that punished the male participant, but not the female accessory, were upheld because they furthered the important state interest in preventing teenage pregnancy [Michael M. v. Sonoma County Superior Court, 450 U.S. 464 (1981)].

3. **Affirmative Action**
   a. Affirmative action measures based on race must pass strict scrutiny.
      (1) The only justification currently allowed for affirmative action is remedying the effects of past or present discrimination in a particular institution.
         (a) Achieving a diverse student body in an institute of higher education, whether private or public, is no longer a valid justification for affirmative action [Students for Fair Admissions, Inc. v. President & Fellows of Harvard College, 143 S. Ct. 2141 (2023)].
      (2) A school district may not assign individual students to schools based on race in order to achieve "voluntary integration" or "racial balancing" when school segregation is caused by social factors (***de facto*** **segregation**) and not caused by past or present government action (***de jure*** **segregation**) [Parents Involved in Cmty. Schools v. Seattle School Dist. No. 1, 551 U.S. 701 (2007)].
         (a) However, a school district is permitted to carry out such voluntary racial balancing by "structural" measures, such as redrawing school zones or building new schools.
      (3) Affirmative action measures based on race must be narrowly tailored to achieve their goals. The institution that adopts such a program must show that available, workable, non-racial alternatives do not suffice.
      (4) In 2014, the Court upheld a Michigan voter initiative that banned taking account of race in admissions to the state's public universities [Schuette v. Coalition to Defend Affirmative Action, 572 U.S. 291 (2014)].

b. Affirmative action based on gender need only pass intermediate scrutiny.

EXAMPLE: Social Security statutes and tax exemptions that entitle women to greater benefits have been upheld [Califano v. Webster, 430 U.S. 313 (1977)].

EXAMPLE: A U.S. navy discharge procedure that required male officers twice denied promotion to be automatically discharged, whereas female officers were not, was upheld because in the past, men had been afforded greater promotional opportunities than women [Schlesinger v. Ballard, 419 U.S. 498 (1975)].

c. In Richmond v. Croson [488 U.S. 469 (1989)], the Supreme Court first held that minority set-asides ("affirmative action") established by state or local governments for construction projects—i.e., programs where a fixed percentage of publicly funded money is awarded to minority-owned businesses—are subject to strict scrutiny review, and must be narrowly tailored to justify a compelling interest.

(1) In Adarand Construction, Inc. v. Pena [515 U.S. 200 (1995)], the Supreme Court set forth a clear rule that any race-based affirmative action program designed to remedy past discrimination—whether enacted by a state municipality or even the federal government—is subject to strict scrutiny.

(2) This rule applies to any "benign," or compensatory, program by any government entity that either favors or discriminates against racial or ethnic minorities. Other general principles include the following:

(a) remedying past discrimination in a particular government institution is generally viewed as a compelling interest, but attempting to remedy general societal injustice through affirmative action is not; and

(b) discrimination by private employers is not subject to equal protection review.

4. **Other Classifications**

a. Age is neither a "suspect" nor a "*quasi*-suspect" classification. Thus, laws and other governmental actions against the elderly are judged by the traditional (or rational basis) test.

EXAMPLE: The Supreme Court upheld the validity of a Massachusetts statute requiring police officers to retire at age 50 even though they may be as physically fit as younger officers [Massachusetts Board of Retirement v. Murgia, 427 U.S. 307 (1976)].

b. The Supreme Court has held that "poverty standing alone is not a suspect classification" [Harris v. McRae, 448 U.S. 297 (1980)].

c. Mental retardation is not a "*quasi*-suspect" classification, and the rational basis standard of review is applicable [City of Cleburne v. Cleburne Living Center, 473 U.S. 432 (1985)].

EQUAL PROTECTION CHALLENGES		
Rational Basis	**Intermediate Scrutiny**	**Strict Scrutiny**
• Age • Alienage (some) • Disability • Wealth • All else	• Gender • Illegitimacy • Undocumented alien children • Sexual orientation	• Alienage • Domestic travel • National origin • Race • Voting

VII. PRIVILEGES AND IMMUNITIES CLAUSES

A. Privileges or Immunities under the Fourteenth Amendment

1. The Fourteenth Amendment provides that no state shall make or enforce any law which abridges the privileges or immunities of citizens of the United States.
2. The Supreme Court ruled early on, in the Slaughter-House Cases [83 U.S. 36 (1873)], that the Privileges or Immunities Clause of the Fourteenth Amendment had very limited application. Among the protected privileges and immunities of national citizenship are the rights [Twining v. New Jersey, 211 U.S. 78 (1908)]:
   a. to travel from state to state;
   b. to petition Congress for redress of grievances;
   c. to vote for national offices;
   d. to enter public lands;
   e. to be protected while in custody of U.S. Marshals; and
   f. to assemble peaceably.

NOTE Corporations and aliens are not protected under the Fourteenth Amendment Privileges or Immunities Clause.

EXAM TIP When an in-state citizen is discriminated against on the basis of the citizen having only resided in the state for a limited time (i.e., a durational residency requirement), this citizen can assert that the Fourteenth Amendment Privileges or Immunities Clause has been violated, insofar as an aspect of a citizen's right to travel (the right to elect to become a permanent resident of a new state) has been violated.

B. Privileges and Immunities under Article IV, Section 2

1. Sometimes referred to as the Comity Clause, Article IV, Section 2 provides: "The Citizens of each State shall be entitled to all Privileges and Immunities of Citizens in the several States."
2. This clause prohibits states from discriminating against citizens who are nonresidents with respect to rights and activities that are fundamental to the national union. Corporations and aliens are not "citizens" for purposes of the Article IV Privileges and Immunities Clause.
   a. The following have been held to be invalid forms of nonresident discrimination:
      (1) a state statute requiring a nonresident commercial fisherman to pay a $2,500 license fee to fish offshore, while a resident fisherman paid only a $25 license fee [Toomer v. Witsell, 334 U.S. 385 (1948)];
      (2) a commuter tax applied to nonresidents who entered New Hampshire to work, while New Hampshire residents were exempt from the tax [Austin v. New Hampshire, 420 U.S. 656 (1975)];
      (3) a state statute imposing residency requirements on women seeking an abortion, which was held invalid because an individual

has a fundamental right to seek medical care [Doe v. Bolton, 410 U.S. 179 (1973)]; and

(4) a state law requiring employers to give hiring preference to state residents [Hicklin v. Orbeck, 437 U.S. 518 (1978)].

b. The Privileges and Immunities Clause does not protect a nonresident against all forms of discrimination. The following types of nonresident discrimination have been upheld:

(1) a state statute requiring a nonresident to pay $225 for a recreational hunting license, while a resident hunter paid only a $9 license fee, because it is within a state's police power to regulate recreational, noncommercial activities [Baldwin v. Montana Fish and Game Commission, 436 U.S. 371 (1978)]; and

(2) discrimination against nonresidents will be given special consideration if its purpose is the preservation of natural, state-owned resources [Sporhase v. Nebraska, 458 U.S. 941 (1982)].

EXAM TIP Discrimination against nonresident citizens in regard to an essential economic right or liberty triggers the Article IV Privileges and Immunities Clause, whereas general economic discrimination against a business or entity is more often viewed using Commerce Clause analysis.

3. In determining whether a state action violates the Privileges and Immunities Clause of Article IV, Section 2, the court will consider [United Bldg. & Constr. Trades Council v. Camden, 465 U.S. 208 (1984); Baldwin v. Montana Fish and Game Comm'n, 436 U.S 371 (1978)]:

a. whether the state has, in fact, discriminated against nonresidents with regard to privileges and immunities it accords its own citizens; and

(1) This factor requires the court to look to see whether the alleged protected right or activity is sufficiently basic to the livelihood of the nation as to fall within the protections of Article IV, Section 2.

b. if so, whether there is sufficient justification for discrimination.

(1) If a challenged restriction does violate the Privileges and Immunities Clause of Article IV, Section 2, the court will hold it invalid unless:

(a) there is a substantial reason for the difference in treatment; and

(b) the discrimination practices against nonresidents bears a substantial relationship to the state's objectives.

VIII. RETROACTIVE LEGISLATION

A. The Contract Clause

1. "No state shall...pass any...Law impairing the Obligation of Contracts" [U.S. Const. art. I, Section 10].
   a. The principal reason for the inclusion of the Contract Clause in the Constitution was to prevent state legislatures from passing retroactive laws impairing an existing contractual obligation. Therefore, the Contract Clause applies only to state legislation and not to state court decisions. Similarly, the Contract Clause does not apply to the federal government.
   b. A private contract can be modified by the legislature under its police power when it is necessary to serve an important and legitimate public interest and the regulation is a reasonable and narrowly tailored means of promoting that interest.
      (1) Thus, during the Great Depression, a statute imposing a moratorium on mortgage foreclosures was upheld [Home Building & Loan Association v. Blaisdell, 290 U.S. 398 (1934)].
      (2) In determining whether a contract may be modified, the Court will consider [Allied Structural Steel Co. v. Spannaus, 438 U.S. 234 (1978)]:
         (a) the severity of the impairment; and
         (b) the importance of the public interest to be served.

         EXAMPLE: New York and New Jersey violated the Contract Clause by permitting the Port Authority to use funds to subsidize public transportation in violation of a previous statutory covenant to private bondholders [United States Trust Co. v. New Jersey, 431 U.S. 1 (1977)].

         EXAMPLE: The Supreme Court recognized the validity of police power limitations on the Contract Clause and invalidated state pension reform legislation which increased the obligation of companies under preexisting pension plans [Allied Structural Steel Co. v. Spannaus, 438 U.S. 234 (1978)].

B. *Ex Post Facto* Laws

1. There are two *Ex Post Facto* Clauses in the Constitution that prevent both the state and federal governments from passing retroactive criminal laws. Article I, Section 9, Clause 3 provides: "No...*ex post facto* Law shall be passed"; and Article I, Section 10, Clause 1 provides: "No State shall pass any...*ex post facto* law."
   a. In general, a statute retroactively alters the criminal law if it:
      (1) makes criminal an act that was not a crime when committed;
      (2) prescribes greater punishment for a crime after its commission;

(3) decreases the amount of evidence required for conviction; or

(4) extends the statute of limitations for a crime as to which the previously applicable statute of limitations has already expired.

C. Bills of Attainder

1. A **bill of attainder** is a legislative act that inflicts punishment without a judicial trial upon named individuals or an easily ascertainable group for past conduct.
2. Article I, Section 9, Clause 3 states: “No bill of attainder…shall be passed”; and Article I, Section 10, Clause 1 provides: “No state shall pass any Bill of Attainder.” These two provisions prevent both federal and state legislatures from passing bills of attainder.
   a. The Supreme Court held that a provision in the Landrum-Griffin Act making it a crime for a member of the Communist Party to act as an officer of a labor union was the equivalent of legislative punishment, and hence a bill of attainder [United States v. Brown, 381 U.S. 437 (1965)].
   b. However, the Court later held that legislation authorizing government control of various presidential papers and tape recordings did not constitute a bill of attainder, because the act was nonpunitive [Nixon v. Administrator of General Services, 433 U.S. 425 (1977)].

IX. FIRST AMENDMENT FREEDOMS

A. Freedom of Religion and Separation of Church and State

1. The First Amendment provides that "Congress shall make no law respecting an establishment of religion, or prohibiting the free exercise thereof."
2. **Establishment Clause**
   a. Where a government program prefers one religion or religious sect over others, strict scrutiny analysis will be applied [Board of Education v. Grumet, 512 U.S. 687 (1994)].
   b. The Supreme Court has held that the appropriate test for a potential Establishment Clause claim is to interpret the Establishment Clause using an originalist approach, examining historical practices and understandings, and including an examination of the potential for coercion [Kennedy v. Bremerton School District, 142 S. Ct. 2407 (2022)].
   c. **Religious Activities Conducted at Public Schools**
      (1) As a general rule, religious activities conducted in public schools violate the Establishment Clause because their primary purpose is to promote religion.
      (2) The following practices in public schools have been held to be invalid:
         (a) prayer and bible reading in public schools [Engel v. Vitale, 370 U.S. 421 (1962)];
         (b) an Alabama law authorizing a period of silence "for meditation or voluntary prayer" [Wallace v. Jaffree, 472 U.S. 38 (1985)];
            1) Note that a truly neutral moment of silence would likely be found constitutional, because it shows no religious preference (or preference for religion over non-religion).
         (c) posting the Ten Commandments on the walls in public school classrooms [Stone v. Graham, 449 U.S. 39 (1980)]; and
         (d) a public school sponsoring a rabbi or other cleric to conduct even a nondenominational prayer as part of a graduation ceremony [Lee v. Weisman, 505 U.S. 577 (1992)].
            1) A state legislature may employ a chaplain to conduct an opening day prayer [Marsh v. Chambers, 463 U.S. 783 (1983)].
            2) However, a state court judge may not conduct such a daily prayer [North Carolina Civil Liberties Union Legal Foundation v. Constangy, 947 F.2d 1145 (4th Cir. 1991)].
      (3) High school students being allowed to vote on whether a student-delivered "invocation" or "message" would take place at school football games is impermissible, as such an activity would be forced on all those present at a school-sponsored event [Santa Fe Independent School District v. Doe, 530 U.S. 290 (2000)].

(4) A state university regulation prohibiting the use of school facilities by a registered student religious organization (whereas facilities were available to other student groups) was held to be in violation of the freedom of free speech under the First Amendment [Widmar v. Vincent, 454 U.S. 263 (1981)].

(5) The Supreme Court has held that prohibiting a religious club from meeting in a public school amounted to religious viewpoint discrimination and violated the Free Speech Clause of the First Amendment. Furthermore, the Court ruled, permitting the club to meet on school grounds would not be in violation of the Establishment Clause [Good News Club v. Milford Central School, 533 U.S. 98 (2001)].

(6) The University of California required student groups to open their membership to "all comers." The university denied funding to the Christian Legal Society on the grounds that it refused membership to gays and lesbians. The Court upheld the university's rule against a First Amendment challenge on the grounds that it was a viewpoint-neutral restriction. The Court ruled that, in the academic context, the rule was reasonable in light of the goals of ensuring all students are included in the student group program, avoiding the need for the University to inquire into the groups' motives for excluding members, bringing together diverse students, and complying with state antidiscrimination rules [Christian Legal Society v. Martinez, 561 U.S. 661 (2010)].

(7) Other decisions regarding religious activities in public schools include:

(a) a prohibition against showing religious films at a school violated free speech [Lamb's Chapel v. Center Moriches Union Free School District, 508 U.S. 387 (1993)];

(b) a university's refusal to fund a student publication because it addressed issues from a religious perspective violated free speech [Rosenberger v. Rector and Visitors of the University of Virginia, 515 U.S. 819 (1995)]; and

(c) a state university's viewpoint-neutral allocation of mandatory student activities fees to political and ideological groups as part of a program to facilitate extracurricular student speech did not violate the First Amendment rights of students who objected to subsidizing those groups' activities [Board of Regents of University of Wisconsin System v. Southworth, 529 U.S. 217 (2000)].

d. **Public School Curriculum**

(1) Anti-evolution laws prohibiting the teaching of Darwinian principles in public schools are unconstitutional [Epperson v. Arkansas, 393 U.S. 97 (1968)].

e. **Other Government Endorsement of Religion**

(1) Displays that celebrate the holiday season without favoring one religion over another are generally upheld. The government

cannot permit the type of display that a reasonable observer would conclude constitutes an endorsement of religion. The context surrounding the display is a key factor in determining its validity [Lynch v. Donnelly, 465 U.S. 668 (1984)].

(2) Placing a cross in a state-owned park immediately in front of the State Capitol was held to not violate the Establishment Clause; there was no endorsement of religion because the park had long been used by a variety of groups to conduct expressive activities [Capitol Square Review Board v. Pinette, 515 U.S. 753 (1995)].

(3) Opening town board meetings with sectarian prayers, where there was no discrimination in the selection of prayer-givers or content, was held to be permissible, with the Court explaining that "[l]egislative bodies do not engage in impermissible coercion merely by exposing constituents to prayer they would rather not hear and in which they need not participate" [Town of Greece v. Galloway, 572 U.S. 565 (2014)].

(4) Having the Ten Commandments carved on a six-foot-high granite monument in a 22-acre park surrounding the Texas State Capital, and surrounded by 37 other monuments, was held to be constitutional [Van Orden v. Perry, 545 U.S. 677 (2005)].

(5) Sunday closing laws have been upheld as a governmental action with a mere incidental benefit to religion [McGowan v. Maryland, 366 U.S. 420 (1961)].

(a) Blue laws or state statutes giving churches and schools the power to veto applications for liquor licenses within a 500-foot radius of the church or school were held unconstitutional because of "excessive government entanglement" [Larkin v. Grendel's Den, Inc., 459 U.S. 116 (1982)].

(6) A city cannot deny a religious organization's request for a ceremonial flag flying if it has accepted all previous (albeit secular) requests [Shurtleff v. Boston, 142 S. Ct. 1583 (2022)].

f. **Tax Deductions for Religious Institutions**

(1) The Supreme Court has upheld the validity of a property tax exemption for religious institutions as the equivalent of exempting other charitable organizations [Walz v. Tax Commission of New York, 397 U.S. 664 (1970)].

(2) A tax exemption from sales and use taxes available only for the sale of religious magazines and books violates the Establishment Clause as an endorsement of religion [Texas Monthly v. Bullock, 489 U.S. 1 (1989)].

g. **Government Aid to Religious Schools**

(1) Most government programs providing direct aid to parochial elementary and high schools have been held to violate the Establishment Clause because they involve "excessive government entanglement" with religion.

(2) Programs that provide aid to all elementary and secondary students (including parochial school students) have been held to "pass" the Establishment Clause test.

(3) Providing bus transportation to and from school for all students (including those attending parochial schools) was held valid [Everson v. Board of Education, 330 U.S. 1 (1947)].

   (a) It was also held that necessary municipal services (e.g., police and fire protection) can be provided to churches and church-related institutions.

(4) If a tax deduction is given to all parents based on actual expenditures for children attending any public, private, or religious school, it will be upheld [Mueller v. Allen, 463 U.S. 388 (1983)].

(5) The Supreme Court permitted the state to furnish textbooks to all students, including those attending parochial schools, because there was little entanglement, and the primary effect was secular [Board of Education v. Allen, 392 U.S. 236 (1968)].

(6) Furnishing standardized secular examinations to parochial school students was held valid because the materials did not contain any religious content [Wolman v. Walter, 433 U.S. 229 (1977)].

(7) Public health services, including a school lunch program, can be provided to all students, since their purpose and effect are secular [Lemon v. Kurtzman, 403 U.S. 602 (1971)].

(8) The Supreme Court stated that Chapter 2 of the 1981 Education Consolidation and Improvement Act, which channels federal funds to local education agencies to acquire, for use in public and private schools, instructional and educational materials, including library and media materials and computer software and hardware, had a secular purpose and did not have the effect of advancing religion either by resulting in governmental indoctrination or by defining recipients by reference to religion, and therefore did not violate the First Amendment's Establishment Clause [Mitchell v. Helms, 530 U.S. 793 (2000)].

(9) A public school may pay for an interpreter for a deaf child at a religious high school in a program that aids both public and private school disabled students without reference to religion [Zobrest v. Catalina Foothills School District, 509 U.S. 1 (1993)].

   (a) Grants to parochial schools for salaries of teachers of secular subjects have been held invalid, because of the risk of "excessive government entanglement" [Lemon v. Kurtzman, 403 U.S. 602 (1971)].

   (b) In contrast, grants to church-related colleges are permissible because their instructors are thought to be restrained by the various academic disciplines (e.g., sociology, biology, etc.), and their students are older, more mature, and less susceptible to indoctrination.

(10) A state statute permitting all parents, in computing their state income tax, to deduct expenses incurred in providing "tuition, textbooks and transportation" for their children in elementary and secondary schools, including parochial schools, was upheld [Mueller v. Allen, 463 U.S. 388 (1983)].

(11) Giving tax deductions or tuition grants only to parents whose children attend parochial schools was held unconstitutional as violating the Establishment Clause [Committee for Public Education v. Nyquist, 413 U.S. 756 (1973)].

(12) A voucher program that allows parents to send their children to parochial or religious schools with state aid instead of to failed public schools is allowed because the aid is neutral with respect to religion to a broad class of citizens, the program is defined without reference to religion, and parents direct aid to religious schools as a result of their own independent and private choice [Zelman v. Simmons-Harris, 536 U.S. 639 (2002)].

(13) The Supreme Court has held that state tax credit-funded voucher programs for private schools that prohibit parents from using those vouchers for religious schools violates the Free Exercise Clause [Espinoza v. Montana Dep't of Revenue, 140 S. Ct. 2246 (2020)].

(a) In its decision, the Court held that school choice programs supporting religious schools do not violate the Establishment Clause, but that such programs that exclude religious schools do violate the Free Exercise Clause.

(14) The Supreme Court has ruled that a state could not exclude religious schools from a school voucher program in which parents chose the school [Carson v. Makin, 142 S. Ct. 1987 (2022)].

h. **Providing Public Services through Religious Institutions**

(1) Federal grants to church-affiliated hospitals for maintenance and care of indigent patients have been held valid [Bradfield v. Roberts, 175 U.S. 291 (1899)].

3. **Free Exercise Clause**

a. A person's religious beliefs are absolutely protected. The government may not punish an individual by denying benefits or imposing burdens based on religious belief [Cantwell v. Connecticut, 310 U.S. 296 (1940)].

(1) A state cannot require a person to carry a message on her license plate (e.g., New Hampshire's "Live Free or Die") which offends her religious belief [Wooley v. Maynard, 430 U.S. 705 (1977)].

(2) The government may not determine the truth or falsity of a person's religious beliefs, but it may determine a person's sincerity in his claim of religious belief [United States v. Ballard, 332 U.S. 78 (1944)].

(3) Public employment may not be conditioned on taking an oath based on a religious belief.

b. Where an individual's conduct is motivated by her religious beliefs, the state may regulate or prohibit the activity if the regulation is neutral in respect to religion and is of general applicability.

(1) In Employment Division v. Smith [494 U.S. 872 (1990)], the State of Oregon criminalized the possession of peyote, and no exemption was made for American-Indians who use peyote for their religious rituals. The Supreme Court upheld the law, and held that a neutral law of general applicability does not violate the Free Exercise Clause, even if it prohibits or punishes conduct engaged in as a religious observance or practice.

c. The approach taken by the Supreme Court in Smith is consistent with all but two of the earlier cases:

(1) a state law outlawing polygamy was upheld [Reynolds v. United States, 98 U.S. 145 (1878)];

(2) the Court struck down a free exercise challenge by a Jewish Air Force doctor who violated uniform dress requirements by wearing a yarmulke while on duty [Goldman v. Weinberger, 475 U.S. 503 (1986)];

(3) the Social Security tax applied to an Amish employer was held constitutional even though his religious beliefs prohibited him from making payments and from receiving benefits [United States v. Lee, 455 U.S. 252 (1982)];

(4) a state cannot deny unemployment compensation benefits to a person whose religious faith commands the observance of Saturday as the Sabbath [Sherbert v. Verner, 374 U.S. 398 (1963)];

(a) This approach by the Supreme Court to denials of unemployment compensation benefits is inconsistent with, but not overruled by, Smith. In light of Smith, it should be viewed as precedent only for cases involving very similar facts.

(5) the Court required that Amish children be exempt from a state law requiring all children to attend high school [Wisconsin v. Yoder, 406 U.S. 205 (1972)];

(a) This case is also inconsistent with Smith, but has not been overruled.

(6) the Court upheld Sunday closing laws because they further the state interest in providing a common day of rest [Braunfeld v. Brown, 366 U.S. 599 (1961)]; and

(7) a state-funded scholarship program for which devotional theology majors were ineligible did not suggest animus toward religion or impose more than a relatively minor burden on program participants [Locke v. Davey, 540 U.S. 714 (2004)].

d. Where the government purposely interferes with particular conduct because it is dictated by religious beliefs, strict scrutiny analysis will be applied and the law will be held unconstitutional unless it can be justified through proof of a compelling state interest served by narrowly tailored means.

EXAMPLE: A city ordinance banned all animal sacrifice done in a public or private ritual not for the primary purpose of food consumption ("kosher" slaughter was permitted). The primary purpose of the law was not to prevent cruelty to animals, but to abolish the sacrificial rituals of a particular Cuban Santeria religious sect. This purposeful interference with religious observance and practice was held unconstitutional by the Court [Church of the Lukumi Babalu Aye, Inc. v. Hialeah, 508 U.S. 520 (1993)].

B. Freedom of Expression

1. The First Amendment provides: "Congress shall make no law...abridging the freedom of speech, or of the press; or the right of the people peaceably to assemble, and to petition the government for a redress of grievances."
   a. The First Amendment was held applicable to the states through the Due Process Clause of the Fourteenth Amendment [Gitlow v. New York, 268 U.S. 652 (1925)].
   b. Freedom of speech encompasses not only the right to communicate a message, but also the right not to be compelled to communicate a message.
2. The government may neither censor all categories of speech nor engage in content-based discrimination among different categories of speech (even if that speech is offensive), with some exceptions.
3. **Exceptions to Freedom of Speech**
   a. **Strict Scrutiny**
      (1) The regulation of speech is allowable if it passes strict scrutiny.

EXAMPLE: A provision of the District of Columbia Code prohibiting signs within 500 feet of a foreign embassy that tended to bring the foreign government into "public odium" or "public disrepute" was held unconstitutional as a content-based regulation of political speech that could not be justified by proof of a compelling governmental interest served by narrowly tailored means [Boos v. Barry, 485 U.S. 312 (1988)].

EXAMPLE: Congress banned corporations and unions from using their general treasury funds to advocate the election or defeat of a candidate within 30 days of an election. Citizens United wanted to run a television show that was critical of presidential candidate Hillary Clinton shortly before the primary election. The Court ruled that corporate spending on speech merits the same First Amendment protection as speech by natural persons. Hence, Congress could not censor such corporate speech [Citizens United v. Federal Election Commission, 558 U.S. 310 (2010)]. However, the Court has held that a state ban on the use of payroll deductions to fund political campaigns is not an abridgement of speech. Thus, unions may engage in political speech, but are barred from enlisting the state's support through payroll deductions [Ysursa v. Pocatello Education Association, 353 U.S. 553 (2009)].

EXAMPLE: In Washington State, citizens may put a referendum on the ballot if they can get a certain number of signatures on a petition. Washington publicly disclosed the signers of a petition seeking a referendum on the rights of same-sex partners. The Court ruled that the First Amendment rights of the signers were not violated, at least in the absence of any showing that the disclosure caused specific harm to the signers. The disclosure requirement served the goal of maintaining the integrity of the electoral process [Doe v. Reed, 561 U.S. 186 (2010)].

b. **Conduct Regulation**

(1) A law which regulates conduct but creates an incidental burden on speech is allowable if [United States v. O'Brien, 391 U.S. 367 (1968)]:

(a) the regulation furthers an important or substantial government interest that is unrelated to the suppression of free expression; and

(b) the incidental restriction on speech is no greater than is essential to the furtherance of that interest.

EXAMPLE: Students wearing black armbands to protest the Vietnam War was held to be protected speech [Tinker v. Des Moines Independent Community School District, 393 U.S. 503 (1969)].

EXAMPLE: A Texas prohibition against desecrating an American flag was held unconstitutional as applied to an individual who burned a flag as a form of political expression. Strict scrutiny was applied because the Texas statute was intended to control expression [Texas v. Johnson, 491 U.S. 397 (1989)].

EXAMPLE: Requiring students to salute the American flag and say the Pledge of Allegiance in school was held unconstitutional [West Virginia State Board of Education v. Barnette, 319 U.S. 624 (1943)].

EXAMPLE: A federal statute, the Flag Protection Act of 1989, was subjected to strict scrutiny and held unconstitutional as a content-based regulation of political speech [United States v. Eichman, 496 U.S. 310 (1990)].

EXAMPLE: Virginia's prohibition of cross-burning with the intent to intimidate was not unconstitutional since it banned conduct rather than expression. While cross-burning could constitute expression, such expressive conduct was not proscribed unless it was done with the intent to intimidate, and targeting cross-burning was reasonable because burning a cross was historically a particularly virulent form of intimidation. A plurality of the Supreme Court, however, found the law to be a facially unconstitutional restraint on speech, to the extent it had the effect that any cross-burning could, *prima facie*, be sufficient evidence from which the jury could infer the required intent to intimidate [Virginia v. Black, 538 U.S. 343 (2003)].

EXAMPLE: An ordinance to keep the streets clean was held as not permissible to justify prohibiting people from handing out literature to others willing to receive it [Schneider v. State of New Jersey, 308 U.S. 147 (1939)].

c. **Government as Speaker**

(1) Where the speaker is the government rather than a private actor, the government may discriminate based on the content of the speech.

EXAMPLE: A city erects several permanent monuments in a public park. Some of the monuments were donated by private organizations. A religious organization asks the city to erect a monument containing the Seven Aphorisms of Summum. The city refuses. The organization sues the city, alleging the violation of the organization's right of free speech. The Supreme Court held that there was no violation of the First Amendment. The permanent monuments constituted speech by the government, even if the monuments were donated by private organizations. When the government speaks, it may favor some views and disfavor others [Pleasant Grove City v. Summum, 555 U.S. 460 (2009)].

EXAMPLE: The Court held that the state of Texas was free to reject specialty license plates bearing the Confederate battle flag [Walker v. Texas Division, Sons of Confederate Veterans, 576 U.S. 200 (2015)].

EXAMPLE: If private individuals or organizations engage in direct communication in a public park (for example, making speeches or distributing leaflets, as opposed to donating permanent monuments) then, of course, the government may not discriminate among the speakers based on the content of their message, since the communication is by private actors and not by the government.

EXAMPLE: Pursuant to the First Amendment, a city must allow the KKK to temporarily erect a cross on a public park when other groups have been permitted to temporarily erect installations. Temporary installations by private organizations constitute private speech, while permanent installations constitute government speech even if donated by private organizations.

(2) When the government sets the overall message to be communicated and approves the message to be disseminated, the speech will be considered government speech even where the government solicits assistance from nongovernmental sources in developing specific messages [Johanns v. Livestock Mktg. Ass'n, 544 U.S. 550 (2005)].

d. **Unprotected Speech**

(1) A regulation which relates to unprotected speech is permissible.

(2) **Unprotected speech** includes:

(a) speech that advocates violence or unlawful action;

1) The constitutional guarantees of free speech do not permit state regulation of the advocacy of the use of force or of violation of law, "except where such advocacy is directed to inciting or producing imminent lawless action and is likely to incite or produce such action" [Brandenburg v. Ohio, 395 U.S. 444 (1969)].

EXAMPLE: A Virginia statute which stated, "Any such burning of a cross shall be *prima facie* evidence of an intent to intimidate a person or group of persons," was found to be unconstitutional. The Court held that this provision was unconstitutional because of its "indiscriminate coverage." However, it ruled that a state "may ban cross burning carried out with the intent to intimidate." The state must prove the intent to intimidate [Virginia v. Black, 538 U.S. 343 (2003)].

(b) fighting words;

1) Words likely to incite an ordinary citizen to acts of immediate physical retaliation may be punished [Chaplinsky v. New Hampshire, 315 U.S. 568 (1942)].

2) To fall within this category, the speech must be more than annoying or offensive; there must be a genuine likelihood of imminent violence by a hostile audience.

3) "Fighting words" statutes are subject to facial invalidity if the conduct proscribed is vague (e.g., a law prohibiting "opprobrious words") or overbroad.

4) "Fighting words" statutes designed to punish certain viewpoints are unconstitutional [R.A.V. v. St. Paul, 505 U.S. 377 (1992)].

(c) hostile audience speech;

1) Speech which elicits an immediate violent response against the speaker by an audience may be grounds for prosecution. The police, however, must make

reasonable efforts to protect the speaker, to guard against a "heckler's veto" of unpopular speech.

(d) true threats;
   1) A statement qualifies as a "true threat," and so is not protected by the First Amendment, if it is a serious expression of an intent to commit an act of unlawful violence to a particular individual or group of individuals [Virginia v. Black, 538 U.S. 343 (2003)].
   2) Statements made in jest, communicated to a large audience, which are political in nature, or which are conditioned on an event that would never happen are more likely to be found to be speech protected by the First Amendment, rather than true threats.

(e) obscene speech; and
   1) For speech to be considered **obscene**, the following three-part test must be satisfied [Miller v. California, 413 U.S. 15 (1975)]:
      a) the average person, applying contemporary community standards, would find that the work, taken as a whole, appeals to the prurient interest (a national standard is not used);
         i) The manner in which allegedly obscene materials are advertised and sold may be probative of their "prurient" appeal [Ginzburg v. United States, 383 U.S. 463 (1966)].
      b) the work depicts or describes, in a patently offensive way, sexual conduct specifically defined by the applicable state law; and
      c) the work, taken as a whole, lacks serious literary, artistic, political, or scientific value.
         i) A national standard is used to determine this value [Pope v. Illinois, 481 U.S. 497 (1987)].
   2) Child pornography is unprotected speech. It may be regulated even without satisfying the Miller test because of the state's compelling interest in protecting minor children.
      a) The sale and distribution of visual depictions of sexual conduct involving children may be prohibited [New York v. Ferber, 456 U.S. 942 (1982)].
      b) A state may criminalize the private possession of child pornography in one's home [Osborne v. Ohio, 495 U.S. 103 (1990)].
      c) Recently, the Supreme Court held that a statute which outlawed not only actual child pornography but also virtual child pornography (in which no real children were depicted) was overly broad and

violated the First Amendment [Ashcroft v. Free Speech Coalition, 535 U.S. 234 (2002)].

i) However, in a follow-up case, the Court upheld a congressional statute that punished those who solicited or distributed pornography while believing it depicted real children, even if in fact it did not [United States v. Williams, 553 U.S. 285 (2008)].

(f) defamatory speech.

1) Constitutional restrictions apply to defamatory speech where the plaintiff is either a public official or public figure, or where the defamatory statement involves a matter of public concern.

2) When the plaintiff is a private person and the subject of the statement is a matter of purely private concern, such as the operations of a credit-reporting agency, the plaintiff need not prove actual malice, and need only show negligence in order to recover according to common law defamation principles [Dun & Bradstreet, Inc. v. Greenmoss Builders, Inc., 472 U.S. 749 (1985)].

a) However, in order to recover presumed or punitive damages, actual malice must be proven.

3) When the plaintiff is a private person and the subject of the statement is a matter of public concern, the plaintiff need not prove actual malice, but must prove negligence about the truth or falsity of the statement.

4) When the plaintiff is a public official or public figure, the plaintiff must prove the state law requirements of defamation plus **actual malice**, defined as knowledge of the falsity or reckless disregard of the truth or falsity of the statement. This rule holds whether the allegedly defamatory statement is a matter of public or private concern [New York Times v. Sullivan, 376 U.S. 254 (1964)].

5) The Supreme Court held that a private plaintiff suing a media defendant for false-light invasion of privacy concerning a matter of public interest must prove actual malice [Time, Inc. v. Hill, 385 U.S. 374 (1967)].

a) Note that this standard is higher than in cases where a private plaintiff sues for defamation over matters of public interest; in the latter cases, the plaintiff need only prove negligence.

b) In addition, the Court has said that a newspaper or broadcaster cannot be held liable for publishing truthful information obtained from the public record through proper means [Cox Broadcasting Co. v. Cohn, 420 U.S. 469 (1975)].

c) However, this does not grant the press greater access to information or exhibits (from a trial) than the public ordinarily has.

EXAMPLE: While the press and public may be entitled to hear a recording played during a trial and report on what was heard, the First Amendment does not provide the press with the right to receive a copy of the recording to broadcast [Nixon v. Warner Communications, 435 U.S. 589 (1978)].

6) Pure opinion may be actionable if it reasonably implies a false and defamatory fact [Milkovich v. Lorain Journal Co., 497 U.S. 1 (1990)].

(3) Certain categories of speech receive lower levels of protection, however, including:

(a) commercial speech;

1) A state may prohibit commercial advertising of matters that are illegal (e.g., prostitution) or advertising that is untruthful, misleading, or deceptive [Pittsburgh Press Co. v. Pittsburgh Commission on Human Relations, 413 U.S. 376 (1973)].

2) Commercial speech is protected by the First Amendment if it is not false or deceptive and does not relate to unlawful activity. If commercial speech satisfies these requirements, government regulation of the speech must satisfy the three-part test set forth in Central Hudson Gas v. Public Service Commission [447 U.S. 557 (1980)]. The regulation must:

a) serve a substantial governmental interest;

b) directly advance the substantial governmental interest; and

c) not be more extensive than is necessary to serve that interest.

3) A state cannot place an absolute ban on the advertisement of drug prices by a pharmacist [Virginia State Board of Pharmacy v. Virginia Citizens Consumer Council, Inc., 425 U.S. 748 (1976)].

4) A federal law making it a crime to send unsolicited advertisements for contraceptive devices was held unconstitutional [Bolger v. Youngs Drug Products Corp., 463 U.S. 60 (1983)].

5) A state cannot prohibit attorneys from advertising routine legal services at stated fees [Bates v. State Bar of Arizona, 433 U.S. 350 (1977)].

a) Similarly, a state supreme court rule prohibiting an attorney from mailing new-office-opening announcements to persons "other than lawyers, clients, friends or relatives" was held to be unconstitutional [In re R. M. J., 455 U.S. 191 (1982)].

6) A state may discipline lawyers for "in-person" solicitation of clients for personal gain because of the potential for overreaching [Ohralik v. Ohio State Bar Association, 436 U.S. 447 (1978)].

7) A state can prevent doctors from claiming to be "board certified" in a medical specialty unless the certifying organization meets certain state standards because the commercial speech doctrine does not protect fraudulent speech, and because such a statute reasonably advances the state's interest in protecting the public [American Academy of Pain Management v. Joseph, 353 F.3d 2020 (9th Cir. 2004)].

8) It is within a state's police power to prohibit billboards carrying commercial advertising [Metromedia, Inc. v. City of San Diego, 453 U.S. 490 (1981)]. It is unclear, however, whether a total ban on billboards would be upheld.

9) A city ban on newsracks placed on sidewalks to distribute commercial publications (while allowing newsracks to sell newspapers) was held invalid, because there was no reasonable "fit" between the type of publication being regulated and the state interest in reducing litter and promoting aesthetics [Cincinnati v. Discovery Network, Inc., 507 U.S. 410 (1993)].

10) Clearly, advertising of unlawful products can be prohibited. However, as to advertising of harmful, yet lawful, products—i.e., "vice advertising," such as advertising for cigarettes, liquor, and gambling—it seems unlikely that the government can completely ban truthful advertising.

    a) The Supreme Court held that a ban prohibiting all advertisement of liquor prices except for price tags displayed on the merchandise, enacted in order to protect the public and decrease alcohol consumption by discouraging price wars, was unconstitutional [44 Liquormart, Inc. v. Rhode Island, 517 U.S. 484 (1996)].

    b) The Twenty-First Amendment, which allows the states to regulate liquor and liquor establishments within the state's borders, may not be used as a constitutional basis to override the protection on commercial speech afforded by the First Amendment.

    c) A federal ban prohibiting beer bottle labels from displaying alcoholic content was held unconstitutional as a violation of the brewer's free speech rights. Because the law applied only to labels, not to advertising, and only to beer, not to wine and spirits, it did not directly advance the government's interest in preventing "strength wars" [Rubin v. Coors Brewing Co., 514 U.S. 476 (1995)].

(b) speech by public employees; and

1) A person does not forgo her right to freedom of speech merely by accepting public employment [Beilan v. Board of Public Ed., School Dist. of Philadelphia, 357 U.S. 399 (1958)]. The employee retains a First Amendment right to speak out on matters of public concern.

a) However, the government, as an employer, has a legitimate interest in regulating the speech of its employees to promote efficiency of its public services [Mandell v. County of Suffolk, 316 F.3d 368 (2d Cir. 2003)].

2) There are two inquiries that determine the level of protection afforded to a public employee's speech [Pickering v. Board of Ed. of Tp. High School Dist. 205, Will County, Illinois, 391 U.S. 563 (1968); Connick v. Myers, 461 U.S. 138 (1983)].

3) First, the court will determine whether the employee spoke as a citizen on a matter of public concern. If not, the employee has no First Amendment cause of action based on the government employer's reaction to the speech.

4) If the employee did speak on a matter of public concern, the question then becomes whether the government employer has an adequate justification for treating the employee differently from any other member of the general public [Garcetti v. Ceballos, 547 U.S. 410 (2006)].

5) In weighing the public employee's First Amendment rights against the public employer's interest in promoting public efficiency, the courts will balance the following factors [Calef v. Budden, 361 F. Supp. 2d 493 (D.S.C. 2005)]:

a) impairs discipline by superiors;

b) impairs harmony among coworkers;

c) has a detrimental impact on close working relationships;

d) impedes the performance of the public employee's duties;

e) interferes with the operation of the agency;

f) undermines the mission of the agency;

g) is communicated to the public or to coworkers in private;

h) conflicts with the responsibilities of the employee within the agency; and

i) makes use of the authority and public accountability which the employee's role entails.

6) While the government entity has broader discretion to restrict speech when it acts in its role as employer, those restrictions imposed must be directed at speech that has some potential to affect the entity's operations [Garcetti v. Ceballos, 547 U.S. 410 (2006)].

(c) sexual speech.

1) Regulation of sexual speech must serve a substantial government interest and leave open reasonable alternative channels of communication.

EXAMPLE: A ban on public nudity, including nude dancing in adult entertainment establishments, was held constitutional, with a plurality opinion focused on the need to protect the important government interests in societal order and morality [Barnes v. Glen Theatres, Inc., 501 U.S. 1030 (1991)].

EXAMPLE: A majority opinion of the Supreme Court held that a similar ban on nude dancing was content-neutral and constitutional because its purpose was to deal with the secondary effects of establishments where there is nude dancing, such as prostitution and other forms of criminal activity [City of Erie v. PAP's A.M., 529 U.S. 277 (2000)].

e. **Time, Place, Manner**

(1) Reasonable regulation of the time, place, or manner of speech is allowed.

(2) A **public forum** is a type of property that has open public access and has historically, traditionally, or explicitly been used for expressive conduct (e.g., streets, sidewalks, and parks).

(a) The government does not create a public forum merely by opening a space to the public. The government must intentionally be opened to the public for the purpose of expressive discourse.

(3) The government may place reasonable restraints on the time, place, and manner of speech in public forums (e.g., picketing, leafleting, and broadcasting). The focus is not on the "content" or "message" of the speech, but rather its "conduct" or "method."

(a) A three-part test is used to determine the constitutionality of time, place, or manner regulations of speech and assembly in public places. The regulation must:

1) be content-neutral as to both subject matter and viewpoint (i.e., the regulation cannot prefer some messages over others);

2) be narrowly tailored to serve a significant (important) government interest; and
3) leave alternative channels of communication open.

NOTE This test is very much like the test for intermediate scrutiny under equal protection.

(b) The Court has held that a complete ban on door-to-door solicitation is unnecessary, because a homeowner can protect his privacy by posting a "No Solicitors" sign [Martin v. Struthers, 319 U.S. 141 (1943)].
(c) An ordinance requiring door-to-door solicitors, or canvassers, to identify themselves to local authorities was upheld in the interests of crime prevention [Hynes v. Mayor of Oradell, 425 U.S. 610 (1976)].
(d) A city may not require persons canvassing door to door to register with the mayor's office and receive a permit where the canvassing consists of religious proselytizing (such as that done by Jehovah's Witnesses), anonymous political speech, or the distribution of handbills [Watchtower Bible & Tract Soc. of N.Y., Inc. v. Village of Stratton, 536 U.S. 150 (2002)].
(e) Charitable solicitations for funds in residential neighborhoods are generally protected [Schaumburg v. Citizens for a Better Environment, 444 U.S. 620 (1980)].
(f) Face-to-face solicitation of funds at an airport terminal, which is a non-public forum, may be prohibited, but a total ban on distribution of literature may not be [International Society for Krishna v. Lee, 505 U.S. 672 (1992)].
(g) The Supreme Court has upheld the constitutionality of a federal law that permits the post office, upon a householder's request, to order a mailer to stop all future mailings to that addressee [Rowan v. United States Post Office, 397 U.S. 728 (1970)].
(h) A public school may not deny use of its facilities to religious groups if other public and private groups are allowed similar access [Lamb's Chapel v. Center Moriches Union Free School District, 508 U.S. 672 (1992)].

(4) A **nonpublic forum** is public property that has not traditionally or explicitly been used as a public forum for discourse, such as military bases, jails, government workplaces, and mailboxes. In a nonpublic forum, the government may restrict access based on the speaker's identity or subject matter, as long as the distinction is viewpoint-neutral and reasonably related to the purpose served by the forum.
(a) Speech-related activities at nonpublic forums can be regulated by reasonable time, place, and manner regulations. The test used by the Court requires a government regulation to be:

1) viewpoint-neutral; and
2) reasonably related to a legitimate interest.

(b) A state may prohibit demonstrations on jailhouse grounds [Adderley v. Florida, 385 U.S. 39 (1966)].

(c) Military bases may be closed to political speeches and distribution of leaflets [Greer v. Spock, 424 U.S. 828 (1976)].

(d) A city may sell space for commercial advertising on city buses but refuse to sell such space for political advertising [Lehman v. Shaker Heights, 418 U.S. 298 (1974)].

(5) A **designated public forum** is a space (not traditionally a public forum) opened by the government for expressive use by the general public or a particular class of speakers, and may limit the forum to discussion of specific subjects or topics.

(a) A designated public forum is evaluated the same as a public forum. Content-based restrictions or the exclusion of a speaker that falls within the class of those to which the designated public forum has been made available are subject to strict scrutiny.

(6) A **limited public forum** is a subset of designated public forums, and arises when the government opens a nonpublic forum but limits the expressive activity to certain kinds of speakers or to the discussion of certain subjects.

(a) Restrictions on speech not within the type of expression allowed in a limited public forum must only be reasonable and viewpoint-neutral.

(b) Additionally, the limitation on the forum must not discriminate against speech on the basis of viewpoint and must be reasonable in light of the purpose served by the forum. In other words, in a limited public forum, a nonpublic forum is opened up to speech on a specific subject or topic but cannot restrict from there on the basis of viewpoint or content without passing strict scrutiny.

(7) The owner of a private shopping center is not required by the Constitution to allow access for purposes of picketing and/or leafleting [Hudgens v. NLRB, 424 U.S. 507 (1976)].

(a) However, a state's constitution may be interpreted to protect such expressive activity [Pruneyard Shopping Center v. Robins, 447 U.S. 74 (1980)].

f. **Public Schools and Student Speech**

(1) Students have a constitutional right to freedom of speech or expression even while attending public school [Tinker v. Des Moines Indep. Cmty. Sch. Dist., 393 U.S. 503 (1969)]. However, that right to free speech is not absolute. Schools are considered, at times, to stand *in loco parentis* (or in place of the parents) and as such, have a limited right to control the

speech of its students [Bethel School Dist. No. 403 v. Fraser, 478 U.S. 675 (1986)].

(2) The Supreme Court has outlined three specific categories of student speech that schools may regulate in certain circumstances:

(a) indecent, lewd, or vulgar speech uttered during a school assembly [Id.];

(b) speech, uttered during a class trip, that promotes illegal drug use [Morse v. Frederick, 551 U.S. 393 (2007)]; and

(c) speech that others may reasonably perceive as bearing the sanction or approval of the school, such as speech included in a school newspaper [Hazelwood School Dist. V. Kuhlmeier, 484 U.S. 260 (1988)].

(3) Additionally, the Supreme Court has held that schools have a special interest in regulating on-campus speech that "materially disrupts classwork or involves substantial disorder or invasion of the rights of others" [Tinker v. Des Moines Indep. Cmty. Sch. Dist., 393 U.S. 503 (1969)].

(a) Though this rule originally applied to on-campus speech, the Supreme Court has ruled that it can extend to off-campus speech as well, though the bar will be higher for the school to establish that the speech is materially disruptive or poses a risk to others. There were three reasons given for the higher bar [Mahanoy Area Sch. Dist. V. B.L., 141 S. Ct. 2038 (2021)]:

1) a school will rarely stand in the place of parents when a student speaks off campus;

2) from the student speaker's perspective, regulating off-campus speech as well as on-campus speech means that the school would regulate all the speech a student utters during a 24-hour day; and

3) the school itself has an interest in protecting a student's unpopular expression, especially when it takes place off campus, because public schools are considered the "nurseries of democracy."

4. **Freedom of Association**

a. There is a close "nexus" between the freedoms of speech and association. The Supreme Court has acknowledged that "state action which may curtail (or have the effect of curtailing) the freedom to associate is subject to the closest scrutiny."

(1) Under the freedom to associate, the Court has struck down laws that prevented the NAACP from assisting individuals and that prevented a labor union from assisting its members in retaining lawyers [NAACP v. Button, 371 U.S. 415 (1963); Brotherhood of Railroad Trainmen v. Virginia, 377 U.S. 1 (1964)].

(2) It is unconstitutional for the government to order the Boy Scouts of America to allow homosexuals to participate in the organization. The organization's view that homosexual conduct was inconsistent with the values it sought to instill in youth members fell within its First Amendment right of expressive association [Boy Scouts of America v. Dale, 530 U.S. 640 (2001)].

(a) The Supreme Court refused to extend First Amendment protection to a high school student's lewd and offensive campaign speech delivered at a school assembly [Bethel School District No. 403 v. Fraser, 478 U.S. 675 (1986)].

5. **Public Employment**

a. In general, an individual cannot be denied public employment based upon membership in a political organization unless the position is a high-level policy-making position [Keyishian v. Board of Regents, 385 U.S. 589 (1967)].

(1) The Court invalidated political patronage dismissals by the Democratic sheriff of Cook County [Elrod v. Burns, 427 U.S. 347 (1976)].

(2) The Court held that party affiliation is not an appropriate requirement for the position of public defender [Brand v. Finkel, 445 U.S. 507 (1980)].

b. An individual may be deprived of public employment for political association if [Scales v. United States, 367 U.S. 203 (1961); Keyishian v. Bd. of Regents, 385 U.S. 589 (1967)]:

(1) she is an active member of a subversive organization;

(2) such membership is with knowledge of the illegal aims of the organization; and

(3) she has a specific intent to further those illegal ends (e.g., violent overthrow of the government).

EXAMPLE: A provision of the Subversive Activities Control Act was held unconstitutionally overbroad by denying members of the Communist Party "employment in any defense facility" [United States v. Robel, 389 U.S. 258 (1967)].

c. In the past, the Court has chosen to deal with loyalty oath qualifications under the "vagueness" and "overbreadth" doctrines.

EXAMPLE: An Arkansas statute requiring teachers to file an affidavit listing "every organization to which they have belonged or regularly contributed within the preceding five years" was invalidated as overbroad [Shelton v. Tucker, 364 U.S. 479 (1960)].

EXAMPLE: Similarly, the Supreme Court invalidated a Florida statute requiring public employees to swear, "I have not and will not lend my aid, support, advice, counsel or influence to the Communist Party" as vague and ambiguous [Cramp v. Board of Public Instruction, 368 U.S. 278 (1961)].

(1) On the other hand, an oath that public employees will "support the Constitution of the United States and will oppose the overthrow of

the government of the United States by force, violence, or by any illegal or unconstitutional means" was held valid in part; the portion of the oath requiring the employees to swear that they would support the Constitution was held constitutionally valid. However, the part of the oath requiring them to swear that they do not believe in the violent overthrow of government was held invalid as providing for the employee's dismissal without inquiry or hearing as required by due process [Connell v. Higginbotham, 403 U.S. 207 (1971)].

6. **Compelled or Coerced Speech**
   a. Compelled speech issues typically fall into two categories:
      (1) compelled speech (where the government requires a person to utter a message); and
      (2) compelled-subsidy speech (where a person is required to fund a message to which he may not agree).
   b. **Compelled Speech**
      (1) The Supreme Court has held that the First Amendment does not "leave it open to public authorities to compel [a person] to utter a message to which he does not agree" [Johanns v. Livestock Mktg. Ass'n, 544 U.S. 550 (2005); West Virginia State Bd. of Educ. v. Barnette, 319 U.S. 624 (1943)].

      EXAMPLE: A state statute requiring every schoolchild to recite the Pledge of Allegiance while saluting the American flag or be expelled from public schools was held unconstitutional because it required a person to utter a message [West Virginia State Bd. of Educ. v. Barnette, 319 U.S. 624 (1943)].

      EXAMPLE: A state statute requiring all license plates in the state to contain the state motto was deemed unconstitutional as an impermissible compulsion of expression [Wooley v. Maynard, 430 U.S. 705 (1977)].
   c. **Compelled-Subsidy Speech**
      (1) With compelled-subsidy speech, a person is being forced to provide funding that supports a message with which the person may not agree.
      (2) Whether or not compelled-subsidy speech is constitutional turns primarily on the identity of the speaker. While a citizen has the right to challenge compelled support of private speech, there is no First Amendment right not to fund government speech [Johanns v. Livestock Mktg. Ass'n, 544 U.S. 550 (2005)].
      (3) If the speaker is a private organization, a member cannot be required to fund speech with which she disagrees. Freedom of association also includes the freedom not to associate, and so if a private organization is engaging in speech, a member who disagrees with that speech is free not to associate with the organization.

(4) When the speaker is the government or a government agency, there is no First Amendment right not to fund such speech. In that the government could subsidize the speech through general taxation and assessments, they can similarly fund such speech "through targeted assessments devoted exclusively to the program to which the assessed citizens object" [Johanns v. Livestock Mktg. Ass'n, 544 U.S. 550 (2005)].

EXAMPLE: Pursuant to a federal act designed to promote and market beef and beef products, the Secretary of Agriculture created a Cattlemen's Beef Promotion and Research Board and an Operating Committee, which imposed an assessment on all sales and importation of cattle. This assessment was used to fund, among other things, beef promotional campaigns approved by the Operating Committee. Various associations whose members paid the assessment challenged the subsidy on the grounds that it subsidizes speech to which they objected. The Supreme Court held that the assessment did not violate the First Amendment, because the government controlled the speech and it did not matter whether it was funded generally, through taxes, or directly, through a targeted assessment [Johanns v. Livestock Mktg. Ass'n, 544 U.S. 550 (2005)].

(a) If the speech being funded is entirely private, commercial speech, a citizen cannot be compelled to pay a subsidy [United States v. United Foods, 533 U.S. 405 (2001)].

(b) However, when the speech is part of a broader regulatory scheme and the government is the speaker, a citizen can be compelled to pay a subsidy to fund the speech [Johanns v. Livestock Mktg. Ass'n, 544 U.S. 550 (2005)].

(5) Similarly, the government cannot force targeted individuals to pay for others to speak. In other words, the government cannot require people to belong in an association engaging in private speech, or require public employees to pay to subsidize a private association's private speech.

EXAMPLE: The State Bar of California was created by law to regulate the state's legal profession, and membership and dues are required as a condition of practicing law in the state of California. However, the legal profession was ultimately governed by the Supreme Court of California—the State Bar of California was an advisory agency that made recommendations as to the admission or discipline of lawyers, formulating rules of professional conduct and preventing unlawful practice of the law. Because membership was compulsory, the Supreme Court held that the use of mandatory dues to fund political and ideological messages and lobbying (in this case, advancing gun control and nuclear weapons freeze initiatives) represented an unconstitutional compelled subsidy and adoption of speech [Keller v. State Bar of California, 496 U.S. 1 (1990)].

(a) This includes requiring public employees to subsidize a union to which they do not belong [Janus v. AFSCME, 138 S. Ct. 2448 (2018)].

(b) Prior to Janus, it was permissible for labor unions to exact "agency fees" from non-union members in the public sector (having the fees deducted directly by the public employer).

7. **Prior Restraint**

a. As a general rule, the government cannot suppress or restrain speech in advance of its publication or utterance.

b. There is a strong presumption against the constitutional validity of any system of prior restraint of expression.

(1) The Supreme Court refused to permit the government to enjoin the publication of the Pentagon Papers [New York Times v. United States, 403 U.S. 713 (1971)].

(2) Confiscation by the post office of mailed materials determined by the postmaster general to be "obscene" was held invalid [Bantam Books, Inc. v. Sullivan, 372 U.S. 58 (1963)].

(3) A restraining order issued by a trial judge to limit media reporting of a criminal trial was held unconstitutional [Nebraska Press Association v. Stuart, 427 U.S. 539 (1976)].

c. There are some exceptional cases in which prior restraints are allowed, including:

(1) a government agency can require prepublication review of writings related to employment of past or present employees where such a review is necessary to protect national security [Snepp v. United States, 444 U.S. 507 (1980)];

(2) classified military information; and

(3) any case involving a search and seizure is governed by the Fourth Amendment.

(a) Thus, any "large scale" seizure of allegedly obscene materials must be preceded by a full adversary hearing, and a judicial determination of obscenity [Quantity of Books v. Kansas, 378 U.S. 205 (1964)].

(b) However, the seizure of a single book or film to preserve it as evidence in a criminal proceeding need only be made pursuant to a warrant based on a determination of probable cause by a neutral magistrate [Heller v. New York, 413 U.S. 483 (1973)].

d. The Supreme Court required trial judges to consider three factors in determining if a restraining order against pretrial publicity is appropriate:

(1) the nature and extent of the pretrial publicity;

(2) the availability of other measures to mitigate the effects of pretrial publicity; and

(3) the likely effectiveness of the restraining order.

e. Another form of prior restraint is the censorship or licensing of motion pictures prior to their exhibition. The Court has held that statutes requiring films to be submitted to a Board of Censors before showing them are constitutional if the following requirements are met [Freedman v. Maryland, 380 U.S. 51 (1965)]:

(1) the standards for the denial of a license are narrowly drawn and reasonable;

(2) when a license is denied, the censor promptly seeks an injunction [Teitel Films v. Cusack, 390 U.S. 139 (1968)];

(3) the burden of proving that the material is "obscene," or otherwise unprotected, is on the censor; and

(4) a prompt judicial determination is provided.

f. A method the government frequently uses for regulating the time, place, and manner of speech is to require a license or permit for such activities as a parade, demonstration, or rally.

(1) Such a licensing statute is valid provided that it:

(a) is content-neutral as applied (i.e., for protected speech, the message of the petitioners cannot be considered in granting or denying the permit); and

(b) does not give licensing officials "unfettered discretion" to determine who may receive a permit.

EXAMPLE: A parade permit that required applicants to pay up to $1,000 per day to cover anticipated costs of police security was held void on its face as a prior restraint. Also, as applied to a white supremacy group, the ordinance was not content-neutral, because unpopular speech is met with greater hostility, thus requiring more police protection [Forsyth County v. Nationalist Movement, 505 U.S. 123 (1992)].

(2) Where a statute is facially void (i.e., it gives the licensing officials unrestricted discretion), a speaker need not even apply for a permit. In this case, one may exercise his First Amendment rights on the public property without a permit [Staub v. Baxley, 355 U.S. 313 (1958)].

(3) On the other hand, if a statute is valid on its face (i.e., it contains narrowly defined standards as to time, place, manner, and duration), then the applicant must seek a permit. If the permit is denied, even arbitrarily, the applicant must appeal the adverse ruling to the proper administrative or judicial body [Poulos v. New Hampshire, 345 U.S. 395 (1953)].

g. As a general rule, if one is enjoined from speaking, she must either obey the injunction or appeal it, unless the licensing statute is facially void or the timing is such that an appeal would effectively frustrate the exercise of her rights [Walker v. City of Birmingham, 388 U.S. 307 (1967)].

8. **Overbreadth**
   a. When a state has the power to regulate an area dealing with free speech, it must not do so "by means which sweep unnecessarily broadly and thereby invade the area of protected freedoms" [NAACP v. Alabama, 377 U.S. 288 (1964)]. Thus, the wording of a statute must be narrow and specific, and not overly broad so as to have a "chilling effect" upon protected speech.
      (1) The Supreme Court has held that "the overbreadth of a statute must not only be real, but substantial as well" [Broadrick v. Oklahoma, 413 U.S. 601 (1973)].
      (2) The Supreme Court further explained that "there must be a realistic danger that the statute itself will significantly compromise recognized First Amendment protections of parties not before the Court for it to be facially challenged on overbreadth grounds" [Members of City Council v. Taxpayers for Vincent, 466 U.S. 789 (1984)].

      EXAMPLE: An ordinance making it unlawful "to curse or revile or to use obscene or opprobrious language toward or with reference" to a police officer performing his duties was held invalid because the ordinance effectively punished all vulgar and offensive speech, even though some of this speech may be protected by the First Amendment [Lewis v. City of New Orleans, 415 U.S. 130 (1974)].

      EXAMPLE: An ordinance prohibiting speech that "stirs the public to anger, invites dispute, brings about a condition of unrest, or creates a disturbance" was held to be overbroad and unconstitutional [Terminiello v. City of Chicago, 337 U.S. 1 (1949)].

9. **Vagueness**
   a. The vagueness doctrine is closely related to the overbreadth doctrine. In NAACP v. Button [371 U.S. 415 (1963)], the Court admonished that governmental regulations must be drawn "with narrow specificity." The following statutes have been ruled "void for vagueness" under due process inquiries:
      (1) a statute making it a crime to "publicly mutilate, trample upon, deface or treat contemptuously the flag of the United States" [Smith v. Goguen, 415 U.S. 566 (1974)];
      (2) a municipal vagrancy ordinance defining vagrants to include "rogues and vagabonds,...lewd, wanton, and lascivious persons,...[and] persons wandering or straying around from place to place without any lawful purpose or objective" [Papachristou v. City of Jacksonville, 405 U.S. 156 (1972)]; and
      (3) a city ordinance that defined loitering as "to remain in any one place with no apparent purpose" and gave police officers absolute discretion to issue dispersal orders to groups of two or more persons seen loitering in a public place if the officer reasonably believed that one of them was a criminal street gang member, and which made it a criminal offense to disobey such order [City of Chicago v. Morales, 527 U.S. 41 (1999)].

10. **Press**

a. The press has no greater freedom to speak than any ordinary member of the general public does. Also, the press has no special right of access to government information.

(1) The First Amendment guarantees both the public and the press a right to attend criminal trials. However, this right is not absolute and may be outweighed where the judge finds an "overriding" interest that cannot be accommodated by less restrictive means [Richmond Newspapers v. Virginia, 448 U.S. 555 (1980)].

(2) A **gag order**—a pretrial order prohibiting the press from publishing certain types of information—will almost never be held constitutional because the trial judge has other alternatives at her disposal (e.g., a change of venue, postponement of the trial, careful *voir dire*, or restricting statements of the lawyers, police, and witnesses) [Nebraska Press Association v. Stuart, 427 U.S. 539 (1976)].

(3) A newsperson has no First Amendment right to refuse to testify before a grand jury [Branzburg v. Hayes, 408 U.S. 665 (1972)].

(4) In general, radio and television broadcasting can be more closely regulated than the press, due to the limited number of airwaves available. A radio broadcast of "patently offensive sexual and excretory speech" (even if not "obscene" under the Miller test) can be sanctioned to protect the privacy interests of children likely to be listening [FCC v. Pacifica Foundation, 438 U.S. 726 (1978)].

(5) The Court has held that cable television receives First Amendment protection somewhere between that of broadcast television and newspapers.

(6) Where cable television operators are subjected to content-neutral regulations, intermediate scrutiny is applied [Turner Broadcasting System, Inc. v. FCC, 512 U.S. 622 (1994)].

(7) On the other hand, where content-specific regulation is imposed, the Court has yet to select a standard of review. However, the Court allows cable television operators the right to ban "indecent" programming that describes sexual activities in a patently offensive manner when in programming on channels that are leased outright to unaffiliated third parties (but not to public access channels) [Denver Area Educational Telecommunications Consortium, Inc. v. FCC, 518 U.S. 727 (1996)].

(8) The Supreme Court held that where a radio commentator played a tape on his talk show that he had legally obtained, but which had been recorded by another person in violation of the law, such a publication was protected under the First Amendment. The Court reasoned that a stranger's illegal conduct does not suffice to remove the First Amendment shield from speech about a matter of public concern [Bartnicki v. Vopper, 535 U.S. 514 (2001)].

(9) As a general rule, any prior restraint of publication will be deemed illegal. This does not mean that, after publication, there may not be civil or criminal consequences from the publication itself. Consider the timing of the action in question and determine if it takes place before or after publication.

11. **Bar Admission**

a. The state is permitted, under the Due Process Clause, to inquire into the qualifications and fitness of candidates for admission to the bar.

(1) A candidate cannot be denied admission for past membership in the Communist Party [Schware v. New Mexico Board of Bar Examiners, 353 U.S. 232 (1957)].

(2) However, the state can refuse bar membership to an applicant who refuses to answer questions (e.g., regarding past Communist Party membership) if his refusal obstructs the bar examiner's investigation of his qualifications [Konigsberg v. State Bar of California, 366 U.S. 36 (1961)].

(3) Reaffirming the validity of Konigsberg, the Court held that a state can inquire into knowing membership in subversive organizations in screening its applicants for the bar. Thus, the First Amendment does not extend unlimited protection to a bar applicant who refuses to disclose her political affiliations [Law Students Civil Rights Research Council, Inc. v. Wadmond, 401 U.S. 154 (1971)].

(4) A residency requirement by the New Hampshire state bar requiring a Vermont resident to establish a home address in New Hampshire prior to being sworn in was held to violate of the Privileges and Immunities Clause of Article IV, Section 2 [Supreme Court of New Hampshire v. Piper, 470 U.S. 274 (1985)].

KAPLAN BAR REVIEW

Contracts

TABLE OF CONTENTS

I. SOURCES OF CONTRACT LAW

In General....176
The Uniform Commercial Code....176
The Common Law of Contracts....177
Basic Definitions and Concepts of Contract Law....178

II. CONTRACT FORMATION: OFFER AND ACCEPTANCE

In General....180
The Offer....180
Acceptance under Common Law....190
Acceptance and the UCC....193

III. CONSIDERATION AND PROMISSORY ESTOPPEL

Consideration and Bargain....200

IV. STATUTE OF FRAUDS

In General....209
The Statute of Frauds in Operation....209
Evaluating Statute of Frauds Issues....209
Analyzing Problems under the Statute of Frauds....210
Analyzing Problems under the UCC Statute of Frauds....216
Effect of Satisfying the Statute of Frauds....223
No Mutuality of Obligation under the Statute of Frauds....223
Limitations on the Statute of Frauds....224

V. GAP-FILLERS, INTERPRETATION, AND THE PAROL EVIDENCE RULE

In General....225
Filling in the Gaps with Default Provisions....225
Interpreting Ambiguous Language....229
Trade Usage, Course of Dealing, and Course of Performance....231
The Parol Evidence Rule....232

VI. PERFORMANCE, MODIFICATION, AND EXCUSE

Obligations under the UCC....239
Modification....242
Excusing Performance Due to Faulty Assumptions....244
Excusing Performance by Agreement of the Parties....251
Conditions....253

VII. DEFENSES

Incapacity....264
Misrepresentation....267
Duress....272
Undue Influence....275
Unconscionability....276
Public Policy....278

VIII. REMEDIES

Monetary Remedies for Breach of Contract....282
Equitable Remedies....294
Other Possible Remedies....298

IX. THIRD-PARTY BENEFICIARIES

In General....301
Classification of the Third-Party Beneficiary....301
Rights of Parties to Enforce the Contract....303

X. ASSIGNMENT OF RIGHTS AND DELEGATION OF DUTIES

Assignment of Rights....306
Delegation of Duties....311

I. SOURCES OF CONTRACT LAW

A. In General

1. There are two principal sources of contract law: Article 2 of the Uniform Commercial Code ("UCC") and state common law.
2. In deciding which source of contract law applies, first look for the subject matter covered by the UCC. If the UCC does not apply, then common law will apply.

B. The Uniform Commercial Code

1. The UCC governs "sales of goods." If the UCC would apply to a contract, then UCC provisions will trump any contrary common law rules.
   a. **Sales** are any transactions in which the seller transfers title of goods to the buyer.
      (1) Leases, bailments, and any other types of transactions that involve goods are not considered sales.
   b. **Goods** are broadly defined under the UCC to mean any "movable item."
      (1) Examples of goods are ball bearings, vehicles, processed foods and produce, the Mona Lisa, clothing, carpeting, furniture, and everything on the shelves of a convenience store. The UCC also specifically defines the following as goods: growing crops, unborn animals, and "identified things attached to realty," such as uncut timber or tobacco.
      (2) Intangibles (e.g., the "goodwill" of a business), currency, stock, bonds and other securities, the assignment of a legal claim, real property, services (e.g., construction and repair projects, landscaping, dry cleaning) are not goods.
   c. Under UCC Section 2-204, a contract for sale of goods may be made in any manner sufficient to show agreement, including conduct by both parties which recognizes the existence of such a contract.
   d. In **hybrid** cases, which involve both the sale of goods and a services contract, the question arises as to which source of contract law should apply.
      (1) The majority rule is that the appropriate source is determined by the predominant purpose of the transaction.
         (a) To determine the predominant purpose of a contract, the following factors are used:
            1) the language of the contract;
            2) the nature of the supplier's business; and
            3) the relative values of the good versus the service.
      (2) The minority rule involves partitioning the contract, applying the UCC to the sale of the goods portion of the contract, and then applying common law to the services portion of the contract.

      EXAMPLE: Both the sale and installation of an audio system for an automobile and the sale of a car with a long-term service agreement involve goods and services.

(3) **Services Contract with Incidental Goods**

(a) A rendition of services with goods incidentally involved, such as a contract with an artist to paint a portrait, would be governed by common law.

(4) **Sale of Goods with Incidental Services**

(a) A sale of goods with services being incidentally involved, such as the sale and installation of a water heater, would be governed by the UCC.

e. **Computer Software and Other Electronic Information**

(1) The majority of courts treat computer software and other electronic information as goods governed by the UCC.

(2) In Maryland and Virginia, the UCC has been displaced by the Uniform Computer Information Transactions Act for transactions involving electronic information.

EXAM TIP The UCC governs the sale of all goods, not just the sale of goods priced at $500 or more. The UCC's Statute of Frauds [§ 2-201] applies only to the sale of goods for a price of $500 or more, requiring that a writing be signed by the party against whom enforcement of the contract is sought, but the rest of the UCC applies to the sale of all goods.

EXAM TIP The UCC governs all sales of goods, not just sales of goods involving merchants. The UCC has a number of provisions that create special rules for merchants (e.g., Section 2-205—only a merchant can make a firm offer; Sections 2-314 and 2-315—the merchant warranty provisions). Although the sale of goods by and between consumers is beyond the scope of the special merchant provisions, such sales are governed by all the other provisions of the UCC.

C. The Common Law of Contracts

1. Contracts that do not involve the sale of goods are covered by the common law of contracts. Frequently encountered examples are service contracts, contracts involving real property, and assignments of legal claims.

2. **Interplay Between Sources**

a. **Common Law Filling in the Gaps of the UCC**

(1) In cases involving the sale of goods, the UCC supplies the primary law and displaces contrary common law rules. However, where the common law rules are not displaced, those rules will supplement the UCC and fill in its "gaps."

EXAMPLE: An example of a UCC provision displacing a common law rule would be Section 2-205, the firm offer rule. The firm offer rule eliminates the common law requirement of consideration by allowing a merchant to make a firm offer that will remain open by requiring a signed writing to that effect.

EXAMPLE: Another example of UCC provisions displacing the common law rules would be Section 2-207, the battle of the forms provision which overrules the common law's mirror image rule, and Section 2-209, the rule governing midterm modifications which eliminates the common law preexisting duty rule.

EXAMPLE: Some examples of common law gap-filling include the common law doctrines of fraud, duress, and incapacity of minors and/or the mentally infirm. These common law rules apply even where the sale is otherwise governed by the UCC.

b. **UCC by Analogy**

(1) For cases that do not involve the sale of goods, the UCC does not apply. However, courts will frequently use its provisions "by analogy" in developing common law.

D. Basic Definitions and Concepts of Contract Law

1. **Contractual Obligations**

a. There are three general categories of contractual obligations:

(1) **Express contractual obligations** are found where the parties make oral or written "expressions" of their commitments.

EXAMPLE: A written contract, an exchange of e-mails, or a face-to-face oral agreement.

(2) **Implied-in-fact contractual obligations** are consensual agreements that fail to express the agreement of the parties in its entirety.

EXAMPLE: The most common implied-in-fact contractual obligation is the duty to pay the "reasonable value" of services rendered or of goods delivered where price is not discussed by the parties in advance.

EXAMPLE: Homeowner hires a plumber to fix a leak, but because of the urgency of the service, the parties do not discuss the price of the work performed. Upon completion of the work, Homeowner has an implied-in-fact obligation to pay the plumber the reasonable value of the services rendered.

(3) An **implied-in-law contractual obligation** arises where there is an equitable imposition of a would-be contract. It is an equitable remedy available to prevent unjust enrichment, and arises in situations where one party bestows a benefit on the other. An implied-in-law obligation is also commonly referred to as a *quasi*-contractual obligation or a restitutionary obligation.

(a) In many cases, the courts will conclude that the bestowal of the benefits unjustly enriched the recipient and will accordingly impose an implied-in-law obligation on the part of the recipient to restore the value of the benefits conferred to the other party.

EXAMPLE: Emergency services are a typical *quasi*-contract area, i.e., a surgeon who performs emergency surgery on an unconscious patient creates an implied-in-law obligation to the patient.

EXAMPLE: Another common situation is where contractual benefits have been conferred by mistake, i.e., a merchant who mistakenly delivers goods to the wrong party may create an implied-in-law obligation on the benefiting party.

EXAMPLE: A third frequent *quasi*-contract situation is where contractual benefits have been conferred via an unenforceable contract, i.e., a would-be buyer of real property who makes improvements on the land before closing and whose oral contract turns out to be unenforceable under the Statute of Frauds may create an implied-in-law obligation on the seller.

b. ***Quantum meruit*** is a means of enforcing both implied-in-fact and implied-in-law contractual obligations.

EXAMPLE: The plumber who was hired to fix Homeowner's leak without first discussing the price may enforce Homeowner's implied-in-fact obligation to pay the reasonable value of the goods delivered via a *quantum meruit* action.

EXAMPLE: A supplier mistakenly delivers goods intended for his buyer to another merchant, who in turn sells them to her customers. The supplier may seek to enforce the merchant's implied-in-law obligation to pay a reasonable value of the goods delivered via a *quantum meruit* action.

c. **Signed Writing Requirements**

(1) A number of rules in contract law require a "signed writing" in order to create an enforceable legal obligation.

EXAMPLE: The Statute of Frauds under both the common law and the UCC bars enforcement of certain contracts unless the party against whom enforcement is sought has signed a writing evidencing the underlying agreement.

EXAMPLE: The UCC requires that firm offers must be made in writing and signed by the offeror in order to be enforceable.

(2) Electronic signatures are legally effective in the vast majority of U.S. jurisdictions under the terms of the Uniform Electronic Transactions Act.

(3) The majority of courts have held that e-mail and the like are sufficient to satisfy the writing requirements of contract law.

II. CONTRACT FORMATION: OFFER AND ACCEPTANCE

A. In General

1. In many cases, parties to a would-be contract negotiate in advance of reaching agreement, engaging in a communications "volley" where inquiries, proposals, and counterproposals are exchanged. The law of "offer and acceptance" provides the rules for determining the point at which the parties have a legally enforceable contract.

B. The Offer

1. In order to constitute an offer, a party's communication must meet two requirements:
   a. an outward manifestation; and
      (1) The manifestation can be oral, written, or made via conduct.

      EXAMPLE: A newspaper seller stands on the corner with a stack of newspapers and hands them to people who pay the posted price.

      (2) Inward thoughts or subjective intentions are irrelevant unless they are reasonably apparent to the other party.

      EXAMPLE: A seemingly serious offer to sell real property made in secret jest is nonetheless an offer.

      EXAMPLE: A proposal to sell at a price that a reasonable person would regard as "too good to be true" (e.g., "new HDTVs for $8.99") does not constitute an offer.

   b. the signal that acceptance will conclude the deal.
      (1) An offer must signal to the would-be offeree that the latter's agreement will conclude the deal. The key inquiry is whether the party making the communication expressed a willingness to commit without further assent.

      EXAMPLE: "I will sell you my car if you'll pay me $2,000 cash." This is an offer because it expresses a willingness to conclude the deal if the other party pays the required $2,000.

      EXAMPLE: "Yes, I'd be willing to sell you my car, but what are you willing to pay for it?" This is not an offer because the communicating party is obviously reserving the right to decide whether she likes the price suggested by the other party. She is thus withholding the privilege of further assent, or she is reserving the right to assent (or not assent) to the other party's proposal.

      (2) Communications that withhold the privilege of further assent fall short of constituting an offer.
         (a) A **preliminary negotiation** is a generic term that applies to the give-and-take that occurs during bargaining.

EXAMPLE: "We're willing to consider that price if you can be more flexible on the warranty and the payment terms."

(b) An **invitation for an offer** is an advanced stage of preliminary negotiations, where the communicating party is closing in on a deal but wants the other party to commit first.

EXAMPLE: "Okay, we're in agreement on everything but price now. What's the best price you can give me?"

2. **Multiple Offerees**

a. When a question involves a party's communication proposing a deal to two or more persons at the same time, a **multiple offeree** issue arises.

b. There are three situations where this can occur:

(1) **commercial advertisements**, where possible offers occur in catalogs, price lists, and circulars;

(a) Under the general rule, advertisements addressed to multiple recipients are treated as invitations for offers rather than offers. The reason is that responses from recipients of the advertisement may exceed the available supply of goods or services; allocating the goods or services among the responding parties will necessitate further assent from the advertising party.

EXCEPTION: Language in the advertisement such as "first-come, first-served," or "first 10 customers only," identifying the means by which the goods or services will be allocated in the event of an excess of demand, eliminates the need for further assent from the advertiser and, thus, constitutes an offer.

(2) **reward offers**, which are general offers that name a price for a service but do not specify an offeree, such as "Will pay $100 reward to the person who finds my lost dog"; and

(a) Generally, reward offers are treated as offers because they are considered communications that promise a bounty in exchange for the performance of a specified task. There are two types of reward offers:

1) **Self-limiting rewards** are reward offers that indicate the task to be rewarded can possibly be performed only once. They are typically treated as offers that can only be accepted by the first person to render the requested performance in accordance with the terms of the offer.

EXAMPLE: "Will pay $100 for finding my lost dog."

2) **Open-field rewards** are reward offers that indicate that the task to be performed can potentially be performed by multiple parties.

EXAMPLE: The Carbolic Smoke Ball case, where the purveyor of a medical preparation promised to pay $100 to anyone who used the preparation as directed and, nonetheless, came down with the flu.

a) Unless otherwise specified in the offer, open-field rewards can be accepted by any and all persons who render the requested performance in accordance with the terms of the reward.

EXAMPLE: "Free Joe Six-Pack Action Figure! Send us proof of purchase labels from six cases of your favorite Anheuser-Busch product together with a self-addressed, stamped envelope. Offer good while supplies last!" Because of the limitation stated in the offer, the power of acceptance exists only so long as supplies last.

(3) **auctions**, which are situations where an item is sold to the highest bidder.

(a) The general rule is that the auctioneer is inviting offers, and the responsive bids are the offers.

EXCEPTION: Where the auction is "without reserve," then the auctioneer is making an offer to sell to the highest bidder.

3. **The Legal Effect of an Offer**

a. An offer creates the power of acceptance in an eligible offeree. This gives the offeree the power to create a contract simply by accepting the offer.

b. When an eligible offeree exercises the power of acceptance before that power is terminated, a legally binding contract is formed between the parties.

c. Generally, there are four ways to terminate the power of acceptance: lapse of time, the death or incapacity of either party, revocation by the offeror, and rejection by the offeree.

(1) **Lapse of Time**

(a) An offeree's power of acceptance terminates at the time stated in the offer. If the offer does not specify the time of termination, then the power of acceptance will terminate after a reasonable time. The reasonable time determination is based on the following factors:

1) subject matter and market conditions; and

a) What is considered a reasonable time will vary depending on the subject matter and the relevant market conditions.

EXAMPLE: A reasonable time would be shorter for an offer to sell stock in a wildly fluctuating market than for an offer to sell real estate in a dormant market.

2) the degree of urgency communicated by the means of transmission.

EXAMPLE: A reasonable time period would be shorter for an offer sent via e-mail than for an offer sent via postal mail.

(b) **Face-to-Face Conversation Rule**

1) An offer made by one person to another in a face-to-face conversation is ordinarily deemed to remain open only until the close of the conversation.

(2) **Death or Incapacity of Either Party**

(a) The supervening death of either the offeror or offeree will terminate the power of acceptance with respect to the offer.

(b) The supervening incapacity of either the offeror or the offeree, as evidenced by adjudication or the appointment of a guardian, will terminate the power of acceptance.

(3) **Revocation by Offeror**

(a) Under the rule of free revocability in American contract law, the offeror is free to revoke an outstanding offer, terminating the offeree's power of acceptance, at any time and for any reason, so long as the revocation:

1) occurs prior to acceptance; and

2) is effectively communicated.

(b) There are two methods of communicating a revocation.

1) **Direct Revocation**

a) Typically, revocation occurs and terminates the offeree's power of acceptance when the offeror communicates directly with the offeree and advises the latter that the offer has been revoked.

2) **Indirect Revocation**

a) In some cases, the offeree will learn of the offeror's intention to abandon the deal from a third-party source, and this will also terminate the offeree's power of acceptance where two conditions are met:

i) the offeror has taken definite action inconsistent with the intention to enter the proposed contract (such as by selling offered real estate to a third party); and

ii) the offeree acquires reliable information of the offeror's inconsistent action (such as learning of the sale from a real estate broker).

(c) **Revocation of an Offer Made to Multiple Offerees**

1) Under the Second Restatement of Contracts, where an offer is made by advertisement in a newspaper or other general notification to the public or some segment

thereof, the power of acceptance is terminated when the notice of revocation is communicated by advertisement or other general notification equivalent to that used for the offer and no better means of notification is reasonably available (the **functional equivalents rule**).

2) In such a case, a particular offeree loses the power of acceptance, even if he is utterly unaware of the revocation.

(d) **Option Contracts and Firm Offers**

1) An offeror is free to revoke an offer any time before acceptance. Under the common law rule of Dickenson v. Dodds (1876), the offeror can revoke even if she has expressly promised the offeree that she would hold the offer open. Under contemporary law, there are two ways to prevent revocation of an offer: a common law option contract or a firm offer under the UCC.

2) Three elements are required for an enforceable option contract:

a) an offer;

b) a subsidiary promise to keep the offer open; and

i) A "sell-by" date in an offer is not necessarily a promise to keep the offer open. It can also constitute an express lapse provision, establishing a deadline for when the power of acceptance will terminate.

EXAMPLE: "I hereby offer to sell you Blackacre for $10,000. This offer expires in 30 days." This language would not indicate an option contract but instead simply an offer with an express date of termination.

c) some valid mechanism for securing enforcement of the subsidiary promise.

i) The most common way to secure enforcement of the subsidiary promise to keep the offer open is by giving consideration in return.

ii) Consideration can be in the form of a performance (e.g., payment for the option) or a promise of performance (e.g., where a buyer of real estate promises his best efforts to obtain financing in exchange for the option).

EXAMPLE: An offer stating, "I hereby offer to sell you Blackacre for $10,000, and in consideration for the $100 received, I hereby grant you a 30-day option on the deal," would meet these three requirements as follows: the offer is the proposal to sell Blackacre for $10,000;

the grant of a 30-day option on the deal; and
the payment of $100 to the offeror.

3) A minority of courts have held that revocation of an offer can be prevented where the offer is in writing and signed by the offeror, recites the purported consideration for the promise to keep the offer open, and proposes an exchange on fair terms within a reasonable time.

EXAMPLE: "I hereby offer to sell you Blackacre for $10,000, and in consideration for the $100 received, I hereby grant you a 30-day option on the deal" will create an enforceable option contract under the minority rule, even if the offeree never paid the $100.

4) Under promissory estoppel, courts will sometimes enforce a subsidiary promise to keep an offer open where the offeree has foreseeably and reasonably relied on the option, and injustice can only be avoided by enforcing the promise.

5) **Special Rule for Construction Contracts**

a) A general contractor bidding on a construction project solicits bids from different subcontractors, such as plumbers, electricians, or glaziers. The general contractor must then use these bids in formulating his own bid, but cannot as a practical matter accept those bids unless and until the general contract is awarded.

b) The problem occurs when a subcontractor revokes her bid (offer) after the general contractor has relied on it to make her own bid on the primary contract, and the general contractor is then awarded the contract based on that bid.

c) The majority rule is that where a general contractor uses a particular subcontractor's bid to formulate his own, an implied option contract is created via promissory estoppel. This prevents the subcontractor from revoking the bid despite the fact that the subcontractor hasn't promised to keep the bid and the general contractor hasn't provided any consideration to keep the bid open.

6) **The UCC "Firm Offer" Rule**

a) Under the UCC, a merchant can make a firm offer (an irrevocable offer) to either buy or sell goods without consideration so long as [§ 2-205]:

i) the offer is made by a merchant;

ii) the offer is made in a writing signed by the merchant; and

iii) the offer expressly states by its terms that it will be held open.

b) Note that the UCC defines a **merchant** in terms of her special knowledge or skill with respect to the practices or goods involved in a transaction. It is important to note that a person may be considered a merchant even if she only has knowledge of the goods, or knowledge of the practices.

c) A firm offer that meets all of the above requirements becomes irrevocable either for the period of time stated in the firm offer or for a reasonable time if no time is specified.

d) Under the UCC, the shelf life of a firm offer can be **no more than three months**. Any firm offers that state a time longer than three months will only be irrevocable for the first three months. The offer would then become revocable, but still enforceable.

e) A merchant selling or buying goods can establish an irrevocable offer for longer than the three-month period stipulated in the UCC by creating a valid common law option contract. This means that the requirements of a subsidiary promise to keep the offer open, as well as some consideration in return, must also be present.

(4) **Rejection by the Offeree**

(a) The power of acceptance can also be terminated if the offeree refuses to accept the offer. There are three ways that rejection can be effected:

1) outright rejection;

a) The offeree's power to accept an offer is terminated by his rejection of the offer. The offeree has the power to accept the offer, but the offeree cannot change his mind and try to accept the offer once he has rejected it.

2) rejection via a counteroffer; and

a) A counteroffer made on the same subject matter operates to simultaneously reject the initial offer.

b) Not all statements or questions about an offer are considered counteroffers. An offeree may test the waters by making a "mere inquiry" about the offeror's willingness to negotiate without creating a counteroffer and terminating the power of acceptance.

<u>EXAMPLE</u>: "I am not willing to pay $10,000 for the car, but I would happily buy your car for $9,000." This statement would rise to the level of a counteroffer because the terms of the initial offer, to purchase the car at $10,000, have been modified by the offeree to $9,000. As a result, the offeree made a counteroffer which at the same time rejected the offeror's initial offer.

EXAMPLE: "$10,000 isn't out of the question, but it is a little high, given the age of the car. Would you be willing to consider a lower offer?" This language would not rise to the level of a counteroffer because the offeree is only asking if the offeror is willing to negotiate the terms, and not proposing a different deal.

3) rejection via nonconforming acceptance.

a) At common law, the **mirror image rule** requires that acceptance must mirror the terms of the offer, and any variation results in a counteroffer and rejection of the initial offer. Despite the mirror image rule, a *de minimis* variation in the terms of the acceptance may likely constitute acceptance in some situations.

i) If a court concludes that the minor variation was implicit in the offer, or merely a suggestion for the addition of a new term, then the response may constitute acceptance mirroring the offer, creating a contract.

ii) If the purpose of raising the issue is to attempt in bad faith to back out of the contract, a *de minimis* variation in the terms of the acceptance may still constitute acceptance.

b) The UCC rejects the common law mirror image rule and recognizes a binding contract despite the presence of a nonconforming acceptance in two sets of circumstances: the shipment of nonconforming goods and the battle of the forms. Each of those circumstances is discussed below.

(b) When the offeror has made a firm offer, the offer will remain open for the stated period even if the offeree makes a counteroffer or outright rejection. The offer will only be considered terminated in this situation if the offeror has changed position in reliance of a rejection made by the offeree.

(c) **Revival of the Offer**

1) The maker is the master of the offer. Therefore, an offeror has the power to revive an offer that the offeree has rejected, and with it the offeree's power of acceptance, and she can likewise revive an offer that has lapsed; all she must do is communicate the revival to the offeree. This can be accomplished by restating the offer or giving the offeree more time to make a decision.

4. **Offer and Acceptance under Unilateral Contracts**

a. An offer can require acceptance by either a promise or a performance.

EXAMPLE: If A makes an offer to sell his car to B for $10,000, A could request a promissory acceptance from B, which would require B to say something to the effect of, "I accept your offer, and promise to pay you $10,000." Alternatively, A could request a performance as acceptance from B, which would require B to pay A the actual $10,000.

(1) An offer seeking a promissory acceptance is an offer to enter into a **bilateral contract**. A promise is being exchanged for a promise. Under a bilateral contract, the offeree can accept the offer by making the requested promise. In this situation, both parties are bound by the terms of the contract once the mutual promises are exchanged.

EXAMPLE: When A promises the car to B, B accepts by promising A the money.

(2) An offer seeking performance in return is an offer to enter into a **unilateral contract**.

EXAMPLE: A promises B the car, and B can only accept the offer by paying A the money directly.

(a) Under a unilateral contract:

1) the offeror is bound only when the offeree completes performance in accordance with the terms of the offer; and

2) the offeree is never bound to perform because she has never promised to perform. It is entirely up to her whether to perform or not, which accounts for the description of the contract being unilateral. However, she will not be entitled to the benefits of the offeror's promise unless and until she renders the required performance.

(3) Where an offer does not specify whether it must be accepted by a promise or a performance, the offeree is free to choose the means of acceptance. However, the offeree must accept via performance where the terms of the offer or the surrounding circumstances make it clear that a performance is required.

EXAMPLE: A says to his old friend B, "I'll sell you my car for $10,000." B may choose the form of acceptance in this case. B is free to accept the car by either promising to pay A the money, or actually paying A the money. In this case, B's acceptance would dictate the type of contract created, because the terms of A's offer did not specify.

(a) In practice, true unilateral contracts, or those stemming from a unilateral offer, are relatively rare and typically fall into two categories.

1) A **reward offer** is a type of unilateral offer where the offeror offers to pay a reward for the successful performance of some act. Ordinarily, the act in question requires some effort on the part of the offeree, and the latter's ability to perform it may be uncertain. The key factor is that the offeror will not settle for a promise and is instead seeking the actual performance before binding himself to the deal.

EXAMPLE: "I'll pay you $100 if you find my lost dog" or "We'll pay $1,000,000 to the first person who proves Fermat's Last Theorem."

2) Rather than a promise to sell a house, most real estate brokerage agreements include a promise by the owner to pay a fee in exchange for the actual sale of the property, which would constitute performance.

(b) **Revocation of the Offer in a Unilateral Contract**

1) Under common law, the offeror was free to revoke the unilateral offer up until the moment that the offeree actually completed performance. The modern majority rule, which also appears in the Second Restatement, is that once the offeree begins performance, an option contract is created and the offeror may not revoke.

EXAMPLE: If A offers to pay B $100 to climb to the top of the flagpole, then once B starts climbing the flagpole, A cannot revoke her offer under the modern rule.

EXCEPTION: An offeror may revoke under the modern rule where the offeree is engaged in "mere preparations" to perform rather than the beginning of performance itself.

EXAMPLE: A offers B $100 if the latter can "ride my horse Bronco" for a full minute, but A revokes when B is saddling the horse. Revocation is permissible because the required performance consisted of riding the horse, and saddling was merely preparation.

2) Although the offeror cannot revoke once the offeree has begun performance, acceptance of the offer is still effective only upon the completion of the performance. The task must be completed in accordance with the terms of the offer in order for the offeree to accept the offer and bind the offeror to his performance obligation. In other words, the offeree who gets close to the top of the flagpole but doesn't actually reach it has not yet accepted the offer, and the offeror need not pay him a penny.

3) The offeree of a unilateral contract is free to abandon the performance at any time and even to not undertake performance at all.

NOTE If an offer to enter a unilateral contract was mailed to the offeree, then the offeror may revoke the offer even if the offeree has placed the acceptance in the mail. The mailbox rule (discussed later in this outline) only applies to bilateral contracts, and so dispatch could not constitute acceptance to create a unilateral contract.

C. Acceptance under Common Law

1. There are only two general requirements to constitute effective acceptance:
   a. under the mirror image rule, the acceptance must mirror the terms of the offer; and
   b. the acceptance must be communicated to the offeror.
2. **Communicating Acceptance**
   a. Once again, the maker is the master of the offer, and if the offer stipulates a particular means of communicating acceptance, then the offeree must utilize those means in order to make an effective acceptance. If the offer is silent as to the means of communication, then the offeree is free to use any reasonable means of transmission.
      (1) Unless the circumstances indicate otherwise, a means of transmission is reasonable if it is:
         (a) the means used by the offeror;
         (b) the means customarily used in similar transactions; or
         (c) a means of communication that is equivalent in expeditiousness and reliability to the means used by the offeror.
   b. There are three instances where the requirement that acceptance be communicated to the offeror may not apply:
      (1) acceptance by silence;
         (a) Generally, an offeree's silence in response to an offer cannot constitute acceptance except in the following three circumstances:
            1) where the offeree takes the benefit of the offeror's services with a reasonable opportunity to reject them and with reason to know the offeror's intention;
            2) where the offeror has given the offeree reason to understand that acceptance may be communicated by silence, in which case the offeree's silence will operate as acceptance if she intends as such; and

            EXAMPLE: An insurance company notifies A that his policy will be automatically renewed unless it hears otherwise from him. A remains silent, intending to accept the offer of renewal. Accordingly, his acceptance is affected by his silence.

            EXAMPLE: Same facts as above, except that A does not intend to accept. In these circumstances, his silence will not operate as acceptance. This is a rare instance in which contractual liability depends on the subjective intentions of the party rather than his outward manifestation.

            3) where, because of previous dealings or other circumstances, it is reasonable that the offeree should notify the offeror if she does not intend to accept, in which case her silence will operate as acceptance.

EXAMPLE: A newspaper sends a written notice that it will continue delivering the paper after the subscription has expired unless it hears otherwise from A. When the subscription has previously been renewed in this manner without incident, A's silence in the face of notice will constitute acceptance.

(2) acceptance by performance; and

(a) The maker is the master of the offer and, accordingly, the maker of an offer to enter a unilateral contract is free to make communication of acceptance a part of the required performance. But if he fails to do so, then acceptance is effective upon the offeree's completion of the requested performance whether or not the offeree so notifies the offeror.

(3) acceptance by mail or other correspondence.

(a) Under the common law **mailbox rule**, which is the rule in every American jurisdiction except the federal court of claims, acceptance by mail is effective upon dispatch so long as the acceptance is properly posted, with the correct address and postage amount.

1) The mailbox rule applies only to acceptances and not to any other communication between contracting parties. Thus, offers, revocations, rejections, and counteroffers are all effective only upon receipt by the other party.

2) Once the offeree dispatches her acceptance, she thereby creates a binding contract.

a) The offeror may not revoke an offer once acceptance has been dispatched.

EXAMPLE: While B was considering A's offer, A had a change of heart and sent B a revocation. However, B dispatched his acceptance before receiving A's revocation. The parties have a contract because A's revocation was not effective until receipt by B and B's acceptance was effective upon dispatch, which was prior to his receipt of the would-be revocation.

b) Once the offeree dispatches her acceptance, the parties have a binding contract and the offeree may not withdraw her acceptance.

EXAMPLE: B dispatches her acceptance of A's offer and then has a change of heart, telephonically notifying A of the fact while the acceptance is still in transmission. The parties have a binding contract because B's acceptance was effective upon dispatch, and it is too late for either party to back out because the contract has been formed.

c) The parties are bound even if the acceptance is lost in transmission and the offeror has no knowledge of that acceptance.

3) The mailbox rule applies to acceptances sent by any means of transmission which involves a foreseeable delay between the time of dispatch by the offeree and the time of receipt by the offeror.

a) This definition would include a private overnight delivery service.

b) This would not include an instantaneous means of communication, such as a facsimile.

c) Its application to e-mail is still undecided.

4) The mailbox rule is only a default rule, meaning that it only applies if the offeror is silent on the question of when acceptance will be effective. As always, the maker is the master of the offer, and thus the offeror is free to establish his own rules for effective acceptance.

EXAM TIP In a situation where the parties simultaneously dispatch identical offers, remember that offers are not effective until received, and the only effect an offer has once received is to create the power of acceptance in the offeree. Accordingly, unless and until one of the parties receives and accepts one of the offers passing in the night, there is no contract.

5) According to the Restatement, acceptance under an option contract is effective upon receipt by the offeror, but the case law on this question is limited. Some authorities have rejected this approach and held that the mailbox rule applies in this context as well.

6) **Mailbox Rule Does Not Apply**

a) Two situations under the mailbox rule involve an offeree who dispatches two responses to an offer: the first purporting to reject the offer, and the second purporting to accept it. In these cases, the mailbox rule does not apply.

b) The parties' obligations will depend on which of the offeree's communications reaches the offeror first:

i) If the acceptance reaches the offeror first, then the acceptance is effective upon receipt and the parties are bound to the contract.

ii) If the rejection reaches the offeror first, then the offeree's power of acceptance is terminated and the subsequently arriving acceptance becomes a counteroffer, which the original offeror is free to accept or reject.

D. Acceptance and the UCC

1. Unless the contract language or circumstances unambiguously indicate otherwise, acceptance may be made in any manner and by any medium reasonable under the circumstances [§ 2-206(1)(a)].
2. The UCC rejects the common law mirror image rule and recognizes a binding contract despite the presence of nonconforming acceptance in two situations: the shipment of nonconforming goods and the so-called "battle of the forms."
3. **Seller's Shipment of Conforming and Nonconforming Goods**
   a. Under the UCC, a seller can accept a buyer's offer to purchase goods for prompt or current shipment in one of three ways:
      (1) a promise to ship goods in conformity with the terms of the offer, such as an acknowledgment of order form sent to the buyer;
      (2) a prompt or current shipment of the goods in conformity with the terms of the offer; or
      (3) the seller can also accept the buyer's offer by shipping nonconforming goods.
         (a) In contrast to common law, under which the nonconforming shipment would have constituted a counteroffer which the buyer would have been free to accept or reject, the UCC specifies that the shipment constitutes a valid acceptance and creates a binding contract between the parties.

         EXCEPTION: Under the UCC, the shipment of nonconforming goods will not constitute acceptance if the seller notifies the buyer that the shipment is offered only as an "accommodation" to the buyer. In such circumstances, the shipment constitutes a counteroffer which the buyer is free to accept or reject.

         EXAMPLE: Buyer orders 1,000 widgets from Seller for immediate delivery. Seller responds by shipping 800 widgets with an accompanying notice to Buyer explaining that Seller did not have adequate inventory to ship 1,000 widgets and was thus shipping 800 widgets as an accommodation to Buyer in light of Buyer's urgent need. The nonconforming shipment would not constitute an acceptance of Buyer's offer in this case.

         (b) Absent accommodation, the seller's shipment of nonconforming goods constitutes acceptance of the buyer's offer under the UCC. It also constitutes a breach of the resulting contract under the perfect tender rule, which is described in detail later.
4. **The Battle of the Forms**
   a. UCC Section 2-207 is designed primarily to deal with difficulties created by the application of the common law mirror image rule to commercial settings, in which parties typically transact business via the use of preprinted forms.

b. A so-called "battle of the forms" may occur when a buyer places an order (the offer) and the seller's acceptance form contains terms which differ from the buyer's order or are not addressed in the order at all.

   (1) Note that these rules apply regardless of which party (buyer or seller) is the offeror or offeree.

c. Because the seller's acceptance contains terms that vary from the buyer's offer, the seller's response constitutes a **nonconforming acceptance**. The UCC deals with two issues in a manner different from the common law.

   (1) First, in many circumstances the UCC rejects the common law mirror image rule and treats a nonconforming acceptance as a legally effective acceptance, thus binding both parties to the contract despite the differing forms.

   (2) Second, the UCC rejects the common law last shot doctrine in determining the terms that will govern a contract formed via mismatching forms.

d. Unless acceptance is expressly made conditional on assent to the additional or different terms (a **conditional acceptance**), the nonconforming acceptance will operate as an effective acceptance of the offer, forming a valid and enforceable contract. Once the contract is formed, the next step is to determine the effect of the new or additional terms.

   EXAMPLE: Buyer sends Seller a purchase order for 1,000 widgets at the advertised price of $10 each. Seller sends Buyer an "Acknowledgment of Order Form" that promises delivery of the widgets at the stated price, but also contains boilerplate language negating warranties and limiting remedies in the event of breach. Seller's form will operate as acceptance of Buyer's offer and create a binding contract despite the presence of terms that vary from Buyer's purchase order.

   (1) **Dickered versus Boilerplate Terms**

      (a) Typically, the forms will be in agreement as to the **dickered terms**—those specific to the transaction—but may vary with respect to the **boilerplate terms**—standard terms that appear on the parties' respective forms regarding issues such as arbitration and warranties.

e. **Nonconforming Acceptance or Confirmation**

   (1) When a contract is formed by an offer followed by a nonconforming acceptance, the treatment of additional or different terms depends on the identities of the parties.

   (2) **Transaction Involving a Consumer**

      (a) When at least one party to the transaction is not a merchant, the additional or different terms are construed as proposals for addition to the contract. Thus, they are not part of the contract unless the offeror expressly agrees to the additional terms [§ 2-207(2)].

(3) **Transactions Where Both Parties Are Merchants**

(a) In a transaction between merchants, there is a distinction between additional terms and different terms.

1) A nonconforming acceptance contains **additional terms** when its provisions address an issue or topic not addressed in the original offer.

EXAMPLE: Buyer's offer is silent on the question of arbitration, and Seller's acceptance purports to require arbitration of all claims.

2) A nonconforming acceptance contains **different terms** when the offer says one thing about a particular issue and the would-be acceptance says something else.

EXAMPLE: Buyer's offer requires arbitration of claims, and Seller's acceptance precludes it.

(b) **Additional Terms**

1) Additional terms become part of the contract unless [§ 2-207(2)]:

a) the offer expressly limits acceptance to the terms of the offer;

EXAMPLE: "This order expressly limits acceptance to the terms stated herein."

b) the offeror objects to the additional terms within a reasonable time after receiving notice of them; or

EXAMPLE: This could be accomplished through language to the effect of: "We do not accept the binding arbitration provision set forth in your Acknowledgment of Order."

c) the additional terms would materially alter the contract.

2) **Materially Altering Terms**

a) Under Section 2-207, terms that **materially alter** the contract are those that would result in surprise or hardship if incorporated without the express awareness of the other party [§ 2-207, cmt. 4].

b) Examples of clauses that would materially alter the contract include [Id.]:

i) a clause negating standard warranties, such as that of merchantability or fitness for a particular purpose in circumstances in which either warranty normally attaches;

ii) a clause requiring that complaints be made in a time materially shorter than customary or reasonable; and

iii) any clause that would vary in a significant way an established usage of trade or a course of past dealing between the parties.

EXAMPLE: Buyer sends Seller a purchase order for 1,000 widgets at the advertised price of $10 each. Seller sends Buyer an Acknowledgment of Order that promises delivery of the widgets at the stated price and includes boilerplate language that negates all warranties and requires payment for the order to be complete within 30 days of delivery, which is standard in the widget trade. The negation of warranties will not be considered part of the contract because it would serve to materially alter the contract. The 30-day payment deadline would be considered part of the contract because it would not materially alter the terms of the contract.

(c) **Different Terms**

1) With respect to different terms, the majority of decisions employ the **knockout rule** and omit both the offeror's original provision and the offeree's differing provision from the resulting contract.

EXAMPLE: Buyer's purchase order contains a choice-of-law provision stating that California law will govern disputes arising from the transaction, and Seller's order acknowledgment states that New York law will govern. Neither provision will be part of the parties' contract; if the parties desire a choice-of-law provision, they will have to negotiate one from scratch.

2) A minority of decisions treat a different term appearing in the acceptance as a mere proposal for alteration of the contract, which the offeror is free to accept or reject.

EXAMPLE: On the same facts as immediately above, the buyer's California law provision would govern the contract unless she expressly agreed to the seller's contrary provision.

(4) **Written Confirmations**

(a) Another situation governed by the battle of the forms rules occurs when parties enter a contract—typically in real-time via face-to-face or telephonic communications—and then one or both of the parties follow up with a written confirmation containing terms additional to or different from the terms of the original deal.

(b) As is the case for a contract formed by an offer followed by a nonconforming acceptance, the treatment of the additional or different terms depends on the identity of the parties.

1) If at least one of the parties to the transaction is a consumer, then any additional or different terms are mere proposals for addition to the contract which the receiving party is free to accept or reject.

2) If the transaction is between merchants:

a) any additional terms are automatically part of the contract unless:

i) they would materially alter the contract; or

ii) the receiving party objects to them within a reasonable time;

b) any terms in a confirmation that differ from the terms of the prior agreement are proposals for inclusion in the contract, which the receiving party is free to accept or reject; and

c) if both merchants send written confirmations and those confirmations contain conflicting terms, then the knockout rule applies and neither party's term is in the contract.

i) All jurisdictions agree that the knockout rule applies to written confirmations.

(c) Because the parties already have a binding contract in this situation—formed prior to the sending of any written confirmation(s)—a written confirmation cannot constitute a conditional acceptance and, accordingly, the parties are bound to the contract irrespective of any differences between their prior agreement and the forms.

f. **Conditional Acceptance**

(1) Under the UCC, a definite and seasonable expression of acceptance will operate as an acceptance even though it states additional or different terms, unless acceptance is expressly made conditional on assent to the additional or different terms [§ 2-207(1)].

(2) However, if the acceptance is made expressly conditional on assent to the additional or different terms, the nonconforming acceptance will not be effective to form a contract.

(a) In this situation, no contract is formed until the offeror expressly assents to the additional or different terms.

(3) **What Constitutes a Conditional Acceptance?**

(a) Under the majority rule, a would-be acceptance which tracks the language of the exception as set out in Section 2-207 constitutes a conditional acceptance if the language in question is clear and conspicuous.

EXAMPLE: Buyer sends Seller a purchase order for 1,000 widgets at the advertised price of $10 each. Seller sends Buyer an Acknowledgment of Order form that promises delivery of the widgets at the stated price, but also contains boilerplate language negating warranties and limiting remedies in the event of breach. Seller's form also contains the following language in large bold font: "Our acceptance of your order is expressly conditional on your assent to the additional or different terms that appear in this acknowledgment." Under the majority rule, Seller's form constitutes a conditional acceptance of Buyer's order, and thus does not operate as a legally effective acceptance. Thus, the exchange of forms does not create a contract. Either party is free to back out of the deal prior to the buyer's assent to the additional or different terms.

(b) Under the minority rule, a would-be acceptance constitutes a conditional acceptance only if it clearly communicates that the offeree is unwilling to do business with the offeror unless and until the offeror agrees to the offeree's terms.

EXAMPLE: Buyer sends Seller a purchase order for 1,000 widgets at the advertised price of $10 each. Seller responds to Buyer's order with an e-mail saying, "We are in receipt of your order for 1,000 widgets at the advertised price of $10 each, and we will be happy to fill it. However, before we can do so, we must require you to agree to the following terms." The message then sets forth terms negating warranties and limiting remedies and concludes, "Upon receipt of your reply to this message stating your agreement to these terms, we will immediately ship your order." Under the minority rule, this exchange of forms would constitute conditional acceptance. By contrast, the proviso tracking language in the form used in the previous example would not constitute conditional acceptance.

g. **Other Situations Governed by the Battle of the Forms Rules**

(1) **Contracts Formed by Conduct**

(a) The UCC also provides that the parties' conduct in recognizing the existence of a contract is sufficient to establish a contract, even though their writings do not otherwise establish a contract [§ 2-207(3)].

EXAMPLE: Buyer sends a purchase order to Seller, Seller responds with a conditional acceptance containing a negation of warranties, and the parties have no further communications. Seller nevertheless ships the ordered goods, and Buyer accepts and pays for them. Although the parties' writings do not form a contract—because Seller sent a conditional acceptance—a binding contract is formed by their conduct.

(b) If a contract is established in this way, the terms of the contract will be the terms on which the writings of the parties agree, together with the implied terms or default rules established by the UCC for warranties, remedies, party performance, and other topics. (The UCC's default rules are discussed at length below in the section on contract interpretation.)

EXAMPLE: On the same facts as above, the parties' contract will include all the terms on which their respective forms agree—typically, the dickered terms such as product description, price, and quantity. Seller's negation of warranties would not be included in the contract because it does not appear in Buyer's form. The UCC's implied warranties would therefore govern the transaction despite Seller's attempt to negate them.

(2) **Transactions without Preprinted Forms**

(a) Although most situations governed by these rules will involve transactions consummated via preprinted forms, the same rules apply to any sale of goods in which an offer is followed by a nonconforming acceptance (e.g., an exchange of transaction-specific e-mails or letters) or a real-time contract is followed by confirmation(s) (e.g., a follow-up letter confirming the details of a deal reached over lunch).

(3) **Shrink-Wrap Contracts**

(a) The authorities are divided on whether the rules of Section 2-207 apply to so-called shrink-wrap contracts (i.e., agreements that consumers find "shrink-wrapped" to computers and other high-tech goods once they open the boxes containing them).

1) The courts that apply Section 2-207 typically conclude that the boilerplate terms in such agreements are mere proposals for additions to the contract, following the usual rules governing transactions that are not "between merchants."

2) Other courts have held that Section 2-207 does not apply and that the consumer's retention and use of the goods constitutes an acceptance of the shrink-wrap terms.

III. CONSIDERATION AND PROMISSORY ESTOPPEL

A. Consideration and Bargain

1. The general rule in American contract law is that a promise is unenforceable unless it is supported by consideration. The promise has some value and must be exchanged for something else of value, such as a counter-promise or performance given to the promisor by the promisee as *quid pro quo* for making the promise.
2. The exchange of promise for consideration is called a **bargain** or **bargained-for exchange**. The requirement of consideration is easily fulfilled in most contract situations, since there is almost invariably a *quid pro quo* (e.g., goods for money) establishing a bargained-for exchange.
3. However, in some promissory transactions, no exchange is contemplated or the existence of *quid pro quo* is questionable. Many of these situations involve intrafamilial transactions, but they occur in the commercial world as well. The problem arises because the promisee has neither promised nor given anything in return to the promisor, leaving the consideration requirement unsatisfied. These transactions are called **gratuitous promises**, which are generally unenforceable under the doctrine of consideration.

   EXAMPLE: A invites his newly widowed sister-in-law, who lives 60 miles from A's farm, to come and live in his guest house without charge so that she'll have a safe place to raise her family, explaining that he is eager to help her in her time of dire need. Because the sister-in-law neither promised nor gave anything in return for A's promise, A's promise is gratuitous and unenforceable.

4. **Insufficient Consideration versus Failure of Consideration**
   a. **Insufficient Consideration**
      (1) A promisor defending against an attempt to enforce a gratuitous promise can state his defense in several ways:
         (a) the promise is not supported by consideration;
         (b) there is a want of consideration, or consideration is lacking; or
         (c) there is legally insufficient consideration.

NOTE These terms are not to be confused with a failure of consideration.

   b. **Failure of Consideration**
      (1) A **failure of consideration** is a claim that the party has not performed in accordance with her promise.

      EXAMPLE: If A promises to deliver a horse to B in exchange for B's promise of payment and A then fails to deliver the horse, then there is a failure of consideration. However, we would not say that the consideration for B's promise was lacking, since A's original promise of performance constituted consideration for B's promise of payment.

c. **The Preexisting Duty Rule**

(1) A promisor cannot provide consideration where that consideration is a duty the promisor is already obligated to perform. This is known as the **preexisting duty rule**.

(2) Preexisting duties are not deemed consideration because the promisor must already perform that duty on the basis of the original contract.

5. **Bargained-For Consideration**

a. The majority of jurisdictions evaluate consideration based on the bargained-for exchange inquiry. A minority of jurisdictions use a benefit/detriment analysis instead. Under this test, consideration is evaluated based on whether there is a benefit to the promisor or a detriment to the promisee.

(1) There are also jurisdictions that use a hybrid evaluation combining the bargained-for exchange inquiry with the benefit/detriment analysis to define consideration as requiring a promise in exchange for a detriment.

(2) Whether courts are applying the benefit/detriment test or the hybrid "promise in exchange for a detriment" test, the question of whether a particular performance by the promise constitutes a "detriment" is answered by the application of the so-called **legal detriment test**.

(a) Under this test, the question is not whether the promisee will actually suffer or end up with some sort of net loss due to the transaction. Rather, the question is whether the promisee is doing something he had a legal right not to do or is forgoing some activity in which he had a legal right to engage.

EXAMPLE: Playing a concert at Carnegie Hall may well be thrilling for a musician, but it would still constitute a legal detriment because the musician has a legal right not to play the concert. Likewise, giving up smoking and drinking may well be good for one's health, but it would still constitute a legal detriment because the abstainer is forgoing activities in which she has a right to engage. Accordingly, promises to pay the musician and the abstainer for their respective efforts would be enforceable under the legal detriment test. These activities would likewise meet the majority bargained-for exchange definition of consideration, for they would each constitute a performance given in exchange for a promise.

6. **Inadequacy of Consideration**

a. The modern rule is that courts do not police the equivalence of bargained-for exchanges via the consideration doctrine. In other words, the supposed inadequacy of consideration is no defense to a breach of contract claim.

EXAMPLE: If A promises his birthright for a mess of pottage from B, B has nonetheless provided consideration for the promised birthright no matter how meager the value of the pottage.

EXCEPTION: If A promised to sell Blackacre to B for a meager sum and then refused to deliver, some courts would refuse to grant B specific performance because of inadequate consideration and, instead, limit B's remedy for breach to money damages.

b. Do not confuse "insufficient consideration" with "inadequate consideration."

(1) **Insufficient consideration** is an increasingly archaic way of saying that there was no consideration for a particular promise.

EXAMPLE: A promises his sister-in-law a place to raise her family and seeks nothing in return.

(2) By contrast, a claim of **inadequate consideration** assumes that there is consideration but argues that it is too small in comparison with the value of the promise for which it is exchanged.

c. Modern courts do not police the fairness of bargains via the consideration doctrine. However, a party may be able to defeat the enforcement of an excessively one-sided bargain through the defense of unconscionability, discussed later.

7. **Illusory Promises**

a. A promise to perform that leaves performance to the discretion of the promising party is an **illusory promise** and won't constitute consideration.

EXAMPLE: Thus, if A says to B, "I'll sell you as many widgets as you want to order within the next two weeks for $5 a piece," and B agrees to buy at that price as many widgets as she decides to order from A, B's promise is illusory and will not constitute consideration for A's promise.

8. **Bargain**

a. Consideration requires a bargain, but does not require bargaining. Thus, there is no requirement that the parties actually negotiate before reaching a deal. "Take it or leave it"-styled transactions are just as enforceable as those following extensive rounds of negotiation. In other words, the bargain requirement refers to the presence (or absence) of an exchange between the parties, not the process of reaching the deal.

b. In contemporary language, bargain may mean that something of greater value was acquired for lesser value, and implies that the transaction was beneficial to the recipient. For purposes of the consideration doctrine, though, **bargain** merely indicates an exchange, which could be beneficial or detrimental.

9. **Gratuitous Promises**

a. **Executed Gifts Distinguished**

(1) Although gratuitous promises are unenforceable under the consideration doctrine, gratuitous transfers are legally binding upon satisfaction of the requirements of a gift.

(2) In most states, delivery of the would-be gift combined with a present intention to bestow the gift constitutes a legally binding gratuitous transfer.

EXAMPLE: If John promises Kirsten a new car for her birthday, that would constitute a gratuitous promise and would be unenforceable if John declines to follow through. However, if John gives Kirsten a new car for her birthday, then the transfer is legally binding, and John cannot later change his mind and take back the car.

b. **Bargains Distinguished**

(1) Certain considerations will determine whether an exchange is a bargain or a gratuitous promise.

(a) **Recitals of Consideration**

1) The requirement of consideration is not satisfied by a false recital.

EXAMPLE: A wants to make a binding promise to give his young granddaughter $10,000 on her 21st birthday and, accordingly, gives her a note that reads: "For value received, I promise you $10,000 upon your 21st birthday." If no value was received in exchange for the promise, the recital would not satisfy the consideration requirement and the promise would be unenforceable.

EXCEPTION: Some courts will enforce option contracts on the basis of a signed writing with a false recital of consideration.

2) A condition on a gratuitous promise also does not satisfy the requirement of consideration. A condition is something a promisee must do to avail himself of the promisor's benevolence.

EXAMPLE: A invites his newly widowed sister-in-law, who lives 60 miles away from his farm, to come and live in his guesthouse without charge so she'll have a safe place to raise her family, explaining that he is eager to help her in her time of need. The promisee here won't be able to take advantage of A's offer unless she moves her family the 60 miles to A's farm. However, the move is merely a condition of the gratuitous promise, not consideration.

3) Distinguishing consideration from a condition on a gratuitous promise can be accomplished using three factors:

a) the language of the parties;

i) Words suggesting benevolence rather than self-interest, such as "gift," may indicate a gratuitous promise that has a condition rather than consideration.

b) commercial versus charitable or familial context; and

i) Bargains are standard operating procedure in the commercial context, and gratuitous promises in that setting are rare. By contrast, gratuitous promises are made in the family and charitable context more regularly.

c) the benefit to the promisor.

i) In case of doubt, the most important factor in determining whether a particular performance is consideration or a mere condition on a gratuitous promise is whether the promisor benefits from the performance.

EXAMPLE: Consider again the situation in which A invites his newly widowed sister-in-law, who lives 60 miles from A's farm, to come live in his guest house without charge so the she'll have a safe place to raise her family, explaining that he is eager to help her in her time of need. The 60-mile move is a condition on a gratuitous promise rather than consideration because A's explanation suggests a benevolent purpose, the transaction occurs in the familial context, and it is the promisee-widow and her family, not A, who will benefit from the move.

10. **Forbearance of a Claim or Defense**

a. Valid consideration exists when a party agrees to forbear a claim or defense in exchange for a promise or performance by the other party. This is so even if the claim or defense proves to be invalid. However, forbearance to assert or the surrender of a claim or defense which proves to be invalid is not consideration unless [Restatement (2d) of Contracts § 74(1)]:

(1) the claim or defense is in fact doubtful because of uncertainty as to the facts or the law; or

(2) the forbearing party believes that the claim or defense may be fairly determined to be valid.

b. The execution of a written instrument surrendering a claim or defense by one who is under no duty to execute it is consideration if the execution of the written instrument is bargained for, even though she is not asserting the claim or defense and believes that no valid claim or defense exists [Id.].

11. **Alternatives in the Absence of Consideration**

a. There are two sets of circumstances in which a promisee may be able to enforce a promise that is not supported by consideration.

(1) **Past or Moral Consideration**

(a) As a general rule, a promise given in exchange for something already given or already performed will not satisfy the bargain requirement.

EXAMPLE: In Mills v. Wyman [20 Mass. (3 Pick.) 207 (1825)], the court refused to enforce the father's after-the-fact promise to compensate a Good Samaritan for nursing his dying son, and the case would likely come out the same way today.

(b) Two exceptions to the past consideration rule were available at common law and continue to apply today:

1) a written promise to pay a debt barred by the statute of limitations is binding; and

2) a written promise to pay all or part of an indebtedness that has been discharged in bankruptcy is binding.

(c) A minority of jurisdictions, supported by Section 86 of the Second Restatement, will enforce a promise made in recognition of a past benefit conferred so long as:

1) the promisee conferred the benefit on the promisor and not on a third party; and

2) the benefit is material.

EXAMPLE: A sees that B is in grave danger and heroically intervenes to save the latter, injuring himself in the process. B gratefully promises to compensate A for his efforts. These are the facts of Webb v. McGowin [168 So. 196 (Ala. Ct. App. 1935)], where the court enforced the promise because A's efforts bestowed a material benefit (the saving of a life) on B.

EXAMPLE: Because the Good Samaritan in Mill*s* v. Wyman bestowed the benefit of nursing services on the promisor's son rather than on the promisor, the promise would not be enforceable.

EXCEPTION: Where the promisor makes a promise in recognition of benefits that the promisor received under the terms of a contract, the promise is not enforceable.

EXAMPLE: Employer promises a retiring employee a pension worth half the latter's salary in recognition of the latter's many years of hard and loyal work. Although the employee's past work no doubt bestowed material benefits on the employer, the work was done under contract (i.e., the employee was paid for it under the terms of the employment agreement), and accordingly, the employer's promise is not enforceable.

(2) **Promissory Estoppel**

(a) A promisee that reasonably relies to his detriment on a gratuitous promise may be able to enforce that promise. The doctrine of **promissory estoppel** allows for the enforcement of certain promises even where there is no consideration in return.

(b) There are four requirements that must be met in order for promissory estoppel to be available:

1) a promise;

a) Clearly, in order for promissory estoppel to be available, there must be a promise on which the claim is based. Statements of present intention or vague statements about the future would not qualify as a promise. The statement must contain an unambiguous assurance of future action to be considered a promise.

EXAMPLE: Statements like "I would like to give you some money to help you with college" would be considered too vague to be an actual promise. Alternately, "I will give $25,000 toward your tuition this fall" would be specific enough to qualify as a promise.

2) foreseeable reliance;

a) The promisee's reliance must be reasonably foreseeable to the promisor at the time of the promise

EXAMPLE: The widow's move to her brother-in-law's farm on the faith of his promise would have been reasonably foreseeable to the brother-in-law at the time he made her the promise. However, if the widow had purchased a high-end SUV to facilitate the move, this would likely not have been foreseeable.

3) actual reliance; and

a) The actual reliance must be induced by the promise. This means that the action or reliance cannot be taken on account of other factors.

EXAMPLE: If the widow had already decided to make the 60-mile move before her brother made her the promise, then this would not be actual reliance.

4) injustice without enforcement.

a) A promise that meets the other elements required by promissory estoppel will be binding if injustice can be avoided only by the enforcement of the promise.

b) Although this requirement may sound vague and open-ended, most courts take it seriously and are willing to use promissory estoppel to depart from the general rule that gratuitous promises aren't enforceable only where the prospect of injustice is convincingly established.

c) There are several factors that a court analyzes.

   i) The court will consider the strength of the case as a whole, and where there is substantial proof of the other elements, the claim that injustice cannot otherwise be prevented is strengthened. Alternately, where there is weak evidence of the other elements, it is less likely that the court will find that injustice could not otherwise be prevented.

   ii) The court will consider the blameworthiness of the breach. Thus, a willful breach provides a stronger case for promissory estoppel than a breach occasioned by circumstances beyond the promisor's control.

   iii) The court will consider the **balance of equities** between the parties. Thus, the requisite injustice is easier to establish the greater the harm of non-enforcement to the promisee is, and more difficult to establish the greater the harm of enforcement to the promisor is.

   EXAMPLE: An uncle's promise to give his nephew $100,000 upon graduation from a specific school is more likely to be enforced if the nephew turned down scholarship opportunities at other schools in order to attend the school of the uncle's choosing, or if the school would have been out of the nephew's reach but for the uncle's promise to pay. It is less likely that a court would enforce an uncle's promise to pay $100,000 upon graduation from law school if the nephew has a lucrative job and the uncle's family has in the meantime suffered serious financial setbacks since making the promise.

   iv) The more detrimental a promisee's reliance, the easier it is to establish the requisite injustice. Some courts treat detrimental reliance as an independent requirement to be established in order to prove promissory estoppel.

   EXAMPLE: Consider an alternative to the preceding example of the uncle who promised to pay the nephew $100,000 upon graduation from law school. The nephew in reliance on the promise decided to borrow his way through a top-ranked school in a distant state, giving up a chance to attend a lesser-ranked, less expensive state school. In this case, it is very possible that the nephew's job prospects and earning potential upon graduation from the high-ranked school are dramatically improved, and a court might find that his reliance on his uncle's promise was, in fact, beneficial and not detrimental. As a result, this would prevent the promise from being enforced.

v) Some courts treat enforcement of a gratuitous promise as a last resort. In those jurisdictions, enforcement via promissory estoppel is barred where other alternatives that could prevent injustice exist. However, all courts would find the existence of options short of enforcement of the promise to be a highly relevant factor in deciding the nature of the injustice at risk.

IV. STATUTE OF FRAUDS

A. In General

1. The general rule in contract law is that a contract need not be in writing and that oral and written agreements are equally enforceable.
2. However, the Statute of Frauds provides an important exception to that rule and makes some classes of contracts unenforceable unless reflected in a signed writing. The Statute of Frauds was originally an English statute and has been adopted in every U.S. jurisdiction through either legislation or common law.
3. The Statute of Frauds can be divided into two general areas of application:
    a. certain sales of goods; and
        (1) The Statute of Frauds governs certain sales of goods in every jurisdiction except Louisiana [§ 2-201].
    b. certain transactions not involving the sales of goods.
        (1) Other types of transactions that do not fall under Section 2-201 of the UCC may still be governed by the Statute of Frauds where states adopted the original Statute of Frauds or some modified version of it.

B. The Statute of Frauds in Operation

1. The Statute of Frauds applies to certain categories of contracts, such as contracts for the sale of real estate or contracts lasting more than one year.
2. For these contracts, the Statute of Frauds requires that the contract be evidenced by a writing signed by the party against whom enforcement is sought.
3. In the context of litigation, the Statute of Frauds is a defense which, if available, may be raised against a party who has claimed breach of contract.
    a. The defense is available to the breaching party when the transaction in question falls within one of the categories governed by the Statute of Frauds, and the required writing is absent or deficient.

C. Evaluating Statute of Frauds Issues

1. The general rule is that a contract within the Statute of Frauds is not enforceable absent a writing signed by the party against whom the enforcement is sought. The most efficient way to analyze a Statute of Frauds problem is by analyzing three questions in the following order:
    a. **Does the agreement fall within the Statute of Frauds?**
        (1) The Statute of Frauds only governs certain categories of contracts/agreements; thus, if the subject matter of the agreement does not fall under the Statute of Frauds, then the Statute of Frauds will not apply.
        (2) If the agreement does fall under the Statute of Frauds, it is necessary to proceed further with the analysis.

b. **Is the Statute of Frauds satisfied?**

(1) If an agreement is within the Statute of Frauds, then the key question is whether the Statute's writing requirement is met.

(a) If the signed writing requirement is met and the Statute is satisfied, then the Statute of Frauds will not render the contract unenforceable.

(b) If the contract is within the subject matter of the Statute of Frauds but the Statute is not satisfied, then the party seeking to enforce the contract will lose.

c. **Is alternative enforcement available?**

(1) If the contract is within the Statute of Frauds, but the Statute is not satisfied, the party seeking to enforce the contract will have to use another theory of enforcement, such as promissory estoppel or *quasi*-contract, in order to protect its interests. The final step in the Statute of Frauds analysis is to look for any of those alternative theories that could apply.

D. Analyzing Problems under the Statute of Frauds

1. Specific Coverage under the Common Law Statute of Frauds

a. In most states, six categories of agreements are governed by the Statute of Frauds:

STATUTE OF FRAUDS
MY LEGS
Marriage, Year, Land, Executor, Guarantee, Sale of goods

(1) a contract upon consideration of marriage;

(2) a contract that will not be completed within one year of the formation of the contract;

(3) a contract for the sale of an interest in land;

(4) a contract of an executor or administrator to answer for a duty of the decedent;

(5) a contract of guarantee or suretyship; and

(6) a contract for the sale of goods at a price of $500 or more.

(a) This category is governed specifically by Section 2-201 of the UCC.

b. Individual states have added additional categories to the six conventional ones. Two common additional categories are real estate brokerage agreements and nonmarital cohabitation agreements.

c. In the typical case, there is little difficulty in determining whether a particular contract falls under the Statute of Frauds. However, some categories have specific limitations within them that narrow the reach of the Statute of Frauds.

d. **Promise to Marry**

(1) Most states have abolished the cause of action for breach of a promise to marry, though it still exists in some jurisdictions. In jurisdictions that recognize this claim, the coverage of the Statute of Frauds has been narrowed as follows:

(a) A promise to marry that has been given in exchange for dowry or other settlement is governed by the Statute, and there must be a signed writing in order to secure enforcement of either party's obligations.

(b) An exchange of promises to marry is not governed by the Statute of Frauds and does not need signed writing to secure enforcement.

e. **Performance within One Year**

(1) The year at issue under the one-year provision is measured from the date of the contract's formation rather than the date of the beginning of performance. A contract that contemplates a duration of less than a year may nonetheless fall under the Statute of Frauds if performance is not to be completed until more than one year after the contract's formation.

EXAMPLE: In June of her first year of law school, Law Student enters an oral agreement with Law Firm to work for the firm during June, July, and August of her second summer. Although the duration of the contemplated performance is only three months, the performance will not be complete until 14 months after the making of the agreement. Accordingly, the contract is governed by the one-year provision, and a signed writing is required in order to secure enforcement.

(2) When a contract does not specify a date by which performance is to be completed, the question of whether a particular contract is to be performed within one year of the making thereof is answered by determining whether it is at all possible to complete the required performance within a year's time.

EXAMPLE: It is highly unlikely that the construction of an oil-producing facility in a war-ravaged country would be completed within a year. But because the performance is possible within that time—even if exceedingly unlikely—the agreement is not governed by the one-year provision, and no signed writing is required.

EXAMPLE: One of the parties to an oral construction agreement attempts to back out 14 months into the project and raises the Statute of Frauds as a defense. Because the prospect of performance is measured from the point of making the contract (when completion within a year was possible) rather than from the time of the dispute (when completion within the first year is clearly no longer possible), the agreement is not governed by the one-year provision and no signed writing is required.

EXAMPLE: A three-year exclusive representation agreement between a professional athlete and his agent cannot be performed within a year, no matter how diligently the agent works. Accordingly, the agreement is governed by the one-year provision, and a signed writing is required.

(3) Virtually any contract can be breached or excused within a year of its formation. However, courts typically hold that a breached or excused contract would not be a fully performed contract for purposes of the one-year provision.

EXAMPLE: Although a two-year contract for an employee's services might be breached by the employee's poor performance at some point during the first year, the contract is nevertheless governed by the one-year provision because full performance will take two years.

(4) Under the majority rule, a lifetime or permanent contract of employment is not governed by the one-year provision because the employee's death is possible within the first year, resulting in termination of the contract without breach. The minority does treat these types of contracts as falling within the one-year provision.

f. **Land-Sale Contracts**

(1) The land provision has been modified under some circumstances.

(2) The land provision governs contracts for the sale of an interest in land, and most courts take the expression "contract for sale" literally, thus distinguishing between a contract for a future sale and a present conveyance.

(a) The contract for future sale is governed by the land provision and requires a signed writing. The present conveyance of land promised for money is held to be outside the land provision.

(3) Although real estate brokerage agreements certainly contemplate the sale of an interest in land, most courts treat brokerage agreements as falling outside of the land provision. The reason is that the brokerage agreement is really a service contract and not a contract for real estate.

(a) Some jurisdictions have resolved this by adding a separate category to their Statute of Frauds specifically for brokerage agreements.

(4) Leases are generally treated as contracts falling within the land provision because a leasehold is an interest in land. Similarly, leases for longer than one year also fall within the one-year provision of the Statute of Frauds.

(a) However, most states except from the land and one-year provisions of the Statute of Frauds short-term leases (for one year or less) or contracts to lease. Where this is the case, leases for greater than one year still need to be in writing to satisfy the Statute of Frauds.

g. **Guaranty / Suretyship Agreements**

(1) The general rule that a promise to answer for the debt of a third party—a suretyship or guaranty agreement—is subject to the Statute of Frauds has two critical exceptions.

(a) When the creditor discharges the original debtor from her obligation on the faith of a guarantee by a third party to pay the debt, these agreements are not governed by the Statute of Frauds and do not require a signed writing by the guarantor.

(b) Under the **main purpose exception**, if the main purpose of the guarantor's promise is to protect or promote his own economic interests, rather than the interests of the debtor, then the agreement is not within the Statute of Frauds and no signed writing is required.

1) The mere presence of a selfish interest is not sufficient to trigger this exception; it must be central to the promise.

h. **Sale of Goods over $500**

(1) This category is discussed under "Analyzing Problems under the UCC Statute of Frauds."

2. **Satisfaction of the Statute of Frauds**

a. If a contract falls within the Statute of Frauds, then the general rule is that the contract is unenforceable unless evidenced by a writing signed by the party against whom enforcement is sought. In essence, there are two requirements for satisfaction of the Statute: a writing, and that the writing be signed.

b. **The Writing Requirement**

(1) There is no requirement that the parties put their actual agreement in writing; rather, all that is necessary is that the writing be a memorandum thereof, which can be prepared before, during, or after contract formation. Under the common law, the following memoranda have been held to satisfy the writing requirement:

(a) a letter from one of the parties to a third party describing the agreement;

EXAMPLE: "Dear Carville: I finally convinced Gregory to repaint my house, and he was willing to do so for only $2,000."

(b) the written offer, acceptance of which formed the contract; and

EXAMPLE: "I will clean your house on the first Friday of each month for the next six months in exchange for $500 per month, payment due by the 15th of each month when such services occur."

(c) a letter from one of the parties to the other party repudiating, and so admitting, the agreement.

EXAMPLE: "Dear Tony: Unfortunately, I regret that I will be unable to build your new shed. The $5,000 you agreed to pay to me was very generous, but I just don't think that I have the time right now, and so I must regretfully bow out."

(2) The memorandum need not document the transaction in detail. Only the following terms are required:

(a) the identity of the parties to the transaction;

(b) the nature and subject matter of the contract; and

(c) the essential terms of the unperformed promises in the agreement.

(3) **Required Description in Cases under the Land Provision**

(a) The case law is split on the kind of description you need to satisfy the land rule under the Statute of Frauds, with some cases holding that an address or its equivalent will do the trick and others requiring a full legal description.

(4) Most courts treat electronic documentation, such as e-mail, as satisfying the writing requirement.

c. **The Signature Requirement**

(1) The actual signature of the party against whom enforcement is sought is not necessary. Any symbol, including initials; typed, stamped, or preprinted signatures; or letterhead, if used with the intention to authenticate the writing, will suffice.

(2) Most states have adopted the Uniform Electronic Transactions Act ("UETA"), pursuant to which electronic signatures are considered to satisfy any legal writing requirements.

(3) **"Tacking Together" Multiple Documents**

(a) The writing need not be a single document; a party may satisfy the Statute by tacking together several documents which, once combined, satisfy all the necessary requirements for the Statute of Frauds.

1) If all of the documents are signed by the party against whom the contract is being enforced, or if a signed document incorporates unsigned documents by reference, then the signature requirement is satisfied.

2) If unsigned documents are not incorporated by reference in a signed document, "tacking together" the signed and unsigned documents to satisfy the Statute of Frauds is nevertheless permissible if:

a) there is at least one signed writing unambiguously establishing a contractual relationship between the parties;

b) the signed and unsigned documents clearly refer to the same subject matter; and

c) there is clear and convincing evidence of acquiescence to the unsigned documents by the party against whom enforcement is sought.

d. **Performance**

(1) The Statute of Frauds may be satisfied with respect to some of the categories of governed contracts via part performance.

(2) **Land Contracts**

(a) Part performance will make an oral contract for the sale of land enforceable in two situations:

1) in an action by the buyer against the seller, but not in an action by the seller against the buyer; and

2) in an action for specific performance, but not in an action for money damages.

(b) Part performance requires a showing of any combination, or all three, of the following:

1) payment of all or part of the purchase price;

2) taking of possession; and

3) making substantial improvements to the property.

(3) **One-Year Contracts**

(a) Full performance of an oral contract for services by the party performing the services will make the contract enforceable against the paying party. On the other hand, part performance is not compensable on the contract. However, the performing party may be able to recover for the reasonable value of the services actually rendered via *quantum meruit*.

(4) **Sale of Goods Contracts**

(a) The UCC Statute of Frauds may be satisfied by part performance of a sale of goods contract, and the rules governing such satisfaction are discussed later.

3. **Enforcement Where the Statute of Frauds Is Not Satisfied**

a. If the contract is within the Statute of Frauds but the Statute is not satisfied because the breaching party never signed a written document, the aggrieved party may nevertheless be able to secure some protection for her interests via an action for restitution or promissory estoppel.

b. **Recovery for Benefits Conferred**

(1) Where one party bestows benefits upon another in connection with an oral contract, even if the enforcement of that contract is barred by the Statute of Frauds, the aggrieved party may recover something. The party has the option of filing a cause of action for restitution, seeking to recover the value of the benefits that he conferred. Alternatively, if services are involved, the party may recover on a theory of *quantum meruit*, meaning he could sue to recover the reasonable value for the services he rendered.

EXAMPLE: A spends three months working for B under an oral two-year employment contract. If B fires A and successfully raises a Statute of Frauds defense against enforcement of the oral contract, A may nonetheless be able to recover from B the reasonable value of the services rendered in *quantum meruit*.

c. **Promissory Estoppel**

(1) Where a party suffers losses in reliance on an oral contract, but the enforcement of that contract is barred under the Statute of Frauds, the party may be able to recover damages via promissory estoppel.

EXAMPLE: Where a party to an oral contract within the Statute of Frauds promises the other party that she has created or will create a signed writing evidencing the parties' agreement, and the other party relies on that assurance by failing to take other steps to satisfy the Statute of Frauds, most courts will find promissory estoppel against the party who falsely made assurances of a signed writing.

EXAMPLE: In many cases, however, there is no assurance that a writing has been or will be created, and the reliance at stake will instead be based on the very contract whose enforcement is barred by the Statute of Frauds—as would be the case, for example, for an employee who leaves his current job and moves across the country based on an oral two-year employment contract, only to be dismissed before he starts his new job. Invoking promissory estoppel in this setting is both more controversial and more difficult.

(2) Some courts hold that promissory estoppel is available to protect reliance on a contract whose enforcement is barred by the Statute of Frauds. Other courts have held that the common law promissory estoppel doctrine is preempted by the Statute of Frauds.

(3) Among those courts that do recognize promissory estoppel, some will impose stiffer requirements on the claimant than those applicable under an ordinary promissory estoppel action. In particular, courts will look for:

(a) the definite and substantial character of reliance, and its relationship to the remedy sought;

(b) the extent to which the reliance is corroborated by the evidence of the formation and terms of the contract; and

(c) the extent to which the formation and terms of the contract are otherwise established by clear and convincing evidence.

E. Analyzing Problems under the UCC Statute of Frauds

1. Specific Coverage under the UCC Statute of Frauds

a. The UCC Statute of Frauds is Section 2-201, which by its terms governs agreements "for the sale of goods for the price of $500 or more."

(1) With regard to agreements for which the price is payable in some form other than money (e.g., goods), the monetary value of the consideration must be determined in order to apply the $500 rule.

(2) For agreements contemplating the sale of multiple goods, calculation of the price will depend on whether the transaction constitutes a single contract or a series of separate contracts. When an agreement falls within the UCC Statute of Frauds and the Statute is not satisfied, the entirety of the contract is unenforceable, not just the portion of the contract which exceeds $499.99.

b. The UCC Statute of Frauds also applies if a contract as modified falls within the Statute (e.g., the contract is modified such that the price of the goods has gone from $300 to $600) [§ 2-209(3)]. By the same token, if the newly modified contract now falls outside of the Statute of Frauds, it does not apply.

2. **Satisfaction of the UCC Statute of Frauds**

a. There are five ways to satisfy the UCC Statute of Frauds.

(1) **Signed Writing**

(a) The easiest way to satisfy the UCC Statute of Frauds, a signed writing requires:

1) a writing;

a) Although the UCC defines **writing** as "any intentional reduction to tangible form," which clearly covers everything from quill and parchment to computer printouts, a more difficult question is presented by electronic documentation (e.g., e-mail). A majority of courts have concluded that electronic documentation satisfies the writing requirement of the UCC.

b) The proposed revisions to UCC Article 2 replace the word "writing" with the word "record" for the express purpose of covering electronic documentation in the UCC Statute of Frauds and other provisions.

2) that is signed by the party against whom enforcement is sought; and

a) The UCC broadly defines "signed" as "any symbol executed or adopted by a party with present intention to authenticate a writing," which covers the same variety of "signings" effective under the common law Statute of Frauds.

EXAMPLE: The party's initials; a typed, stamped, or printed signature; or a memorandum written on preprinted letterhead would all suffice.

b) Most states have adopted the UETA, under which electronic signatures satisfy legal writing requirements.

3) which is "sufficient to indicate that a contract for sale has been made between the parties."

a) The Official Comment to UCC Section 2-201 states, "All that is required is that the writing afford a basis for believing that the offered oral evidence rests on a real transaction," a very relaxed standard.

<u>**EXAMPLE**</u>: A enters an oral agreement with B to sell the latter a speedboat for $10,000. B writes a check that contains A's name as the payee, B's name as payor, $10,000 as the amount, and the word "speedboat" in the notation space. Although the writing does not use the word "agreement" or "contract," it is clearly "sufficient to indicate that a contract of sale has been made" between A and B and would, therefore, satisfy the writing requirement of the UCC Statute of Frauds against B, the signing party.

(b) Satisfaction of the UCC Statute of Frauds requires the term indicating the quantity of goods sold in the transaction.

1) The contract is unenforceable beyond the quantity of goods shown in the writing, irrespective of the parties' actual agreement.

2) If there is no quantity term, the contract is altogether unenforceable, subject to two exceptions:

a) where other language in the writing provides an unambiguous basis for measuring quantity; and

<u>**EXAMPLE**</u>: "My 2009 sweet basil crop" or "my 1998 Honda Odyssey."

b) in the case of output and requirements contracts, the expression "output," "requirements," or their equivalent satisfies the quantity requirement under the UCC.

3) Apart from the quantity term, no other term is required in the writing. Moreover, it doesn't matter if a term is incorrectly stated. However, a writing can have so few terms that it will no longer be "sufficient to indicate that a contract for sale has been made between the parties."

<u>**EXAMPLE**</u>: A and B enter an oral agreement under the terms of which A is to sell B five tobacco barns for a total of $5,000. After they shake hands, A takes out a piece of paper, writes "five barns," signs it, and gives it to B. If A subsequently backs out of the deal, she will have a successful Statute of Frauds defense against B despite the fact that she signed a writing with a quantity term, because the writing, taken as a whole, is insufficient to indicate that a contract for sale has been made between A and B.

(c) Despite the fact that the rules under the UCC Statute of Frauds are generally more easily satisfied than the common law Statute of Frauds rules, a written offer that will satisfy the latter may not be enough under the UCC.

1) Because the UCC's writing requirement says that the writing must be "sufficient to indicate that a contract for sale has been made between the parties," the plain language suggests that only a writing that is contemporaneous with or subsequent to contract formation will satisfy the test.

2) However, a written offer that proposes a sale of goods at a price of $500 or more that meets the requirements of the UCC firm offer rule is enforceable against the signing merchant. In such a case, the UCC Statute of Frauds is irrelevant, despite the fact that without documentary proof of acceptance, the offer is not sufficient to indicate that a contract for sale has actually been made.

(2) **Merchant's Confirmation**

(a) The UCC Statute of Frauds may be satisfied when two merchants enter an oral agreement and one of them sends the other a written confirmation of the agreement. In such a circumstance, the Statute is satisfied against the recipient merchant if the latter fails to object to the confirmation in a timely fashion.

(b) A valid merchant's confirmation requires a writing that [§ 2-201(2)]:

1) is "sufficient against the sender";

a) The question here is whether the confirmation meets the requirements of Section 2-201(1) (i.e., it must be signed by the sender, it must contain a quantity term, etc.).

2) is "in confirmation of the contract";

a) The authorities are divided on whether this language imposes a requirement on valid merchants' confirmations in addition to the requirement that the writing be "sufficient against the sender." Some courts hold that a writing that is sufficient against the sender under Section 2-201(1) is all that is necessary; other courts stress the "and" term and require express language confirming the existence of a prior oral agreement.

EXAMPLE: During a telephone conversation on March 8, A places an order and B agrees to fulfill it. A sends a signed letter to B that outlines the price, quantity, and delivery terms "per 3/8 discussion," and ends with the following language: "We look forward to you fulfilling our order per these terms." Because the signed writing would be sufficient to satisfy the UCC Statute of Frauds against sender A, some courts would hold that it would also be sufficient against the recipient. Other courts would require an express reference to the parties' preexisting "agreement" or "contract" in order to satisfy the "writing in confirmation of the contract" requirement of Section 2-201(2).

3) is "sent within a reasonable time" of the making of the oral agreement; and

4) the contents of which the receiving merchant has "reason to know."

(c) A confirmation that never reaches the intended recipient's place of business (e.g., because of postal misdirection) would not be valid against the recipient, since the latter would have no "reason to know" its contents. On the other hand, a confirmation that reaches the intended recipient's place of business but remains unopened through some neglect would meet the "reason to know" test.

(d) A confirmation that meets the foregoing requirements will satisfy the UCC Statute of Frauds against the recipient unless the recipient provides written notice of objection to the confirmation's contents within 10 days of receipt, but a would-be objection that is itself sufficient against the objector under Section 2-201(1) will satisfy the Statute against the objector.

EXAMPLE: A and B enter an oral agreement under the terms of which A is to sell B five tobacco barns for a total of $5,000. The following day, B sends a written confirmation of the agreement to A, and two days later B receives a signed reply that reads in pertinent part: "My understanding is that we don't have a contract between us, for as I mentioned, I am still entertaining other offers for the barns. My apologies for any confusion that may have been caused." Because A's reply objects to the confirmation's contents, the confirmation does not satisfy the UCC Statute of Frauds against A.

EXAMPLE: A's signed reply to B's confirmation reads: "I regret that I can't go through with the sale of my barns to you. Although the $5,000 you agreed to pay is very generous, my accountant has advised me of certain tax implications of the transaction that I hadn't considered, and I must therefore bow out." Because A's signed reply is itself sufficient to indicate that a contract for sale had been made between the parties—a contract from which A is now seeking to escape—the reply satisfies the UCC Statute of Frauds against A.

(3) **In-Court Admission**

(a) A third means of satisfying the UCC Statute of Frauds occurs when a party against whom enforcement is sought "admits in his pleading, testimony, or otherwise in court that a contract for sale was made."

1) This exception applies whether the admission in question is voluntary (as in pleadings) or involuntary (as on cross-examination).

2) A number of courts have held that the existence of this exception requires that Statute of Frauds claims be resolved at trial rather than at the pleadings stage, since the party against whom enforcement is sought might be persuaded to admit to the existence of a contract in open court.

3) Other courts have concluded that it would defeat the purpose of the Statute of Frauds to permit a party attempting to enforce a contract to "badger the defendant through discovery and trial simply because of the possibility of obtaining an admission."

4) The in-court admission exception will not secure enforcement of the contract in question "beyond the quantity of goods admitted."

(4) **Part Performance**

(a) Despite the absence of a signed writing, an otherwise valid contract is enforceable "with respect to goods for which payment has been made and accepted or which have been received and accepted."

(b) The part performance exception does not apply unless there are actions by both parties indicating that a contract for sale exists. Thus, a payment can constitute part performance only if the buyer makes the payment and the seller accepts it, and delivery of goods can constitute partial performance only if the seller makes the delivery and the buyer accepts the goods.

1) If a buyer pays cash, there is seldom any question whether payment has been made and accepted. Payment by check, however, is more complicated, with some courts holding that receipt of a check without indorsement or negotiation does not constitute acceptance, and other courts holding that mere retention of the check for a reasonable period constitutes acceptance.

2) Any act of dominion inconsistent with a seller's continued ownership of goods (e.g., moving them from the warehouse receiving area to a retail store) will constitute acceptance of the goods.

(c) **Divisible versus Indivisible Goods**

1) If the contract in question involves divisible goods (e.g., widgets), part performance secures enforcement for any quantity that has already been paid for by the buyer or

delivered by the seller; the contract is not enforceable beyond that quantity.

2) If the contract in question involves an indivisible good (e.g., a speedboat) the majority rule holds that partial payment secures enforcement of the entire contract, though a minority of courts refuses enforcement unless full payment has been made.

(5) **Substantial Reliance by the Seller of Specially Manufactured Goods**

(a) A seller is unlikely to be able to sell specially manufactured goods to other buyers if a would-be buyer backs out, thus leaving the seller with a potentially large reliance loss. Also, the fact of manufacture according to specifications attributable to the buyer provides strong evidence that an oral contract actually exists between the parties.

(b) Accordingly, an aggrieved seller can secure enforcement of an oral contract by establishing the following five elements:

1) the goods are to be specially manufactured for the buyer;

2) the goods are not suitable for sale to others in the ordinary course of the seller's business;

3) the seller has substantially begun to manufacture, or made commitments to procure, the goods;

4) the actions undertaken to begin to manufacture or procure occurred under circumstances that reasonably indicate that the goods are for the buyer; and

5) the actions undertaken to begin to manufacture or procure occurred before the seller received notice of the buyer's revocation.

b. Authorities are divided on whether a party seeking enforcement of a sale of goods contract that is also within the common law one-year provision must satisfy both the UCC and the common law Statute of Frauds.

EXAMPLE: Merchants A and B enter an oral installment contract calling for A's delivery to B of 1,000 widgets per month for two years at a price of $1.00 per widget. A sends B a written confirmation of the oral agreement that meets the requirements of UCC Section 2-201(2), to which B does not respond. B backs out of the deal, A sues for breach of contract, and B defends via the Statute of Frauds. Although the written confirmation clearly satisfies the UCC Statute of Frauds, the contract will be nevertheless unenforceable in some jurisdictions because the agreement is also governed by the common law one-year provision, which is not satisfied because the party against whom enforcement is sought (B) did not sign the writing.

3. **Enforcement Where the UCC Statute of Frauds Is Not Satisfied**

a. If a party has relied to its detriment on an oral contract whose enforcement is barred by the UCC Statute of Frauds, the aggrieved party may be able to secure a remedy via promissory estoppel.

(1) While some courts hold that promissory estoppel is available in appropriate circumstances to secure enforcement of a promise otherwise barred by the Statute of Frauds, other courts point to the express language of the UCC Statute of Frauds ("[e]xcept as otherwise provided in this section, a contract . . . is not enforceable"), and conclude that it precludes promissory estoppel, since that doctrine is not mentioned in Section 2-201.

(2) Among those courts that do recognize promissory estoppel, some impose enhanced proof requirements on the claimant, such as proving unconscionable injury or that the other party would be unjustly enriched without enforcement of the contract.

(3) Because of the unique vulnerability of construction contractors to revocation by their subcontractors, virtually all courts have protected a general contractor via promissory estoppel even if the oral subcontract in question is for goods at a price of $500 or more.

F. Effect of Satisfying the Statute of Frauds

1. An otherwise perfectly valid contract, possessing offer, acceptance, and consideration, can still be unenforceable under the Statute of Frauds. This can happen if the contract is covered by the Statute of Frauds, but does not satisfy the Statute.
2. On the other hand, satisfaction of the Statute of Frauds does not ensure a "win"; the aggrieved party must still go on to establish both a valid contract and a breach thereof to succeed on his claim.
3. Thus, satisfying the Statute of Frauds is necessary but not sufficient alone to enforce a contract.

EXAMPLE: A sues B for breach of an oral contract for the sale of land, and B raises the Statute of Frauds defense. A adduces the written offer signed by B and thus establishes that the Statute is satisfied. A may still lose on her breach of contract claim, however, if it turns out that the offer lapsed or was revoked before A accepted it or if for any other reason A fails to persuade the trier of fact that a valid contract existed between the parties.

G. No Mutuality of Obligation under the Statute of Frauds

1. It is possible for one party to prevail under a Statute of Frauds defense while, for the same transaction, the other party would be fully liable under the contract. This is a result of the fact that the Statute of Frauds does not require that both parties have signed a writing, only that the party against whom enforcement of the contract is sought has signed. If the writing evidencing the contract is signed by only one of the parties, the contract will be enforceable against the signing party but not against the non-signing party.

EXAMPLE: A and B enter an oral contract for the sale of land and the only signed writing between them is an offer signed by B. If B breaches, he will not have a Statute of Frauds defense because A will be able to adduce a writing signed by B. If A breaches, however, she will be able to raise a successful Statute of Frauds defense because she is the party against whom enforcement is sought and she didn't sign the writing.

a. An exception to this principle is created by the merchant's confirmation provision of UCC Section 2-201, under which a signed written confirmation sent by one party to the other will defeat a Statute of Frauds claim by the receiving party as well as by the sending party unless certain conditions are met.

H. Limitations on the Statute of Frauds

1. The only effect of a successful Statute of Frauds defense is to defeat enforcement of the contract against the non-signing party. The contract may still be valid and enforceable for other purposes, such as:

 a. the contract may provide evidence in establishing an element of a legal claim apart from breach of contract;

 EXAMPLE: A brings an action against C for tortious interference with A's oral land contract with B. Although B would have a successful Statute of Frauds defense in a breach of contract action brought by A, the Statute will be irrelevant in A's tortious interference claim against C.

 b. the contract may provide evidence establishing a defense to a legal claim apart from breach; and

 EXAMPLE: Under an oral contract for the sale of A's land to B, B takes possession. A reneges and brings a trespass action against B. Although A would have a successful Statute of Frauds defense in a breach of contract action brought by B, the Statute would be irrelevant to the validity of B's defense to A's trespass claim.

 c. the contract may provide evidence of the value of the services already rendered.

 EXAMPLE: A spends three months working for B under an oral two-year employment contract. If B fires A and successfully raises a Statute of Frauds defense against enforcement of the oral contract, A may nonetheless be able to recover from B the reasonable value of the services rendered in *quantum meruit*. Moreover, he may offer the price agreed to in the oral contract as evidence of the value of the services rendered.

V. GAP-FILLERS, INTERPRETATION, AND THE PAROL EVIDENCE RULE

A. In General

1. Parties to a contract ordinarily reach explicit and unambiguous agreements on the essential issues of the contract, such as quantity and price. However, they frequently fail to be as explicit as to the details. This can result in either gaps in the contract or contractual language that is subject to more than one interpretation. This section deals with the rules courts use to fill contractual gaps and resolve contractual ambiguities.

B. Filling in the Gaps with Default Provisions

1. One of the principal ways that contract law deals with gaps in a contract is by supplying terms that govern areas where the contract is silent. Just as a word processing program has default settings for the margins and layout, the body of contract law has default provisions for contracts.
2. These provisions can be overridden where the parties provide for a different procedure, but if they do not, the default contract terms will supplement their contract. Standard rules automatically supply contract terms unless they are set aside by party action or agreement.
3. **UCC Default Rules for the Sales of Goods**
   a. **Implied Warranties**
      (1) **Warranty of Title and against Infringement**
         (a) For the sale of all goods, there is an implied warranty of good title to the goods, of the rightful transfer of the goods, and that no liens or other security interests are attached to those goods [§ 2-312].
         (b) This warranty can only be excluded or modified by [§ 2-312(2)]:
            1) specific language; or
            2) circumstances which give the buyer reason to know that the seller does not claim unencumbered title.
         (c) Unless otherwise agreed, a merchant regularly dealing in goods of the kind warrants that they are free of any rightful claim of a third person by way of infringement. However, a seller is not liable for such a claim if the buyer provides specifications to the seller and the claim arises out of compliance with the specifications [§ 2-312(3)].
      (2) **Warranty of Merchantability**
         (a) If the seller of the goods is a merchant with respect to goods of that kind under the UCC, then there is a warranty of merchantability for the sale of goods. The warranty guarantees that the goods are fit for the ordinary purposes for which those goods would be used [§ 2-314].

(3) **Warranty of Fitness for a Particular Purpose**

(a) This warranty grants that the goods being sold are fit for the particular purpose for which the buyer intends to use them. The warranty only applies where, at the time of contracting, the seller has good reason to know [§ 2-315]:

1) the particular purpose for which the goods are required; and

2) that the buyer is relying on the seller's skill or judgment to select or furnish reasonable goods.

(4) **Excluding or Modifying Implied Warranties of Merchantability and Fitness**

(a) The **implied warranty of merchantability** may be excluded or modified by language mentioning "merchantability" and need not be in a writing. However, if it is in a writing, it must be conspicuous [§ 2-316(2)].

(b) An **implied warranty of fitness** may be excluded or modified by language in a writing that is conspicuous. Language to exclude all implied warranties of fitness is sufficient if it states, for example, that "There are no warranties which extend beyond the description on the face hereof" [§ 2-316(2)].

(c) However, the above language is not necessary to exclude or modify the warranty if [§ 2-316(3)]:

1) the contract includes an expression like "as is" or "with all faults" or other similar language that in common understanding calls the buyer's attention to the exclusion of warranties and makes plain that there is no implied warranty;

2) the buyer has fully examined the goods before entering into the contract, or has refused to do so, in which case there is no implied warranty as to defects that should have been apparent from the examination; or

3) course of dealing, course of performance, or usage of trade indicate that the warranty is excluded or modified.

b. **Express Warranties**

(1) Note that the UCC also provides that a contract can create express warranties. Express warranties by the seller are created as follows [§ 2-313(1)]:

(a) any **affirmation of fact or promise** made by the seller to the buyer that relates to the goods and becomes part of the basis of the bargain creates an express warranty that the goods will conform to the affirmation or promise;

(b) any **description of the goods** that is made part of the basis of the bargain creates an express warranty that the goods will conform to the description; or

(c) any **sample or model** that is made part of the basis of the bargain creates an express warranty that the whole of the goods will conform to the sample or model.

(2) The seller need not use formal words such as "warrant" or "guarantee," nor must the seller have a specific intention to make a warranty in order to create an express warranty. However, a mere affirmation of the value of the goods or a statement of the seller's opinion does not create a warranty [§ 2-313(2)].

(3) Words or conduct relevant to the creation of an express warranty and words or conduct tending to negate or limit warranty shall be construed wherever reasonable as consistent with each other [§ 2-316(1)].

(a) Where an express warranty conflicts with a limitation or disclaimer, the express warranty will prevail [Id.].

(4) The measure of damages for breach of warranty is the difference at the time and place of acceptance between the value of the goods accepted and the value they would have had if they had been as warranted [§ 2-714(2)].

c. **Missing Terms**

(1) Under the UCC, where there are pertinent terms missing, the following provisions will supplant the contract:

(a) The default rule for a missing **price term** is the reasonable price at the time established by the contract for the delivery of goods.

(b) A missing **time term** exists if the contract is silent as to the date of delivery or any other date by which action must be taken under the contract. The default rule for a missing time term is that contractual action must be performed within a reasonable time.

(c) The default rule for a missing **place of delivery term** is that the place of delivery will be the seller's place of business unless otherwise agreed.

4. **Common Law Default Rules for Service and Employment Contracts**

a. **Missing Price Term**

(1) If one party performs services at the request of another but no price is discussed in advance, then the default rule under common law will apply. The default rule for a missing price term is the reasonable value of the services rendered. This is typically available based on *quantum meruit*.

b. **Missing Duration Term**

(1) In practically every jurisdiction, the employment-at-will rule is the default rule for duration of an employment contract; absent an agreement to the contrary, an employer may dismiss, and an employee may quit, at any time for any reason.

(2) In a majority of jurisdictions, oral or written assurances of job security made to an individual employee, as well as assurances

contained in policy documents distributed to the workforce, may suffice to take the contract out of the default rule.

EXAMPLE: Statements made during a recruiting interview that make assurances of job security would displace the at-will rule. Alternatively, similar written assurances contained in a personnel handbook would also displace the rule.

EXCEPTION: Most courts will enforce a clear and conspicuous declaration in a personnel handbook or other employer policy statement to the effect that the employment relationship is "at will." However, a conflict between such a disclaimer and other written or oral representations by the employer will create a jury question on whether the employer has successfully opted out of the at-will default.

5. **The Obligation of Good Faith and Fair Dealing**
   a. Another source of gap-filling is the obligation of good faith and fair dealing. Both the UCC and the Restatement impose an obligation of good faith in the performance and enforcement of contracts. **Good faith** is generally defined as "honesty in fact in the conduct or transaction concerned" and, in the case of a merchant, good faith means "honesty in fact and the observance of reasonable commercial standards of fair dealing in the trade."
   b. The obligation of good faith may only be raised in regard to the performance and enforcement of contracts, but not to negotiations or other precontractual conduct. Challenges to unfair dealing in those settings must be made via claims of fraud, duress, or other defenses, discussed later.
   c. The good-faith obligation will also operate to ensure good faith where the terms of the contract leave a critical term, such as the price, satisfaction, or quantity, open to the determination of one party.
      (1) **Open Price Term**
         (a) If a contract leaves the price to be fixed by one of the parties, then the specified party must fix the price in good faith [§ 2-305(2)].
      (2) **Satisfaction Term**
         (a) A contract may contain a satisfaction clause, or similar term, whereby the determination as to whether a party's performance obligation is complete is left to the discretion of the other party. In those contracts, the good-faith obligation operates to require the party making that determination do so in good faith.

         EXAMPLE: A commercial developer and the seller of a piece of land enter into a contract. The developer places a condition on his purchase of the land that the seller first acquires "satisfactory leases" for the future occupancy of the land. The developer must determine in good faith whether or not the future leases are "satisfactory."

(3) **Open Quantity Term: Output and Requirements Contracts**

(a) An **output contract** is a contract in which the buyer agrees to purchase all of a seller's output for a particular good.

(b) A **requirements contract** is a contract in which the seller agrees to supply the buyer with all of the buyer's requirements for a particular good.

(c) Under the UCC, the party entitled to determine the particular quantity of goods to be sold—either the buyer demanding delivery of her requirements or the seller demanding purchase of his output—must make that determination in good faith [§ 2-306].

(d) In addition to the good-faith requirement, the UCC prohibits any unreasonably disproportionate demand or tender, if there was either [§ 2-306(1)]:

1) a stated estimate made between the parties; or

2) in the absence of a stated estimate, any comparable prior outputs or requirements.

EXAMPLE: Seller and Buyer are parties to a three-year contract obligating Seller to supply Buyer with the latter's upsidasium bearing requirements for Buyer's turbojet engine manufacturing plant. The market price for upsidasium suddenly skyrockets, and Buyer greatly increases its demand for bearings with the intention of selling them at great profit to third parties. Seller is not obligated to fill the order because Buyer's requirements demand was made in bad faith.

EXAMPLE: The upsidasium market remains stable, but because of a decline in the commercial aviation industry, the demand for Buyer's engines declines precipitously and accordingly Buyer reduces its monthly demand for bearings by 90% in comparison with the previous 24 months. Although Buyer's reduced demand was made in good faith, it is unreasonably disproportionate to its prior requirements and, accordingly, violates Section 2-306.

C. Interpreting Ambiguous Language

1. Where the parties did not fail to address an issue, but instead drafted the contract's language in such a way that the language could be subject to more than one interpretation, then a different type of analysis is needed in order for the courts to properly determine the meaning.

a. **Objective versus Subjective Meaning**

(1) The objectively reasonable meaning of a term at the time of contracting would control over a contrary subjective understanding of the term by one of the parties.

EXAMPLE: Contractor and Homeowner enter a contract for renovations to Homeowner's home. The contract incorporates by reference "the specifications dated 1/11/07," which had been prepared by Homeowner and were attached to the contract before signing. Contractor mistakenly thinks that the specifications referenced were an earlier version prepared by Contractor, and she signs the contract on that understanding. The specifications prepared by Homeowner and referenced in the contract are binding on both parties.

(2) This rule is subject to two exceptions.

(a) Where one party harbors a subjective understanding of a term that differs from the objectively reasonable meaning, typically the objective understanding will prevail. However, if the other party knows or has reason to know of the first party's subjective understanding, then that subjective interpretation will control.

EXAMPLE: The facts being otherwise as stated in the previous example, just before the parties sign the contract, Homeowner overhears Contractor tell her business partner that she was glad Homeowner had agreed to Contractor's version of the specifications. Because Homeowner knew of Contractor's understanding of the contractual terms, that understanding controls.

(b) Where the evidence demonstrates that both parties shared the subjective understanding of the term at the time of contracting, the mutual subjective understanding will control.

EXAMPLE: A general contractor is building a bridge. He hires a paving subcontractor to do work at a price to be calculated in accordance with the dimensions of the "concrete surface of the bridge deck." At the time of contracting, both of the parties understand that the concrete work included the sides and bottom as well as the "surface" of the bridge deck and, accordingly, that interpretation would be the controlling interpretation.

b. ***Contra Proferentem* and the Doctrine of Reasonable Expectations**

(1) Under the **rule of *contra proferentem***, if an ambiguous term is included in the contract, then it will be interpreted against the party who supplied the term during negotiations or drafting. Thus, if more than one meaning is possible, then the meaning more favorable to the other party will control.

(a) This rule of construction applies to contracts between bargaining equals as well as to contracts of adhesion, which are standard form (take-it-or-leave-it) contracts that a party with superior bargaining power uniformly imposes on its trading partners.

(2) Under the **doctrine of reasonable expectations**, even unambiguous terms may be interpreted against the drafting party if they conflict with the reasonable expectations of the other party.

(a) Most courts will apply the doctrine of reasonable expectations to insurance contracts, but its application is potentially available to all adhesion contracts.

(b) Under the doctrine, courts make a distinction between the dickered terms, which discuss the transaction-specific terms negotiated by the parties, and boilerplate terms, or those terms appearing in fine print. The court will apply the doctrine only to the boilerplate terms.

EXAMPLE: In an insurance contract, the coverage, deductibles, premium amounts, and policy periods are typically the dickered terms. The rest of the agreement, including specification of the claims process and exclusions, are typically set forth in boilerplate and are therefore subject to the doctrine of reasonable expectations.

(c) Under this doctrine, the parties' obligations consist of the dickered terms and only the boilerplate terms that would be consistent with the reasonable expectations of the purchaser. Unreasonable boilerplate terms are unenforceable.

EXAMPLE: Fertilizer Co. purchased from Allied Insurance Co. an insurance policy covering burglary with fine-print boilerplate language defining "burglary" as requiring "visible marks on" or "physical damage to" the exterior of the insured building. During the policy term, Fertilizer Co. was the victim of a theft in which the perpetrators were able to force open a Plexiglas door without leaving marks or damage, and Allied refused payment on the policy. Because the definition of "burglary" was a boilerplate term inconsistent with the reasonable expectations of the insured, the court interpreted the policy to cover the theft.

D. Trade Usage, Course of Dealing, and Course of Performance

1. Extrinsic evidence of trade usage, course of dealing, or course of performance will be available as an additional means of filling contractual gaps or resolving contractual ambiguities.
2. **Definitions under the UCC**
   a. A **usage of trade** is any practice or method of dealing having such regularity of observance in a place or trade as to justify an expectation that it will be observed with respect to the transaction in question.
   b. A **course of dealing** is a pattern of conduct concerning previous transactions between the parties that is fairly to be regarded as establishing a common basis of understanding for interpreting their subsequent expressions and other conduct.
   c. A **course of performance** is present when a particular contract involves repeated occasions for performance by a party and the other party, with knowledge of the nature of the performance and opportunity for objection to it, accepts the performance or acquiesces in it without objection.

3. Evidence of trade usage, course of dealing, or course of performance is admissible under the UCC and is typically available in common law cases as well.

   a. Such evidence may be used to supplement the express terms of a contract or to give meaning to a particular ambiguous term. However, it is not admissible to contradict the express terms of a contract.

      EXCEPTION: Course of performance evidence may be available to establish the waiver or modification of an express term.

   b. In the event of a conflict, course of performance prevails over course of dealing and usage of trade, and course of dealing prevails over usage of trade.

      EXAMPLE: A is one of many suppliers of upsidasium, and B is one of A's long-standing customers. A fills an order by B and demands immediate payment; B refuses. It is standard practice in the upsidasium industry for purchasers to pay invoices upon delivery, and, therefore, B's refusal to do so is in violation of the parties' contract.

      EXAMPLE: Same facts as the previous example except that in the past, A has regularly given B 30 days to pay for deliveries. Because this course of dealing between the parties trumps the payment-upon-delivery usage of trade, B has 30 days within which to make the required payment.

      EXAMPLE: Same facts as the previous example except that the parties' contract contains a provision requiring payment within seven days of delivery. Because the express terms of a contract override both course of dealing and usage of trade, B has seven days within which to make payment despite the past practice of paying in 30 days and the industry practice of immediate payment.

      EXAMPLE: Same facts as the previous example except that A and B are parties to an installment contract and B has paid 30 days after multiple deliveries without objection by A. This evidence of the parties' course of performance is admissible to establish that A has waived its contractual right to payment within seven days of delivery and/or that the parties have mutually modified that obligation.

E. The Parol Evidence Rule

1. In General

   a. Another source of evidence shedding light on the meaning of an agreement is the negotiations of the parties leading up to the execution of a written contract. The **parol evidence rule** governs efforts to introduce such evidence [§ 2-202].

   b. The rule governs:

      (1) both oral and documentary evidence of negotiations and other communications between the parties (e.g., an exchange of letters between the parties); and

(2) communications that took place prior to or contemporaneously with the execution of the written contract.

NOTE For ease of reference, courts refer to all such evidence as "parol evidence."

2. **Approaching a Parol Evidence Analysis**
   a. When a party seeks to introduce parol evidence, the court will determine the admissibility of the evidence based on two questions:
      (1) First, what is the purpose for which the evidence is being introduced?
      (2) Second, does the evidence relate to a term or contract which is integrated?
         (a) The integration analysis may focus on the term itself or the contract as a whole, depending on the purpose for which the parol evidence is being introduced.
3. **Integration**
   a. While the first step in the analysis is to determine the purpose for which the evidence is being introduced, the effects of these different purposes will depend upon the level of integration in the contract.
   b. **Full versus Complete Integration**
      (1) When a particular contract is **fully integrated** (sometimes referred to as partial integration), it means that the terms contained within the contract are intended to be the final discussion of the parties as to those specific terms. It does not, however, mean that the parties have specifically excluded any provisions not contained within the agreement.
      (2) On the other hand, when a contract is **completely integrated**, the parties intend the contract to represent a "complete and exclusive statement of all the terms" [§ 2-202(3)]. When this is the case, only the terms contained within the written agreement are considered part of the contract.
   c. **Determining Full Integration and Complete Integration**
      (1) The question of whether the terms of a contract are fully integrated (i.e., final) and whether an integration is complete (i.e., exhaustive) is for the judge, not the jury, to decide.
      (2) In reaching decisions regarding whether the terms of a contract are fully integrated, the judge will rely on the following evidence:
         (a) The thoroughness and specificity of the written instrument in connection with the terms at issue are strong indicators that the parties intended the writing to represent their final agreement.
         (b) Parol and other extrinsic evidence are admissible. The determination is not made on the basis of an examination of the writing alone; "all the circumstances"—including the proffered parol evidence and other evidence extrinsic to the written contract—must be considered.

(3) In reaching decisions regarding the complete integration of a contract, the judge will rely on the following evidence:

(a) **Merger Clause**

1) The most important evidence that the parties intended their written agreement to represent an exhaustive account of their contractual obligations is the presence in the contract of a merger clause reciting that the writing "contains the complete and entire agreement of the parties" or other words to that effect. The authorities are divided, however, on whether a merger clause is conclusive or merely persuasive on the question of complete integration.

(b) **Other Evidence**

1) Additional factors which are important for determining whether a contract as completely integrated include the detail with which the contract sets forth its provisions, as well as the length of the agreement itself.

(c) **Parol and Other Extrinsic Evidence Admissible**

1) Once again, the question is subject to an "all the circumstances" test, and the proffered parol evidence as well as other extrinsic evidence may be considered in that connection.

EXAMPLE: A and B have a written contract under the terms of which A agrees to sell B "all the uncut timber on my property." Evidence of conversations between the parties during a visit to the timber site is admissible to explain that "property" means A's country cottage and not A's home in the suburbs.

EXAMPLE: A and B have a written contract under the terms of which A agrees to sell B "all the uncut timber on my property." Evidence of an exchange of letters between the parties in which they agreed that their agreement would not include the shady trees in the immediate vicinity of A's country cottage would contradict the written expression (i.e., that A had agreed to sell B "all the uncut timber on my property") and would therefore be admissible only if the court concluded that the quoted provision was not intended by the parties to be the final word with respect to which timber would be cut (i.e., that the writing was not integrated). In making that determination, the court is free to consider the exchange of letters and other extrinsic evidence.

EXAMPLE: A and B had a written contract under the terms of which A agrees to sell B "all the uncut timber on my property," and the contract contained detailed terms with respect to the felling and transportation of the timber as well as a merger clause stating that the contract was "a complete and exhaustive account of the obligations between the parties." Evidence of an oral agreement between the parties at the time of signing the contract that A would pay to have the trees inspected for termites before cutting would be admissible to supplement the agreement only if the court concluded that the contract was partially (rather than completely) integrated. Some courts would consider the merger clause to be conclusive on the question of complete integration and thus bar the evidence, but other courts would treat it as persuasive only, evaluate the proffered evidence of the supplemental oral agreement, and admit it if they concluded that the parties did not intend the previously drafted merger clause to bar it, despite their subsequent signatures on the contract.

EXAMPLE: Same facts as in the previous example, except A and B are logging companies, and B offers evidence that sellers doing business in the commercial lumber trade invariably pay to have the trees inspected for termites before cutting. This evidence would be admissible even if the court concluded that the contract was completely integrated because, under the UCC, uncut timber equals "goods," and usage of trade evidence is admissible to supplement a written agreement.

4. **Purpose for Which Evidence Is Introduced**
   a. The effect of the rule depends on the purpose for which the parol evidence is being introduced:
      (1) to explain or interpret the terms of the written contract;
      (2) to supplement the terms of the written contract; or
      (3) to contradict the terms of the written contract.
   b. **To Explain or Interpret Terms of a Written Contract**
      (1) In a majority of jurisdictions, parol evidence is always admissible for this purpose.
      (2) A minority of jurisdictions follow the traditional common law rule and require a threshold showing that the term in question is patently ambiguous (i.e., ambiguous on its face) before admitting parol evidence for this purpose.
   c. **To Supplement Terms of a Written Contract**
      (1) Parol evidence is admissible for this purpose unless the contract is completely integrated.
         (a) A completely integrated contract is intended by the parties to represent an exhaustive as well as final account of the parties' obligations.

(2) **UCC Distinction**

(a) Usage of trade, course of dealing, and course of performance evidence are admissible in sale of goods cases to supplement the terms of a written agreement.

d. **To Contradict Terms of a Written Contract**

(1) Parol evidence is admissible for this purpose unless the term(s) in question are fully integrated.

(a) Integrated terms are terms intended by the parties to represent their final agreement on the subjects in question.

(2) **UCC Distinction**

(a) Course of dealing or course of performance evidence may be admissible in sale of goods cases to "qualify" the meaning of an integrated term.

5. **When the Parol Evidence Rule Will Not Apply**

a. The parol evidence rule will not apply to the following types of evidence:

(1) **Subsequent Agreements**

(a) The parol evidence rule only applies to oral or written communications made prior to or contemporaneously with the execution of a written agreement. This means that it will not apply to subsequent agreements entered into after the execution of the written document.

EXAMPLE: Buyer and Seller enter into a written agreement for the sale of 1,000 widgets. Two months before delivery is to be made, the parties orally agree to modify the agreement and specify the goods as nonstandard type-Y widgets, with Buyer agreeing to pay an additional cost. Evidence of this modification would not fall within the parol evidence rule, as it was made subsequent to the execution of the written agreement.

(2) **Collateral Agreements**

(a) The parol evidence will not affect agreements between the parties that are entirely distinct from the written agreement of the contract at issue. Evidence offered to prove or enforce such "collateral agreements" is admissible.

EXAMPLE: A and B execute a detailed written contract, complete with a merger clause, by which A agrees to sell A's car to B. As part of the transaction, the parties orally agree that B may park the automobile in A's garage for one year, paying $25 per month. Despite the completely integrated writing, either A or B may adduce evidence of the parking arrangement under the collateral agreement rule.

(3) **Attacks on the Validity of the Written Agreement**

(a) The key predicate to the application of the parol evidence rule is that there is a valid written agreement. As a result, the parol evidence rule will not bar efforts to prove that the written agreement is invalid or unenforceable. The absence of an enforceable agreement may be proved by parol evidence or any other extrinsic evidence.

(b) A party can assert such a claim in one of the following ways:

1) **Failure of an Oral Condition Precedent to the Agreement**

a) Evidence that the parties orally agreed to a condition precedent to the contract taking effect as well as further evidence that the condition failed would not be barred by the parol evidence rule where both parties' obligations would be discharged by the failure of that condition.

EXAMPLE: The parties to a written contract for the sale of artwork orally agree that the sale will not take effect unless and until a certificate of authenticity is issued by a named art expert. Because authentication is a condition precedent to the sale, the parol evidence rule will not bar proof of the oral agreement.

2) **Absence of Consideration**

a) Evidence that a written agreement lacks consideration or that there was a false recital of consideration is not barred by the parol evidence rule.

3) **Mistake or Duress**

a) Evidence that the written agreement was formed from mistake or duress may be admissible to prove that there was never a contract.

4) **Fraud**

a) The majority rule is that the parol evidence rule will not bar extrinsic evidence of fraud.

b) The minority rule is that extrinsic evidence is inadmissible to prove fraud where the written contract expressly eliminates an element of the claim (e.g., "the parties agree that neither party relied in any way on representations made outside the four corners of this agreement").

5) **Reformation**

a) The parol evidence rule is also inapplicable where a party to a written agreement alleges facts entitling him to reformation of the agreement. Reformation is based on the premise that the parties had reached an agreement concerning the instrument, but while reducing their agreement to written form, and as the result of mutual mistake or fraud, some provision or language was omitted from, inserted, or incorrectly stated in the instrument intended to be the expression of the actual agreement of the parties.

b) For the plaintiff to obtain reformation, it must be shown:

i) that there was an antecedent valid agreement;

ii) which is incorrectly reflected in the writing (e.g., by mistake); and

iii) proof of these elements is established by clear and convincing evidence.

VI. PERFORMANCE, MODIFICATION, AND EXCUSE

A. Obligations under the UCC

1. **In General**
   a. The seller's obligation is to transfer and deliver, and the buyer's obligation is to accept and pay in accordance with the contract [§ 2-301].
2. **Seller's Obligations**
   a. **Non-Carrier Cases**
      (1) **Non-carrier cases** are contracts in which it appears that the parties do not intend for the goods to be moved by common carrier.
      (2) In non-carrier cases, the seller has an obligation to tender delivery—that is, to put and hold conforming goods at the buyer's disposition and give the buyer any notification reasonably necessary to enable her to take delivery [§ 2-503(1)].
      (3) Tender must be at a reasonable hour, and the goods must be kept available for the period reasonably necessary to enable the buyer to take possession [§ 2-503(1)(a)].
         (a) However, unless otherwise agreed-upon, the buyer must furnish facilities reasonably suited to receiving the goods [§ 2-503(1)(b)].
   b. **Carrier Cases**
      (1) **Carrier cases** are contracts in which, due to express terms or due to the circumstances, it appears that the parties intend for the goods to be moved by common carrier.

      <u>EXAMPLE</u>: Common carrier may include such means as freight train, boat, or parcel delivery service.

      (2) Absent some other agreement, there is a presumption that the contract is a **shipment contract**, under which the seller is not obligated to deliver at a named destination, and bear the concurrent risk of loss until arrival, unless he has specifically agreed to do so or the commercial understanding of the terms used by the parties contemplates such delivery [§ 2-503, cmt. 5].
         (a) Under a shipment contract, the seller need only put the goods in the possession of a carrier and make appropriate arrangements for them to be sent to the buyer, provide the buyer with any document necessary to enable her to obtain possession of the goods, and promptly notify the buyer that the goods have been shipped [§ 2-504].
         (b) The seller's failure to notify the buyer of the shipment or to make a proper contract for the shipment is only grounds for rejection if material delay or loss ensues [Id.].
      (3) In a **destination contract**, the seller has agreed to tender the goods at a particular destination.

(a) If the contract requires the seller to tender delivery of the goods at a particular destination, the seller must, at the destination, put and hold conforming goods at the buyer's disposition [§ 2-503(1)].

(b) The seller must also give the buyer any notice of tender that is reasonably necessary and provide the buyer with any documents of title necessary to obtain delivery. Tender of documents through ordinary banking channels is sufficient [§ 2-503].

(4) In contracts that specify that delivery is **free on board** ("F.O.B."), the F.O.B. point is the delivery point.

(a) If the contract is F.O.B. the seller's place of shipment, the seller need only, at his expense and risk, put the goods in the possession of the carrier.

EXAMPLE: Seller is a shirt manufacturer with a factory in Baltimore. She contracts to sell 2,000 shirts to Buyer, who runs a retail clothing store in Las Vegas. If their contract states that the goods are "F.O.B. Baltimore," Seller's risk and expense would end once she puts it in the possession of the carrier (e.g., The Quick-Ship Co.).

(b) If the contract is F.O.B. the destination, the seller must, at his expense and risk, tender delivery of the goods at the destination location [§ 2-319(1)].

EXAMPLE: If in the above example, the contract states that the goods are "F.O.B. Las Vegas," the Seller would continue to bear the expense and risk while the goods are being shipped by The Quick-Ship Co., until the goods are actually tendered for delivery at the destination location.

(5) In contracts that specify the delivery is **free alongside** ("F.A.S."), the seller must deliver the goods alongside the vessel (in the manner usual at the port of delivery) or on a dock designated by the buyer and obtain and tender a receipt for the goods [§ 2-319(2)].

3. **Buyer's Obligations**

a. Unless otherwise agreed-upon, the buyer's tender of payment is a condition to the seller's duty to tender and complete delivery [§ 2-511(1)].

b. A tender of payment is sufficient when it is made by any means or in any manner current in the ordinary course of business, unless the seller demands payment in cash and gives the buyer a reasonable extension of time to procure it [§ 2-511(2)].

c. A buyer's payment by check is conditional and will be defeated if the check is not honored upon presentment [§§ 2-511(3); 2-511, cmt. 5].

d. **Inspection of the Goods**

(1) Generally, unless the parties agree otherwise, the buyer has a right to inspect goods upon tender or delivery before making payment or acceptance [§ 2-513(1)].

(2) If the contract requires payment before inspection, nonconformity of the goods will not excuse the buyer from making payment unless [§§ 2-512(1), 5-109(b)]:
  (a) the nonconformity appears without inspection (i.e., it is evident merely from taking delivery); or
  (b) despite tender of the required documents, the documents are forged or materially fraudulent such that an injunction against the issuer would be justified.

(3) Note that payment before inspection will not constitute an acceptance of the goods or impair the buyer's right to inspect or any of her remedies [§ 2-512(2)].

4. **Risk of Loss**

a. If the seller is required or authorized to ship the goods by carrier, the risk of loss passes to the buyer [§ 2-509(1)]:
  (1) when the goods are delivered to the carrier if the contract does not require the seller to deliver the goods at a particular destination (i.e., under a shipment contract, which is the default presumption in carrier cases); or
  (2) when the goods are tendered at a particular destination by the carrier so that the buyer is able to take delivery if the contract requires the seller to deliver the goods at a particular destination (i.e., under a destination contract).

b. If the goods are held by a bailee to be delivered without being moved, the risk of loss passes to the buyer [§ 2-509(2)]:
  (1) when the buyer receives a negotiable document of title covering the goods;
  (2) when the bailee acknowledges the buyer's right to possess the goods; or
  (3) after the buyer receives a nonnegotiable document of title or other written direction to deliver the goods to the buyer, once the buyer has had a reasonable time to present the document or direction to the bailee.

c. In any other case [§ 2-509(3)]:
  (1) if the seller is a merchant, the risk of loss passes to the buyer when the buyer receives (i.e., takes physical possession of) the goods; and
  (2) if the seller is not a merchant, the risk of loss passes to the buyer upon tender of delivery.

d. **Effect of Breach on Risk of Loss**
  (1) If the seller breaches the contract by making a nonconforming tender or delivery, the risk of loss remains on the seller until cure or acceptance [§ 2-510(1)].
  (2) If the buyer rightfully revokes acceptance (as described below), the buyer may—to the extent of any deficiency in his effective

insurance coverage—treat the risk of loss as having been on the seller from the beginning [§ 2-510(2)].

(3) If the buyer breaches before the risk of loss passes to the buyer, the seller may—to the extent of any deficiency in her effective insurance coverage—treat the risk of loss as resting on the buyer for a commercially reasonable time [§ 2-510(3)].

B. Modification

1. At common law, parties were free to enter a contract on virtually any terms that they wished. Once they had entered the contract, however, the law made it very difficult for them to modify those terms.
2. The contemporary rules allowing for modification under the UCC and common law are more flexible. However, effective modification of a valid contract is still a burdensome project.
3. **Modification at Common Law**

a. **The Preexisting Duty Rule**

(1) At common law, a promise to increase compensation under an existing contract is an unenforceable modification to an existing contract because there is no consideration offered for the modification under the preexisting duty rule.

EXAMPLE: The captain of a fishing vessel promised to pay $100 to each of the sailors for their work on a fishing voyage. Midway through the voyage, the sailors threatened to cease work unless they were promised an additional $50 each, and the captain reluctantly agreed. At the end of the voyage, the captain paid each of them the originally promised $100 but refused to pay the $50 increase, so the sailors sued to recover the additional amount. Because the sailors were already obliged to perform the work in question under the terms of their original contract with the captain, his promise of an additional $50 is unenforceable under the preexisting duty rule.

b. **Exceptions to the Preexisting Duty Rule**

(1) **Mutual Modification**

(a) A promise to increase compensation under an existing contract is enforceable as a mutual modification to the contract if:

1) both parties agree to a performance that is different from the one required by the original contract; and

2) the difference in performance is not a mere pretense of a newly formed bargain.

EXAMPLE: During the course of the fishing voyage, the ship's cook takes ill, and the captain instructs the youngest of the sailors to perform the cook's duties in addition to her fishing duties. The sailor refuses to perform the work unless the captain promises her an additional $50 in compensation, and the captain reluctantly agrees.

The promise of additional compensation is enforceable as part of a "mutual modification" of the original contract.

EXAMPLE: Midway through the voyage, the sailors threaten to cease work unless they are promised an additional $50 each. The captain reluctantly agrees, and in exchange, the sailors promise to wake him each morning with a chorus of "Rule Britannia." Although there appears on the surface to be a "mutual modification" of the original contract, it is a "mere pretense" of a new bargain and, accordingly, the promised increase in compensation is unenforceable under the preexisting duty rule.

(2) **Unforeseen Circumstances**

(a) Where a promise of increased compensation is given in exchange for a performance, and that performance is rendered substantially more burdensome than reasonably anticipated by the parties when they entered the contract, then the preexisting duty rule will not apply.

EXAMPLE: Same basic facts as in the previous examples, but the fishing nets provided by the captain turn out to be defective and thus increase the workload of the sailors in a manner substantially in excess of what was reasonably contemplated under the original contract. The sailors threaten to cease the fishing unless they are promised an additional $50 each, and the captain reluctantly agrees. The promise is enforceable despite the preexisting duty rule in view of circumstances not reasonably anticipated by the parties at the time of contracting.

4. **Modification and the Sales of Goods under the UCC**

a. Under the UCC, the preexisting duty rule is abolished and an agreement modifying an existing contract for the sale of goods needs no consideration to be binding. Modifications must, however, meet the UCC's **good-faith test**, and a failure to do so will render them unenforceable.

(1) Good faith means honesty in fact and the observance of reasonable commercial standards of fair dealing [§ 1-201(b)(20)].

(2) With respect to modifications, the obligation of good faith means "[t]he effective use of bad faith to escape performance on the original contract terms is barred, and the extortion of a 'modification' without legitimate commercial reason is ineffective as a violation of the duty of good faith" [§ 2-209, cmt. 2].

b. The good-faith test for modifications applies even to modifications that are supported by consideration. Similar to the contemporary common law rule that requires more than mere pretense of a new bargain to secure enforcement of a mutual modification, a bargained-for modification is unenforceable under the UCC if the appearance of the mutual bargain is merely a pretext to hide a bad faith change of terms.

5. **Duress and Midterm Modifications**
    a. In addition to challenging a midterm modification under the rules just discussed, a party who agrees to a contractual modification in commercially extortionate circumstances may also be able to raise the defense of duress, discussed later in this outline.
    b. The duress defense is available not only in common law cases, but also in sales of goods cases governed by the UCC.
6. **Effect of "No Oral Modifications" Clauses**
    a. Unless required by the Statute of Frauds, modifications can generally be oral or written. However, the enforceability of an oral modification to an agreement may depend upon whether the contract contains a "no oral modifications" clause.
        (1) There is no specific language required for this type of provision. "No oral modifications," "all modifications must be in writing," or any such similar language would suffice.
    b. **Common Law Cases**
        (1) Originally, there was a common law rule that made oral modification clauses invalid, and even today most courts will refuse to enforce them where a party has reasonably relied on the oral agreement at issue. However, their enforcement is becoming more likely in modern cases, particularly in the construction context.
    c. **UCC Cases**
        (1) Under Section 2-209, clauses prohibiting subsequent oral modifications are presumptively valid.
        (2) An oral modification made in violation of such a clause may nevertheless be enforceable if the disadvantaged party relies on the modification or the parties perform in accordance therewith.

C. Excusing Performance Due to Faulty Assumptions

1. A party entering a contract is susceptible to making countless assumptions about the present and future circumstances in which performance will take place. When such assumptions turn out to be faulty, the doctrines of mistake, impossibility, impracticability, and frustration of purpose may be available to excuse the parties' obligations.

    EXAMPLE: A faulty assumption about the facts at the time of contracting would be that the stone in a ring the seller is selling is a diamond and not a topaz.

    EXAMPLE: A faulty assumption about the future facts in a contract would be the assumption that the cost of fuel won't increase beyond a certain range and triple the costs of the busing service whose bid was accepted by the school district.

2. Faulty assumptions about present facts, or the facts as they exist at the time of contracting, are dealt with under the doctrine of mistake. Faulty assumptions about future facts are dealt with via the doctrines of impossibility, impracticability, and frustration of purpose.

3. **Mistake**

   a. When a party or parties make a faulty assumption about the present circumstances, and thus enter a contract on that basis, this is known as a **mistake**.

   b. A mistake regarding the facts that exist at the time of contracting will excuse performance only where the mistaken facts are material to that contract. This requires that the mistaken facts will significantly impact the value of the transaction to one or both parties.

   c. When only one of the parties to a contract is operating under a faulty assumption about material facts as they exist at the time of contracting, the situation is governed by the rules of unilateral mistake. When both parties labor under a common faulty assumption, the situation is governed by the rules of mutual mistake.

      (1) **Unilateral Mistake**

         (a) Under the rules governing unilateral mistake, a party operating under a faulty assumption about material facts as they exist at the time of contracting is not excused from his contractual performance unless:

            1) the other party knew or had reason to know of the mistake; or

               EXAMPLE: A agrees to sell B a cow, which A knows to be barren and, as the parties are writing up and signing the agreement, B asks A a series of questions about the care and feeding of pregnant cows. Because A has reason to know that B is mistaken with respect to the cow's capacity to bear calves, B's obligation to purchase the cow is excused on account of unilateral mistake.

            2) the mistake was based on a clerical error.

               a) The clerical error exception is not available in all jurisdictions, and where available, it is subject to the following exceptions:

                  i) where the error was caused by extreme negligence on the part of the party making the error; or

                  ii) where the other party has relied on the clerical error.

      (2) **Mutual Mistake**

         (a) Where both parties have labored under a common faulty assumption regarding the present facts, there is a mutual mistake. Under the rules of mutual mistake, the contract will be voidable by the disadvantaged party where:

            1) the fact about which the parties were mistaken is essential to the contract (i.e., it goes to the very heart of the exchange);

            2) both parties were mistaken; and

            3) the disadvantaged party did not bear the risk of mistake under the parties' agreement.

EXAMPLE: A agrees to sell B a cow at beef cow prices because at the time of contracting, both parties were under the assumption that the cow was barren. A short time later, the cow was discovered to be with calf, which greatly increased her resale value. The contract is voidable at the option of A.

EXAMPLE: A agrees to sell B a cow at beef cow prices. At the time of contracting, both parties share the mistaken impression that the cow is barren. B tells A that she is still going to try to breed the cow in any case. In this case, A bears the risk of B's efforts succeeding, because if B succeeds, it will prove the parties' assumption that the cow was barren wrong. So A is accordingly bound by the contract even if the cow turns out to be fertile.

(3) **Application under the Common Law and the UCC**

(a) The doctrine of mistake originated under common law, but is also available in sales of goods cases governed by the UCC.

4. **Impossibility, Impracticability, and Frustration of Purpose**

a. Where the faulty assumptions of the parties relate to future facts, as opposed to existing facts, these issues are dealt with under the doctrines of impossibility, impracticability, and frustration of purpose.

b. These doctrines may be used as a defense to a breach of contract claim. However, they can also be raised affirmatively for claims of rescission or cancellation of the contract.

c. **Impossibility**

(1) The **doctrine of impossibility** excuses both parties from their obligations under a contract if the performance has been rendered impossible by events occurring after the contract was formed.

(2) Application of the doctrine of impossibility requires:

(a) objectively impossible performance; and

1) Objective impossibility occurs when the performance under the contract becomes literally impossible because of circumstances beyond the control of the parties.

EXAMPLE: If X promises to sell Y his horse, but the horse dies before X can deliver it, then X's performance has become objectively impossible.

2) Subjective impossibility occurs when the performance under the contract becomes impossible because of some failure or fault on the part of the performing party. Under those circumstances, the performance obligation is not excused and will be considered as a breach of the contract.

EXAMPLE: The failure of a party to have enough money either to make a promised payment or to obtain the components required for the production of a promised product would be subjective impossibilities.

EXAMPLE: Dealer promises to sell Buyer 200 bushels of wheat, expecting to procure the wheat from Farmer. Just before harvest, Farmer's crop fails due to wheat blight. The impossibility of Dealer's performance is subjective. While it may be impossible for Dealer to deliver the promised bushels in a timely fashion, because her expected source dried up at the last minute, under the contract she was free to secure the wheat from any source. It was Dealer's selection of Farmer, and her failure to have a backup plan, that gave rise to the resulting situation. Accordingly, Dealer does not meet the legal test of impossibility.

(b) the occurrence of the contingency must not be known to the parties at the time of contracting. This can occur in one of two ways:

1) it may be a supervening contingency, whereby the performance was possible at the time of contracting, but afterward a contingency occurs that renders the performance impossible; or

2) it may be an existing contingency, whereby a contingency existed at the time of contracting, but was unknown to the parties until after the contract was formed.

(3) **Exceptions**

(a) The doctrine of impossibility will not apply where the parties have allocated the risk of the contingency and provided remedial measures in the event of its occurrence.

(b) If events render performance only temporarily impossible, then this will typically only suspend the obligations of the parties until the impossibility ends.

(4) **Types of Impossibility**

(a) There are three main categories of impossibility:

1) destruction of the subject matter of the contract;

a) Where the contract performance involves particular goods, a building or structure, or any other tangible item, the destruction of which occurs without the fault of either party, then the contract is discharged.

EXAMPLE: Buyer promises to buy Farmer's 2008 wheat crop, the entirety of which is destroyed just before harvest by wheat blight. Farmer's performance is excused on the basis of impossibility.

2) death or incapacity; and

a) If the existence of a particular person is necessary for the performance of a contract (e.g., personal performance by an individual is required, or performance is to be rendered to a specific person) then that person's death or incapacity will trigger the doctrine of impossibility, and the parties' obligations will be dismissed.

3) illegality.

a) The doctrine of impossibility will discharge the parties' obligations if performance is prohibited by a change in a constitution, statute, administrative regulation, or municipal ordinance, or by judicial order.

d. **Impracticability**

(1) Courts are reluctant to excuse performance for any reason other than impossibility. However, under the **doctrine of impracticability**, a promisor may be excused from performance where unforeseen difficulties have made performance prohibitively expensive or otherwise extremely burdensome.

(2) The doctrine of impracticability has its source in Section 2-615 of the UCC, but has since been adopted in the common law of contracts as well.

(3) The following elements are required to show that performance under a contract would be impracticable:

(a) the impracticability of the performance was caused by some unforeseen contingency;

(b) the risk was neither assumed nor allocated by the parties; and

(c) the increase in the cost of performance would be far beyond what either party anticipated.

1) Even the courts that have allowed relief due to impracticability have held that increased cost alone is not sufficient as an excuse.

(4) **Impracticability under the UCC**

(a) Under the UCC, a number of examples of contingencies that would not excuse performance are listed.

1) Increased cost alone does not excuse performance unless the rise in cost is due to an unforeseeable contingency and alters the essential nature of performance.

2) A rise or collapse in the market will not justify impracticability because those contingencies are exactly the types of business risks that fixed-price contracts are intended to account for.

(b) The UCC also lists the following examples of contingencies that would trigger impracticability. All involve a severe shortage of raw materials or supplies:

1) where the shortage is caused by:

a) war or embargo;

b) local crop failure; or

c) unforeseen shutdown of major sources of supply; or

2) the shortage either caused a marked increase in cost or prevents the seller from securing the supplies necessary for his performance.

(5) **Contractual Allocation of the Risk of Non-Performance**

(a) The parties are free to allocate the risk of a contingency or to specify the remedial measure to dictate performance in the event of a contingency. Where they do so, the performance that would otherwise be excused by impracticability will be governed by their contractual agreement.

(b) The doctrine of impracticability thus operates as a default rule where the contract is silent as to the occurrence of a contingency.

(c) Whether the parties have provided for the contingency will depend on all of the circumstances, but some specific guidelines apply.

1) If the contingency was foreseeable at the time of contract and the contract is silent, it may suggest that the absence of a term excusing the performance was an affirmative decision to allocate the risk to the performing party.

2) The payment of a supra-market premium by the non-performing party might also reflect that the parties bargained for the contingency, and that the consideration in exchange for the premium would be the performance of the party in spite of the contingency.

3) Where evidence of a course of dealing or of trade usage reveals that it is customary for the performing party or others in a similar position to assume the risk of such contingencies.

(6) A performance obligation may be excused when the failure to perform is based on a good faith compliance with a foreign or domestic regulation or order.

e. **Frustration of Purpose**

(1) Where a contingency occurs that dramatically reduces the value of performance to the receiving party, the **doctrine of frustration of purpose** may be available to excuse the receiving party from its contractual obligations.

EXAMPLE: The doctrine of frustration of contractual purpose has as its source the famous case of Krell v. Henry, which involved the owner of a London flat with a "ringside" view of the forthcoming coronation parade who agreed to lease the flat at premium prices to a lessee eager to witness the festivities. The parade was canceled when the king became ill, and the lessee's contractual obligations to the owner were excused on the grounds that going through with the rental agreement in the absence of its *raison d'être* "cannot reasonably be said to have been in the contemplation of the parties at the date of the contract."

(2) **Modern Test**

(a) The contemporary version of this rule will discharge a party's contractual obligations when the following three conditions are met:

1) the party's principal purpose in entering the contract is frustrated;

a) This means that the frustration of incidental or non-material purposes would not qualify.

2) there is substantial frustration; and

a) Thus, a variation on Krell v. Henry in which the town erected bleachers that only partially obstructed the parade view from the apartment would not justify a finding of frustration.

3) non-occurrence of the event precipitating frustration was a basic assumption of the contract.

a) Frustration of purpose does not apply where the risk of the supervening event was reasonably foreseeable and the parties could and should have anticipated and made provision for it in the agreement. In other words, the frustration must be so severe that it is not fairly regarded as being within the risks assumed under the contract.

(3) **Contractual Allocation of the Risk**

(a) Where the parties contractually allocate the risk of the non-occurrence of the event, the doctrine of frustration of purpose will not be available.

EXAMPLE: The facts otherwise being as they were in Krell v. Henry, assume that the parties' written agreement contained the following language: "The parties understand and agree that the flat owner will be arranging at great expense to move himself and his family to the countryside in order to permit occupancy by lessee and accordingly that lessee will be obligated under this agreement irrespective of whether the coronation parade takes place during the lease period." Since the contract allocated the risk of the contingency to the lessee, his obligations under the contract were not excused for frustration of purpose when the parade was postponed.

EXAMPLE: The facts otherwise being as they were in Krell v. Henry, assume that all of London was abuzz with news of the new king's possibly serious illness during the days before the parties entered into their agreement. Because a postponement of the coronation parade was therefore foreseeable, the lessee's failure to secure language in the parties' agreement discharging his duties in the event of postponement constitutes evidence that the lessee bore that risk and remained fully obligated under the contract when it came to fruition.

(4) **Application under Common Law and the UCC**

(a) The frustration of purpose doctrine is followed under common law.

(b) The frustration of purpose doctrine is available to supplement the UCC in sales of goods contracts.

D. Excusing Performance by Agreement of the Parties

1. **Rescission**

a. The parties may also agree to discharge each other's remaining duties of performance under an existing contract that is at least partly executory on each side [Restatement (Second) of Contracts § 283(1)]. Typically, consideration will be provided by each party's discharge of the other's duties [Restatement (Second) of Contracts § 283, cmt. a].

b. The Statute of Frauds will not prevent an oral agreement of rescission that discharges unperformed duties from being enforced unless rescission of a transfer of property is involved [Restatement (Second) of Contracts § 283, cmt. b, 148].

2. **Accord and Satisfaction**

a. The parties may make an **accord**, which is a contract under which the obligee promises to accept substituted performance in satisfaction of the obligor's existing duty. **Satisfaction**—performance of the accord—will discharge the original duty [Restatement (Second) of Contracts § 281].

b. Accord alone will not discharge the original duty, but once the accord is made, the original duty will be suspended subject to the terms of the accord until the obligor has the chance to make the substituted performance [Restatement (Second) of Contracts § 281, cmt. b].

(1) If there is such a breach of the accord by the obligor as to discharge the obligee's duty to accept the substituted performance in satisfaction, the obligee is no longer bound under the accord, and he may choose between enforcing the original duty or the duty under the accord [Id.].

(2) If the obligee breaches the accord, the original duty is not discharged, but the obligor can seek specific performance of the accord (in addition to damages for partial breach) [Id.].

c. **Validity of Accord—Consideration Required**

(1) General contract law applies to accords, such that consideration is required [Restatement (Second) of Contracts § 281, cmt. d].

(2) There may be sufficient consideration if the substituted consideration differs significantly from that required by the original duty, or because the original duty was doubtful or the obligor believed it to be doubtful [Id.].

(3) Generally, there may be an accord and satisfaction when a creditor agrees to accept part payment of an unliquidated debt

that the debtor tenders in full satisfaction of the debt; however, in order for part payment to constitute sufficient consideration on its own, there must be a *bona fide* or good faith dispute as to the debt [see 1 Am. Jur. 2d. Accord & Satisfaction § 39].

3. **Anticipatory Repudiation**
   a. Anticipatory repudiation occurs when, prior to the time that performance is due under the contract, a party announces his intention not to perform, or circumstances make such an intention reasonably clear to the aggrieved party.
   b. Technically, anticipatory repudiation is not the same as a breach of contract because the party has not yet failed on its promise of performance. However, the aggrieved party is given the option to immediately treat the anticipatory repudiation as a breach of contract and to be entitled to the same rights and remedies.
   c. Anticipatory repudiation may be established by:
      (1) a party's definitive statement indicating that she will commit a breach of contract; or
      (2) a party's voluntary or affirmative act that renders the party unable to perform or apparently unable to perform (e.g., the sale of the contracted-for item to a third party).
   d. **Adequate Assurance of Performance**
      (1) If anticipatory repudiation cannot be established but there are reasonable grounds for insecurity (i.e., reasonable grounds to believe that the other party is unwilling or unable to perform), the insecure party may make a demand for **adequate assurance of performance**.
      (2) Adequate assurance of performance must be provided in the following forms:
         (a) the UCC requires that a demand for adequate assurance of performance on a sale of goods contract be made in writing [§ 2-609(1)]; and
         (b) under the Restatement of Contracts, an adequate assurance of performance may be made either:
            1) by oral communication; or
            2) in writing.
      (3) **Suspension of Performance by the Insecure Party**
         (a) Upon making a demand for assurances, a party with reasonable grounds for insecurity may suspend its own contractual performance so long as:
            1) suspension is commercially reasonable; and
            2) the insecure party has not yet received the agreed-upon return for the performance in question.

            EXAMPLE: If a seller reads about a planned bankruptcy filing by a buyer, the seller may, after demanding assurances, suspend delivery of goods for which the buyer has not already paid.

(b) The insecure party may also suspend his own performance where the performing party:

1) does not respond to a demand for assurances within a reasonable time (30 days under the UCC); or

2) does not respond in a manner that provides reasonable assurance to the other party.

a) In this situation, the reasonableness of an assurance of performance is determined by:

i) the circumstances;

ii) the relationship between the parties;

iii) the parties' past dealings; and

iv) the nature of the insecurity requiring assurance.

(c) The failure to respond with reasonable assurances constitutes a repudiation of the contract by the non-responding party.

e. **Rights of the Aggrieved Party upon Repudiation**

(1) If the aggrieved party chooses to treat the anticipatory breach as a breach of contract, she may:

(a) cancel the contract and terminate all rights and obligations under it; or

(b) bring an action for damages or specific performance.

(2) The aggrieved party may immediately resort to one of these remedies upon repudiation, or he may wait until performance should have occurred.

(3) If an aggrieved party chooses to ignore a repudiation, then she is prevented from continuing to perform on the contract if performance would increase her damages from the contract.

(4) If the aggrieved party can prove to the court that he was willing, ready, and able to render performance had the anticipatory repudiation not occurred, then the aggrieved party is relieved of:

(a) performance of contractual obligations; and

(b) performance of any conditions precedent.

f. **Retraction of Repudiation**

(1) A party who has made an anticipatory repudiation to the other party may retract the repudiation unless and until the other party:

(a) acts in reliance on the repudiation;

(b) positively accepts the repudiation by signifying this to the breaching party; or

(c) commences a suit for damages or specific performance.

E. Conditions

1. In some contracts, the obligation to perform is conditioned upon the happening of some event or upon action by the other party. The law regarding conditions governs two distinct issues: the order of parties' performances and the remedies where conditions to the contract have failed.

2. **Promissory versus Pure Conditions**
   a. A condition to contractual performance can be a condition controlled by the parties or can be a condition outside of either party's control.
      (1) A **promissory condition** is where the contract performance is conditioned on the occurrence of the promised performance by the other party.

      EXAMPLE: A publication contract contains the following language: "Publisher's duty of payment is expressly conditioned on Author's timely completion of the promised manuscript." In this case, Author's timely delivery of the manuscript is a promissory condition on Publisher's contractual obligation of payment.

      (2) **Pure conditions** are typically where contract performance is conditioned on the occurrence of events beyond the control of either party.

      EXAMPLE: Skyblasters, Inc. agrees by contract to provide a fireworks display for a holiday celebration sponsored by the Village of Remulak, and the contract contains a "weather permitting" provision. In this case, good weather is a pure condition on Skyblasters' performance obligation.

3. **Express versus Implied Conditions**
   a. **Express conditions** are those which the parties expressly include in provisions of the contract.

   EXAMPLE: "Publisher's duty of payment is expressly conditioned on Author's timely completion of the promised manuscript." This would be an express condition to contract performance of payment because it is listed within the contract.

   b. **Implied conditions** are those created under common law or the UCC to address order of performance and rights upon breach when the parties haven't done so expressly. Implied conditions are those fairly to be inferred from evidence of the parties' intentions. They are often referred to as implied-in-fact, since their existence is determined by the process of contract interpretation rather than the express language of the contract.

4. **Rules Governing the Order of Performance**
   a. The rules regarding order of performance are dependent on whether the contract falls under common law or the UCC.
      (1) **Cases Governed by Common Law**
         (a) If the contract contains express conditions specifying the order of performance, then those specifications will control the order of performance.
         (b) If the contract is silent as to order of performance:
            1) Where one party's performance requires a period of time to be completed and the other party's performance does not, then the performance over time is treated as an implied condition of the latter.

2) Where the parties can exchange performance more or less simultaneously, then the performances are treated as concurrent conditions of each other.

(2) **Sales of Goods under the UCC**

(a) Under the UCC, the parties are free to specify the order of performance, and where the contract contains those specifications, the performance obligations under that contract will be performed according to the contractual terms.

(b) Because sales contracts most commonly involve delivery and payment of goods, performance is treated as concurrent, and so each performance is conditioned on the performance of the other.

5. **Rules Governing the Failure of a Condition**

a. The default rules for a failed condition of the contract performance are dependent on whether the contract falls under the common law rules of contracts or under the UCC.

b. **Cases Governed by the Common Law**

(1) In common law cases, the rights of the parties in the event of a failed condition depend on whether the condition is express or implied.

(2) **Express Conditions**

(a) Where a party's performance under the contract is subject to an express condition, the failure of that condition will discharge the party's obligation to perform.

(b) **Identifying Express Conditions**

1) In some cases, the parties will use the magic words to describe a particular performance or event as a condition on a return performance.

EXAMPLE: "The party's duty to perform is expressly conditioned on the promised performance."

2) The term "expressly conditioned" does not have to be included, but language conveying the same idea will constitute an express condition as well.

EXAMPLE: "No obligation to proceed unless and until franchisee takes the following steps" or "payment due upon completion of second benchmark."

3) In the absence of clear language, an express condition may be established by trade usage, course of dealing, or course of performance evidence.

(c) **Excusing Failed Express Conditions**

1) Generally, a failure of the occurrence of an express condition will discharge the performance obligation of the party who stood to benefit from the condition.

2) Nevertheless, there are three situations in which the failure of the condition may be excused without discharging the beneficiary's performance obligation.

3) **Waiver**

   a) The party who has been discharged from performing by the failed condition may waive the right to discharge and perform anyway. When the party waives the condition, the waiving party's obligation becomes absolute because it is no longer subject to the condition.

   b) Some courts treat a waiver of condition as a midterm modification to the contract and require that additional consideration be given by the other party to give the waiver effect.

4) **Bad Faith Conduct**

   a) A condition will be excused on the basis of bad faith conduct by the beneficiary of the condition. Thus, bad faith conduct will excuse the condition where the benefitting party interferes with the fulfillment of a contract, or where the benefitting party fails to take steps necessary for the condition's fulfillment.

   EXAMPLE: In a contract for the sale of real property, a buyer's performance obligation is conditioned on his success in securing financing. If the buyer fails to apply for financing, this would be considered conduct in bad faith, and the buyer's performance obligation would become absolute.

5) **Avoiding Forfeiture**

   a) In some situations the fulfillment of a condition may result in a forfeiture or great loss to one of the parties. In those cases a court may excuse the condition to avoid forfeiture.

   b) In deciding to excuse a condition, the court will consider:

      i) whether the party favoring excuse will suffer a loss greatly disproportionate to the actual prejudice to the other party;

      ii) whether the failure of the condition is due to willfulness or serious neglect;

      iii) whether the other party played a role in bringing that failure about;

      iv) whether the condition relates to a minor term in the contract as opposed to a material one; and

      v) whether the fulfillment of the condition has not failed completely but has merely been delayed.

NOTE There is another consideration that applies to insurance contracts only. In deciding to excuse a condition, courts will consider whether, where a contract for insurance benefits conditions benefits payments on timely notice of covered events, such notice is not provided because of circumstances outside the insured's control.

EXAMPLE: A failure to provide notice of a covered disability, where the disability itself has caused the failure of timely notice, would be a condition that would be excused.

EXAMPLE: Failure to provide timely proof of death, where the body is not discovered for an extended period of time, would be an excusable condition.

(3) **Implied Conditions**

(a) When the breach in question relates to an express condition, courts will enforce the condition to the letter and discharge the conditioned performance obligation, absent an excuse such as waiver or bad faith.

(b) When the possibility of breach is not addressed by an express condition, it is still a breach; however, under the law of implied conditions, courts can treat that breach in one of two ways: either as a material breach or as substantial performance.

(c) **Material Breach versus Substantial Performance**

1) If the breach is serious enough, the court will treat the breach in the same way it would treat a breach of an express condition (i.e., as relieving the aggrieved party of her own performance obligation). This is called **material breach**, and the aggrieved party is free to walk away from her own obligations and sue the breaching party for damages.

2) In certain cases, if the breach is less serious, the court will treat the party's performance as "close enough," meaning that the party has rendered **substantial performance** of the condition. In these cases, the aggrieved party will not be discharged of his performance obligation. The doctrine of substantial performance applies to contracts for services and, in particular, to construction contracts.

3) Even where the court finds substantial performance of a condition, the aggrieved party may still sue for damages as remedy for the breach.

4) The Restatement of Contracts lists five factors that can help to distinguish between material breach and substantial performance:

a) the extent to which the aggrieved party will be deprived of the benefit, which she reasonably expected under the terms of the contract;

b) the extent to which the aggrieved party can adequately be compensated via damages for the defective performance;

c) the extent to which the breaching party will suffer forfeiture if a material breach is found;

d) the extent to which the breach was willful or in bad faith, rather than merely negligent or innocent; and

e) the likelihood that the breaching party will cure her failure within a reasonable time and in a manner consistent with the reasonable purposes of the contract.

i) The likelihood that the failure will be cured is a significant circumstance in determining whether the breach is material or non-material [Restatement (Second) of Contracts § 241].

EXAMPLE: Contractor builds a house for Landowner and—unbeknownst to Contractor—the plumbing subcontractor installs a brand of pipe that differs from the brand specified in the contract but is in every important respect the same quality. It would be an extremely expensive and burdensome task for Contractor to remove and replace the pipe. The use of the substitute pipe is a breach of the parties' contract, but Contractor has substantially performed because Landowner is deprived of merely a *de minimis* benefit since the substitute pipe is the functional equivalent of the brand required by the contract. Contractor will suffer an enormous loss if he is required to remove and replace the errant pipe; and the breach was at most negligent if the Contractor did not monitor the subcontractor closely enough, but in no way was the Contractor's breach willful or in bad faith.

EXAMPLE: Contractor builds a house for the Yuppies, a young couple who are foodies and love to entertain and, accordingly, their plans include a spacious kitchen. The Yuppies spend the year in Paris while the house is under construction, and in their absence and without prior consultation, Contractor decides to deviate from the plans and build a smaller kitchen, thus enabling Contractor to save significant construction costs. Contractor's improvisation is a material breach because it would deprive the Yuppies of a substantial benefit for which they had contracted; because money would not adequately compensate them for the diminished kitchen that was to be the centerpiece of their dream home; and because Contractor's breach was willful and in bad faith.

5) **Total Breach versus Partial Breach**

a) A material breach can be treated as either a partial breach or a total breach.

i) A claim for damages for **total breach** is one for damages based on all of the injured party's remaining rights to performance [Restatement (Second) of Contracts § 236].

ii) A claim for damages for **partial breach** is one for damages based on only part of the injured party's remaining rights to performance [Id.].

b) However, a non-material breach can only be a partial breach.

(4) **Failed Condition That Cannot Be Excused**

(a) Where a condition has failed and cannot be excused, there are other methods of enforcement available to mitigate the consequences for the breaching party.

(b) If a contract requires both parties to render a series of performances over a period of time, the contract may be divisible in the event of a failed condition.

1) The failed condition must not be material to the contract itself, but must relate to a small portion of the contract performance in order for the contract to be severable into separate transactions, allowing the breaching party to recover for portions properly performed.

2) The legal test for determining whether a contract is divisible is:

a) Can the performance in question be apportioned into corresponding pairs of parties' performances?

b) Can each pair be properly regarded as agreed equivalents?

NOTE A helpful way to look at divisibility is by asking whether the contract is nothing more than the sum of its parts. If so, then the contract is divisible. If the contract involves more than the sum of its parts, then it is unlikely to be divisible.

EXAMPLE: A one-year cleaning service contract would be divisible if the services were provided and paid for on a monthly basis, as it would be easy to apportion the larger exchange into "pairs of part performance" that are "properly regarded as agreed equivalents" (i.e., a month's worth of cleaning in exchange for a month's pay). To put it another way, the one-year contract is merely the sum of the 12 monthly exchanges.

EXAMPLE: A contracts to build a house for B for $100,000, with progress payments of $5,000 due in monthly installments during construction and a balloon payment upon the architect's certificate of satisfactory completion. The contract is not divisible, for the performances and the progress payments are not "agreed equivalents," and the whole is greater than the sum of the parts, since no reasonable person would enter a freestanding contract for a month of construction work.

(c) Where a party has failed to fulfill an express condition or is in material breach of the contract, she may still be able to recover in *quantum meruit* the value of benefits she has conferred to the aggrieved party during performance.

1) The breaching party may recover the reasonable value of the benefits conferred under a theory of *quantum meruit*.

2) The reasonable value of the benefits conferred will be reduced by the damages suffered by the aggrieved party due to the breach.

c. **Sales of Goods Contracts under the UCC**

(1) **Express and Implied Conditions in Relationship to the Perfect Tender Rule**

(a) Under the **perfect tender rule**, the terms of a contract for the sale of goods are enforced exactly. Every contract term is thus treated as an express condition, and a breach of the performance obligation by the seller will relieve the payment obligation of the buyer.

1) As a result, there is no need to distinguish between express and implied conditions because they will be treated in the same fashion.

(b) The perfect tender rule enables a buyer to reject a seller's goods "if the goods or the tender of delivery fail in any respect to conform to the contract." Under this rule, any deviation from the performance specified by the contract (e.g., regarding the quality or quantity of the goods, or the time or manner of delivery) constitutes a breach by the seller.

(c) If the seller fails to make perfect tender, the buyer has three courses of action available [§ 2-601]:

1) **Reject the Goods**

a) For a buyer to reject the goods, the buyer must exercise the right of rejection within a reasonable time after delivery and notify the seller of the rejection within a reasonable period of time [§ 2-602(1)].

b) If the buyer rejects the goods, the buyer may bring an action for damages against the seller for imperfect tender, and the buyer must use reasonable care with respect to holding the goods for a time sufficient for the seller to remove them [§ 2-602].

   i) If the seller gives no instructions within a reasonable time after notification of rejection, the buyer may store the goods for the seller's account, reship them to the seller, or resell them for the seller's account [§ 2-604].

   ii) However, if the buyer is a merchant and the seller has no agent or place of business in the place where the goods were rejected, the buyer must follow any reasonable instructions received from the seller, and if none, must make reasonable efforts to sell the goods if they are perishable or their value will decline quickly [§ 2-603(1)].

   iii) A merchant buyer who resells the goods after a rightful rejection is entitled to reimbursement for the reasonable expenses of caring for and selling the goods [§ 2-603(2)].

c) If the buyer fails to state in connection with the rejection a particular defect, the buyer will be precluded from relying on the unstated defect to justify rejection if the defect is ascertainable by reasonable inspection, where [§ 2-605(1)]:

   i) the seller could have cured the defect if it was stated seasonably; or

   ii) between merchants, the seller after rejection made a written request for a written full and final statement of all defects on which the buyer proposes to rely.

d) If a buyer does not effectuate rejection in the manner specified above, then the buyer has made a failed rejection. A failed rejection will be deemed to be acceptance of the goods by the buyer.

2) **Accept the Goods**

a) The buyer may accept the goods, despite the improper tender. Acceptance occurs when the buyer has had a reasonable opportunity to inspect the goods and signifies acceptance either through:

   i) stating to the seller that the goods conform to the contract;

ii) taking the goods despite their non-conformance;

iii) failing to make an effective rejection of the goods; or

iv) taking any action that would be inconsistent with the seller's ownership of the goods.

EXAMPLE: Buyer puts the goods on display in the showroom.

b) If the buyer accepts the goods, he has the following rights and duties:

i) he must pay contract price for the goods;

ii) he may seek damages against the seller for the nonconformity if he notified the seller of the nonconformity within a reasonable time after discovering it, the seller is not prejudiced by the lack of notice, or his rights would not be affected; and

iii) he may revoke his acceptance if the nonconformity substantially impairs the value of the goods, and he was initially unaware of the nonconformity because of the difficulty of discovery or because his acceptance was predicated on the seller's assurances of conformity or that nonconformity would be cured.

NOTE The buyer must revoke his acceptance within a reasonable time after the buyer discovers or should have discovered the grounds for revocation, and before there is any substantial change in the condition of the goods (unless caused by their own defect). The revocation is only effective once the buyer notifies the seller of it [§ 2-608(2)].

3) **Reject Part and Accept Part of the Goods**

a) A buyer who has received improper tender may accept some of the commercial tender and reject the rest.

b) The buyer will then have the rights and duties of acceptance for the goods she accepted, and the rights and duties of rejection for the goods she rejected (though this picking and choosing is limited to "commercial units"—e.g., a buyer of bread can reject individual loaves but not half loaves).

EXAMPLE: Buyer's contract guaranteed that Seller would deliver 10 gross of quart-sized Mason jars, which are invariably boxed and sold by the gross in the Mason jar trade. If Seller's tender is imperfect (e.g., it is late or short), Buyer is free to accept some of the jars and reject the rest, but he must do so "by the gross."

(d) **Seller's Ability to Cure**

1) If a seller makes a nonconforming tender but the time of performance has not yet expired under the contract, then the seller may substitute conforming goods so long as:

a) the seller gives the buyer seasonable notice of her intention to substitute; and

b) the seller makes conforming delivery within the time specified in the contract.

2) If a seller makes a nonconforming delivery and had reasonable grounds to believe that delivery would be acceptable to the buyer, then he may substitute a conforming delivery if:

a) the seller gives the buyer reasonable notice of his intention to substitute; and

b) the seller makes conforming delivery within a reasonable time.

3) **Proof of Reasonable Grounds by Seller**

a) A seller may prove that she had reasonable grounds to believe that the buyer would accept nonconformity if she has evidence of:

i) express assurances to that effect from the buyer; or

ii) trade usage, course of dealing, or course of performance evidence to that effect.

(2) **Special Rules for Installment Contracts**

(a) Under the UCC, **installment contracts** are contracts that contemplate the delivery of goods in separate lots to be separately accepted by the buyer.

(b) Because such contracts are performed in installments, the occasion of a nonconforming tender will almost invariably occur in connection with a particular installment. When that occurs, the rights of the buyer are as follows:

1) If the nonconforming installment substantially impairs the value of the whole contract, there is a breach of the whole contract [§ 2-612(3)].

2) If the nonconforming installment substantially impairs the value of that installment, and the seller cannot cure, the buyer may reject the installment. However, if the nonconforming installment does not substantially impair the value of the contract as a whole, and the seller gives adequate assurance that he will cure, the buyer must accept the installment [§ 2-612(2)].

VII. DEFENSES

A. Incapacity

1. Infancy

a. Infancy is the time period before a person reaches the age of majority. An infant, commonly referred to as a minor, is any person who is under the age of 18.

b. At common law, minors lacked the capacity to enter into a contract. The modern rule is that a minor may enter into a contract, but the contract is voidable at the option of the minor. However, in certain circumstances the contract may be ratified, or alternately, the minor may still be liable for the benefits received.

EXCEPTION: In most states, minors enjoy the power of avoidance even if they are married or emancipated. However, a minority of jurisdictions deprive married or emancipated minors of the power of avoidance, making all contracts they enter into enforceable against them.

c. **Power of Avoidance**

(1) While minors have the capacity to enter a contract before they reach the age of majority, they also have the power to disaffirm contracts they enter into (the power of avoidance), with some exceptions.

(2) The **power of avoidance** means that the minor has the option of voiding the contract. However, the contract is not void against the other parties to a contract, and so is enforceable against everyone but the minor.

(a) There is an increasing trend toward limiting minors' use of the power of avoidance to a defense only. The minor is allowed to disaffirm a contract that the other party seeks to enforce against him. However, he may not use the defense to bring suit against the other party to secure restitution of monies already paid.

(3) Upon exercising the right to disaffirm a contract, the minor is obligated to return to the other party any goods received under the contract.

(a) The minor must return the goods if they are in her possession when she disaffirms the contract. However, she is not liable for damage, wear and tear, or any other depreciation in value of the goods.

(b) If the minor is not in possession of the goods at the time of disaffirming the contract because she sold the goods, then the minor will be obligated to turn over the proceeds of the sale of the goods to the other party.

(c) A contract between a minor and another party may be for something that cannot be returned, such as a services contract or a lease. In such a case, where the subject matter of the contract is non-returnable, the minor is under no further obligation to return or compensate the other party.

(d) In a minority of jurisdictions, a minor can only disaffirm a contract by making the other party whole. In these jurisdictions, the minor would be liable for depreciation, as well as compensating the other party for the services or other non-returnable items, in addition to returning possession or the proceeds of a sale for returnable items.

d. **Ratification**

(1) For most contracts that minors enter into before reaching the age of majority, the minor may **ratify** that contract upon reaching the age of majority.

(2) A minor may ratify most transactions entered into during infancy by making any manifestation to the other party of an intention to be bound by the original contract.

(a) The minor's silence regarding the contract after reaching the age of majority is not sufficient to constitute a ratification unless the minor continues to take advantage of goods or services provided under the contract.

(b) In a minority of jurisdictions, if a minor fails to disaffirm the contract within a reasonable time after reaching the age of majority, then the contract will be deemed ratified.

(c) Once a minor disaffirms a contract, a majority of jurisdictions consider the contract void, with title to the property revesting in the other party (where possible). Once disaffirmed, a minor can no longer ratify the contract. Ratification must occur prior to the minor's avoidance of the contract.

e. **Exceptions**

(1) **Necessaries**

(a) A minor's contract for necessaries is voidable. However, the other party has the right in *quasi*-contract to recover for the reasonable value of the goods or services provided.

(b) **Necessaries** are those items considered necessary for survival. Most basic categories of necessaries include things like food, clothing, shelter, and medical care.

1) In some jurisdictions, these items are only considered necessaries if provided to an emancipated minor whose parents cannot or will not provide them.

2) Courts are split on whether to include automobiles and/or education in the category of necessaries.

(c) The other party may secure the reasonable value of the goods or services only, not the contract price. Additionally, if the minor paid more than the reasonable value, then the minor is entitled to a refund of the difference between the amount paid and the reasonable value.

(2) **Misrepresentation by Minor**

(a) In a minority of jurisdictions, if a minor has misrepresented his age to the contracting party in order to obtain the goods or services of the contract, he may be equitably estopped from proving his real age in court. This would deny the minor the defense of infancy and make the contract enforceable.

2. **Mental Incompetence**

a. At common law, an insane person did not have capacity to enter a contract, and any contracts she made were void. Under modern rules, the bar for establishing mental incompetence is lower—a party need not be "insane" to invoke the doctrine—and the consequences of invocation depend on multiple factors.

(1) The key in all cases is whether the person was incompetent at the time of contracting.

(2) The party who becomes incompetent after entering a contract can escape contractual liability—if at all—via impossibility and related doctrines, discussed earlier.

b. **Requirements for Mental Incompetence**

(1) If a party is adjudicated incompetent and a guardian is appointed, then this adjudication will be sufficient to establish mental incompetence for contract cases.

(2) Where there is no adjudication of mental incompetence by a court, then a party may still be declared mentally incompetent for the purposes of contract formation under the following circumstances:

(a) **Cognitive Defects**

1) In almost every jurisdiction, a person will be deemed mentally incompetent and lacking capacity to enter a contract if the person is unable to understand in a reasonable manner the nature and consequences of the transaction.

EXAMPLE: A person who is operating under the influence of delusions or hallucinations will be deemed mentally incompetent based on cognitive defects.

(b) **Volitional Defects**

1) In many jurisdictions, mental incompetence can be established if:

a) a person is unable to act in a reasonable manner in relation to the transaction; and

b) the other party has reason to know of this condition.

EXAMPLE: A person who is a manic depressive would be able to avoid a contract if he was in a manic phase at the time of contract formation and if the other party had reason to know of that person's state based, for example, on his erratic behavior.

c. **Legal Consequences**

(1) In most jurisdictions, a contract entered into by an incompetent person is voidable. This means that the contract is enforceable at the option of the incompetent party, rather than void, which would make it unenforceable by either party.

(a) Some jurisdictions, as well as the Second Restatement, hold that a person adjudicated incompetent and under guardianship has no capacity to incur contractual duties, making such contracts void.

(2) A party who is mentally incompetent at the time of contract may ratify the contract if she becomes competent at a later time. Ratification may be accomplished by an oral or written manifestation of the intention to be bound by the original contract.

(3) If the mentally incompetent person exercises her power of avoidance and has received some benefit under the contract, then she is required to make the other party whole by paying the reasonable value of the goods or services rendered.

(a) A mentally incompetent party will be responsible for damage, wear and tear, or any other depreciation in value of the goods.

EXCEPTION: If the other party takes unfair advantage of the mentally incompetent person, and has knowledge of the person's incompetence, then the other party is entitled only to a return "as is" of any goods still in the possession of the mentally incompetent party and will have no right of recovery for goods or services already consumed.

(4) The rules governing the liability of a mentally incompetent party for contracts for necessaries are the same as for minors. The mentally incompetent party will be liable to the other party for the reasonable value of those goods and services.

(a) For mentally incompetent persons, necessaries include the retention of legal services in connection with adjudicating mental incompetence.

B. Misrepresentation

1. Misrepresentation can play two roles in contract cases: it may be a "sword," as the basis for affirmative relief, or a "shield," a defense to enforcement.

a. Misrepresentation can be used as a basis for affirmative relief under a tort claim brought by the aggrieved party in the form of an action for rescission and damages.

b. Misrepresentation can be used as a defense to an effort to enforce the contract.

2. **Misrepresentations** are untrue statements or assertions that relate to existing facts.

a. Misrepresentations relate to existing facts, not to future conduct or action. If one says, "I'm going to do something," and doesn't do it, that's a broken promise, not a misrepresentation. But, if one says, "I'm going to do X," and at the time he makes that promise he actually doesn't intend to do X, that may be actionable as promissory fraud.

b. Misrepresentations must relate to facts, not opinions. A statement that is based on a party's mere opinion, guess, or supposition will not be considered a misrepresentation.

(1) Where one party disguises a fact as an opinion, then this will constitute a misrepresentation.

EXAMPLE: An automobile dealer who tells a buyer that she thinks the car runs pretty well, even though she knows that the car does not run well, would be disguising a fact as an opinion, and thus be making a misrepresentation to the buyer.

(2) Where a party holds himself out to have knowledge or special skill, and asserts an opinion on the basis of the skill or knowledge, then his assertions are held to relate to the underlying facts and, therefore, sufficient to establish misrepresentation.

EXAMPLE: A certified mechanic who tells a buyer that he thinks the car runs pretty well, even though he knows that the car does not run well, would, in effect, be asserting facts about the state of the car and, thus, making a misrepresentation to the buyer.

3. **Types of Misrepresentation**

a. **Fraudulent Misrepresentation**

(1) To establish fraudulent misrepresentation, the following must be proved:

(a) the defendant must have made an assertion that was inconsistent with existing facts;

1) Most claims of fraudulent misrepresentation are based on oral or written statements.

a) Statements that are "half-truths" can be misrepresentations as well.

EXAMPLE: An advertisement for real estate "suitable for commercial development," where applicable zoning regulations would prohibit such use.

2) Misrepresentations can also be made through conduct.

EXAMPLE: When a payor issues a check for a specified amount despite insufficient funds, she is representing that she has funds on deposit to cover the instrument.

a) Active efforts to "cover up" the truth (termed **fraudulent concealment**) likewise constitute misrepresentations.

EXAMPLE: A seller of real estate undertakes efforts to hide termite damage from potential buyers.

(b) the state-of-mind element requires that there was both:

1) scienter; and

a) The scienter requirement relates to the defendant's state of mind with respect to the assertion. The defendant will satisfy the scienter requirement if either:

i) he made the assertion knowing it to be false; or

ii) he made the assertion knowing that he had no idea whether it was true or false.

EXAMPLE: Scienter would be present where the auto dealer says, "This baby can go from zero to 70 in six seconds flat," if she either knows that the car can't accelerate that quickly or has no basis for knowing whether the car can accelerate that quickly.

2) intent to mislead.

a) The defendant will meet the requirement for intent to mislead if:

i) he made the assertion for the purpose of misleading the aggrieved party; or

ii) he made the assertion knowing there was a substantial likelihood that the aggrieved party would be misled.

(c) the misrepresentation must be material to the contract; and

1) Materiality can be shown by either an objective standard or a subjective standard:

a) Under an objective standard, a misrepresentation is material where such an assertion was likely to induce a reasonable person to enter into the contract.

EXAMPLE: An assertion that a used car has been carefully inspected by an independent auto mechanic would appeal to a reasonable person and, thus, satisfy the objective materiality test.

b) A misrepresentation is material under a subjective standard if assertion of such a fact was likely, for reasons known to the defendant, to induce the aggrieved party specifically into entering the contract.

EXAMPLE: An assertion that the car was owned by Salman Rushdie when he was living incognito in the U.K. would be material if made to an individual whom the seller knew to be a Rushdie enthusiast.

(d) there must have been reasonable reliance on the representation.

1) The standard for determining whether an aggrieved party's reliance on the defendant's misrepresentation is reasonable

is whether, under all of the same circumstances, a reasonable person would have relied on the assertion.

EXAMPLE: Reliance would be unreasonable if the aggrieved party has independent knowledge or reason to know that the perpetrator's statement is false.

EXAMPLE: Reliance would be unreasonable if the aggrieved party has reason to believe that the perpetrator is unreliable.

EXAMPLE: Reliance would be unreasonable if no reasonable person would have believed the assertion.

EXAMPLE: Reliance would be unreasonable if the aggrieved party could have easily ascertained the truth by cursory inspection of the goods.

2) Because of the "duty to read," it is generally not reasonable to rely on a trading partner's characterization of a writing's content. However, two situations in which reliance on the contents of a writing would be reasonable are:

   a) if the defendant is a merchant and the aggrieved party is a customer; or

   b) if the defendant induces the aggrieved party not to read the writing by some devious means.

   EXAMPLE: The perpetrator induces the victim to sign a contract that the perpetrator knows to contain terms of which the victim is unaware and in circumstances in which the perpetrator knows the victim won't have time to read the contract.

b. **Non-Fraudulent Misrepresentation**

(1) Non-fraudulent misrepresentation may either be negligent or innocent misrepresentation. For either claim, the following elements must be established:

   (a) the defendant must have made an assertion that was inconsistent with existing facts;

   (b) the misrepresentation must be material to the contract; and

   (c) there must have been reasonable reliance on the misrepresentation.

(2) Because negligent or innocent misrepresentation is not intentional, there is no need to make a showing of the defendant's state of mind. Instead, the following factors are required:

   (a) For negligent misrepresentation, the aggrieved party must show that the perpetrator would have known that the assertion was false had she exercised reasonable care.

   (b) For innocent misrepresentation, the aggrieved party need only show that the perpetrator made an assertion not in accord with existing fact.

(3) The same remedies are available to the victim of either negligent or innocent misrepresentation, so the difference between them is merely descriptive (i.e., what to call a particular misrepresentation) but has no further legal consequence.

c. **Fraudulent Nondisclosure**

(1) The wrong that must be committed under a claim of fraudulent nondisclosure relates not to an assertion made by the defendant, but to the defendant's silence where there was a duty to disclose.

(2) To prove fraudulent nondisclosure, one must show that:

(a) the nondisclosure was material to the contract, under either an objective standard or a subjective standard; and

(b) there was reasonable reliance on the nondisclosure.

NOTE Because fraudulent nondisclosure is based on the defendant's silence rather than an assertion, there is no requirement that the defendant make an assertion.

(3) Although there is generally no duty of disclosure to trading partners, if a party is aware of material facts that are unlikely to be discovered by the other party in the exercise of ordinary care and diligence, then there will be a duty to disclose that information in these circumstances:

(a) where the parties enjoy a relationship of trust and confidence;

EXAMPLE: A relationship between family members or a professional's relationship with a client would be a relationship of trust and confidence.

(b) if a party has made an assertion that was true at the time but has been rendered untrue by intervening events; or

EXAMPLE: If a person makes an assertion that an individual plans to keep property in an undeveloped state and later learns that the individual no longer intends to keep the property undeveloped, he would need to disclose this change.

(c) if the obligation of good faith would require that the party disclose the information.

EXAMPLE: A seller of residential real estate who learns of a termite infestation would have a good-faith obligation to disclose the infestation to the buyer.

4. **Remedies**

a. Victims of fraudulent misrepresentation, non-fraudulent misrepresentation, and fraudulent nondisclosure may use those claims in two ways:

(1) avoidance; or

(a) All three claims give the victim the power of avoidance, which may be exercised to defend against a breach of contract claim brought by the misrepresenting party.

(2) rescission and reliance damages.

(a) All three claims enable the victim to bring a tort action to rescind the contract and collect damages for reliance on the misrepresentation, including consequential damages.

b. Victims of fraudulent and non-fraudulent misrepresentation have a third option: they may live with the contract and sue for the benefit of the bargain.

(1) The victim of fraudulent misrepresentation may bring a tort action seeking the benefit of the bargain. This would allow the victim to recover the difference between the value of the goods or services actually received and the value of the promised goods or services. This tort remedy is the functional equivalent of expectation damages, discussed later in this outline.

(2) This remedy of bringing a tort action for the benefit of the bargain is not available for claims of negligent or innocent misrepresentation. However, parties bringing such claims may be able to characterize the assertion contrary to fact as a warranty and thus obtain expectation damages by asserting breach thereof.

c. Because fraudulent misrepresentation is an intentional tort, the aggrieved party may secure punitive damages against the defendant to penalize the defendant on the basis of the fraudulent intention.

(1) Punitive damages are not available for claims of negligent or innocent misrepresentation or fraudulent nondisclosure.

C. Duress

1. At common law, the defense of duress was available in two circumstances:

a. physical compulsion; and

(1) A party could claim duress as a defense to contract liability if the party signed the contract under force of physical compulsion.

b. unlawful threat.

(1) A party could claim duress as a defense to contract liability if the party signed the contract under threat of unlawful activity against herself or her family.

2. Although the above two circumstances still constitute duress, the contemporary definition of the term has been relaxed to cover less egregious instances of coercive persuasion. Thus, under modern law, there are three elements to a defense of duress:

a. a threat;

(1) A **threat** made by the perpetrator is a manifestation of intent to inflict harm on the other person, made in words or by conduct.

EXAMPLE: The words "your money or your life" would be considered a threat.

EXAMPLE: An example of conduct considered a threat is the scene in *The Godfather* where the man wakes up with a horse's head in bed, which was placed there to induce him to sign the contract.

b. that is wrongful in nature; and

(1) A threat is wrongful in nature if it involves criminal or tortious conduct, whether the threat is itself unlawful (e.g., extortion or blackmail) or whether it is merely a threat to engage in future unlawful action (e.g., causing harm to a party's person, family member, or property).

(2) A threat to pursue criminal charges constitutes a wrongful threat, even if the perpetrator honestly believes that the target is guilty of that crime.

(3) A threat to bring a civil action is wrongful only if made in bad faith—that is, if the perpetrator does not honestly and reasonably believe that the target has civil liability.

(4) A threat is sufficient to constitute duress if what is threatened is a bad faith breach of contract. This is commonly known as economic duress.

(a) If a party refuses to perform unless he is awarded additional benefits, this may constitute a bad faith breach of contract.

1) Economic duress will usually arise where the threatened party acquiesces to the other party's demands at the time but then refuses to confer the additional benefits.

EXAMPLE: Sailors on a fishing voyage cease their work midway through the voyage and refuse to resume their duties unless the captain agrees to give them a raise. At the end of the voyage, the captain refuses to pay the higher amount, and the sailors sue.

(b) Not every demand for a change in contract price will be considered a bad faith demand. If the demand for a change in contract terms is due to the fact that performance under the terms of the contract has become extremely burdensome because of unanticipated circumstances, then there is no duress.

EXAMPLE: The sailors' demand for additional compensation in response to an unanticipated expansion of their workload due to faulty fishing nets would be a good-faith demand.

c. that leaves the aggrieved party with no reasonable choice but to succumb to the threat.

(1) The third element of duress is that the wrongful threat must leave the aggrieved party with the absence of reasonable choice except to agree to the contract or modification on which the perpetrator is insisting. This is seldom an issue when what is threatened is a crime or a tort, a criminal prosecution, or a bad faith civil suit, for risking the eventuality of any of those is scarcely a reasonable choice.

(2) Hard cases often arise in the context of economic duress (i.e., threatened breach of contract). Three common situations where this will arise are:

(a) when there are no adequate and reasonably priced substitutes for the services or goods the perpetrator is threatening to withhold;

EXAMPLE: The ship's captain is not in a position to find replacement sailors when already at sea, and so no adequate substitutes would be available.

(b) when the threatened breach would cause the aggrieved party to break his own contracts, especially if there is a prospect of substantial consequential or liquidated damages; or

EXAMPLE: If the purchaser of upsidasium bearings needed for use in the manufacture of turbo-jet engines would, on account of the breach, be forced to breach its contract with an aircraft manufacturer.

(c) when the alternative of acquiescing to the threat and then suing for damages is inadequate to redress substantial harms to the aggrieved party.

EXAMPLE: Where the threatened breach would cause the aggrieved party to renege on its own commitments and thus harm its reputation and opportunities for future business, damages would be inadequate as a remedy.

NOTE A minority of jurisdictions add another element to the requirements for economic duress: the aggrieved party must protest the threatened breach rather than acquiesce without complaint in the demand for additional payment or other benefits with the secret intention of refusing to make the newly promised payment at contract's end. The courts that impose this additional requirement hold that the obligation of good faith requires the aggrieved party to speak up at the time of the threat.

3. **Third-Party Duress**

a. If the wrongful threat is made by a third party, rather than the other party to the contract, the aggrieved party will still have a valid claim of duress unless:

(1) the other party gives value or relies materially on the transaction; and

(2) the other party is proceeding in good faith without reason to know of the duress.

4. **Remedies**

a. Contracts made under physical compulsion are void.

b. Contracts entered into under other forms of duress are voidable at the option of the aggrieved party.

c. The aggrieved party is:

(1) entitled to restitution of any benefits conferred under duress; and

(2) required to return excess value of benefits to the perpetrator.

5. The common law defense of duress can be used in cases arising under the UCC as a supplementary provision.

D. Undue Influence

1. An aggrieved party may avail herself of the defense of undue influence when the circumstances reveal a vulnerable, but not incapacitated, party who succumbs to untoward bargaining tactics and pressures from the other party, where those pressures or tactics fall short of fraud or duress.
2. **Elements**
    a. There are two elements to the defense of undue influence:
        (1) unfair persuasion was used; and
            (a) Although the test for unfair persuasion is one that looks at all of the circumstances, courts have looked in particular to the following indicia of untoward pressure:
                1) discussion of the transaction at an unusual or inappropriate time;
                2) consummation of the transaction at an unusual place;
                3) insistent demands that the transaction or business be finished immediately;
                4) extreme emphasis on the untoward consequences of delaying the transaction;
                5) the use of multiple persuaders against the target of persuasion;
                6) absence of third-party advisers to the target of persuasion; and
                7) statements that there is no time to consult financial advisers or attorneys.
        (2) the other party was vulnerable to such persuasion.
            (a) A vulnerable party can be established in any of the following ways:
                1) where the mental infirmity is due to age or illness but falls short of mental incompetence;
                2) where the vulnerability is due to some recent trauma or event; or
                3) where the vulnerable party is reliant on the other party because of some relationship of trust or confidence with the other party.
3. **Remedies**
    a. Contractual obligations assumed under undue influence are voidable at the option of the aggrieved party.
    b. The aggrieved party is entitled to restitution of any benefits conferred on the other party, but must return the value in excess of those benefits to the other party.

c. Where the vulnerable party suffers undue influence at the hands of a third party rather than the other party to the contract, the aggrieved party has the power to avoid the contract at his option, unless two conditions are met:
   (1) the other party gives value or relies materially on the transaction; and
   (2) the other party is proceeding in good faith without reason to know of the undue influence.

4. Like the other defenses, the common law claim of undue influence is available in cases arising under the UCC as a supplementary provision.

E. Unconscionability

1. Just as with undue influence, the defense of unconscionability may be available when a party uses inappropriate bargaining tactics to take unfair advantage of a vulnerable party. Unconscionability, however, focuses not only on the unfair process but also on the unfair results.
2. **Elements**
   a. There are two elements to a defense of unconscionability. In most jurisdictions, both of the following elements must be proved in order to succeed on a defense of unconscionability. However, where there is an extremely strong showing of one element, the party may be able to succeed on a defense of unconscionability despite a weaker showing of the other element. The elements are:
      (1) **procedural unconscionability**; and
         (a) This element can be met where the bargaining process that produced the contract in question created an absence of meaningful choice for the aggrieved party. The following are circumstances that may establish the absence of a meaningful choice:
            1) near-miss cases;

               EXAMPLE: When a party is vulnerable to the pressure of the other party, such as because of language barriers or advanced age, but the vulnerability falls short of mental incompetence or duress.

               EXAMPLE: When the victim is subjected to misleading or coercive sales tactics that fall short of actual fraud or duress.

            2) absence of bargaining power; and

               EXAMPLE: When the party is forced to accept proposed terms, as may be the case in standard form contracts with "take it or leave it" provisions which sellers and suppliers impose on all customers and that cannot be varied by bargaining, greatly limiting the other party's power to bargain.

EXAMPLE: Where one party is weakened by poverty or language barriers, which greatly limits his ability to shop for alternative terms particularly with respect to necessaries.

3) fine-print terms.

EXAMPLE: Where the contract included complex or arcane terms hidden in the maze of the fine print in a lengthy standard form contract.

(2) **substantive unconscionability**.

(a) The second element of unconscionability is met when the contract terms are unreasonably unfavorable to the aggrieved party.

(b) Typical examples include:

1) grossly excessive price;

EXAMPLE: Where a pay-over-time plan requires the consumer to pay a total sum that is many times the value of the purchased goods, or where a bank charges an overdraft fee that is many times the bank's actual processing costs.

2) grossly disproportional consequences for a minor breach;

EXAMPLE: An add-on clause, pursuant to which a merchant is entitled to repossess multiple household items, including furniture, bedding, and a stereo, when a consumer missed a payment, despite the fact that the consumer had already paid nearly 80% of the monies owed for the various purchases.

3) provisions binding one party but not the other; and

EXAMPLE: An arbitration provision in an employment contract that requires the employee but not the employer to arbitrate any disputes, or that permits the employer but not the employee to amend the provisions of the agreement at will.

4) provisions which are grossly unfair.

EXAMPLE: In Brower v. Gateway 2000 [676 N.Y.S.2d 569 (N.Y. App. Div. 1998)], the court found unconscionable a binding arbitration clause that required consumers pursuing disputes with a merchant to pay a nonrefundable advance fee that exceeded the purchase price of the goods, travel to a distant city for the proceeding, pay the merchant's legal fees in the event of a loss, and file all correspondence in a foreign country.

3. **Remedies**

a. Upon a finding of unconscionability, a court may:

(1) refuse to enforce the contract;

(2) excise the offending clause and enforce the remainder of the contract; or

(3) limit the application of the offending clause as to avoid any unconscionable result.

4. **Application**
   a. The question of whether or not unconscionability is present is a question of law to be decided by the courts.
   b. The question of whether a particular contract or clause is unconscionable is to be determined by the circumstances existing at the time of contract formation, not at the time the dispute arose.
   c. A party claiming or resisting a claim of unconscionability is entitled to present evidence of the allegedly offending provision's commercial setting, as well as its purpose and effect.
      (1) To refuse a party the opportunity to present such evidence before granting summary judgment is a reversible error.

5. **Unconscionability under the UCC**
   a. The defense of unconscionability is specifically recognized as a defense under the UCC, and applies in the same manner as under the common law [§ 2-302].

F. Public Policy

1. The last of the defenses is called the public policy defense. It is a claim that courts should not enforce a contract because doing so would violate or undermine some important public policy.
2. Public policy may be raised as a defense to the enforcement of a contract in the following four contexts:
   a. where the subject matter of the contract itself is specifically prohibited by law;

      EXAMPLE: In most jurisdictions, a contract for prostitution, gambling, or bribery is illegal under the law and, accordingly, unenforceable in court.

   b. where a contract is formed for the purpose of committing a crime or violating a legal regulation;

      EXAMPLE: A contract between an employer and a hired assassin would be a contract for the commission of a crime.

   c. where the contract performance would not constitute a crime, but would constitute a tort; or

      EXAMPLE: A publicist being hired for the express purpose of spreading a defamatory story about a private citizen would be a contract for the commission of a tort.

   d. where the contract performance would violate certain values and freedoms designated by the state or jurisdiction.

      EXAMPLE: A contract that prohibits one party from marrying for an extended period of time would violate the public policy of promoting free and consent-based marriages.

3. **Sources of Public Policies**
   a. **Legislation**
      (1) Legislation is frequently the source of the "policy" invoked under the public policy defense.

      EXAMPLE: Cases involving contracts prohibited by statutory law and cases involving contracts for the commission of a crime or the violation of a legal regulation.

   b. **Judicial Decision**
      (1) Where the subject matter of the contract is not specifically prohibited under law, then the public policy defense may operate to:
         (a) fill gaps where there is no direct legislative warrant on point; and
         (b) in most jurisdictions, promote larger notions of the public good.
      (2) Judicially developed public policies include:
         (a) policies grounded on moral and social values, such as the policy against the impairment of family relationships;
         (b) policies based on economic considerations, such as the policy against restraints of trade; and
         (c) policies designed to protect governmental processes and institutions, such as the policy of protecting the integrity of voting and elections.

         EXAMPLE: A contract under which a private citizen agrees to vote a certain way in exchange for a year's supply of beer would violate the public policy of free and unrestricted exercise of the right to vote.

4. **Operation of the Defense of Public Policy**
   a. The public policy defense is almost invariably invoked as a defense in an action by one of the parties seeking enforcement of a contract against the other. When it is successful, the defendant will win irrespective of whether she was the party who promised to perform the public policy violation or the party paying for it.
   b. The idea here is not that the courts have any special solicitude for defendants, but rather that courts will refuse to play any role whatsoever in the enforcement of contracts violating public policy, with the result that the party attempting to enforce the contract will be out of luck.

      EXCEPTION: An exception to the public policy defense may exist where one of the parties is more egregiously "in the wrong" than the other party. In the language of the courts, in such cases the parties are not *in pari delicto* ("equally at fault"), and the more innocent party may be able to secure restitution of any benefits conferred on the guiltier party despite the fact that the contract itself remains unenforceable.

(1) The *in pari delicto* defense is most commonly available when a particular statute has been enacted to protect a particular class of persons or actions.

EXAMPLE: A debtor may be entitled to restitution of insurance premiums, where the creditor coerced the debtor to purchase credit insurance and there is a statute on point that is designed to protect debtors from such creditor coercion.

c. A contract that is subject to the defense of public policy is not itself void as a matter of public policy. The defense only operates to treat the contract as voidable at the option of the defending party.

5. **Contracts Frequently Falling under the Public Policy Defense**

a. **Noncompetition Agreements**

(1) Many employment contracts, as well as contracts for the sale of a business, contain a provision that prevents one party from competing for a certain period of time or in a certain area. Where this provision is reasonable, the court will generally enforce it.

(a) However, where the noncompete provision imposes an unreasonable geographical barrier, duration, or term, then the enforcement of such a provision may be considered a violation of the public policy of promoting a citizen's freedom to work.

(b) Under the **blue pencil rule**, most jurisdictions remove the offending portion of the noncompetition clause while enforcing the remainder of it.

EXAMPLE: A court may enforce only the first two years of a five-year noncompete clause.

(c) A minority of jurisdictions will hold that the inclusion of such a provision invalidates the entire noncompetition clause.

b. **Sales of Goods via Bribery**

(1) If a contract for the sale of goods was based on bribery by any party, then the public policy defense could be used by the victim of the bribe to make the contract unenforceable.

EXAMPLE: Buyer sues Seller for breach of contract when Seller refuses to supply the specified quantity to Buyer at the agreed-upon price. Seller raises the defense of public policy because after the fact, Seller learns that Buyer bribed Seller's agent with a car in order to secure the unreasonably favorable contract terms.

c. **Sales of Goods Intended for Unlawful Use**

(1) If a contract is for the sale of goods that the seller knows the buyer intends for an unlawful use, then the public policy defense would be available to defeat an action either by the seller seeking payment or by the buyer seeking delivery.

d. **Liability-Limiting Provisions**

(1) When the provisions of a contract would limit a party's liability for tortious behavior by restricting the right of the injured party to pursue claims against the reckless or intentional harms caused by the party, the provision would not be upheld, because to do so would violate public policy.

(a) Provisions that limit liability for negligent (rather than reckless or intentional) tortious conduct are generally permissible.

e. **Unlicensed Goods or Services**

(1) When a contract is for unlicensed goods or services, then the contract may be rendered unenforceable by the public policy defense.

EXAMPLE: An unlicensed contractor could be prevented from recovering payment for his services if the homeowner invokes a public policy defense.

EXCEPTION: Because the homeowner is not *in pari delicto* with the unlicensed contractor, an action by the homeowner against the contractor for shoddy work might survive the public policy defense.

VIII. REMEDIES

A. Monetary Remedies for Breach of Contract

1. Monetary Damages at Common Law

a. A party aggrieved by a breach of contract may be able to recover money damages calculated to protect that party's expectation interest, reliance interest, or restitutionary interest. A party may elect only one of these three remedies.

(1) To compensate a party for her **expectation interest**, the court will calculate money damages designed to put the aggrieved party where she would be if the other party had fully and properly fulfilled the contract terms.

EXAMPLE: A patient with a hand injury contracts with his doctor for hand surgery. The doctor promises him a "100% perfect" hand, but instead, the surgery makes the hand worse. The expectation interest of the patient is measured by the difference between the value of the promised "100% perfect" hand and the value of the hand worsened by surgery.

(2) To protect an aggrieved party's **reliance interest**, a court will calculate the money damages designed to put the aggrieved party in the position she was before the contract was made.

EXAMPLE: A agrees to buy B's car. On the faith of the promise, A pays B a $2,000 down payment for the car and enters a 12-month lease agreement with C for a parking space for $2,400. The reliance interest of A would be $4,400, the amount it would take to compensate A for what he's lost on the faith of B's promise.

(3) To protect an aggrieved party's **restitutionary interest**, a court will calculate money damages designed to return to the aggrieved party the value of the benefit she conferred on the breaching party.

b. **Expectation Damages**

(1) The default rule for the proper measurement of damages in breach of contract cases is the expectation interest of the aggrieved party. This means the aggrieved party will be entitled to the amount that will restore him to the position he would have been in had the contract been fully performed.

(2) The formula for expectation damages is:

	Loss of value of the breaching party's performance
+	any incidental and consequential costs generated by the breach
-	any payments received from the breaching party
-	any costs saved as a result of the breach
=	Expectation Damages of the Aggrieved Party

EXAMPLE: General Contractor repudiates its contract with Subcontractor when Subcontractor is halfway finished with its work under the subcontract. Subcontractor is entitled to seek from the breaching General Contractor an amount equal to: the contract price or the unrealized value of General Contractor's promised performance plus costs associated with storing, insuring, and/or returning materials and equipment secured by Subcontractor in the course of contractual performance (i.e., incidental costs generated by the breach), minus any progress payments already made by General Contractor and minus money Subcontractor may have saved on salaries and equipment rental by not having to complete performance.

(3) **Limitations on Recovery for Expectation Damages**

(a) The aggrieved party may not be able to recover the full amount of expectation damages in the following situations:

1) where the cost of performance greatly exceeds the market value of the performance;

a) **Cost of performance** is the cost that would be incurred in an effort to perform as promised under the contract.

b) **Market value of performance** is the net increase in the market value of finding substitute performance of the contract.

EXAMPLE: In the infamous case of Peevyhouse v. Garland Coal & Mining Co. [382 P.2d 109 (Okla. 1962)], landowners entered into a contract with a coal-mining firm permitting the latter to strip-mine their farmland but requiring the firm to restore the land to its original state once the mining project was complete. When the firm breached by refusing to do the restoration work, there were two ways to measure the resulting expectation damages: the cost of performance (i.e., the costs that would be incurred in an effort to restore the land as promised in the contract), or the net increase in the market value of the property that would be realized if the restorative work had been completed as promised. Because restoration would have cost the mining firm $29,000 but increased the market value of the land by only $300, the court limited the landowners' recovery to the latter figure. This was based on the determination that the restoration work was incidental to the main purpose of the contract (which was a lease to strip-mine the land for coal), the main purpose had been fully performed, and the cost of performance would have been disproportionately costly.

c) Many courts would award cost of performance despite the disparity with market value on the view that expectation damages should be calculated, in the words of the Second Restatement, "on the basis of the value of performance to the injured party himself and not on its value to some hypothetical reasonable person or on some market."

d) Where the breach of the contract is willful and the performance was not incidental to the agreement, damages may be measured by cost of completion despite it being disproportionate to the value of the performance.

EXAMPLE: The plaintiff operated a manufacturing plant which, after decades of operation, the plaintiff decided to close. The plaintiff agreed to convey the structures and equipment to the defendant in exchange for $275,000 and the defendant's agreement to remove the equipment, demolish the structures, and grade the property as specified. The defendant made the cash payment, removed the equipment, and demolished the structures, but did not grade the property as required by the contract. The plaintiff sued for $110,500, constituting the cost of performance. The defendant argued that damages should be limited to $3,000, representing the difference between the fair market value of the property and the price that the plaintiffs sold the property for. The court determined that the performance was part of the main purpose of the contract (rather than incidental), the defendant's breach was willful, and the appropriate measure of damages was the cost of performance, despite the disproportionate difference [American Standard, Inc. v. Schectman, 80 A.D.2d 318 (1981)].

2) where expectation damages cannot be calculated with reasonable certainty;

a) While an aggrieved party does not have to calculate with mathematical precision to receive expectation damages, there must be some reasonable basis for calculation.

b) Doubts in calculations will be resolved in favor of the aggrieved party.

c) Requiring reasonable certainty of expectation damages may leave the aggrieved party uncompensated for losses that cannot be easily valued.

EXAMPLE: A new business is unable to open because of a breach by a key supplier who has not completed promised work. Because there is no proven track record for the new business, it is difficult to establish with any certainty what profits would have been realized had it opened on time.

d) Some jurisdictions apply the "new business" rule and automatically bar recovery, but most jurisdictions will evaluate the facts on a case-by-case basis and award expectation damages if a reasonable calculation is possible (e.g., on the basis of profit records for similarly situated ventures).

3) where damages are unforeseeable; and

a) Under the **Hadley rule**, a breaching party will be liable for general damages (those damages that naturally flow from the breach) but not for special or consequential damages, which are those damages that result from the particular circumstances of the aggrieved party unless, at the time of contracting, the breaching party knew or had reason to know that the consequential damages would result from breach. A common type of consequential damages is lost profits.

b) The Hadley rule operates as another limitation on the right of an aggrieved party to recover expectation damages by denying recovery to the aggrieved party for unforeseeable consequential damages, even though those damages would not have occurred if the breaching party had fully performed on the contract.

c) The rule barring recovery for unforeseeable consequential damages is a default rule, and the parties may opt out of its application to their contract and instead allow liability for all consequential damages whether foreseeable or unforeseeable.

4) where damages can be mitigated.

a) The aggrieved party may not recover for any losses it could have avoided without unreasonable risk, burden, or humiliation.

b) The aggrieved party's duty to mitigate damages is limited to taking reasonable efforts to mitigate. If such reasonable mitigation efforts fail or cause additional expense, then the breaching party will be fully liable.

EXAMPLE: The liability of a breaching buyer of produce would be reduced if the seller permitted the produce to rot after breach rather than selling it to third parties; but if the seller is forced by the breach into a "fire sale" because of the short shelf life of the produce in question, then the breaching buyer will be fully liable for expectation damages—that is, for any difference between what the seller nets from the "fire sale" and what it stood to earn but for the broken contract.

EXAMPLE: The liability of an employer is reduced if an employee dismissed in breach of contract takes an extended vacation rather than seeking other work. But the aggrieved employee need only make reasonable efforts to secure a position that is reasonably equivalent to the job lost and, accordingly, she need not accept substitute work when it: is in a different field; offers significantly lower pay or less desirable terms and conditions of employment than those of the lost job; would entail more burdensome responsibilities than those of the lost job; or would damage the aggrieved party's career prospects (e.g., an A-list movie star would not be required to mitigate damages for a film producer's breach of contract by taking a lesser role in a B-grade film).

EXAMPLE: The liability of a breaching landowner to a construction contractor hired to erect a structure on the property is reduced where the contractor continues the building project after the landowner has repudiated the contract. But the liability of a buyer of goods ordered for special manufacture would not be reduced if the seller continues the manufacturing process after breach in order to finish the goods for possible sale to third parties.

c. **Reliance Damages**

(1) Reliance damages may be available where expectation damages are not available.

(2) The measurement of damages for the reliance interest of an aggrieved party is calculated by determining the amount of money necessary to restore the aggrieved party to the position he was in prior to the contract.

(a) The reliance interest is compensated by the value lost to the breaching party, as well as any other value lost from the aggrieved party's reliance on the breaching party.

(3) The aggrieved party's reliance interest is measured by any expenditures made in preparation for performance or in actually performing, less any loss which the breaching party can prove, with reasonable certainty, that the aggrieved party would have suffered even if the contract had been fully performed.

(4) The most common use of reliance damages arises when the expectation damages would be uncertain or speculative, as where the breach would deprive the aggrieved party of opportunities to enter potential transactions with third parties.

EXAMPLE: Inventor signs a contract with Railroad Co. for shipment of a new stove Inventor plans to display at a manufacturers' convention, and she pays fees to the convention hotel for a room and for display space, as well as an exhibition fee to the convention sponsor. If Railroad Co. breaches the contract by failing to deliver the stove until after the convention, Inventor will be unable to recover damages for opportunities she may have lost due to his inability to showcase the stove, as calculating the probability and value of those opportunities would be too speculative. However, Inventor would be entitled to reliance damages (i.e., a return of Railroad Co.'s fee, plus compensation for the amounts she paid to the hotel and convention sponsor).

d. **Restitutionary Damages**

(1) A party aggrieved by a breach of contract is entitled to restitutionary damages rather than expectation damages at his option. If chosen, the aggrieved party may choose to recover the value of the benefits conferred on the breaching party by the aggrieved party during the course of the contract.

(a) Restitutionary damages are available to both the breaching and aggrieved parties.

(2) The aggrieved party's restitutionary interest will be measured by either:

(a) the reasonable value of the benefit conferred upon the breaching party; or

1) This is measured by the market value of the service(s) rendered, and not the price established by the parties in the contract.

2) The contract price may be admissible as evidence in calculating the restitutionary damages, as evidence of the price of retaining those services on the market.

EXAMPLE: Where General Contractor dismisses Subcontractor halfway through Subcontractor's performance, Subcontractor's restitutionary interest is measured by the market value of the services rendered thus far. The contract price may be admitted as relevant evidence for determining the market value for these services.

(b) the extent to which the breaching party's property has increased in value based upon the aggrieved party's performance.

EXAMPLE: Contractor built a Turkish bathhouse on Homeowner's property. The market value of the services is the cost to Homeowner of hiring another contractor to do the work, which equals $30,000. The value added to Homeowner's property is the net increase in the home's value from the addition of the bathhouse, which equals $20,000. A court calculating Contractor's restitutionary interest could award him either amount, considering what relevant precedents permit and what justice requires.

(3) An aggrieved party is likely to make this election if the restitutionary recovery would exceed the amount recoverable based on her expectation interest, and that situation is most likely to arise in the context of a "losing contract" (i.e., where the expectation interest would be less than zero because the aggrieved party would have actually lost money had the other party not breached).

EXAMPLE: General contractor breaches its contract with Subcontractor when Subcontractor is halfway finished with its work under the subcontract. Subcontractor is entitled to seek from the breaching General either expectation damages or restitutionary damages (i.e., the market value of the services already rendered at the time of breach). Even if Subcontractor had a "losing contract," it is nevertheless entitled to recovery of its restitutionary interest.

(4) In order to secure restitutionary damages, the party seeking the remedy must have conferred some benefit on the other party through either part performance or reliance.

(a) If the aggrieved party has fully performed under the contract, then the aggrieved party is limited to expectation damages.

EXAMPLE: Subcontractor completes contractual performance and General Contractor refuses to pay. Subcontractor has no right to seek restitutionary damages and is entitled to recovery of the contract price only.

e. **Liquidated Damages Provisions**

(1) Parties are free to include among the terms of their contract a **liquidated damages clause** designed to provide for damages of their own choosing in the event of breach.

(2) Such a provision is enforceable if the court finds it to be a valid liquidated damages clause, and unenforceable if the court finds that it constitutes a penalty.

(3) The basic idea here is that the parties are free to establish a regime of "home-made" damages designed to reflect the likely consequences of a breach in a manner suited to the peculiarities of their transaction, but that the parties are not free to threaten to punish a breach with harsh measures designed to give a potentially breaching party no choice but to perform.

(a) A basic axiom of American contract law is that a party has a right either to perform on a contract or to pay damages, and a penalty clause is seen as interfering with that right.

(4) The test for determining whether a clause in a particular contract is a valid liquidated damages provision has three prongs:

(a) Did the parties intend for the clause to operate as a liquidated damages clause or as a penalty?

1) Evidence of specific or camouflaged effort to punish breach would support a claim that the clause was intended as a penalty.

2) Modern decisions downplay the importance of this prong and emphasize the other two.

(b) Was the clause reasonable at the time of contracting in relation to the anticipated harm?

1) The key question is whether there was an anticipated harm that would be difficult to prove or for which no adequate remedy would be available.

EXAMPLE: Repudiation of a commercial lease by an "anchor" tenant in a shopping mall is likely to cause reductions in pedestrian traffic to other stores as well as harm to the mall's reputation and attractiveness as a shopping "destination." Because the extent and monetary value of those harms would be difficult to establish in court, a liquidated damages clause designed to award the mall owner a sum that represents an inexact but reasonable forecast of those harms would be appropriate.

(c) Was the clause reasonable in relation to the harm and losses that actually occurred due to the breach?

EXAMPLE: If the shopping mall tenant repudiates the contract shortly after entering it, and the mall owner is able to secure a substitute "anchor" with minimal delay, a clause guaranteeing the owner significant liquidated damages would be unreasonable in relation to the actual harms caused by the breach.

(5) **Anticipated versus Actual Harm**

(a) When a particular clause satisfies the second prong of the test (it was reasonable at the time of contracting in relation to anticipated harms) but not the third prong of the test (it wasn't reasonable in relation to the harms actually suffered), some courts will uphold the challenged clause as a valid liquidation of damages with the view that a clause that satisfies either one of the prongs will be valid.

1) Those courts would uphold the clause in the example immediately above because it was reasonable in relation to anticipated harms even though it wasn't reasonable in relation to the actual harms caused by the breach.

(b) Other courts, however, will conclude that the clause is a penalty if it specifies damages that are "grossly disproportionate" to the actual harm, even if the clause was reasonable at the time of contracting.

1) Those courts would declare the clause in the example immediately above to be a penalty, because it was excessive in relation to the actual harms, despite the fact that it was reasonable in relation to the harms anticipated at the time of contracting.

(6) The party attempting to show that the liquidated damages clause is actually an unenforceable penalty has the burden of proof.

(a) If the party fails to offer evidence of the unreasonableness of the provision, then the liquidated damages provision will be upheld.

(7) If the court concludes that the liquidated damages clause is, in fact, a penalty, then the clause will be stricken from the contract.

(a) If the clause is stricken from the contract, the aggrieved party is still entitled to recover whatever legal or equitable relief it would be entitled to under law.

2. **Monetary Damages under the UCC**

a. Most of the rules governing remedies under the UCC reflect the same underlying principles that apply in common law cases—in particular, the right of an aggrieved party to expectation damages and the duty of an aggrieved party to mitigate damages—but they differ in their details because they are specifically designed for application to the sales of goods context.

b. **Seller's Remedies**

(1) Upon a buyer's breach of a contract for the sale of goods, the seller is free to cancel the contract and to withhold delivery of any yet to be delivered goods. In addition, the seller may have a right to recover money damages from the breaching buyer.

(2) The nature of the seller's right to recover depends on whether the goods have been delivered.

(a) **Action for the Price**

1) If some or all of the goods have been delivered and accepted, the seller is entitled to collect the contract price for those goods [§ 2-709].

(b) **Damages for Nonacceptance or Repudiation**

1) If some or all of the goods have not been delivered—either because the buyer has rejected them, or in the context of anticipatory repudiation—the seller can recover damages with respect to them.

2) The measure of recovery will depend on whether the seller resells the goods to a third party.

a) **Seller Resells**

i) If the seller resells, he can recover the **contract-resale differential**—that is, the difference between the contract price and the resale price [§ 2-706].

ii) In order for the seller to recover, the resale must be made in good faith and in a commercially reasonable manner.

EXAMPLE: A seller may not make a "sweetheart" deal to sell the goods at a below-market discount to a friend or a relative.

iii) The seller is not accountable to the buyer for any profit made on any resale [§ 2-706(6)].

b) **Seller Does Not Resell**

i) If the seller does not resell, he can recover the **contract-market differential**—that is, the difference between the market value of the goods at the time and place of the promised delivery and the contract price [§ 2-708].

3) **Whether or Not the Seller Resells**

a) Whether or not the seller resells, he is also entitled to recover **incidental damages**—that is, the costs associated with getting stuck with goods the seller thought he had sold as well as the costs of resale.

EXAMPLE: Incidental costs associated with the seller remaining in possession of the goods include such things as storage and insurance. Incidental costs associated with the resale of the goods include costs incurred in the form of new advertisements and sales commissions.

b) However, the seller's damages will be reduced by an amount reflecting expenses avoided on account of the breach.

EXAMPLE: If the seller had expected to pay shipping costs in connection with the original contract, and instead incurs substantial savings by reselling to a local buyer, the seller's recovery will be reduced.

(3) **Lost Profits for Lost Volume Sellers**

(a) In the ordinary case, a seller's profit is built into the contract price and, accordingly, either the contract-market differential (if there is no resale) or the contract-resale differential (if there is a resale) will fully protect the seller's right to that profit in the event of breach by the buyer.

EXAMPLE: If Seller contracts to sell a boat to Buyer, Buyer subsequently reneges, and Seller's resale results in a lower price, Seller will get her anticipated profit by requiring the breaching Buyer to pay the difference between the contract price and the resale price.

(b) A different problem arises if the seller is a volume seller (i.e., if, instead of having a single object to sell, he makes repeated sales of the same goods, such as widgets). When a particular buyer breaches in this context, the seller has a "lost volume" problem—even if he sells the particular widget he expected to sell to the breaching buyer to another customer; but for the breach, at the end of the day, the seller would have made and profited from two sales rather than only one.

1) A **lost volume seller** is one whose supply of goods exceeds the demand for the same; that is, the seller can satisfy all potential buyers who may seek to deal with her.

EXAMPLE: BigBox, an electronics store, purchases from the manufacturer a particular brand of new televisions for $200, and resells them for $400. Buyer visits the store and, after shopping around, decides to purchase one of these new televisions as a gift for a friend. Buyer requests that the television be gift-wrapped, and the parties agree that Buyer will pay for the television two hours later, when he returns to pick up the television after it has been gift-wrapped. Buyer never returns. BigBox, the near the end of the day, sells a television of the same model to another purchaser for the same price. But for Buyer's breach, BigBox would have sold two televisions that day, rather than one.

(c) The UCC accordingly permits lost volume sellers to recover the profit they would have made on the lost sale rather than relegating them to either the contract-market or contract-resale differential.

(d) To recover lost profits, the seller must be able to show:

1) that he could have made the sale to both the breaching buyer and resale buyer;

2) that it would have been profitable for the seller to make both sales; and

3) that he probably would have made the additional sale to the resale buyer even absent the buyer's breach.

c. **Buyer's Remedies**

(1) Upon a seller's breach of a contract for the sale of goods, a buyer can either recover damages or seek specific performance.

(2) There are two ways to measure a buyer's damages under the UCC, and the key factor is whether the buyer has **covered** (purchased replacement goods).

(a) **If Buyer Covers**

1) If the buyer covers, her damage measure is the **contract-cover differential**—that is, the difference between what the buyer would have paid under the contract and what he actually paid to secure cover [§ 2-712(2)].

2) Cover must be made "in good faith and without unreasonable delay" [§ 2-712(1)].

EXAMPLE: An aggrieved buyer cannot purchase substitute widgets from his brother-in-law at premium prices nor wait around until the market price of widgets has skyrocketed and purchase then.

(b) **If Buyer Does Not Cover**

1) If the buyer does not cover, she is entitled to the **contract-market differential**—that is, the difference between what the buyer would have paid under the contract and the market price of the goods at the time the buyer learned of the breach [§ 2-713].

(c) **Whether or Not Buyer Covers**

1) Whether or not the buyer covers, she is also free to seek incidental damages—the costs associated with securing cover—and consequential damages, as discussed earlier [§§ 2-712, 2-713].

2) However, the buyer's damages will be reduced by an amount reflecting expenses avoided because of the breach.

(3) **Difference in Value Damages**

(a) This measure of damages available under the UCC is similar to the common law's expectation damages. It is available if the buyer receives nonconforming goods from the seller. The buyer is entitled to recover damages for nonconforming goods based on the following:

(b) The difference in value damages does not require a showing of foreseeability—only that the goods did not conform to the goods specified in the contract.

	Value of Goods Contracted For
–	Value of Goods Received
=	Buyer's Recovery under Difference in Value Damages

(4) **Deduction of Damages from Price Still Due**

(a) A buyer may deduct all or any part of the damages resulting from the seller's breach of contract from any part of the price still due under the same contract. In order to make the deduction, the buyer must give notice to the seller of her intention to withhold all or part of the price [§ 2-717, cmt. 2].

B. Equitable Remedies

1. The typical remedy for contract claims is to award monetary damages. However, where an award of money damages would be inadequate to compensate the aggrieved party, a court may instead award an equitable remedy.
2. The most common equitable remedies in contracts cases are **specific performance** (which requires the breaching party to take some particular action), **negative injunctions** (which prohibit the breaching party from a particular action), and **rescission** (which amounts to a cancellation of the contract).
3. **Specific Performance**
    a. Specific performance is an extraordinary remedy that is available to order a breaching party's performance only where a monetary award would be inadequate to grant relief to the aggrieved party.
    b. As a practical matter, specific performance is a remedy for paying, rather than performing, parties (e.g., buyers who pay money for goods, purchasers who pay money for real estate, and parties who pay money for services rendered).
        (1) When the paying party breaches, the remedy of money damages will, in the ordinary case, give the performing party the promised money, and so the availability of specific performance is a nonissue.
        (2) When the performing party breaches, however, the paying party may prefer to secure the promised performance itself rather than money damages; this raises the question of whether specific performance is available.
    c. **Cases Where Specific Performance is Generally Available**
        (1) At common law, money damages are presumed to be inadequate when a party is purchasing either:
            (a) unique objects; or

            EXAMPLE: Works of art and precious heirlooms.

            (b) real property.

            EXAMPLE: At common law, Blackacre was presumed to be "unique," and such factors as location, natural resources, climate, and permissible uses justify that characterization even in contemporary real estate markets.

        (2) **Equity Considerations**
            (a) Specific performance is an equitable remedy, and a decision to grant or deny it is, accordingly, a decision for the court and not the jury.
            (b) Whether to grant or deny specific performance is committed to the court's remedial discretion based on the competing equities in particular cases, and is not bound by hard-and-fast rules (such as those governing money damages).
            (c) The court's determination is likely to take into account some or all of the following factors:

1) whether the aggrieved party has **clean hands** (has dealt fairly and in good faith with the breaching party);
2) whether the terms of the contract in question are sufficiently definite;
    a) Because a decree of specific performance is enforceable via contempt, courts are reluctant to issue an order that doesn't give the parties adequate guidance as to the conduct required.
3) whether performance by the aggrieved party can be reasonably assured;
    a) For example, performance could be assured by requiring tender of the aggrieved party's performance as a condition of the breaching party's obligations under the decree.
4) whether the terms of the contract are fair; and
    a) A court may deny specific performance where the underlying exchange is unfair even if the unfairness falls short of unconscionability or other doctrines that would excuse contractual performance altogether by the breaching party.
    b) In some jurisdictions, a party seeking specific performance of a contract for real property must plead and prove adequate consideration, despite the general rule that courts don't police the adequacy of contractual consideration.
5) whether specific performance would be in the public interest.
    a) Specific performance may be denied, for example, where the decree might have anticompetitive results.

d. **Contracts for Which Specific Performance is Not Available**

(1) **Contracts for Personal Services**

(a) Specific performance is not available to require a breaching employee or contractor to perform. Specific performance in such a case would violate the public policy prohibiting involuntary servitude, and it would be difficult to enforce.

(2) **Contracts Requiring Ongoing Cooperation between Parties**

(a) Specific performance is likewise disfavored in the context contracts that are not capable of immediate enforcement. Contracts that require a continuing series or acts or continuing cooperation between the parties for successful performance would present courts ordering specific performance with daunting problems of supervision similar to those in the personal services context.

e. **Sale of Goods Contracts under the UCC**

(1) The UCC liberalizes the rules governing the availability of specific performance for sales of goods in two ways:

(a) Specific performance may be permitted if the goods are unique or in "other proper circumstances" [§ 2-716(1)].

1) Thus, the subject matter of a contract does not have to be unique in order to obtain specific performance; if the buyer has adequately searched but is unable to cover the breach, "other proper circumstances" may be present [§ 2-716, cmt. 2].

(b) Specific performance is available even where ongoing cooperation would be required between the parties (e.g., in output or requirements contracts) so long as the requisite inability of a party to cover can be established.

(2) **Replevin**

(a) The buyer also has a right of **replevin**—which is an action to repossess property—for goods identified in the contract if [§ 2-716(3)]:

1) after reasonable effort, the buyer is unable to cover;

2) the circumstances reasonably indicate that an effort to cover will be unavailing; or

3) if the goods have been shipped under reservation (i.e., the seller has reserved a security interest in the goods) and satisfaction of the security interest in them has been made or tendered.

4. **Negative Injunctions**

a. Negative injunctions are orders by the court prohibiting the breaching party from taking particular action. The limitations that apply to specific performance also apply to negative injunctions. Most commonly, negative injunctions are used to prevent employees from going to work for a competitor or competing with their former employer.

b. The availability depends on whether the former employer is seeking mid-term or post-employment relief.

(1) **Midterm Relief**

(a) When an employee is under contract for a specified period of time and the employee breaches the contract by departing before the end of that period, a negative injunction will be available to prevent the employee from competing directly or indirectly with his former employer if the employee's services are unique or extraordinary.

(b) Most of the cases finding that services meet this test involve professional athletes and entertainers.

1) Although the presence of a specific contractual provision establishing exclusive employment during the period of time in question will aid the employer in securing a negative injunction, most courts will imply such a term for the period of employment specified in the contract.

EXAMPLE: In the famous case of Lumley v. Wagner, an opera singer under contract to sing at Her Majesty's Theatre for a three-month period was persuaded to depart mid-contract to begin a concert series at a competing venue. Because her services were unique and extraordinary, the court granted a negative injunction barring her from performing at any competing venue for the duration of the contract term.

(2) **Post-Employment Relief**

(a) Enforcement of employment contract provisions that prohibit post-employment competition against the employer have become a common source of negative injunctions.

(b) The validity of such noncompetition clauses will depend on three factors:

1) most courts require a significant business justification for enforcing post-employment restraints;

a) An employer's need to protect confidential information would qualify, but some courts will allow little or no justification for enforcing such a provision.

2) most jurisdictions limit the scope of the enforcement of noncompetes to reasonable duration and geographical restrictions; and

a) However, the advent of the information age has prompted courts to broaden the definition of a reasonable geographical restraint, but at the same time, to lessen the amount of time considered to be a reasonable duration of restraint.

3) most courts will issue a negative injunction against a competing employee only if the employment contract contains an express noncompetition agreement, but some courts have granted relief in the absence of such a provision based on the tort theory of inevitable disclosure of trade secrets.

5. **Rescission**

a. Rescission is an equitable remedy that cancels the contract (and forms the basis for restitution). Both parties are placed back where they were before the contract was executed.

b. Rescission of a contract is available:

(1) by consent of both parties;

(2) for mistake (either unilateral or mutual);

(3) for fraud, misrepresentations, and nondisclosures;

(4) for duress or undue influence;

(5) for illegality; or

(6) for failure of consideration (which would also be a material breach).

c. A party seeking rescission must be ready to return to the other party all benefits received.

C. Other Possible Remedies

1. **Promissory Estoppel**

   a. The type of interest a party may recover under a claim of promissory estoppel depends on the jurisdiction in which it brings suit. Courts are split:

      (1) some courts award expectation damages;

      (2) other courts, instead, favor reliance damages; and

      (3) other courts award damages on a case-by-case basis and tailor the remedy to the injustice at issue, where possible.

         (a) In doing so, the court will focus on:

            1) the strength of the proof for each of the individual elements of the claim;

            2) the blameworthiness of the breach;

            3) the extent of the detrimental reliance by the aggrieved party;

            4) the relative positions of the parties; and

            5) the availability of alternative options to granting full enforcement of the promise.

2. **Restitution and Unjust Enrichment**

   a. A party who bestows benefits on another may seek to recover the value of those benefits in an action for restitution. A party aggrieved by a breach of contract may have the option of electing a restitutionary, rather than expectation, recovery. However, there are many other contexts in contract law in which a party may be entitled to restitution pursuant to the policy of avoiding unjust enrichment.

   b. The following are contexts where restitution might be available:

      (1) **Benefits Conferred under a Failed Contract**

         (a) When a party bestows benefits on her trading partner in connection with what turns out to be a "failed" contract (e.g., unenforceable because of the Statute of Frauds or a failed condition, or voidable because of incapacity, fraud, duress, undue influence, or unconscionability), the party bestowing the benefits may ordinarily recover their value via restitution, subject to offset by any benefits received from the other party.

         EXAMPLE: A enters an oral contract to sell land to B, and prior to closing, B makes improvements on the land. If A reneges, B may be unable to enforce the contract because of the Statute of Frauds. However, B is entitled to recover the value of the improvements via an action for restitution.

      (2) **Benefits Conferred by a Breaching Party**

         (a) At common law, the breaching party was not entitled to receive any recovery for the benefits it may have conferred under the contract. The modern rule is that such a recovery is possible.

1) A breaching party may recover the amount of benefit he conferred on the aggrieved party less any damages to the aggrieved party as a result of the breach (otherwise known as the **right of offset**).

EXAMPLE: A works for B under a 12-month contract and, without advance notice, breaches the contract after 11 months in order to accept other employment. A is entitled to restitution of the reasonable value of the services rendered, subject to offset for B's damages—that is, the cost of hiring a replacement for A at the last minute.

(3) **Emergency Benefits Conferred by a Health Care Professional**

(a) The general rule is that a person who bestows benefits without request from the benefiting party is considered a volunteer or officious intermeddler who will not be entitled to any recovery.

(b) However, an exception applies to doctors and other health care professionals who provide emergency health care to a patient who is unable to consent. These health care professionals are entitled to the reasonable value of those services they have rendered, even where their efforts were unsuccessful.

NOTE This exception does not apply to non-medical persons whose life-saving efforts are deemed "gratuitous."

(4) **Benefits Conferred by Mistake**

(a) A party who mistakenly confers benefits to another party may be entitled to restitution. In this situation, the following will be considered:

1) the blameworthiness of the error;
2) whether the recipient was aware of the error in time to prevent it; and
3) whether the recipient availed herself of the benefits at issue.

EXAMPLE: After a hurricane, Owner hires Contractor to perform repairs on his storm-damaged home. Because of confusion caused by damage to street signs and mailboxes, Contractor performs the repairs on the wrong house. Contractor is entitled to restitution from the benefiting homeowner if the latter was aware of Contractor's mistaken efforts and remained silent.

3. **Agreed-To Remedies**

a. Parties to a contract may also contract out of the legal and equitable remedies available under the law, by specifying agreed-to remedies in the contract.

b. These remedies typically take two forms: liquidated damages provisions and provisions limiting or excluding damages.

c. **Provisions Limiting or Excluding Damages**

(1) The parties to a contract may limit or exclude the availability of certain damages. Thus, parties can limit their remedial rights to those provided for in the contract or exclude rights to remedies that they would otherwise be entitled to under law.

(2) There are different types of exclusive remedies provisions, including:

(a) provisions that limit or alter the measure of damages available; and

EXAMPLE: A provision limiting or excluding consequential damages.

(b) exclusive remedies provisions, in which the parties expressly agree that only one remedy, or certain specified remedies, will be available in the event of a breach.

EXAMPLE: A provision that limits the remedy available to the buyer for replacement goods or a "do-over" of services.

(3) Such provisions are enforceable unless they are unconscionable. Under the UCC, limitation of consequential damages for personal injury in the case of consumer goods is *prima facie* unconscionable [§ 2-719(3)].

IX. THIRD-PARTY BENEFICIARIES

A. In General

1. In a typical contract, the parties promise performances to each other. If one party refuses to perform, the other has standing to bring a claim for breach because the parties are in contractual privity. In some contracts, however, one of the parties promises a performance that will benefit a third party (a third-party beneficiary).

   EXAMPLE: In exchange for B's promise of payment, A promises to deliver widgets to C. C is the third-party beneficiary of the contract between A and B.

2. The critical issue in third-party beneficiary law is the circumstances under which the third-party beneficiary has standing to enforce the contract against the promisor.
   a. Under common law, courts traditionally held that a third-party beneficiary did not have standing to sue the promisor because there was no contractual privity between them; however, under contemporary law, the privity requirement has been relaxed and third-party beneficiaries may have standing to sue the promisor for breach, even though the promise was made to the promisee and not to the third-party beneficiary.

B. Classification of the Third-Party Beneficiary

1. The right of an aggrieved third-party beneficiary to bring an action for breach of contract against a breaching promisor or promisee will depend upon the classification of the beneficiary. The First Restatement and Second Restatement each classify beneficiaries differently.
   a. While the two Restatements use different terminology, the practical effect is the same under both nomenclatures.
2. **First Restatement**
   a. The First Restatement placed third-party beneficiaries into one of three categories:
      (1) when a promisee seeks a performance from the promisor that will benefit a third party, and the promisee's purpose is to satisfy a debt or other obligation owed by the promisee to the third party, the third-party beneficiary is a **creditor beneficiary**;

      EXAMPLE: A owes B $100 and enters a contract with C to whitewash C's fence in exchange for C's promise to pay B the $100. B is a creditor beneficiary because A's purpose in contracting with C is to satisfy her debt to B.

      (2) when a promisee seeks a performance from the promisor that will benefit a third party, and the promisee's purpose is to make a gift of that performance to the third party, the third-party beneficiary is a **donee beneficiary**; and

EXAMPLE: Desiring to make a graduation gift to A, B agrees to pay C $100 in exchange for C's promise to whitewash A's fence. A is a donee beneficiary because B's purpose in contracting with C is to make a gift to A.

(3) third parties who will benefit from a promisor's performance as a practical matter, but who may not meet the test for creditor or donee beneficiaries under the First Restatement are **incidental beneficiaries**.

EXAMPLE: A enters a contract with B whereby B is to erect a house on A's land. C owns land next to A, and the value of C's land will be enhanced by the building. C is an incidental beneficiary of B's promise to construct the house, and C has no rights under the contract.

3. **Second Restatement**

a. The Second Restatement eliminates the "creditor" and "donee" beneficiary terminology, and instead puts third-party beneficiaries into one of two possible categories: intended beneficiaries and incidental beneficiaries.

b. **Intended beneficiaries** broadly fall into the same two categories utilized by the First Restatement, where the promised performance will satisfy an obligation of the promisee to pay money to the beneficiary (creditor beneficiaries) and where the promisee intends to give the beneficiary the benefit of the promised performance (donee beneficiaries). Many courts continue to use the older terms, however.

(1) The key factor in determining whether a party is an intended beneficiary is whether the promised performance is intended to benefit the third-party beneficiary. Courts are divided over whether the test for determining intent to benefit requires a mutual intention of the parties (the Second Restatement test) or merely a reasonably apparent purpose of the promisee (the First Restatement test).

EXAMPLE: A hires Attorney B to draft A's will in accordance with A's instructions, which include a wish to make A's stepdaughter, C, a residual heir. Attorney B breaches the contract by neglecting to include the requested provision, and upon A's death, C brings a third-party beneficiary action against Attorney B for his breach. The intention of A to benefit C was "reasonably apparent" to Attorney B and, accordingly, would satisfy the "intent to benefit" test under the First Restatement. But because the benefit to C was a matter of indifference to Attorney B, there would be no "intent to benefit" her under the Second Restatement "intention of the parties" test.

c. **Incidental beneficiaries**, as under the First Restatement, are third parties who will benefit from a promisor's performance as a practical matter, but who may not meet the test for intended beneficiaries under the Second Restatement.

C. Rights of Parties to Enforce the Contract

1. Third-Party Beneficiary's Rights

a. Under both the First and Second Restatement, an incidental beneficiary does not enjoy any right to seek enforcement of the contract from either the promisor or promisee to the original agreement.

b. **Third-Party's Rights against the Promisor**

(1) Any third-party beneficiary, other than an incidental beneficiary, has a right to secure enforcement of the agreement from a breaching promisor.

(a) This applies to creditor and donee beneficiaries under the First Restatement and intended beneficiaries under the Second Restatement.

c. **Third-Party's Rights against the Promisee**

(1) Although a third-party beneficiary has rights against the promisor in connection with the promised performance, she has no rights against the promisee in the event that the performance is not forthcoming.

EXAMPLE: Desiring to make a graduation gift to A, B agrees to pay C $100 in exchange for C's promise to whitewash A's fence. If C fails to whitewash A's fence, A has no recourse against B.

(2) Instead, a third-party beneficiary will only have rights against the promisee resulting from the promisor's failure to perform based on whether or not there is an independent obligation between the promisee and the third-party beneficiary.

(a) Thus, a First Restatement creditor beneficiary can elect to sue either the promisee on the prior obligation between the beneficiary and the promisee or the promisor on the third-party beneficiary contract. However, satisfaction of the claim by one operates as a release of the other's obligation.

(b) Similarly, a Second Restatement intended beneficiary can only sue the promisee if the beneficiary would have fallen into the First Restatement's definition of a creditor beneficiary. That is, the intended beneficiary can only sue the promisor on the third-party beneficiary contract or the promisee if the promisee owes a separate obligation to the beneficiary, which the third-party beneficiary contract was intended to satisfy.

EXAMPLE: A owes B $100 and enters into a contract with C to whitewash C's fence in exchange for C's promise to pay B the $100. In the event of nonpayment, B can elect to sue either A on the preexisting obligation or C as a third-party beneficiary, but payment of the $100 by either A or C will release the other from any further performance obligation to B.

(3) The promisee's preexisting obligations to a creditor or intended beneficiary are not discharged by the formation of a third-party

beneficiary contract under which the promisor promises to fulfill the promisee's obligation to the beneficiary.

EXAMPLE: A owes B $100 and enters a contract with C to whitewash C's fence in exchange for C's promise to pay B the $100. C's obligation to pay B the $100 does not discharge A's preexisting obligation to B.

d. **Vesting of the Right to Sue**

(1) A third-party beneficiary does not automatically have the right to seek enforcement of the contract, or prevent the contract from being modified by the original parties, purely by virtue of the third-party beneficiary contract having been made.

(2) The parties to a contract are free to modify or rescind it by mutual consent, and they may modify or rescind a third-party beneficiary provision without the beneficiary's consent unless and until the beneficiary's rights under the contract have vested.

(a) Once the third-party beneficiary's rights vest, the ability of the original parties to make any future rescissions or modifications will be terminated.

(b) If the third-party beneficiary's rights under the contract vest before he is notified of any modification or rescission of the contract, the modification or rescission will be ineffective.

(3) Vesting occurs with regard to an intended beneficiary when:

(a) the beneficiary brings suit on the matter;

EXAMPLE: A contracts with B to pay B $2,000 in exchange for B doing renovations to C's house. B begins to perform, but ceases midway and informs C that she does not intend to complete the work. A and B agree to modify the original contract to instead have B do the renovation work on A's house, thereby eliminating C from the arrangement. Before being notified of the modification, C sues B to enforce the original contract based on B's anticipatory repudiation. C's filing suit vests his rights in the agreement, and A and B's modification will be ineffective.

(b) the beneficiary changes his position in justifiable reliance on the contractual promise;

EXAMPLE: As a birthday gift for his son B, A hires Contractor C to renovate B's home and advises B of the "gift" at a family party. In reliance on his father's promise, B lets an option expire on a new home he and his wife were intending to purchase. A and Contractor C can no longer modify B's rights under the contract.

(c) the beneficiary manifests his assent to the contract at the request of either the promisee or the promisor; or

EXAMPLE: A owes B $100 and agrees to whitewash C's fence in exchange for C's promise to pay B the $100. A asks B to assent to the contract; once B does so, A and C can no longer modify B's rights.

(d) the rights of the beneficiary have vested under an express term of the contract providing for such vesting.

EXAMPLE: Under the terms of her life insurance policy with Hartford Insurance, A's designations of beneficiaries become irrevocable upon A's demise or adjudication of incompetence. The rights of C, a designated beneficiary, against Hartford Insurance will vest upon the occurrence of either event.

e. **Defenses Available to Promisor**

(1) Because a third-party beneficiary's rights are entirely dependent on the underlying contract, any valid defenses the reneging promisor would have to the enforcement of the contract, such as impracticability, the failure of a condition, or a breach of the contract by the promisee, would also be effective against the beneficiary.

(2) The promisor may not assert defenses based on separate transactions with the promisee, such as a right to setoff arising in connection with a deal unrelated to the contract at issue, unless the contract expressly subjects the rights of the beneficiary to such a claim.

2. **Promisee's Rights against the Promisor**

a. When the promisor does not perform, the promisee has a claim for breach of contract against the promisor.

b. If the promisor's performance is intended to benefit a donee beneficiary, the promisee ordinarily will not have suffered any economic loss for the nonperformance and, therefore, may be unable to recover more than nominal damages. As a result, however, some courts consider the damage remedy inadequate and will order specific performance.

EXAMPLE: Desiring to make a donation to her alma mater, Laurie Lawyer promised to provide legal services to Nellie Merchant, a seller of computer hardware, in exchange for Merchant's promise to provide 100 free laptops to Nutmeg Law School. If Merchant fails to deliver the promised laptops, Lawyer can sue her for breach of contract, but because Lawyer has suffered no economic loss on account of the breach, Lawyer may be able to secure specific performance.

c. If the promisor's performance is intended to benefit a creditor beneficiary, the promisee may secure specific performance of the promisor's obligation.

(1) A claim for money damages would, however, expose the promisor to the possibility of double liability, since the promisor is also liable to the third-party beneficiary. Accordingly, some courts refuse to allow the promisee to recover damages against the promisor unless the promisee has already made payment to the beneficiary to cover the default.

X. ASSIGNMENT OF RIGHTS AND DELEGATION OF DUTIES

A. Assignment of Rights

1. An **assignment** is a transfer of a right to receive a performance under a contract.
2. Assignments typically have three relevant parties in a basic factual scenario: A and B have a valid contract, and B subsequently assigns his rights under the contract to C. In this scenario:
   a. A is the **obligor** (the party with the obligation to perform);
   b. B is the **assignor** (the party who assigned the right); and
   c. C is the **assignee** (the party to whom the right was assigned).

   EXAMPLE: A and B have a contract whereby B agrees to provide services to A in exchange for A's payment. B's right to A's payment may be assigned to C, a third party. Upon assignment, A has a payment obligation to C. In this transaction, B is the assignor, who assigned the right to receive payment; C is the assignee, to whom that right was assigned; A is the obligor, the party with the obligation to perform (here, to make the payment).

3. To make an effective assignment of a contract right [Restatement (2d) of Contracts §§ 324, 327]:
   a. the owner must manifest an intention to make a present transfer of the right without further action by the owner or the obligor; and
      (1) There are no "magic words"—not even an express reference to "assignment"—required to make a manifestation effective.
      (2) Oral assignments are effective unless there is some independent applicable writing requirement, such as an assignment of a right to real property under a contract of sale, which must be in writing under the Statute of Frauds.
      (3) A promise to transfer a currently existing right at a future date is not an effective assignment.
      (4) A promise to transfer a right that the assignor expects to acquire in the future is not an effective assignment.

      EXAMPLE: The statement "I will assign you 10% of the royalties when I obtain them" is not an assignment, as it expresses only an intent to assign in the future.

   b. a manifestation of assent by the assignee is essential, unless:
      (1) a third person gives consideration for the assignment; or
      (2) the assignment is irrevocable by virtue of the delivery of a writing to a third person.
         (a) An assignee who has not manifested assent to an assignment may, within a reasonable time after learning of its existence and terms, render it inoperative from the beginning by disclaimer.

         EXAMPLE: A contracts to buy $200 worth of widgets from B. B delivers the widgets, but requests that A pay C the $200 as a gift, without C's knowledge. When C learns of the gift, she refuses it. The assignment is ineffective due to C's disclaimer.

NOTE An "order" by an obligee directing an obligor to pay the debt to a third party is not an assignment. The most common example of an order is a check, which, under both common law and the UCC, does not operate as an assignment of the drawer's rights against the bank.

4. **Partial Assignments**
   a. A partial assignment is valid. Hence, there can be an assignment of a fraction of the assignor's rights.

      EXAMPLE: If A owes B $10,000 for goods B delivered to A, B may assign his right to $5,000 of that money to C.

   b. When suit is brought, however, all of the parties owning rights after the assignment must be joined in the action, unless joinder is not feasible and it is equitable to proceed without joinder.

5. **Rights to Be Assigned**
   a. The general rule is that all rights are assignable, subject to the following exceptions:
      (1) a right is not assignable if the assignment would materially alter the risks to or obligations of the other party to the contract;

      EXAMPLE: A and B are parties to a requirements contract under the terms of which A is obligated to supply B with B's monthly requirements for widgets. B's rights under the contract are not assignable to C if C's monthly requirements would greatly exceed B's.

      (2) a right is not assignable if the obligor has a personal interest in rendering the performance in question to the obligee and not to a third party;

      EXAMPLE: Nanny A's obligation under a contract to provide child-care services to B's family is not assignable to another family.

      (3) a right is not assignable if assignment would materially impair the obligor's chance of obtaining return performance or materially reduce the value of that return performance to the obligor;
      (4) a right is not assignable if assignment would violate applicable law or public policy; and

      EXAMPLE: A state statute prohibiting assignment of wages.

      (5) a right is not assignable if assignment is prohibited by the contract. (Note that such provisions are strictly construed in both scope and effect.)
         (a) Although there is older precedent invalidating an assignment when the contract expressly states that attempted assignments are "void," most courts will treat an assignment in violation of contractual restriction as a breach of contract by the assignor—making her liable for any damages to the

obligor—but not as a basis for nullifying the obligor's performance obligation to the assignee.

(b) Absent contractual language or circumstances suggesting a contrary intention of the parties, a contractual prohibition against "assignment of the contract":

1) will bar a delegation of contractual duties but not an assignment of contractual rights;

2) will not apply to:

a) rights that accrue to the assignor as a result of a breach of contract by the obligor; or

EXAMPLE: If A agrees to sell and B agrees to buy widgets under a contract prohibiting assignment, and A fails to deliver the promised widgets, giving rise to a claim for breach by B, B can assign his rights upon breach to C.

b) rights that accrue to the assignor upon complete performance by the assignor; and

EXAMPLE: If A agrees to sell and B agrees to buy widgets under the terms of a contract prohibiting assignment, and A delivers the promised widgets, A can assign her rights to B's payment to C.

3) can be invoked by the obligor (to resist making performance to the assignee) but not by the assignor (in an action brought by the assignee).

NOTE An offer cannot be assigned, although an option can be.

EXAMPLE: If A has agreed to sell land to B and B has paid consideration to keep the offer open for six months, B can assign the option to C.

EXAM TIP The right of a partner to share in the management of the partnership is not assignable, but the right to profits and to the partner's share in a dissolution is assignable.

6. **Assignment for Value Contrasted with Gratuitous Assignment**

a. An **assignment for value**, where the assignee acquires the assignor's contractual right(s) in exchange for payment or a promise thereof to the assignor, is valid against the obligor and cannot be revoked by the assignor, although it may be modified like any other contract via mutual consent of the parties.

b. A **gratuitous assignment**, where the assignor assigns contractual rights to the assignee without consideration for such transfer, has the following legal effects:

(1) A gratuitous assignment is valid and binding against the obligor, who cannot raise the absence of consideration between the assignor and the assignee as a defense to any breach of his obligations to the assignee.

(2) Between the assignor and the assignee, the law of gifts governs the question of whether the assignor can revoke the assignment. A gift requires that there be donative intent and delivery.

(a) Because the assignment is a transfer of legal rights under a contract, it is impossible to physically deliver an intangible right. However, delivery of something representative or symbolic of an intangible right, such as a savings account book, is held to be sufficient to meet the delivery requirement.

(3) Even if there is no delivery, the assignment becomes irrevocable once payment of the obligation is made to the assignee.

(4) The assignor will be estopped from revoking the assignment if the assignee acts to his detriment in reliance upon the assignment.

7. **Rights and Obligations of the Parties after Assignment**

a. **Rights of Assignee against the Obligor**

(1) The basic rule is that:

(a) an assignee gets whatever rights to the contract her assignor had; and

(b) the assignee takes subject to whatever defenses the obligor could have raised against the assignor, such as a lack of consideration, incapacity, fraud, duress, or mistake.

(2) **Payment to Assignor**

(a) If the obligor pays the assignor, this defense can be raised against the assignee, provided that payment was made before notice of the assignment was given to the obligor.

(b) Once notice of the assignment is given, payment to the assignor is no defense.

(c) If the obligor doubts whether the assignment was made, he can pay the money into court and interplead the assignor and assignee.

(3) **Setoffs and Counterclaims**

(a) If the obligor has a right of setoff that could be raised against the assignor, such right can always be raised against the assignee if the alleged setoff arises out of the same transaction.

(b) If, however, the setoff arises out of a separate transaction, it is available against the assignee only if the transaction which gave rise to the setoff arose before notice of the assignment was given to the obligor.

(c) The obligor and the assignor may agree to an adjustment of their rights without consent of the assignee up until the time that the assignee has given notice of the assignment to the obligor.

(4) **Waiver of Defenses**

(a) If one of the original parties to the contract agrees that she will not raise defenses against an assignee in the event that the rights are assigned, the agreement is enforceable with two limitations:

1) defenses that are in the nature of "real defenses" under Article 2 of the UCC can still be raised; and

a) These defenses include infancy, other incapacity that voids a contract, fraud in the execution, duress (when it removes the parties' capacity to contract), discharge in bankruptcy, and any other discharge of which the assignee has reason to know.

2) the agreement not to raise defenses is invalid if the obligor who signed the waiver was the buyer or lessee of consumer goods.

b. **Rights of Assignee against Assignor**

(1) Unless a contrary intention is manifested, one who assigns or purports to make an assignment for value impliedly warrants to the assignee:

(a) that he will do nothing to defeat or impair the value of the assignment and has no knowledge of any fact that would do so;

(b) that the right as assigned actually exists and is not subject to any limitations or defenses against the assignor other than those stated or apparent at the time of the assignment; and

(c) that any writing evidencing the rights that are being delivered to the assignee to induce her to accept the assignment is genuine.

NOTE An assignment does not, in and of itself, operate as a warranty that the obligor is solvent or that the obligor will perform his obligation.

c. **Rights among Successive Assignees**

(1) A problem of rights among successive assignees may arise when the assignor, who is owed money by the obligor, assigns her right to the money to the first assignee, and then later assigns the same right to a second assignee. The assignor is liable to both assignees for assigning the same right twice.

(2) However, if the assignor is bankrupt or has fled the jurisdiction and both assignees attempt to collect from the obligor, the majority rule is that the first assignee prevails.

(a) There are various exceptions to the majority rule. In several jurisdictions, and under the Second Restatement, a subsequent assignee who has paid value and took the assignment in good faith will prevail if he [Restatement (Second) of Contracts § 342]:

1) obtains payment from the obligor;

2) recovers a judgment on the debt;

3) enters into a new contract with the obligor; or
4) receives delivery of a tangible token or writing from the assignor, the surrender of which is required by the obligor's contract.

B. Delegation of Duties

1. A **delegation** occurs when a third party agrees to satisfy a performance obligation owed by one of the parties to a contract.
2. Delegations typically have three relevant parties in a basic factual scenario: A and B have a valid contract, and B subsequently delegates duties under the contract to C. In this scenario:
   a. A is the **obligee** (the party for whom the performance obligation is owed);
   b. B is the **obligor** (the party with a performance obligation), and is also the **delegator** (the party who delegated his performance to a third party); and
   c. C is the **delegatee** (the party to whom the performance obligation was delegated).
3. **Rights of the Obligee against the Delegator**
   a. A delegation does not relieve the delegator from her obligations under the contract. Despite the delegator's delegation to the delegatee of the performance obligation owed to the obligee, the delegator remains liable for the performance.
      (1) Thus, while an assignment of rights effectuates a transfer of those rights to a third party (upon assignment, the assignee and not the assignor has rights under the original contract), a delegation of duties does not operate as a "transfer" of those duties from the delegator to the delegatee.
   b. **Novation**
      (1) If there is a novation, the delegator is relieved from the obligations under the contract. This requires a clear promise by the obligee to release the delegator in return for the liability of the delegatee.
      (2) Simple assent to the delegation is not enough to effectuate a novation; there must also be a promise to release the delegator.
4. **Liability of the Delegatee**
   a. When the delegatee has agreed to perform the delegator's contract obligations, he is liable to the delegator if he does not do so.
   b. Under the third-party beneficiary theory, the delegatee is also liable to the obligee, because the obligee is an intended beneficiary of the promise made to the delegator.

   EXAMPLE: Joe Plumbing Co. enters a contract to provide plumbing services for Mondo Condo Association and subsequently hires a plumbing subcontractor, Elite Plumbers Inc., to perform the services in question. If Elite Plumbers Inc. fails to perform the delegated duties, it would be liable for breach of contract to both Joe Plumbing and Mondo

Condo. Elite Plumbers would be liable to Mondo Condo because it is a third-party beneficiary of the Joe Plumbing-Elite Plumbers contract.

5. **Delegable Duties**
   a. The general rule is that all obligations can be delegated.
   b. The exceptions fall into the following two categories:
      (1) when the performance in question is personal and the recipient must rely on qualities such as the character, reputation, taste, skill, or discretion of the party who is to render the performance; or

      EXAMPLE: Nanny A is under contract to provide childcare services to B's family. Her performance obligation cannot be delegated to a third party.

      (2) when the contract prohibits delegation.
         (a) Unlike prohibitions against assignments, contract provisions barring delegation are fully enforceable.
   c. The effect of a party's attempt to delegate nondelegable duties differs depending on whether the contract is governed by the common law or the UCC.
      (1) At common law, an attempted delegation of a nondelegable duty operates as an immediate breach of the contract and gives the other party an immediate right to sue.
      (2) Under the UCC, the other party may treat any assignment which delegates performance as creating reasonable grounds for insecurity, and the other party has a right to demand adequate assurances from the assignee without prejudicing his rights against the assignor [§ 2-210(5)].

KAPLAN BAR REVIEW

Criminal Law

TABLE OF CONTENTS

I. GENERAL PRINCIPLES

Classifying Crimes....316
Elements of Crimes....318

II. HOMICIDE

In General....323
Murder....326
Manslaughter....333

III. OTHER CRIMES AGAINST THE PERSON

Criminal Battery....337
Criminal Assault....338
Mayhem....339
Kidnapping....340
False Imprisonment....340
Rape....341
Statutory Rape....343
Other Crimes against the Person....343

IV. CRIMES AGAINST PROPERTY

Theft Crimes....344
Theft by Trespass, Force, or Threat....344
Theft by Fraud, Deceit, or Misrepresentation....350
Other Theft-Related Crimes....352
Crimes against the Habitation....355
Possession Offenses....359

V. INCHOATE CRIMES

Introduction....362
Solicitation....362
Attempt....363
Conspiracy....365

VI. PARTIES TO CRIME AND ACCOMPLICE LIABILITY

Accomplice....369
The Common Law Approach....371

VII. DEFENSES

Types 372
Excuse Defenses 372
Justification Defenses 376
Other Considerations 381

I. GENERAL PRINCIPLES

EXAM TIP Unless otherwise instructed, directly or indirectly, applicants should apply MODERN (majority) rules to Criminal Law questions on the MBE®. In most cases, the common law rule and the modern rule are the same. Where the outline indicates that the modern majority rule is NOT the common law rule (e.g., burglary, conspiracy, larceny), applicants should apply the modern majority rule on the exam.

A. Classifying Crimes

1. Felonies versus Misdemeanors

a. This classification scheme focuses on the punishment that may be imposed.

b. A **felony** is a crime punishable by death or by imprisonment for more than one year.

(1) At common law, burglary, arson, robbery, rape, larceny, murder, manslaughter, and mayhem were considered felonies.

c. A **misdemeanor** is a crime punishable by imprisonment for no more than one year or by a fine only.

(1) At common law, crimes not considered felonies were deemed misdemeanors.

2. *Malum Prohibitum* versus *Malum in Se*

a. This classification scheme focuses on the nature of the criminal act.

b. ***Malum prohibitum*** refers to criminal conduct that is wrongful only because it violates a statute (e.g., illegal drug use, driving without a license, or failing to register a firearm).

c. ***Malum in se*** refers to conduct that is deemed to be inherently wrongful (e.g., murder, rape, robbery, battery, or larceny).

3. Classification Based on Intent

a. This classification scheme focuses on the mental state of the criminal defendant at the time of the alleged crime.

b. A **specific intent crime** is a crime in which the defendant's guilt requires proof that the defendant intended to bring about a specifically prohibited harm.

c. A **general intent crime** is a crime in which the defendant's guilt requires proof that the defendant committed a criminal act while possessed of a generally bad state of mind.

(1) A person whose criminal acts are reckless or criminally negligent is possessed of a generally bad state of mind even though that person does not intend to bring about a specific harm.

(a) **Criminal negligence**, also called gross or culpable negligence, requires negligence that causes a greater risk of harm than ordinary negligence, or ordinary negligence that occurs where a defendant is consciously aware of the risk. It is more than ordinary tortious negligence.

(2) A person who intentionally commits a criminal act without also intending to bring about a specific harm is said to possess a generally bad state of mind.

d. A **strict liability crime** is a crime in which the defendant's guilt requires proof only that the defendant voluntarily engaged in conduct that is prohibited by statute. There is no particular mental state that must also be proven.

EXAMPLE: State A has a statute that makes having sex with a minor under the age of 17 a strict liability crime. Joe meets Sarah in a bar and assumes that she is 21 because 21 is the drinking age in State A. Sarah also tells Joe that she is 21, and nothing about her appearance suggests she may be lying. She also presents to Joe a completely convincing piece of false identification that states a birth date that would make her 21. However, in reality, Sarah is only 15. If Joe has sex with her, he is guilty of violating the State A statute.

e. A **malice crime** is a crime in which the defendant acts intentionally or with reckless disregard of an obvious or known risk that the particular harmful result will occur.

CLASSIFICATION OF CRIMES

Specific Intent Crimes	General Intent Crimes	Malice Crimes	Strict Liability Crimes
• Attempt • Solicitation • Conspiracy • Larceny • Larceny by Trick • False Pretenses • Embezzlement • Forgery • Burglary • Assault • Robbery • Intent-to-Kill Murder • Voluntary Manslaughter	• Battery • Rape • Kidnapping • Involuntary Manslaughter • Depraved-Heart Murder • False Imprisonment	• Arson • Common Law Murder	• Regulatory Offenses (e.g., traffic violations, vehicle offenses, or administrative statutes) • Public Welfare Offenses (e.g., selling alcohol to minors, or other regulations of firearms, food, and drugs) • Morality Crimes (such as statutory rape, or bigamy)

EXAM TIP If, on the exam, you encounter a criminal activity that does not appear to involve specific intent, the malice standard, or strict liability, and the question does not indicate or supply a mental state requirement, you should assume that for criminal culpability, general intent would be required. General intent is the "catch-all."

B. Elements of Crimes

1. ***Actus Reus*** **(Guilty Act)**

   a. In general, a prosecutor will satisfy this element of a crime by showing that the defendant committed the "guilty act" voluntarily.

      (1) Habitual acts that one is simply "unaware of" are considered conscious and voluntary.

      EXAMPLE: A chain smoker who lights a cigarette in a no-smoking area without realizing it can be successfully prosecuted.

      (2) Acts that are reflexive, convulsive, or performed while unconscious are deemed to be involuntary and are insufficient to satisfy this element.

      (3) Mere bad thoughts, unaccompanied by action, will always be insufficient to satisfy this element.

   b. In rare instances, a prosecutor will satisfy this element of a crime by showing a defendant's voluntary omission to act in circumstances where the defendant had a legal duty to act.

      (1) An omission to act can be the basis of a guilty verdict only if the defendant:

         (a) had a legal duty to act; and

         (b) was physically able to perform the act.

      (2) A legal duty to act may arise in the following ways:

         (a) by statute (e.g., failure to file a tax return);

         (b) by contract (e.g., failure of a lifeguard, nurse, or guide on a hiking or river-rafting expedition to rescue);

         (c) based upon a relationship (e.g., a parent for a child or a spouse for a spouse);

         (d) where a voluntary undertaking is begun (e.g., unreasonable abandonment of a rescue that could worsen a victim's plight is sufficient, even if done by a Good Samaritan); or

         (e) where someone creates a risk of peril to another.

         EXAMPLE: If a defendant pushes a victim into a swimming pool as a joke, but then realizes that the victim can't swim when the victim begins to drown, the defendant can be prosecuted for murder for failing to throw the victim a life preserver or otherwise trying to rescue the victim.

   c. Under the principle of vicarious liability, a prosecutor may satisfy the *actus reus* element of a crime by showing that the defendant was responsible for the criminal acts of another party.

2. ***Mens Rea*** **(Guilty Mind)**

   a. Except for strict liability crimes, a prosecutor must show that, concurrent with the "guilty act," the defendant acted with a "guilty mind."

(1) **Concurrence** requires a showing that the criminal act occurred while the defendant was possessed of the requisite criminal state of mind.

EXAMPLE: Common law burglary is the unlawful breaking and entering of the dwelling of another at night with the intent "to commit a felony or larceny therein." If a defendant breaks into a house to escape from the rain, and then, having already entered the dwelling, decides to steal a valuable item from the dwelling before leaving, this is not burglary. The intent to steal was formed after the entry, and so the "guilty act" (breaking and entering) did not occur at the same time that the defendant possessed the requisite "guilty mind" (intent to commit larceny). Absent the concurrence of burglary's *actus reus* with its *mens rea*, there is no burglary.

(2) Strict liability crimes have no *mens rea* element.

b. **Types of *Mens Rea***

(1) A person acts **purposely** when that person acts with a conscious motivation or desire to bring about a specific result.

(2) A person acts **knowingly** when that persons acts with knowledge or substantial certainty that the action will produce a certain result.

(3) A person acts **intentionally** when that person acts purposely or knowingly.

(4) A person acts **willfully** when that person acts purposely or knowingly and with moral turpitude.

(a) While intentional acts may be committed with moral turpitude, willful acts are always characterized as such.

(5) A person acts **recklessly** when that person acts with conscious disregard of the substantial and unjustifiable risk created by the action.

(a) Reckless conduct involves a gross deviation from the conduct of law-abiding persons.

(6) A person acts in a **criminally negligent** manner when that person should have known of the high degree of risk created by the action.

(a) While reckless conduct requires awareness of the risks created, criminally negligent conduct does not.

(b) Criminally negligent conduct is more unreasonable than ordinarily negligent behavior, and it is less deviant than reckless, wanton behavior.

c. **The Doctrine of Transferred Intent**

(1) The **transferred intent doctrine** operates when a defendant intends criminal conduct against one party, but instead harms another party.

(2) Pursuant to this doctrine, the defendant's mental state as it pertained to the intended victim can be used to satisfy the *mens rea* element of the crime committed against the actual victim.

(3) This doctrine applies only to completed crimes, and not to attempt crimes.

EXAMPLE: A defendant fired a gun with an intent to kill. The shot missed the intended victim, and nearly hit an unintended victim. The defendant is guilty of only one count of attempted murder—the attempted murder of the intended victim. Because the transferred intent doctrine does not apply to attempt crimes, the defendant will not also be guilty of attempted murder of the unintended victim.

3. **Causation**

a. For crimes that require that the criminal act bring about a specifically prohibited harm, the defendant's conduct must be both the actual and proximate cause of that harm.

b. **Actual Cause**

(1) Actual cause (also called cause-in-fact) may be satisfied by any of three tests.

(2) **But-For Causation**

(a) If the criminal result would not have occurred absent the defendant's act, then the defendant's act is the actual cause of the criminal result.

(b) In other words, "but for" the defendant's actions, the criminal result would not have occurred.

(3) **Substantial Factor Test**

(a) When there are multiple causes or multiple parties responsible for the criminal result, courts will still find a defendant criminally responsible if the defendant's act was a substantial factor causing the criminal result.

EXAMPLE: D1 stabs the victim in the heart with a knife. Simultaneous with this stabbing, D2 shoots the victim in the head. Medical testimony conclusively establishes that either the knife or bullet wound alone was sufficient cause to instantly kill the victim. Both D1 and D2's act can be considered the actual cause of the victim's death.

(4) **Acceleration of Result**

(a) When a defendant's conduct speeds up or hastens an inevitable death, even by a very brief amount of time, the defendant is considered an actual cause of the victim's death.

EXAMPLE: D1 shoots the victim in the chest. D2 then runs over the victim with a car, killing the victim instantly. Medical evidence establishes that the victim would have died from the gunshot wound, but that she died more quickly as the result of being run over. Both D1 and D2 are substantial factors, and D2 is also an accelerating factor.

c. **Proximate Cause**

(1) **Proving Proximate Cause**

(a) In crimes involving criminal negligence or recklessness, a finding of proximate cause requires a showing that the resultant harm was within the risk created by the defendant's conduct.

(b) In crimes involving an intent to bring about a prohibited result, a finding of proximate cause requires a showing that the resultant harm is sufficiently similar to that which was intended.

(2) **Intervening Causes**

(a) When an intervening event occurs between the defendant's conduct and the criminal result of that conduct, the question arises as to whether the defendant's responsibility for that result is superseded, or cut off, by that intervening event.

(b) **Foreseeable Intervening Causes**

1) If an intervening cause is foreseeable, it is not superseding and the defendant remains criminally responsible for the resulting harm.

2) Foreseeable intervening causes include the following:

a) a third party's ordinary negligence;

b) a victim's special sensitivities or vulnerabilities, even if unknown to the defendant; and

EXAMPLE: The victim is a hemophiliac, or suffers from another medical condition causing his level of harm to be increased.

c) conduct by a victim or third party that is dependent on or responsive to the defendant's conduct, so long as it is not an abnormal response.

EXAMPLE: During a robbery, the defendant severely beat the victim, including major blows to the victim's head, before the defendant fled the scene. The victim got into her car and started to drive to a nearby hospital. However, the victim had suffered a concussion which, combined with blood loss, caused the victim to pass out. The victim's car went off the road and into a tree, and the victim died from the car crash. It is established at trial that, had the victim called an ambulance and received some on-site care, she would have survived. Because the victim's actions were not an abnormal response to the defendant's conduct, the defendant will still be responsible for the victim's death.

(c) **Unforeseeable Intervening (Superseding) Causes**

1) If an intervening cause is unforeseeable, it is superseding, and the defendant is relieved of criminal responsibility for the harm caused.

EXAMPLE: The defendant sees the victim on an ocean pier and begins shooting at him. In order to avoid harm, the victim dives into the ocean. However, the currents are unexpectedly strong, and the victim drowns. This is not an abnormal response to the defendant's conduct, and therefore would be considered foreseeable. The defendant is the proximate cause of the victim's death.

2) Unforeseeable intervening causes include the following:

a) a third party's criminally negligent or reckless conduct; and

b) conduct by a victim or third party that is coincidental or independent of the defendant's conduct.

EXAMPLE: A bank customer is shot in the toe by the defendant during a robbery. While waiting for the EMT to dress the wound and transport her to the hospital, the bank customer is killed by a serial killer who happens to be walking past the bank. The serial killer is unrelated to the robbery. This is not foreseeable, and the independent intervening cause superseded the defendant's act and broke the causal connection to the victim's death. The defendant will not be considered the proximate cause of the victim's death.

II. HOMICIDE

A. In General

1. A **homicide** results when a human being unlawfully causes the death of another human being.
   a. The killing of another human being is not always criminal.
      (1) A death that results from another person's ordinary negligence will subject that person to tort liability, but not criminal punishment.
      (2) A death that results from another person's conduct in circumstances that are fully exculpatory (e.g., where the killing was justified as an act of self-defense) is deemed a lawful—not criminal—killing.
   b. Homicides are criminal when the killer acted with a criminal state of mind (*mens rea*) and without any legal justification or excuse that would fully exculpate the killer's conduct.
2. In criminal law, homicides are typically categorized in two different ways.
   a. Homicides can be classified as either malicious (murders) or not malicious (manslaughters).
   b. Homicides can also be classified as either intentional or unintentional.
3. ***Actus Reus***
   a. For purposes of proving homicide, a prosecutor must show that the defendant's act caused the death of another living person.
      (1) Criminal liability for a homicide usually requires that the defendant's conduct be the actual cause of another person's death.
      (2) Criminal liability for a homicide always requires that the defendant's conduct be the proximate cause of another person's death.
   b. **Actual ("But For") Cause**
      (1) For purposes of **actual** (or "but for") **causation**, a prosecutor need only show that the defendant's actions contributed to or hastened the victim's death.

      EXAMPLE: A defendant is on trial for the death of a terminally ill patient. The defendant had disconnected life support from this patient, and the patient died more quickly as a result. This defendant's conduct constitutes an actual cause of the patient's death.

      EXAMPLE: A defendant is on trial for the death of a shooting victim. The defendant had shot the victim in the shoulder, causing a serious, but not life-threatening, injury. Shortly thereafter, another person attacked the victim with a knife. The victim's stab wounds were not, by themselves, life-threatening. However, the combination of the bullet and knife wounds caused excessive bleeding, which proved fatal to the victim. Here, both the defendant's conduct and the other attacker's conduct are actual causes of the victim's death.

EXAMPLE: A defendant stabbed a victim, causing an injury that would usually not be life-threatening. However, the victim had hemophilia. As a result, the stabbing proved to be fatal. Admittedly, but for the victim's preexisting medical condition, the victim would not have died. Nevertheless, it is also true that but for the defendant's conduct, the victim would not have died. Consequently, the defendant actually caused the victim's death. (As with defendants in a civil action, criminal defendants take their victims as they find them.)

(2) **Exceptions to the "But For" Requirement**

(a) A defendant who was an accomplice to the killer can be guilty of a homicide even though only the killer actually caused the victim's death.

(b) A defendant who committed or attempted to commit an inherently dangerous felony can be guilty of a felony murder even though it was a co-felon (or in some cases, a non-felon) whose actions actually caused the victim's death.

(c) When the reasonably foreseeable consequence of a conspiracy is a homicide, all members of the conspiracy can be found guilty of the homicide, regardless of which of the conspirators actually caused the victim's death.

c. **Proximate (Legal) Cause**

(1) When a victim's death is a foreseeable consequence of the defendant's conduct, the defendant's conduct is deemed to be a proximate cause of that death.

(2) For purposes of establishing proximate cause, prosecutors need only show that the victim's death was the "natural and probable" consequence of the defendant's conduct; they do not need to show that the defendant foresaw the exact chain of events that resulted in the victim's death.

EXAMPLE: From outside a ballroom window, a defendant aimed and fired a rifle at a crowd that had gathered inside for an event. The defendant had no experience handling firearms, and so the bullet went astray, hitting the top of the chandelier hanging over the middle of the ballroom. The chandelier then fell from the ceiling and crashed on top of an elderly guest. The guest's injuries proved to be fatal. While this defendant may not have foreseen this exact chain of events, it is still the case that a foreseeable consequence of shooting a rifle at a crowd of people is that the bullet will hit someone or something with fatal consequences. Here, the bullet hit the chandelier, causing it to fall and kill a guest. Thus, this defendant will be deemed to have proximately caused the guest's death.

(3) When an intervening act occurs that is outside the universe of "foreseeable" events caused by the defendant's conduct, such an intervening act will sever the chain of proximate causation.

EXAMPLE: Same basic facts as above, only this time, the bullet missed the chandelier and simply struck the far wall of the ballroom, harming no one. However, when the bullet shattered the ballroom window, the crowd inside rushed out of the ballroom into the parking lot. In the panic to evacuate, a guest was knocked to the ground and stepped on by many others, causing injuries to the guest which proved fatal. Because it is foreseeable that, after shooting a firearm into a crowd indoors, the crowd would then rush to leave the building, the defendant will be considered the proximate cause of the guest's death.

EXAMPLE: Same basic facts as above, only this time, the entire crowd evacuated without injuries. Shortly thereafter, a drunk driver drove into the parking lot and struck a light post. When the post fell over, it crashed on top of a guest's head, causing a fatal injury. Here, the drunk driver's collision with a light post is not a "natural and probable" consequence of shooting a rifle into a crowd. Thus, on these facts, the defendant will not be deemed to have proximately caused the guest's death.

(4) At common law, the proximate cause of a person's death could not be the conduct of a defendant if that conduct occurred more than one year and one day before the death. However, the majority of modern jurisdictions have done away with this rule.

d. **Miscellaneous Considerations**

(1) The *actus reus* may be a voluntary act, an involuntary act arising from a voluntary act (such as when a person who has frequent seizures kills someone as a result of having a seizure while driving a car), or an omission to act when there is a legal duty to act.

(2) For purposes of homicide, the defendant's conduct must have caused the death of another living person.

(a) At common law, a living person was one "born alive" and so would not include a fetus.

(b) Conduct inflicted upon a person already dead cannot be the basis of a homicide conviction.

(3) **Suicide**

(a) Persons who commit suicide have not committed a homicide because their conduct did not cause another person's death.

(b) A defendant who persuaded or aided another to commit suicide can be charged and convicted of a homicide.

4. ***Mens Rea***

a. For purposes of proving homicide, a prosecutor must show that, contemporaneous with the defendant's guilty act, the defendant was possessed of a guilty mind.

b. The different types of homicide are mainly distinguishable by their different *mens rea*.

(1) The *mens rea* for the different types of murder are all characterized by malice; the presence of malice is what distinguishes murder from manslaughter.

(2) The presence or absence of an intent to kill does not distinguish murder from manslaughter; some intentional killings qualify only as manslaughters and some unintentional killings qualify as murders.

c. **Proving Intent to Kill**

(1) An **intent to kill** exists when a defendant purposely or knowingly kills—that is, when the defendant consciously desires to kill another person or makes the resulting death inevitable.

(2) Under the **deadly weapons doctrine**, the finder of fact may infer an intent to kill when the defendant intentionally uses any instrument that, judging from its manner of use, is calculated to produce death or serious bodily injury.

EXAMPLE: At trial, a defendant admits to violently swinging a baseball bat at the victim's head. However, according to the defendant's testimony, the defendant intended to only slightly injure the victim. Despite this testimony, the jury can infer an intent to kill from the manner in which the defendant used the baseball bat.

B. Murder

1. At common law, **murder** is defined as the unlawful killing of a human being with malice aforethought.

a. At common law, the *mens rea* for murder was malice.

b. With respect to common law murder, there are four distinct mental states sufficient to meet the malice standard required. Each corresponds to a different type of murder. The four mental states are:

(1) intent to kill;

(2) intent to inflict serious bodily injury;

(3) depraved heart or extreme recklessness; and

(4) felony murder.

2. **Types of Common Law Murder**

   a. **Intent-to-Kill Murder**

      (1) Intent-to-kill murder is a specific-intent crime.

      (2) A person who, without legal justification or excuse, intentionally causes the death of another human being has committed murder.

      (3) ***Mens Rea***

         (a) An "intent to kill" mental state satisfies the common law's malice standard for murder.

         (b) An intent to kill exists when a defendant purposely or knowingly kills—that is, when the defendant consciously desires to kill another person or makes the resulting death inevitable.

   b. **Intent-to-Cause-Serious-Bodily-Injury Murder**

      (1) Intent-to-cause-serious-bodily-injury murder is an example of an unintentional killing; it is also a specific-intent crime and constitutes a second-degree murder.

      (2) A person who, with an intent to inflict serious bodily injury upon another human being, causes the death of that human being has committed murder.

         (a) **Serious bodily injury**, also called "great bodily injury" or "grievous bodily injury," means a significant but nonfatal injury.

      (3) ***Mens Rea***

         (a) An "intent-to-inflict-serious-bodily-injury" mental state satisfies the common law's malice standard for murder.

         (b) Like intent-to-kill malice, intent-to-inflict-serious-bodily-injury malice can arise from a conscious desire or substantial certainty that the defendant's actions will result in the victim's injury.

         (c) Like intent-to-kill malice, intent to inflict serious bodily injury must be proved by examination of all the surrounding circumstances, including the words and behavior of the defendant.

         (d) The use of any instrument in a way that is likely to cause serious injury allows the trier of fact to infer an intent to inflict serious bodily injury.

         EXAMPLE: The defendant swung a heavy sledgehammer at the victim's leg. The victim's leg was severely broken. As a result of complications from this injury, the victim died a week later. On these facts, the trier of fact may not be able to infer an intent to kill, but can infer an intent to inflict serious bodily injury.

   c. **Depraved-Heart Murder**

      (1) Depraved-heart murder is an example of an unintentional killing; it is also a general-intent crime and constitutes a second-degree murder.

(2) A person commits **depraved-heart murder** when he engages in extremely reckless conduct that causes another person's death.

(3) ***Mens Rea***

(a) The mental state for depraved-heart murder is extreme recklessness, and this *mens rea* satisfies the common law's malice standard for murder.

1) It is not the gruesomeness of the killing that manifests the malice of a depraved-heart murder.

EXAMPLE: A person intentionally pushed the victim into an industrial-sized compactor designed to compress the metal remains of junked cars. The victim's death was gruesome, and the killing constitutes a murder. However, on these facts, we can infer an intent to kill.

(b) A person acts with extreme recklessness when her conduct is characterized by a wanton indifference to human life and a conscious disregard of an unusually high risk of death or serious bodily injury.

EXAMPLE: A person thought it would be amusing to drive on the wrong side of the street, "like they do in England." He did so, at high speed, and crashed into an oncoming car. The driver of that car died as a result. This killing constitutes depraved-heart murder.

EXAMPLE: A parent drove frantically to the nearest hospital, because the parent's child was bleeding profusely from an accidental gunshot. En route, the parent ignored a stop sign and crashed into another car crossing the intersection. The driver of this other car died as a result of injuries incurred in the accident. On these facts, the parent's driving did not manifest a wanton indifference to human life. Consequently, this killing would not constitute depraved-heart murder.

d. **Felony Murder**

(1) Felony murder is a specific-intent crime and constitutes a first-degree murder.

(2) A defendant commits felony murder if that person intended to commit an inherently dangerous felony (or a predicate felony as defined by statute) and, during the commission or attempted commission of this felony, proximately caused another person's death, whether intentionally or not.

EXAMPLE: Two co-felons committed a robbery. During the robbery, one of the co-felons got angry and intentionally killed the robbery victim. The second co-felon had no such intention. While the first co-felon is guilty of an intent-to-kill murder, the second co-felon is guilty of a felony murder.

(a) Any successful defenses to the underlying felony will preclude a conviction for felony murder.

EXAMPLE: A defendant is on trial for burglary and felony murder for the death of the homeowner during the burglary. At the conclusion of the trial, the jury acquitted the defendant on the charge of burglary. Because the defendant was found not guilty of burglary, the felony underlying the felony murder, the defendant cannot be convicted for felony murder.

(b) However, the defendant does not have to be charged or convicted of the underlying felony in order to be charged and convicted with felony murder. The jury can convict a defendant of felony murder if the prosecution proves beyond a reasonable doubt that the felony occurred, even if the felony is not separately charged.

EXAMPLE: A defendant is on trial for felony murder as a result of the death of a homeowner occurring during a burglary. However, the prosecution chose not to separately charge the defendant with burglary. After trial, if the prosecution nevertheless proves beyond a reasonable doubt that the burglary occurred and that the death occurred during the commission of the burglary, the jury may find the defendant guilty of felony murder.

(3) ***Mens Rea***

(a) The mental state required for felony murder is the intent to commit an inherently dangerous felony, and this *mens rea* satisfies the common law's malice standard for murder.

(4) **Inherently Dangerous Felonies**

(a) A jurisdiction's criminal code may identify certain felonies as inherently dangerous so as to trigger possible criminal liability for a felony murder.

(b) In the absence of such a statutory designation, the majority of courts will determine whether an offense is inherently dangerous by applying a test that considers only the elements of the felony in the abstract.

a) In other words, for most courts making this determination, the factual context or circumstances of the felony as committed are irrelevant.

EXAMPLE: A person pretended to be a doctor with a cancer cure and fraudulently induced the victim to pay $5,000 for an ointment that actually had no medical value or purpose. As a result, the victim did not seek competent medical treatment in a timely fashion and died of cancer in a matter of weeks instead of months or years. On these facts, a felony murder was not committed because, absent a statutory designation, fraud is not inherently dangerous.

b) A minority of courts apply a contextual test, looking at the particular circumstances of the case to determine whether the underlying offense should be considered inherently dangerous.

EXAMPLE: Same facts as above. In a minority jurisdiction, the court may find the defendant guilty of felony murder.

(c) At common law and still today, the "BARRK" offenses (burglary, arson, robbery, rape, and kidnapping) are deemed inherently dangerous felonies that trigger possible criminal liability for felony murder.

(5) **Proximate Causation**

(a) For purposes of felony murder, the resulting death must be a foreseeable outgrowth of the defendant's actions.

(b) Although many courts have leniently applied this foreseeability requirement, the majority of jurisdictions limit the application of felony murder by following the **agency theory** of felony murder.

1) Pursuant to this theory, only a death caused by the defendant or the defendant's co-felon can be the basis for a felony murder conviction.

2) Any death caused by a non-felon (e.g., a police officer, victim of the predicate felony, witness, or bystander) cannot be the basis for a felony murder conviction.

3) It is worth noting that agency theory is distinct from the rule at common law, which provided that felons could be guilty of felony murder even if the death was caused by a non-felon.

(c) In those jurisdictions that do not follow the agency theory of felony murder, many have adopted the **Redline limitation**.

1) According to this limitation, deaths caused by a non-felon can be the basis of a felony murder conviction only if the killing was not justifiable or excusable.

2) A justifiable or excusable killing caused by a non-felon cannot be the basis for a felony murder conviction.

EXAMPLE: Two co-felons commit armed robbery of a bank, during which a shootout with police occurs. As a result, one of the co-felons is killed by the police. In a jurisdiction that has adopted the Redline limitation, the surviving co-felon would not be subject to felony murder liability.

EXAMPLE: Similar facts as above but now, during the shootout, a witness to the robbery is unintentionally killed by the police. In a jurisdiction that has adopted the Redline limitation, the surviving co-felon would be subject to felony murder liability.

(6) **Commission or Attempted Commission of the Felony**

(a) The felony murder rule requires that the harm that causes the victim's death must have occurred during the commission or attempted commission of the predicate felony.

1) Note that only the death-causing injury has to occur during the commission or attempted commission of the felony. The victim does not need to actually die during the felony. The death of a victim who succumbs to her wounds after the felony has concluded will still support a conviction of felony murder.

(b) **Timing**

1) For purposes of felony murder, the felony starts when a person could be convicted of attempting the underlying felony.

2) The felony or attempted felony continues even while the felon is in immediate flight from the scene of the felony, but is considered "complete" once the defendant has reached a place of temporary safety.

a) This "place" does not need to be a fixed locale, such as a hideout or home.

(7) **Independent Predicate Felony and the Question of Merger**

(a) Most states will apply felony murder only when the underlying (predicate) felony is independent of (or collateral to) the homicide, so that every felonious attack on an individual which proves fatal does not become escalated by the felony murder rule.

(b) When the felony is independent of the homicide, the underlying felony and the homicide do not merge. The felon is guilty of both the underlying felony and felony murder.

1) This is because felony murder and the underlying felony do not share any elements such that the underlying felony would merge as a lesser-include offense. It is only the case that, as an element of felony murder, the injury causing the death must occur during the commission or attempted commission of another inherently dangerous felony.

EXAMPLE: The victim of a kidnapping was unintentionally killed during the commission of the kidnapping. Because homicides can occur without a kidnapping, kidnapping is independent of (or collateral to) the homicide. As such, the kidnapping will not merge with the homicide, and this victim's kidnapper is guilty of both kidnapping and felony murder.

(c) When the felony is not independent of the homicide—that is, when the underlying felony is inextricable from the homicide—the felony merges into the appropriate homicide charge (not felony murder). In such an instance, the perpetrator is guilty only of the homicide.

EXAMPLE: The victim of an aggravated battery was unintentionally killed during the commission of the battery. Because the elements of battery are subsumed by the elements of murder, the battery merges with the murder, and the perpetrator is guilty only of the (intent-to-inflict-serious-bodily-injury) homicide.

3. **Murder by Degrees**

a. While degrees of murder were not recognized at common law, most jurisdictions distinguish between different degrees of murder based on criteria identified in the given state's murder statute.

b. **First-Degree Murder**

(1) **First-degree murder** includes intent-to-kill murder committed with premeditation and deliberation and, in most jurisdictions, felony murder.

(a) If an unjustified, intentional killing is committed in the "spur of the moment" but not in circumstances sufficient to negate malice, the killing still constitutes murder, but not murder in the first degree.

EXAMPLE: While on a business trip, a man was approached by his trusted business partner, who told him that she in fact had been cheating him out of millions of dollars. Upon hearing this, the unsuspecting man immediately became outraged and, in that instant, pushed the business partner over the balcony of his 10th-floor hotel room. If charged with murder, the man can argue that this was not a first-degree murder because the victim's death was not premeditated.

(2) If the defendant was voluntarily intoxicated—but still sober enough to form the intent to kill—the defendant may be able to avoid liability for first-degree murder by proof that the intoxication precluded premeditation or deliberation.

(3) A statute may specify the felonies which support a first-degree murder charge for felony murder. If such a statute exists, a killing

which occurs during any other inherently dangerous felony would be considered a lesser degree of murder, such as second-degree murder.

EXAM TIP In the absence of such a statute on the bar exam, assume that the BARRK offenses support a first-degree murder charge for felony murder, and any other inherently dangerous felony leads to second-degree murder for felony murder.

(4) **Premeditation and Deliberation**

(a) **Premeditation** is more than just an intent to kill, it is a fully formed conscious desire or purpose to kill.

(b) There is no specific period of time required to form such a purpose; it could arise in a fraction of a second. To establish premeditation for purpose of first-degree murder, the prosecution must prove that the defendant acted with the requisite intent or knowledge and that such intent or knowledge existed for a period of time permitting reflection.

(c) Premeditation does not exist where the defendant acts in the spur of the moment—that is, where the defendant commits an instantaneous, intentional act of taking another's life.

EXAMPLE: The defendant was crossing a bridge when the victim approached from the other direction. When the victim got close to the defendant, the defendant was able to read the text on the victim's shirt. Offended by what the shirt said, the defendant impulsively shoved the victim over the railing, causing the victim to fall to his death. Because the defendant acted in the spur of the moment—instantaneously and impulsively—the defendant would not be guilty of first-degree murder, despite the fact that the defendant acted intentionally.

c. **Second-Degree Murder**

(1) **Second-degree murder** is any murder that does not count as first-degree murder, including intent-to-kill murders that lack premeditation and deliberation because they were acted on in the spur of the moment, intent-to-inflict-serious-bodily-harm murder, and depraved-heart murder.

C. Manslaughter

1. **Manslaughter** refers to unlawful killings of another person that are accomplished, unlike murder, in the absence of malice.

2. **Voluntary Manslaughter**

a. Voluntary manslaughter, which is commonly referred to as a heat-of-passion killing, is a specific-intent crime.

b. A person commits **voluntary manslaughter** when, without justification, that person intentionally causes the death of another human being in mitigating circumstances that are sufficient to negate malice aforethought.

   (1) Mitigating circumstances sufficient to negate malice aforethought include adequate provocation and imperfect self-defense.

c. **Adequate Provocation**

   (1) For adequate provocation to exist, the following must be true:

      (a) the circumstances of the killing must be such that, when considered objectively, a reasonable person would lose self-control;

      (b) a causal connection must exist between the legally adequate grounds for provocation and the provocation subjectively experienced by the killer; and

      (c) the time period between the provocation and the intentional killing must not be long enough for a reasonable person to have cooled off or for the killer to have subjectively cooled off.

   (2) Courts will commonly find that adequate provocation existed in the following circumstances:

      (a) the defendant was an unsuspecting spouse who killed immediately after finding the other spouse engaged in sexual conduct with another person; or

      (b) the defendant killed immediately after suffering a serious battery.

   (3) "Mere words" are insufficient to establish adequate provocation.

      EXAMPLE: An acquaintance approached a person and said that she had an affair with this person's spouse. Upon hearing this, the person immediately became enraged and, in that split second, decided to beat the acquaintance to death. As a result of the beating, the acquaintance did in fact die. Because the person was provoked by "mere words," this killing was not adequately provoked. As a result, it will not constitute a voluntary manslaughter, but rather, murder.

      EXAMPLE: A co-worker angrily approached a person and said, "I'm going to kill you." The co-worker made no other threatening action and was not armed with a weapon. Upon hearing this, the person immediately became enraged and, in that split second, decided to beat the co-worker to death. As a result of the beating, the co-worker did in fact die. Because the person was provoked by mere words, this killing was not adequately provoked. It will not constitute a voluntary manslaughter, but rather, a murder.

(4) Defendants who killed after having actually cooled off or while otherwise not in the heat of passion will not have their culpability reduced from murder to voluntary manslaughter even if the circumstances were such that a reasonable person would have been adequately provoked at the time of the killing.

d. **Imperfect Self-Defense**

(1) For **imperfect self-defense** to exist, at least one of the following must be true:

(a) the defendant killed in self-defense but did so after having started the altercation;

(b) the defendant killed in self-defense but did so after the initial aggressor had withdrawn from the attack; or

(c) the defendant killed in the honest, but unreasonable, belief that serious harm was imminent and deadly force was necessary.

e. A minority of states allow diminished mental capacity short of insanity to reduce murder to manslaughter.

3. **Involuntary Manslaughter**

a. Involuntary manslaughter is a general-intent crime.

b. A person commits **involuntary manslaughter** when that person unintentionally causes the death of another human being through criminally (or grossly) negligent conduct or by an unlawful act other than a predicate felony for felony murder.

c. **Criminally Negligent Manslaughter**

(1) Criminal (or gross) negligence requires more than the sort of simple carelessness or inattentiveness that qualifies in tort law as ordinary negligence.

(2) **Criminal** (or gross) **negligence** requires a reckless disregard for the high risks created by one's conduct.

EXAMPLE: While driving home, a man was momentarily distracted and did not notice a stop sign. As a result, he entered the intersection when another car with the right of way was also entering the intersection. The cars collided and the driver of the other car died from the injuries sustained in the accident. Here, the man's inattentiveness was a manifestation of ordinary—not criminal—negligence. As such, this man will not be guilty of involuntary manslaughter.

EXAMPLE: A woman was in a rush to get home after a very long day at work. As she approached an intersection, she decided not to stop at the stop sign, figuring she could "beat" any other car through the intersection. She figured wrong. In the resulting crash, the driver of the other car was killed. Here, the woman's reckless disregard of the stop sign would justify a conviction for involuntary manslaughter.

d. **"Unlawful Act" Manslaughter**

(1) Pursuant to the **misdemeanor-manslaughter rule**, a person has committed involuntary manslaughter when that person intended to commit an unlawful act other than an inherently dangerous felony and the commission of this unlawful act unintentionally, but proximately, causes another person's death.

(2) Despite its name, the misdemeanor-manslaughter rule applies when the unlawful act is a felony that is not also a predicate felony for felony murder (in other words, for felonies that are not inherently dangerous).

(3) When the unlawful act is a *malum in se* misdemeanor, the misdemeanor-manslaughter rule will apply even if the misdemeanor is not independent of the homicide or cause of death.

EXAMPLE: A defendant commits a misdemeanor assault (or battery) that proximately but unintentionally causes another person's death. Here, there is no merger, and the perpetrator is guilty of both assault (or battery) and involuntary manslaughter.

(4) When the unlawful act is a *malum prohibitum* misdemeanor, the misdemeanor-manslaughter rule applies only if the unintentional killing was a foreseeable consequence of the unlawful conduct or the consequence of the defendant's criminal (or gross) negligence.

EXAMPLE: A defendant unintentionally but proximately caused another person's death while driving five miles per hour above the speed limit. This unlawful act is a mere infraction, and not a misdemeanor. As such, the misdemeanor-manslaughter rule will not apply.

EXAMPLE: A defendant unintentionally but proximately caused another person's death while driving 60 miles per hour in a school zone with a posted speed limit of only 15 miles per hour. In this jurisdiction, driving 35 miles per hour or more above the posted speed limit is a misdemeanor. Arguably, on these facts, the misdemeanor-manslaughter rule will apply. While excessive speeding is a *malum prohibitum* misdemeanor, the conduct here is readily described as criminally negligent.

EXAMPLE: A defendant unintentionally but proximately caused another person's death while driving with a suspended license. This unlawful act is a *malum prohibitum* misdemeanor. However, because the defendant's unlawful act does not qualify as criminal or gross negligence and because another person's death is not a foreseeable consequence of the defendant's unlawful act, the misdemeanor-manslaughter rule will not apply.

III. OTHER CRIMES AGAINST THE PERSON

A. Criminal Battery

1. Simple Battery

a. Simple battery is a misdemeanor; it cannot be the basis for a felony murder indictment or conviction.

b. **Simple battery** is committed when a person, without consent, causes a harmful or offensive contact with another person and does so by the purposeful, knowing, reckless, or criminally negligent use of force.

(1) Criminal battery is a specific-intent crime when the harmful or offensive contact is caused purposefully.

(2) Criminal battery is a general-intent crime when the harmful or offensive contact is caused knowingly, recklessly, or in a criminally negligent manner.

c. **Causes Harmful or Offensive Contact by Use of Force**

(1) To prove that a defendant caused a harmful or offensive contact by use of force, a prosecutor must show that the defendant put a force in motion and that, as a result of this force, the victim's person was harmfully or offensively touched.

(2) The prosecutor does not need to show that the defendant directly applied this force to the victim's person.

EXAMPLE: John tells his dog to attack a stranger and, as a result, the dog bites the stranger's leg. John is guilty of battery, even though John himself did not make physical contact with the stranger. It is enough that John's conduct put a force (the attacking dog) in motion that itself made the unlawful contact with the stranger.

(3) The prosecutor does not need to show that the force put into motion by the defendant made direct contact the victim's person.

EXAMPLE: John, in a fit of rage, fires a gun at his ex-wife's new house. The bullet smashes the window and a shard of glass hits the ex-wife's new boyfriend in the eye. Regardless of whether John intended to shoot someone, this act would likely rise at least to the level of criminal negligence (creating a high degree of risk of death or serious injury) or even recklessness (conscious disregard of a substantial and unjustifiable risk). John would be guilty of battery. Even though the bullet that John's conduct directly and purposely put into motion made no direct contact with the boyfriend's person, it is enough that the bullet indirectly caused a harmful or unlawful contact with that person.

2. Aggravated Battery

a. Aggravated battery is a felony.

b. A simple battery is elevated to an **aggravated battery** when:
   (1) the defendant causes the victim serious bodily injury;
   (2) the defendant uses a deadly weapon to commit the battery; or
   (3) the defendant batters a woman, child, or law enforcement officer.

3. **Defenses**
   a. A defendant can avoid a conviction on a battery charge by proving any of the following:
      (1) the alleged victim consented to the contact, and this consent was not obtained by means of coercion or fraud;
      (2) when the defendant caused contact with the alleged victim, the defendant was acting in self-defense or in defense of a third person; or
      (3) when the defendant caused contact with the alleged victim, the defendant was trying to prevent the commission of a crime.

B. Criminal Assault

1. **Simple Assault**
   a. Simple assault is a misdemeanor; it cannot be the basis for a felony murder indictment or conviction.
   b. **Simple assault** is committed when a person attempts to commit a battery or intentionally causes the victim to fear an immediate battery.
   c. **Attempting to Commit Battery**
      (1) At common law, this was the only way to commit criminal assault.
      (2) Because "attempt" is a specific-intent crime, a defendant is guilty of this type of assault when she has purposely tried to cause a harmful or offensive contact with the victim's person. A defendant's reckless or criminally negligent conduct cannot lead to an assault conviction based upon an attempt to batter.

      EXAMPLE: A defendant pulled the trigger on a gun, intending only to slightly injure the victim. Even if there were no bullets in the chamber of the gun, this defendant will be guilty of assault. The gun's incapacity to fire a bullet is irrelevant. The defendant is guilty of assault because the defendant attempted to use force for the purpose of causing a harmful or offensive contact with the victim's person.

      (3) The fact that the victim was not aware of the attempted battery is no defense to this type of assault.
   d. **Intentionally Causing the Victim to Fear an Immediate Battery**
      (1) This type of assault did not exist at common law.
      (2) In this type of assault, the defendant must act with threatening conduct intended to cause the victim to feel reasonable apprehension of imminent harm. A conditional threat is generally

insufficient unless accompanied by an overt act to accomplish the threat.

EXAMPLE: Defendant points a gun at Victim and says, "If you don't get over here right now, I am going to shoot you." Defendant has committed an assault.

(3) **Reasonable Apprehension**

(a) When a reasonable person would not expect imminent bodily harm, there is no criminal assault.

EXAMPLE: Words alone are generally held insufficient to constitute an "apprehension" assault.

(b) The element of **apprehension** in this type of assault connotes "expectation" more than "fear" (though the term "fear" is employed frequently in assault crime statutes). The victim does not have to actually be afraid, but rather, to simply (and reasonably) anticipate or expect that the defendant's act(s) will result in immediate bodily harm.

(c) Note that in this type of assault (unlike attempted battery assault), the fear or apprehension piece is a key element, so no assault has been committed where the victim is unaware of the threat of harm.

(d) The threat must be to commit a present battery; a promise of future action is generally not an assault.

(e) Any threatened contact, including one that is offensive or insulting, is sufficient to constitute an "apprehension" assault. There need be no actual pain or injury threatened.

(4) If the feared battery is accomplished, the assault and battery merge and the defendant is found guilty only of the battery.

2. **Aggravated Assault**

a. Aggravated assault is a felony.

b. A simple assault is elevated to an **aggravated assault** when:

(1) the defendant commits an assault with a dangerous weapon; or

(2) the defendant acts with the intent to seriously injure, rape, or murder the victim.

C. Mayhem

1. Mayhem is a felony.
2. Mayhem is committed when a person maliciously uses physical force that causes the dismemberment of a victim's limbs or the permanent disabling or disfiguring of a victim's limbs or face.
3. **Maliciously Uses Physical Force**

a. For purposes of mayhem, the maliciousness of the act causing the victim's injuries is proven by showing that the defendant acted with an unlawful intent to vex, annoy, or injure another person.

4. At common law, the crime required an intent to maim or do bodily injury and the causing of injuries that substantially reduced the victim's fighting capability (e.g., dismemberment of the disabling of a body part useful in fighting); mere disfigurement would not be sufficient to prove mayhem.

   EXAMPLE: A student spat a spitball at a classmate, hitting this classmate in the eye. As a result, the classmate was permanently disfigured. Because this involved the disfigurement but not the disabling of a body part, this would not have constituted mayhem at common law. However, under the modern majority rule, the student would be guilty of mayhem.

D. Kidnapping

1. Kidnapping is a felony and can be the predicate felony for a felony murder conviction.
2. **Kidnapping** is committed when a person intentionally abducts another by means of force or the threat of force.
3. **Abduction**
   a. To prove the victim was abducted, a prosecutor must show that, without consent, lawful authority, or warrant, the defendant restrained the victim's liberty so that the victim could be concealed or taken to another place.
      (1) This element can be met where the victim is taken from one place to another or when they are secretly confined where the person is not likely to be found.
   b. Under the Model Penal Code, a person is guilty of kidnapping if the defendant unlawfully removes another from his place of residence or business, or a substantial vicinity where he is found, or if the defendant unlawfully confines another for a substantial period in a place of isolation, with any of the purposes:
      (1) to hold for ransom or reward, or as a shield or hostage;
      (2) to facilitate the commission of any flight or felony thereafter;
      (3) to inflict bodily injury on or to terrorize the victim or another; or
      (4) to interfere with the performance of any governmental or political function.
4. **Aggravated Kidnapping**
   a. **Aggravated kidnapping** occurs when the kidnapping is committed to obtain a ransom or to further the commission of another felony.
5. The crime of abduction, when distinguished from kidnapping, does not require a showing that the defendant used or threatened to use force.

E. False Imprisonment

1. False imprisonment is a misdemeanor.
2. **False imprisonment** is committed when a person intentionally and unlawfully confines another.

3. **Confinement**
   a. To prove confinement, the defendant must intend to preclude any reasonable means of escape and the victim must subjectively believe that there is no reasonable means of escape.
   b. Victims are not required to try to resist or attempt escape where the defendant has the apparent ability to effectuate threats.

   EXAMPLE: After discovering Diane cheating on him with another man, Jack left Diane in the bedroom and slammed the door, yelling, "Stay there until you're sorry. If you beg, I may let you out for breakfast." Though Jack intended to lock the bedroom door, he was so upset that he accidentally released the lock before slamming the door. Diane believed that she was locked in and never checked the door herself. Jack is guilty of false imprisonment.

   c. For purposes of false imprisonment, the confinement can be accomplished by erecting physical barriers, applying force, threatening to apply immediate physical force, or invalidly asserting authority.
   d. Victims are not "confined" if they are aware of a reasonable means of escape, but are not required to affirmatively search for potential escape routes.
4. **Distinguished from Kidnapping**
   a. False imprisonment is generally considered a lesser-included offense of kidnapping, such that if a defendant is convicted of kidnapping, the lesser charge of false imprisonment merges into the kidnapping charge.
   b. Kidnapping is accomplished by abduction, whereas false imprisonment requires only restraint. Factors which distinguish whether a defendant committed kidnapping as opposed to false imprisonment may include:
      (1) whether the victim was moved;
      (2) the required intent of the jurisdiction's kidnapping statute;
         (a) If a statute requires a particular intent for a kidnapping charge and the defendant lacks that element, the defendant may still be charged with false imprisonment.
      (3) the purpose of the confinement; or
      (4) in some jurisdictions, whether the confinement involved aggravating factors, such as the use of a deadly weapon or the risk of bodily injury.

F. Rape

1. Rape is a felony.
2. **Rape** occurs when a person has sexual intercourse with or commits a sexual intrusion against another person without this other person's consent.

3. At common law, rape could only be committed by a male person against a female person. Today, rape can be committed by any person against any other person, regardless of sex or gender.
4. At common law, a husband could not rape his wife. Today, rape can occur between married persons.
5. **Sexual Intercourse and Sexual Intrusions**
    a. To prove that there was sexual intercourse or a sexual intrusion, the prosecutor must show that there was penetration, even to the slightest degree, of the nonconsenting person's vagina or anus with any body part or object or show that there was oral penetration with a sex organ.
    b. Other nonconsensual sexual contacts are generally covered under a separate crime of sexual assault, sexual contact, or sexual battery.
6. **Lack of Consent**
    a. A prosecutor can prove the victim's lack of consent by showing that, at the time of the alleged rape, the victim was unconscious or otherwise physically incapable of consenting due to the effects of drugs or intoxicating substances.
    b. A prosecutor can also prove the lack of consent by showing either:
        (1) that it was verbally communicated by the victim; or
        (2) that it was implied by the victim's physical resistance to the sexual intercourse or intrusion.
7. **Defenses**
    a. If the defendant can prove that the alleged victim actually consented to the sexual intercourse or sexual intrusion, rape's lack-of-consent element is rebutted and the prosecutor's case-in-chief is defeated.
    b. Even when prosecutors can prove the elements of rape, including lack of consent, defendants can avoid criminal liability by showing that they reasonably and honestly—albeit mistakenly—believed the alleged victim had consented.
        (1) In determining whether the prosecution has proven its case-in-chief, a jury first considers the alleged victim's state of mind and decides whether there was actual consent to the alleged acts. If the jury decides that no actual consent was given and that the prosecution has proven its case, the jury would then view the events from the defendant's perspective to determine whether the manner in which the victim expressed their lack of consent was so equivocal as to cause the defendant to reasonably and honestly believe that there was consent when, in fact, there was not.
        (2) The defendant's affirmative defense has both an objective (reasonableness of the defendant's belief from the perspective of a reasonable person) and subjective (honesty of the defendant's belief) component.

G. **Statutory Rape**

1. In general, when a person is under the statutorily prescribed age of consent (usually 16), an act of intercourse constitutes rape despite their apparent or actual consent.
    a. However, a person cannot be convicted of "statutory" rape of their spouse.
2. A defendant's mistake as to the age of consent is no defense to statutory rape.
3. A defendant guilty of both statutory and forcible rape will be sentenced to the more serious crime of forcible rape, because the less serious crime of statutory rape would merge.

H. **Other Crimes against the Person**

1. **Bigamy** is the crime of marriage by one individual to more than one other person.
2. **Incest** is the crime of sexual relations between individuals who are closely related to one another. The degree of relationship required varies by state.

IV. CRIMES AGAINST PROPERTY

A. Theft Crimes

1. Theft crimes are crimes that involve some taking of property from the victim by the defendant. The key to analyzing theft crimes and to distinguishing among them often depends on two things:
   a. the nature of the taking; and
   b. whether the defendant acquired custody, possession, or title to the property.

      EXAMPLE: Larceny requires that the defendant obtain possession unlawfully. False pretenses that the defendant obtain title falsely. Embezzlement requires that the defendant convert (misuse) property that has already been entrusted to her.

2. **Nature of the Taking**
   a. Theft offenses typically occur in one of two ways. Either the property can be taken:
      (1) by trespass, force, or threat; or
      (2) by fraud, deception, or misrepresentation.
   b. Takings by trespass, force, or threat include larceny, robbery, and blackmail.
   c. Takings by fraud, deception, or misrepresentation include larceny by trick, false pretenses, and embezzlement.

3. **What the Defendant Acquires**
   a. A person is said to have **custody** of property when the property has been left with him, but he has no rights over the property.

      EXAMPLE: Low-level employees are typically considered to only have custody of their employer's property.

   b. A person has **possession** of property when she has custody and the authority to exercise discretion over the property, or limited rights to use the property. When property is loaned to another person to use, that person is considered to have possession.

      EXAMPLE: An auto mechanic has possession over a car left with him for repairs, because he has the right to open it, repair it, drive it around in order to test it, etc.

   c. A person has **title** to property when she is the legal owner of the property.

B. Theft by Trespass, Force, or Threat

1. **Larceny**
   a. Larceny is a specific-intent crime. At common law, larcenies were classified as misdemeanors. At modern law, they may be classified as felonies by statute, depending on the value of the property taken.

b. **Larceny** occurs when a person:
   (1) unlawfully takes and carries away property possessed by another; and
   (2) does so with the intent to permanently deprive that person of possession.

c. ***Actus Reus***
   (1) The *actus reus* of larceny consists of the unlawful taking and carrying away of property possessed by another.
   (2) **Taking**
      (a) For purposes of larceny, a "taking" occurs when a person, without consent or right, exercises dominion and control over another's property.
      (b) When a taking occurs without consent or right, this is also known as a trespassory taking.
   (3) **Carrying Away**
      (a) Any movement—even the slightest movement—of another's property will satisfy the "**carrying away**" **(asportation)** element of larceny.
   (4) **Property Possessed by Another**
      (a) Larceny is a crime against possessors of property. It is enough for larceny to establish that someone other than the defendant had the right to possess the property to the exclusion of the defendant at the time of the taking.
         1) Because the property must be "of another," a good-faith claim of right rebuts the prosecutor's larceny case. Larceny is a crime of possession, as opposed to ownership.
      (b) The victim of a larceny does not need to own or have title to the property. The victim need only have possession, control, and custody of the property.

      EXAMPLE: A person had a one-year lease on a car owned by a dealership. During the lease period, the car was stolen by a thief. Both the dealership and the lessee are victims of the larceny.

      (c) For purposes of larceny, anyone having a possessory interest in property through title or possession, even illegally, or who possesses a greater right of possession than the defendant, can be considered an "owner" of the property.

      EXAMPLE: The victim acquired a stolen painting off the black market, and proudly displayed it on a wall for many years. One day, a thief broke into the house and took the painting. The thief has committed larceny, despite the fact that the victim was not the lawful owner of the painting.

(d) The perpetrator of a larceny can be the lawful owner of that stolen property, provided that the named victim had a greater right to the care, custody, control, or management of the stolen property (i.e., the taking violated the right of another to the exclusive possession of the property at the time).

EXAMPLE: The owner of a car entered into a contract with a co-worker whereby the car was loaned to the co-worker for a one-month period in exchange for $1,000. During the loan period, after they got into a workplace dispute, the owner went out to the parking lot, got into the car, and drove away. Because the co-worker had lawful possession of the car, the owner will be guilty of larceny.

(e) A bailee generally has lawful possession of bailed property. However, if that property is a closed container with other items inside, the property inside the container is only in the bailee's custody because the bailor has constructive possession of it.

EXAMPLE: A person stored several boxes in a commercial storage facility. Inside the boxes were other items owned by this person. The owner of the facility opened these boxes and misappropriated some of their contents. The owner of the facility—the bailee, in this scenario—has committed a larceny.

(f) At modern law, the kinds of property that can be the subject of larceny include not only tangible personal property, but also services and other intangibles (such as gas and electrical power and written instruments that represent property rights).

1) At common law, larceny was limited to tangible personal property.

(g) Lost or mislaid property can be the subject of larceny. However, abandoned property cannot, because by abandoning the property, the owner has relinquished his rights in the property.

1) In order to be guilty of larceny for lost or mislaid property, there are two requirements. The finder:

a) must intend to permanently deprive the owner of it; and

b) must either know who the owner is or have reason to believe (from earmarkings on the property or from the circumstances of the finding) that she can find out the owner's identity.

d. ***Mens Rea***

(1) Larceny requires that the intent to permanently deprive the owner accompany the taking.

(2) The taking and carrying away (asportation) must generally concur in time with the intent to permanently deprive.

(3) However, under the **doctrine of continuing trespass**, a person who wrongfully takes another's property intending only to use it temporarily before restoring it unconditionally to its owner may nevertheless be guilty of larceny if that person later has a change of mind and decides not to return the property after all.

(a) In such instances, the trespassory taking is said to continue until the time the intent to permanently deprive is formed.

(b) For the doctrine to apply, the initial taking must be trespassory, or wrongful. A taking with permission from the owner will not satisfy the continuing trespass doctrine if the taker then decides not to return the property at a later date.

(4) The intent to keep, destroy, or hold property for ransom will suffice to prove this element.

(5) When a defendant recklessly exposes property to loss or deals with property in a manner involving a substantial risk of loss, the intent to permanently deprive is satisfied.

(6) When a defendant intends to use the property temporarily and then abandon it, hoping someone will return it to the victim, even if the property somehow does return to the victim, the intent to permanently deprive is satisfied.

EXAMPLE: The defendant robs a bank, but did not make any specific plans for how to get away afterward. On leaving the bank, the defendant steals a car and drives it to within a mile of his hideout, before then leaving the car on the side of the road. The defendant has committed larceny of the car by wrongfully taking it and then abandoning it.

(7) If, during the time of taking, the defendant continuously intends to return the property to the victim unconditionally and within a reasonable time, there is no intent to permanently deprive.

(a) Evidence that a defendant actually returned the property to the victim does not conclusively prove that, during the taking, the defendant had always intended to return it.

(8) Defendants who pawn property may negate the intent to permanently deprive element by proof that, at the time of taking, they intended to redeem the property and return it to the victim.

(9) When the defendant takes property with the intent to later pay for it or later replace it, such intent may negate the intent to permanently deprive element if, for example, the property is easily replaceable (i.e., not unique).

EXAMPLE: Bill broke into Steve's home and took a computer. Bill took the computer and dumped it in a nearby alley, smashing it to pieces. Bill is guilty of larceny.

EXAMPLE: Same case, but Bill left the computer in his yard, where it got rusted and dirty. One year later, Bill, feeling remorse, returned the computer to Steve. Bill will be guilty of larceny.

(10) Where a defendant, at the time of the taking, has a good-faith belief that she is entitled to possession, there is no intent to permanently deprive, even if that belief is both incorrect and unreasonable.

EXAMPLE: Dana accidentally takes someone else's umbrella upon leaving a restaurant. She is not guilty of larceny if she honestly (even if unreasonably) believed that it was not the property of another.

2. **Robbery**

a. Robbery is a specific-intent crime, and is classified as a felony.

b. Larceny, assault, and battery are all lesser-included offenses of robbery, which means that they all merge with the robbery upon the completion of the offense.

c. Robbery occurs when a person commits a larceny and:

(1) the property unlawfully taken was on the victim's person or in the victim's presence; and

(2) the taking was accomplished by force or intimidation.

d. **Person or Presence**

(1) "Presence" refers to the area within the victim's protection or control.

(2) Property is in a person's presence for purposes of robbery if it is within the area within which the victim could reasonably be expected to exercise some physical control, but for the fact that the victim was overcome by force or prevented by the fear or intimidation.

e. **Accomplished by Force or Intimidation**

(1) This refers to violence or the threat of violence and, for purposes of robbery, must occur contemporaneously with the taking.

EXAMPLE: The defendant breaks into the victim's house and, pointing a gun at the victim, demands the combination for the victim's safe, which was located in the victim's office on the other side of town. The defendant then goes to the office and takes the property found inside the safe. The defendant has not committed robbery, because the taking was not contemporaneous with the intimidation (nor was the property taken from the presence of the victim).

(2) **Robbery by Force**

(a) The force or violence can be slight, but must be more than what is necessary to simply move the property.

EXAMPLE: As a woman was walking down the sidewalk, a thief came up from behind her, grabbed her purse, and ran off. The thief has committed larceny, not robbery.

EXAMPLE: As a man was walking down the sidewalk, a thief came up from behind him and took the man's wallet out of his back pocket without the man even noticing. The thief has committed larceny, not robbery.

(b) For a sudden "snatching" of property to constitute robbery, it must be accompanied by more force or violence than is necessary to remove the property from the person, or must be accompanied by a simultaneous act of intimidation or violence.

EXAMPLE: As a woman was walking down the sidewalk, a thief came up from behind her and pushed her down to the ground. While the woman was stunned from the sudden violence, the thief grabbed her purse and ran away. The thief has committed robbery.

(3) **Robbery by Intimidation**

(a) The threat of violence must place the victim in actual fear, and this fear must also exist during the taking.

(b) Even an empty threat that produces actual fear during the taking is sufficient.

f. The Model Penal Code definition of robbery requires that the theft be accompanied by serious bodily injury upon another, or by threatening or placing another in fear of immediate serious bodily injury.

3. **Extortion, Coercion, and Blackmail**

a. Extortion, coercion, and blackmail are statutorily defined as felonies.

b. In general, extortion and coercion are different names for the same crime, while blackmail is often considered a form of each.

c. As distinct from blackmail, **extortion** (or **coercion**) generally occurs when a person threatens to physically harm another person or to destroy the property of another person for the purpose of obtaining something of value from this other person.

(1) Similar to robbery, extortion involves unlawful threats.

(2) Unlike robbery, extortion does not require threats of immediate or imminent physical harm, and property does not need to be taken from the victim's person or presence.

d. As distinct from extortion, **blackmail** occurs when a person threatens to make accusations or share information that will expose another to criminal prosecution or public ridicule for the purpose of obtaining something of value from this other person.

e. Because extortion, coercion, and blackmail statutes criminalize the taking of a victim's property by threat, it is no defense to these crimes to argue that the defendant's threat was to reveal factually correct information that the defendant was entitled to reveal.

C. Theft by Fraud, Deceit, or Misrepresentation

1. Larceny by Trick

a. **Larceny by trick** is a form of larceny whereby the defendant obtains possession of the personal property of another by means of a representation or promise that the defendant knows to be false at the time of the taking.

b. Like larceny but unlike false pretenses, larceny by trick is a crime of possession, not ownership. The defendant's fraud is used to cause the victim to convey possession, not title, of the property to the defendant.

c. Unlike larceny, larceny by trick does not entail a trespassory taking. Instead, possession of the victim's property is conveyed to the perpetrator as a result of a fraud committed by the perpetrator against the victim.

2. Embezzlement

a. **Embezzlement** occurs when a person in lawful possession of another person's property engages in the fraudulent conversion or misappropriation of that property.

b. **Lawful Possession**

(1) Unlike larceny, whose victims are the possessors of property, embezzlement is a crime against the owners of property.

(2) While larceny is committed by someone who unlawfully possesses the victim's property, embezzlement can only be committed by someone in lawful possession of the victim's property.

(3) Generally, employees are said to have custody (not possession) over their employer's property, which makes a wrongful taking by the employee a larceny. However, the employee has possession—and thus could commit embezzlement—if:

(a) a third party gives property directly to an employee for the benefit of the employee's employer; or

(b) the employee is in a high-level position (e.g., an office manager, bank president, or corporate official).

(4) Many embezzlement statutes require that the property be "entrusted" to the defendant. Such statutes have been construed as not applicable to defendants who come into lawful possession of property by finding it or by mistaken delivery (i.e., the property was not "entrusted" to the defendant because it was never intended that he be given possession). Fraudulent conversion by a co-owner of property is not embezzlement.

c. **Property of Another**

(1) Embezzlement is a crime against tangible personal property. It does not concern intangible property, real estate, or services.

d. **Fraudulent Conversion or Misappropriation**

(1) Unlike larceny, which involves the taking of property, embezzlement involves the fraudulent conversion or misappropriation of property.

(2) **Fraudulent conversion** or misappropriation occurs when a person seriously interferes with another person's ownership rights.

(a) Actions that "seriously interfere" with another person's ownership rights are actions that deprive such a person of a significant portion of the property's usefulness or value.

1) The following actions, if taken with regard to another person's property, can "seriously interfere" with this other person's ownership rights: selling, consuming, pledging, donating, discarding, heavily damaging, or claiming title.

(b) While slight movement or limited use will not "seriously interfere" with another person's ownership rights, more substantial movement or use of another person's property can do so.

(c) Proving fraudulent conversion does not require proof that the defendant's actions led directly to the defendant's personal gain.

(d) While a conversion is still fraudulent even if the defendant intended to later substitute it for equivalent property, a conversion is not fraudulent if the defendant intended to restore the exact property.

(e) A conversion is not fraudulent if the defendant took actions that the defendant honestly believed were consistent with the defendant's right to possess the owner's property.

3. **Theft by False Pretenses**

a. This is a statutory crime that, depending upon the value of the property stolen, may be a misdemeanor or felony.

b. **Theft by false pretenses** occurs when a person, with the intent to defraud the victim of title to personal property, knowingly makes a false representation of a present or past material fact that causes the victim to transfer title to the defendant.

c. **Intent to Defraud**

(1) The intent to defraud must exist at the time the victim transfers title to the defendant.

d. **Title to Personal Property**

(1) The modern scope of false pretenses includes written instruments, stocks, bonds, notes, and deeds, as well as money and credit cards.

e. **Knowingly Making a False Representation**

(1) The defendant must know that her representation is false at the time that the title is transferred.

f. **Material Fact**

(1) Puffery and statements of opinion cannot be the basis of a false pretenses conviction, because these are not representations of fact.

g. **Causes the Victim to Transfer Title**

(1) The victim's reliance upon the false representation must be a reason—but not necessarily the only reason—for why the victim transferred.

(2) While title is transferred, the title is voidable because of the defendant's fraud.

4. **Distinguishing Theft by False Pretenses from Embezzlement and Larceny by Trick**

a. Unlike embezzlement, which involves the interference of another person's ownership rights, false pretenses involves the transfer of title.

b. Unlike larceny by trick, whereby the defendant acquires only possession of the stolen property, false pretenses is a crime in which the defendant acquires title to the stolen property.

EXAMPLE: As a result of a defendant's fraud, the victim entered into a sale or trade with the defendant and, as part of this sale or trade, delivered money to the defendant. Because title generally passes when payment is made, this defendant is guilty of false pretenses.

EXAMPLE: A defendant pays for property with a worthless check. Because title does not pass until the check is cashed, the defendant is guilty of larceny by trick.

EXAMPLE: A defendant acquired the victim's money by cheating the victim in a game of cards. In this situation, the defendant acquired possession of, but not title to, the money. Thus, this defendant is guilty of larceny by trick.

c. When a victim pledges money for security, bails money for safekeeping, or gives money to be used only for a specific purpose, and the victim takes such action as a result of the defendant's misrepresentations, the defendant acquires only possession, and thus, is guilty of larceny by trick.

(1) If, however, in response to the defendant's false representations, the victim lends money or grants title, the defendant is guilty of false pretenses.

D. Other Theft-Related Crimes

1. **Receiving Stolen Property**

a. Receiving stolen property was a common law misdemeanor but, as a statutory crime, is either a misdemeanor or felony depending on value of the stolen property received.

b. A defendant is guilty of **receiving stolen property** when he receives property that he knows to be stolen and intends to permanently deprive the owner thereof.

c. **Receiving Stolen Property**

(1) A person has "received" stolen property if she has physical possession of that property or exercises control over it.

EXAMPLE: A person who arranges the sale of goods known to be stolen exercises control over those goods, and so has "received" them.

EXAMPLE: A person who has a thief place goods known to be stolen in a designated place exercises control over those goods and so has "received" them.

d. **Known to be Stolen**

(1) The defendant must either actually know or constructively know that the property is stolen at the time that the defendant received the property.

(2) Constructive knowledge exists when the facts and circumstances surrounding the receipt of the property leave no reasonable doubt that the receiver must have known, without further inquiry, that it was stolen.

e. **Intent to Permanently Deprive the Owner**

(1) The defendant must, at the time of receiving the stolen property, have the specific intent to permanently deprive the owner of that property.

(a) The defendant does not have to be acting for personal gain.

(2) When, at the time of receipt of the stolen property, a defendant intends to unconditionally return the property to its owner, the defendant is not guilty of receiving stolen property, because the requisite *mens rea* cannot be proven.

(3) When, at the time of receipt of the stolen property, a defendant intends to conditionally return the property (such as upon payment of a reward), this may be used as nonconclusive evidence that the defendant intended to permanently deprive the owner.

2. **Forgery**

a. **Forgery** occurs when a person fraudulently makes a false writing with apparent legal significance with the intent to make wrongful use of the forged document.

b. **Fraudulent Making**

(1) The making element will be satisfied by the creation of a new document, the altering of an existing document (including improperly filling in a form), or by inducing someone to sign a

document knowing that the person is unaware of the document's significance.

c. **False Writing with Apparent Legal Significance**

   (1) Forgery requires more than including false information in an otherwise genuine document. It requires that the document itself not be genuine.

   (2) For an alteration to qualify as a fraudulent making of a forged document, the alteration must be material—that is, it must change the legal meaning or effect of the document.

   (3) For a writing to be one with apparent legal significance, the writing must have some effect on legal rights or duties (e.g., a contract, a will, a negotiable instrument, a deed, or a mortgage).

d. **Intent to Make Wrongful Use of the Forged Document**

   (1) An intent to reimburse the victim or to collect on a good-faith claim of debt does not negate a forger's intent to make wrongful use of the forged instrument.

   (2) A forger who is not motivated by the desire for monetary gain can still intend to make wrongful use of the forged instrument.

e. Completion of the "making" element completes the crime; the defendant does not have to actually use the forged document to be found guilty of forgery.

   EXAMPLE: Dylan wrote a will and signed the name of his ailing Aunt Bunny. He then signed the names of two other family members whom Bunny would likely have chosen as witnesses. Dylan intended to use the document after Aunt Bunny died to claim a large part of her estate. The fake will is discovered before Bunny dies. Dylan is guilty of forgery.

f. A defendant who actually acquires property by use of the forged document may additionally be guilty of another crime, such as false pretenses.

3. **Bad Checks**

   a. All jurisdictions have enacted bad check legislation to deal with no-account or insufficient-funds checks given with the intent to defraud. The giving of the check is an implied representation of sufficient funds, absent postdating or some other means of notification of inadequate credit by the drawer.

   b. Bad check statutes generally do not require that any property be obtained from the victim as a result of issuing the bad check.

   c. However, the requisite mental state of the drawer is often required to be that of knowledge of the insufficient funds and the intent to defraud.

4. **Credit Card Fraud**

   a. Obtaining property by means of a stolen or unauthorized credit card is also a statutory crime in most jurisdictions.

False Pretenses	Larceny by Trick	Credit Card Fraud	Check Fraud
• Obtains title • By representation or promise the defendant knows is fake	• Obtains possession • By representation or promise the defendant knows is fake	• Obtains title • By stolen or unauthorized credit card	• Obtains title • By stolen check or on non-sufficient funds account

E. Crimes against the Habitation

1. **Burglary**

   a. Burglary is a felony. It is also deemed an inherently dangerous felony, such that it can trigger felony murder liability.

   b. **Burglary** occurs when a person breaks and enters into a structure of another with an intent to commit a felony or theft crime therein.

   c. **Breaking**

      (1) For purposes of burglary, the "breaking" must be trespassory—that is, accomplished by someone who lacks authority or consent.

      (2) The breaking element can be proven by a showing of an actual breaking or a constructive breaking.

      (3) An **actual breaking** occurs when the defendant uses force—even slight force—to create an opening that permits entry into a structure.

         (a) The force necessary for an actual breaking can be slight, and includes such actions as turning a key, opening an unlocked door or window, or pushing open a door or window that is already partially open.

      (4) Under both the common law and modern statutes, a **constructive breaking** occurs when the defendant uses fraud, deception, or the threat of force to gain entry into a structure.

      EXAMPLE: While walking down the street, the defendant noticed a house with its front door open. Seeing the opportunity, the defendant entered the house, grabbed a wallet off a front table, and left. Because the defendant entered through an already open door and did not use any force to effect an entry, the defendant's actions will not support a conviction for burglary.

      EXAMPLE: The defendant walked up to a house and rang the doorbell. When the occupant opened the door a couple of inches to see who was there, the defendant shoved the door open further and entered the house, intending to steal whatever could easily be grabbed. The defendant has committed burglary.

   d. **Entering**

      (1) For purposes of burglary, the "entering" must be trespassory—that is, accomplished by someone who lacks authority or consent.

(2) The entering element can be proven by showing that any part of the defendant's body was placed inside the structure.

(3) The entering element can also be proven by showing that the defendant inserted a tool inside the structure, so long as that tool was inserted for the purpose of accomplishing the felony or theft within.

EXAMPLE: The defendant used a crowbar to smash the glass on a bedroom window, and then reached inside with the crowbar in order to pry the window open, intending to then climb inside and steal the occupant's jewelry. However, once the window was opened, an alarm went off, and the defendant abandoned his plans and ran away. Even though the crowbar was inserted into the structure, its purpose was to effectuate the breaking (by opening the window), not the actual underlying felony (stealing the jewelry). As such, the defendant has not satisfied the "entering" element of burglary.

EXAMPLE: After opening a window, the defendant inserted a coat hanger inside of the victim's bedroom in order to hook onto the victim's necklace and pull it outside of the house. However, the coat hanger knocked over a bottle beneath the window, causing the victim to wake up and the defendant to run away. Because the tool (the coat hanger) was inserted into the house for the purpose of accomplishing the underlying felony or theft offense (stealing the necklace), the defendant's actions satisfy the "entering" element of burglary.

(4) For purposes of burglary, the entering need not occur at the same time as the breaking, but it must be related to the breaking.

EXAMPLE: The defendant broke the window of a structure with her gun. Before entering through that broken window, the defendant left the scene, returning several hours later wearing a heavy jacket that would better protect her from the broken glass. Only then did the defendant climb through the same broken window and into the structure. For purposes of proving a burglary, this defendant's entering of the structure is sufficiently related to the breaking.

EXAMPLE: After breaking a window of a structure with his gun, the defendant saw an open window and climbed through it into the structure. On these facts, a prosecutor would not be able to prove burglary because the entering is not sufficiently related to the breaking.

e. **Structure of Another**

(1) This element includes most any structure, and is not limited to dwellings or structures within the curtilage of a dwelling.

(2) At common law, this element was more narrowly defined to include only dwellings and structures within the curtilage of a dwelling.

f. **Intent to Commit a Felony or Theft Offense Therein**

(1) In general, burglary requires that the breaking and entering be accompanied by a simultaneous intent to commit a felony or theft offense therein.

(2) An intent formed after an initial entry will satisfy the *mens rea* element of burglary only if it is simultaneous with an additional "entry" once inside the structure.

EXAMPLE: A defendant breaks into and enters a neighbor's home with the intent only to trespass. However, once inside the home, the defendant forms an intent to steal, opens a bedroom door, and enters the bedroom intending to steal items from inside that room. The opening of the bedroom door and entering into that room constitutes an additional entry. Because the defendant had an intent to steal at the time of this additional entry, a breaking and entering have occurred for purposes of committing a burglary.

g. The burglary is complete once the defendant enters with sufficient criminal intent, regardless of whether the defendant commits or even attempts to commit the intended felony or theft crime therein.

EXAMPLE: The defendant breaks into and enters a house with the intent of stealing money and jewelry from within. However, while looking for anything to take, the defendant is startled by the homeowner and runs out of the house without taking anything. While the defendant has not committed the intended crime of larceny (because no property was taken), the defendant can nevertheless be convicted of burglary, which was completed once the defendant entered the house with the requisite intent.

h. **No Merger of Crimes**

(1) A defendant who commits or attempts to commit burglary, and commits or attempts to commit the felony or theft offense within, can be charged and convicted with both crimes (burglary as well as the other felony or theft offense).

EXAM TIP A crime will only merge with another crime as a lesser-included offense if the greater offense includes all elements of the lesser-included offense, plus at least one additional element (e.g., larceny merging into robbery). Burglary and the underlying offense do not actually share any elements. Rather, burglary requires, as an element, the intent to commit another felony or theft offense within the structure. This is not the same thing, and does not result in the crimes merging together.

i. **Other Common Law Distinctions**

(1) As distinct from the modern majority rule, the common law rule was limited to breaking and enterings that occurred between sunset and sunrise ("at night").

(2) The common law further limited burglary to dwelling houses and structures within the curtilage of a dwelling house.

2. **Arson**

a. Arson is a felony. It is also deemed an inherently dangerous felony, which means that it can trigger felony murder liability.

b. Arson occurs when a person maliciously burns property.

c. **Malicious**

(1) This element of arson can be satisfied by actions that intentionally or recklessly cause property to burn.

(2) An intentional burning is a burning done purposely or knowingly.

(3) A reckless burning is an unintentional burning that results from actions taken with a conscious disregard of the substantial and unjustifiable risks that a burning would occur.

d. **Burning**

(1) This element is satisfied by evidence of charring.

(2) To satisfy this element, there is no requirement that the structure be extensively damaged or seriously charred.

(3) However, charring is not satisfied where the damage to the surface of the structure is merely discoloration ("blackening") or warping.

EXAMPLE: The defendant started a fire in a trash receptacle kept inside a structure. As a result, the walls of the structure suffered smoke damage and the ceiling of the structure became blackened and warped. On this evidence, the defendant will not be guilty of arson.

EXAMPLE: The defendant intentionally caused an explosion that damaged a structure. As a result of the explosion, a fire started that further damaged the structure. If the fire damage was not limited to the surface of the structure—that is, if there was charring and not merely scorching—the defendant can be found guilty of arson.

e. **Property**

(1) For purposes of arson, the property burned need not be property owned by someone other than the defendant. A defendant can burn her own property and be guilty of arson.

EXAMPLE: The defendant set fire to his own business, intending to collect the insurance proceeds. In addition to committing insurance fraud, the defendant would be guilty of arson.

(2) The property burned can be a dwelling, building, structure, vessel, or even personal property.

f. At common law, arson required the malicious burning of the dwelling of another.

(1) As distinct from the modern majority rule, the common law rule was limited to dwellings of another person.

F. Possession Offenses

1. Controlled Substances

a. The Uniform Controlled Substances Act ("UCSA") was first published in 1970, and was adopted by almost every state as the basis for state drug laws. The UCSA was most recently revised in 1994, and this version has been adopted by more than half of the states.

b. Under the Uniform Controlled Substances Act, except as otherwise authorized, a person may not knowingly or intentionally manufacture, distribute, or deliver a controlled substance, or possess a controlled substance with intent to manufacture, distribute, or deliver [UCSA § 401(a)].

c. At federal law, except as otherwise authorized, it is unlawful for any person knowingly or intentionally [21 U.S.C. § 841(a)]:

(1) to manufacture, distribute, or dispense, or possess with intent to manufacture, distribute, or dispense, a controlled substance; or

(2) to create, distribute, or dispense, or possess with intent to distribute or dispense, a counterfeit substance.

d. It is also unlawful for any person knowingly or intentionally to possess a controlled substance unless such substance was obtained directly, or pursuant to a valid prescription or order, from a practitioner, while acting in the course of her professional practice, or except as otherwise authorized by statute [21 U.S.C. § 844(a)].

e. Both state and federal laws vary in level of offense and severity of punishment depending on the substance and amount involved.

2. Firearms

a. The National Firearms Act [26 U.S.C. §§ 5801, *et seq.*] prohibits the possession of certain firearms and accessories in violation of the registration, authorization, and notification requirements that the Act sets forth.

b. **Registration of Importers, Manufacturers, and Dealers**

(1) On first engaging in business and thereafter on or before the first day of July of each year, each importer, manufacturer, and dealer in firearms must register with the state in which the business is located his name, including any trade name, and the address of each location in the district where he will conduct such business [26 U.S.C. § 5802].

(2) An individual required to register under this section shall include a photograph and fingerprints of the individual with the initial application.

(3) Where there is a change during the taxable year in the location of, or the trade name used in, such business, the importer, manufacturer, or dealer shall file an application to amend her registration.

(4) Firearms operations of an importer, manufacturer, or dealer may not be commenced at the new location or under a new trade name prior to approval of the application.

c. **Prohibited Acts**

(1) It is unlawful for any person [26 U.S.C. § 5861]:

(a) to engage in business as a manufacturer or importer of, or dealer in, firearms without having paid the special (occupational) tax required by Section 5801 for his business or having registered as required by Section 5802;

(b) to receive or possess a firearm transferred to him in violation of the provisions of Chapter 53;

(c) to receive or possess a firearm made in violation of the provisions of Chapter 53;

(d) to receive or possess a firearm which is not registered to him in the National Firearms Registration and Transfer Record;

(e) to transfer a firearm in violation of the provisions of Chapter 53;

(f) to make a firearm in violation of the provisions of Chapter 53;

(g) to obliterate, remove, change, or alter the serial number or other identification of a firearm required by Chapter 53;

(h) to receive or possess a firearm having the serial number or other identification required by Chapter 53 obliterated, removed, changed, or altered;

(i) to receive or possess a firearm which is not identified by a serial number as required by Chapter 53;

(j) to transport, deliver, or receive any firearm in interstate commerce which has not been registered as required by this Chapter 53;

(k) to receive or possess a firearm which has been imported or brought into the United States in violation of Section 5844; or

(l) to make, or cause the making of, a false entry on any application, return, or record required by Chapter 53, knowing such entry to be false.

(2) In order to be convicted, the defendant must be aware that she in fact possesses something, whether the possession be actual or constructive, and that the thing possessed is in fact a "firearm" of some sort. However, it is unnecessary that the accused know

either that the item possessed is unregistered or even subject to registration [United States v. Freed, 401 U.S. 601 (1971); United States v. Javino, 960 F.2d 1137 (2d Cir. 1992)].

(3) Actual possession of a firearm exists when a person has direct physical control over the firearm. Constructive possession is established when a person, though lacking physical custody of the firearm, still has the power and intent to exercise control over the firearm [Henderson v. United States, 575 U.S. 622 (2015)].

V. INCHOATE CRIMES

A. Introduction

1. The category of inchoate crimes refers to those crimes that are committed when an intended crime, often referred to as the "target offense," is not fully completed or accomplished.
2. The basic inchoate crimes are solicitation, attempt, and conspiracy.
3. **Merger Doctrine**
   a. According to this doctrine, when a person's conduct simultaneously satisfies the elements of two crimes, the perpetrator will only be charged or convicted of the more serious crime; the lesser offense is said to have merged with the greater offense.
   b. With respect to inchoate crimes, if the target offense is completed or accomplished, the crimes of solicitation and attempt merge with the target offense, but the crime of conspiracy does not.

B. Solicitation

1. A person (the solicitor) commits the crime of **solicitation** when he requests or encourages another person (the solicitee) to commit a criminal offense and does so with the intent that the person solicited commit the crime.
   a. The crime of solicitation is complete at the time the solicitation is made.
   b. If the solicited party completes the target offense, the crime of solicitation merges with the crime solicited and the solicitor is guilty as an accessory before the fact of the crime committed by the solicitee.
      (1) Because solicitation is a specific-intent crime, only the actual completion of the target offense will result in merger. If the solicitor requests a completed crime but the solicitee only manages to attempt the target offense, the solicitation will not merge with the attempted crime, and the solicitor can be charged with both.

      EXAMPLE: A contacts B and requests that B kill C. B tries, but does not manage to kill C. A can be charged and convicted with both solicitation to commit murder and attempted murder.

      EXAMPLE: A contacts B and requests that B kill C. B succeeds and kills C. A can be convicted of murder but not solicitation to commit murder as well, because the crime of solicitation merged into the completed offense.
2. Solicitation was a common law misdemeanor, but now can be a felony depending on the crime solicited.
   a. Generally, the more serious the felony, the harsher the punishment.
3. ***Actus Reus***
   a. **Request or Encourage**
      (1) This element is broadly understood to include enticements, urgings, advisements, and demands.

b. **To Commit a Criminal Offense**

(1) This element encompasses both misdemeanors and felonies.

(2) At common law, this element only encompassed felonies.

4. ***Mens Rea***

a. This element is satisfied if the alleged solicitor specifically intends that the solicitee perform the target offense.

b. A defendant's mere approval of the criminal acts performed by another party is not enough to satisfy this element.

5. **Response by Solicited Party**

a. It is unnecessary that the person solicited enter into an agreement to commit the requested crime. Indeed, a person solicited to do a crime may not even respond, but the solicitor will still be guilty of solicitation.

b. If the request by the solicitor is for the solicitee to commit a crime jointly with the solicitor, the act of making the request constitutes a solicitation, but if the solicitee agrees and an overt act is later committed in furtherance of the crime, the proper charge becomes conspiracy, rather than solicitation.

6. A solicitor may not be guilty of the offense if she could not be convicted of the underlying crime—for instance, where the solicitor is a member of the class of persons the law seeks to protect (e.g., a minor, in relation to statutory rape).

7. **Defenses**

a. At common law, there were no defenses to solicitation if the elements were present. However, under modern statutes, specific-intent defenses such as voluntary intoxication and unreasonable mistake of fact are legitimate defenses to solicitation.

b. Even where it would be impossible for the solicited party to carry out the target offense, such impossibility provides no defense to the soliciting party.

c. Because the crime of solicitation is complete as soon as the solicitation is made, renunciation or withdrawal by the soliciting party cannot be a defense to the crime of solicitation, even if it might serve as a defense to the target offense.

C. Attempt

1. A person is guilty of **attempt** if he specifically intended to bring about a criminal result and took a significant overt act in furtherance of that intent.

a. Once a person completes the target offense, the attempt merges into the target crime.

2. **Significant Overt Act**

a. To prove this element, a prosecutor must show that the defendant engaged in an act of perpetration, and not merely an act of preparation.

b. **Competing Approaches**

(1) At common law, proof of this element required a showing that the defendant performed the "last act" necessary to achieve the intended result.

(2) Some modern courts use a "**proximity**" **test** to determine whether this element has been satisfied. Per this test, the court's determination is based on how close in time and physical distance a defendant was to the time and place the target crime was to be committed.

(3) Some modern courts use an "**equivocality**" **test**, which requires that the defendant's conduct be such that it can have no other purpose than the commission of the crime attempted.

(4) Some modern courts follow the Model Penal Code and deem this element satisfied if the defendant took a step toward the offense substantial enough to corroborate the defendant's criminal intent.

EXAMPLE: Defendant intends to kill Victim by tying her up and pushing her into the pool. At common law, Defendant likely would have to push the tied-up Victim into the pool to be guilty of attempted murder. Today, tying up the Victim next to the pool without pushing her in would likely be sufficient under all of the tests discussed above.

3. The **specific intent** requirement for attempt liability—the requirement that the defendant specifically intended to bring about a criminal result—means that, in some cases, an attempt conviction requires more proof than a completed offense.

EXAMPLE: A and B attack C. A intends to kill C, but B intends only to seriously injure him. If C does not die, then only A can be convicted of attempted murder. Even in a jurisdiction that recognizes murder based on a *mens rea* which itself does not require the specific intent to kill (e.g., murder based on the intent to seriously injure), to be guilty of attempted murder, one still must have a specific intent to kill.

4. **Defenses**

a. **Legal Impossibility**

(1) Legal impossibility is a defense to attempt crimes.

(2) **Legal impossibility** requires a showing that, even if the defendant had accomplished what had been intended, the defendant would have committed no crime.

b. **Factual Impossibility**

(1) While legal impossibility is a defense to attempt crimes, factual impossibility is not.

(2) **Factual impossibility** occurs when the defendant attempts to undertake a criminal act, but the present facts at the time prevent the crime from being completed.

EXAMPLE: The defendant fired a powerful weapon into a neighbor's home. The defendant's intent was to kill the neighbor. However, unbeknownst to the defendant, the neighbor was away on vacation and the home was left unoccupied. Even though the circumstances were such that the defendant could not have killed anyone, the defendant will be guilty of attempted murder.

c. **Abandonment or Withdrawal**

(1) Abandonment (or withdrawal) is not a defense to a charge of attempt once the attempt is complete.

(2) If the elements of attempt have been proven, evidence that the defendant thereafter decided to not carry through with the target offense is inconsequential; the defendant will still be guilty of attempt.

(3) A minority of jurisdictions (including MPC jurisdictions) recognize a voluntary and complete abandonment as a defense.

(a) **Voluntary** means a true change of heart, not simply giving up in the face of difficulties or an increased likelihood of being caught.

(b) **Complete** means that the defendant is not merely postponing commission of the crime.

D. Conspiracy

1. Conspiracy is graded a felony when the target offense is a felony, and is graded a misdemeanor when the target offense is a misdemeanor.

   a. At common law, conspiracy was a misdemeanor regardless of the severity of the target offense.

2. A person engages in a criminal **conspiracy** when that person agrees with one or more other persons to commit a crime, and any of the conspirators then takes an overt act in furtherance of that agreement.

   a. At common law, conspiracy was defined more broadly. There was no "overt act" requirement; proof of the requisite "agreement" would suffice.

   (1) The requisite "agreement" was not limited to agreements to commit a crime; it also applied to agreements with others to commit a lawful act by unlawful means (e.g., by dishonesty or fraud).

3. Unlike solicitation and attempt, when the target offense of a conspiracy is committed, the crime of conspiracy does not merge into the target offense. In other words, a defendant can be found guilty of both the target offense and the conspiracy to commit the target offense.

4. ***Actus Reus***

   a. For purposes of a conspiracy charge, a prosecutor must show that at least two people shared an intent to commit a crime.

b. A feigned agreement by all other parties will not suffice; an actual agreement between two people is required.

EXAMPLE: As part of an undercover operation, a police officer and the defendant agreed to rob a bank. The police officer had no intention of actually robbing the bank. Therefore, this "agreement" cannot support a conviction for conspiracy.

(1) The MPC, followed by a minority of courts, allows for the concept of **unilateral conspiracies**. This approach dispenses with the requirement that there be an actual agreement; if the defendant agrees and intends to commit the crime but the other party does not intend to actually follow through, the defendant can still be found guilty of conspiracy.

c. The agreement between the conspirators need not be express; it may be proved circumstantially, such as by conduct where the conspirators demonstrate over time that they intended to achieve the same objective and agreed to work together toward that end.

d. **Overt Act in Furtherance of the Agreement**

(1) For conspiracy, the overt act requirement can be satisfied by an action that is itself not criminal or unlawful.

(2) The overt act requirement can also be satisfied by an act of a co-conspirator; the act need not be an action taken by the defendant.

(3) Unlike the overt act requirement for attempt crimes, the overt act requirement for conspiracies can be satisfied by an act of mere preparation.

EXAMPLE: The defendant entered into an actual agreement to commit an arson. In preparation for this crime, one of the parties to the agreement purchased an ignition device and some cans of accelerant. On these facts, all parties to the agreement, including the defendant, would be guilty of conspiracy.

EXAMPLE: The defendant entered into an actual agreement to steal a co-worker's prized stamp collection. In preparation of the theft, one of the parties to the agreement drove by the co-worker's house to scout the co-worker's home and its perimeter. On these facts, all parties to the agreement, including the defendant, would be guilty of conspiracy.

5. ***Mens Rea***

a. The mental state for conspiracy requires both the intent to agree and the intent to achieve the objective of the agreement.

b. Conspiracy is a specific-intent crime.

6. **Vicarious Liability of a Co-Conspirator**
   a. **Accomplice Liability**
      (1) According to the general rules of accomplice liability, when the defendant's co-conspirator commits the target offense, the defendant will be guilty of the target offense as well, because the conspirator aided or abetted the co-conspirator in the commission of the target offense.
   b. **The Pinkerton Doctrine**
      (1) Per the Pinkerton doctrine, a conspirator's accomplice liability can extend to other crimes besides the target offense.
      (2) The **Pinkerton doctrine** provides that each conspirator is liable for any crime committed by any co-conspirator so long as:
         (a) the defendant was a party to the conspiracy;
         (b) the offense was within the scope of the conspiracy;
         (c) the offense was committed in furtherance of the conspiracy; and
         (d) the defendant could have reasonably foreseen the offense as a "necessary or natural consequence of the unlawful agreement."
      (3) The Pinkerton doctrine is followed by a majority of jurisdictions.
7. **Miscellaneous Considerations**
   a. Because a corporation and its agent are considered one person, no conspiracy can exist between them.
   b. **The Wharton Rule**
      (1) According to the **Wharton Rule**, when a crime is so defined as to require two or more people to commit it, a conspiracy to commit such a crime requires the involvement of an additional person beyond that number required by definition to commit it.

      EXAMPLE: If two persons engage in a duel, they are guilty of the crime of dueling, but not of conspiracy to duel.
      (2) Wharton Rule crimes include, besides dueling, the following offenses:
         (a) bigamy;
         (b) incest;
         (c) gambling;
         (d) giving and receiving bribes; and
         (e) adultery.
   c. **Single versus Multiple Conspiracies**
      (1) The nature of the agreement determines whether there is a single conspiracy or multiple conspiracies.
      (2) In a **chain relationship**, where several crimes are committed under one large scheme in which each member knows generally

of the other parties' participation and a community of interest exists, one single conspiracy results.

(3) Alternatively, in the so-called **hub-and-spoke relationship**, where one common member enters into agreements to commit a series of independent crimes with different individuals, multiple conspiracies exist.

d. **Procedural Issues**

(1) It is not necessary to try more than one conspirator; a single conspirator could be tried and convicted of conspiracy.

(2) However, if all other alleged co-conspirators are acquitted of the conspiracy charge, the remaining alleged co-conspirator must also be acquitted, because a conspiracy presumes the participation of at least two parties.

8. **Defenses**

a. **Protected Class**

(1) A member of a class that is sought to be protected by the criminalizing of certain conduct may avoid a conspiracy charge for engaging in that conduct.

EXAMPLE: A minor is charged with conspiracy to commit a statutory rape. However, if the defendant is the alleged victim of the statutory rape, then she cannot be convicted on the conspiracy charge.

b. **Impossibility**

(1) Impossibility is not a defense to conspiracy.

c. **Abandonment (or Withdrawal)**

(1) Abandonment (or withdrawal) is not a defense to a charge of conspiracy. If the elements of conspiracy have been proven, evidence that the defendant thereafter decided to not carry through with the target offense is inconsequential; the defendant will still be guilty of conspiracy.

(2) Although not a defense to the conspiracy charge, abandonment (or withdrawal), when communicated to all co-conspirators, will cut off further liability for crimes committed in furtherance of the conspiracy.

(a) The withdrawal does not have any effect on the defendant's liability for any crimes already committed, or for the crime of conspiracy itself. It only severs the defendant's liability for any crimes committed after the withdrawal.

(3) Under the MPC, which is a minority rule, withdrawal by a co-conspirator may be a valid affirmative defense to the charge of conspiracy itself where the renouncing party gives timely notice of his plans to all members of the conspiracy and performs an affirmative act to "thwart" the success of the conspiracy.

VI. PARTIES TO CRIME AND ACCOMPLICE LIABILITY

A. Accomplice

1. Modern law distinguishes only between accomplices to a crime and accessories after the fact. Under the modern approach, an accomplice to a crime is fully liable for the crime being committed.
2. A person is criminally liable as an **accomplice** if, with an intent to effectuate the commission of a crime, that person:
   a. assists or encourages another person committing that crime; or
   b. fails to oppose another person committing that crime despite having a legal duty to do so.
3. An accomplice to a crime is fully liable for the crime committed. In other words, an accomplice is punishable to the same extent as would be the principal. However, an accomplice can be convicted before the principal is convicted.
   a. Because accomplices help to effectuate a crime, they are akin to accessories before the fact but distinct from accessories after the fact, whose assistance is provided only after the crime has been committed.

      EXAMPLE: The getaway driver for a bank robbery would be considered an accomplice, and would be culpable for the bank robbery, even if the driver never left the vehicle at any time.
4. ***Actus Reus***
   a. To be an accomplice, a person must actually assist or encourage the perpetrator of a crime, even if only to a slight degree.
      (1) Under the MPC, an attempt to assist or encourage the principal is sufficient, even if the principal is not actually assisted or encouraged by the defendant.

      EXAMPLE: A person, intending to encourage a bully to beat up the victim, flashed a thumbs-up sign at the bully, who then proceeded to beat up the victim. However, the bully had not noticed the thumbs-up sign and so was not encouraged by it. While this attempt to "give assistance or encouragement" would suffice under the MPC, the majority rule requires more than an attempt to assist or encourage; it requires that the principal be actually assisted or encouraged. Thus, on these facts, a prosecutor in a jurisdiction following the majority rule would not be able to prove that the alleged accomplice "gave assistance or encouragement" to the bully.
   b. A person can be guilty as an accomplice even if the principal would have committed the crime without that person's assistance or encouragement. In other words, an accomplice's assistance or encouragement need not be an actual ("but for") cause of the principal's crime.

EXAMPLE: A person flashed a thumbs-up sign to a bully just before the bully beat up the victim. The bully would have beaten up the victim regardless. However, having seen the thumbs-up sign, the bully felt encouraged to do so. On these facts, a prosecutor could prove that the alleged accomplice had "given assistance or encouragement."

c. A person's mere presence will not be sufficient to prove that this person gave assistance or encouragement to the perpetrator of a crime.

d. A person's mere words may be sufficient to prove that this person assisted or encouraged the principal to commit a crime.

e. An individual is not liable as an accomplice for the acts of a "false accomplice" (e.g., an undercover police officer).

5. ***Mens Rea***

a. For purposes of accomplice liability, it must be shown that the defendant intended to commit the acts of assistance or encouragement and further intended to assist or encourage another to commit the crime charged.

b. A minority of modern statutes create accomplice liability with a lower mental state—that of knowingly assisting or encouraging a crime, such as in cases where a seller, knowing of the buyer's intent to commit arson, sells him an explosive device.

6. An accomplice is responsible not just for the crime assisted and encouraged, but also for other crimes that are the natural and probable consequences of the crime assisted or encouraged.

a. The MPC, in contrast, limits accomplice liability to only the crime assisted or encouraged.

EXAMPLE: An accomplice assisted and encouraged a felon to commit an armed bank robbery. During the robbery, the felon shot and killed a bank teller. Although the MPC rule would limit the accomplice's liability to armed robbery, the majority rule provides that the accomplice can also be held responsible for the killing of the bank teller.

7. **Renunciation**

a. An accomplice may avoid accomplice liability if, before the crime begins, that accomplice:

(1) stopped assisting and encouraging the principal; and

(2) effectively communicated to the principal the accomplice's intention to withdraw.

b. A minority of jurisdictions require the accomplice to neutralize her prior assistance or encouragement. However, these jurisdictions do not additionally require the accomplice to try to thwart the commission of the crime.

B. The Common Law Approach

1. The common law distinguished between four categories of criminals: principals in the first degree, principals in the second degree, accessories before the fact, and accessories after the fact.
2. **Principals in the First Degree**
   a. Any and all perpetrators who performed the criminal act with the requisite mental state were known as **principals in the first degree**.
3. **Principals in the Second Degree**
   a. Any and all persons who were present at the scene of the felony and aided, abetted, or otherwise encouraged the commission of the crime with the requisite intent were known as **principals in the second degree**.

   EXAMPLE: During a bank robbery, a getaway car driver waits outside. This driver is present at the scene and, by providing the robbers inside the bank with the expectation that they can make a successful escape from the scene of the crime, has aided, abetted, and encouraged the robbery to occur. At common law, with respect to this robbery, the driver would be a principal in the second degree.

   b. A principal in the second degree was punishable to the same extent as the perpetrator (or principal in the first degree).
4. **Accessories before the Fact**
   a. Any and all persons not present at the scene of the felony but who nevertheless aided, abetted, or encouraged the commission of the crime were known as **accessories before the fact**.
   b. An accessory before the fact was punishable to the same extent as the principal; as such, the common law's "accessory before the fact" was akin to today's "accomplice."
      (1) At common law, unlike today's majority rule, conviction of the principal was required for conviction of an accessory.
5. **Accessory after the Fact**
   a. A defendant was guilty as an **accessory after the fact** if:
      (1) a felony had been committed;
      (2) the defendant knew of the commission of this crime; and
      (3) the defendant personally aided any perpetrator of this crime with the intent to hinder the principal's apprehension, conviction, or punishment.
   b. Unlike accomplices (or accessories before the fact), accessories after the fact were not punishable to the same extent as the perpetrators of the crime.
   c. The common law's accessory after the fact is usually treated by modern statutes as a person guilty of the crime of "obstruction of justice."

VII. DEFENSES

A. Types

1. Fully Exculpatory versus Partially Exculpatory

a. A **fully exculpatory defense** relieves the defendant of any guilt or blame for the alleged crime. As a result, the defendant is deemed "not guilty" and is not subject to criminal punishment.

EXAMPLE: Insanity, (perfect) self-defense, and involuntary intoxication.

b. A **partially exculpatory defense** reduces the criminal defendant's blameworthiness such that the defendant is deemed "guilty" of a lesser crime or is subject to a lesser punishment.

EXAMPLE: Adequate provocation, imperfect self-defense, and voluntary intoxication.

2. Excuse versus Justification

a. An **excuse defense** is one which acknowledges that the defendant's conduct was wrongful and blameworthy, but asserts that the circumstances of the crime were such that the defendant should not be held fully responsible for the consequences of that conduct.

EXAMPLE: Insanity, intoxication, and adequate provocation.

b. A **justification defense** is one which asserts that the alleged criminal act was warranted, given the circumstances, and so not wrongful or blameworthy.

EXAMPLE: (Perfect) self-defense and necessity.

B. Excuse Defenses

1. Insanity

a. If the defendant is insane at the time of his criminal act, no criminal liability will be imposed for the criminal act. Four tests for insanity are followed in various jurisdictions.

b. The **M'Naghten test** focuses on the defendant's reasoning abilities.

(1) Per the M'Naghten test, a defendant can successfully assert an insanity defense if, at the time of the commission of the crime, she was laboring under a defect of reason from a disease of the mind, which caused her to not know the nature and quality of their actions or to not know that her actions were wrong.

(a) **Disease of the mind** includes all mental abnormalities, but not a psychopathic personality.

(2) There is a split of authority in M'Naghten jurisdictions as to whether "wrong" includes both legal and moral wrongs. Some jurisdictions will find that a defendant is not insane where, even

though the defendant believes the act was not morally wrong, he knows it to be illegal. Others will find defendants who do not know an act was morally wrong to be insane, regardless of his belief as to the act's legality.

c. Under the **irresistible impulse test**, a defendant can successfully assert an insanity defense when, at the time of the commission of the crime, she had a mental disease that kept her from controlling her conduct.

d. Under the **Durham** (or **New Hampshire**) **rule**, also known as the "product" rule, a defendant can successfully assert an insanity defense when, but for his mental defect or disease, the crime would not have been committed.

e. Under the **Model Penal Code test**, a defendant can successfully assert an insanity defense if, at the time of the crime and because of a mental disease or defect, she lacked the substantial capacity to either appreciate the criminality (wrongfulness) of her conduct or conform her conduct to the requirements of the law.

    (1) The MPC test is distinct in that it combines a cognitive component (not knowing) with a volitional component (not controlling) and allows a verdict of insanity for either one.

    (2) It is typically easier to establish MPC insanity because it does not require the total or absolute loss of cognitive ability or volition, only that the defendant lacked substantial capacity in these areas.

    (3) "Mental disease or defect" does not include abnormalities manifested only by repeated criminal or otherwise antisocial conduct.

    EXAMPLE: Kleptomania (a compulsion to steal) will not constitute a mental disease or defect under the MPC test.

    (4) Pursuant to federal law, it is an affirmative defense to a prosecution under any federal statute that, at the time of the commission of the acts constituting the offense, the defendant, as a result of a severe mental disease or defect, was unable to appreciate the nature and quality or the wrongfulness of his acts [18 U.S.C. § 17(a)].

f. **Procedural Issues**

    (1) A defendant is presumed sane; the burden is on the defendant to prove otherwise.

        (a) Under federal law, a defendant has the burden of proving insanity by clear and convincing evidence in federal court [18 U.S.C. § 17(b)].

        (b) In the majority of states, the defendant has the burden of proving insanity by a preponderance of the evidence in state court.

(2) A not guilty plea at arraignment does not waive the right to raise the insanity defense at a later time.

2. **Competency**

a. Competency to stand trial is very different from a mental incapacity.

b. **Incompetency** typically refers to a doctrine that prevents defendants from being tried, convicted, or punished unless they have the sufficient present ability to consult counsel with a reasonable and rational understanding of the proceedings.

c. If a defendant is found incompetent, she can later be tried and punished if competency is restored.

(1) Insanity concerns the defendant's mental state at the time the offense is committed; competency is assessed at any time during the pendency of the criminal case in court.

d. **Burden of Proof**

(1) The burden of proof in all courts is a preponderance of the evidence, pursuant to 18 U.S.C. § 4241 and its interpretive case law.

(2) If, after the hearing, the court finds by a preponderance of the evidence that the defendant is presently suffering from a mental disease or defect rendering him mentally incompetent to the extent that he is unable to understand the nature and consequences of the proceedings against him or to assist properly in his defense, the court shall commit the defendant to the custody of the Attorney General.

(3) In the federal system, the burden of proof falls on the party making the motion to determine competence.

(4) However, the Supreme Court has ruled that the state may place the burden of proof on the defendant when determining competency, but for due process reasons, it cannot increase the level of evidence required to be proved. Therefore, whether in federal court or state court, the burden of proof when determining competency is a preponderance of the evidence [Cooper v. Oklahoma, 517 U.S. 348 (1996); Medina v. California, 505 U.S. 437 (1992)].

3. **Diminished Capacity**

a. A minority of jurisdictions allow the defense of **diminished capacity**, which is short of insanity, to prove that as a result of a mental defect, the defendant did or did not have a state of mind that is an element of the offense.

b. When pleading diminished capacity, the defense is used to negate a specific mental state required for the particular crime.

4. **Intoxication**

a. Voluntary or involuntary intoxication—whether brought about by alcohol or by narcotic drugs—can be a defense to a crime.

b. **Voluntary Intoxication**

(1) Voluntary intoxication is never a defense to a strict liability crime or a general-intent crime; it can never negate recklessness or criminal negligence.

(2) **Voluntary intoxication** is a valid defense to a specific-intent crime when it negates the requisite mental state.

(3) It operates as an affirmative defense insofar as the burden of proof is on defendants to show that they were intoxicated and that their intoxication prevented them from forming the requisite "purposeful" or "knowing" mental state.

c. **Involuntary Intoxication**

(1) Involuntary intoxication is never a defense to a strict liability crime, but can be a defense to both general-intent and specific-intent crimes.

(2) **Involuntary intoxication** is a valid defense when, at the time of the crime, it negated the requisite mental state or it caused a temporary insanity.

(a) In the latter instance, it is not a mental disease or defect, but rather, an intoxicated condition that causes the insanity. Regardless, the rules of insanity would otherwise govern.

5. **Infancy**

a. At common law, a complete defense due to incapacity existed for children under seven years of age. Children between the ages of seven and 14 were rebuttably presumed to lack criminal capacity. Children over age 14 were held responsible as adults.

b. Most states have abolished the common law presumptions and established a specific minimum age required for a criminal conviction.

6. **Duress (or Coercion)**

a. The defense of **duress** excuses criminal conduct when the defendant reasonably believes that the only way to avoid unlawful threats of great bodily harm or imminent death is to engage in unlawful conduct.

(1) For duress, unlike necessity, the threat must come from human forces rather than from forces of nature.

(2) While self-defense or defense of others justifies the use of force against an aggressor, duress provides an excuse for unjustified criminal conduct.

(3) When successfully asserted, a defendant can fully or partially excuse her responsibility for her criminal actions, and so mitigate or avoid criminal punishment.

b. Duress, or coercion, is not available as a defense to murder. However, it can be a defense to manslaughter, and could excuse a charge of felony murder if it operates as a defense to the underlying felony.

7. **Entrapment**
   a. A defendant can successfully assert the defense of **entrapment** upon a showing that he was in no way predisposed to commit the crime, and that the criminal act was the product of creative activity originating with law enforcement officials.
   b. To prove entrapment, it is not sufficient to prove that government officials encouraged criminal activity by providing the opportunity or the equipment for the commission of a crime. If the defendant did have a predisposition to commit the crime, the entrapment defense would fail.
   c. For purposes of proving the defendant's "predisposition" to commit the alleged crime, a defendant's past criminal record is relevant.
8. **Mistake of Fact**
   a. **Mistake of fact** is a defense when the mistake negates the existence of a mental state required to establish a material element of the crime.
      (1) In other words, mistake of fact applies where, if the facts were as the defendant thought them to be, there would have been no crime.

      EXAMPLE: A defendant is on trial for receiving stolen property—specifically, a painting. The defendant was given the painting as a gift from a friend, who told the defendant that it was a limited edition print that the friend had recently purchased. However, the friend had actually stolen the painting from a private collection. The defendant will be able to assert the defense of mistake of fact, because if the facts were as the defendant believed them to be, there would have been no crime.

   b. A mistake of fact is a defense to a general-intent crime only if the mistake of fact was reasonable (viewed objectively).
   c. A mistake of fact can be a defense to a specific-intent crime even if the mistake of fact was not reasonable, so long as the mistake of fact was honest.
   d. Mistake or ignorance of fact is never a defense to a strict liability crime, which itself requires no mental state.

   EXAMPLE: A defendant is on trial for statutory rape. At trial, the defendant asserts that she honestly—albeit mistakenly—believed that the victim was of age. This mistake provides the defendant with no defense, because statutory rape is a strict liability crime.

C. **Justification Defenses**
1. **Self-Defense**
   a. **Definitions**
      (1) An **initial aggressor** is the person who strikes the first blow or commits a crime against another person.

(2) **Deadly force** is force that is likely to cause death or serious bodily harm.

(3) **Non-deadly force** is force that is likely to cause bodily harm that is less than serious bodily harm.

b. In general, when a person reasonably believes that he is in imminent danger of unlawful bodily harm, he has a right of self-defense that permits the use of reasonably necessary force to prevent such harm.

c. **Belief of Necessity**

(1) Self-defense has both a subjective and objective component.

(2) In order to assert self-defense:

(a) the person asserting the defense must actually and honestly believe that the use of force was necessary to protect herself (the subjective component); and

(b) the belief must be one that a reasonable person would have under the circumstances (the objective component).

d. An initial aggressor does not have a right of self-defense unless the victim of the initial aggression:

(1) observes the initial aggressor's complete withdrawal; or

(2) escalates the force level by responding with a disproportionate amount of force.

e. Victims of an initial aggression will lose their right of self-defense when they use disproportionate force.

f. **Imminent Danger**

(1) Once an unlawful attack is over, subsequent acts of retaliation or revenge are not justifiable as self-defense because such acts are not in response to a threat of imminent danger.

(2) Preemptive attacks in anticipation of some future threat of bodily harm are not justifiable as self-defense because they are not in response to a threat of imminent danger.

g. **Reasonably Necessary Force**

(1) For purposes of self-defense, force is reasonably necessary when it is proportional to the unlawful attack that the defender seeks to thwart and necessary to avoid the harm threatened by that attack.

EXAMPLE: The victim started punching the defendant, who countered with a punch to the victim's jaw. The victim fell backward, awkwardly hitting his head against a wall, and subsequently died as a result. Here, both the victim and the defendant used non-deadly force. While a punch is likely to cause bodily injury, a punch—even a punch to the jaw—is not likely to cause serious bodily injury or death Thus, although the victim died as a result of the punch to the jaw, the punch constituted a non-deadly force that was justified in the circumstances. This defendant would not be guilty of a criminal homicide.

EXAMPLE: The victim attacked the defendant with a butcher knife. To thwart the victim's use of deadly force, the defendant's only available recourse was to shoot the victim with a gun. Here, the defendant's use of deadly force is proportional and warranted. As such, the defendant is not guilty of a criminal homicide.

(2) **Use of Deadly Force**

(a) For purposes of self-defense, deadly force is reasonably necessary only when it is used to thwart an unlawful attack that threatens death or serious bodily injury.

(b) In other words, if non-deadly force would stop a deadly attack, responding with deadly force is not reasonable.

(3) **Retreat**

(a) In general, a person has no duty to retreat from an attack that threatens deadly force.

(b) A minority of jurisdictions require a defendant to retreat if it is feasible and can be done in safety before using deadly force. These jurisdictions do not require a defendant to retreat if it cannot be done safely or if the defendant is in her own home, vehicle, or workplace.

(1) Even if in one of those places, however, a defendant in a retreat jurisdiction must retreat before using deadly force if the defendant is the aggressor.

2. **Defense of a Third Person**

a. Generally, a person is justified in using force to defend a third person to the same extent that the third person would be justified in using force to defend himself.

b. Defense of a third person can be successfully asserted even when a defendant reasonably but mistakenly believed that a third person was a non-aggressor being unlawfully attacked by another.

c. Defense of a third person can be successfully asserted even when the third person being threatened with harm has no special relationship with the defendant.

3. **Defense of Property**

a. Reasonable, non-deadly force is justified in defending one's property from theft, destruction, or trespass where the defendant has a reasonable belief that the property is in immediate danger and no greater force than necessary is used.

(1) This means that the use of non-deadly force is improper where a request to desist would suffice.

b. Reasonable, non-deadly force is also justified when used to reenter real property or regain possession of wrongfully taken personal property upon "immediate pursuit."

c. Force may not be used to protect property after the necessity or threat has passed.

d. **Deadly Force**

(1) Deadly force is never justified when used merely to defend or retrieve property.

(2) However, deadly force may be justified where the defender reasonably believes an entry will be made or attempted in her dwelling by one intending to commit a felony therein.

4. **Necessity**

a. In general, when a person reasonably believes that a perilous circumstance has created an imminent threat of bodily harm, he is justified to use reasonably necessary force to cause a lesser harm so as to avoid the greater harm.

EXAMPLE: The defendant is walking down the street when she notices an air conditioner start to fall from a window of a building several floors high. Below the window is a young man wearing large headphones. The defendant rushes forward and pushes the young man out of the way moments before the air conditioner smashes to the ground where the man had been standing. The defendant will be justified in the use of force in pushing the man aside, and will not be guilty of battery because of the defense of necessity.

b. **Distinguished from Other Defenses**

(1) Self-defense (and defense of others) justifies the use of force against an unlawful actor. However, when the threat of imminent danger is not caused by an unlawful actor, the appropriate justification to appeal to is necessity.

(2) Necessity, unlike duress, the threat must come from natural, or non-human, forces.

EXAMPLE: The defendant's brother is kidnapped, and the defendant is told that, unless he breaks the legs of a gambler in debt to the kidnapper, the defendant's brother will be killed. This situation involves the defense of duress, not necessity, because the greater harm is threatened by a human, rather than by a non-human force.

c. A defendant can avail herself of the necessity defense even if the imminent threat of bodily harm concerned only a harm to others.

d. **Reasonably Necessary Force**

(1) For the defendant's force to be reasonably necessary, it must be the case that no less harmful alternative course of action was available to the defendant.

e. This defense protects, among others, military personnel acting within their duties, as well as public executioners.

f. **Exception**

(1) A defendant cannot successfully assert the defense of necessity when the defendant was at fault in creating the perilous situation.

EXAMPLE: In an attempt to save the lives of all 10 passengers on a plane, a pilot crash landed the plane on a stretch of roadway outside the populated areas of town. As a result, only one passenger died. However, two other people also died when the car they were in swerved off the road to avoid the plane. If the pilot was not at fault for causing the plane to crash, the pilot can successfully assert a necessity defense. However, if the plane crash was caused by the pilot's recklessness or the pilot's criminally negligent failure to maintain the plane's engine, then a necessity defense would be unsuccessful.

5. **Law Enforcement Defenses**

a. **Police**

(1) A police officer may use that amount of non-deadly force that he reasonably believes necessary to effect a lawful arrest or prevent the escape of the arrestee.

(2) A police officer may use deadly force only to prevent the commission of a dangerous felony or to effectuate an arrest of a person reasonably believed to have committed a felony where it reasonably appears necessary to the officer.

b. **Private Citizens**

(1) A private citizen is privileged to use that amount of non-deadly force that reasonably appears necessary to prevent the commission of a felony or a misdemeanor amounting to a breach of the peace.

(2) A private citizen may use non-deadly force to make an arrest if the crime was, in fact, committed, and she reasonably believes the person against whom she uses the force committed the crime.

(3) A private citizen may use the same amount of deadly force as a police officer only if a dangerous felony is involved and the person against whom he used the force is actually guilty of the crime.

(4) A proper mistake—meaning one that is both made in good faith and reasonable—as to the use of lethal force may justify a homicide committed in self-defense or to prevent the commission of a dangerous felony. However, a private citizen-defendant who mistakenly uses deadly force to prevent the escape of a fleeing felon is not justified. Thus, if no dangerous felony has actually been committed, or if the victim was not actually the felon, the defendant will be criminally liable.

NOTE: Unlike private citizens, police officers who mistakenly use deadly force in such fleeing felon situations may be justified.

c. **Public Duty**

(1) A public official, police officer, or private citizen offering assistance is justified in using reasonable force against another or in taking the property of another provided that she is acting within her authority pursuant to a law, court order, or process that is valid or that she reasonably believes to be valid.

6. **Resisting Unlawful Arrest**

a. A defendant may use reasonable, non-deadly force to resist an unlawful arrest.

(1) A minority of jurisdictions do not permit even non-deadly force in order to resist an unlawful arrest.

b. Most jurisdictions permit an individual to use force to resist an arrest made with excessive force, especially if the individual fears injury.

c. An individual may only resist a lawful arrest by a police officer where the individual does not know that the other person is a police officer.

7. **Domestic Authority**

a. The parents of a minor child, or one *in loco parentis*, may justifiably use reasonable force on the child to promote the child's welfare.

b. **Reasonableness** is determined in light of the child's age, sex, health, and particular misconduct based on the totality of the circumstances.

c. This defense is available in some other situations where similar responsibility lies, such as a ship's captain for his crew or a warden for her prisoners.

D. Other Considerations

1. **Consent**

a. Consent of the victim is not a defense to a crime except when it negates a specific element of the offense, such as in rape or kidnapping.

2. **Condonation**

a. Subsequent forgiveness by the victim is generally not a defense to the commission of a crime.

3. **Mistake of Law**

a. Generally, when a defendant is unaware that his acts are criminally proscribed, such ignorance of the law provides no defense.

EXAMPLE: A homeowner puts a sign on her front lawn advertising her new realty business, unaware that there is a criminal statute in the city prohibiting commercial advertising on residential property. The homeowner is fined for violation of the statute. The fact that the homeowner was unaware of the statute will not be a defense.

b. **Exceptions**

(1) When a statute proscribing the defendant's conduct has not been made reasonably available, the defendant's mistake or ignorance of law can be the basis of a successful defense.

(2) When the defendant has reasonably relied on a statute or judicial decision that was later overruled or declared unconstitutional, the defendant's mistake or ignorance of law can be the basis of a successful defense.

EXAMPLE: A city had an ordinance prohibiting homeowners from putting up signs on their front lawns and imposing criminal penalties on homeowners who violated the statute. The city later amended the ordinance to permit signage up to a certain size and shape. The amended ordinance was challenged in local court, and the judge found it constitutional. A homeowner then put a sign on his front lawn which was within the parameters allowed by the statute. Later, an appellate court ruled that the amended ordinance was unconstitutional and reinstated the original ordinance, and the homeowner removed the sign. The homeowner then received notice of a fine for the period in which the sign was up, per the terms of the original ordinance. Because the homeowner relied on the lower court ruling in putting up the sign, he will be able to assert mistake of law as a defense.

(3) When a defendant relies in good faith upon an erroneous statement of law contained in an administrative order or in an official interpretation by a public officer or department, the defendant's mistake or ignorance of law can be the basis of a successful defense.

(4) When some element of the alleged crime specifically involves knowledge or awareness of the law by the defendant, the defendant's mistake or ignorance of law can be the basis of a successful defense.

KAPLAN BAR REVIEW

Criminal Procedure

TABLE OF CONTENTS

I. INTRODUCTION TO CRIMINAL PROCEDURE

Systems of Criminal Procedure....386
Exclusionary Rule....386

II. THE FOURTH AMENDMENT

Government Action....391
Arrests and Other Detentions....391
Evidentiary Search and Seizure....396
Warranted Actions....400

III. STATEMENTS AND CONFESSIONS

In General....417
Involuntary Statements....417
Inadmissible Statements....417

IV. IDENTIFICATIONS

The Two Bases to Attack Identifications of a Defendant....427

V. PRETRIAL PROCEDURES: CHRONOLOGY FROM ARREST TO TRIAL

Grand Jury Indictment....429
Information....429
Booking....430
Bail Hearing....430
Preliminary Hearing....431
Arraignment....431
Motions....432
Plea Bargaining....432
Collateral Attacks on Guilty Pleas after Sentencing....433

VI. PRETRIAL RIGHTS

The Right to a Speedy Trial....434
Rights during Discovery Stage....434

VII. DOUBLE JEOPARDY

In General....436
When Jeopardy Attaches....436
Same Offense....436
Separate Sovereignties Doctrine....437
Retrial after Jeopardy Attaches....437

Appeal by the Prosecution 438
Application of Double Jeopardy in Sentencing 438
Collateral Estoppel 439

VIII. GUARANTEES OF A FAIR TRIAL

Right of Severance 440
Impartiality 440
The Right to Counsel at Trial 440
Competency 443
Jury Trial 443
The Right to a Public Trial 446
Right of Confrontation 446
Right to Compulsory Process 447
Procedural Rights for Conviction 448

IX. POST-TRIAL STAGE

Defendant's Rights during Sentencing 449
Punishment 450
Appeal 451
Habeas Corpus 452

X. RIGHTS OF PRISONERS, JUVENILES, AND ALIENS

Prisoners' Rights 454
Juveniles' Rights 455
Aliens' Rights 455

XI. MISCELLANEOUS PROCEDURAL CONSIDERATIONS

Retroactivity of New Decisions 456
Ex Post Facto Crimes 456
Independent State Grounds 456
Privilege against Self-Incrimination 456
Exceptions to the Privilege against Self-Incrimination 458

I. INTRODUCTION TO CRIMINAL PROCEDURE

A. Systems of Criminal Procedure

1. **Federal and State Systems**
   a. While provisions in the United States Constitution are the highest sources of criminal procedure law, these provisions (including the Fourth, Fifth, Sixth, and Fourteenth Amendments) create only a floor, not a ceiling, as to the rights that states must extend to their citizens. States may create more extensive (but never less extensive) rights under their own constitutions, which are subject to ultimate review by their own state supreme courts.
2. **The Fourth, Fifth, and Sixth Amendments**
   a. The Fourth Amendment protects the people and their papers, houses, and effects from unreasonable searches and seizures, and requires particularized, as opposed to general, warrants that are supported by probable cause.
   b. The Fifth Amendment requires that no person be denied her life, liberty, or property without due process of law, and grants each person a privilege against compelled self-incrimination.
   c. The Sixth Amendment requires, in relevant part, that in all criminal prosecutions, the accused has a right to counsel to assist in his defense.

B. Exclusionary Rule

1. The **exclusionary rule** is a procedural rule of federal constitutional law used to deter unlawful police conduct. Under this rule, all evidence seized in violation of the Fourth Amendment, including physical evidence and statements, is inadmissible in a criminal proceeding. This rule was made applicable to the states under Mapp v. Ohio [367 U.S. 643 (1961)].
   a. The exclusionary rule is not meant as a remedy for a violation of the defendant's Fourth Amendment rights. Rather, this rule is aimed at the deterrence of Fourth Amendment violations by the police.
   b. The exclusionary rule has also been extended to violations of the Fifth Amendment [Murphy v. Waterfront Comm'n of New York Harbor, 378 U.S. 52 (1964)] and Sixth Amendment [United States v. Wade, 388 U.S. 218 (1967); Nix v. Williams, 467 U.S. 431 (1984)].
   c. The exceptions which apply to the Fourth Amendment exclusionary rule (independent evidence, inevitable discovery, and attenuation) also apply to violations of the Fifth and Sixth Amendments.
2. A criminal defendant must have standing to raise a Fourth Amendment violation claim. This is a threshold issue for any criminal defendant seeking to have evidence suppressed under the exclusionary rule. The defendant asserting the Fourth Amendment violation must personally be the victim of the police's unreasonable conduct. In analyzing standing to contest a search, a court must determine "whether the person who claims the protection of the Amendment has a legitimate expectation of privacy in the invaded place" [Rakas v. Illinois, 439 U.S. 128 (1978)].

3. In addition to excluding all evidence that has been illegally obtained, any additional evidence, including oral statements and physical objects acquired either directly or indirectly from the illegal arrest, search, or seizure, must also be excluded as tainted **fruit of the poisonous tree** [Wong Sun v. United States, 371 U.S. 471 (1963)].
   a. The fruit of the poisonous tree doctrine is not (or is to a very limited extent) applicable to Miranda violations.

      EXAMPLE: A criminal defendant is arrested lawfully but not read her Miranda warnings. After being subjected to custodial interrogation, she confesses to being a runner for a drug ring and tells the police where the drugs are manufactured and stored. Her confession is inadmissible under Miranda, but the drugs seized are likely admissible because their seizure is subject to Miranda and not Fourth Amendment analysis.

4. Subsequently seized evidence, otherwise inadmissible under the fruit of the poisonous tree doctrine, may still be admitted into evidence provided the taint is dissipated or purged by:
   a. **independent evidence**, which is evidence obtained from a source independent of the original illegality [Murray v. United States, 487 U.S. 533 (1988)];
      (1) In Murray, the police officers' illegal entry into a warehouse did not require suppression of evidence (marijuana) later discovered as a result of a search warrant obtained using information that was completely unconnected to the initial, unlawful entry, even where those officers seeking the warrant did not inform the issuing magistrate of the first entry.
   b. **inevitable discovery**, which is evidence that would have been discovered regardless of the illegality [Nix v. Williams, 467 U.S. 431 (1984); Wong Sun v. United States, 371 U.S. 471 (1963)]; or
      (1) In Nix, the Supreme Court adopted the inevitable discovery exception to the exclusionary rule where a conversation with a suspect, in violation of his right to counsel, ended with the suspect's leading police to a murder victim's body. The Court reasoned that because the police were systematically searching in the same area, they would have found the body quickly and in virtually the same condition, and therefore, the fairness and deterrent intents of the exclusionary rule would not be served by suppressing evidence of the body or its condition upon discovery.

         EXAMPLE: Defendant is arrested for driving under the influence. He voluntarily gets out of his car and, after failing the field sobriety test, is handcuffed and placed in a police car. His car is then locked and left by the side of the road until the police are able to come back to tow the car back to the police station for an inventory search. However, before the tow truck comes to collect the car, the police officers search the entire car, including the trunk and glove compartments, without a warrant and find in the trunk evidence of a gambling ring's being run by the defendant. This evidence would most likely not be suppressed under the doctrine of inevitable discovery.

c. **attenuation**, where a confession or consent to an illegal search is obtained after an illegal detention or entry, but is distant enough from the initial illegality that it is considered voluntary and not a product of the Fourth Amendment violation. While no single factor is dispositive, the factors a court will consider include [Brown v. Illinois, 422 U.S. 590 (1975)]:
   (1) whether Miranda warnings were given;
   (2) the temporal proximity of the arrest and the confession or consent;
   (3) the presence of intervening circumstances; and
   (4) the purpose and flagrancy of the official misconduct.
      (a) In Hudson v. Michigan [547 U.S. 586 (2006)], Justice Scalia added the "social costs" of suppressing evidence, including the "risk of releasing dangerous criminals into society," into the analysis of the exclusionary rule when the Court determined that a violation of the knock-and-announce rule did not require the suppression of all the evidence found in the search.

5. A defendant may challenge the affidavit upon which a warrant was issued by proving by a preponderance of the evidence the following conditions [Franks v. Delaware, 438 U.S. 154 (1978)]:
   a. a substantial showing that the affidavit contained false statements;
   b. the statements were made intentionally, knowingly, or in reckless disregard for the truth; and
   c. the magistrate's finding of probable cause could not have been made without the false statements.
      (1) If the defendant cannot prove these conditions, the warrant will be upheld if there was a "substantial basis" to issue the warrant in the first instance [Massachusetts v. Upton, 466 U.S. 727 (1984)].

6. The Supreme Court has held that where an officer makes an unconstitutional investigatory stop, learns during the stop that the suspect is subject to a valid arrest warrant, arrests the suspect, and then seizes incriminating evidence during a search incident to that arrest, the evidence seized is admissible under the Fourth Amendment. The Court held that the outstanding arrest warrant was a critical intervening circumstance wholly independent of the illegal stop [Utah v. Strieff, 579 U.S. 232 (2016)].
   a. It is important to note that the Court found it especially significant that there was no evidence that the officer's stop reflected flagrantly unlawful police misconduct [Id.].

7. **Balancing Approach on the Exclusionary Rule**
   a. The court sees that the only benefit of the exclusionary rule is to prevent future violations by law enforcement officers, and therefore will consider the benefit of the deterrence with the benefit of the remedy.

(1) The exclusionary rule precludes only the use of suppressed evidence in the prosecution's case-in-chief and does not apply to the use of evidence for impeachment.

(a) However, confessions which have been coerced [Mincey v. Arizona, 437 U.S. 385 (1978)] or immunized [New Jersey v. Portash, 440 U.S. 450 (1979)] are inadmissible for any purpose.

b. **Good Faith Exception**

(1) Evidence obtained pursuant to an invalid warrant will not be excluded if a reasonably well-trained officer would have believed that the warrant was valid [United States v. Leon, 468 U.S. 897 (1984)].

(2) Aspects for considering the good faith exception include:

(a) whether the police were acting on a good faith reliance of a facially valid warrant;

(b) whether the police were acting in reliance of a valid statute; and

(c) whether the police were acting in reliance of a court official rather than a police officer.

(3) The good faith exception to the exclusionary rule does not apply, however, when:

(a) the police lie or mislead the court in attaining a warrant;

(b) the magistrate is not neutral or detached; and

(c) no reasonable police officer would have believed the warrant was valid.

(4) The good faith exception has been extended to police negligence.

(a) In Herring v. United States [555 U.S. 135 (2009)], the Supreme Court held that the exclusionary rule did not apply when an illegal arrest was the result of isolated negligence attenuated from the arrest, but suggested that the exclusionary rule might apply to evidence resulting from gross or systemic negligence on the part of the police. In Herring, the defendant was arrested pursuant to an arrest warrant that had been recalled by the court, but that the police had negligently failed to remove from its computer system.

8. **Limitations on the Exclusionary Rule**

a. The exclusionary rule has not been extended to grand jury proceedings, and evidence at issue may be considered in granting an indictment [United States v. Calandra, 414 U.S. 338 (1974)].

(1) A grand jury indictment may be based on illegally obtained evidence [United States v. Calandra, 414 U.S. 338 (1974)] or even on hearsay evidence [Costello v. United States, 350 U.S. 359 (1956)].

b. Evidence obtained under the reasonable reliance of the validity of a search warrant issued by a detached and neutral magistrate is not subject to the exclusionary rule [United States v. Leon, 468 U.S. 897 (1984); Arizona v. Evans, 514 U.S. 1 (1995)].

c. Evidence excluded by the rule from use by one sovereign may be used in the civil proceedings of another sovereign [United States v. Janis, 428 U.S. 433 (1976)].

d. Evidence excluded by the rule for violating the Fourth, Fifth, or Sixth Amendments may be used to impeach testimony given on either direct examination or cross-examination [United States v. Havens, 446 U.S. 620 (1980)].

e. A confession obtained without giving Miranda warnings may be used to impeach a defendant's testimony [Harris v. New York, 401 U.S. 222 (1971)], unless it is:

   (1) coerced [Mincey v. Arizona, 437 U.S. 385 (1978)]; or

   (2) immunized [New Jersey v. Portash, 440 U.S. 450 (1979)].

f. The Court has also held that the exclusionary rule is unavailable in, among other types, deportation and parole revocation hearings [Immigration & Naturalization Service v. Lopez-Mendoza, 468 U.S. 1032 (1984); Pennsylvania Bd. of Probation and Parole v. Scott, 524 U.S. 357 (1998)].

9. **Procedural and Enforcement Considerations**

a. A defendant has a right to a suppression hearing, at which time the judge, as a matter of law, determines the admissibility of the evidence out of the jury's presence [Jackson v. Denno, 378 U.S. 368 (1964)].

   (1) The government's burden is to establish admissibility of the evidence by a preponderance [Lego v. Twomey, 404 U.S. 477 (1972)].

   (2) The defendant's testimony at the suppression hearing may not be used against her at trial on the substantive issue of guilt [Simmons v. United States, 390 U.S. 377 (1968)].

b. Admission of illegally obtained evidence constitutes reversible error unless the error is "harmless." Under this standard, the government must prove beyond a reasonable doubt that the error did not contribute to a conviction [Chapman v. California, 386 U.S. 18 (1967)]. In effect, the government must prove beyond a reasonable doubt that it still would have obtained a conviction without the error.

II. THE FOURTH AMENDMENT

A. Government Action

1. The Fourth Amendment applies only to government, not private, conduct. This amendment was intended as a restraint on the activities of sovereign authorities only [Burdeau v. McDowell, 256 U.S. 465 (1921)].
2. Where the actor is an agent of the federal, state, or local government (as well as some civil authorities), this requirement is met.
3. When a private party acting on his own acquires evidence that the government later seeks to introduce in a criminal prosecution, neither the Fourth Amendment nor the exclusionary rule is triggered. However, when a private party acts at the direction of a government agent or pursuant to an official policy, any search conducted and evidence seized is subject to Fourth Amendment scrutiny [Skinner v. Railway Labor Executives Association, 489 U.S. 602 (1989)].

   EXAMPLE: A police officer's demand that an airline employee inspect a passenger's bag before flight will make the actions of the private actor a public action and, therefore, subject to the Fourth Amendment.

B. Arrests and Other Detentions

1. **General Principles**
   a. Arrest warrants are generally not required before arresting someone in a public place [United States v. Watson, 423 U.S. 411 (1976)].
      (1) However, the nonemergency arrest of an individual in her own home requires an arrest warrant.
   b. To determine whether a person is in custody, the Supreme Court has adopted a two-step approach [Howes v. Fields, 565 U.S. 499 (2012)].
      (1) The initial step is to ascertain whether, in light of the objective circumstances of the interrogation, a reasonable person would have felt he was not at liberty to terminate the interrogation and leave.
         (a) In order to determine how a suspect would have gauged his freedom of movement, courts must examine all of the circumstances surrounding the interrogation. Relevant factors include [Id.]:
            1) the location of the questioning [Stansbury v. California, 511 U.S. 318 (1994)];
            2) the duration of the questioning [Berkemer v. McCarty, 468 U.S. 420 (1984)];
            3) statements made during the interview [Oregon v. Mathiason, 429 U.S. 492 (1977)];
            4) the presence or absence of physical restraints during the questioning [New York v. Quarles, 467 U.S. 649 (1984)]; and
            5) the release of the interviewee at the end of the questioning [California v. Beheler, 463 U.S. 1121 (1983)].

(2) The second step is to determine whether the relevant environment "presents the same inherently coercive pressures as the type of station house questioning at issue in Miranda" [Howes v. Fields, 565 U.S. 499 (2012)].

(3) Whether a person is in custody depends on the objective circumstances of the interrogation, and not on the subjective views harbored by either the interrogating officers or the person being questioned. In other words, it is determined based on what a reasonable person in the suspect's position would believe, and not on the actual mindset of the particular suspect being questioned [J. D. B. v. North Carolina, 564 U.S. 261 (2011)].

c. When a person is taken into custody for the purpose of commencing a criminal action, an **arrest** has occurred [Dunaway v. New York, 442 U.S. 200 (1979)].

(1) More than a stop-and-frisk is required. Although brief detentions by police are permissible for the purpose of questioning, even without probable cause that the person has committed a crime, such a "stop" is not considered an arrest [Terry v. Ohio, 392 U.S. 1 (1968)].

d. In 2012, the Court held that officials may strip-search individuals who have been arrested for any crime, even without reasonable suspicion that they are dangerous or carrying contraband items [Florence v. Board of Chosen Freeholders, 566 U.S. 318 (2012)], and in 2013, the Court held that the police may collect DNA samples from arrestees [Maryland v. King, 569 U.S. 435 (2013)].

e. An unlawful arrest is no defense to a subsequent conviction of the crime charged.

2. **Warrant Requirement**

a. A valid arrest may occur either with or without a warrant. Generally, no warrant is required for an arrest; the police need only possess probable cause.

(1) The police may come into possession of the requisite facts and circumstances for probable cause from their own observations of the suspect or through information obtained from third parties.

(a) If a police officer personally witnesses a crime, probable cause exists to arrest the suspect(s) observed committing the crime.

(b) Police observations prior to a stop may provide the objective basis for a reasonable belief that the suspect is engaged in criminal activity, and thus justify limited detention and questioning. Any facts and circumstances derived from such a limited stop may then escalate reasonable belief or suspicion to probable cause sufficient to justify an arrest.

(2) Probable cause to arrest may also be obtained indirectly through an informant. The tip may serve as a basis for a valid probable cause arrest if reliability is established by:

(a) the informant's tip containing specific details; and

(b) the reliability of both the details and the informant being confirmed prior to the moment of arrest.

b. An arrest warrant is required before police can arrest an individual in her own home, absent exigent circumstances or consent [Payton v. New York, 445 U.S. 573 (1980)].

NOTE The requirements for an arrest warrant are virtually identical to the requirements for a search warrant.

(1) Warrantless in-home arrests may be justified by consent or exigent circumstances when [United States v. Santana, 427 U.S. 38 (1976)]:

(a) an arrest attempt outside the home is thwarted because the suspect retreats into the home;

(b) there is insufficient time to secure a warrant because the delay would allow the suspect to evade arrest or destroy evidence; or

(c) the arresting officer is in "hot pursuit" and has probable cause to effect a valid arrest of the suspect.

EXAMPLE: While on a routine patrol, the police observe an apparent sale of illegal narcotics taking place in the front yard of a residence. When the suspects look up and spot the officers, they immediately run into the residence carrying what appear to be illegal narcotics. The police may follow the suspects into the residence in order to commence an arrest because they have probable cause to arrest the suspects and there is insufficient time to obtain an arrest warrant before the suspects destroy the evidence.

c. Police generally may not legally search for the subject of an arrest warrant in the home of a third party absent exigent circumstances or consent without first obtaining a search warrant for those premises [Steagald v. United States, 451 U.S. 204 (1981)].

d. Unless exigent circumstances exist, the arresting officers must "knock and announce" their identity before entering to make the arrest [Richards v. Wisconsin, 520 U.S. 1154 (1997)]. The violation of the **knock-and-announce rule** does not automatically trigger the automatic exclusion of evidence seized after the violation [Hudson v. Michigan, 547 U.S. 586 (2006)].

(1) An exigent circumstance would include reasonable suspicion that knocking and announcing would be dangerous or futile, or would inhibit effective investigation.

e. An arresting officer may break windows or other property only if reasonably required to execute the warrant [United States v. Ramirez, 523 U.S. 65 (1998)].

3. **Warrantless Arrests at Common Law**
   a. Both police officers and private citizens may make arrests for felonies committed in their presence.
      (1) A police officer may arrest a person for a felony not committed in his presence when he has reasonable grounds to believe the person did, in fact, commit the felony.
      (2) A private citizen may arrest a person, but it will be valid only if the felony is found to have actually been committed.
   b. Police officers and private citizens may make arrests for misdemeanors when:
      (1) the crime is committed in their presence; and
      (2) the misdemeanor amounts to a breach of the peace.
   c. A warrant is required for a misdemeanor that the police officer did not personally observe, regardless of whether the arrest takes place inside or outside the suspect's home.
   d. The use of deadly force to prevent the escape of a felony suspect is allowed if [Tennessee v. Garnor, 471 U.S. 1 (1985)]:
      (1) the suspect poses a threat of serious physical harm to the officer or to others; or
      (2) the suspect has committed a crime involving such infliction of harm, if some feasible warning has been given.
4. **Probable Cause**
   a. **Probable cause**, which is required at the time of the arrest, is the measure of justification that applies to full-scale intrusions—searches, seizures, and arrests. It is defined as that quantity of facts and circumstances within the police officer's knowledge that would warrant a reasonable person to conclude that the individual in question has committed a crime (for an arrest) or that specific items related to criminal activity can be found at a particular location (for a search).
   b. Probable cause is evaluated in terms of what was known at the moment of the government intrusion. A police officer may establish probable cause by considering events leading up to the moment of arrest [Maryland v. Pringle, 540 U.S. 366 (2003)].
      (1) Subjective intentions play no role in ordinary, probable cause Fourth Amendment analyses [Whren v. United States, 517 U.S. 806 (1996)]. In Whren, the Court held that the detention of a motorist, where the police had probable cause to believe he had committed a traffic violation, was adequate for the subsequent search and seizure regardless of any other motive the police officer may have had in making the stop. This is true even where the stop was for a misdemeanor, such as the failure to wear a seatbelt [Atwater v. City of Lago Vista, 532 U.S. 318 (2001)].
   c. **Anticipatory** or **conditional warrants** are warrants that are conditioned on an event occurring, such as the delivery of a package. The

Court requires the following two showings to issue such a warrant [United States v. Grubbs, 547 U.S. 90 (2006)]:

(1) if the triggering condition occurs, there must be a fair probability that evidence of a crime or contraband will be found at a particular location; and

(2) there is probable cause that the triggering condition will occur.

5. **Reasonable Suspicion**

a. **Reasonable suspicion** is a belief based upon articulable information that is more than a mere hunch used by a reasonable person or police office that the suspect has or is about to engage in illegal or criminal activity.

b. Courts must look to the totality of the circumstances of each case to see whether the police officer has a "particularized and objective basis" for suspecting legal wrongdoing [United States v. Arvizu, 534 U.S. 266 (2002)].

c. Persons present on the premises during a valid search pursuant to a search warrant may be detained [Michigan v. Summers, 452 U.S. 692 (1981)].

6. **Terry Standard**

a. In order to take the next intrusive step of patting down or frisking a criminal suspect, the police officer must be able to articulate more than a reasonable suspicion that criminality is afoot.

(1) In order to frisk a stopped individual, the police must articulate reasonable suspicion that the suspect is armed and dangerous [Terry v. Ohio, 392 U.S. 1 (1968)].

(a) Sudden flight from a high-crime area may be an adequate reasonable suspicion for an investigative stop [Illinois v. Wardlow, 528 U.S. 119 (2000)].

(b) An anonymous tip alone is inadequate. However, under the totality of the circumstances, an anonymous tip coupled with police corroboration of some of the information contained in the tip shows sufficient indicia of reliability to justify an investigative stop [Alabama v. White, 496 U.S. 325 (1990)].

b. **Stop-and-Frisk**

(1) If a police officer reasonably believes, based upon the officer's own observations or those of an informant, that criminal activity may be afoot, then the officer may stop and briefly question a criminal suspect.

(2) The required reasonable belief or reasonable suspicion must be supported by some objective evidence that the suspect is engaged or about to become engaged in criminal activity, or is a wanted criminal [United States v. Hensley, 469 U.S. 221 (1985)].

(3) The police may do a limited pat-down of the suspect's outer garments (a "frisk") for weapons if they have a reasonable and articulable suspicion that the person detained may be "armed and dangerous," despite the lack of probable cause or a warrant [Terry v. Ohio, 392 U.S. 1 (1968)].

(a) The frisk may also extend to the interior of a car where the suspect is sitting [Michigan v. Long, 463 U.S. 1032 (1983)].

(b) If, during the frisk for weapons, the officer feels items that reasonably feel like a weapon or contraband, such as crack cocaine, the officer may seize the items, even if they turn out to be something other than weapons or contraband [Minnesota v. Dickerson, 508 U.S. 366 (1993)].

(c) A minimum level of justification must exist for reasonable suspicion; presence in an area alone is not enough, but common sense behaviors can be enough to warrant a stop-and-frisk [Illinois v. Wardlow, 528 U.S. 119 (2000)].

NOTE Flight is not enough for probable cause but is enough for reasonable suspicion.

(d) A police officer is justified in requesting a suspect's name as identification during a Terry stop as long as the request has an immediate relation to the purpose of the stop [Hiibel v. Nevada, 542 U.S. 177 (2004)].

(e) The fact that an officer may have also had some improper subjective basis for the stop will not result in a finding that the stop was illegal, as long as the stop was supported by an objectively reasonable belief that the suspect was engaged or about to engage in criminal activity [Whren v. United States, 517 U.S. 806 (1996)].

(f) The officer's reasonable belief may be based upon hearsay, such as an informant's tip [Adams v. Williams, 407 U.S. 143 (1972)]. However, the objective evidence requirement mandates that the information be confirmed as reliable prior to actually conducting the stop. The tip must contain some predictive information so that the police may test the tip.

EXAMPLE: A tip that a person is standing by a pay phone with a plaid jacket does not provide reasonable suspicion because there is no predictive information other than the physical description to prove that the tip is correct [Florida v. J.L., 529 U.S. 266 (2000)].

(g) A Terry stop based on less than full probable cause is permitted when the detainee is suspected of involvement in a past crime constituting a felony or a threat to public safety [United States v. Hensley, 469 U.S. 221 (1985)].

C. Evidentiary Search and Seizure

1. Expectation of Privacy

a. A person may assert her Fourth Amendment rights only when there is a government intrusion into her reasonable expectation of privacy, or when the government's investigatory conduct results in a physical trespass against her person, home, papers, or effects. When government action qualifies as a search pursuant to either of these tests, a defendant may seek the remedy of exclusion of the evidence discovered during the search, but only if the defendant has standing to object to the government conduct.

(1) **Standing**

(a) A defendant whose rights are violated must establish standing to assert a Fourth Amendment claim.

1) An ownership or possessory interest in the premises is sufficient.

2) A passenger in an automobile lacks standing to challenge the validity of a search of the vehicle [Rakas v. Illinois, 439 U.S. 128 (1978)].

a) In Rakas, passengers in a car, who did not claim to own the car and did not even claim to own the property seized (in this case, guns found under the passenger seat of the car) did not have standing to object to the legality of the search simply because they were present at the time of the search.

b) Mere lawful presence in the car is only one factor the courts consider in determining existence of a legitimate expectation of privacy.

3) However, a car passenger does have standing to challenge a police stop of an automobile. In Brendlin v. California [551 U.S. 249 (2007)], the Supreme Court held that all occupants of a car are "seized" for purposes of the Fourth Amendment during a traffic stop, not just the driver. So when police unlawfully make a random stop of an automobile, the passenger has standing to challenge the search and seizure of items inside the vehicle as a fruit of the wrongful stop.

4) A defendant who is an overnight guest in another's home has standing [Minnesota v. Olson, 495 U.S. 91 (1990)].

a) However, short-term guests, non-overnight social guests, and commercial guests have no reasonable expectation of privacy in a host's home [Minnesota v. Carter, 525 U.S. 83 (1998)].

(b) Standing based on a legitimate expectation of privacy is not necessarily determined by mere ownership of the items seized.

(c) Where a defendant is charged with possession of an illegal item, Fourth Amendment standing is not automatic.

1) The defendant must show a legitimate expectation of privacy in the items seized or in the premises searched [United States v. Salvucci, 448 U.S. 83 (1980)].

2) There must be a fairly substantial nexus between the defendant and the place searched [Rawlings v. Kentucky, 448 U.S. 98 (1980)].

EXAMPLE: A defendant had no legitimate expectation of privacy, and thereby no standing, where illegal drugs were found in a companion's purse, even though the defendant immediately claimed ownership.

(2) A defendant has a reasonable expectation of privacy when the objects identified by the government investigation are not "held out to the public."

(a) A defendant has no expectation of privacy in things held out in public.

(b) Furthermore, a defendant does not have a reasonable expectation of privacy in the following items, even if they are not held out in public:

1) handwriting exemplars [United States v. Mara, 410 U.S. 19 (1973)];
2) voice exemplars [United States v. Dionisio, 410 U.S. 1 (1973)];
3) bank records [United States v. Miller, 425 U.S. 435 (1976)];
4) pen registers, which record telephone numbers dialed [Smith v. Maryland, 442 U.S. 735 (1979)]; and
5) private conversations, including eavesdropping [Hoffa v. United States, 385 U.S. 293 (1966)].

NOTE A person in a closed telephone booth does have an actual (subjective) and reasonable expectation of privacy such that the attachment of electronic eavesdropping devices on the exterior of the phone booth constitutes an impermissible search [Katz v. United States, 389 U.S. 347 (1967)].

2. When the government uses a device or technology that is not in general public use that enables it to observe the interior of a private home when it would be unable to observe that area with the naked eye, the surveillance falls under the Fourth Amendment and is presumptively unreasonable without a warrant [Kyllo v. United States, 533 U.S. 27 (2001)].

EXAMPLE: The government's attachment of a GPS device to a vehicle, and its use of that device to monitor the vehicle's movements, also constitutes a search under the Fourth Amendment [United States v. Jones, 565 U.S. 400 (2012)].

EXAMPLE: In 2013, the Court held that the use by police of a trained detection dog to sniff for narcotics on a front porch is also a search under the Fourth Amendment [Florida v. Jardines, 569 U.S. 1 (2013)].

3. Under the open fields doctrine, any unoccupied or undeveloped area outside of the **curtilage**, the living space directly around the home, is not extended Fourth Amendment protection. The protection also does not apply

to naked-eye observations of private property by air [California v. Ciralo, 476 U.S. 207 (1986)]. These areas are not considered part of the "home" within the meaning of the Fourth Amendment so a physical trespass into open fields does not qualify as a search.

a. In Ciralo, the court upheld observations made from aircraft of marijuana crops growing in a secluded area of the suspect's property.

NOTE The open fields away from a home are not close or "intimate" enough to the home to provide protection from government interference or surveillance [Oliver v. United States, 466 U.S. 170 (1984)].

EXAMPLE: Aerial photography of the outdoor areas around a large fenced-in industrial complex was not a search [Dow Chemical Co. v. United States, 476 U.S. 227 (1986)].

4. A defendant loses any privacy right that may have existed with discarded property, such as commingled garbage and abandoned rental premises.

5. **Search and Seizure and the Use of Police Dogs**

a. In general, a canine search does not constitute an unreasonable search unless the canine physically intrudes upon a constitutionally protected area (e.g., home, curtilage, or person).

b. In Florida v. Jardines [569 U.S. 1 (2013)], the Supreme Court held that police use of a trained detection dog to sniff for narcotics on the front porch of a private home is a "search" within the meaning of the Fourth Amendment to the United States Constitution, and therefore, without consent, requires both probable cause and a search warrant. The rationale was that this was a physical intrusion on constitutionally protected property—an area in which the homeowner had a reasonable expectation of privacy.

c. **Automobile Exception**

(1) The use of drug-sniffing dogs trained to detect contraband, but not other items, does not invade the privacy rights of the suspect [Illinois v. Caballes, 543 U.S. 405 (2005)].

d. **Administrative Searches**

(1) To protect airline passengers from weapons and explosives, warrantless administrative searches are permitted at airports. A passenger may avoid being searched by declining to board the plane.

(2) Although narcotics-sniffing dogs may smell a passenger's luggage, any resulting detention must be brief, and luggage seizure is subject to Fourth Amendment limitations [United States v. Place, 462 U.S. 696 (1983)].

e. **Traffic Stops**

(1) Illinois v. Caballes [543 U.S. 405 (2005)] allowed drug-sniffing dog use during traffic stops, holding that brief prolongations of those stops to allow for such inspections did not violate the Fourth Amendment.

(2) Rodriguez v. United States [575 U.S. 348 (2015)] held that the police may not prolong traffic stops to wait for drug-sniffing dogs to inspect

vehicles. A police stop exceeding the time needed to handle the matter for which the stop was made violates the Fourth Amendment.

D. Warranted Actions

1. The Fourth Amendment prohibits only federal law enforcement officials from conducting unreasonable searches and seizures. The prohibition is equally applicable to state law enforcement personnel by virtue of the Fourteenth Amendment. However, the Fourth Amendment allows federal and state law enforcement officers to conduct reasonable searches and seizures.
2. A search conducted by a government authority without a warrant is presumptively invalid unless it falls within a specifically carved-out exception [Katz v. United States, 389 U.S. 347 (1967)]. Thus, a reasonable search under the Fourth Amendment must be conducted either pursuant to a warrant or under an exception to the warrant requirement.
3. **Search and Arrest Warrants**
    a. A **warrant** is a judicial authorization for police action, either to search a particular place (**search warrant**) or to arrest a particular person (**arrest warrant**).
        (1) A search warrant must be issued by a neutral and detached magistrate after an adequate showing of probable cause, and must describe with particularity the place to be searched and items to be seized.
            (a) Illegally obtained probable cause will not support a search warrant or warrantless search.
        (2) An arrest warrant also must be issued by a neutral and detached magistrate after an adequate showing of probable cause, and must describe the identity of the suspect either by name or a reasonably specific description, so that the officers may locate the suspect with reasonable effort.
4. **Searches Pursuant to a Warrant**
    a. **Warrant Requirements**
        (1) The warrant must be issued by a neutral and detached magistrate who reviews evidence submitted by police officers and determines that there is probable cause to issue the warrant [Giordenello v. United States, 357 U.S. 480 (1958)].
            (a) A justice of the peace who also happens to be the state attorney general is not neutral and detached [Coolidge v. New Hampshire, 403 U.S. 443 (1971)].
            (b) However, a court clerk is a neutral judicial officer regarding warrants for city ordinance violations [Shadwick v. City of Tampa, 407 U.S. 345 (1972)].
            (c) A warrant is invalid if the magistrate takes a monetary reward in return for issuing the warrant [Connelly v. Georgia, 429 U.S. 245 (1977)].
            (d) A neutral magistrate may not "supervise" the scope of the search [Lo-Ji Sales, Inc. v. New York, 442 U.S. 319 (1979)].

(2) Either oral testimony or an affidavit must set forth the facts or circumstances relied upon by the magistrate, who must then make an independent judgment of the reasonableness of the requested search or seizure to determine if there is probable cause [Shadwick v. City of Tampa, 407 U.S. 345 (1972)].

(3) The Federal Rules of Criminal Procedure allow a warrant to be issued based on information submitted by reliable electronic means (e.g., fax or email) [Fed. R. Crim. P. 4.1].

(4) The warrant must describe with particularity the place to be searched and the item or person to be seized. Absent independent justification, a search warrant confers upon police only the authority to search named places or persons.

   (a) Where only the search of one apartment is required, a warrant authorizing the search of the entire apartment building is imprecise and thus invalid [United States v. Hinton, 219 F.2d 326 (7th Cir. 1955)].

   (b) The scope of the search is limited to the premises described in the warrant [Marron v. United States, 275 U.S. 192 (1927)]. Nonetheless, contraband not named in the warrant may be lawfully seized under the **plain view doctrine** where the police are acting under a valid warrant [Harris v. United States, 331 U.S. 145 (1947)].

   (c) A location owned by nonsuspects may be searched upon obtaining a warrant [Zurcher v. Stanford Daily, 436 U.S. 547 (1978)].

   (d) A warrant properly issued for the search of contraband carries with it the implicit authority to detain occupants on the premises during the search [Michigan v. Summers, 452 U.S. 692 (1981)].

(5) The warrant must be based upon probable cause.

   (a) **Probable cause** is satisfied when the following two-prong test is met [Carroll v. United States, 267 U.S. 132 (1925)]:

      1) the testimony or affidavit presented to the magistrate contains facts or circumstances that are still relevant and not out of date; and

      2) it must be sufficient that a reasonable person would conclude it to be more probable than not that evidence of named items or persons will be found.

   (b) A warrant based on an informant's tip will be issued when probable cause is established under the "totality of the circumstances" [Illinois v. Gates, 462 U.S. 213 (1983)]. The relevant factors taken into account are:

      1) credible information;

      2) reliable informant;

      3) police corroboration; and

      4) declaration against interest.

(c) Generally, informants need not reveal their identity, and the government will not be required to disclose the identity of an informant if disclosure will jeopardize the informant's physical safety or the integrity of a pending investigation [McCray v. Illinois, 386 U.S. 300 (1983)].

(6) It is improper to issue a warrant, even when there is probable cause, if the intrusion is unreasonable.

EXAMPLE: It is improper to require the removal of a bullet from an individual suspected of robbery when the bullet is deeply embedded in the body, removal would damage the body, and the removal would require general anesthesia [Winston v. Lee, 470 U.S. 753 (1985)].

(7) A defendant may challenge the affidavit upon which a warrant was issued by proving by a preponderance of the evidence the following conditions [Franks v. Delaware, 438 U.S. 154 (1978)]:

(a) a substantial showing that the affidavit contained false statements;

(b) the statements were made intentionally, knowingly, or in reckless disregard for the truth; and

(c) the magistrate's finding of probable cause could not have been made without the false statements.

1) If the defendant cannot prove these conditions, the warrant will be upheld if there was a "substantial basis" to issue the warrant in the first instance [Massachusetts v. Upton, 466 U.S. 727 (1984)].

b. **Execution of Warrant**

(1) A search warrant need not specify the precise manner for its execution, yet limitations do apply, as follows [Ker v. California, 374 U.S. 23 (1964)]:

(a) only the police, not private citizens, may execute a warrant;

(b) a search warrant must be executed promptly while probable cause still exists; and

(c) absent exigent circumstances, a police officer must knock and announce his presence before attempting a forcible entry.

1) A violation of the **knock-and-announce rule** does not require the automatic suppression of all evidence found in the subsequent search [Hudson v. Michigan, 547 U.S. 586 (2006)].

(2) Persons unnamed in a warrant may not be searched merely because of their presence at a search location [Ybarra v. Illinois, 444 U.S. 85 (1979)].

(3) In general, private citizens may not execute warrants with the police. It is a violation of the Fourth Amendment for police to bring members of the media or other third parties into a home

during the execution of a warrant when the presence of the third parties in the home is not in aid of execution of the warrant. Where the police enter a home under the authority of a warrant to search for stolen property, the presence of third parties for the sole purpose of identifying the stolen property is proper [Wilson v. Layne, 526 U.S. 603 (1999)].

(4) When police do not obtain a search warrant or an arrest warrant until after they enter the defendant's home and conduct a search, such a search is not permissible under the Fourth Amendment absent exigent circumstances, even when the police believe that they have probable cause to search [Kirk v. Louisiana, 536 U.S. 635 (2002)].

(5) Unless an exception to the warrant requirement is applicable, a search (or arrest) conducted pursuant to an invalid warrant will generally constitute a violation of the Fourth Amendment.

(a) A search conducted pursuant to an invalid warrant does not always make the evidence inadmissible under the exclusionary rule. Evidence seized by police acting in good faith on the basis of an objectively valid warrant is admissible if the actual invalidity is due to an error by the issuing magistrate [United States v. Leon, 468 U.S. 897 (1984); Massachusetts v. Sheppard, 468 U.S. 981 (1984)].

EXAM TIP Warrantless searches are generally unconstitutional unless they fall within one of the following warrant exceptions, which are described further below: (1) searches incident to a lawful arrest; (2) automobile exception; (3) plain view; (4) consent; (5) searches pursuant to a stop; (6) hot pursuit; or (7) exigent circumstances.

5. **Exceptions to Warrant Requirement**

a. Because the warrant requirement is central to the Fourth Amendment protection against unreasonable searches and seizures, warrantless searches are unconstitutional unless they fall within one of the eight exceptions discussed below.

(1) **Searches Incident to a Lawful Arrest**

(a) To protect the arresting police officers and to prevent the destruction of evidence, the defendant's person, as well as the area within her immediate control (usually referred to as the wingspan) may be searched incident to a lawful arrest.

1) A search incident to arrest includes a cursory scan or "protective sweep" of adjoining rooms, and the entire domicile may be scanned, provided there is reasonable suspicion of an armed accomplice [Maryland v. Buie, 494 U.S. 325 (1990)].

2) However, a warrantless search of the entire house following a lawful arrest is unconstitutional [Chimel v. California, 395 U.S. 752 (1969)].

3) If a custodial arrest is effected while the defendant is in a car, the police may search the passenger compartment of the vehicle only if it is reasonable to believe that the defendant might access the vehicle at the time of the search or that the vehicle contains evidence of the offense of arrest [Arizona v. Gant, 556 U.S. 332 (2009)].

(b) When police officers merely issue a traffic citation and do not make an arrest, they may not search the driver or the car for contraband [Knowles v. Iowa, 525 U.S. 113 (1998)].

(c) A search incident to a lawful arrest must be contemporaneous to the arrest [United States v. Chadwick, 433 U.S. 1 (1977)] and may even precede it [Rawlings v. Kentucky, 448 U.S. 98 (1980)].

(d) When the offense in question authorizes a full custodial arrest, a search incident to that arrest may follow, even when the police do not fear for their safety or believe contraband will be found.

EXAMPLE: A search of a defendant's pack of cigarettes which contained heroin was held to be lawful as incident to his arrest for a traffic violation [United States v. Robinson, 414 U.S. 218 (1973)].

EXAMPLE: A driver was ordered out of his vehicle and a full search of his person was held lawful, even though the arrest was only for a traffic violation, where the police officer noticed a bulge in the defendant's jacket and believed that it might be a weapon. The police had a reasonable suspicion that the defendant was armed, and so the search was lawful to ensure the safety of the officers [Pennsylvania v. Mimms, 434 U.S. 106 (1977)].

(e) The warrantless search and seizure of digital contents of a cell phone during an arrest is unconstitutional [Riley v. California, 573 U.S. 373 (2014)].

(2) **Automobile Exception**

(a) The automobile exception is based on the idea that a lesser expectation of privacy exists in an automobile, boat, or airplane than in one's home or personal property [United States v. Chadwick, 433 U.S. 1 (1977)]. Additionally, the inherent mobility of vehicles requires prompt action by law enforcement.

1) The use of drug-sniffing dogs trained to detect contraband, but not other items, does not invade the privacy rights of the suspect [Illinois v. Caballes, 543 U.S. 405 (2005)]. A trained dog's alert provides probable cause to search a vehicle for narcotics [Florida v. Harris, 568 U.S. 237 (2013)].

(b) The Supreme Court has ruled that once the police have probable cause to search the moving or temporarily stopped vehicle, they may seize the vehicle and search it later, even if there is sufficient time to obtain a warrant between the seizure of the vehicle and the subsequent search [Chambers v. Maroney, 399 U.S. 42 (1970)].

(c) The police may inspect a container within an automobile if they have probable cause to believe the container has contraband or evidence, even where the police do not have probable cause to search the entire car [California v. Acevedo, 500 U.S. 565 (1991)].

(d) Warrantless search and seizure of items from an automobile may be justified under several scenarios, including [United States v. Martinez-Fuerte, 428 U.S. 543 (1976)]:

1) a search incident to a lawful arrest;
2) plain view;
3) an inventory search following a lawful impounding; or
    a) If the police lawfully impound a vehicle, they may conduct a routine inventory search. Because the reason for the search is not criminal investigation, the police do not need probable cause or a warrant to justify the search [South Dakota v. Opperman, 428 U.S. 364 (1967)]. Such a search is justified:
        i) to safeguard the defendant's property; and
        ii) to protect the police against false claims of theft.
    b) However, in some jurisdictions, the police must give the subject the option of having someone pick up the car for her or allowing her to park and secure it herself, instead of conducting an inventory search.
4) a border search.
    a) Congress has granted the executive plenary authority to conduct routine searches and seizures at the border, or at fixed checkpoints near the border, without probable cause or a warrant, in order to regulate the collection of duties and to prevent the introduction of contraband into the United States [United States v. Flores-Montano, 541 U.S. 149 (2004)].
    b) Reasonable suspicion is required for searches that are unusually intrusive, such as a body cavity search or a search that results in destruction of property [Id].

(e) There are only limited circumstances under which the police may conduct a warrantless search of a parked vehicle. In such a case, because of the decreased threat of mobility, there would likely be ample time to obtain a search warrant. Thus, a search warrant must be obtained unless the purpose of the search is not criminal investigation.

(f) Where probable cause to conduct a warrantless search exists, the police may search the entire vehicle, including closed containers and luggage, to find the objects for which the probable cause existed [United States v. Ross. 456 U.S. 798 (1982)].

1) The Supreme Court has held it to be an improper invasion of privacy to open a footlocker without a warrant, even though the item was obtained from an automobile over which the police had custody [United States v. Chadwick, 433 U.S. 1 (1977)].

(g) A mere lawful stop based on reasonable suspicion of a criminal violation can ripen into probable cause sufficient for a warrantless search.

EXAMPLE: A lawful vehicle stop for speeding developed into probable cause to search when officers observed fruits of a crime they had learned of through a police broadcast [Colorado v. Bannister, 449 U.S. 1 (1980)].

1) The Fourth Amendment does not require police officers to advise bus passengers of their right not to cooperate and to refuse consent to searches, provided that a reasonable person would feel free to decline the request to search or otherwise terminate the encounter [United States v. Drayton, 536 U.S. 194 (2002)].

(h) **Automobile Stops**

1) Police officers not set up at a checkpoint may not randomly stop a vehicle to check the license and registration without a reasonable suspicion of wrongdoing. Such a stop is unconstitutional because it leaves too much discretion to the police officer [Delaware v. Prouse, 440 U.S. 648 (1979)].

2) The police, operating at a checkpoint, may stop traffic to check the vehicle registration and drivers' licenses of automobile drivers, as long as the stops:

a) are random; and

b) are based on some fixed formula, such as every vehicle or every fifth vehicle.

i) If a formula is used, there is no requirement of reasonable belief or objective basis for stopping any particular vehicle [Michigan Department of Police v. Sitz, 496 U.S. 444 (1990)].

3) Sobriety or drunk-driving checkpoints are permissible [Michigan v. Sitz, 496 U.S. 444 (1990)].

4) When police set up a checkpoint to search vehicles for evidence of illegal drugs, the checkpoint violates the Fourth Amendment because its primary purpose is indistinguishable from the general interest in crime control and because the checkpoint is not based on individualized suspicion of wrongdoing [Indianapolis v. Edmond, 531 U.S. 32 (2000)].

5) A police highway checkpoint set up to obtain information from motorists about a recent crime does not violate the Fourth Amendment [Illinois v. Lidster, 540 U.S. 419 (2004)].

6) Police officers who lawfully stop a vehicle may ask all of the occupants to exit the vehicle, even without any individualized suspicion that any occupant has been or is engaged in criminal activity [Maryland v. Wilson, 519 U.S. 408 (1997)].

7) Customs officials may stop vehicles at permanent checkpoints located at or near the border. Such a stop does not constitute an unreasonable seizure. Therefore, there is no requirement of reasonable belief or objective basis that a vehicle's occupants or contents are illegally entering the country before this type of stop may occur.

(3) **The Special Needs Doctrine**

(a) The **special needs doctrine** is an exception to the general requirement of individualized suspicion of searches. The Supreme Court has held that a warrantless, suspicionless search may be justified when special needs, beyond the normal need for law enforcement, make the warrant and probable-cause requirement impracticable [Griffin v. Wisconsin, 483 U.S. 868 (1987)].

1) Police are permitted to use checkpoints to conduct brief seizures and/or limited searches with no individualized suspicion or warrant in response to a public safety danger that cannot be addressed by complying with the normal individualized suspicion/warrant requirements.

EXAMPLE: Common special needs checkpoint searches include sobriety checkpoints, searches for recently escaped prison inmates, counterterrorism checkpoints, and checkpoints to search for suspects of a recent crime.

(b) If the court finds that the primary purpose of a program of searches is a special need and not a general interest in crime control, the court must then conduct a context-specific inquiry into the reasonableness of the program.

(c) The court will use the following balancing test to weigh the special need against the privacy interest advanced [Lynch v. City of New York, 589 F.3d 94 (2d Cir. 2009)]:

1) the nature of the privacy interest involved;

2) the character and degree of the governmental intrusion; and

3) the nature and immediacy of the government's needs and the efficacy of the program in addressing those needs.

EXAMPLE: Police set up a checkpoint to search vehicles for evidence of illegal drugs. The checkpoint violates the Fourth Amendment because its primary purpose is indistinguishable from the general interest in crime control and because the checkpoint is not based on individualized suspicion of wrongdoing.

(d) A special needs search or seizure must be based on a fixed formula that deprives individual officers of the discretion to select the subjects.

EXAMPLE: In response to heightened intelligence reports of possible terrorist subway bombings, police may establish checkpoints to randomly search bags of subway passenger. Police may only look in bags capable of concealing a bomb.

(e) Police may seize any contraband that comes into plain view while searching within the scope of the special needs inspection, even if the contraband is unrelated to the public safety concern.

(f) Police officers may not randomly stop a vehicle to check the license and registration without a reasonable suspicion of wrongdoing.

EXAM TIP Because a special needs stop is a seizure, if it is unreasonable (not based on a valid special needs justification), any evidence it leads to will be tainted by the stop. However, if it is reasonable, any subsequent search or seizure will be unaffected by the stop, even if the evidence is unrelated to the special need.

(4) **Plain View**

(a) The police may seize property that is clearly visible in plain view without a warrant if [Coolidge v. New Hampshire, 403 U.S. 443 (1971); Horton v. California, 496 U.S. 128 (1990)]:

1) the police are lawfully present at the place where the object can be seen;

2) the officers have a lawful right of access to the object; and

3) it is "immediately apparent" that the object is incriminating.

(b) A police officer may follow an arrestee into his house and then lawfully seize any contraband evidence that is in plain view [Washington v. Chrisman, 455 U.S. 1 (1982)].

(c) The police officer may not move objects to get a better view [Arizona v. Hicks, 480 U.S. 321 (1987)].

(d) Courts have held that where a police officer sees contraband through the window of a vehicle, the officer is considered to have lawful access to seize the contraband.

(5) **Consent**

(a) **Consent** is a warrantless intrusion requiring no justification; an individual may simply waive her Fourth Amendment rights as long as that waiver is voluntary. Because a consent search is made pursuant to a valid consent, it does not invade a defendant's privacy.

(b) To justify a search based on consent, police must establish the following three elements:

1) voluntariness;
   a) To be effective, the defendant's consent must be a voluntary decision made without coercion [Schneckloth v. Bustamonte, 412 U.S. 218 (1973)].
   b) The police need not inform the defendant that he has a right to withhold consent [Id.].
   c) Voluntariness is determined by the **totality of the circumstances**.
   d) Consent given pursuant to an invalid warrant is deemed involuntary [Bumper v. North Carolina, 391 U.S. 543 (1968)].
   e) The consent cannot be obtained by duress (such as police demanding entry to the location), fraud occurring when the police either claim to have a warrant or pose as repairmen, or coercion on the part of the police.
   f) In certain situations, voluntariness is assumed by virtue of engaging in specific behavior, such as traveling by airplane or engaging in a regulated business.
   g) Consent may be revoked at any time, in which case the search must cease.
   h) When a person on probation agrees, as a condition of that probation, to submit to random, unannounced warrantless searches that are not based on probable cause, such searches are valid, especially where they are actually based on reasonable suspicion [United States v. Knights, 534 U.S. 112 (2001)].
2) proper scope; and
   a) The consenting party controls the scope of the search, and any conduct exceeding the scope of the consent is unlawful. The scope is defined by the explicit or implicit terms of the consent.

      EXAMPLE: Aida Fellon, eager to show that she did not have anything to hide and to get the police off of her back, invites them to check the car expecting the police to only look in the passenger compartment. The police were justified in arresting her when they found heroin around the transmission because she gave the police permission to check the car and never limited the scope of the search.
   b) However, once a suspect has granted permission to search a car for narcotics, the containers within the car may also be searched [Florida v. Jimeno, 500 U.S. 258 (1991)].

3) third-party consent.
   a) The person consenting must have either actual or apparent authority to consent, such as a person who [Illinois v. Rodriguez, 477 U.S. 177 (1990)]:
      i) truly may consent (such as the owner or occupant of the particular premises); or
      ii) has apparent authority to consent, such as having a key or knowing where things are on the premises—even if it later turns out the person lacked the actual authority to consent.

      EXAMPLE: A landlord may not consent to the search of a tenant's apartment [Chapman v. United States, 365 U.S. 610 (1961)].

      EXAMPLE: A motel owner may not consent to the search of a guest's room [Stoner v. California, 376 U.S. 483 (1964).

      EXAMPLE: An employer may not consent to the search of an employee's private storage area.
   b) The general rule is that any person who has joint control or use of shared premises may consent to a valid search, and any evidence obtained may be used against the other occupants [Frazier v. Cupp, 394 U.S. 731 (1969)].
      i) Such consent applies to common areas, but not to private, reserved areas where the defendant has exclusive control [United States v. Matlock, 415 U.S. 164 (1974)].
      ii) The prosecution has the burden of proving that the co-occupant had authority to grant access by virtue of "joint access or control" over the area [Illinois v. Rodriguez, 497 U.S. 177 (1990)].
   c) A co-occupant's refusal to a search request is controlling over himself and renders a warrantless entry and search invalid against him [Georgia v. Randolph, 547 U.S. 103 (2006)].
   d) A present co-tenant who is silent (and does not object) does not have standing to object to the reasonableness of the search.
   e) A co-tenant who is absent does not have any standing to object to the search. This is the case even where the police are responsible for the co-tenant's absence (e.g., because of a detention or arrest) [Fernandez v. California, 571 U.S. 292 (2014)].

(6) **Searches Pursuant to a Stop**

(a) A **stop** is the momentary detention, often accompanied by very limited questioning, of a criminal suspect. The stop may take place in the suspect's home or vehicle or upon the street.

(b) A stop is a **seizure** within the meaning of the Fourth Amendment. Thus, the seizure must be reasonable to satisfy the constitutional requirements. Whether this seizure is unreasonable, and therefore violative of the Fourth Amendment, depends upon the type of stop conducted.

1) Probable cause is not required for a short, investigatory stop. Instead, the Fourth Amendment is satisfied if the stop is supported by the reasonable suspicion to believe that criminal activity may be afoot. However, as the scope of the stop increases, so should the justification for the stop.

a) **Reasonable suspicion** is a belief based upon articulable information that is more than a mere hunch used by a reasonable person or police officer that the suspect has or is about to engage in illegal or criminal activity.

b) Courts must look to the totality of the circumstances of each case to see whether the police officer has a "particularized and objective basis" for suspecting legal wrongdoing [United States v. Arvizu, 534 U.S. 266 (2002)].

(c) Persons present on the premises during a valid search pursuant to a search warrant may be detained [Michigan v. Summers, 452 U.S. 692 (1981)].

(7) **Hot Pursuit**

(a) A warrantless search is lawful when police are in actual "hot pursuit" of a fleeing suspect to apprehend her; they may seize "mere" evidence as well as any contraband they find [Warden v. Hayden, 387 U.S. 294 (1967)].

(b) Police may enter and search a private dwelling while in reasonable pursuit of the fleeing suspect [United States v. Santana, 427 U.S. 38 (1976)].

1) Police may enter the private dwelling of the suspect or of another person.

(c) The hot pursuit exception does not apply categorically when police are chasing someone for a suspected misdemeanor. Whether a police officer can enter a fleeing misdemeanant's home without a warrant is based on the totality of the circumstances, and whether they show an emergency such as imminent harm to others, a threat to the officer personally, destruction of evidence, or escape from the home [Lange v. California, 141 S. Ct. 2011 (2021)]. This includes flight from the officer, but not every instance of a suspected misdemeanant fleeing will trigger the hot pursuit exception.

(d) The police may use force reasonable under the particular circumstances of the situation, including deadly force, to stop a fleeing suspect who may be endangering innocent bystanders, even if it places the suspect in serious risk of death [Scott v. Harris, 550 U.S. 372 (2007)].

EXAMPLE: A police officer who pushed a car off the road and potentially harmed the fleeing suspect did not violate the suspect's Fourth Amendment rights because the facts demonstrated that innocent bystanders were in danger.

(8) **Exigent Circumstances**

(a) In certain emergency situations where evidence may be lost or destroyed before a warrant can be obtained, a warrantless search and seizure is permitted [Illinois v. McArthur, 531 U.S. 326 (2001); Schmerber v. California, 384 U.S. 757 (1966)].

(b) The police may conduct a warrantless search and seizure of evidence in or on a suspect's body provided that:

1) there is probable cause to believe that the nature of the evidence renders it easily destroyed or likely to disappear before a warrant can be obtained; and

2) the procedure for seizing the evidence is reasonable.

EXAMPLE: An individual suspected of murder by strangulation may have evidence under his fingernails that he may easily remove. This evidence is easily destroyed or likely to disappear, and thus may be obtained from the suspect's body by reasonable means. However, note that a similar type of evidence—the blood-alcohol level of a drunk-driving suspect, which will diminish over time—may not be treated the same way. Police must generally obtain a warrant before taking the blood of a drunk-driving suspect; the natural metabolism of blood alcohol does not justify a blood draw without consent [Missouri v. McNeely, 569 U.S. 141 (2013)].

EXAMPLE: Pummeling a suspect's stomach with nightsticks and then pumping it medically to retrieve illegal drugs swallowed is not considered a reasonable procedure for obtaining evanescent evidence. Such techniques "shock the conscience" and violate due process [Rochin v. California, 342 U.S. 165 (1952)].

(c) Police may enter a home without a warrant when they objectively have a reasonable belief that an occupant is in serious imminent harm [Utah v. Stewart, 547 U.S. 398 (2006)].

(d) No general emergency exception exists, so courts are cautious not to over-expand the areas permissible for warrantless searches.

EXAMPLE: A warrantless search of a fire scene was permitted at the scene and a few hours later to determine the cause of the fire. However, a search several days later to investigate the fire scene for evidence of arson was held illegal without a warrant [Michigan v. Tyler, 436 U.S. 499 (1978)].

(e) Although there is no exception to the warrant requirement for searches at the scene of a crime, police may search a crime scene without a warrant to seek other victims or a remaining killer [Mincey v. Arizona, 437 U.S. 385 (1978); Thompson v. Louisiana, 469 U.S. 17 (1984)].

6. **Administrative Searches and the Balancing Justification**

a. Administrative searches are conducted by an administrative agency for the enforcement of the regulations granted to that specific agency, with a lesser showing of probable cause required.

b. An administrative warrant will generally be required for administrative inspectors to search private homes or businesses with some exceptions, as follows:

(1) warrantless searches of businesses that are traditionally subject to extensive regulation and affect important public interests are not unreasonable within the meaning of the Fourth Amendment;

(2) the search of a locked storeroom of a firearms warehouse is permitted during reasonable hours because of the public interest involved [United States v. Biswell, 406 U.S. 311 (1972)]; and

(3) a search for highly contaminated food is justified without a warrant [North American Cold Storage v. City of Chicago, 211 U.S. 306 (1908)].

c. Examples of extensively regulated industries include pharmacies, liquor distributors, and businesses that must receive and maintain a license specific to their business to operate.

d. To protect airline passengers from weapons and explosives, warrantless administrative searches are permitted at airports. A passenger may avoid being searched by declining to board the plane.

(1) Although narcotics-sniffing dogs may smell a passenger's luggage, any resulting detention must be brief, and luggage seizure is subject to Fourth Amendment limitations [United States v. Place, 462 U.S. 696 (1983)].

(2) Seizure of a disembarking passenger by narcotics agents, who took a suspect's ticket and identification and then escorted the passenger to a detention room, violated the Terry stop standard for reasonable suspicion and was held unconstitutional [Florida v. Royer, 460 U.S. 491 (1983)].

e. When issued, an administrative warrant holds a lesser showing of probable cause [Camara v. Municipal Court, 413 U.S. 266 (1973)].

   (1) Strict probable cause is not required for issuance of an administrative warrant:

      (a) where reasonable standards exist for inspecting buildings involving municipal, health, or safety functions [Camera v. Municipal Court of San Francisco, 387 U.S. 523 (1968)];

      (b) if the search is not for the purpose of gathering a criminal investigation;

      (c) for drug testing of railroad employees associated with an accident or customs agents seeking promotion [Skinner v. Railway Labor Executives' Assoc., 489 U.S. 602 (1989); Nat'l Treasury Employees Union v. Von Raab, 489 U.S. 656 (1989)]; and

      (d) within schools, where officials have the right to conduct searches as long as there are "reasonable grounds for suspecting that the search will turn up evidence that the student has violated or is violating either the law or the rules of the school" [New Jersey v. T.L.O., 469 U.S. 325 (1985)].

   (2) It is still unresolved whether a student has a legitimate expectation of privacy in lockers, desks, and other school property. However, drug testing of students who participate in competitive extracurricular activities does not violate the Fourth Amendment [Board of Educ. of Indep. Sch. Dist. No. 92 of Pottawatomie County v. Earls, 536 U.S. 822 (2002)].

      EXAMPLE: Child and social services officers are allowed to inspect a home without a warrant because they are not conducting a criminal investigation.

7. **Border Crossings and Checkpoints**

   a. As an incident of national sovereignty, customs and immigration searches, when conducted by government agents in a routine manner and not particularized for a specific person or specific property, are not an invasion of privacy and do not require probable cause [United States v. Flores-Montano, 541 U.S. 149 (2004); Alameida-Sanchez v. United States, 413 U.S. 266 (1973)].

   b. The search may be conducted upon crossing any port of entry into the United States, such as international borders, international airports, and post offices where foreign mail enters.

   c. Government officials may make routine searches of items and people crossing the border and at fixed checkpoints near the border. The Court has concluded that searches made by government officials at the borders are reasonable by virtue of occurring at the national border, and do not require probable cause or reasonable suspicion [United States v. Flores-Montano, 541 U.S. 149 (2004)].

d. Reasonable suspicion is required for an unusually intrusive search, such as a body cavity search or a search that results in destruction of property [Id.].

e. Where a suspect refuses to submit to an X-ray by customs agents at the border, and reasonable justification for detention initially exists, the detention may continue until a bowel movement occurs [United States v. de Hernandez, 473 U.S. 531 (1985)].

8. **Other Searches**

a. **Wiretapping**

(1) **Wiretapping** is the use of an electronic surveillance device without the suspect's knowledge or consent. Any form of electronic surveillance, be it voice recording or otherwise, violates a defendant's right to a reasonable expectation of privacy [Katz v. United States, 389 U.S. 347 (1967)]. A warrant must, therefore, be issued, demonstrating that:

(a) probable cause has been shown that a crime has been or is being committed;

(b) the warrant names the suspects and describes the particular conversation to be overheard; and

(c) the wiretap is valid only for a brief period, after which time it will be terminated and the recorded conversations returned to the court.

(2) In foreign matters of national security, warrantless wiretaps are allowed.

(3) However, in domestic matters, even the president cannot request such surveillance without a warrant being issued upon approval by a neutral magistrate [United States v. U.S. District Court (Eastern District of Michigan), 407 U.S. 297 (1972)].

EXAMPLE: A state hospital's performance of a diagnostic test to obtain evidence of a patient's criminal conduct for law enforcement purposes is an unreasonable search if the patient has not consented to the procedure. The interest in using the threat of criminal sanctions to deter pregnant women from using cocaine is not adequate to justify a departure from the general rule that a nonconsensual search is unconstitutional if it is not authorized by a valid warrant [Ferguson v. City of Charleston, 532 U.S. 67 (2001)].

b. Conversations are not privileged because listening to a conversation does not invade a person's reasonable expectation of privacy.

(1) Each party to a conversation assumes the risk that the other party will reveal, transmit, or tape record the substance of the conversation [Hoffa v. United States, 385 U.S. 293 (1966)]. The assumption also includes eavesdropping.

(2) There is no constitutional right to protect misplaced confidences. A defendant has no basis under the Fourth Amendment for objection as an unlawful warrantless search, even if the person turns out to be a police informer [United States v. White, 401 U.S. 745 (1971)].

NOTE A participant in a conversation is not eavesdropping.

c. **Government Employers**

(1) The Supreme Court has held that, when conducted for a "non-investigatory, work-related purpose" or for the "investigation of work-related misconduct," a government employer's warrantless search employee electronic communications is reasonable if it is "justified at its inception" and if "the measures adopted are reasonably related to the objectives of the search and not excessively intrusive in light of the circumstances giving rise to the search" [City of Ontario v. Quon, 560 U.S. 746 (2010); O'Conner v. Ortega, 480 U.S. 709 (1987) (plurality opinion)].

EXAMPLE: In City of Ontario v. Quon [560 U.S. 746 (2010)], the city of Ontario, California issued pagers to its police department. The contract with the service provider specified a monthly character limit for the pagers, with extra fees incurred for going over. After several months of overages by Quon and others, the police chief requested from the service provider, and received, transcripts of the pagers from Quon and another employee. The purpose of this request was to determine whether the messages were work-related—and so the monthly character limit was too low—or whether the overages were for personal messages. The transcripts revealed many messages that were not work-related, and some that were sexually explicit, and the officers in question were disciplined. The officers filed suit alleging that the city violated their Fourth Amendment rights by obtaining the transcripts. The Supreme Court held that while Quon had a reasonable expectation of privacy in the text messages, because the search was reasonable and for a work-related purpose under the O'Conner approach, it did not violate the petitioners' Fourth Amendment rights.

III. STATEMENTS AND CONFESSIONS

A. In General

1. The Supreme Court uses several approaches to determine the admissibility of statements and confessions made by a defendant and the propriety of both pre-indictment and post-indictment identification procedures. A defendant's rights in these areas derive from the Fourth, Fifth, and Sixth Amendments.

B. Involuntary Statements

1. A statement is generally considered involuntary when the police subjected the suspect to coercive conduct, and that conduct, under the totality of the circumstances, was sufficient to overcome the will of the suspect (given her particular vulnerabilities and the conditions of the interrogation).
2. This standard is by its nature subjective, and requires a case-by-case analysis to determine voluntariness. Thus, a statement made by a suspect of average intelligence who is comfortable in his surroundings when the statement is made is likely, but not assumed, to be considered voluntary.

FOUR BASES TO EXCLUDE STATEMENTS AND CONFESSIONS	
Approach	**Constitutional Basis**
Voluntariness Approach—To be admissible, a statement must be voluntarily made based on the totality of the circumstances.	Due Process Clause of Fifth and Fourteenth Amendments
Right to Counsel Approach—Statements made during any "critical stage" of a criminal proceeding are inadmissible unless the defendant is afforded the right to counsel.	Sixth Amendment Right to Counsel
Miranda Standard—Statements made during custodial interrogation are inadmissible in the absence of Miranda warnings.	Fifth Amendment Privilege against Self-Incrimination
Fruits of Illegal Conduct—Even voluntary statements obtained as fruits of prior illegal searches and seizures are inadmissible.	Fourth Amendment Exclusionary Rule

C. Inadmissible Statements

1. A statement may be found inadmissible if it is:
   a. involuntary under the Due Process Clauses of the Fifth and Fourteenth Amendments;
      (1) The voluntariness standard is based on the trustworthiness and reliability of the proffered evidence and is used to determine the admissibility of a confession based on the totality of

the circumstances [Brown v. Mississippi, 297 U.S. 278 (1936)]. Factors of coercion include the defendant's:

(a) age;

(b) sex;

(c) education; and

(d) mental and physical health.

(2) Although the police have broad rein to trick and deceive the defendant during interrogation, they may not offer false promises of dropping charges to elicit a confession [Spano v. New York, 360 U.S. 315 (1959)].

(3) Coercion may take the form of physical abuse, threats, or promises of leniency.

(4) If the defendant's confession is the product of coercion, it may not be introduced at trial as either direct evidence or for impeachment purposes.

(5) However, admission of an involuntary confession no longer results in automatic reversal. Rather, the harmless error rule is now applicable to the admission of involuntary confessions [Arizona v. Fulminante, 499 U.S. 279 (1991)]. Under this standard, the government must prove beyond a reasonable doubt that the introduction of the confession into evidence did not contribute to the verdict of guilt.

b. in violation of the Sixth Amendment right to counsel under the Massiah rule;

(1) Under the Sixth Amendment, a suspect has a right to counsel during questioning by police. The accused must make the request unambiguously to the interrogator, at which time the questioning must cease.

(2) The Sixth Amendment right to counsel is offense-specific, and the police may continue to question on other offenses, even those that are factually related to the charged offense.

EXAMPLE: Police were allowed to question a defendant without counsel about the murders of a homeowner and his daughter, even after the defendant had been indicted on burglary charges (and represented by counsel on these charges) relating to the victims' home [Texas v. Cobb, 532 U.S. 162 (2001)].

(3) In Montejo v. Louisiana, the U.S. Supreme Court explicitly overturned Michigan v. Jackson [475 U.S. 625 (1986)], which had prohibited law enforcement, pursuant to the Sixth Amendment's guarantee of counsel to all criminal defendants, from questioning a defendant who has counsel or who has requested counsel.

(a) In overturning Michigan v. Jackson, the Court held that a defendant's rights are adequately protected by the rules announced in Miranda and Edwards v. Arizona [451 U.S. 477 (1981)] (under which a defendant in custody cannot be interrogated once he has asserted his right to counsel unless he initiates further communications with police)].

(b) The Court stated that the constitutional protections granted in Miranda, Edwards, and Minnick (though they generally address Fifth Amendment rights) were sufficient to protect a defendant's Sixth Amendment rights from police badgering that might elicit culpable evidence [Montejo v. Louisiana, 556 U.S. 778 (2009)].

(4) Counsel must be present at all questioning until the accused waives the right.

(5) Absent an effective waiver once formal charges have been filed, the deliberate eliciting of any incriminating statements from a defendant without the assistance of an attorney violates the Sixth Amendment right to counsel.

(6) The police agents' secret recording of a suspect's conversations while out on bail violated his right to counsel [Massiah v. United States, 377 U.S. 201 (1964)].

(a) The right to counsel extends not only to noncustodial settings, but also to the beginning of the adversarial court process. The initial appearance in a court will trigger this right because it signals the government's intent to prosecute [Rothgery v. Gillespie County, 554 U.S. 191 (2008)].

EXAMPLE: A violation of the right to counsel occurred when the defendant himself initiated a conversation with his co-defendant, who, by the time of the meeting, had become a police agent [Maine v. Moulton, 474 U.S. 159 (1985)].

(b) Although the police cannot knowingly exploit or intentionally create an opportunity to confront the accused without counsel absent a waiver, passive listening by a cellmate informant does not violate the right to counsel. The defendant must demonstrate that the police and their informant took some action, beyond merely listening, that was designed deliberately to elicit incriminating remarks [Kuhlmann v. Wilson, 477 U.S. 436 (1986)].

c. in violation of the Fifth Amendment privilege against self-incrimination as applied by the Miranda rule; or

(1) The Fifth Amendment states that "no person shall be compelled in a criminal case to be a witness against himself."

(2) The Fifth Amendment privilege against self-incrimination, which applies only to natural persons, must be asserted to be effective.

(3) The privilege applies only to "compelled" self-incriminating testimony [California v. Byers, 402 U.S. 424 (1971)]. A defendant may never be compelled to testify against herself [Chavez v. Martinez, 538 U.S. 760 (2003)].

(4) When a witness has reason to fear that answers to possible questions might tend to incriminate him or subject him to other prosecution within the United States, he has a valid Fifth Amendment

privilege against self-incrimination [Ohio v. Reiner, 532 U.S. 17 (2001); United States v. Balsys, 524 U.S. 666 (1998)].

(5) The privilege may be asserted in any criminal, civil, or administrative proceeding where incriminating testimony can be used in a subsequent prosecution, such as in a grand jury proceeding where a trial may result.

(6) The privilege against self-incrimination protects against admission of evidence that is testimonial in nature, but not against the admission of real or physical evidence (i.e., blood, hair, and handwriting samples).

EXAMPLE: A lie detector test will be protected testimonial evidence, whereas blood, hair, and handwriting samples are not.

(7) The privilege does not prevent the government from seeking information.

(8) The accused has a right to waive his privilege and give testimony.

(9) When the government questions an individual outside the trial setting, the purpose of the questioning determines whether the individual's failure to affirmatively invoke the privilege constitutes a valid waiver.

(a) The more criminally investigative the government's purpose, the more likely the court will be to require a knowing, intelligent, and voluntary waiver from the individual questioned.

(b) The defendant's silence may be used as an adoptive admission in a precustodial situation [Jenkins v. Anderson, 447 U.S. 231 (1980)].

(10) When either use or transactional immunity has been granted to a defendant, the privilege against self-incrimination is eliminated [Kastigar v. United States, 406 U.S. 441 (1972)].

(11) Immunized testimony cannot be used to impeach [New Jersey v. Potash, 440 U.S. 450 (1979)], but it can be used to prove perjury [United States v. Apfelbaum, 445 U.S. 115 (1980)].

(12) **Miranda**

(a) The Miranda rule states that no statement made by a defendant will be admitted into evidence unless, prior to custodial interrogation, the defendant is given certain warnings [Miranda v. Arizona, 384 U.S. 436 (1966)].

(b) The Miranda rule is now the main basis for excluding a confession, but does not replace the case-by-case analysis used in the "voluntariness approach" [Dickerson v. United States, 530 U.S. 428 (2000)]. An involuntary confession, to which Miranda did not apply, would still be excluded on due process grounds as described above.

(c) **Miranda Warnings**

1) Miranda warnings need not be given verbatim, provided the defendant is sufficiently informed of her rights [California v. Prysock, 453 U.S. 355 (1981)]. Miranda requires that the suspect be given the following four warnings:

a) he has a right to remain silent;
b) anything he says can be used against him in court;
c) he has the right to the presence of an attorney; and
d) if he cannot afford an attorney, one will be provided for him.

2) **Interrogation**

a) Miranda only applies when an interrogation occurs. For the purposes of Miranda, an interrogation occurs where police know or should reasonably know that their actions or inquiries are reasonably likely to elicit an incriminating response from the suspect [Rhode Island v. Innis, 446 U.S. 291 (1980)].
b) Volunteered, spontaneous, or unsolicited statements are not considered the product of an interrogation and thus are admissible.
c) The test focuses on the susceptibility of the suspect. Thus, if there are no objective indications of particular susceptibility, such as youth, then the police may talk in the presence of the suspect provided there is no direct questioning, even though such conversations in the presence of a juvenile suspect could constitute a Miranda violation.
d) Miranda bars only "official" interrogation. Thus, informant questioning in jail does not require giving Miranda warnings [Illinois v. Perkins, 496 U.S. 292 (1990)]. Miranda also does not apply to questioning by private security guards [People v. Baugh, 311 N.E.2d 607 (Ill. 1974)].

3) **Custody**

a) The Miranda rule applies only to statements made during custodial interrogation where the suspect experiences significant deprivation of freedom of movement and may not leave. Courts apply objective criteria to determine whether the suspect is in custody [Yarborough v. Alvarado, 541 U.S. 652 (2004)].
b) The following objective factors must be considered in determining whether the suspect was in custody for Miranda purposes:
    i) when and where it occurred;
    ii) how long it lasted;
    iii) how many police officers were present;
    iv) what the officers and the defendant said and did;
    v) the presence of physical restraint or the equivalent, such as a drawn weapon or a guard stationed at the door; and

vi) whether the defendant was being questioned as a suspect or as a witness.

c) Subjective factors are not considered. This means that neither the subjective beliefs of the police nor the suspect determine whether the interrogation was, in fact, custodial. Whether the suspect actually believed she was free to leave or not, or whether the police actually would have allowed the suspect to leave or not, does not matter. What matters is whether the suspect experienced a significant deprivation of freedom of movement from an objective perspective.

d) For Miranda purposes, a Terry stop is not considered to be custodial; therefore, Miranda warnings are not required [Berkemer v. McCarty, 468 U.S. 420 (1984)].

e) During a roadside stop, a Miranda warning is not required because a person is not considered to be in custody because the person being stopped is not considered to have given up his freedom.

f) On-the-scene questioning is not necessarily custodial.

g) Statements made before a grand jury investigation are not the products of custodial interrogation [United States v. Mandujano, 425 U.S. 564 (1976)].

h) Interrogation of a taxpayer during a criminal investigation by the IRS is not custodial interrogation [Beckwith v. United States, 425 U.S. 341 (1976)].

(d) **Special Exceptions**

1) Miranda does not apply to [Oregon v. Mathiason, 429 U.S. 492 (1977)]:

a) questions by police officers regarding age, date of birth, height, weight, and the like; and

i) A slurred response when answering a question is admissible in a drunk-driving case [Pennsylvania v. Muniz, 496 U.S. 582 (1990)].

b) questioning by a parole officer when the defendant was free to leave the police station.

2) The right to receive Miranda warnings may in some cases be outweighed by the immediate threat posed to the public safety [New York v. Quarles, 467 U.S. 649 (1984)].

(e) **Admissibility**

1) Statements obtained in violation of Miranda may not be used in the prosecution's case-in-chief.

2) Statements obtained from the defendant in violation of her Miranda rights are admissible to impeach the defendant's testimony at trial [Harris v. New York, 401 U.S. 222 (1971)].

3) The Miranda warnings do not necessarily prevent the inclusion of physical evidence, even if oral statements are not allowed [United States v. Patane, 542 U.S. 630 (2004)].

4) A co-conspirator does not have automatic standing to challenge the seizure of illegally obtained evidence from another co-conspirator. To have authority or standing to challenge the lawfulness of a search or seizure by a government agent, an individual's personal privacy rights must be invaded (rather than those of a third party).

5) Admission of evidence in violation of a person's Miranda rights does not result in automatic reversal, but may be harmless error [Milton v. Wainwright, 407 U.S. 371 (1972)].

(f) **Waiver of Miranda Rights**

1) A knowing and intelligent waiver of one's Miranda rights is permitted, but the prosecution has a "heavy burden" to prove that there was compliance with the warnings requirement and that the waiver was voluntary, knowing, and intelligent.

2) The waiver need not be in writing [North Carolina v. Butler, 441 U.S. 369 (1979)].

3) The waiver can be express or implied, but it ordinarily cannot be presumed from a defendant's silence [Fare v. Michael C., 442 U.S. 707 (1979)].

4) An admission from a mentally disabled person may be used because the general inquiry is whether there was police over-reaching [Colorado v. Connelly, 479 U.S. 157 (1986)].

   a) However, if the mental disability is such that it made the defendant unable to understand the meaning of the warnings, the waiver cannot be intelligent.

5) Miranda waivers have been upheld even when obtained after police had misrepresented the strength of the case or the seriousness of the crime being investigated.

EXAMPLE: A defendant can effectively waive her rights and talk to the police about a robbery without knowing specific facts, such as not knowing that the robbery victim is now dead, and no new Miranda warnings regarding the nature of the charges are required. Although trickery will not invalidate a waiver *per se* under Miranda, the use of police deception may, in some circumstances, rise to the level of a due process violation under the voluntariness approach.

EXAMPLE: A defendant's waiver of counsel was sufficiently "knowing and intelligent" when police withheld from the defendant information that an attorney had sought to consult with him [Moran v. Burbine, 475 U.S. 412 (1986)].

6) A waiver is valid as long as the defendant was aware of the Miranda rights and understood the waiver. The defendant need not be warned of possible charges facing her [Colorado v. Spring, 479 U.S. 564 (1987)].

   a) A defendant validly waived his Miranda rights when making oral statements, even though he refused to sign a statement without benefit of counsel [Connecticut v. Barrett, 479 U.S. 523 (1987)].

(g) **Invocation of Miranda Rights and Repetition of Warnings**

1) Special rules have developed to deal with how often the police need to give warnings during prolonged interrogations and what the police can and cannot do under Miranda once a suspect has invoked one of his Miranda rights.

2) If a defendant either requests an attorney or states that she wishes to remain silent, all interrogation must stop. These requests can be made at any point during the course of the interrogation.

   a) Just saying the word "lawyer" (or similar) is not enough to invoke the right to counsel for Miranda purposes. Invocation of the right "requires, at a minimum, some statement that can reasonably be construed to be an expression of a desire for the assistance of an attorney" [Davis v. United States, 512 U.S. 452 (1994); McNeil v. Wisconsin, 501 U.S. 171 (1991)].

   b) In order to unambiguously request counsel, a suspect must "articulate his desire to have counsel present sufficiently clearly that a reasonable police officer in the circumstances would understand the statement to be a request for an attorney" [Davis v. United States, 512 U.S. 452 (1994)].

      i) On the other hand, if the request is ambiguous or equivocal, the police do not need to cease questioning. An ambiguous request is one that "a reasonable officer in light of the circumstances would have understood only that the suspect might be invoking the right to counsel" [Id.].

3) The general rule is that a defendant's right to terminate interrogation, at any time and in any manner, must be scrupulously honored.

   a) To resume questioning anew, the police must allow for a significant period of time to elapse and must provide a fresh set of Miranda warnings.

b) A defendant who has exercised his right to remain silent may properly be questioned about an unrelated crime following a significant lapse of time, provided a new set of warnings is given [Michigan v. Mosely, 423 U.S. 96 (1975)].

c) A defendant who has requested an attorney may not be further questioned until either counsel is furnished or the defendant voluntarily initiates a discussion beyond a "necessary inquiry arising out of the incidents of the custodial relationship" [Oregon v. Bradshaw, 462 U.S. 103 (1983)].

d) The Supreme Court has held that if a suspect has been released from interrogative custody, the police obligation to honor an invocation of the Miranda right to counsel expires after 14 days [Maryland v. Shatzer, 559 U.S. 98 (2010)].

i) However, when an inmate is questioned, the Court held that releasing the inmate from interrogation back into the general prison population ends the inherently compelling pressures of custodial interrogation, and so constitutes a break in custody [Id.].

4) Provided there is no Fourth Amendment violation, admissions obtained after the giving of Miranda warnings are admissible, even if prior admissions on the same matter were obtained in violation of Miranda [Oregon v. Elstad, 470 U.S. 298 (1985)].

a) However, the police may not give a Miranda warning in the middle of questioning and then ask the defendant to repeat the statements made before the Miranda warning was given [Missouri v. Siebert, 542 U.S. 600 (2004)].

5) However, a suspect does not invoke her right to remain silent by simply not answering questions. The Supreme Court has recently held that a suspect must unambiguously invoke her right to remain silent before the police are required to end their questioning [Berghuis v. Thompkins, 560 U.S. 370 (2010)].

6) Miranda warnings need not be repeated because of a short (as opposed to "significant") break in interrogation or because a new police agent begins questioning [Westover v. United States, 384 U.S. 436 (1966)].

7) When inmates are offered minimal incentives (such as visitation rights, work opportunities, ability to send money to family, canteen expenditures, access to a

personal television, or incarceration in a lower-level security facility) to participate in a sexual abuse treatment program in which they "accept responsibility" for and admit to their crimes and any uncharged sexual criminal offenses, such statements are not compelled self-incrimination prohibited by the Fifth Amendment [McKune v. Lile, 536 U.S. 24 (2002)].

d. the fruit of an illegal arrest or search under the Fourth Amendment exclusionary rule.

(1) Even a voluntary statement or confession made after a waiver of Miranda rights may be inadmissible if it is the fruit of an illegal arrest, search, or seizure [Wong Sun v. United States, 371 U.S. 471 (1963)].

(2) Entrapment will result in the exclusion of a confession or statement to police only when the origin of intent was in the police. Thus, if the defendant was personally predisposed to commit the crime, entrapment is not a defense.

(3) However, remember that in order to have authority or standing to challenge the lawfulness of a search or seizure by a government agent, an individual's personal privacy rights must have been involved (and not those of a third party).

IV. IDENTIFICATIONS

A. The Two Bases to Attack Identifications of a Defendant

1. Pre-Indictment Identifications: The Due Process Standard

a. Any lineup, show-up, or photo identification will be inadmissible as violative of due process when the identification is unnecessarily suggestive and likely to produce an irreparable mistaken identification [Stovall v. Denno, 388 U.S. 293 (1967)].

(1) However, the Supreme Court has sharply narrowed a defendant's ability to successfully object to any identification as a violation of due process to cases where the defendant can also prove that the unnecessarily suggestive circumstances were arranged by law enforcement [Perry v. New Hampshire, 565 U.S. 228 (2012)].

b. Three issues ordinarily bear on whether the prosecution can properly introduce identification evidence [Perry v. New Hampshire, 565 U.S. 228 (2012)]:

(1) whether the police were involved in arranging the procedure;

(2) whether the identification process was highly suggestive, and therefore unreliable; and if so,

(3) whether the suggestive procedure was necessary under the circumstances.

EXAMPLE: A photo identification that includes repetitive display of a photo or distinctive marks upon the photo.

c. One-on-one identifications require very close judicial scrutiny because of the high likelihood of misidentification. Courts have adopted a specific approach for both out-of-court and in-court identifications: where an identification is both suggestive and unnecessary, it can still be admissible if it is reliable based on a **totality of the circumstances** approach [Manson v. Brathwaite, 432 U.S. 98 (1977)]. The following factors are considered and then balanced against the degree of suggestiveness:

(1) the opportunity to view the criminal at the scene;

(2) the witness's degree of attention;

(3) the accuracy of the witness's description;

(4) the degree of certainty of the witness; and

(5) the time interval between the crime and the identification.

EXAMPLE: An unnecessarily suggestive show-up seven months after the crime was held proper because it satisfied the criteria for reliability [Neil v. Biggers, 409 U.S. 188 (1972)].

EXAMPLE: The showing of a single photograph to a police officer two days after a crime was admissible [Manson v. Brathwaite, 432 U.S. 98 (1977)].

EXAMPLE: In a lineup where the defendant was six inches taller than the other suspects, was the only suspect in the lineup wearing clothes similar to those the thief was described as wearing, and was the only suspect to reappear in the second lineup, a due process violation was found [Foster v. California, 394 U.S. 440 (1969)].

d. When an out-of-court identification is excluded for suggestiveness or unreliability, a subsequent in-court identification will not be allowed.

2. **The Right to Counsel in Post-Indictment Lineups**

a. The right to counsel attaches upon the start of adversary proceedings, to which an indictment would qualify [Moore v. Illinois, 434 U.S. 220 (1977)].

b. After formal charges are filed, the defendant has a right to have counsel present at a lineup [United States v. Wade, 388 U.S. 218 (1967)].

NOTE Still unresolved is the point at which counsel may be present at a lineup—after a defendant is in custody under an arrest warrant (i.e., a formal charge), or only upon indictment.

c. No right to counsel exists at police lineups conducted before the accused is indicted [Kirby v. Illinois, 406 U.S. 682 (1972)].

d. The inadmissibility of a previous out-of-court identification made at a lineup, based on a violation of the defendant's right to counsel, does not bar the witness from making an in-court identification of the accused at trial when the prosecution can clearly and convincingly show that the subsequent identification stemmed from an independent, "purging" source [Gilbert v. California, 388 U.S. 263 (1967)].

3. Improper admission of an identification will result in overturning a conviction, unless the prosecution can show harmless error [Chapman v. California, 386 U.S. 18 (1967)].

V. PRETRIAL PROCEDURES: CHRONOLOGY FROM ARREST TO TRIAL

A. Grand Jury Indictment

1. The **indictment** is a written accusation of charges against the defendant issued by a grand jury after it reviews the prosecution's evidence.
2. A Fifth Amendment right to a grand jury exists in all federal felony cases.
    a. In federal court, the accused can waive a grand jury hearing except in capital offenses.
3. The right to indictment by a grand jury for capital and infamous crimes has not been held binding on the states [Hurtado v. California, 110 U.S. 516 (1884)], although several states require it in felony cases.
4. A federal grand jury is composed of between 16 and 23 persons, 12 of whom must agree to issue an indictment.
5. The grand jury—for its foreperson or deputy foreperson—must return the indictment to a magistrate judge in open court. To avoid unnecessary cost or delay, the magistrate judge may take the return by video teleconference from the court where the grand jury sits [Fed. R. Crim. P. 6(f)].
6. Special grand juries that investigate unlawful activity on their own, such as political corruption, may bring an indictment to commence a proceeding.
7. Grand juries are conducted in secret; the accused has no right to be present.
    a. The accused usually has no right to know that a grand jury is considering evidence against her.
8. The grand jury has the power to subpoena evidence or testimony it wishes to consider as part of its investigation.
    a. An accused may not challenge a grand jury subpoena for lack of probable cause.
9. The accused may not be present, confront witnesses, or introduce evidence in a federal grand jury proceeding.
10. A grand jury witness has no right to counsel, except for consultation outside the grand jury room.
11. Miranda warnings need not be given to potential defendants testifying at a grand jury proceeding [United States v. Mandujano, 425 U.S. 564 (1976)].
12. Grand jury witnesses are sworn and thus subject to penalty of perjury [United States v. Wong, 431 U.S. 174 (1977)].
13. If the grand jury pool was chosen in a racially discriminatory manner, reversal of a subsequent conviction on an indictment issued by that grand jury is the proper course [Vasquez v. Hillery, 474 U.S. 254 (1986)].

B. Information

1. An **information** is a written accusation of charges filed in the name of the state by a prosecutor based on information submitted by police or private citizens.
2. The information is an alternative to an indictment, used when a grand jury indictment is not required or has been waived.
    a. An information is almost always used in misdemeanors.

3. A preliminary judicial hearing on probable cause prior to filing an information is afforded in most states, but it is not an explicit constitutional right [Gerstein v. Pugh, 420 U.S. 103 (1975)].

C. Booking

1. **Booking** generally occurs when a defendant first arrives at the police station or jail. The defendant is often photographed, fingerprinted, informed of the criminal charges, and allowed to make a phone call.
2. Criminal defendants may not be compelled to testify against themselves, but the booking procedures, photographs, and inventory searches that compel only physical evidence are not protected by the Fifth Amendment.
   a. Also, a defendant accused of driving while intoxicated may be forced to submit to a blood-alcohol test without Fifth Amendment implications, and his refusal to submit to such testing may be used against him at trial [South Dakota v. Neville, 459 U.S. 553 (1983)].
   b. The Supreme Court has held that the Fourth Amendment does not bar the fingerprinting of a properly seized person, because it "involves none of the probing into an individual's private life and thoughts that marks an interrogation or search" [Davis v. Mississippi, 394 U.S. 721 (1969)]. However, a detention for the sole purpose of obtaining fingerprints is subject to the constraints of the Fourth Amendment.
   c. When a person is arrested and taken to jail for incarceration, it is standard procedure for jail employees to conduct a warrantless search of the arrestee and take custody of her clothes and personal effects. The items found on the person of the arrestee are typically placed in an envelope, which is sealed and taken to the property room of the jail for safekeeping. This warrantless inventory search has consistently been upheld as constitutional. After booking, the defendant may be allowed to post bail and obtain immediate release, or the defendant will be thoroughly searched and placed in a cell pending her court appearance.

D. Bail Hearing

1. The defendant is entitled to an individualized hearing to determine whether bail should be granted or denied.

NOTE A bail hearing is not yet considered to be among those "critical stages" where the defendant has a right to counsel—although counsel is usually present.

2. A bail hearing will be set and conducted during or soon after the arraignment.
3. The purpose of bail is to assure the presence of the defendant at trial [Stack v. Boyle, 342 U.S. 1 (1951)].
4. A denial of bail may be raised at any time during criminal proceedings.
5. The Eighth Amendment prohibits "excessive bail," but there is no explicit constitutional right to bail.

NOTE Most states, however, grant a right to bail in their constitutions.

6. Eighth Amendment challenges arise when "significant restraints" on the defendant's liberty exist, such as being held in jail or released only upon posting bail, and those restraints exceed the safety interest in holding the defendant [Gerstein v. Pugh, 420 U.S. 103 (1975)].

E. Preliminary Hearing

1. The **preliminary hearing** is an adversarial procedure used to determine probable cause to prosecute. While no constitutional right for a preliminary hearing *per se* exists, in situations where a defendant is arrested without a warrant or a prior indictment, such as a grand jury indictment, there will exist a Fourth Amendment right to a probable cause hearing.
2. Presentation of evidence is allowed by both sides, and the defendant may assert any of his defenses.

NOTE Though it is a strategic choice as to whether defense counsel opts to cross-examine the prosecution's witnesses at this time, the defendant's Sixth Amendment right to confront and cross-examine opposing witnesses who are unavailable at trial will be deemed protected if the defense counsel had a fair opportunity to cross-examine the witnesses at the preliminary hearing [California v. Green, 399 U.S. 149 (1970)].

3. A defendant may waive her right to a preliminary hearing.
4. A delay between arraignment and the preliminary hearing is normal. The police and prosecutor may continue their investigation during this time. Plea bargain negotiations are allowed and proper.

F. Arraignment

1. During the arraignment, the defendant is given formal notice of the charges against him and advised by the court of his rights.
2. The defendant has a right to counsel at this stage, although the defendant may be entitled to counsel earlier [Coleman v. Alabama, 399 U.S. 1 (1970)].
3. The defendant is called upon to answer the indictment, elect a trial by judge or jury, and enter his plea. In felony cases, indigent defendants are usually appointed counsel at this time.
4. If the defendant pleads not guilty, or remains silent, a preliminary motion and trial dates are set.
5. By pleading *nolo contendere*, or "no contest," a defendant can forgo a trial without admitting guilt. Note that such a plea is not admissible to prove guilt in subsequent criminal and civil cases.
6. If the defendant pleads guilty and thus waives a jury trial, the judge then determines if the plea was voluntarily and intelligently made [McCarthy v. United States, 394 U.S. 459 (1969)].

a. To be voluntary and intelligent, the plea must be taken on the record and the judge must personally be certain that the defendant understands [Boykin v. Alabama, 395 U.S. 238 (1969)]:
   (1) the nature of the charge against him [Henderson v. Morgan, 426 U.S. 637 (1976)];
   (2) the maximum possible sentence and any mandatory minimums;
   (3) the fact that he has a right not to plead guilty; and
   (4) that by pleading guilty, the right to a jury trial is waived.

7. A guilty plea is valid to impose criminal punishment, even when the defendant never makes a formal admission of his guilt [North Carolina v. Alford, 400 U.S. 25 (1970)].
8. The defendant must be advised of his right to counsel. The entry of a guilty plea requires the assistance of counsel, unless the defendant has voluntarily waived this right.
9. A defendant may withdraw her guilty plea and plead again when any form of error occurs during the taking of the plea [McCarthy v. United States, 394 U.S. 459 (1969)].
10. A withdrawn guilty plea is inadmissible in a subsequent civil trial.

G. Motions

1. Following the formal indictment, a defendant may raise motions to dismiss, motions to suppress evidence, or motions to compel discovery.
2. The defendant's chief "remedy" for enforcing his Fourth Amendment right to a reasonable expectation of privacy, Fifth Amendment right against self-incrimination, and Sixth Amendment right to counsel is to bring a motion to suppress the evidence, generally pursuant to either the exclusionary rule or the fruit of the poisonous tree doctrine.
3. Motions can be filed to compel the prosecution to provide discovery that the defense believes is relevant and available to the prosecution.
4. Before trial, motions can be filed to keep the prosecution from presenting evidence that, although obtained legally, may not be admissible because of a variety of evidentiary rules, such as the rule against hearsay.

H. Plea Bargaining

1. A defendant may agree to plead guilty to an offense in return for the prosecutor's recommendation of a lesser sentence or dismissal of a charge.
2. A defendant has a right to enforce her plea bargain once the court accepts the plea.
   a. Failure to enforce the bargain can result in either specific performance of the plea or withdrawal of the guilty plea by the defendant [Santobello v. New York, 404 U.S. 257 (1971)].
   b. The plea bargain is enforceable against the prosecutor, not the judge. Because the plea bargain is viewed as a contract negotiation, it is permissible for the prosecution to drive a hard bargain and even to

threaten the defendant with a more serious charge if he does not plead guilty [Bordenkircher v. Hayes, 434 U.S. 357 (1978)].

3. A prosecutor need not reveal information about the impeachment of witnesses or affirmative defenses (including information that may tend to impeach the credibility of a prosecution witness, such as a plea agreement or conflicting statements) before the defendant enters into a binding plea agreement [United States v. Ruiz, 536 U.S. 622 (2002)].

I. Collateral Attacks on Guilty Pleas after Sentencing

1. On the theory that the defendant knew the risks involved before choosing to waive a jury trial, the defendant does not have a right to collaterally attack a guilty plea for prior constitutional violations [Brady v. United States, 397 U.S. 742 (1970); Tollett v. Henderson, 411 U.S. 258 (1973)].
2. However, the defendant who pleads guilty is allowed to file a collateral attack [Santobello v. New York, 404 U.S. 257 (1971); Blackledge v. Perry, 417 U.S. 21 (1974)]:
   a. when the prosecutor fails to keep her promise;
   b. when the court lacks jurisdiction; or
   c. when ineffective assistance of counsel occurs.

VI. PRETRIAL RIGHTS

A. The Right to a Speedy Trial

1. The Sixth Amendment guarantees a criminal defendant the right to a speedy trial in both federal courts and state courts (through the Fourteenth Amendment) [Klopfer v. North Carolina, 386 U.S. 213 (1967)]. A violation of this right results in a complete dismissal of the charges against the defendant [Strunk v. United States, 412 U.S. 434 (1973)].
2. The right to a speedy trial attaches once a defendant is "accused," such as upon arrest or filing of charges.
   a. Pre-arrest delays may violate due process only if sufficient prejudice is found [United States v. Lovasco, 431 U.S. 783 (1977)].
3. Conversely, a long interval between arrest and indictment raises the inference of a violation, even if the defendant was released after the arrest [Dillingham v. United States, 423 U.S. 64 (1975)].
4. The Speedy Trial Act of 1974 requires federal indictment within 30 days of arrest and trial within 70 days of indictment.
5. The court judges violations of the right to a speedy trial by balancing the following factors [Barker v. Wingo, 407 U.S. 514 (1972)]:
   a. the length of the delay;
   b. the reason for the delay;
      (1) The right is waived when a defendant willfully delays the trial by filing a pretrial motion or seeking a suppression hearing.
      (2) If the prosecution delays, courts evaluate the good faith and the justifiability of the delay.
   c. the defendant's assertion of his right to a speedy trial; and
   d. the prejudice to the defendant, which may include oppressive incarceration, memory loss by witnesses, loss of evidence, and anxiety to the defendant.

B. Rights during Discovery Stage

1. The defendant must be informed of the charges against her in sufficient detail so that an adequate defense is possible [Russell v. United States, 369 U.S. 749 (1962)].
2. Although state courts are not required to permit liberal pretrial discovery, they must grant the defense the same discovery rights given to the prosecution [Wardius v. Oregon, 412 U.S. 470 (1973)].
3. The prosecution has a limited right to compel disclosure of some information by the defendant.
   a. The defendant may be compelled to notify the prosecution in advance of an alibi defense, including the names and addresses of any alibi witnesses and any witnesses refuting the alibi [Williams v. Florida, 399 U.S. 78 (1970)].

(1) The prosecutor may not comment on the defendant's failure at trial to either present the alibi or produce an alibi witness.

(2) However, a defendant may be impeached when he has given notice of one alibi, but then testifies as to a different alibi.

b. The privilege against self-incrimination is not violated by this disclosure.

c. If a defense witness has made a pretrial statement or report, there is some authority that the prosecution can require the defendant to disclose at the trial those portions of the statement or report relevant to the witness's testimony at trial. This rule also applies to expert witnesses who may be used to establish an affirmative defense, such as insanity.

4. **Exculpatory Information**

a. It is a violation of due process for the prosecution to fail to disclose, prior to trial, evidence that is both favorable and material to the defense.

b. Favorable evidence, subject to the disclosure obligation, includes:

(1) when the defense makes a specific request, evidence that is responsive to the request [Brady v. Maryland, 373 U.S. 83 (1963)]; or

(2) when the defense fails to make a specific request, or makes a general "Brady" request, evidence that is clearly exculpatory [United States v. Bagley, 473 U.S. 667 (1985)].

c. The disclosure obligation applies prior to trial, and there is no constitutional obligation to disclose such evidence prior to plea bargaining [United States v. Ruiz, 536 U.S. 622 (2002)].

d. If the prosecution discloses evidence prior to trial, the obligation is satisfied.

e. If, after trial, the defendant learns that favorable information had not been disclosed, the defense must prove the evidence was also material in order to have the conviction (or sentence, when the evidence relates only to the sentence) reversed.

f. Evidence is considered material if, considering the entire record of trial, it creates a reasonable probability of a different outcome.

(1) In other words, had the evidence been disclosed as required, it would have created reasonable doubt.

VII. DOUBLE JEOPARDY

A. In General

1. The **Double Jeopardy Clause** is intended to prevent undue harassment and expense by eliminating the risk of a defendant being punished twice for the same offense. The Fifth Amendment provision, which states, "... nor shall any person be subject for the same offense to be twice put in jeopardy of life or limb," applies to the states through the Due Process Clause of the Fourteenth Amendment [Benton v. Maryland, 395 U.S. 784 (1969)]. The Double Jeopardy Clause applies to all crimes, even ones punishable only by fine.

B. When Jeopardy Attaches

1. In a nonjury trial, jeopardy attaches when the first witness is sworn and the court begins to hear the evidence.
2. In a jury trial, jeopardy attaches when the jury is impaneled and sworn [Christ v. Bretz, 437 U.S. 28 (1978)].
3. If a civil fine is truly a punishment, then the Double Jeopardy Clause is triggered [United States v. Halper, 490 U.S. 435 (1989)].
4. When a grand jury fails to indict a defendant, or hands down a no bill or no true bill, that defendant may again be indicted for the same offense, as jeopardy has not yet attached.

C. Same Offense

1. Crimes constitute the same offense for double jeopardy purposes if one set of facts proves them both.
2. When a second offense contains all of the elements of a first offense, plus additional elements, then the first offense is a **lesser-included offense** of the second.

   EXAMPLE: Robbery contains all the elements of larceny. Larceny is classified as a lesser-included offense of robbery.

   a. Once jeopardy has attached for the lesser-included offense, retrial is barred for the greater offense [Brown v. Ohio, 432 U.S. 161 (1977)].
   b. Likewise, once jeopardy has attached for the greater offense, retrial is barred for the lesser-included offense [Harris v. Oklahoma, 433 U.S. 682 (1977)].
   c. The order of trials is irrelevant, as is the determination of whether the defendant was acquitted or convicted for the first offense.
3. **Exceptions to Lesser-Included Offenses**
   a. When at the time jeopardy attaches for the first offense all the elements of the second offense have not occurred, a later trial for the greater offense is permitted.
   b. If the prosecution wishes to try closely related charges together, the defendant may make a motion for separate trials. However, if this request is granted, the defendant has waived any claim to double jeopardy [Jeffers v. United States, 432 U.S. 137 (1977)].

c. Separate trials and separate punishments do not violate double jeopardy and are proper when one unlawful act produces more than one separate criminal offense.

EXAMPLE: No violation of double jeopardy occurred when cumulative sentences for two offenses were imposed for conduct arising from one criminal act [Missouri v. Hunter, 459 U.S. 359 (1983)].

d. The following would constitute separate offenses:

(1) burglary and conspiracy to commit burglary;

(2) driving while intoxicated and involuntary manslaughter; and

(3) murder of more than one victim.

D. Separate Sovereignties Doctrine

1. The double jeopardy prohibition does not prevent dual prosecution by separate sovereigns. Therefore, a defendant may be prosecuted for the same criminal conduct by [Bartkus v. Illinois, 359 U.S. 121 (1959); Abbate v. United States, 359 U.S. 187 (1959)]:

a. a federal court and then by a state court, or vice versa; or

b. state courts in two separate states.

2. Inasmuch as a municipality is not considered a separate sovereign, a local conviction would bar a state prosecution for the same offense [Waller v. Florida, 397 U.S. 387 (1970)].

E. Retrial after Jeopardy Attaches

1. Despite the rule against double jeopardy, retrial is permitted if:

a. the defendant successfully appeals her conviction because of an error made at trial; or

(1) The defendant's appeal is considered a waiver of a double jeopardy claim [Burks v. United States, 437 U.S. 1 (1978)].

b. the appeal was granted because of the amount of evidence supporting the conviction.

(1) In such a case a retrial following reversal of a conviction due to insufficient evidence is prohibited by the Double Jeopardy Clause [Hudson v. Louisiana, 450 U.S. 40 (1981)].

(a) However, a retrial following reversal due to the conviction being against the weight of the evidence is not barred [Tibbs v. Florida, 457 U.S. 31 (1982)].

2. Retrial for a greater offense is unconstitutional after a conviction for a lesser-included offense, because the conviction of the lesser crime implies acquittal of the greater [Price v. Georgia, 398 U.S. 323 (1970)].

3. **Retrial after Mistrial**

a. Retrial is permitted in situations where a mistrial has been granted on the defendant's motion [United States v. Dinitz, 424 U.S. 600 (1976)].

b. Retrial is not permitted when the defendant objects to a mistrial, unless in the discretion of the court a manifest necessity exists that justice can only be served by declaring a mistrial [Illinois v. Somerville, 410 U.S. 458 (1973)].

EXAMPLE: A jury that fails to agree on a verdict is a proper basis to find "manifest necessity" and permit retrial.

NOTE If a judge grants an acquittal instead of a mistrial following a hung jury, retrial is not permitted [United States v. Martin Linen Supply, 430 U.S. 564 (1977)].

EXAMPLE: Improper conduct by the defendant or improper remarks by defense counsel are sufficient grounds to declare a mistrial and permit retrial [Arizona v. Washington, 434 U.S. 497 (1978)].

EXAMPLE: Illness or death of the judge, jurors, or the defendant may result in mistrial without double jeopardy barring retrial [United States v. Sanford, 429 U.S. 14 (1976)].

NOTE Necessity caused by the prosecution may be invalid grounds to declare a mistrial [Downum v. United States, 372 U.S. 734 (1963)].

F. Appeal by the Prosecution

1. The prosecution's right to appeal an adverse ruling is more limited than the defendant's right to appeal. The prosecution may appeal without the bar of double jeopardy in two situations, as follows:
   a. when a judge grants an acquittal on an issue not related to the guilt or innocence of the defendant, the prosecution may appeal the dismissal [United States v. Scott, 437 U.S. 82 (1978)]; and

   EXAMPLE: When the judge sets aside a jury's guilty verdict as a matter of law, the prosecution may appeal [United States v. Wilson, 420 U.S. 332 (1975)].

   b. the prosecution is allowed to appeal whenever the appeal can be decided without subjecting the defendant to a second trial.

   EXAMPLE: Following a guilty verdict, an appeal by the prosecution challenging the leniency of the sentence was found not to be in violation of the Double Jeopardy Clause [United States v. DiFrancesco, 449 U.S. 117 (1980)].

G. Application of Double Jeopardy in Sentencing

1. When a defendant appeals his conviction, receives a new trial, and is then reconvicted for the same offense, double jeopardy is not an absolute bar to the imposition of a harsher sentence.
   a. However, due process requires that a more severe sentence can be given upon reconviction only when the judge makes an affirmative showing of new information on the record [North Carolina v. Pearce, 395 U.S. 711 (1969)].

   b. Also, the Double Jeopardy Clause does apply to capital-sentencing proceedings when such proceedings "have the hallmarks of the trial on guilt or innocence" [Bullington v. Missouri, 451 U.S. 430 (1981)].

2. The limitation preventing more serious punishment upon resentencing is inapplicable following:
   a. a jury sentence [Chaffin v. Stynchcombe, 412 U.S. 17 (1973)]; and
   b. a trial *de novo* [Colten v. Kentucky, 407 U.S. 104 (1972)].
3. When a defendant is convicted of murder and sentenced to life imprisonment but successfully appeals the conviction, jeopardy has not terminated and the life sentence initially imposed does not raise a double jeopardy bar to a death sentence on retrial [Sattazhan v. Pennsylvania, 537 U.S. 101 (2003)].
4. A court can reduce a sentence on appeal to the sentence of a non-jeopardy-barred crime [Jones v. Thomas, 491 U.S. 376 (1989)].

H. Collateral Estoppel

1. The **doctrine of collateral estoppel**, which precludes relitigation between the same parties of issues actually determined at an earlier trial, is embodied in the guarantee against double jeopardy [Ashe v. Swenson, 397 U.S. 436 (1970)].
2. Collateral estoppel will only be applicable when the very issue sought to be precluded in the later prosecution has been necessarily determined in the earlier trial.

VIII. GUARANTEES OF A FAIR TRIAL

A. Right of Severance

1. When two defendants are tried together, if either co-defendant is unfairly prejudiced at any stage of a joint trial, a right of severance may be granted.
2. In a joint trial where a co-defendant's confession implicates the other defendant, the right to confrontation prohibits the use of such a confession and dictates that the defendants are entitled to separate trials [Bruton v. United States, 391 U.S. 123 (1968)].
3. The traditional approach of giving the jury instructions to consider the confession only against the confessing defendant is constitutionally inadequate, unless:
   a. incriminating portions of the confession can be adequately deleted;
   b. the co-defendant takes the witness stand after making a confession and is subject to cross-examination; or
      (1) This applies even when the co-defendant testifies at trial that she never made the confession [Nelson v. O'Neil, 402 U.S. 622 (1971)].
   c. the co-defendant's statement is subject to the harmless error rule.

B. Impartiality

1. The due process right to an unbiased judge requires the defendant to be tried before a magistrate who is neither prejudiced against the defendant nor financially interested in the outcome of the trial [Ward v. City of Monroeville, 409 U.S. 57 (1972)].

C. The Right to Counsel at Trial

1. The Sixth Amendment provides that "the accused shall enjoy the right to have the assistance of counsel for his defense." This right has been applied to the states through the Fourteenth Amendment [Gideon v. Wainwright, 372 U.S. 335 (1963)].
2. The right to counsel means the right to effective counsel. The law presumes that legal counsel is effective, and it is the duty of the defendant to demonstrate otherwise. This claim is often raised on collateral appeal, but may be raised in any appeal. Under Strickland v. Washington [466 U.S. 668 (1984)], a defendant making this claim must prove both:
   a. that counsel was ineffective—for example, because she deviated from reasonably prevailing norms; and
   b. there is a reasonable probability that the verdict would have been not guilty had counsel been effective.

   EXAMPLE: Where counsel is inexperienced and has little time to prepare in relation to the complexity of the case, reversal is not proper unless both prongs of Strickland are satisfied. There must be a particular allegation of specific attorney errors [United States v. Cronic, 466 U.S. 648 (1984)].

EXAMPLE: Ignoring the defendant's requested appellate issues and arguing issues of the attorney's choosing is not ineffective [Jones v. Barnes, 463 U.S. 745 (1988)].

EXAMPLE: Effective assistance of counsel was denied when the government tapped into conversations between the defendant and his attorney [Beach v. United States, 386 U.S. 26 (1966)].

EXAMPLE: Ineffective counsel occurs when a government informant reveals accounts of the defendant's conversation with her attorney [Weatherford v. Bursey, 429 U.S. 545 (1977)].

EXAMPLE: In a capital punishment case, the trial counsel's failure to investigate the accused's background and to present mitigating evidence of the accused's unfortunate life history at the sentencing proceedings violated the accused's Sixth Amendment right to the effective assistance of counsel [Wiggins v. Smith, 539 U.S. 510 (2003)].

EXAMPLE: In the sentencing phase of a death penalty proceeding, assistance of counsel was deemed effective when the defendant's lawyer urged a life sentence during opening statements, called attention to the mitigating evidence introduced during the guilt phase of the proceedings, and cross-examined prosecution witnesses, but called no witnesses for the defendant and declined to make a closing statement (thereby preventing the lead prosecutor from making one). The Supreme Court found that this was a decision as to trial strategy, and not an ineffective assistance of counsel [Bell v. Cone, 535 U.S. 685 (2002)].

NOTE In two analogous situations, the Strickland test is not to be used: (1) If there is an actual conflict that adversely affects the attorney's performance, reversal is proper [Cuyler v. Sullivan, 446 U.S. 335 (1980)]; (2) If the defense attorney indicates to the court that such a conflict exists, the defense must be severed [Holloway v. Arkansas, 435 U.S. 475 (1978)].

c. A defendant may waive the right to counsel when he does so knowingly and intelligently [Faretta v. California, 422 U.S. 806 (1975)].

d. The defendant has the right to represent himself.

  (1) Although a defendant has the right to represent himself, the court is permitted to appoint a stand-by counsel, even over the defendant's objection, provided the defendant maintains actual control of his case [McKaskle v. Wiggins, 465 U.S. 168 (1984)].

  (2) If the court appoints an attorney for a defendant who is representing himself, the defendant may not divide the actual representation between himself and the attorney [United States v. Conder, 423 F.2d 904 (5th Cir. 1970)].

  (3) Even though a defendant is deemed by the court to be competent to stand trial, the trial court may still deem the defendant incompetent to defend himself [Indiana v. Edwards, 554 U.S. 164 (2008)].

e. Although an intelligent waiver of the right to counsel will generally be recognized and approved, there is no absolute right to waive counsel at the appellate level [Martinez v. Court of Appeal of California, Fourth Appellate Dist., 528 U.S. 152 (2000)].

3. Absent waiver, a defendant may not be "imprisoned for any offense, whether classified as petty, misdemeanor, or felony unless he was represented by counsel" [Argersinger v. Hamlin, 407 U.S. 25 (1972)].
   a. An uncounselled conviction cannot be used in recidivist sentencing [Baldasur v. Illinois, 446 U.S. 222 (1980)].
   b. A suspended sentence that may result in the "actual deprivation of a person's liberty" may not be imposed unless the defendant was provided assistance of counsel in the prosecution for the crime charged [Alabama v. Shelton, 535 U.S. 654 (2002)].
4. The right to counsel includes the right to be provided with free counsel when the accused cannot afford an attorney.
   a. An indigent must be informed of her right to free counsel before a valid waiver can arise [Kitchens v. Smith, 401 U.S. 847 (1971)].
   b. There is no constitutional standard for indigency, although some states do require a defendant to repay the amount of attorney's fees at a later time, if possible [Fuller v. Oregon, 417 U.S. 40 (1974)].
   c. An attorney must be appointed when there is a colorable issue in controversy [Penson v. Ohio, 488 U.S. 75 (1988)], although the attorney may withdraw if he feels there are no valid issues in controversy [Anders v. California, 386 U.S. 738 (1967)].
5. It is a violation of the Sixth Amendment to represent more than one defendant whenever a conflict of interest is shown to exist that jeopardizes the rights of any defendant or adversely affects the attorney's performance, although co-defendants may choose to share counsel [Cuyler v. Sullivan, 446 U.S. 335 (1980)].
   a. Either the defendant or the court may raise an attorney's conflict of interest.
   b. To demonstrate that a violation of the Sixth Amendment right to counsel resulted from counsel's conflict of interest, the defendant must show that the conflict adversely affected counsel's representation [Mickens v. Taylor, 535 U.S. 162 (2002)].
   c. The Supreme Court discourages multiple representation of defendants in the same case because if one defendant later decides to cooperate and testify against the co-defendant, the attorney must be disqualified in both cases, due to the fact that the attorney-client privilege will prevent the attorney from using information obtained during the representation to zealously cross examine the cooperating defendant [Wheat v. United States, 486 U.S. 153 (1988)]. The Sixth Amendment requires zealous representation.
6. Failure to provide counsel at trial results in an automatic reversal.
   a. The harmless error rule applies, however, to the denial of counsel at criminal proceedings other than trial [United States v. Wade, 388 U.S. 218 (1967)].

7. The right to counsel attaches to all critical stages of the proceedings that affect the defendant's right to a fair trial, including [Gilbert v. California, 388 U.S. 263 (1967)]:
    a. custodial interrogations [Miranda v. Arizona, 384 U.S. 436 (1966)];
    b. post-indictment lineups [Kirby v. Illinois, 406 U.S. 682 (1972)];
    c. preliminary hearings [Coleman v. Alabama, 399 U.S. 1 (1970)];
    d. arraignments [Hamilton v. Alabama, 368 U.S. 52 (1961)];
    e. felony trials [Gideon v. Wainwright, 372 U.S. 335 (1963)];
    f. sentencing [Mempa v. Rhay, 389 U.S. 128 (1967)]; and
    g. appeals as a matter of right [Douglas v. California, 372 U.S. 353 (1963)].
8. The following stages are not deemed "critical" because they are easily re-created and no right to counsel exists:
    a. preliminary identification procedures [Schmerber v. California, 384 U.S. 757 (1966); Gilbert v. California, 388 U.S. 263 (1967); United States v. Ash, 413 U.S. 300 (1973)];
    b. pre-indictment lineups [Kirby v. Illinois, 406 U.S. 682 (1972)];
    c. non-adversarial detention hearings [Gerstein v. Pugh, 420 U.S. 103 (1975)];
    d. grand jury proceedings [United States v. Mandujano, 425 U.S. 564 (1976)];
    e. discretionary appeals [Ross v. Moffitt, 417 U.S. 600 (1974)];
    f. parole revocations [Gagnon v. Scarpelli, 411 U.S. 778 (1973)]; and
    g. *habeas corpus* proceedings.

D. Competency

1. A defendant must be able to understand the nature of the charges against her and have the capacity to consult with her lawyer in preparing her defense.
2. The defendant must be oriented as to time and place and also must have a fair recollection of the events surrounding the charge [Dusky v. United States, 362 U.S. 402 (1960)].
3. The defendant has a right to a hearing by a judge to determine competency, but it is often determined by a jury. Competency to stand trial cannot be waived.
    a. Competency is determined by a defendant's mental condition at the time of trial, not at the time of the crime (as insanity is), and may be raised after the completion of the trial [Pate v. Robinson, 383 U.S. 375 (1966)].
4. A defendant found to be incompetent is generally committed for treatment, but cannot remain indefinitely in a mental hospital. The criminal proceedings are suspended until the defendant regains competence.
5. The government may administer antipsychotic drugs to a mentally ill defendant against the defendant's will for the purpose of rendering the defendant competent to stand trial on serious criminal charges [Sell v. United States, 539 U.S. 166 (2003)].

E. Jury Trial

1. The right to a jury trial in criminal prosecutions was held applicable to the states as being "fundamental to the American scheme of justice" [Duncan v. Louisiana, 391 U.S. 145 (1968)].

2. The right to a jury trial attaches in any criminal proceeding where the defendant faces a potential sentence of longer than six months [Baldwin v. New York, 399 U.S. 66 (1970)].
   a. The right to a jury trial was extended to criminal contempt cases in which the punishment imposed exceeded six months in jail [Frank v. United States, 395 U.S. 147 (1969)].
   b. In a civil contempt case, no right to a jury trial exists.
3. The defendant can expressly and intelligently waive his right to a jury trial [Singer v. United States, 380 U.S. 24 (1965)].
4. **Size of the Jury**
   a. A six-member jury is upheld in noncapital cases in state courts as long as the jury functions as a representative cross-section of the community [Williams v. Florida, 399 U.S. 78 (1970)].
      (1) A unanimous verdict is required with a six-person jury [Burch v. Louisiana, 441 U.S. 130 (1979)].
      (2) Five-person juries are held unconstitutional as a denial of due process [Ballen v. Georgia, 435 U.S. 223 (1978)].
   b. Federal trials require unanimous verdicts from 12-member juries. The Supreme Court has held that the Sixth Amendment right to a jury trial, as incorporated against the states through the Fourteenth Amendment, requires a unanimous verdict to convict a defendant of a serious offense [Ramos v. Louisiana, 140 S. Ct. 1390 (2020)]. In other words, where a federal trial requires a unanimous verdict to convict, a state jury must also be unanimous to convict.
5. **Makeup of the Jury**
   a. The defendant has a right to a jury selected from a cross-section of the community; this cross-section, however, need not include members of all minority groups [Carter v. Green City Jury Commissioner, 396 U.S. 320 (1970)].
   b. During the jury selection process, each side is permitted to request the removal of any juror for cause if the juror does not appear capable of rendering a fair and impartial verdict. The request to strike for cause must state a specific reason and be granted by the trial judge.
   c. In addition, each side gets a certain number of peremptory challenges, which allow them to dismiss a juror without stating a reason. Peremptory challenges can be exercised for any rational or irrational reason (other than race, ethnicity, or gender). The number of peremptory challenges varies by state, but in federal criminal court, each side is entitled to the following number of peremptory challenges [Fed. R. Crim. P. 24(b)]:
      (1) in a capital case, 20 peremptory challenges when the government seeks the death penalty;
      (2) in any other felony case, the government has six peremptory challenges and the defendant or defendants jointly have 10 peremptory challenges; and

(3) in a misdemeanor case, three peremptory challenges.

d. The exclusion of prospective jurors based on race, ethnicity, or gender violates the Equal Protection Clause [J.E.B. v. Alabama, 511 U.S. 127 (1994)].

(1) A *prima facie* showing of purposeful racial discrimination in jury selection can be established solely on the prosecutor's exercise of peremptory challenges at the defendant's trial, placing the burden on the state to prove otherwise [Batson v. Kentucky, 476 U.S. 79 (1986)]. A pretextual reason for exercising a peremptory challenge given by the prosecution gives rise to an inference of discriminatory intent [Miller-El v. Dretke, 545 U.S. 231 (2005); Snyder v. Louisiana, 552 U.S. 472 (2008)].

(2) The underrepresentation of a distinct and significant racial group from the number of individuals sequestered for jury selection provides adequate grounds for a *prima facie* showing of discriminatory jury selection [Taylor v. Louisiana, 419 U.S. 522 (1975)].

(3) To rebut a charge of racial discrimination, the state must show it followed racially neutral selection procedures [Alexander v. Louisiana, 405 U.S. 625 (1972)].

(4) The defendant has standing to challenge jury selection even if she is not a member of the excluded group [Peters v. Kiff, 407 U.S. 493 (1972)].

NOTE Statutes giving women, but not men, the right to exempt themselves from jury duty are invalid [Taylor v. Louisiana, 419 U.S. 522 (1975); Duren v. Missouri, 439 U.S. 357 (1979)].

e. It is reversible error to exclude jurors merely because they have misgivings about imposing capital punishment [Witherspoon v. Illinois, 391 U.S. 510 (1968)].

(1) In a capital case, a prospective juror is subject to a challenge for cause if their views about capital punishment would "prevent or substantially impair the performance of his duties as a juror in accordance with his instructions and...oath" [Wainwright v. Witt, 469 U.S. 412 (1985)].

(2) Merely being opposed to capital punishment is not enough to excuse the juror for cause. The juror's personal beliefs must substantially limit their ability to follow the court's instructions during a capital sentencing hearing or otherwise prevent the juror from fairly considering the imposition of a death sentence [Id.].

f. The exclusion of prospective jurors based on race, ethnicity, or gender violates the Equal Protection Clause. A Batson challenge can remedy this situation. In a Batson challenge, based on race, nationality, gender, religion, or some other cognizable group [Batson v. Kentucky, 476 U.S. 79 (1986)]:

(1) the party opposing the peremptory challenge must establish a "prima facie case" of discrimination;

(2) the proponent of the strike must offer a neutral explanation for choosing to strike the juror; and

(3) the court will decide whether the party raising the Batson challenge has proved purposeful discrimination [Purkett v. Elem, 514 U.S. 765, 767 (1995)].

g. The party making the Batson challenge has the burden of persuasion. Equal protection applies to civil and criminal trials equally [Edmonson v. Leesville Concrete Company, 500 U.S. 614 (1991)].

F. The Right to a Public Trial

1. Under the Sixth Amendment, the defendant has the right to a public trial in all criminal prosecutions.
2. Because the Sixth Amendment right to a public trial belongs to the defendant, not the public, the defendant may choose to waive this right and exclude the press and public [Gannett Co. v. De Pasquale, 443 U.S. 368 (1979)].
3. Members of the press and general public have a Sixth Amendment right to be present at all criminal proceedings except the grand jury, unless the judge specifically finds some overriding interest to necessitate a closed trial [Globe Newspaper Co. v. Superior Court, 457 U.S. 596 (1982)].
    a. This right can supersede the defendant's waiver of a public trial.
    b. The trial judge has the right to place limitations on the public and media, but public and media exclusion must be to protect the defendant's right to a fair trial [Irwin v. Dowd, 366 U.S. 717 (1961); Groppi v. Wisconsin, 400 U.S. 505 (1971)].
    c. In states that use preliminary hearings instead of grand juries, there is no general right for the media to be present at those proceedings—even those that take place in a courtroom.

G. Right of Confrontation

1. The defendant has a fundamental right of confrontation, meaning he may confront all witnesses against him in any criminal prosecution, federal or state [Pointer v. Texas, 380 U.S. 400 (1965)].
2. The primary purpose of the right of confrontation is to give the defendant an opportunity to cross-examine witnesses at trial; this right does not apply at a grand jury proceeding.
3. Although the defendant has the right to be present at the trial, this right is not absolute and may be waived.
    a. A waiver of the right to confrontation occurs when a defendant voluntarily leaves the trial [Taylor v. United States, 414 U.S. 17 (1973)].
    b. The court may first warn and then physically remove a disorderly defendant from the courtroom [Illinois v. Allen, 397 U.S. 337 (1970)].

NOTE The trial judge may bind and gag the defendant, cite her for contempt, or remove her from the courtroom for disruptive behavior.

c. Placing a screen between a child-abuse victim and the defendant is a violation of the confrontation clause [Coy v. Iowa, 487 U.S. 1012 (1988)], but excluding the defendant and transmitting the child's testimony to him via television is permissible [Maryland v. Craig, 497 U.S. 836 (1990)].

4. The right of confrontation is vital to allow for impeachment of both prosecution and defense witnesses so that a court may determine the credibility of the witness and discover possible bias.

5. The introduction of out-of-court statements must not deny the defendant the right of confrontation. The Sixth Amendment issue predominates over the hearsay question. However, the Confrontation Clause does not automatically exclude all hearsay evidence.

   a. The prosecution must demonstrate that the witness is unavailable after good-faith efforts have been made, and that the hearsay statement is trustworthy. Trustworthiness is shown when the hearsay statement either [Mancuri v. Stubbs, 408 U.S. 204 (1972)]:

      (1) falls within one of the recognized hearsay exceptions; or

      (2) is made under oath, and the defendant had the opportunity to cross-examine the witness at the time it was made.

   b. Out-of-court statements that are **testimonial** in nature, such as statements made to the police or 911 after an emergency has ceased, are inadmissible under the Confrontation Clause, even if such statements would be considered to be excited utterances [Crawford v. Washington, 541 U.S. 36 (2004)]. Statements, however, are considered nontestimonial and admissible when made in the course of police investigation under circumstances "objectively indicating that the primary purpose of the interrogation is to enable police assistance to meet an ongoing emergency" [Davis v. Washington, 547 U.S. 813 (2006)].

   EXAMPLE: A statute allowing post-indictment co-conspirator admissions does not violate the Sixth Amendment, meaning an incriminating hearsay statement of a co-conspirator is properly admitted at trial despite the defendant's absence [Dutton v. Evans, 400 U.S. 74 (1970)].

   EXAMPLE: The right to confrontation is satisfied when the defendant had the right to cross-examine at an earlier hearing [Barber v. Page, 390 U.S. 719 (1968); California v. Green, 399 U.S. 149 (1970)].

   EXAMPLE: A co-defendant's confession cannot be used against the defendant at a joint trial unless the co-defendant takes the stand, the defendant makes a similar confession, or references to the defendant are omitted [Richardson v. Marsh, 481 U.S. 200 (1988)].

H. Right to Compulsory Process

1. The right to compulsory process gives a defendant the power to present her own witnesses and a fair opportunity to present a defense free from intimidation or prejudicial exclusion of material evidence [Washington v. Texas, 388 U.S. 14 (1967)].

2. The Sixth Amendment right to compulsory process for obtaining witnesses has been incorporated to apply to state criminal proceedings [Washington v. Texas, 388 U.S. 14 (1967)].

I. Procedural Rights for Conviction

1. The prosecution must prove beyond a reasonable doubt, but not beyond all doubt, that the defendant is guilty of each element of the crime charged to satisfy the due process requirement of a fair trial [Speiser v. Randall, 358 U.S. 860 (1958); Taylor v. Kentucky, 436 U.S. 478 (1978)].
2. The defendant may be required to prove an affirmative defense, such as self-defense, by a preponderance of evidence [Leland v. Oregon, 343 U.S. 790 (1952)].
    a. However, in insanity cases in federal court, the defendant must prove the affirmative defense of insanity by clear and convincing evidence [18 U.S.C. § 17(b)]. In state courts, the majority rule is that the defendant must prove insanity by a preponderance of the evidence.

    EXAMPLE: To reduce a charge of murder to voluntary manslaughter, the defendant may be required to prove an affirmative defense, such as extreme emotional disturbance, by a preponderance of the evidence [Patterson v. New York, 432 U.S. 197 (1977)].
3. Because there is no absolute right to a jury instruction on the presumption of innocence, failure to so instruct the jurors cannot, by itself, amount to a denial of a fair trial [Kentucky v. Whorton, 441 U.S. 786 (1979)].
4. A mandatory presumption, which the jury must accept, is unconstitutional in a criminal case because it violates the defendant's right to due process [Sandstrom v. Montana, 442 U.S. 510 (1979)].
5. A permissive presumption, which the jury may accept, is allowed in criminal proceedings only when a "rational connection" exists between the prosecution's proof of the basic fact and the jury's inference of the ultimate fact or element of the crime [Ulster County Court v. Allen, 442 U.S. 140 (1979)].

IX. POST-TRIAL STAGE

A. Defendant's Rights during Sentencing

1. A defendant's case is ready for sentencing once a verdict or plea of guilty is entered. The sentence is determined according to applicable sentencing statutes, which must comply with the Eighth and Fourteenth Amendments.
2. The accused has a right to counsel during the sentencing hearing.
3. For misdemeanor offenses—offenses punishable by fine, by imprisonment for not more than one year, or both—if the defendant gives written consent, the court will permit sentencing to occur by video teleconferencing or in the defendant's absence [Fed. R. Crim. P. 43(b)(2)].
4. A defendant in a sentencing hearing has a Fifth Amendment right to remain silent, and no adverse inference may be drawn from the exercise of that right [Mitchell v. United States 526 U.S. 314 (1999)].
5. During sentencing, the court may use hearsay evidence and testimony not subject to cross-examination, or evidence obtained in violation of the Fourth Amendment [Williams v. New York, 333 U.S. 241 (1949)].
   a. When the death penalty is involved, however, the defendant is given greater confrontation rights [Gardner v. Florida, 430 U.S. 349 (1977)].
6. Other than the fact of a prior conviction, any fact that increases the penalty for a crime beyond the prescribed statutory maximum must be submitted to the jury and proved beyond a reasonable doubt [Apprendi v. New Jersey, 530 U.S. 466 (2000)]. These rights may be waived by a defendant being sentenced by a judge (sitting without a jury) or subsequent to a plea [Blakely v. Washington, 542 U.S. 296 (2004)].
   a. A sentencing judge, sitting without a jury, may not find an aggravating circumstance necessary for imposition of the death penalty [Ring v. Arizona, 536 U.S. 584 (2002)].
   b. A jury must be able to consider and give effect to a defendant's mitigating evidence in imposing the sentence [Penry v. Johnson, 532 U.S. 782 (2001)].
   c. A defendant's Sixth Amendment rights are, however, violated when a sentencing judge enhances a sentence based on facts that are neither admitted by the defendant nor found by a jury [Blakely v. Washington, 542 U.S. 296 (2004)].
   d. With regard to the Federal Sentencing Guidelines, a sentence outside the advisory Guidelines range does not require extraordinary circumstances and is reviewed under an "abuse of discretion" standard, regardless of whether the sentence falls above or below the Guidelines range [Gall v. United States, 552 U.S. 38 (2007)].
7. Generally, if a defendant wins on appeal and is then reconvicted, a more severe penalty may not be imposed on retrial [North Carolina v. Pearce, 395 U.S. 711 (1969)].
   a. To prevent vindictive punishment, a harsher sentence may only be imposed when it is based on new, objective information of the defendant's conduct occurring after the first sentence was decreed.

NOTE In a trial *de novo*, where no review of the original trial or appeal is considered in reaching a new verdict, an increased punishment can result because a different court is rendering the sentence [Colten v. Kentucky, 407 U.S. 104 (1972)].

B. Punishment

1. The Eighth Amendment guarantee against cruel and unusual punishment is applicable to the states via the Fourteenth Amendment [Francis v. Resweber, 329 U.S. 459 (1946)].
2. **Requirement**
   a. In order to comply with the Eighth Amendment, the sentence must be proportional to the crime committed and the sentences of other similarly situated criminals having conducted similar crimes.
      (1) The concept of imposing harsher sentences for repeat offenders has been held constitutional [Rummel v. Estelle, 445 U.S. 263 (1980)].
      (2) Excessive jail terms that are grossly disproportionate to the crime committed violate the Eighth Amendment [Weems v. United States, 217 U.S. 349 (1910)].
      (3) Imposition of the death penalty for the crime of rape is grossly disproportionate to the offense and unconstitutional under the Eighth Amendment [Coker v. Georgia, 433 U.S. 584 (1977); Kennedy v. Louisiana, 554 U.S. 407 (2008)].
   b. A defendant cannot be imprisoned because of his inability to pay a fine [Tate v. Short, 401 U.S. 395 (1971)].
   c. Doubling up inmates into one jail cell is neither cruel nor unusual [Rhodes v. Chapman, 450 U.S. 906 (1981)].
   d. Conviction of an individual because she is addicted to narcotics is a cruel and unusual punishment [Robinson v. California, 370 U.S. 660 (1962)].

NOTE Being an addict or an alcoholic cannot in and of itself be criminal; however, being drunk in public can be a punishable crime [Powell v. Texas, 392 U.S. 514 (1968)].

   e. Mandatory capital punishment for specified crimes, such as shooting a police officer, is unconstitutional because it precludes consideration of mitigating factors [Woodson v. North Carolina, 428 U.S. 280 (1976); Lockett v. Ohio, 438 U.S. 586 (1978); Eddings v. Oklahoma, 469 U.S. 368 (1986)].
3. **The Death Penalty**
   a. The death penalty is not considered cruel and unusual punishment nor grossly disproportionate to the crime, provided the court's review procedure affords procedural safeguards to prevent arbitrary or discriminatory sentencing [Gregg v. Georgia, 428 U.S. 153 (1976)].
   b. The following procedural safeguards exist to prevent violations of the Eighth Amendment:
      (1) a bifurcated trial, where one jury determines guilt and a second jury recommends the sentence, was established to lessen the likelihood of discriminatory sentencing;

(2) evidence concerning aggravating circumstances must be presented before imposing the death penalty;

(a) Furthermore, a killing cannot be raised to a capital offense under a vague state statute when none of the express aggravating factors are proved [Godfrey v. Georgia, 446 U.S. 420 (1980)].

(3) the court must review mitigating factors before imposing the death penalty, although a jury need not receive instructions on the concept of mitigation or mitigating factors allowed by a state [Buchanan v. Angelone, 522 U.S. 269 (1998)];

(4) a jury may not impose a death sentence unless it is also permitted to return a verdict of guilty to a lesser-included offense supported by the evidence [Beck v. Alabama, 447 U.S. 625 (1980)];

(a) A state court need not instruct the jury on offenses that, under state law, are not considered lesser-included offenses of the crime charged [Hopkins v. Reeves, 524 U.S. 88 (1998)].

(5) when a capital defendant's future dangerousness is at issue, and the only sentencing alternative to death is life imprisonment without possibility of parole, due process entitles the defendant to tell the jury that he is ineligible for parole [Kelly v. South Carolina, 534 U.S. 246 (2002)]; and

(6) there must be a review procedure to prevent imposition of the death penalty for arbitrary or discriminatory reasons.

c. A disproportionate use of capital punishment on one race does not violate the Eighth Amendment.

d. Execution of individuals who were under 18 years of age at the time of their capital crimes is prohibited by the Eighth and Fourteenth Amendments [Roper v. Simmons, 543 U.S. 551 (2005)].

e. Execution of mentally retarded defendants is cruel and unusual punishment under the Eighth Amendment [Atkins v. Virginia, 536 U.S. 304 (2002)].

4. **The Jury's Role in Punishment**

a. There is no right to have a jury determine a sentence. Even the death penalty may be imposed by a judge acting alone or with jury advisement as to sentence [Spaziano v. Florida, 468 U.S. 447 (1984)].

b. A state statute may not exclude from a jury all individuals who express some opposition to the death penalty. The state may exclude all potential jurors who indicate that they would never, under any circumstances, impose the death penalty [Witherspoon v. Illinois, 391 U.S. 510 (1968)].

C. Appeal

1. The U.S. Constitution does not guarantee the right to an appeal. States may provide such a right by statute as long as access to appellate review is afforded in a nondiscriminatory manner [Griffin v. Illinois, 351 U.S. 12 (1956)].

a. Where a state grants a first appeal to all individuals, such as an appeal as a matter of right, indigents must be provided with appointed counsel to satisfy equal protection requirements [Douglas v. California, 372 U.S. 353 (1963)].

b. Consequently, indigents are entitled on appeal to be provided free transcripts of trial proceedings [Mayer v. City of Chicago, 404 U.S. 189 (1971)].

2. Recovery of defense costs is constitutional provided it is achieved in a nondiscriminatory manner. A state can recover legal costs from an indigent who is convicted on appeal and is subsequently able to pay [Fuller v. Oregon, 417 U.S. 40 (1974)].

3. Following an automatic first appeal, some jurisdictions provide a second discretionary avenue of appeal. The right to counsel for indigents does not attach during this proceeding, nor does the right attach for a writ of *certiorari* to the U.S. Supreme Court [Ross v. Moffitt, 417 U.S. 600 (1974)].

4. A motion to grant acquittal will only be granted if it is established that the evidence provided in the prosecution's case-in-chief is so insufficient that guilt is not even a rational option among a range of options. This is known as the "rational result" test.

   a. The standard of proof is whether the evidence, viewed in the light most favorable to the prosecution, supports a rational finding that all of the elements of the offense have been established.

5. Following a reversal of a conviction on appeal, a defendant can be retried. However, on retrial, it is prejudicial error and a violation of both due process and double jeopardy to be tried for any crime more serious than the crime for which the defendant was convicted [Price v. Georgia, 398 U.S. 323 (1970)].

D. *Habeas Corpus*

1. Following an unsuccessful appeal, a defendant may, in certain instances, collaterally attack the lawfulness of her detention by filing a writ of *habeas corpus*.

2. **Procedural Considerations**

   a. The defendant-petitioner must prove an unlawful detention by a preponderance of the evidence.

   b. Indigents have no right to appointed counsel, inasmuch as a *habeas corpus* petition is a civil suit.

   c. To bring a timely writ of *habeas corpus*, the petitioner must be in custody, which includes those out on bail, on probation, or parole.

   d. Although a state prisoner may seek a writ in either state or federal court, the following requirements must be satisfied before a state prisoner can bring a petition for *habeas corpus* in a federal court:

      (1) the petitioner must show that the detention violates the U.S. Constitution;

      (2) a state petitioner must have followed all state procedural rules at trial or been denied relief, absent a showing of cause for noncompliance and resulting prejudice [Francis v. Henderson, 425 U.S. 536 (1976)];

      (3) all available state remedies must have been exhausted before the federal court may consider the petition [Fay v. Noia, 372 U.S. 391 (1963)];

(4) the petitioner must show clear and convincing evidence of error before the federal court will review factual findings of the state court [Sumner v. Mata, 449 U.S. 539 (1981)]; and

(5) a petitioner who had a full and fair opportunity to raise a Fourth Amendment violation previously in state court will not be permitted to seek a writ in federal court based on the alleged allegation [Stone v. Powell, 428 U.S. 465 (1976)].

EXAMPLE: Claims challenging the sufficiency of the evidence may be reviewed to satisfy due process, if it is found that no rational trier of fact could have found the defendant guilty after viewing the evidence as favorably as possible for the prosecution [Jackson v. Virginia, 443 U.S. 307 (1979)].

e. Federal prisoners may bring *habeas corpus* proceedings only in federal court. In seeking federal *habeas corpus*, a federal prisoner must show both cause as to why an objection was not made at trial to the alleged constitutional violation and a resulting actual prejudice [United States v. Frady, 456 U.S. 152 (1982)].

f. The state may appeal the granting of a writ, and the defendant may be retried for the same offense without violating the prohibition against double jeopardy.

X. RIGHTS OF PRISONERS, JUVENILES, AND ALIENS

A. Prisoners' Rights

1. Generally, prisoners' constitutional rights are more limited in scope than those held by individuals in society at large [Shaw v. Murphy, 532 U.S. 223 (2001)]. The test for prisoner rights is whether restrictions are reasonably related to legitimate penological interests [Turner v. Safley, 482 U.S. 78 (1987)].
2. **Parole or Probation**
   a. No federal constitutional right to parole or probation exists. However, where state law provides for a right to parole, a prisoner denied parole must be granted notice of the reasons for denial and an opportunity to be heard [Greenholtz v. Inmates of Nebraska, 442 U.S. 1 (1979)].
      (1) Revocation of probation entitles the prisoner to the right to counsel if a new sentence is imposed [Mempa v. Rhay, 389 U.S. 128 (1967)]; otherwise, the right to counsel is limited and determined on a case-by-case basis.
      (2) Due process affords a prisoner the right to both a prerevocation hearing and a revocation hearing. At this latter hearing, evidence may be presented and confrontation of witnesses is allowed, subject to the discretion of the court [Morrissey v. Brewer, 408 U.S. 471 (1972)].
3. **Other Specific Rights**
   a. Prisoners must have reasonable access to the courts and legal counsel as well as some form of communication with the press [Bounds v. Smith, 430 U.S. 817 (1977); Pell v. Procunier, 417 U.S. 817 (1974)].
   b. The state may not refuse to provide prisoners with medical care [Estelle v. Gamble, 429 U.S. 97 (1976)].
   c. A prisoner must be given notice of the forfeiture of property through a certified letter addressed to him at the facility where he is confined [Dusenbery v. United States, 534 U.S. 161 (2002)].
4. **Limits on Prisoner Rights**
   a. Prisoners have no right to unionize [Jones v. North Carolina Prisoners' Labor Union, Inc., 443 U.S. 119 (1977)].
   b. Mail may be censored subject to strict guidelines [Procunier v. Martinez, 416 U.S. 396 (1974)], and letters to inmates from their attorneys may be opened, but not read, by prison authorities [Wolff v. McDonnell, 418 U.S. 539 (1974)].
   c. Inmates have no right to provide legal service to fellow inmates.
   d. A private corporation operating a correctional facility through a contract is not subject to suit for allegedly violating a prisoner's constitutional rights [Correctional Services Corp. v. Malesko, 534 U.S. 61 (2001)].
   e. Visiting regulations are usually viewed as reasonably related to legitimate penological interests and are, therefore, constitutional [Overton v. Bazzetta, 539 U.S. 126 (2003)].

B. Juveniles' Rights

1. Juvenile offenders must receive due process of the law under the following recognized procedural safeguards [In re Winship, 397 U.S. 358 (1970)]:
   a. the right to written notice of the charges;
   b. the right to counsel;
   c. the right to confront and cross-examine witnesses;
   d. the privilege against self-incrimination;
   e. the right to have guilt proved beyond a reasonable doubt; and
   f. the right not to be placed in jeopardy twice for the same offense once adjudicated a delinquent [Breed v. Jones, 421 U.S. 519 (1975)].
2. The following constitutional rights have not been extended to juvenile proceedings [McKeiver v. Pennsylvania, 403 U.S. 528 (1971)]:
   a. the right to a jury trial;
   b. the right to bail; and
   c. the right to a public trial.
3. The Eighth and Fourteenth Amendments forbid imposition of the death penalty on offenders who were under the age of 18 when their crimes were committed [Roper v. Simmons, 543 U.S. 551 (2005)].

C. Aliens' Rights

1. Under the U.S. Constitution, an alien's detention is limited to the time reasonably necessary to accomplish that alien's removal from the United States. Indefinite detention is not allowed [Zadvydas v. Davis, 533 U.S. 678 (2001)].

XI. MISCELLANEOUS PROCEDURAL CONSIDERATIONS

A. Retroactivity of New Decisions

1. A Supreme Court case creating a new constitutional right is fully retroactive to all defendants whether the case is pretrial, at trial, or in the process of direct appeal.
2. However, a collateral petitioner using a writ of *habeas corpus* will receive the benefit of a new decision only if [Trague v. Lane, 489 U.S. 288 (1989); Saffle v. Parks, 494 U.S. 484 (1990)]:
   a. the crime is itself decriminalized; or
   b. the prosecution was fundamentally unfair and the new rule maximizes the truth-finding function of trial.

B. *Ex Post Facto* Crimes

1. A crime must be law at the time of the offense in order to punish the defendant. The basic *ex post facto* protections include prohibition of the following [Collins v. Youngblood, 497 U.S. 37 (1990)]:
   a. retroactive criminal statutes;
   b. increasing the punishment after the commission of the offense;
   c. removing a defense that was viable at the time of the offense; and
   d. applying rules of procedure or evidence retroactively if those rules would make it easier to convict a defendant.
2. A state may not enact a statute that extends the limitations period for a crime when the previously applicable limitations period has already expired [Stogner v. California, 539 U.S. 607 (2003)].

C. Independent State Grounds

1. In accordance with the Tenth Amendment, all powers not expressly given to the federal government by the U.S. Constitution reside in the states. Thus, state courts, pursuant to their own constitutions and cases interpreting their constitutions, can give to the criminally accused greater procedural protections than are federally required.
   a. However, if they so proceed, they must indicate that such a decision is based on "adequate and independent state grounds" and must not entangle state and federal bases [Michigan v. Long, 463 U.S. 1032 (1983)].
2. Thus, in any state prosecution, a competent defense will make a separate set of solely state constitutional arguments.

D. Privilege against Self-Incrimination

1. The Fifth Amendment provides that no person shall be compelled in any criminal case to be a witness against herself, and that this privilege belongs to the accused and to all witnesses. This right

is binding upon the states through the Due Process Clause of the Fourteenth Amendment.

a. The privilege against self-incrimination applies to all proceedings, both civil and criminal, where formal testimony is received.

b. However, the holder of the privilege must be a natural person or a sole proprietorship. Partnerships, corporations, and other business entities are not entitled to assert the privilege; officials for such entities must submit to subpoenas for business records and testimony that might incriminate the entity. Such an official may, however, refuse to provide evidence that might tend to incriminate himself.

c. The Fifth Amendment privilege applies to questions posed by the government during a criminal trial and in any situation where the individual's response might be used to incriminate that person in a future criminal trial [Lefkowitz v. Turley, 414 U.S. 70 (1973)].

2. The evidence protected by the Fifth Amendment privilege must be self-incriminating.

3. The privilege against self-incrimination protects individuals only from being compelled to provide testimonial or communicative evidence. Thus, the Fifth Amendment privilege does not protect against compulsion to perform physical acts or submit physical evidence [Schmerber v. California, 384 U.S. 757 (1966); Pennsylvania v. Muniz, 496 U.S. 582 (1990)]. There is no Fifth Amendment right to refuse to:

   a. give a urine sample;

   b. submit to fingerprinting, photography, or measurements;

   c. write, speak, or wear particular clothes;

   d. assume a stance or walk; or

   e. make a particular gesture for identification or court appearances.

4. The defendant has no obligation to testify, and the prosecution may not comment on the defendant's failure to testify [Griffin v. California, 380 U.S. 609 (1965)].

   a. A criminal defendant need not be warned of the right not to testify. Therefore, a response to questions asked by the government will constitute a valid waiver of the privilege.

   b. The defendant may ask the judge to instruct the jury not to draw an adverse inference from the defendant's failure to testify [Carter v. Kentucky, 450 U.S. 288 (1981)].

   c. When a prosecutor argued during summation that the testifying defendant's presence at trial afforded an opportunity to tailor the testimony of other witnesses, there was no Fifth Amendment violation [Portuondo v. Agard, 529 U.S. 61 (2000)].

5. When a defendant has pled guilty, she does not waive her Fifth Amendment rights in the sentencing hearing, and the sentencing judge may not draw adverse inferences from the defendant's silence at sentencing [Mitchell v. United States, 526 U.S. 314 (1999)].

E. Exceptions to the Privilege against Self-Incrimination

1. Testimony for which the individual has been granted use, derivative use, or transactional immunity is not self-incriminating and hence eliminates the privilege.
   a. **Use immunity** ensures that the testimony of the witness will not be used against that witness.
      (1) Use immunity alone is not enough protection to overcome an individual's invocation of the Fifth Amendment privilege against self-incrimination. As a result, it is rarely given alone.
   b. **Derivative use immunity** goes one step further than use immunity, and protects the witness from having any information or leads that the prosecution derives from his testimony used against him.
      (1) Use and derivative use immunity, granted together, meet the minimum threshold for overcoming an individual's Fifth Amendment privilege against self-incrimination. As a result, they are usually granted together.
   c. **Transactional immunity** is extremely broad and ensures that the witness will not be prosecuted for any crimes related to the entire transaction.
2. Testimony regarding acts for which the applicable statute of limitations has run is also not self-incriminating.

   EXAMPLE: The witness does not want to answer a prosecutor's question because the answer will implicate her in a non-adulterous, but nonetheless embarrassing, situation. Because the evidence would not be "incriminating," the witness has no Fifth Amendment right to refuse to answer.
3. Once a defendant decides to take the stand and permit questioning on direct examination, he may be cross-examined regarding the substance of his testimony [Brown v. United States, 356 U.S. 148 (1958)]. Generally, the defendant is thought not to waive the Fifth Amendment privilege in total, but to grant a waiver to the extent necessary for reasonable scrutiny by the prosecution.
4. The Fifth Amendment privilege does not protect volunteered information, regardless of how incriminating. The government is only prohibited from compelling or coercing an individual into incriminating herself.

EXAM TIP Examine the factual setting in which the questions are asked and the purpose for which the government is asking them in order to determine whether "compulsion" exists.

KAPLAN BAR REVIEW

Evidence

TABLE OF CONTENTS

I. GENERAL PROVISIONS

Federal Rules of Evidence 462
Scope 462
Rulings on Evidence 462
Preliminary Questions 464
Limited Admissibility 464
Remainder of or Related Writings or Recorded Statements 465

II. JUDICIAL NOTICE

In General 466

III. PRESUMPTIONS

Presumptions in Civil Cases in General 467
Applying State Law to Presumptions in Civil Cases 468

IV. RELEVANCY AND ITS LIMITS

Admissibility 469
Admissibility of Specific Types of Evidence 470

V. PRIVILEGES

In General 479
Privilege under Common Law 479

VI. WITNESSES

In General 490
Impeachment 492
Examination of Witnesses 495

VII. OPINIONS AND EXPERT TESTIMONY

Acceptable Testimony 498
Bases of Expert's Opinion Testimony 499
Opinion on an Ultimate Issue 499
Disclosing the Facts or Data Underlying an Expert's Opinion 499
Court-Appointed Expert Witnesses 499

VIII. HEARSAY

Definitions........501
Analysis of Hearsay Issues........501
Hearsay Exemptions........503
Hearsay Exceptions........505

IX. AUTHENTICATION AND IDENTIFICATION

Authenticating or Identifying Evidence........520
Self-Authenticating Evidence........522
Subscribing Witness's Testimony........524

X. CONTENTS OF WRITINGS, RECORDINGS, AND PHOTOGRAPHS

Definitions........525
Requirement of the Original........525
Admissibility of Duplicates........526
Admissibility of Other Evidence of Content........526
Copies of Public Records to Prove Content........527
Summaries to Prove Content........527
Testimony or Statement of a Party to Prove Content........527
Functions of the Court and Jury........527

I. GENERAL PROVISIONS

A. Federal Rules of Evidence

1. The Federal Rules of Evidence were adopted in 1978; before this time, the rules of evidence were governed by common law.

B. Scope

1. The Federal Rules of Evidence apply in all federal civil and criminal cases, including bankruptcy proceedings [Fed. R. Evid. 101, 1101(a)–(b)].
2. The Federal Rules of Evidence do not apply to [Fed. R. Evid. 1101(d)]:
   a. preliminary determinations of fact by a judge;
   b. grand jury proceedings;
   c. probation and sentencing hearings;
   d. obtaining a warrant;
   e. bail proceedings; or
   f. other proceedings that Congress has exempted from the Federal Rules of Evidence.

C. Rulings on Evidence

1. Specific requirements must be met for an appellate court to reverse a trial court's admission or exclusion of evidence. The analysis upon appellate review depends on whether the trial court admitted or excluded evidence, and the existence of prejudicial error [Fed. R. Evid. 103].
   a. An evidentiary ruling may be reversed for error only if [Fed. R. Evid. 103(a)]:
      (1) prejudicial error exists; and
         (a) If the jury's verdict would not have been affected by the trial court's ruling, then only harmless error has occurred. The **harmless error standard** applies to Rule 103. However, when a substantial right is found (i.e., the outcome of the trial), then **prejudicial error** has occurred.

         EXAMPLE: Snow White is being tried for robbery. The prosecution calls seven diminutive eyewitnesses to the stand, all of whom testify that they saw Snow White grab Stepmother's purse and run away. The defense seeks to impeach the fourth witness, Dopey, with evidence of his prior conviction for obtaining prescriptions by fraud, but the judge upholds the prosecution's objection to this evidence. Though exclusion of this evidence may have been improper, the error will be found to be harmless because it is highly unlikely that allowing the defense to impeach Dopey would have resulted in a verdict of "not guilty," given the testimony of six other eyewitnesses.

(2) proper objection or an offer of proof is made.

(a) For rulings admitting evidence, a timely objection or motion to strike must appear of record, and state the specific ground of the objection, if it is not apparent from the context [Fed. R. Evid. 103(a)(2)].

1) A timely objection is one made as soon as the opposing attorney reasonably knows that valid grounds for an objection exist. An objection made after the answer is given is usually made in the form of a motion to strike with a request to the judge for an instruction to the jury that they disregard the evidence objected to. In extraordinary circumstances an appellate court can reverse even in the absence of an objection if the error is obvious and causes a miscarriage of justice [Fed. R. Evid. 103(e)].

2) When an objection states the precise legal ground on which it is based, it is sufficient to preserve an issue for appeal; however, to obtain a reversal on appeal, the specific objection must have been valid on the ground stated. If the judge reserves ruling on a specific objection to a later point in the trial, counsel must raise the objection at that later point or the objection is waived.

(b) For rulings excluding evidence, an oral or written explanation of the excluded evidence must be made on the record. This offer of proof, or **proffer**, must address the relevancy and the admissibility of such evidence [Fed. R. Evid. 103(a)(2)].

EXAMPLE: At Cinderella's trial, the defense seeks to have Fairy Godmother testify that Cinderella was at the ball with her when Stepmother's purse was snatched. However, the trial court will not allow Fairy Godmother to testify because, as a fairy, she will not swear on the Bible to tell the truth. The defense must admit into the record what Fairy Godmother would have testified to, had she been allowed to testify, if Cinderella is to later appeal on the grounds that Fairy Godmother's testimony was improperly excluded.

1) Offers of proof are generally not required where the substance of the evidence is apparent from the context [Id.].

2) If the trial court excluded evidence, reversal can occur only where no valid grounds for objection existed, resulting in prejudicial error, and an offer of proof was made to establish relevancy of the excluded evidence.

3) In jury trials, proceedings shall be conducted, to the extent practicable, so as to prevent inadmissible evidence from being suggested to the jury by any means, such as making statements or offers of proof, or asking questions, in the hearing of the jury [Fed. R. Evid. 103(d)].

D. Preliminary Questions

1. The party seeking admission of evidence (the proponent) has the burden to establish preliminary facts such as competency, qualification of witnesses, unavailability, or privilege by a preponderance of the evidence. The trial judge makes a preliminary factual determination on admissibility of evidence; the jury then determines the weight and credibility of the evidence. When making the determination of admissibility, the judge is not bound by the rules of evidence except for those addressing privileges, and thus may rely on affidavits or hearsay statements [Fed. R. Evid. 104].

   EXAMPLE: Davis is on trial for the murder of his wife, Violet. At trial, the prosecution seeks to introduce testimony that Walter had told his best friend, Bruce, that Walter, not Davis, was the real father of Violet's newborn son. Such testimony falls under a Rule 804 exception to the hearsay rule, but only if Walter is unavailable to testify himself. When determining whether or not the testimony is admissible, the judge may hear evidence that Walter told Bruce, "I'm leaving the country and going into hiding, and I'll never come back for any reason," itself hearsay, to determine whether or not Walter is truly unavailable.

2. If the relevance of a particular piece of evidence depends on a particular finding of fact by the jury, the court will admit the evidence, as long as the judge determines that a reasonable jury could find the necessary fact, with the instruction to the jury to disregard the evidence absent a finding of the required fact [Fed. R. Evid. 104(b)].

   EXAMPLE: The prosecution seeks to admit into evidence a letter allegedly written by Davis that reads in part, "I killed her, and I'm glad I did it and she's gone. Nobody will ever catch me." If the letter was not written by Davis, however, it is not relevant to the case at hand. As long as the judge determines that a reasonable jury could find that Davis wrote the letter, he will admit the evidence and instruct the jury that they are only to consider the letter if they find that Davis did, in fact, write the letter.

3. The trial judge is given discretion to excuse the jury while determining the admissibility of a preliminary fact whenever evidence may have a prejudicial impact (i.e., a confession in a criminal case) [Fed. R. Evid. 104(c)].
4. A decision by the accused to testify on a preliminary issue does not waive her Fifth Amendment privilege against self-incrimination as to other issues in the case. The accused testifies for the limited purpose of addressing the preliminary issue and cross-examination is limited to that area of inquiry [Fed. R. Evid. 104(d)].

E. Limited Admissibility

1. If evidence is admitted as to one party or for one purpose, but is inadmissible as to another party or for another purpose, the court, upon request, shall restrict the evidence to its proper scope and instruct the jury accordingly [Fed. R. Evid. 105].
2. Counsel must request the limiting instruction [Id.].

EXAMPLE: A prior inconsistent statement may be used merely to impeach, but not as substantive evidence.

EXAMPLE: A statement by one defendant may be admitted as an admission, but inadmissible as hearsay against other parties (when offered for its truth).

EXAMPLE: Character evidence may be offered for a non-character purpose, such as admitting evidence of the victim's reputation for violence to show defendant's reasonable belief that self-defense was necessary.

F. Remainder of or Related Writings or Recorded Statements

1. If a party introduces all or part of a statement, an adverse party may require the introduction, at that time, of any other part—or any other statement—that in fairness out to be considered that the same time. The adverse party may do so over a hearsay objection [Fed. R. Evid. 106]. This rule is sometimes referred to as the **rule of completeness** or the completeness doctrine.
    a. The purpose of this rule is to prevent a party from misleading the jury about the content of writings or recorded statements by taking something out of context.

II. JUDICIAL NOTICE

A. In General

1. Judicial notice is a substitute for evidence whereby the court accepts certain matters as true without the requirement of formal proof.
2. Under the Federal Rules, legislative facts are not recognized within the subject of judicial notice, but are considered instead to be part of the overall judicial process [Fed. R. Evid. 201(a)].
   a. Legislative facts are those used by courts to interpret statutes and make policy decisions (e.g., the fact that hiring based on nepotism promotes racial inequality) [Fed. R. Evid. 201, cmt.].
3. A judicially noticed (or adjudicative) fact must be one which is not subject to reasonable dispute because it [Fed. R. Evid. 201(b)]:
   a. is generally known within the trial court's territorial jurisdiction; or
   b. can be accurately and readily determined from sources whose accuracy cannot reasonably be questioned.

   EXAMPLE: A judge may take judicial notice of the fact that the New England Patriots had an 18–1 record for the 2007 football season, or that Central Park is in Manhattan.
4. The judge may not take judicial notice of a fact merely because it is within his knowledge.
5. A court **may** choose to take judicial notice, whether or not requested by a party, in the following situations:
   a. laws of foreign countries;
   b. regulations of private agencies;
      (1) Judicial notice of the regulations of a private agency is only appropriate where those regulations have the force of law [Getty Petroleum Mktg., Inc. v. Capital Terminal Co., 391 F.3d 312 (1st Cir. 2004)].
   c. municipal ordinances; and
   d. matters of local geography.
6. A court **must** take judicial notice if it is requested by a party and the court is supplied with the necessary information [Fed. R. Evid. 201(c)(2)].
7. Courts **must** take judicial notice of the following situations without request by either party:
   a. federal and state law (constitutions, case law, procedural rules, etc.); and
   b. indisputable facts and scientific propositions.
8. As a general rule, once a fact is judicially noticed, no contradictory evidence is permitted on that issue.
   a. A civil jury will be instructed that it **must** accept as conclusive any fact judicially noticed [Fed. R. Evid. 201(f)].
   b. A criminal jury will be instructed that it **may**, but is not required to, accept as conclusive any fact judicially noticed [Id.].

III. PRESUMPTIONS

A. Presumptions in Civil Cases in General

1. The party having the burden of persuasion generally has the initial burden of producing such legally sufficient evidence as to each element of a claim or defense that a reasonable trier of fact could infer proof of the facts alleged [Fed. R. Evid. 301]. Failure to meet this burden results in a judgment as a matter of law against the party [Fed. R. Civ. P. 50]. When considering such evidence for purposes of a motion for judgment as a matter of law, the judge will interpret the evidence in the light most favorable to the non-moving party.
   a. The general civil standard of persuasion is by a **preponderance of the evidence**—enough evidence, that is, to tip the balance in favor of the fact. The preponderance standard applies to most civil cases, preliminary fact determinations by the court, and some criminal issues such as venue, statutes of limitations, and voluntariness of a confession.
   b. A second and stricter civil standard is that of **clear and convincing evidence**, which demands that the evidence support a finding that the fact is significantly more likely to be true than to not be true—a "high probability of truth." This degree of persuasion is used in such instances as fraud, disbarment, and the validity of a deed or will.
   c. In a criminal trial, the accused must be proven guilty of each element of a crime, as well as absence of mitigating factors, **beyond a reasonable doubt**. This standard requires that any doubt that exists would not affect a reasonable person's belief that the fact is true.
2. A **presumption** is a procedural device that shifts the burden of going forward to the opposing party. A presumption may be defined as an inference that may be drawn when one set of facts (basic facts) establishes a very high probability of the existence of another set of facts (ultimate or presumed facts), absent a contrary showing. Upon introduction of this contrary evidence, the Federal Rules follow the Thayer majority view (the "bursting bubble" theory) that the presumption disappears at this point and the jury determines the weight and credibility of the evidence.

   <u>**EXAMPLE**</u>: Proof that a letter was duly mailed (basic fact) establishes a presumption that the letter was received (presumed fact), unless some evidence (i.e., a scintilla—less than a preponderance) is introduced to refute receipt of delivery, such as the fact that on the day the letter would likely have been delivered, a bucket of mail was stolen out of the mail truck.

   a. **Conclusive** (irrebuttable or irrefutable) **presumptions** are those that are conclusively established once a set of basic facts is proven. The presumption is then treated as a rule of substantive law rather than a presumption.

      <u>**EXAMPLE**</u>: There is an irrebuttable presumption that a child under seven is incapable of negligence. Upon proof that Danny is six years old, it is conclusively established that Danny cannot be held liable for his negligence.

B. Applying State Law to Presumptions in Civil Cases

1. Where the rule of decision regarding a claim or defense arises under state law, the Federal Rules follow the Erie Doctrine and apply the substantive law of the state court.
2. An unrebutted presumption may not be used in a criminal case to direct a verdict against the accused because of the Sixth Amendment right to a jury trial. The jury may, but is not required to, use the basic facts to find the presumed facts. Furthermore, if the presumed facts establish guilt, they must do so beyond a reasonable doubt.

IV. RELEVANCY AND ITS LIMITS

A. Admissibility

1. Test for Relevant Evidence

a. Evidence is **relevant** if [Fed. R. Evid. 401]:

(1) it has any tendency to make a fact more or less probable than it would be without the evidence; and

(2) the fact is of consequence in determining the action.

EXAMPLE: Evidence that the defendant maintained an insurance policy on his spouse before her death is relevant to whether or not he is guilty of her murder. While the insurance policy certainly does not prove, or even make it extremely likely, that he is guilty, it makes his guilt slightly more likely by providing a possible motive.

b. The Federal Rules of Evidence deal with twin concepts of relevance: logical and legal.

(1) Rule 401 addresses **logical relevance**. Establishing the logical relevancy of evidence is a threshold question that must be answered prior to the consideration of other evidentiary principles or exclusionary rules. In order for evidence to be logically relevant, it must have some logical tendency to prove or disprove a fact of consequence (some probative value). This is a very low standard to apply, and in most instances logical relevance is relatively easy to establish [Fed. R. Evid. 401].

(2) Rule 403 addresses **legal relevance**. In order for evidence to be legally relevant, it must be actually helpful to deciding the case. Evidence that is too minimally logically relevant, or that is logically relevant but also carries a high probability of being misused, by the finder of fact, may not help to resolve the issues in question and thus may not be legally relevant [Fed. R. Evid. 403].

c. Direct evidence is evidence that, if believed, proves a fact or set of facts without the need to draw another inference [Fed. R. Evid. 401, cmt.].

EXAMPLE: Witness's testimony that he saw Defendant shoot Victim will constitute direct evidence.

d. Evidence is considered to be circumstantial when, in order to prove one set of facts, an inference must be drawn from another set of facts [Id.].

EXAMPLE: Witness's testimony that she saw Defendant fight with Victim a week before the murder will constitute circumstantial evidence.

NOTE Circumstantial evidence is generally inadmissible to prove the non-existence of a dangerous condition by a lack of similar accidents.

2. **General Admissibility of Relevant Evidence**
   a. Relevant evidence is admissible unless any of the following provides otherwise [Fed. R. Evid. 402]:
      (1) the United States Constitution;
      (2) a federal statute;
      (3) the Federal Rules of Evidence; or
      (4) other rules prescribed by the Supreme Court.
   b. Irrelevant evidence is not admissible [Id.].
3. **Excluding Relevant Evidence for Prejudice, Confusion, Waste of Time, or Other Reasons**
   a. The court may exclude relevant evidence if its probative value is substantially outweighed by a danger of one or more of the following [Fed. R. Evid. 403]:
      (1) unfair prejudice;
      (2) confusing the issues;
      (3) misleading the jury;
      (4) undue delay;
      (5) wasting time; or
      (6) needlessly presenting cumulative evidence.

NOTE All evidence presented against a defendant will prejudice a jury. Remember that Rule 403 is concerned only with unfair prejudice.

   b. Rule 403 is commonly referred to as the balancing test rule because it requires the judge to balance competing interests of probative value and other concerns. The key analytical focus when dealing with this test is the language "substantially outweighed by a danger of." Rule 403 will thus only exclude that evidence that is significantly more prejudicial than probative, and sets a low bar for admissibility.

      EXAMPLE: Paula sues Diana for negligently rear-ending Paula's automobile, giving Paula whiplash and a concussion. The judge may refuse to allow Paula to present evidence that Diana works as a topless dancer because it is of low probative value to the issue of negligence and has a substantial risk of prejudicing the jury against her.

B. Admissibility of Specific Types of Evidence

1. **Character Evidence**
   a. **Crimes or Other Acts**
      (1) The general rule is that evidence of a person's character or character trait is inadmissible to prove that on a particular occasion he acted in accordance with that character or trait.

      EXAMPLE: Evidence that Defendant is generally violent is not admissible as evidence to prove she is guilty of an assault.

(a) In a criminal case, while the prosecution may not initially show the defendant's bad character traits to make an inference that he is more likely to have committed the crime charged, the accused may introduce evidence of character traits inconsistent with the crime charged (e.g., honesty, peacefulness). However, once the door to character evidence has been opened by the defendant, the prosecution may rebut evidence that has been admitted [Fed. R. Evid. 404(a)(2)(A)].

(b) In order to place his character in issue, the accused must establish the pertinence of the character trait to the charged offense(s). In other words, the accused must show how the proffered character trait is inconsistent with the charged offense [Fed. R. Evid. 404, cmt.].

EXAMPLE: Where an accused charged with criminal fraud offers evidence that she is a non-violent person, such evidence will not be admissible because criminal fraud is not itself a violent crime; the accused's character for nonviolence is not pertinent.

(c) There are several types of character evidence that defendants generally offer, including:

1) previous acts pertinent to the character trait in question;
2) opinion testimony given by one or more witnesses who know the accused and who testify as to his (pertinent) good character; and
3) testimony of witnesses familiar with his (pertinent) good reputation.

(d) Courts have generally permitted an accused to introduce evidence of a victim's character when the asserted defense makes it relevant [Fed. R. Evid. 404(a)(2)(B)]. Under Rule 405(a), both opinion and reputation testimony are allowed. When the accused presents testimony of the victim's character trait(s), the prosecutor may cross-examine the reputation or opinion witness and may present witnesses of her own [Id.].

EXAMPLE: Defendant is on trial for the murder of Victim. Evidence of Victim's reputation for being violent is admissible under Rule 404(a)(2) to show that he was the first aggressor. Additionally, to the extent Defendant was aware of Victim's reputation for violence, it is also relevant with respect to the reasonableness of the amount of force Defendant used in self-defense.

(2) Evidence of character may be admissible when offered for a purpose other than to show conduct in conformity with one's character.

(a) Such evidence is admissible where a person's character is an ultimate issue–an essential element of a cause of action, claim, or defense. This evidence may be submitted in the form of reputation, opinion, or specific acts [Fed. R. Evid. 404, cmt.].

1) Examples of these types of cases include:
   a) defamation;
   b) deceit (usually as an element of the defense);
   c) misrepresentation (usually as an element of the defense);
   d) negligent entrustment; and
   e) child custody.

NOTE In a majority of jurisdictions, with assault and battery, the victim's character is not in issue in the strict sense, based on the defendant's reasonable belief that force was necessary.

(b) Reputation, opinion, and specific acts are also admissible to prove that one person knew or should have known of the character of another in cases where the knowledge of the character of another is in issue, such as in cases of negligent entrustment or self-defense [Id.].

EXAMPLE: Doreen is being sued for negligent entrustment in lending her car to Thomas, who ran over three pedestrians while using her car to drag race. The plaintiff may introduce evidence of Thomas's reputation for being a careless driver, and the opinions of others regarding Thomas's driving skills, to show that Doreen should have known that Thomas was a reckless driver. Thomas's prior speeding tickets may also be introduced to show that Thomas was a reckless driver, which is an ultimate issue in a negligent entrustment case.

NOTE A reputation witness may be cross-examined in good faith as to whether or not she has heard of specific acts of a party bearing on reputation. This example of using specific acts for the limited purpose of impeachment rather than substantive evidence is heavily tested.

(c) Whether or not the defendant in a criminal case introduces evidence of good character, the prosecution may introduce circumstantial evidence of other crimes, wrongs, or acts for the very narrow purpose of proving [Fed. R. Evid. 404(b)(2)]:
   1) motive;
   2) intent;
   3) absence of mistake;
   4) identity;
   5) knowledge;
   6) opportunity;
   7) preparation;
   8) plan; or
   9) scheme.

NOTE This exception is often simplified and referred to as the **MIMIC Rule** (**M**otive, **I**ntent, absence of **M**istake, **I**dentity, or **C**ommon plan or scheme).

NOTE Admission of MIMIC evidence under Rule 404(b) is subject to a determination under Rule 403 that the substantial danger of unfair prejudice does not outweigh the probative value of the evidence.

(3) In a criminal case, the prosecutor must [Fed. R. Evid. 404(b)(3)]:

(a) provide reasonable notice of any such evidence that the prosecutor intends to offer at trial, so that the defendant has a fair opportunity to meet it;

(b) articulate in the notice the permitted purpose for which the prosecutor intends to offer the evidence and the reasoning that supports the purpose; and

(c) do so in writing before trial—or in any form during trial if the court, for good cause, excuses lack of pretrial notice.

(4) Character evidence may be used to impeach witnesses, as provided in Rules 607, 608, and 609 [Fed. R. Evid. 404(a)(3)].

(a) Ways to impeach include prior felony convictions, misdemeanor convictions, or reputation or opinion evidence for untruthfulness [Fed. R. Evid. 608-609].

(5) Specific instances of animal behavior are generally admissible to prove conduct in conformity therewith. Thus, evidence that a dog has bitten others is relevant to show the likelihood of its biting a particular victim on a later occasion.

b. **Methods of Proving Character**

(1) Rule 405 controls the form that character evidence takes at trial, not its admissibility. If character evidence is admissible for any reason, it may be proven in the form of reputation testimony or opinion testimony [Fed. R. Evid. 405(a)]. If character is not at issue in the case, then specific instances of conduct may only be addressed during cross-examination to test the validity of the reputation or opinion testimony [Michelson v. United States, 335 U.S. 469 (1948)].

EXAMPLE: If Susan is called to the stand to testify that in her opinion, Doug is honest, she may not testify on direct examination about him finding a stranger's wallet and returning it. She may, however, be asked on cross-examination about an earlier incident in which Doug stole and used someone's credit card, for the purpose of challenging the credibility of her opinion of Doug's honesty.

(a) Relevant specific acts may also be admitted to show character if character is an essential element of a charge, claim, or defense [Fed. R. Evid. 405(b)].

EXAMPLE: In a defamation case, Plaintiff denies a statement made by Defendant calling him a thief. A defense witness may then properly testify that Plaintiff was convicted of burglary 13 years ago.

2. **Habit and Routine Practice**
    a. **Habit evidence** refers to a narrow range of highly probative traits, namely, automatic, invariable patterns of behavior that could be characterized by the words "always" or "invariably." Actions performed "frequently" or "often" do not constitute habits. A **habit** is a regular response to a given situation that is done without a high degree of forethought. Habit evidence does not need to be corroborated [see, e.g., Weil v. Seltzer, 873 F.2d 1453 (D.C. Cir. 1989); Fed. R. Evid. 406].

    EXAMPLE: Stopping and checking both ways before making a turn at a particular intersection, wearing one's seat belt on every car trip, and taking vitamins every morning are all habits that may be admissible in court.

    b. Evidence of a person's habit or an organization's routine practice is admissible to show that on a particular occasion the person or organization acted in accordance with the habit or routine practice [Fed. R. Evid. 406]. A habit or routine practice may be proved by testimony in the form of an opinion or by specific instances of conduct sufficient to show that the habit existed or the practice was routine.

    EXAMPLE: The receptionist for a company may testify that it was routine practice for all mail placed in the outgoing mail basket to be taken to the post office each day between 2:00 p.m. and 3:00 p.m.

3. **Subsequent Remedial Measures**
    a. Evidence of remedial measures taken subsequent to an injury or harm is not admissible to prove [Fed. R. Evid. 407]:
        (1) negligence;
        (2) culpable conduct;
        (3) a defect in a product;
        (4) a defect in a product's design; or
        (5) a need for warning or instruction.
    b. Evidence of remedial measures may be admitted for another purpose, such as impeachment, or, if disputed, proving [Id.]:
        (1) ownership;
        (2) control; or
        (3) the feasibility of precautionary measures.

        EXAMPLE: Paula slips on a loose brick on the steps of her apartment building, breaking her arm. The next day, the owner of the building sends someone out to repair the loose brick. If Paula sues the owner of the building and the management company for negligence, evidence of the repair is not admissible to show negligence or that the brick was in fact loose. It will, however, be admissible to show the owner's control of the building.

4. **Compromise Offers and Negotiations**
    a. Evidence of an offer to settle a claim, and any statements or conduct accompanying the offer, is not admissible to prove the validity or

amount of a disputed claim. Such evidence also may not be used for impeachment through a prior inconsistent statement or contradiction [Fed. R. Evid. 408(a)].

EXAMPLE: Donald is involved in an automobile accident with Peter. As Donald and Peter exit their vehicles, Peter says, "I can't believe you did this! I am going to sue you!" Donald says, "Oh, no! My insurance will skyrocket if they find out I caused another accident! I'll just write you a check for the damage—will $1,000 cover it?" At trial, Donald claims Peter caused the accident, and that the damages to Peter's car were only $500. Peter may not rely on Donald's statement to show that Donald was at fault, or that Peter's damages were greater than $500.

EXAM TIP A commonly tested issue is that statements made in connection with an offer to settle are inadmissible to prove fault or value of the claim; an admission or other form of otherwise relevant evidence cannot be severed and admitted from the offer to settle.

b. The court may admit this evidence for another purpose, such as [Fed. R. Evid. 408(b)]:
   (1) proving a witness's bias or prejudice;
   (2) negating a contention of undue delay; or
   (3) proving an effort to obstruct a criminal investigation or prosecution.

   EXAMPLE: The next week, Donald rear ends Percy and Peggy. Donald runs up to the cars and wails, "Not again! I'll never be able to get insurance if they find out about this! I'll give you each $2,000 to cover whatever damage I've done." Peggy takes $2,000 from Donald, but Percy says, "I'm sure I have whiplash and a concussion. I'll see you in court!" At trial, Peggy testifies that Percy backed into Donald and that Donald did not rear-end Percy. Percy's attorney may introduce Peggy's acceptance of a settlement with Donald to show Peggy's bias.

5. **Offers to Pay Medical and Similar Expenses**
   a. Evidence of offering or promising to pay medical, hospital, or similar expenses resulting from an injury is not admissible to prove liability for the injury [Fed. R. Evid. 409].
   b. Unlike statements made in conjunction with an offer to compromise, under the Federal Rules of Evidence an admission made in connection with offers to pay medical or hospital expenses is admissible and may be severed from the offer itself. Rule 409 only protects the offer and the payment itself [Fed. R. Evid. 409, cmt.].

   EXAMPLE: Three weeks after the events of the above example, Donald drives through a red light and sideswipes Petunia, who is severely injured. While Petunia is being loaded into the ambulance, Donald says, "I'm so sorry; I was thinking about something else and just didn't notice the red light. I feel awful about this, but don't worry; I will pay for the best doctors in the state." At trial, Petunia may not admit Donald's offer to pay her medical bills to show that he is responsible, but she may admit the first part of his statement: "I was thinking about something else and just didn't notice the red light."

6. **Pleas, Plea Discussions, and Related Statements**
   a. In a civil or criminal proceeding, evidence of the following are not admissible against the defendant who made the plea or participated in plea discussions [Fed. R. Evid. 410(a)]:
      (1) a guilty plea that was later withdrawn;
      (2) a plea of *nolo contendere*;
      (3) a statement made during a proceeding on either of those pleas under Federal Rule of Criminal Procedure 11 or a comparable state procedure; or
      (4) any statement made during plea discussions with an attorney for the prosecuting authority if the discussions did not result in a guilty plea or they resulted in a later-withdrawn guilty plea.
         (a) However, a statement described above, made during a proceeding or plea discussion, is admissible [Fed. R. Evid. 410(b)]:
            1) in any proceeding in which another statement made during the same plea or plea discussions has been introduced, if in fairness the statements ought to be considered together; or
            2) in a criminal proceeding for perjury or false statement, if the defendant made the statement under oath, on the record, and with counsel present.
   b. Rule 410 does not apply to statements made to law enforcement, only where the bargaining is done with an attorney for the government [Fed. R. Evid. 410, cmt.].

7. **Liability Insurance**
   a. Evidence that a person was or was not insured against liability is not admissible to prove whether the person acted negligently or otherwise wrongfully [Fed. R. Evid. 411].
   b. Evidence of insurance against liability may be admitted for another purpose, such as proving a witness's bias or prejudice or proving agency, ownership, or control [Id.].
   c. **Severance**
      (1) Statements made in connection with evidence of insurance coverage may be severed and are admissible.

      EXAMPLE: Bart, driving the brand new Porsche his father Homer purchased for him as a graduation gift, drives through the window of the local Kwik-E-Mart. The owner of the Kwik-E-Mart sues both Bart and Homer for damages. Homer claims that Bart, not Homer, owns the car and thus Homer is not liable. Owner may introduce evidence of the $500,000 auto insurance policy Homer maintains on the Porsche to indicate that Homer, in fact, owns the automobile, but Owner may not use such evidence to suggest that Homer took out a large insurance policy because he knew Bart to be a dangerous driver.

8. **Sexual Conduct**

a. **Sex-Offense Cases: The Victim's Sexual Behavior or Predisposition**

(1) In any civil or criminal proceeding involving alleged sexual misconduct, reputation and opinion evidence is generally inadmissible to prove [Fed. R. Evid. 412(a)]:

(a) that a victim engaged in other sexual behavior; or

1) Note that for purposes of this rule, **victim** is defined as including an alleged victim [Fed. R. Evid. 412(d)].

(b) a victim's sexual predisposition.

(2) **Exceptions**

(a) In a criminal case, the following evidence is admissible (absent other reasons for inadmissibility) [Fed. R. Evid. 412(b)(1)]:

1) evidence of specific instances of a victim's sexual behavior, if offered to prove that someone other than the defendant was the source of semen, injury, or other physical evidence;

2) evidence of specific instances of a victim's sexual behavior with respect to the person accused of the sexual misconduct, if offered by the defendant to prove consent or if offered by the prosecution; and

3) evidence whose exclusion would violate the defendant's constitutional rights.

(b) In a civil case, the court may admit evidence (reputation, opinion, or specific acts) offered to prove a victim's sexual behavior or sexual predisposition (absent other reasons for inadmissibility) if its probative value substantially outweighs the danger of harm to any victim and of unfair prejudice to any party. This standard sets a high bar for admission of the evidence. Evidence of a victim's reputation is admissible only if the victim has placed it in controversy [Fed. R. Evid. 412(b)(2)].

(c) **Motion**

1) If a party intends to offer evidence under Rule 412(b), the party must [Fed. R. Evid. 412(c)(1)]:

a) file a motion that specifically describes the evidence and states the purpose for which it is to be offered;

b) do so at least 14 days before trial unless the court, for good cause, sets a different time;

c) serve the motion on all parties; and

d) notify the victim or, when appropriate, the victim's guardian or representative.

(d) **Hearing**

1) Before admitting evidence under this rule, the court must conduct an in camera hearing and give the victim and parties a right to attend and be heard. Unless the court orders otherwise, the motion, related materials, and the record of the hearing must be and remain sealed [Fed. R. Evid. 412(c)(2)].

b. **Similar Crimes in Sexual-Assault Cases**

(1) In a criminal case in which a defendant is accused of a sexual assault, the court may admit evidence that the defendant committed any other sexual assault. The evidence may be considered on any matter to which it is relevant [Fed. R. Evid. 413(a)].

c. **Similar Crimes in Child-Molestation Cases**

(1) In a criminal case in which a defendant is accused of child molestation, the court may admit evidence that the defendant committed any other child molestation. The evidence may be considered on any matter to which it is relevant [Fed. R. Evid. 414(a)].

d. **Similar Acts in Civil Cases Involving Sexual Assault or Child Molestation**

(1) In a civil case involving a claim for relief based on a party's alleged sexual assault or child molestation, the court may admit evidence that the party committed any other sexual assault or child molestation. The evidence may be considered on any matter to which it is relevant [Fed. R. Evid. 415(a)].

e. **Notice to Judge and Discretion**

(1) Under Rules 413, 414, and 415, specific acts are admissible. However, notice to the judge is required, and the court has discretion to exclude.

V. PRIVILEGES

INTRODUCTION TO PRIVILEGES AND BAR EXAM IMPLEMENTATION	
Procedure	**Substance**
General Rule: In federal court (and as a default on the MBE®), apply the FRE. **Exception**: In federal diversity cases (wherein state law will govern the substantive claims), still apply the FRE as to procedure, but apply state law with respect to: • Privileges; • Burdens of Proof and Presumptions; and • Dead Man's Statutes. **Note**: If tested on the MBE®, the question must give an indication of the law in the state (because all states are different).	**General Rule**: Federal courts recognize the following privileges: • Attorney-Client; • Spousal (Husband-Wife) (including both the testimony privilege and confidential communication privilege); • Clergy-Penitent; and • Psychotherapist-Patient. **Main Distinction**: Federal common law does not recognize a physician-patient privilege, whereas most states do.

EXAM TIP While most states recognize the physician-patient privilege, federal common law does not. Federal common law recognizes only a psychotherapist-patient privilege in this area. Therefore, on the MBE®, do not presume that the physician-patient privilege applies (but always look to see if the question gives some other indication that it may apply).

A. In General

1. A claim of privilege will be governed by the principles of common law, subject to any superseding state law, unless any of the following provides otherwise [Fed. R. Evid. 501]:
   a. the U.S. Constitution;
   b. a federal statute; or
   c. rules prescribed by the Supreme Court.
2. In a civil case, state law governs privilege regarding a claim or defense for which state law supplies the rule of decision [Id.]. In a federal court case arising under a federal right or defense, the court may make individual determinations regarding privilege using its "reason and experience."
   a. The development of generally applicable rules of evidence in federal courts is reserved for Congress.

B. Privilege under Common Law

1. Except as otherwise provided by constitution or statute or by these or other rules promulgated by a state, no person has a privilege to:
   a. refuse to be a witness;
   b. refuse to disclose any matter;

c. refuse to produce any object or writing; or

d. prevent another from being a witness or disclosing any matter or producing any object or writing.

2. **Attorney-Client Privilege**

a. A client has a privilege to refuse to disclose, and to prevent any other person from disclosing, confidential communications made for the purpose of facilitating the rendition of professional legal services to the client:

(1) between herself or her representative and her lawyer or her lawyer's representative;

(2) between her lawyer and her lawyer's representative;

(3) by herself, her representative, her lawyer, or her lawyer's representative to a lawyer or a representative of a lawyer representing another party in a pending action and concerning a matter of common interest therein;

(4) between representatives of the client or between the client and a representative of the client; or

(5) among lawyers and their representatives representing the same client.

b. A client is a person, public officer, corporation, association, or other organization or entity, either public or private, who is provided professional legal services by a lawyer or who consults a lawyer with a view to obtaining professional legal services from him.

c. A communication is confidential if it is not intended to be disclosed to third persons.

(1) The privilege is limited to communications which the client either expressly made confidential or which she could reasonably assume under the circumstances would be understood by the attorney as so intended. A mere showing that the communication was from the client to her attorney does not suffice. Rather, circumstances indicating the intention of secrecy must appear.

d. A lawyer is a person authorized, or reasonably believed by the client to be authorized, to engage in the practice of law in any state or nation.

e. A representative of the lawyer is one employed by the lawyer to assist the lawyer in the rendition of professional legal services.

f. The traditional view, which protected only verbal communications, has been expanded to include spoken or written words and acts that intend to convey a message.

EXAMPLE: Exhibition of one's arm to display a physical characteristic.

(1) However, preexisting written documents (i.e., contract, leases, and memos) do not become privileged merely because they are given to the attorney. Basic facts, such as name, occupation, address, etc., of the client and the identity of the lawyer are never privileged.

g. The privilege may be claimed by the client, her guardian or conservator, the personal representative of a deceased client, or the successor, trustee, or similar representative of a corporation, association, or other organization, whether or not in existence. The person who was the lawyer or the lawyer's representative at the time of the communication is presumed to have authority to claim the privilege, but only on behalf of the client.
   (1) The client is holder of the privilege. Thus, the power to waive is hers, and only she or her attorney or agent acting with her authority may exercise this power. According to the prevailing view, the client, merely by voluntarily taking the stand as a witness in a suit to which she is party and testifying to facts that were the subject of consultation with her counsel, does not waive the privilege for secrecy of the communications to his lawyer.

h. There is no privilege:
   (1) if the services of the lawyer were sought or obtained to enable or aid anyone to commit or plan to commit what the client knew or reasonably should have known to be a crime or fraud;
   (2) as to a communication relevant to an issue between parties who claim through the same deceased client, regardless of whether the claims are by testate or intestate succession or by *inter vivos* transaction;
   (3) as to a communication relevant to an issue of breach of duty by the lawyer to his client or by the client to her lawyer;
   (4) as to a communication relevant to an issue concerning an attested document to which the lawyer is an attesting witness;
   (5) as to a communication relevant to a matter of common interest between two or more clients, if the communication was made by any of them to a lawyer retained or consulted in common, when offered in an action between any of the clients; or
   (6) as to a communication between a public officer or agency and its lawyers, unless the communication concerns a pending investigation, claim, or action and the court determines that disclosure will seriously impair the ability of the public officer or agency to process the claim or conduct a pending investigation, litigation, or proceeding in the public interest.

3. **Physician- and Psychotherapist-Patient Privilege**

a. A patient has a privilege to refuse to disclose, and to prevent any other person from disclosing, confidential communications made for the purpose of diagnosis or treatment of his physical, mental, or emotional condition, including alcohol or drug addiction.
   (1) This privilege extends to communications the patient has with his physician or psychotherapist, as well as with persons who are participating in the diagnosis or treatment under the direction of the physician or psychotherapist, including members of the patient's family.

(2) A physician-patient privilege will only be enforced in federal court where state law provides rules for decision and where state law recognizes a physician-patient privilege (there is no federal common law recognizing physician-patient privilege).

b. A **patient** is a person who consults, is examined, or is interviewed by a physician or psychotherapist.

c. A **physician** is a person authorized to practice medicine in any state or nation, or reasonably believed by the patient to be so.

d. A **psychotherapist** is:

(1) a person authorized to practice medicine in any state or nation, or reasonably believed by the patient to be so authorized, while engaged in the diagnosis or treatment of a mental or emotional condition, including alcohol or drug addiction; or

(2) a person licensed or certified as a psychologist under the laws of any state or nation, while similarly engaged.

NOTE The psychotherapist-patient privilege also includes licensed social workers.

e. A communication is confidential if it is not intended to be disclosed to third persons, except:

(1) persons present to further the interest of the patient in the consultation, examination, or interview;

(2) persons reasonably necessary for the transmission of the communication; or

(3) persons participating in the diagnosis and treatment under the direction of the physician or psychotherapist, including members of the patient's family.

EXAMPLE: Victor visits his orthopedist for treatment of injuries suffered in a car accident caused by Derrick. When his name is called, Victor goes to the front desk and says to the receptionist, "You know, I'm really not feeling that bad, but my attorney suggested that I come in and get checked out." Walter, a patient sitting in the waiting room, hears Victor. Victor later repeats the same sentiment to his doctor while the nurse practitioner is in the examination room. Victor's first statement is not privileged because it was made within Walter's presence, but Victor's second statement is privileged.

f. The physician-patient privilege is a statutory privilege that did not exist under common law. It applies when the patient consults the doctor for purposes of diagnosis or treatment. Examinations made in preparation for litigation or by court-appointed attorneys do not fall within the privilege. Autopsy reports are likewise unprivileged. Observations and impressions made by the physician are protected. The amount of the fee paid is not privileged. The privilege was extended to psychotherapists in Jaffe v. Redmond [518 U.S. 1 (1996)].

g. Examples of privileged information include:
   (1) x-rays and lab tests; and
   (2) opinions of the physician made during diagnosis or treatment.

h. Examples of unprivileged information (i.e., exceptions) include:
   (1) personal injury suits brought by the patient; and
   (2) malpractice suits brought against the physician.

i. The privilege may be claimed by the patient, his guardian or conservator, or the personal representative of a deceased patient. The person who was the physician or psychotherapist at the time of the communication is presumed to have authority to claim the privilege, but only on behalf of the patient.

j. There is no privilege:
   (1) for communications relevant to an issue in proceedings to hospitalize the patient for mental illness, if the psychotherapist in the course of diagnosis or treatment has determined that the patient is in need of hospitalization;
   (2) if the court orders an examination of the physical, mental, and/or emotional condition of a patient, whether a party or a witness—communications made in the course thereof are not privileged under this rule with respect to the particular purpose for which the examination is ordered, unless the court orders otherwise; or
   (3) as to a communication relevant to an issue of the physical, mental, and/or emotional condition of the patient in any proceeding in which he relies upon the condition as an element of his claim or defense, or, after the patient's death, in any proceeding in which any party relies upon the condition as an element of his claim or defense.

   EXAMPLE: A defendant claiming insanity as a defense to a criminal charge may not claim privilege with respect to her treatment by a psychiatrist.

RELATIONSHIP BETWEEN PHYSICIAN-PATIENT PRIVILEGE AND ATTORNEY-CLIENT PRIVILEGE	
When a client is examined by a doctor at an attorney's request, consider the primary purpose:	
If the primary purpose is for the medical treatment of the client… …it is likely that the physician-patient privilege would be applicable (if the jurisdiction so allows), and such privilege would be waived if the client puts his medical condition at issue (e.g., sues for personal injury).	However, if the primary purpose of retaining the doctor is to render an expert opinion to the attorney so that the attorney may better conduct litigation or advise her client on the client's legal rights… …the physician-patient privilege would likely not apply (because no treatment is contemplated), but the attorney-client privilege may cover the communications between the client and the doctor because the examination is necessary for the attorney's ability to conduct the case (i.e., it is necessary to help the client communicate his condition to the attorney). Note, however, that the attorney-client privilege in this situation would be waived if the doctor were later called as an expert witness by the same client.

4. **Spousal Privileges (or Husband-Wife Privileges)**
   a. The spousal privilege has two separate and distinct parts:
      (1) the **spousal testimony privilege** (or spousal immunity), which, in criminal cases, encompasses the right of a witness-spouse not to be forced to testify against their current spouse; and
      (2) the **spousal communication privilege** (or confidential communication privilege), which protects confidential communications made during a legally valid marriage.

SPOUSAL PRIVILEGES	Type of Case It Applies in	Protects	Must Be Married at the Time of the...	May Be Waived...
Spousal Testimony	Criminal	Testimony Against Spouse	Trial	By the Witness-Spouse
Spousal Communications	Any	Confidential Communications	Communication	Only by Both Together

   b. **Spousal Testimony Privilege**
      (1) Under common law, a married person whose spouse is the defendant in a criminal case may not be called as a witness by the prosecution, and a married person may not be compelled to testify against his spouse in any criminal proceeding. Note that this "privilege" is not really a privilege, since it does not apply to any particular information. Rather, it is the incapacity of one spouse to testify against the other in a criminal case.
      (2) Federal courts, as well as most state courts, now follow the view of Trammel v. United States [445 U.S. 40 (1980)] that the witness-spouse, rather than the party-spouse, holds the privilege. This is based on the rationale that a criminal defendant cannot keep his spouse off the stand. The modern view prevails, and when in doubt, attorneys should rely upon the U.S. Supreme Court jurisprudence.
      (3) The spousal privilege extends to all communications made before or during a valid marriage. However, the privilege lasts only during the marriage and terminates upon divorce or annulment.
      (4) The common law privilege preventing adverse testimony of a spouse was subject to an exception in cases of prosecution of the husband for violent offenses committed against the wife.
   c. **Spousal Communication Privilege**
      (1) In any civil or criminal case, either spouse—whether or not a party—has a privilege to refuse to disclose, and to prevent another from disclosing, a confidential communication made between the spouses while they were married. The rationale is to encourage open communication, trust, and confidence between spouses.

(2) The privilege for marital communications extends to any confidential statement made between spouses during the existence of a legal marriage. The widely accepted rule is that the "quality" of the marriage will not be inquired into—communications intended to be confidential are privileged unless and until a divorce decree has been entered.

(a) A substantial number of recent cases remove from the privilege those communications made in furtherance of an ongoing crime or tort. Today, most jurisdictions do recognize this "joint participants" exception.

(3) In contrast to the spousal testimony privilege, the spousal communication privilege protects only communications made during—not before—a valid marriage. However, upon divorce, the marital privilege endures as to those confidential communications made during the marriage.

(a) A communication is confidential if it is made privately to one's spouse and is not intended for disclosure to any other person.

PRIVILEGE AT ISSUE:	Time Communications Made:		
	Before Marriage	**During Marriage**	**Upon Divorce**
Spousal Testimony Privilege	Protected	Protected	Entire privilege is lost.
Spousal Communication Privilege	Not Protected	Protected	Privilege exists as to confidential communications made during the marriage.

d. **Spousal Privileges Exceptions**

(1) While exceptions to privileges vary from state to state, as a general rule, neither the spousal communication privilege nor the spousal testimony privilege will cover communications or acts:

(a) in furtherance of a future crime or fraud (i.e., joint criminal activity); or

(b) destructive of the family unit (e.g., cases of spousal or child abuse).

(2) The privilege does not apply to communications made:

(a) in order to enable or aid anyone to commit or plan to commit a crime or a fraud;

(b) in a proceeding brought by or on behalf of either spouse to establish his competence; nor

(c) in a criminal proceeding where the marital communication was offered in evidence by a defendant who is one of the spouses between whom the communication was made, pursuant to the defendant's Sixth Amendment rights.

5. **Clergy-Penitent Privilege**
   a. A person has a privilege to refuse to disclose, and to prevent another from disclosing, a confidential communication made by the person to a clergyman in her professional character as spiritual adviser.
      (1) A clergyman is a minister, priest, rabbi, accredited Christian Science practitioner, or other similar functionary of a religious organization, or an individual reasonably believed to be so by the person consulting her.
      (2) A communication is confidential if made privately and not intended for further disclosure except to other persons present in furtherance of the purpose of the communication.
   b. The privilege may be claimed by the person, by his guardian or conservator, or by his personal representative if he is deceased. The person who was the clergyman at the time of the communication is presumed to have authority to claim the privilege, but only on behalf of the communicant.
6. **Political Vote**
   a. Every person has a privilege to refuse to disclose the tenor of her vote at a political election conducted by secret ballot.
   b. This privilege does not apply if the court finds that the vote was cast illegally or determines that the disclosure should be compelled pursuant to the election laws of the state.
7. **Trade Secrets**
   a. A person has a privilege, which may be claimed by himself, his agent, or his employee, to refuse to disclose, and to prevent other persons from disclosing, a trade secret he owns, if the allowance of the privilege will not tend to conceal fraud or otherwise work injustice. If disclosure is directed, the court shall take such protective measures as the interest of the holder of the privilege and of the parties and the interests of justice require.
8. **Secrets of State and Other Official Information**
   a. If the law of the United States creates a governmental privilege that the courts of a state must recognize under the U.S. Constitution, the privilege may be claimed as provided by the law of the United States.
   b. No other governmental privilege is recognized except as created by the U.S. Constitution or statutes of a state.
   c. If a claim of governmental privilege is sustained and it appears that a party is thereby deprived of material evidence, the court shall make any further orders that the interests of justice require, including striking the testimony of a witness, declaring a mistrial, finding upon an issue as to which the evidence is relevant, or dismissing the action.
9. **Identity of Informer**
   a. The United States, or a state or subdivision thereof, has a privilege to refuse to disclose the identity of a person who has furnished information relating to or assisting in an investigation of a possible violation of

a law to a law enforcement officer or member of a legislative committee or its staff conducting an investigation.

b. The privilege may be claimed by an appropriate representative of the public entity to which the information was furnished.

c. In Branzburg v. Hayes [408 U.S. 665 (1972)], the Court declined to allow a First Amendment privilege for newsmen to refuse to reveal their sources. However, several state courts have enacted "shield" laws allowing a qualified privilege (the **newsman's privilege**) in this area.

d. In United States v. Nixon [418 U.S. 683 (1974)], the Supreme Court recognized a constitutional privilege for the president to refuse disclosure of information (the **executive privilege**). As to matters of national security, this privilege is absolute. However, other information is given only a qualified protection, wherein disclosure is required upon a showing of special need (i.e., evidence found necessary for a pending criminal proceeding).

e. There is no privilege:

   (1) if the identity of the informer has been disclosed by the government or by the informer, or if the informer appears as a witness for the government; or

   (2) if it appears in the case that an informer may be able to give testimony relevant to any issue in a criminal case, or to a fair determination of a material issue on the merits in a civil case to which a public entity is a party, and the informed public entity invokes the privilege.

      (a) In this situation, the court shall give the public entity an opportunity in camera to show facts relevant to determining whether the informer can, in fact, supply that testimony. The showing will ordinarily be in the form of affidavits, but the court may direct that testimony be taken if it finds that the matter cannot be resolved satisfactorily upon affidavit.

      (b) In criminal cases, if the court finds there is a reasonable probability that the informer can give the testimony and the public entity elects not to disclose her identity, the court, on motion of the defendant or on its own motion, shall grant appropriate relief, which may include one or more of the following:

         1) requiring the prosecuting attorney to comply;

         2) granting the defendant additional time or a continuance;

         3) relieving the defendant from making disclosures otherwise required of him;

         4) prohibiting the prosecuting attorney from introducing specified evidence; or

         5) dismissing charges.

      (c) In civil cases, the court may make any order the interests of justice require.

      (d) Evidence submitted to the court shall be sealed and preserved to be made available to the appellate court in the event of an appeal, and the contents shall not otherwise be revealed without consent of the informed public entity.

10. **Fifth Amendment Privilege against Self-Incrimination**

    a. The accused in a criminal trial has a Fifth Amendment privilege to refuse to take the stand.

        (1) This privilege does not prevent cross-examination once voluntary testimony has been given upon direct examination. Refusal to be cross-examined permits the judge to strike from the record any direct testimony previously given. When an accused waives the Fifth Amendment privilege, she may be questioned to the extent reasonably necessary for adequate cross-examination by the prosecution (i.e., regarding impeachment and matters related to the testimony on direct examination, but not a total or "blanket" waiver).

    b. Testimony given at a preliminary hearing does not waive the privilege of the accused not to take the stand at trial. Furthermore, evidence of a defendant's attempt to enforce his constitutional rights (e.g., by motion to suppress) given at a preliminary hearing is inadmissible at trial, and the prosecution may not comment on it [Simmons v. United States, 390 U.S. 377 (1968)].

    c. A witness also has a Fifth Amendment privilege to refuse to answer questions if the answers would expose the witness to criminal liability. Unlike the accused, a witness may not refuse to take the stand.

    d. The privilege against self-incrimination applies only to evidence that is testimonial in nature. Presentation of real and demonstrative forms of evidence are not protected.

        EXAMPLE: An accused can be compelled to give writing, hair, and blood samples, fingerprints, and to stand in a lineup.

    e. Where immunity has been granted, no Fifth Amendment privilege exists.

    f. Transactional immunity prevents a witness from being prosecuted for any crime referred to in the testimony. This broad type of immunity provides greater protection than that conferred by the Fifth Amendment and is not constitutionally required.

        (1) The witness may still be prosecuted for perjury. In addition, the immunity does not extend to a transaction noted in an answer which is totally unresponsive to the question asked.

            EXAMPLE: Vinnie is granted transactional immunity for his testimony that he committed a mob hit on Tony "The Tiger" at the direction of Sal "The Shark." At trial, the prosecutor asks Vinnie, "What happened to Tony 'The Tiger'?" and Vinnie responds, "I killed him, just like I killed a whole lot of guys for a whole lot of other guys," and proceeds to rattle off a list of missing Mafioso, finishing up with "Nyah, nyah, I'm immune, and you can't put me away for any of those now." Vinnie may be prosecuted for the other murders; his immunity only extends to the murder of Tony.

g. Immunity from using the actual testimony of the witness and any evidence derived therefrom (i.e., "derivative use") is sufficient to compel testimony without jeopardizing the Fifth Amendment privilege.

11. **Effect of Privilege**

a. A person who holds a privilege against disclosure waives the privilege if she voluntarily discloses, or consents to the disclosure of, any significant part of the privileged matter. This rule does not apply if the disclosure itself is privileged.

b. A claim of privilege is not defeated by a disclosure which was:

(1) compelled erroneously; or

(2) made without opportunity to claim the privilege.

EXAMPLE: At Darryl's first trial for murder, the judge forces Darryl's wife Wanda to testify that Darryl told her, before Vincent's murder, "I'm going to get him, and he'll be sorry he ever messed with me," by threatening to charge Wanda with contempt of court if she does not testify. Darryl's trial results in a hung jury. The fact that Wanda was compelled to testify at the first trial will not constitute a waiver of her privilege not to testify at the second trial.

c. Neither the judge nor counsel should comment upon a claim of privilege, regardless of whether such claims arise from the present proceeding or a prior occasion. No inference may be drawn from the assertion of a privilege.

(1) The prosecutor can comment on a failure by the accused to present evidence to support an alibi or failure to submit to reasonable tests (i.e., giving blood or urine specimens). Also, where prior notice of an alibi defense is required, the prosecution can impeach a defendant who testifies to a different alibi at trial.

d. In jury cases, proceedings shall be conducted, to the extent practicable, so as to facilitate the making of claims of privilege without the knowledge of the jury.

e. It is permissible to draw an adverse inference from an assertion of the Fifth Amendment privilege in a civil case where probative evidence has been presented against the witness, although it is not permissible to do so in a criminal case [Baxter v. Palmigiano, 425 U.S. 308 (1976)].

VI. WITNESSES

A. In General

1. **Competency to Testify**
    a. Unless otherwise provided in the Federal Rules of Evidence, every person is competent to be a witness. However, in a civil case, state law governs the witness's competency regarding a claim or defense for which state law supplies the rule of decision [Fed. R. Evid. 601].
2. **Need for Personal Knowledge**
    a. A witness may testify to a matter only if evidence is introduced sufficient to support a finding that the witness has personal knowledge of the matter. Evidence to prove personal knowledge may consist of the witness's own testimony. This rule does not apply to a witness's expert testimony under Rule 703 [Fed. R. Evid. 602].
3. **Oath or Affirmation to Testify Truthfully**
    a. Before testifying, a witness must give an oath or affirmation to testify truthfully. It must be in a form designed to impress that duty on the witness's conscience [Fed. R. Evid. 603].
4. **Interpreter**
    a. An interpreter must be qualified and must give an oath or affirmation to make a true translation [Fed. R. Evid. 604].
5. **Judge's Competency as a Witness**
    a. The presiding judge may not testify as a witness at the trial. A party need not object to preserve the issue [Fed. R. Evid. 605].
6. **Juror's Competency as a Witness**
    a. A juror may not testify as a witness before the other jurors at the trial. If a juror is called to testify, the court must give a party an opportunity to object outside the jury's presence [Fed. R. Evid. 606(a)]. The purpose of using this evidence is to overturn a jury verdict.
    b. During an inquiry into the validity of a verdict or indictment, a juror may not testify about [Fed. R. Evid. 606(b)(1)]:
        (1) any statement made or incident that occurred during the jury's deliberations;
        (2) the effect of anything on that juror's or another juror's vote; or
        (3) any juror's mental processes concerning the verdict or indictment.
    c. The court also may not receive a juror's affidavit or evidence of a juror's statement on any of these matters [Id.].
    d. This is collectively known as the "no-impeachment" rule. However, the Supreme Court has held that "where a juror makes a clear statement that indicates he or she relied on racial stereotypes or animus to convict a criminal defendant, the Sixth Amendment requires that the no-impeachment rule give way in order to permit the trial court to consider the evidence of the juror's statement and any resulting

denial of the jury trial guarantee" [Pena-Rodriguez v. Colorado, 580 U.S. 206 (2017)].

(1) However, not every comment indicating racial bias or hostility will allow further judicial inquiry. For the court to set aside the no-impeachment bar, "there must be a showing that one or more jurors made statements exhibiting overt racial bias that cast serious doubt on the fairness and impartiality of the jury's deliberations and resulting verdict" [Id.].

(2) The statement must tend to show that racial animus was a significant motivating factor in the juror's vote to convict.

e. A juror may, however, testify about whether [Fed. R. Evid. 606(b)(2)]:

(1) extraneous prejudicial information was improperly brought to the jury's attention;

(2) an outside influence was improperly brought to bear upon any juror; or

(3) a mistake was made in entering the verdict on the verdict form.

EXAM TIP As a general rule, jurors will not be allowed to testify as to matters occurring within the jury room, although an irregularity occurring within the jury room (i.e., one of the jurors bringing a prejudicial newspaper article to the deliberation) is within the scope of permissible testimony.

COMPETENCY OF WITNESS

	Common Law	Federal Rules
Mental Capacity	Witness must have capacity to accurately observe, remember, and relate the facts.	Requirements of capacity to perceive and tell the truth are abandoned; questions of mental competence (based on age, illness, use of drugs) go to weight rather than admissibility.
Grounds for Disqualification	Felons, atheists, infants, mental incompetents, financially interested parties, and spouses of parties are disqualified.	Every person is competent, except where the case turns on state law (i.e., diversity cases), in which case the Erie doctrine requires the state rule of competence to control [Fed. R. Evid. 601].
Affirmation of Truthfulness	Witness must not only declare he will testify truthfully, but must show the mental capacity that he understands the obligation to tell the truth.	Witness must declare to testify truthfully by oath or affirmation in a form designed to impress that duty on the witness's conscience [Fed. R. Evid. 603].
Judge as Witness	Judge not disqualified, although the court may exercise discretion to avoid prejudice.	Presiding judge is absolutely disqualified [Fed. R. Evid. 605].

COMPETENCY OF WITNESS		
	Common Law	**Federal Rules**
Jurors as Witnesses	Traditionally, jurors are competent to testify.	Jurors disqualified as witnesses if either party objects [Fed. R. Evid. 606(a)].
Attorney as Witness	Competent, subject to ethical standards.	Competent, subject to ethical standards.
Juror Testimony	Jurors incompetent to impeach a verdict or testify as to matters occurring during jury deliberations.	Juror testimony or affidavits admissible to show **extraneous prejudicial information** (i.e., personal threats), **improper outside influence** (i.e., news media information), or **mistake** in entering the verdict [Fed. R. Evid. 606(b)].
Financial Interest in Outcome	Dead Man's Statutes disqualify financially interested witnesses in civil suits from testifying as to any conversations or transactions with the decedent.	The Federal Rules have abandoned Dead Man's Statutes, except where the Erie doctrine requires state law to be followed.

B. Impeachment

1. Who May Impeach a Witness

a. Any party, including the party that called the witness, may attack the witness's credibility [Fed. R. Evid. 607].

<u>**EXAMPLE**</u>: The defense attorney calls Defendant's wife to the stand to testify that her husband was at home watching television with her at the time of the murder. To the surprise of Defendant's attorney, Wife instead testifies that her husband arrived at home significantly later than the time of the murder, appearing disheveled and upset. The defense may impeach the credibility of Wife.

2. A Witness's Character for Truthfulness or Untruthfulness

a. A witness's credibility may be attacked or supported by [Fed. R. Evid. 608(a)]:

(1) testimony about the witness's reputation for having a character for truthfulness or untruthfulness; or

(2) testimony in the form of opinion about that character.

(a) Evidence of truthful character is admissible only after the witness's character for truthfulness has been attacked [Id.].

1) Opinion evidence of this nature was not permitted under common law; only reputation evidence was allowed.

(b) However, evidence of bias or interest does not constitute such an attack so as to allow evidence of the witness's character for truthfulness to be introduced.

EXAMPLE: Glenda testifies at trial that Damian was with her at the movies at the time of the burglary he is accused of committing. The prosecution then introduces evidence that Glenda is well known in the neighborhood to be a liar. The defense may introduce other opinion or reputation testimony of Glenda's honesty. If, instead, the prosecution introduces evidence that Glenda and Damian have been secretly dating for several months, this will not allow the defense to introduce evidence of Glenda's reputation for honesty, as her relationship with Damian goes to her potential bias, but not to her veracity.

b. Except for a criminal conviction under Rule 609, extrinsic evidence is inadmissible to prove specific instances of a witness's conduct in order to attack or support the witness's character for truthfulness [Fed. R. Evid. 608(b)].

(1) However, the court may, on cross-examination, allow such specific instances to be inquired into if they are probative of the character for truthfulness or untruthfulness of [Id.]:

(a) the witness; or

(b) another witness whose character the witness being cross-examined has testified about.

(2) By testifying on another matter, a witness does not waive any privilege against self-incrimination for testimony relating only to the witness's character for truthfulness [Id.].

EXAMPLE: John testifies at his trial that he is not guilty of embezzlement. His neighbor, Melissa, takes the stand to testify in John's defense. The prosecution may cross-examine Melissa about her own acts of untruthfulness, and, if Melissa has testified as to John's character, she may be cross-examined as to John's specific acts (i.e., her knowledge of his involvement in other fraudulent activities).

c. Credibility of witnesses under Rule 608 is considered a collateral matter, in that, if the witness lies about the credibility issue on cross-examination, counsel does not have the ability to prove the lie with extrinsic evidence and must accept the witness's answer. This is commonly referred to as the **collateral matter doctrine**, and is motivated by the potential waste of time if such evidence were to be allowed.

EXAMPLE: If Glenda claims to have graduated from Yale, and the prosecution, under cross-examination, is unable to obtain an admission from Glenda that she did not complete her degree, the prosecution may not introduce testimony by the dean of Yale to prove Glenda is lying.

3. **Impeachment by Evidence of a Criminal Conviction**

a. Under common law, the conviction of a person of treason or any felony, a misdemeanor involving dishonesty, or the obstruction of justice rendered the convicted person altogether incompetent as a witness. Those were said to be "infamous" crimes.

b. By contrast, under the Federal Rules of Evidence, such a witness may testify, but the opposing party may bring up the witness's past crimes to undermine her credibility [Fed. R. Evid. 609].

c. The following rules apply to attacking a witness's character for truthfulness by evidence of a criminal conviction [Fed. R. Evid. 609(a)]:

   (1) for a crime that, in the convicting jurisdiction, was punishable by death or by imprisonment for more than one year, the evidence:

      (a) must be admitted, subject to Rule 403, in a civil case or in a criminal case in which the witness is not a defendant; and

      (b) must be admitted in a criminal case in which the witness is a defendant, if the probative value of the evidence outweighs its prejudicial effect to that defendant; and

   (2) for any crime regardless of the punishment, the evidence must be admitted if the court can readily determine that establishing the elements of the crime required proving—or the witness's admitting—a dishonest act or false statement.

d. **The 10-Year Rule**

   (1) If more than 10 years have passed since the witness's conviction or release from confinement for it, whichever is later, evidence of the conviction is admissible only if [Fed. R. Evid. 609(b)]:

      (a) its probative value, supported by specific facts and circumstances, substantially outweighs its prejudicial effect; and

         1) Note that, unlike the Rule 403 balancing test, this test requires that the conviction be highly probative; the balancing will skew heavily toward a default of rejecting the conviction, to the extent that a non-*crimen falsi* conviction that is more than 10 years old is presumptively inadmissible.

      (b) the proponent gives an adverse party reasonable written notice of the intent to use it so that the party has a fair opportunity to contest its use.

e. **Juvenile Adjudications**

   (1) Evidence of a juvenile adjudication is admissible under this rule only if [Fed. R. Evid. 609(d)]:

      (a) it is offered in a criminal case;

      (b) the adjudication was of a witness other than the defendant;

      (c) an adult's conviction for that offense would be admissible to attack the adult's credibility; and

      (d) admitting the evidence is necessary to fairly determine guilt or innocence.

f. **Pendency of an Appeal**

   (1) A conviction is admissible even if an appeal is pending, but evidence of the pendency is also admissible [Fed. R. Evid. 609(e)].

g. Convictions in another state or in a federal court are usable to impeach. Though a judgment against a lawyer of suspension or disbarment for criminal misconduct is not technically a conviction, it has been held to be provable to impeach.

h. A *nolo contendere* plea, which does not admit culpability, may be used to impeach in a subsequent civil or criminal proceeding [United States v. Williams, 642 F.2d 136 (5th Cir. 1981)].

4. **Religious Beliefs or Opinions**

a. Evidence of a witness's religious beliefs or opinions is not admissible to attack or support the witness's credibility [Fed. R. Evid. 610].

C. Examination of Witnesses

1. **Mode and Order of Examining Witnesses and Presenting Evidence**

a. The court should exercise reasonable control over the mode and order of examining witnesses and presenting evidence so as to [Fed. R. Evid. 611(a)]:

(1) make those procedures effective for determining the truth;

(2) avoid wasting time; and

(3) protect witnesses from harassment or undue embarrassment.

b. Cross-examination should not go beyond the subject matter of the direct examination and matters affecting the witness's credibility. The court may allow inquiry into additional matters as if on direct examination [Fed. R. Evid. 611(b)].

c. Leading questions should not be used on the direct examination except as necessary to develop the witness's testimony. Ordinarily, the court should allow leading questions [Fed. R. Evid. 611(c)]:

(1) on cross-examination; and

(2) when a party calls a hostile witness, an adverse party, or a witness identified with an adverse party.

d. Other circumstances in which leading questions may be appropriate on direct examination include:

(1) to establish preliminary background information about a witness;

(2) to jog a witness's memory;

(3) to lay a foundation; or to facilitate a young or timid witness.

2. **Writing Used to Refresh a Witness's Memory**

a. On direct examination, the examiner may jog the memory of a witness who has some knowledge of the purported testimony, but whose memory is incomplete, upon laying a proper foundation.

b. Any writing, photograph, further questioning, or other form of evidence will suffice. After the memory has been "refreshed," the witness must testify without having the refreshing evidence present.

EXAMPLE: Philip O'Malley, a traffic cop, is called to testify about the scene of the accident between Donald and Petunia. When questioned about the length of the skid marks left by Petunia's vehicle, Philip is unable to remember. The accident report may be used to refresh Philip's memory.

c. When a witness uses a writing to refresh memory, the Federal Rules of Evidence give an adverse party certain options, which are available [Fed. R. Evid. 612(a)]
   (1) while testifying; or
   (2) before testifying, if the court decides that justice requires the party to have those options.

d. Unless otherwise provided by law in a criminal case [18 U.S.C. § 3500], an adverse party is entitled to [Fed. R. Evid. 612(b)]:
   (1) have the writing produced at the hearing;
   (2) inspect it;
   (3) cross-examine the witness about it; and
   (4) introduce in evidence any portion that relates to the witness's testimony.

e. If the producing party claims that the writing includes unrelated matter, the court must examine the writing in camera, delete any unrelated portion, and order that the rest be delivered to the adverse party. Any portion deleted over objection must be preserved for the record [Id.].

f. If a writing is not produced or is not delivered as ordered, the court may issue any appropriate order. However, if the prosecution does not comply in a criminal case, the court must strike the witness's testimony or—if justice so requires—declare a mistrial [Fed. R. Evid. 612(c)].

g. Where privileged material is used to refresh, most courts hold a waiver to have occurred and allow inspection by the adverse party [see, e.g., Wheeling-Pittsburgh Steel Corp. v. Underwriters Laboratories, Inc., 81 F.R.D. 8 (N.D. Ill. 1978)].

3. **Witness's Prior Statement**

a. When examining a witness about the witness's prior statement, a party need not show it or disclose its contents to the witness. However, the party must, on request, show it or disclose its contents to an adverse party's attorney [Fed. R. Evid. 613(a)].

b. Extrinsic evidence of a witness's prior inconsistent statement is admissible only if the witness is given an opportunity to explain or deny the statement and an adverse party is given an opportunity to examine the witness about it, or if justice so requires [Fed. R. Evid. 613(b)].
   (1) This provision does not apply to an opposing party's statements under Rule 801(d)(2) (discussed below) [Id.].

4. **Court's Calling or Examining a Witness**

a. The court may call a witness on its own or at a party's request. Each party is entitled to cross-examine the witness [Fed. R. Evid. 614(a)].

b. The court may examine a witness regardless of who calls the witness [Fed. R. Evid. 614(b)].

5. **Excluding Witnesses**

a. At a party's request, the court must order witnesses excluded so that they cannot hear other witnesses' testimony, or the court may do so on its own [Fed. R. Evid. 615(a)]. This rule does not authorize excluding:

(1) a party who is a natural person;
(2) an officer or employee of a party that is not a natural person, after being designated as the party's representative by its attorney;
(3) a person whose presence a party shows to be essential to presenting the party's claim or defense; or
(4) a person authorized by statute to be present.

b. An order under Rule 615(a) operates only to exclude witnesses from the courtroom. However, the court may also, by order [Fed. R. Evid. 615(b)]:
(1) prohibit disclosure of trial testimony to witnesses who are excluded from the courtroom; and
(2) prohibit excluded witnesses from accessing trial testimony.

FOUNDATIONAL REQUIREMENTS FOR IMPEACHMENT EVIDENCE		
Manner of Impeachment	**Applicable Rule of Evidence**	**Foundational Requirements**
Character for Truthfulness	Reputation for credibility [Fed. R. Evid. 608(a)]. Opinion about credibility [Fed. R. Evid. 608(a)].	Familiarity with the witness.
	Crimen falsi convictions [Fed. R. Evid. 609]. Non-*crimen falsi* convictions [Fed. R. Evid. 609].	Must be shown to the witness. Introduction of certified copy sufficient.
	Misdemeanors involving dishonesty or false statements [Fed. R. Evid. 609].	No special foundation necessary.
	Specific instances of uncharged conduct [Fed. R. Evid. 608(b)].	No extrinsic evidence allowed.
Bias or Interest	Questioning concerning favoritism, hostility, or financial interest. Introduction of extrinsic evidence is allowed.	Although bias is always material, most courts require a factual basis to be laid prior to introduction of extrinsic evidence.
Sensory Defect	Either questioning or extrinsic evidence relating to the witness's inability to observe, remember, and relate the evidence.	Questioning regarding deficiency is necessary prior to introduction of extrinsic evidence.
Prior Inconsistent Statement	Questioning as to prior oral or written statements contradictory to testimony given on the stand is admissible to impeach [Fed. R. Evid. 613(a)], and as substantive evidence only if the prior statement was made at a sworn proceeding (i.e., subject to penalty of perjury) [Fed. R. Evid. 801(d)(1)].	Under common law, a foundation was required. The Federal Rules require only that the witness be afforded an opportunity to explain or deny the inconsistency.

VII. OPINIONS AND EXPERT TESTIMONY

A. Acceptable Testimony

1. Opinion Testimony by Lay Witnesses

a. If a witness is not testifying as an expert, testimony in the form of an opinion is limited to one that is [Fed. R. Evid. 701]:

(1) rationally based on the witness's perception;

(2) helpful to clearly understanding the witness's testimony or to determining a fact in issue; and

(3) not based on scientific, technical, or other specialized knowledge within the scope of Rule 702.

b. The proper scope of non-expert opinion includes such perceptions as speed and other measurements; physical states such as intoxication or injury; personal emotions of others (fear, sorrow); sensory descriptions (taste, sound, smell); value of one's own land; and sanity of the testator (where the opinion is given by a subscribing witness of the will). Legal conclusions must be avoided (i.e., schizophrenic, or an alcoholic, or testifying that an accident victim fractured his spine). Evidence of the witness having a truthful character is admissible only after the witness's character for truthfulness has been attacked. Law enforcement personnel exist in a gray area when it comes to lay witness opinion; sometimes their testimony falls into lay opinion and sometimes it is qualified as expert testimony [Fed. R. Evid. 701, cmt.].

2. Testimony by Expert Witnesses

a. A witness who is qualified as an expert by knowledge, skill, experience, training, or education may testify in the form of an opinion or otherwise if the proponent demonstrates to the court that it is more likely than not that [Fed. R. Evid. 702]:

(1) the expert's scientific, technical, or other specialized knowledge will help the trier of fact to understand the evidence or to determine a fact in issue;

(2) the testimony is based on sufficient facts or data;

(3) the testimony is the product of reliable principles and methods; and

(4) the expert's opinion reflects a reliable application of the principles and methods to the facts of the case.

b. Federal courts assess the reliability of scientific evidence by asking (among other questions) the following [Daubert v. Merrell Dow Pharmaceuticals, Inc., 509 U.S. 579 (1993)]:

(1) Has the methodology been tested?

(2) Are there known rates of error?

(3) Has the methodology been generally accepted?

(4) Has the methodology been subject to peer review?

c. Depending on the particular circumstances of the case at issue, these factors might also be applicable in assessing the reliability of non-scientific expert testimony as well [see Id.; Fed. R. Evid. 702; Kumho Tire Co. v. Carmichael, 526 U.S. 137 (1999)].

B. Bases of Expert's Opinion Testimony

1. An expert may base an opinion on facts or data in the case that the expert has been made aware of or personally observed. If experts in the particular field would reasonably rely on those kinds of facts or data in forming an opinion on the subject, they need not be admissible for the opinion to be admitted [Fed. R. Evid. 703].
2. However, if the facts or data would otherwise be inadmissible, the proponent of the opinion may disclose them to the jury only if their probative value in helping the jury evaluate the opinion substantially outweighs their prejudicial effect [Id.].
    a. The opponent, however, is allowed to bring out such facts without this special balancing test [Fed. R. Evid. 703, cmt.].
3. The expert's opinion must reliably fit the theory and methods on which the opinion is based.

C. Opinion on an Ultimate Issue

1. As a general rule, an opinion is not objectionable just because it embraces an ultimate issue [Fed. R. Evid. 704(a)].
2. There is, however, an exception to this rule. In a criminal case, an expert witness must not state an opinion about whether the defendant did or did not have a mental state or condition that constitutes an element of the crime charged or of a defense. These matters are for the trier of fact alone [Fed. R. Evid. 704(b)].

   EXAMPLE: An expert witness may testify that the defendant suffers from schizophrenia, but may not testify that the defendant was legally insane.

D. Disclosing the Facts or Data Underlying an Expert's Opinion

1. Unless the court orders otherwise, an expert may state an opinion—and give the reasons for it—without first testifying to the underlying facts or data, but the expert may be required to disclose those facts and data on cross-examination [Fed. R. Evid. 705].
2. Experts may be properly cross-examined as to [Fed. R. Evid. 705, cmt.]:
    a. qualifications;
    b. subject matter and basis of an opinion; and
    c. compensation.
3. Experts (like other witnesses) are subject to impeachment by any of the usual methods, including prior inconsistent statements, truthfulness, and bias.
    a. A commonly employed impeachment technique is to show that the expert is biased. For example, the cross-examiner may prove that the expert is receiving a large fee to testify, or that she always aligns himself with a particular point of view or with a particular litigant.

E. Court-Appointed Expert Witnesses

1. On a party's motion or on its own, the court may order the parties to show cause why expert witnesses should not be appointed and may ask the parties to submit nominations. The court may appoint any expert that the parties agree on and any of its own choosing, but the court may only appoint someone who consents to act [Fed. R. Evid. 706(a)].

2. The court must inform the expert of the expert's duties, either in writing with a copy filed with the clerk or orally at a conference in which the parties have an opportunity to participate. The expert [Fed. R. Evid. 706(b)]:
   a. must advise the parties of any findings the expert makes;
   b. may be deposed by any party;
   c. may be called to testify by the court or any party; and
   d. may be cross-examined by any party, including the party that called the expert.
3. The expert is entitled to a reasonable compensation, as set by the court. The compensation is payable as follows [Fed. R. Evid. 706(c)]:
   a. in a criminal case or in a civil case involving just compensation under the Fifth Amendment, from any funds that are provided by law; and
   b. in any other civil case, by the parties in the proportion and at the time that the court directs—and the compensation is then charged like other costs.
4. The court may authorize disclosure to the jury that the court appointed the expert [Fed. R. Evid. 706(d)].
   a. The parties are not limited by Rule 706 in calling expert witnesses of their own selection [Fed. R. Evid. 706(e)].

	COMMON LAW	FEDERAL RULES OF EVIDENCE
Basis of Expert Opinion—Rule 703	Expert must disclose assumed facts upon which opinion is based.	Prior disclosure of underlying facts not required absent request by court [Fed. R. Evid. 705].
	Opinion must be based on admissible evidence.	Basis of opinion may be assumed facts, facts not in evidence, or even otherwise inadmissible hearsay, provided it is of a type reasonably relied upon by experts in the field [Fed. R. Evid. 703]. Note: While an expert may rely on information gained from another expert, he may not merely serve as a conduit of the other expert's opinion (i.e., testify as to what the other expert thought).
Ultimate Issues	No opinions are permitted.	Testimony on an ultimate issue is not objectionable (examples include that a medical procedure was necessary, that a building was earthquake-proof, or that a doctor was negligent). However, expert testimony as to the mental state of a defendant in a criminal case is not permitted.
Cross-Examination of Experts	No inquiry is allowed regarding a publication unless the writing was referred to or relied on at trial, or the expert wrote the publication, or the writing was admitted into evidence; such statements relied on or referred to may only be used to impeach.	Hearsay exception—Rule 803(18) allows an expert to be cross-examined as to statements contained in any published treatise of reliable authority; such evidence may be admitted substantively and for purposes of impeachment.

VIII. HEARSAY

A. Definitions

1. A **statement** is a person's oral assertion, written assertion, or nonverbal conduct, if the person intended it as an assertion [Fed. R. Evid. 801(a)].
2. A **declarant** is the person who made a statement [Fed. R. Evid. 801(b)].
3. **Hearsay** is a statement that [Fed. R. Evid. 801(c)]:
   a. the declarant does not make while testifying at the current trial or hearing; and
   b. a party offers in evidence to prove the truth of the matter asserted in the statement.
      (1) Any statement not made in court, regardless of who says it, is potentially hearsay if offered for the truth contained therein.

      EXAMPLE: David is on trial for the murder of his wife, Veronica, who was last seen alive on August 25 and whose body was never found. The prosecution seeks to call Wendy to testify that Veronica called her on August 30 and said, "I'm terrified of David; he's threatened to kill me." This testimony is hearsay if offered to prove that David actually threatened Veronica, but is not hearsay if offered to establish that Veronica was still alive on August 30.

B. Analysis of Hearsay Issues

1. Hearsay is not always inadmissible; the finding that a statement is hearsay merely requires further analysis of its admissibility. When analyzing the admissibility of potential hearsay evidence:
   a. determine the assertion or conduct serving as the out-of-court statement;
      (1) An oral or written assertion includes verbal communication such as a tape recording or videotape.
      (2) Nonverbal conduct intended as an assertion qualifies as a statement and is considered hearsay [Fed. R. Evid. 801(a)].

      EXAMPLE: Gestures (such as pointing a finger, nodding the head, "thumbs up"), silence where it is intended to communicate, and sign language.

      (3) Under the Federal Rules, non-assertive conduct is non-hearsay because it is not intended as an assertion [Fed. R. Evid. 801, cmt.].
      (4) In addition to the traditional forms of evidence classified above as non-hearsay, the Federal Rules specifically exempt certain statements as non-hearsay (discussed below) [Fed. R. Evid. 801(d)].

NOTE Note that this treatment under the Federal Rules of Evidence is contrary to common law.

   b. determine who is the declarant;
      (1) Distinguish between the person who made the statement (the declarant) and the witness presently testifying. Also, determine

whether the declarant is a party or non-party—a statement of a party offered against him by his opponent is admissible as non-hearsay, whereas a similar statement made by a non-party is inadmissible as hearsay unless a hearsay exception applies.

c. determine the purpose for which the evidence is offered; and

(1) If the evidence is being offered for its truth, it is hearsay.

(2) If is it being offered for some other non-truth purpose, it is not hearsay.

(a) **Legally Operative Facts**

1) Where words themselves have legal significance apart from their truth (i.e., at issue is whether or not the words were actually spoken), the fact of independent probative value makes them non-hearsay [Fed. R. Evid. 801, cmt.]. The two main categories are:

a) tortious words, including the actual words of slander or libel in defamation actions; and

b) transactional words, including the actual words of offer and acceptance in a contract or the words of intent in a donative transfer, sale, will, or deed.

(b) **Verbal Acts**

1) Explanatory words that accompany ambiguous physical actions are termed verbal acts. As such, their legal significance is independent of their truth [Fed. R. Evid. 801, cmt.]. An example of this would be if A hands B a pen and says, "This is a gift." Without these words, it is unclear whether A is returning B's pen to him, lending him a pen, or giving him a pen.

EXAMPLE: A bus passenger yelling, "Look out!" prior to an accident is admissible as non-hearsay to prove the driver had notice of the danger.

(c) **State of Mind**

1) Statements offered to prove a relevant attitude, belief, or intent of either the declarant or the listener are admissible circumstantially as non-hearsay [Fed. R. Evid. 801, cmt.].

EXAMPLE: The defendant's knowledge that the victim made threats to attack her is admissible as non-hearsay in a claim of self-defense to prove defendant's fearful state of mind.

(d) **Impeachment**

1) Statements of the witness offered merely to challenge credibility or show perjury (irrespective of their truth) are non-hearsay.

(e) **Statement of Ability to See, Hear, or Comprehend**

1) An out-of-court statement is not offered for its truth if it is offered to show that the declarant was able to see, hear, smell, speak, understand a language, etc.

(f) **Effect on the Listener**

1) A statement is not hearsay when it is offered not for its truth, but instead, to show what the listener knew or to explain their motive, intent, belief, or actions. This is the case when what matters isn't whether the statement was true, but that the listener believed the statement was true.

EXAMPLE: A defendant is on trial for murder. To support her claim of self-defense, the defendant takes the stand and testifies that, the day before the killing, the victim said to her, "When I see you tomorrow, I'm going to kill you." This statement is not being offered to prove that the victim actually intended to kill the defendant. Rather, it is being offered to prove that the defendant was under the belief that the victim intended to kill her.

d. apply possible hearsay exceptions.

(1) If the statement in question constitutes hearsay, it must be determined whether or not the statement falls under a hearsay exception as defined in the rules. If it does not, the statement will be inadmissible.

C. Hearsay Exemptions

1. The Federal Rules specifically exempt some out-of-court statements from being hearsay, even though they are offered for their truth. These fall under two broad categories: certain prior statements of a declarant-witness and certain statements made by the opposing party [Fed. R. Evid. 801(d)].

2. **Declarant-Witness's Prior Statement**

a. A statement is not hearsay when the declarant testifies and is subject to cross-examination about a prior statement, and the statement is either [Fed. R. Evid. 801(d)(1)]:

(1) a prior sworn inconsistent statement;

(a) A **prior sworn inconsistent statement** is a statement inconsistent with the declarant's testimony and which was given under penalty of perjury at a trial, hearing, or other proceeding or in a deposition [Fed. R. Evid. 801(d)(1)(A)].

(2) a prior consistent statement; or

(a) A **prior consistent statement** is a statement consistent with the declarant's testimony and which is offered either to rebut an express or implied charge that the declarant recently fabricated it or acted from a recent improper influence or motive in so testifying; or to rehabilitate the declarant's credibility as a witness when attacked on another ground [Fed. R. Evid. 801(d)(1)(B)].

(b) When introduced to rebut charges of recent fabrication or improper motive, the prior consistent statement has to predate the motive for the alleged fabrication or improper motive.

(3) a prior identification.

(a) A **prior identification** is a statement which identifies a person as someone the declarant perceived earlier [Fed. R. Evid. 801(d)(1)(C)].

3. **Opposing Party's Statement**

a. A statement is not hearsay when the statement is offered against an opposing party, and the statement is [Fed. R. Evid. 801(d)(2)]:

(1) made by the party in an individual or representative capacity;

(2) one the party manifested that it adopted or believed to be true;

(3) made by a person whom the party authorized to make a statement on the subject;

(a) Under this exemption, the statement must be considered, but does not by itself establish the declarant's authority.

(4) made by the party's agent or employee on a matter within the scope of that relationship and while it existed; or

(a) Under this exemption, the statement must be considered, but does not by itself establish the existence or scope of the relationship between the party and the declarant.

(5) made by the party's co-conspirator during and in furtherance of the conspiracy.

(a) Under this exemption, the statement must be considered, but does not by itself establish the existence of the conspiracy or participation in it.

NON-HEARSAY CATEGORIES	
Opposing Party's Statement **[Fed. R. Evid. 801(d)(2)(A)]**	• A statement of a party offered by his opponent. • Unavailability and personal knowledge of the declarant are not required. • Statement need not be against interest when made. • Guilty pleas are included as admissions, but final judgments of criminal convictions are hearsay exceptions under Rule 803(22).
Adoptive Statement (or Statement by Silence) **[Fed. R. Evid. 801(d)(2)(B)]**	Circumstances must be such that a reasonable person would have denied the assertion.
Authorized Statement **[Fed. R. Evid. 801(d)(2)(C)]**	• Authority to speak may be express or implied. • Independent proof may be required to show extent of agent's authority in partnership situations—including statements of predecessors-in-interest during the time of ownership of land.
Vicarious Statement of an Agent or Employee **[Fed. R. Evid. 801(d)(2)(D)]**	• Common law refused to admit statements of employees where no authority to speak existed. • Federal Rules allow such statements if made during the employment and concerning a matter within the scope of employment. • No authority to speak is required.

NON-HEARSAY CATEGORIES	
Co-Conspirator's Statement **[Fed. R. Evid. 801(d)(2)(E)]**	• The content of the statement of a co-conspirator may be taken into account in proving the existence of the relationship, but other independent is required. • Scope of conspiracy must be ascertained to determine whether statement made by co-conspirator after arrest is inadmissible, since not made during the conspiracy.
Prior Sworn Inconsistent Statements **[Fed. R. Evid. 801(d)(1)(A)]**	• Prior inconsistent statements are not hearsay when offered to impeach (to show inconsistency as opposed to being offered for their truth). • Under Rule 801(d)(1)(A), prior sworn inconsistent statements are non-hearsay and are admissible as substantive evidence. • **Sworn** means subject to penalty of perjury, and includes depositions and grand jury testimony, but not an affidavit. It must be under oath and subject to cross-examination.
Prior Consistent Statements **[Fed. R. Evid. 801(d)(1)(B)]**	Admissible as substantive evidence to rebut charge against the declarant of recent fabrication or improper influence or motive.
Prior Identifications **[Fed. R. Evid. 801(d)(1)(C)]**	A prior identification will be admissible non-hearsay only where the declarant (eyewitness) is presently testifying at the trial (i.e., available).

D. Hearsay Exceptions

1. The Rule against Hearsay

a. Hearsay is not admissible unless any of the following provides otherwise [Fed. R. Evid. 802]:

(1) a federal statute;

(2) the Federal Rules of Evidence; or

(3) other rules prescribed by the Supreme Court.

b. Exceptions to the hearsay exclusion are fall within two general categories:

(1) those which are admissible regardless of whether the declarant is available as a witness [Fed. R. Evid. 803]; and

(2) those which require that the declarant be unavailable for the evidence to be admissible [Fed. R. Evid. 804].

2. Regardless of Whether Declarant Is Available as a Witness

a. The following are not excluded by the rule against hearsay, regardless of whether the declarant is available as a witness [Fed. R. Evid. 803]:

(1) **Present Sense Impression**

(a) A statement describing or explaining an event or condition, made while or immediately after the declarant perceived it [Fed. R. Evid. 803(1)].

<u>**EXAMPLE**</u>: Wanda testifies that Victor looked up and screamed, "That crane is about to fall!" right before the crane fell on him.

(2) **Excited Utterance**

(a) A statement relating to a startling event or condition, made while the declarant was under the stress of excitement that it caused [Fed. R. Evid. 803(2)].

(b) The exception for an excited utterance requires that the declarant speak while under the stressful influence of a startling event or condition. The necessary state of excitement may embrace the consequent shock or emotional distress that may persist even after "excitement," in the narrow sense, has subsided. The rationale supporting admission is that emotional stress suspends the process of reflective thought necessary for conscious fabrication, and that the recent nature of the exciting event minimizes the danger of faulty memory.

(c) A present sense impression requires spontaneity, due to the fact that the statement must be made while or immediately after the declarant perceived the event. On the other hand, an excited utterance does not require spontaneity, provided the statement was made under the stress of excitement.

(3) **Then-Existing Mental, Emotional, or Physical Condition**

(a) A statement of the declarant's then-existing state of mind (such as motive, intent, or plan) or emotional, sensory, or physical condition (such as mental feeling, pain, or bodily health), but not including a statement of memory or belief to prove the fact remembered or believed unless it relates to the validity or terms of declarant's will [Fed. R. Evid. 803(3)].

(b) The existence of an injury to a party (or in some cases to a non-party) may be an element of a cause of action. The exception for present physical condition admits relevant hearsay declarations in which the declarant, either by exclamation or by narration, indicates her then-existing bodily condition. Thus, a declarant's out-of-court statements that she was having difficulty hearing and that she was experiencing headaches would be admissible under the exception. There is no danger of a defect in memory and only a minimal danger of erroneous perception.

EXAMPLE: Wanda testifies that after the car accident, the driver of the school bus said to her, "I can't feel my toes."

(4) **Statement Made for Medical Diagnosis or Treatment**

(a) A statement that [Fed. R. Evid. 803(4)]:

1) is made for—and is reasonably pertinent to—medical diagnosis or treatment; and

2) describes:

a) medical history;

b) past or present symptoms or sensations;

c) their inception; or

d) their general cause.

(b) The Federal Rule is explicit in its provision that statements of past symptoms are admissible when made for, and reasonably pertinent to, medical diagnosis or treatment. The rule allows admission of remarks made to other medical attendants. The wording of the rule is broad enough to admit statements made to a physician consulted for the purpose of enabling him to testify, even if no treatment is contemplated [Fed. R. Evid. 803, cmt.].

EXAMPLE: Dr. Doolittle, who happened to be at the scene of the accident, testifies that Cindy, one of the children on the bus, told him she was "seeing stars."

(c) Statements made to medical providers that do not relate to diagnosis or treatment, but which are relevant only with respect to liability issues, are not admissible [Id.].

(d) Rule 803(4) does not specify to whom the statements must be made to fall under the exception. However, the Official Comments say that such statements do not need to be made to a physician, and could include statements made to hospital attendants, ambulance drivers, or even members of the family [Fed. R. Evid. 803, cmt.].

(5) **Recorded Recollection**

(a) A record that [Fed. R. Evid. 803(5)]:

1) is on a matter the witness once knew about but now cannot recall well enough to testify fully and accurately;

2) was made or adopted by the witness when the matter was fresh in the witness's memory; and

3) accurately reflects the witness's knowledge.

(b) If admitted, the record may be read into evidence. However, it may only be received as an exhibit if offered by an adverse party [Id.].

1) A **record** is defined as including a memorandum, report, or data compilation, and includes electronically stored information [Fed. R. Evid. 101(b)(4), (6)].

(c) Usually, the witness will have herself written the memorandum or record that is offered as recorded recollection, but Rule 803(5) expressly takes account of the case in which the witness was not the author. It is enough that the witness adopted the writing which, in this context, means that she examined the writing and affirmed its correctness at a time when memory was fresh. There is no particular time after the event during which the recording must be made (or if made by another, its accuracy affirmed), but there should be proof that recollection was clear when the writing was made or verified [Fed. R. Evid. 803, cmt.].

(d) Under the Federal Rule, applicability of the exception hinges upon a finding that the witness "once knew but now cannot recall well enough to testify fully and accurately." There is still disagreement among some state jurisdictions as to whether impaired memory is essential to the applicability of the present exception and, if so, whether there must be a complete inability to remember the pertinent event before the prior writing may be introduced.

EXAMPLE: The inventory of an illegal drug lab as noted in a police report, which the officer read and signed.

(6) **Records of a Regularly Conducted Activity**

(a) A record of an act, event, condition, opinion, or diagnosis if [Fed. R. Evid. 803(6)]:

1) the record was made at or near the time by—or from information transmitted by—someone with knowledge;

2) the record was kept in the course of a regularly conducted activity of a business, organization, occupation, or calling, whether or not for profit;

3) making the record was a regular practice of that activity;

4) all these conditions are shown by the testimony of the custodian or another qualified witness, or by a certification that complies with the rules for domestic or foreign records under Rule 902(11) or (12) or with a statute permitting certification; and

5) neither the source of information nor the method of circumstances of preparation indicates a lack of trustworthiness.

(b) The term **business** includes a business, institution, association, profession, occupation, and calling of every kind, whether or not conducted for profit [Fed. R. Evid. 803, cmt.].

(c) The Federal Rule and its various counterparts in state jurisdictions contemplate that the person(s) who provides the basic information for the entry will have personal knowledge of the act or event that is recorded. There is no requirement, however, that this person be called to testify; it suffices that the custodian or other qualified witness states that it is the business practice to base the entry upon data supplied by one with personal knowledge.

(d) It is essential under the Federal Rule and its state counterparts that the report was made in the regular course of business, that it was the regular practice to make the kind of entry in question (thus ensuring that entries were not made simply for litigation purposes), and that the entry was made "at or near the time" of the condition or event described in the entry [Id.].

EXAMPLE: The hospital admission records may be admitted to show that a party did, in fact, seek medical treatment for his injuries.

(7) **Absence of a Record of a Regularly Conducted Activity**

(a) Evidence that a matter is not included in a record of a regularly conducted activity if [Fed. R. Evid. 803(7)]:

1) the evidence is admitted to prove that the matter did not occur or exist;

2) a record was regularly kept for a matter of that kind; and

3) neither the possible source of the information nor other circumstances indicate a lack of trustworthiness.

EXAMPLE: The absence of hospital admission records showing that the party sought treatment for her injuries may be used as evidence that she did not, in fact, seek treatment at the hospital.

(8) **Public Records**

(a) A record or statement of a public office if [Fed. R. Evid. 803(8)]:

1) it sets out:

a) the office's activities;

b) a matter observed while under a legal duty to report, but not including, in a criminal case, a matter observed by law-enforcement personnel; or

i) This section embraces records of "matters observed" pursuant to a public duty to observe and report as, for example, an induction officer's observation that an individual refused to take a required oath.

ii) However, records of matters observed by law enforcement personnel are inadmissible in criminal cases, at least when offered by the government against the accused. Thus, for example, recorded observations made by the police at the scene of an arrest would not come within the public records exception. The basis for this special restriction is the assumption that the adversarial relationship between law enforcement officials and criminal defendants casts doubt on the objectivity of these officials' public entries detailing observations pertinent to the defendant's guilt. Further, the admission of these entries would raise difficulties under the Confrontation Clause of the U.S. Constitution, if the officer making them were not available for cross-examination by the defendant. Generally speaking, if the police observations recorded in the public record are to be introduced, they must be presented by the observing officer, not by offering the public records as a substitute for the officer's testimony [Fed. R. Evid. 803, cmt.].

c) in a civil case or against the government in a criminal case, factual findings from a legally authorized investigation; and

2) neither the source of information nor other circumstances indicate a lack of trustworthiness.

EXAMPLE: The conclusions of an investigator regarding whether the cause of an airplane crash was equipment malfunction or pilot error are admissible.

(9) **Public Records of Vital Statistics**

(a) A record of a birth, death, or marriage, if reported to a public office in accordance with a legal duty [Fed. R. Evid. 803(9)].

EXAMPLE: A birth certificate or a marriage license.

(10) **Absence of a Public Record**

(a) Testimony—or a certification under Rule 902—that a diligent search failed to disclose a public record or statement if the testimony or certification is admitted to prove that [Fed. R. Evid. 803(10)]:

1) the record or statement does not exist; or

2) a matter did not occur or exist, if a public office regularly kept a record or statement for a matter of that kind.

EXAMPLE: The lack of a birth certificate in the usual place a birth certificate would be registered is admissible.

(11) **Records of Religious Organizations Concerning Personal or Family History**

(a) A statement of birth, legitimacy, ancestry, marriage, divorce, death, relationship by blood or marriage, or similar facts of personal or family history, contained in a regularly kept record of a religious organization [Fed. R. Evid. 803(11)].

EXAMPLE: Record of a marriage maintained by the church.

(12) **Certificates of Marriage, Baptism, and Similar Ceremonies**

(a) A statement of fact contained in a certificate [Fed. R. Evid. 803(12)]:

1) made by a person who is authorized by a religious organization or by law to perform the act certified;

2) attesting that the person performed a marriage or similar ceremony or administered a sacrament; and

3) purporting to have been issued at the time of the act or within a reasonable time after it.

EXAMPLE: The date of marriage contained in marriage certificate.

(13) **Family Records**

(a) A statement of fact about personal or family history contained in a family record, such as a Bible, genealogy, chart, engraving on a ring, inscription on a portrait, or engraving on an urn or burial marker [Fed. R. Evid. 803(13)].

EXAMPLE: A family tree written in the front of a family Bible may be admitted to prove ancestry.

(14) **Records of Documents That Affect an Interest in Property**

(a) The record of a document that purports to establish or affect an interest in property if [Fed. R. Evid. 803(14)]:

1) the record is admitted to prove the content of the original recorded document, along with its signing and its delivery by each person who purports to have signed it;

2) the record is kept in a public office; and

3) a statute authorizes recording documents of that kind in that office.

EXAMPLE: A real property deed.

(15) **Statements in Documents That Affect an Interest in Property**

(a) A statement contained in a document that purports to establish or affect an interest in property if the matter stated was relevant to the document's purpose—unless later dealings with the property are inconsistent with the truth of the statement or the purport of the document [Fed. R. Evid. 803(15)].

EXAMPLE: Boundaries contained in a real property deed.

(16) **Statements in Ancient Documents**

(a) A statement in a document that was prepared before January 1, 1998, and whose authenticity is established [Fed. R. Evid. 803(16)].

(b) The common law required the document to be at least 30 years old. The Federal Rules previously required that the document have been in existence for at least 20 years. However, the rule was amended to include a specific date, due to the risk that the exception would be used to admit large amounts of unreliable electronically stored information.

(c) A document is "prepared" when the statement proffered was recorded in that document [Fed. R. Evid. 803, Notes]. The relevant date is the one on which the information was recorded, not when the information was prepared for trial.

EXAMPLE: A hardcopy document was prepared in 1996. A party can admit a scanned copy of that document under the ancient documents exception even though the scan occurred much more recently. The subsequent scan does not alter the document.

(17) **Market Reports and Similar Commercial Publications**

(a) Market quotations, lists, directories, or other compilations that are generally relied on by the public or by persons in particular occupations [Fed. R. Evid. 803(17)].

EXAMPLE: The price of IBM stock at the close of the New York Stock Exchange on June 1, 2005.

(18) **Statements in Learned Treatises, Periodicals, or Pamphlets**

(a) A statement contained in a treatise, periodical, or pamphlet if [Fed. R. Evid. 803(18)]:

1) the statement is called to the attention of an expert witness on cross-examination or relied on by the expert on direct examination; and

2) the publication is established as a reliable authority by the expert's admission or testimony, by another expert's testimony, or by judicial notice.

(b) If admitted, the statement may be read into evidence, but not received as an exhibit [Id.].

(c) This exception under the Federal Rules did not exist at common law. A learned treatise may only be used after an expert witness has relied on the document, or it has been called to his attention on cross-examination. The document must be established as "authoritative" by testimony or judicial notice. The treatise is not itself admitted as an exhibit; however, the parts that are read into evidence may be used as substantive evidence, as well as for impeachment [Fed. R. Evid. 803, cmt.].

(19) **Reputation Concerning Personal or Family History**

(a) A reputation among a person's family by blood, adoption, or marriage—or among a person's associates or in the community—concerning the person's birth, adoption, legitimacy, ancestry, marriage, divorce, death, relationship by blood, adoption, or marriage, or similar fact of personal or family history [Fed. R. Evid. 803(19)].

EXAMPLE: A witness may testify as to her date of birth without having to rely on her birth certificate.

(20) **Reputation Concerning Boundaries or General History**

(a) A reputation in a community—arising before the controversy—concerning boundaries of land in the community or customs that affect the land, or concerning general historical events important to that community, state, or nation [Fed. R. Evid. 803(20)].

(21) **Reputation Concerning Character**

(a) A reputation among a person's associates or in the community concerning the person's character [Fed. R. Evid. 803(21)].

(22) **Judgment of a Previous Conviction**

(a) Evidence of a final judgment of conviction if [Fed. R. Evid. 803(22)]:

1) the judgment was entered after a trial or guilty plea, but not a *nolo contendere* plea;

2) the conviction was for a crime punishable by death or by imprisonment for more than a year;

3) the evidence is admitted to prove any fact essential to the judgment; and

4) when offered by the prosecutor in a criminal case for a purpose other than impeachment, the judgment was against the defendant.

(b) The pendency of an appeal may be shown, but does not affect admissibility [Id.].

(c) Judgments of previous convictions, punishable by death or imprisonment in excess of one year, are admissible under this hearsay exception (unless offered by the government against a person other than the accused). Note, however, that although a criminal judgment is admissible in a subsequent civil proceeding, a civil judgment may not be so used in a later criminal proceeding, due to the higher criminal burden of proof.

NOTE Although evidence of judgments (under Rule 803(22)) and guilty pleas (as an opposing party's statement under Rule 801(d)(2)) are admissible, pleas of *nolo contendere*, withdrawn guilty pleas, and offers to plead guilty are inadmissible under Rule 410.

(23) **Judgments Involving Personal, Family, or General History, or a Boundary**

(a) A judgment that is admitted to prove a matter of personal, family, or general history, or boundaries, if the matter [Fed. R. Evid. 803(23)]:

1) was essential to the judgment; and

2) could be proved by evidence of reputation.

3. **When the Declarant Is Unavailable as a Witness**

a. **Criteria for Being Unavailable**

(1) A declarant is considered to be unavailable as a witness if the declarant [Fed. R. Evid. 804(a)]:

(a) is exempted from testifying about the subject matter of the declarant's statement because the court rules that a privilege applies;

(b) refuses to testify about the subject matter despite a court order to do so;

(c) testifies to not remembering the subject matter;

(d) cannot be present or testify at the trial or hearing because of death or a then-existing infirmity, physical illness, or mental illness; or

(e) is absent from the trial or hearing and the statement's proponent has not been able, by process or other reasonable means, to procure:

1) the declarant's attendance, in the case of a hearsay exception under Rule 804(b)(1) (involving former testimony) or 804(b)(6) (involving a statement offered against a party that wrongfully caused the declarant's unavailability); or

2) the declarant's attendance or testimony, in the case of any other hearsay exception under Rule 804(b).

3) A declarant is not unavailable as a witness if the statement's proponent procured or wrongfully caused the declarant's unavailability as a witness in order to prevent the declarant from attending or testifying [Id.].

b. The following are not excluded by the rule against hearsay if the declarant is unavailable as a witness [Fed. R. Evid. 804(b)]:

(1) **Former Testimony**

(a) Testimony that [Fed. R. Evid. 804(b)(1)]:

1) was given as a witness at a trial, hearing, or lawful deposition, whether given during the current proceeding or a different one; and

2) is now offered against a party who had—or, in a civil case, whose predecessor in interest had—an opportunity and similar motive to develop it by direct, cross-, or redirect examination.

EXAMPLE: In Trial #1, Defendant was charged with reckless driving, a misdemeanor that carried a maximum fine of $500. At trial, the officer who followed Defendant and arrested him testified that she saw Defendant throw something out the car window while driving. Defendant's attorney did not cross-examine the officer. In Trial #2, Defendant was charged with murder. At the trial, the prosecution seeks to introduce the former (Trial #1) testimony of the police officer (now deceased) to prove that Defendant threw the murder weapon from the car (other evidence having established that the weapon was recovered near the location where Defendant was arrested for reckless driving). The former testimony is not admissible because Defendant's attorney had no real motive to develop or cross-examine the officer at Trial #1, given that the event had little to do with reckless driving and the fine for reckless driving was small.

(2) **Statement under the Belief of Imminent Death**

(a) In a prosecution for homicide or in a civil case, a statement that the declarant, while believing the declarant's death to be imminent, made about its cause or circumstances [Fed. R. Evid. 804(b)(2)].

EXAMPLE: A decedent's last words, which were, "A blue van hit me."

(b) This has also been referred to as a **dying declaration**.

(3) **Statement against Interest**

(a) A statement that [Fed. R. Evid. 804(b)(3)]:

1) a reasonable person in the declarant's position would have made only if the person believed it to be true because, when made, it was so contrary to the declarant's proprietary or pecuniary interest or had so great a tendency to invalidate the declarant's claim against someone else or to expose the declarant to civil or criminal liability; and

EXAMPLE: The statement of a doctor, which was, "I usually have a few drinks before surgery."

2) is supported by corroborating circumstances that clearly indicate its trustworthiness, if it is offered in a criminal case as one that tends to expose the declarant to criminal liability.

HEARSAY EXCEPTION/ EXEMPTION	DISTINGUISHING CHARACTERISTICS
Statement against Interest **[Fed. R. Evid. 804(b)(3)]**	• Unavailability required. • Statement of a person, usually a non-party, against interest (proprietary, pecuniary, or penal) when made. • Statement was made such that a reasonable person would not have made it unless he believed it to be true. Personal knowledge is required.
Opposing Party's Statement **[Fed. R. Evid. 801(d)(2)]**	• Unavailability not required. • Statement of a party need not be against interest when made. • Personal knowledge of declarant not required.

(4) **Statement of Personal or Family History**

(a) A statement about [Fed. R. Evid. 804(b)(4)]:

1) the declarant's own birth, adoption, legitimacy, ancestry, marriage, divorce, relationship by blood, adoption, or marriage, or similar facts of personal or family history, even though the declarant had no way of acquiring personal knowledge about that fact; or

EXAMPLE: A woman's statement of her birth date.

2) another person concerning any of these facts, as well as death, if the declarant was related to the person by blood, adoption, or marriage or was so intimately associated with the person's family that the declarant's information is likely accurate.

(5) **Statement Offered against a Party that Wrongfully Caused the Declarant's Unavailability**

(a) A statement offered against a party that wrongfully caused—or acquiesced in wrongfully causing—the declarant's unavailability as a witness, and did so intending that result [Fed. R. Evid. 804(b)(6)].

(b) This has also been referred to as forfeiture by wrongdoing.

HEARSAY EXCEPTIONS; DECLARANT UNAVAILABLE
San Francisco Fire Department
Statement against Interest, Former Testimony, Family, Dying Declaration

HEARSAY EXCEPTIONS REQUIRING UNAVAILABILITY		
Hearsay Exception	**Common Law**	**Federal Rule**
Former Testimony **[Fed. R. Evid. 804(b)(1)]**	Parties and issues must be identical.	Party (or predecessor-in-interest in a civil case) against whom evidence is now offered must have been a party in the former proceeding, and must have had an opportunity and similar motive to develop testimony. NOTE: Actual cross-examination is not required, only the opportunity to cross-examine. Additionally, criminal cases do require parties be identical.
Statement under the Belief of Imminent Death **[Fed. R. Evid. 804(b)(2)]**	Applies only in homicide cases; declarant must be dead.	Applies in all civil cases and criminal homicide cases; declarant need not die but still must be unavailable.
Statement against Interest **[Fed. R. Evid. 804(b)(3)]**	Limited to statements against a pecuniary or proprietary interest.	Includes statements that subject declarant to civil liability or render invalid a claim by him against another, as well as statements against penal interest. Where declarant's statement is offered to exculpate the defendant, corroborating circumstances must be shown to indicate trustworthiness.

4. **Confrontation Clause**

a. Under the Confrontation Clause of the Sixth Amendment, testimonial hearsay is inadmissible against a criminal defendant who has not had an opportunity to cross-examine the declarant.

(1) **Testimonial evidence** in this context refers, at a minimum, to [Crawford v. Washington, 541 U.S. 36 (2004)]:

(a) prior testimony at a preliminary hearing, before a grand jury, or at a former trial; and

(b) police interrogations.

(2) A criminal defendant forfeits his Confrontation Clause rights if he causes the unavailability of the declarant with the intent to prevent that declarant from testifying [Giles v. California, 554 U.S. 353 (2008)].

(3) The Supreme Court held that it was a violation of the Sixth Amendment right of confrontation for a prosecutor to submit affidavits of state laboratory analysts (regarding whether material connected to the petitioner was cocaine) without the analysts testifying at the trial [Melendez-Diaz v. Massachusetts, 557 U.S. 305 (2009)].

(4) In Davis v. Washington [547 U.S. 813 (2006)], the Supreme Court drew a distinction between statements made to the police to assist in an investigation and prosecution, which it considered to be testimonial, and statements made to police to enable them to meet an ongoing emergency, which the Court held should be considered nontestimonial.

(a) In particular, statements made to the police "under circumstances objectively indicating that the primary purpose of the interrogation is to enable police assistance to meet an ongoing emergency" should be considered nontestimonial [Id.].

EXAMPLE: Statements made during an emergency 911 call would be considered nontestimonial, and therefore not subject to the Sixth Amendment Confrontation Clause.

(b) However, the Supreme Court has also held that statements made at a crime scene to police during an investigation of the crime (and for that purpose) are testimonial in nature, and so subject to the Confrontation Clause [Hammon v. Indiana, 547 U.S. 813 (2006)].

1) In Hammon v. Indiana, the Supreme Court found that the declarant faced "no emergency in progress" and "no immediate threat to her person." Instead, the relative safety of the conversation between the declarant and the officer made it "formal enough" to qualify as a "testimonial" statement intended as evidence of the past crime [Id.].

(c) The Supreme Court later noted that the "primary purpose of the interrogation" standard requires "a combined inquiry that accounts for both the declarant and the interrogator" and set forth a range of factors that may be used to determine the existence of an ongoing emergency, including [Michigan v. Bryant, 562 U.S. 344 (2011)]:

1) the nature of the dispute;
2) the scope of the potential harm to the victim;
3) the threat to additional identifiable victims;
4) the existence of a more generalized threat to the public;
5) the suspect's choice of weapon; and
6) whether the suspect remains "at large" or had been located (but not yet apprehended) by the police and/or any other first responders.

(d) In making this determination, the Court has emphasized that "the question is whether, in light of all the circumstances, viewed objectively, the 'primary purpose' of the conversation was to 'creat[e] an out-of-court substitute for trial testimony'" [Ohio v. Clark, 576 U.S. 237 (2015)].

5. **Hearsay within Hearsay**

a. Where one out-of-court statement offered for its truth contains another such out-of-court statement ("double hearsay"), each layer of hearsay must be examined separately and a hearsay exception found. Justification for admissibility of each statement is required; otherwise, the entire statement is inadmissible [Fed. R. Evid. 805].

EXAMPLE: The custodian of a business record could introduce into evidence an entry made by her employer recording a statement made to him by the defendant, which said, "The goods I sold you were not up to our usual quality." The entry itself would be a business record and the statement included therein would be an admission.

6. **Attacking and Supporting the Declarant's Credibility**

a. When a hearsay statement—or a statement defined in Rule 801(d)(2)(C), (D), or (E)—has been admitted in evidence, the declarant's credibility may be attacked, and then supported, by any evidence that would be admissible for those purposes if the declarant had testified as a witness [Fed. R. Evid. 806].

b. The court may admit evidence of the declarant's inconsistent statement or conduct, regardless of when it occurred or whether the declarant had an opportunity to explain or deny it [Id.].

c. If the party against whom the statement was admitted calls the declarant as a witness, the party may examine the declarant on the statement as if on cross-examination [Id.].

7. **Residual Exception**

a. Under the following circumstances, a hearsay statement is not excluded by the rule against hearsay even if the statement is not specifically covered by a hearsay exception in Rule 803 or 804 [Fed. R. Evid. 807(a)]:

(1) the statement has equivalent circumstantial guarantees of trustworthiness;

(2) it is offered as evidence of a material fact;

(3) it is more probative on the point for which it is offered than any other evidence that the proponent can obtain through reasonable efforts; and

(4) admitting it will best serve the purposes of the Federal Rules of Evidence and the interests of justice.

b. The statement is admissible only if, before the trial or hearing, the proponent gives an adverse party reasonable notice of the intent to offer the statement and its particulars, including the declarant's name and address, so that the party has a fair opportunity to meet it [Fed. R. Evid. 807(b)].

IX. AUTHENTICATION AND IDENTIFICATION

A. Authenticating or Identifying Evidence

1. To satisfy the requirement of authenticating or identifying an item of evidence, the proponent must procure evidence sufficient to support a finding that the item is what the proponent claims it is [Fed. R. Evid. 901(a)].
2. All evidence, whether direct or circumstantial, may be classified as either testimonial or tangible.
   a. Tangible evidence is of three types:
      (1) real evidence;
         (a) **Documentary evidence** includes writings such as letters, contracts, books, newspapers, motion pictures, tape recordings, X-rays, photographs, ancient writings, computer printouts, "self-authenticating" documents, and handwriting specimens.
         (b) Voice samples including voice identifications and telephone conversations.
         (c) Physical objects include such items as weapons, drugs, and clothing.
         (d) Such displays as the in-court exhibition of a body part or physical disability (i.e., a limp), a view of the scene by the jury, or a comparison of physical characteristics in a paternity case are also classified as real evidence.
      (2) demonstrative evidence; or
         (a) **Demonstrative evidence** is a term of art given to certain types of evidence whose relevance depends on its ability to explain or simulate material facts in the case. Maps, charts, diagrams, and scale models are common examples of visual aids included in this category.
            1) Although demonstrative evidence requires a testimonial foundation to establish admissibility, it is generally used only for explanatory purposes and is generally not offered as substantive evidence.
      (3) scientific evidence.
         (a) Scientific tests and experiments include such evidence as psychiatric testing, chemical analyses, blood tests, ballistics and forensic analyses, radar, voiceprints, and fingerprinting.
            1) Scientific tests require minimum foundational safeguards of reliability. Proffered experiments and theories must be recognized and accepted in the given scientific field, test conditions must show substantial similarity to the conditions at issue, and the person performing the experiments must be qualified and attest to the proper working order of any equipment used.

NOTE Polygraph tests are generally inadmissible (but some jurisdictions allow the use of polygraphs upon written stipulation, subject to judicial discretion and limiting instructions).

3. After the relevancy of a given piece of non-testimonial evidence is determined, it must be authenticated prior to being admitted into evidence. **Authentication** is accomplished by laying a foundation of preliminary evidence sufficient to sustain a finding that the matter is what it purports to be [Fed. R. Evid. 901, cmt.].
   a. In addition to direct identification or testimony to authenticate a writing, circumstantial evidence is also admissible [Id.].

      EXAMPLE: Where X mails a letter to Y and Y then sends a reply letter back to X in which he makes reference to X's letter, sufficient circumstantial evidence has been established to authenticate Y's reply letter as having been written by him (this is known as the "reply letter" doctrine).
4. Physical objects may be authenticated:
   a. by testimony of personal knowledge showing familiarity with the object;

      EXAMPLE: A police officer's testimony that the gun offered in evidence is the same one she saw at the scene of the crime.
   b. by distinctive markings or characteristics; or
   c. by chain of custody.
      (1) Where an object, such as a bullet, can easily be confused with another object, a strict method of authentication is used whereby testimonial evidence must account for the whereabouts of the object from the time at issue until trial.
5. A writing that has been in existence for a number of years will frequently be difficult to authenticate by direct evidence. Where the maker of an instrument, or those persons who witnessed the making, or even those familiar with the maker's handwriting, have died or become unavailable, the need to resort to authentication by circumstantial evidence is apparent. The frequent necessity of authenticating ancient writings by circumstantial evidence has thus given rise to the **ancient document rule**.
   a. Under this rule, a document or data compilation is sufficiently authenticated as an ancient document if the party who offers it satisfies the judge that the evidence is [Fed. R. Evid. 901(b)(8)]:
      (1) is in a condition that creates no suspicion about its authenticity;
      (2) was in a place where, if authentic, it would likely be; and
      (3) is at least 20 years old when offered (30 years old under common law).
6. The following are examples only—and not a complete list—of evidence that satisfies the requirement [Fed. R. Evid. 901(b)]:
   a. the testimony of a witness with knowledge that an item is what it is claimed to be;

b. a non-expert's opinion that handwriting is genuine, based on a familiarity with it that was not acquired for the current litigation;

c. a comparison with an authenticated specimen by an expert witness or the trier of fact;

d. the appearance, contents, substance, internal patterns, or other distinctive characteristics of the item, taken together with all the circumstances;

e. an opinion identifying a person's voice—whether heard firsthand or through mechanical or electronic transmission or recording—based on hearing the voice at any time under circumstances that connect it with the alleged speaker;

f. for a telephone conversation, evidence that a call was made to the number assigned at the time to:

(1) a particular person, if circumstances, including self-identification, show that the person answering was the one called; or

(2) a particular business, if the call was made to a business and the call related to business reasonably transacted over the telephone;

g. evidence that:

(1) a document was recorded or filed in a public office as authorized by law; or

(2) a purported public record or statement is from the office where items of this kind are kept;

h. evidence describing a process or system and showing that it produces an accurate result; or

i. any method of authentication or identification provided by act of Congress or other rules prescribed by the Supreme Court pursuant to statutory authority.

B. Self-Authenticating Evidence

1. The following items of evidence are self-authenticating; they require no extrinsic evidence of authenticity in order to be admitted [Fed. R. Evid. 902]:

a. a document that bears [Fed. R. Evid. 902(1)]:

(1) a seal purporting to be that of the United States, or of any state, district, commonwealth, territory, or insular possession thereof; and

(2) a signature purporting to be an execution or attestation;

b. a document that bears no seal if [Fed. R. Evid. 902(2)]:

(1) it bears the signature of an officer or employee of an entity named in Rule 902(1)(A); and

(2) another public officer who has a seal and official duties within that same entity certifies under seal—or its equivalent—that the signer has the official capacity and that the signature is genuine;

c. a document purporting to be signed or attested by a person who is authorized by a foreign country to do so [Fed. R. Evid. 902(3)];

(1) The document must be accompanied by a final certification that certifies the genuineness of the signature and official position of

the signer or attester—or of any foreign official whose certificate of genuineness relates to the signature or attestation or is in a chain of certificates of genuineness relating to the signature or attestation [Id.].

(2) If all parties have been given a reasonable opportunity to investigate the document's authenticity and accuracy, the court may, for good cause, either [Id.]:

(a) order that it be treated as presumptively authentic without final certification; or

(b) allow it to be evidenced by an attested summary with or without final certification.

d. a copy of an official record—or a copy of a document that was recorded or filed in a public office as authorized by law—if the copy is certified as correct by [Fed. R. Evid. 902(4)]:

(1) the custodian or another person authorized to make the certification; or

(2) a certificate that complies with Rule 902(1), (2), or (3), a federal statute, or a rule prescribed by the Supreme Court;

e. a book, pamphlet, or other publication purporting to be issued by a public authority [Fed. R. Evid. 902(5)];

f. printed material purporting to be a newspaper or periodical [Fed. R. Evid. 902(6)];

g. an inscription, sign, tag, or label purporting to have been affixed in the course of business and indicating origin, ownership, or control [Fed. R. Evid. 902(7)];

h. a document accompanied by a certificate of acknowledgment executed that is lawfully executed by a notary public or another officer who is authorized to take acknowledgments [Fed. R. Evid. 902(8)];

i. commercial paper, a signature on it, and related documents, to the extent allowed by general commercial law [Fed. R. Evid. 902(9)];

j. a signature, document, or anything else that a federal statute declares to be presumptively or *prima facie* genuine or authentic [Fed. R. Evid. 902(10)];

k. the original or a copy of a domestic record that meets the requirements of Rules 803(6)(A)-(C), as shown by a certification of the custodian or another qualified person that complies with a federal statute or a rule prescribed by the Supreme Court [Fed. R. Evid. 902(11)];

(1) Before the trial or hearing, the proponent must give an adverse party reasonable notice of the intent to offer the record—and must make the record and certification available for inspection—so that the party has a fair opportunity to challenge them [Id.].

l. in a civil case, the original or a copy of a foreign record that meets the requirements of Rule 902(11), except that the certification, rather than complying with a federal statute or Supreme Court rule, must be signed in a manner that, if falsely made, would subject the maker to a criminal penalty in the country where the certification is signed [Fed. R. Evid. 902(12)];

(1) The proponent must also meet the notice requirements of Rule 902(11) [Id.].

m. a record generated by an electronic process or system that produces an accurate result, as shown by a certification of a qualified person that complies with the certification requirements of Rule 902(11) or (12), and the proponent also meets the notice requirements of Rule 902(11) [Fed. R. Evid. 902(13)]; or

   (1) There is no intent to require, or permit, a certification under this Rule to prove the requirements of Rule 903(6). This rule is solely limited to authentication, and any attempt to satisfy a hearsay exception must be made independently [Fed. R. Evid. 902, Notes].

n. data copied from an electronic device, storage medium, or file, if authenticated by a process of digital identification, as shown by a certification of a qualified person that complies with the certification requirements of Rule 902(11) or (12), and the proponent meets the notice requirements of Rule 902(11) [Fed R. Evid. 902(14)].

C. Subscribing Witness's Testimony

1. A subscribing witness's testimony is necessary to authenticate a writing only if required by the law of the jurisdiction that governs its validity [Fed. R. Evid. 903].

X. CONTENTS OF WRITINGS, RECORDINGS, AND PHOTOGRAPHS

A. Definitions

1. A **writing** consists of letters, words, numbers, or their equivalent set down in any form [Fed. R. Evid. 1001(a)].
2. A **recording** consists of letters, words, numbers, or their equivalent recorded in any manner [Fed. R. Evid. 1001(b)].
3. A **photograph** means a photographic image or its equivalent stored in any form [Fed. R. Evid. 1001(c)].
4. An **original** of a writing or recording means the writing or recording itself or any counterpart intended to have the same effect by the person who executed or issued it [Fed. R. Evid. 1001(d)].
   a. For electronically stored information, "original" means any printout—or other output readable by sight—if it accurately reflects the information [Id.].
   b. An "original" of a photograph includes the negative or a print from it [Id.].
5. A duplicate means a counterpart produced by a mechanical, photographic, chemical, electronic, or other equivalent process or technique that accurately reproduces the original [Fed. R. Evid. 1001(e)].

B. Requirement of the Original

1. An original writing, recording, or photograph is required in order to prove its content unless the Federal Rules of Evidence or a federal statute provides otherwise [Fed. R. Evid. 1002].
2. The **best evidence rule** applies only where the contents of a writing are at issue.
   a. When a witness without personal knowledge introduces the contents of a document into evidence as proof of what it says, the best evidence rule applies.

      EXAMPLE: A receipt to prove payment; a transcript to prove testimony at a former trial.

   b. The best evidence rule also applies in situations where the content of a writing directly affects legal rights that are at issue in the case.

      EXAMPLE: Defamatory writings and recordings, a book, photograph, or film in an obscenity or pornography action, or a contract, will, or deed where the document is the subject of the lawsuit.

   c. If the witness's testimony is reliant on the writing (the testimony is derived from the writing itself, not from personal knowledge), the best evidence rule applies.

      EXAMPLE: Testimony based on the findings of an x-ray, microscope slide, letter, recording, or other document.

NOTE The underlying writing itself is usually hearsay, and will be inadmissible unless it comes within an exception.

d. When first-hand testimony, rather than the record of the event, is used to prove the content of the record, the best evidence rule does not apply. This result follows where the event (i.e., the examination) is in issue, not the record of it (i.e., the report). But if the plaintiff seeks to introduce the findings of a medical report, and does not have first-hand knowledge, then the best evidence rule applies [Fed. R. Evid. 1002, cmt.].

EXAMPLE: A buyer of goods may testify that he paid for them without producing a receipt to that effect.

EXAMPLE: A mother who gave birth may testify to that fact without showing a birth certificate for her child.

EXAMPLE: A doctor who performed an examination may testify as to his findings without producing the medical report.

e. Physical objects—including the inscription on a tombstone—are not within the best evidence rule, unless the item can easily be brought into court and the exact wording is necessary to the case.

f. Additionally, secondary evidence of a writing is allowed where the fact at issue is not material to the litigation [Fed. R. Evid. 1004(d)].

C. Admissibility of Duplicates

1. A duplicate is admissible to the same extent as an original unless [Fed. R. Evid. 1003]:
   a. a genuine question is raised about the original's authenticity; or
   b. the circumstances make it unfair to admit the duplicate.

   EXAMPLE: A duplicate of a property deed may be inadmissible where the copy is missing key information necessary to the current litigation.

2. Under common law, photocopies (unless made in compliance with the business records exception) were not treated as originals.

NOTE The Federal Rules do not include a document hand-copied from an original as a duplicate.

D. Admissibility of Other Evidence of Content

1. An original is not required and other evidence of the content of a writing, recording, or photograph is admissible if [Fed. R. Evid. 1004]:
   a. all the originals are lost or destroyed, and not by the proponent acting in bad faith;
   b. an original cannot be obtained by any available judicial process;
   c. the party against whom the original would be offered:
      (1) had control of the original;
      (2) was at that time put on notice, by pleadings or otherwise, that the original would be a subject of proof at the trial or hearing; and
      (3) fails to produce it at the trial or hearing; or

   d. the writing, recording, or photograph is not closely related to a controlling issue.

2. Where the original is unavailable under Rule 1004, the Federal Rules allow any form of secondary evidence (even oral testimony) [Fed. R. Evid. 1004, cmt.]. Under common law, a copy of the original was the preferred form of secondary evidence; however, where the writing is a public record or official document, the Federal Rules require a certified copy.

E. Copies of Public Records to Prove Content

1. The proponent may use a copy to prove the content of an official record—or of a document that was recorded or filed in a public office as authorized by law—if the following conditions are met [Fed. R. Evid. 1005]:
   a. the record or document is otherwise admissible; and
   b. the copy is certified as correct in accordance with Rule 902(4) or is testified to be correct by a witness who has compared it with the original.
2. If no such copy can be obtained by reasonable diligence, then the proponent may use other evidence to prove the content [Id.].

F. Summaries to Prove Content

1. The proponent may use a summary, chart, or calculation to prove the content of voluminous writings, recordings, or photographs that cannot be conveniently examined in court [Fed. R. Evid. 1006].
2. The proponent must make the originals or duplicates available for examination or copying, or both, by other parties at a reasonable time and place. Additionally, the court may order the proponent to produce them in court [Id.].

G. Testimony or Statement of a Party to Prove Content

1. The proponent may prove the content of a writing, recording, or photograph by the testimony, deposition, or written statement of the party against whom the evidence is offered. The proponent need not account for the original [Fed. R. Evid. 1007].

H. Functions of the Court and Jury

1. Ordinarily, the court determines whether the proponent has fulfilled the factual conditions for admitting other evidence of the content of a writing, recording, or photograph under Rule 1004 or Rule 1005. However, in a jury trial, the jury determines—in accordance with Rule 104(b) regarding preliminary questions—any issue about whether [Fed. R. Evid. 1008]:
   a. an asserted writing, recording, or photograph ever existed;
   b. another one produced at the trial or hearing is the original; or
   c. other evidence of content accurately reflects the content.

KAPLAN BAR REVIEW

Real Property

TABLE OF CONTENTS

I. OWNERSHIP OF REAL PROPERTY

Present Possessory Estates 532
Future Interests 536
Cotenancy 547
Landlord-Tenant 550
Special Problems 562

II. RIGHTS IN LAND

Covenants at Law and Equity 571
Easements, Profits, and Licenses 574
Fixtures 579
Zoning 581
Support Rights 587
Water Rights 587

III. CONTRACTS

Creation and Construction 589
Marketability of Title 592
Equitable Conversion and Risk of Loss 593
Options and Rights of First Refusal 594
Fitness and Suitability 594
Merger 595

IV. MORTGAGES/SECURITY DEVICES

Types of Security Devices 597
Some Security Relationships 600
Transfers by Mortgagor 602
Transfers by Mortgagee 603
Discharge 603
Foreclosure 604

V. TITLES

Adverse Possession 608
Transfer by Deed 611
Transfer by Operation of Law and Will 618
Title Assurance Systems 619
Special Problems 625

I. OWNERSHIP OF REAL PROPERTY

NOTE An estate in land is an interest in real property that is presently or may become possessory.

A. **Present Possessory Estates**

1. A freehold estate gives the owner of the estate title to or a right to hold the property. A non-freehold estate gives mere possession.
2. **Types of Freehold Estates**
   a. **Fee Simple Absolute**
      (1) A **fee simple absolute** is the largest possible estate in land, denoting the aggregate of all possible rights that a person may have in that parcel of land, including:
         (a) the unimpeded right to sell or convey all or part of the property; and
         (b) the unimpeded right to devise the property.

NOTE A fee simple absolute may last in perpetuity. If the owner of a fee simple absolute dies intestate, the property will pass to the owner's heirs by intestacy.

      (2) The following words are traditionally used to create a fee simple absolute: O conveys "to A and his heirs."
         (a) **Words of purchase** describe the persons, called "purchasers," who take an interest under a grant or device. **Words of limitation** describe the nature of the estate taken by the purchasers.

         EXAMPLE: O conveys "to A and her heirs." The words "to A" are words of purchase because they indicate that A takes an interest under the grant from O. The words "and her heirs" are words of limitation because they describe the nature of the estate taken by A—in this case, a fee simple absolute.

         (b) At early common law, the words "to A and his heirs" were required to create a fee simple absolute.
         (c) However, under modern law, a fee simple absolute is generally presumed when the words "to A" are used.
   b. **Defeasible Estates**
      (1) A defeasible estate is an estate that may terminate before its maximum duration has run.
      (2) **Fee Simple Determinable**
         (a) A determinable estate terminates automatically on the happening of a named future event.
         (b) A determinable estate is described with the following words:
            1) for so long as;

2) during;

3) while; or

4) until.

(c) A determinable estate is created:

1) in one clause; and

2) with a limitation built into that one clause.

EXAMPLE: O conveys "to A and her heirs for so long as the premises are used for educational purposes." This creates a determinable estate.

(d) A determinable estate is followed by a possibility of reverter, which may be implied.

(3) **Fee Simple Subject to a Condition Subsequent**

(a) An **estate subject to a condition subsequent** may be cut short if the estate is retaken by the grantor on the happening of a named future event.

1) The condition only gives the grantor the right to take the estate, however. It does not automatically terminate the estate (as distinguished from a determinable estate).

(b) An estate subject to a condition subsequent is described with the following words:

1) provided, however;

2) however if;

3) but if;

4) on condition that; or

5) in the event that.

(c) An estate subject to a condition subsequent is created:

1) in two separate clauses; and

2) with a condition stated in the second clause.

EXAMPLE: O conveys "to A and his heirs, but if the premises are not used for educational purposes, then O has the right to reenter the premises and terminate A's estate." This creates a fee simple subject to a condition subsequent.

EXAMPLE: O conveys "to A for life; provided, however, that if the premises are not used for charitable purposes, O may reenter and retake the premises." This creates a life estate subject to a condition subsequent.

(4) **Fee Simple Subject to Executory Interest**

(a) A **fee simple subject to an executory interest** is an estate that is automatically divested in favor of a third person on the happening of a named event.

EXAMPLE: O conveys "to A for so long as the premises are used for charitable purposes, but if the premises cease to be used for charitable purposes, then to B."

EXAMPLE: O conveys "to A, but if the premises cease to be used for educational purposes, then to B."

1) A fee simple subject to an executory interest is followed by a shifting executory interest.

NOTE This is subject to the Rule Against Perpetuities.

(5) **Fee Tail**

(a) At early common law, a **fee tail** was a freehold estate that descended to the grantee's lineal descendants (children) only.

(b) The following words are used to create a fee tail general: O conveys "to A and the heirs of his body."

1) In a fee tail general, children of the grantee take when the grantee dies.

(c) The following words are used to create a fee tail male or female: O conveys "to A and the heirs [male]/[female] of his body."

1) In a fee tail male or female, descent is limited to the male or female heirs of the grantee.

(d) The following words are used to create a fee tail special: O conveys "to the heirs of his body by his wife B."

1) In a fee tail special, descent is limited to the grantee's descendants by a specific spouse.

(e) The fee tail is followed by a reversion in the grantor or a remainder in a third party. That future interest becomes possessory if and when the grantee's lineal line has failed.

(f) Fee tails are disfavored in modern law. Today, if the words "to A and the heirs of his body" are used:

1) in most states, the grantee gets a fee simple absolute; and

2) in some states, the grantee has a life estate, with a remainder *per stirpes* in the grantee's lineal descendants in being at the time of the life tenant's death.

(6) **Unclear Grants**

(a) If the words of the grant are not clear:

1) a covenant is preferred over a defeasible estate because the award is money damages rather than forfeiture; and

2) a fee simple subject to a condition subsequent is preferred over a fee simple determinable because in the former, forfeiture is not automatic.

c. **Life Estate**

(1) A **life estate** lasts for the duration of the grantee's life.

(2) The following words are used to create a life estate: O conveys "to A for life."

(3) A **life estate *pur autre vie*** is an estate where the duration is measured by the life of someone other than the grantee.

EXAMPLE: O conveys "to A for the life of B." If B predeceases A, A's estate ends at B's death. If A predeceases B, under the modern rule, A's heirs are entitled to the use of the land until B dies.

(4) Life estates can be made defeasible.

(5) **Duty to Repair**

(a) A life tenant has a duty to maintain the property in a reasonable state of repair, ordinary wear and tear excepted. This duty is limited to the extent of the income derived or, if she personally occupies the premises, to the extent of the reasonable rental value of the land.

(b) A tenant for a term of years also has a duty to maintain the property in a reasonable state of repair, ordinary wear and tear excepted. However, this duty is not limited to the extent of income derived or reasonable rental value discussed above. Further, the lessee's duty is now largely governed by statutes that tend to relieve at least the residential lessee of the duty to repair.

(6) **Mortgages**

(a) The life tenant has a duty to pay the interest on a mortgage to the extent of profits derived from the property. A tenant for years or a periodic tenant has no common law duty to make mortgage payments. However, commercial leases often require a nonresidential tenant to pay taxes, mortgages, etc., and to make specific repairs.

(7) **Taxes**

(a) The life tenant must pay all ordinary taxes, to the extent of profits derived from the property. A tenant for years or a periodic tenant has no common law duty to pay property taxes unless:

1) the lease is "perpetual" or for a long term with an option in the tenant and his successors to renew "forever";

2) the tenant holds without any obligation to pay rent; or

3) the tenant has erected improvements on the leased premises for his own benefit.

(8) **Special Assessments**

(a) The life tenant must pay the full cost of special assessments (apparently to the extent of income derived) if the life of the public improvement is less than the duration of the life tenant's estate. Equitable apportionment is applied for improvements likely to last longer (e.g., curbs and streets).

A tenant for years or a periodic tenant has no common law duty to pay carrying charges such as special assessments or insurance premiums.

d. **Non-Freehold Estates**

(1) **Leasehold Estate**

(a) A **leasehold estate** is an estate that is limited in duration.

EXAMPLE: O transfers "to A for a term of 10 years."

(b) Traditionally, the landlord was said to maintain the fee, subject to the leasehold interest.

(c) The modern approach provides that the landlord holds a reversion following the leasehold estate.

B. Future Interests

1. **Reversionary Interest**

a. A **reversion** is a future interest retained by the grantor when the grantor transfers less than a fee interest to a third person.

b. Under the majority rule, a reversion is transferable, devisable, and descendible.

NOTE A reversion is not subject to the Rule Against Perpetuities.

EXAMPLE: O conveys "to A for life, then to B for life, then to C for life." The entire fee simple absolute is not accounted for in this transaction. Therefore, following all of these life estates, O has a reversion.

EXAMPLE: O conveys "to A for a term of 10 years." A has an estate for a term of 10 years. O retains a reversion.

EXAMPLE: O conveys "to A for life." O retains a reversion. If O conveys her reversion to C, C's interest is still defined as a reversion, even though it is now in a third party.

EXAMPLE: T devises "Blackacre to A for life." When T dies, A gets a present possessory life estate. T's reversion passes by the terms of his will or to T's heirs by the laws of intestacy if there is no will.

EXAMPLE: T devises Blackacre "to A for life," and T also devises "the rest and residue of my estate to B." When T dies, A gets a present possessory life estate. B gets the residue of T's estate, which includes the reversion to Blackacre.

2. **Remainders**

a. A **remainder** is a future interest created in a third person that is intended to take effect after the natural termination of the preceding estate.

b. **Contingent Remainders**

(1) A remainder will be contingent if:

(a) the takers are unascertained; or

(b) the interest is subject to a condition precedent and, therefore, does not fall in automatically on the natural termination of the previous estate.

(2) At strict common law, a contingent remainder could descend and be devised but could not be transferred *inter vivos*.

(3) Under modern law, a contingent remainder is transferable, descendible, and devisable (except, possibly, when the contingent remainder is in an unascertained person).

(4) A contingent remainder is subject to the Rule Against Perpetuities.

EXAMPLE: T devises "to A for life, remainder to A's widow and her heirs." If A is living at the time of creation, whether married or unmarried, A has a life estate and A's widow (if any) has a contingent remainder in fee simple because the taker is not yet ascertained or ascertainable. Therefore, T's estate retains a reversion.

EXAMPLE: O conveys "to A for life, remainder to B and her heirs if B reaches 21." If, at the time of creation, B is already 21, A has a life estate and B has a vested remainder in fee simple. If instead, at the time of creation, B is not yet 21, A has a life estate and B's remainder is contingent because B has not yet fulfilled the condition precedent, which is B reaching 21. Therefore, O retains a reversion.

(5) **Doctrine of Destructibility of Contingent Remainders**

(a) At common law, a contingent remainder in real property is destroyed by any of the following:

1) if it fails to vest by the natural termination of the prior vested estate;

EXAMPLE: O conveys "to A for life, remainder to B and her heirs if B reaches 21." A has a life estate. If B is not yet 21, B has a contingent remainder (contingent on B reaching 21), and O retains a reversion. Assume that A dies and B is not yet 21. B's contingent remainder cannot fall in naturally at the termination of A's life estate because B has not yet met the condition precedent to vesting. B's contingent remainder is destroyed. Therefore, O's reversion will become possessory.

2) the **doctrine of merger**; or

a) Merger occurs, and the holder of the present and future interest takes a fee simple absolute, when one party who possesses a present or future interest in the subject realty, by subsequent transactions, obtains all outstanding present and vested estates in that property. Situations in which this may occur include:

i) by surrender of the present estate to the owner of a future estate;

ii) by release of a future estate to the owner of a present estate; or

iii) when all holders of present and future vested interests convey all of these interests to a third party.

EXAMPLE: O conveys "to A for life, remainder to B if B earns a law degree." A has a life estate. If B has not yet earned a law degree, B has a contingent remainder in fee simple absolute. O retains a reversion. Assume that, one year later, O conveys her reversion to A, and B still has not earned a law degree. A now has both a life estate and a reversion. At common law, A's two interests merge because they are not separated by a vested estate. A gets a fee simple absolute. B's contingent remainder is destroyed.

EXAMPLE: O conveys "to A for life, remainder to B's first-born daughter." A has a life estate. If B does not yet have a daughter, B's unborn daughter has a contingent remainder. O retains a reversion. Assume that O later devises his reversion to A and that B still does not have a daughter at the time of O's death. At O's death, A receives O's reversion. A also has her life estate. A's two interests merge because they are not separated by a vested estate. A gets a fee simple absolute, and B's first-born daughter's contingent remainder is destroyed.

3) if the holder of the present possessory estate surrenders his interest before the contingent remainder vests.

EXAMPLE: T devises "to A for life, remainder to B's widower." Assume that T's will creates this devise but does not expressly dispose of the reversion. However, T's will leaves the residue of T's estate to A. Assume further that, at the time the will takes effect (when T dies), B is alive and married. At T's death, A has a life estate and a reversion. B's widower has a contingent remainder because a person cannot have a widower until she dies. B's widower's contingent remainder is not destroyed by merger because A's interests were created at the same time and by the same instrument.

EXAMPLE: Assume that one year after T dies, A conveys her life estate and the reversion to C. C gets a life estate and a reversion. The life estate and the reversion merge. C gets a fee simple absolute. B's widower's contingent remainder is destroyed.

(6) Under modern law, many jurisdictions have abolished the rule of destructibility of contingent remainders. In those jurisdictions, if a contingent remainder has not vested at the natural termination of the prior vested estate, the contingent remainder will become an executory interest, subject to the Rule Against Perpetuities.

(7) In jurisdictions that have retained the destructibility rule, it is important to distinguish between contingent remainders, which are destructible, and executory interests, which are not destructible. If a future interest is created such that it may in some case fall in automatically at the natural termination of the previous estate, an irrebuttable presumption will arise, causing the interest to be treated for all purposes as a contingent remainder.

EXAMPLE: O conveys "to A for life, remainder to B and his heirs if B reaches 21." A has a life estate. If B is not yet 21 at the time of creation, B may not be ready to take when A dies. However, B could possibly turn 21 before A dies. Therefore, B's interest is treated as a contingent remainder rather than an executory interest and thus may be destroyed in states in which contingent remainders are still destructible.

EXAMPLE: O conveys "to A for so long as liquor is not served on the premises, but if liquor is served on the premises then to B and her heirs." A has a fee simple subject to an executory limitation. B will take only if A's estate is cut short by the service of liquor on the premises. Thus, B cannot possibly take at the natural termination of A's estate. Therefore, B has a shifting executory interest rather than a contingent remainder.

c. **Vested Remainders**

(1) A **vested remainder** requires its takers to be ascertained or ascertainable at the time that the remainder is created. A vested remainder also must fall in automatically at the natural termination of the previous estate, meaning there can be no conditions precedent to taking.

(2) A vested remainder is transferable, descendible, and devisable.

(3) A fully vested remainder is not subject to the Rule Against Perpetuities. However, a remainder that is vested subject to open is subject to the Rule Against Perpetuities.

EXAMPLE: Testator devises "to A for life, remainder to B and his heirs." A has a life estate. B has a vested remainder in fee simple because the taker is identified, and B's interest falls in automatically at the natural termination of the previous estate (when A dies).

EXAMPLE: O conveys "to A for life, remainder to B for life, remainder to C and her heirs." A has a life estate, B has a vested remainder for life, and C has a vested remainder in fee simple.

(4) **Special Types of Vested Remainders**

(a) A remainder that is **vested subject to open**, sometimes called **vested subject to partial divestment**, is a remainder that:

1) has been made to a class (e.g., "my children"); and
2) has at least one member who is ascertainable and who has satisfied any conditions precedent to vesting, but may have other members join the class later.

EXAMPLE: T devises "to A for life, remainder to A's children and their heirs." Assume that at the time of creation (T's death), A is living and has one child, B. A has a present possessory life estate and B has a vested remainder subject to open, because A could have more children. T retains nothing.

EXAMPLE: Assume further that one year later, a second child, C, is born to A. A has a life estate, B and C together have a vested remainder subject to open, and T retains nothing.

(b) A **vested remainder subject to total divestment** is presently vested but may be terminated on the happening of a future event.

EXAMPLE: O conveys "to A for life, remainder to B for so long as the premises are used for educational purposes." A has a life estate, and B has a vested remainder subject to total divestment. O retains a possibility of reverter.

3. **Executory Interests**

a. An **executory interest** is a future interest in a third person that cuts short the previous estate before it would have naturally terminated.

(1) Since a fee estate has the potential to last forever, any interest created in a third party that follows the granting of a fee will always be an executory interest.

(2) There are two types of executory interests.

(a) A **shifting executory interest** is an interest that cuts short a prior estate created by the same conveyance. The interest passes from one grantee to another.

(b) A **springing executory interest** is an interest that follows a gap in possession or divests the estate of the transferor. The interest passes from a grantor to a grantee.

b. An executory interest is transferable, descendible, and devisable.

c. An executory interest is subject to the Rule Against Perpetuities.

EXAMPLE: O conveys "to A, but if liquor is served on the premises, then to B and his heirs." A has a fee simple subject to an executory limitation. B has a shifting executory interest because his interest may cut short A's estate.

EXAMPLE: O conveys "to A for life, remainder to B and her heirs one month after A's death." A has a life estate. B has a springing executory interest because her interest cannot become presently possessory until one month after the natural termination of A's life estate. O retains a reversion. After A's death, O's reversion becomes possessory. Then, one month after A's death, the fee simple springs out of O to B.

4. **Possibility of Reverter and Powers of Termination**

a. **Possibility of Reverter**

(1) A **possibility of reverter** is a future interest in the grantor that follows a determinable estate.

(2) The creation of a fee simple determinable estate automatically creates the possibility of reverter in the grantor.

(3) At strict common law, a possibility of reverter could descend through intestacy but could not be devised or transferred *inter vivos*.

(4) Today, under the modern trend, a possibility of reverter is transferable, devisable, and descendible (it can be transferred by law, will, or intestacy).

(5) The statute of limitations begins to run on a possibility of reverter as soon as the limitation occurs, because the property automatically reverts to the grantor on the occurrence of the limitation.

(6) A possibility of reverter is not subject to the Rule Against Perpetuities.

EXAMPLE: O conveys "to A and her heirs for so long as liquor is not served on the premises." A has a fee simple determinable. O has a possibility of reverter, which becomes possessory automatically if liquor is served. If O then conveys her possibility of reverter to C, C's interest is still defined as a possibility of reverter, even though it is now in a third party.

b. **Power of Termination**

(1) A **power of termination** (formerly called a "right of re-entry") is a future interest in the grantor that follows a fee simple or life estate subject to a condition subsequent.

(2) The creation of the power of termination requires a grantor to reserve this right in the conveyance either expressly or by necessary implication.

(a) While there is no definitive rule on this point, courts tend to show a constructional preference against finding a defeasible estate where the language is ambiguous.

(b) As a result, where the language is ambiguous or doubtful, courts generally treat a provision in a deed as a covenant, and not a condition subsequent.

(3) Upon the happening of the event, the property will not automatically revert back to the grantor. The grantor has to exercise the power of termination through an affirmative action to retake the property.

(4) At strict common law, a power of termination could descend through intestacy but could not be devised or transferred *inter vivos*.

(5) Today, under modern law, all states agree that a power of termination is descendible, and a majority of states agree that a power of termination is devisable, but the majority rule is that a power of termination is not transferable *inter vivos*.

(6) The statute of limitations does not begin to run against a power of termination until the grantor attempts to exercise the right. However, in some states, the statute of limitations begins to run against a power of termination when the condition occurs.

(7) A power of termination is not subject to the Rule Against Perpetuities.

EXAMPLE: O conveys "to A and his heirs, but if liquor is served on the premises, then O and his heirs may reenter and terminate A's estate." A has a fee simple subject to a condition subsequent, and O has a power of termination. If liquor is served, O must take affirmative steps before A's estate is terminated. If O transfers his power of termination to C, C's interest is still defined as a power of termination, even though it is now in a third party.

EXAMPLE: O conveys "to A; provided, however, that liquor may not be served on the premises." No power of termination has been reserved. Therefore, O cannot take the property back if liquor is served on the premises. The condition subsequent language will be stricken. Therefore, A is left with a fee simple absolute.

5. **Rules Affecting These Interests**

a. **Rule in Shelley's Case**

(1) Also known as the rule against remainders in grantee's heirs, the Rule in Shelley's Case arises in grants such as the following: O conveys "to A for life, remainder to the heirs of A."

(2) The requirements for applicability of the Rule in Shelley's Case are:

(a) A must get a freehold estate (a life estate or a fee tail);

(b) A's heirs must get a remainder in fee (or in tail);

(c) the same instrument must create both A's and A's heirs' interests; and

(d) both estates must be legal or both must be equitable.

(3) If all of these requirements are met:

(a) A gets both a life estate and a remainder; and

(b) by merger, A gets a fee simple and thus A's heirs take nothing by virtue of the grant itself.

(4) The Rule in Shelley's Case is a rule of law, which the court must treat as creating an irrebuttable presumption.

(5) The Rule in Shelley's Case has been abolished by statute or judicial decision in most states.

b. **Doctrine of Worthier Title**

(1) Also known as the rule against remainders in grantor's heirs, the Doctrine of Worthier Title arises in grants such as the following: O conveys "to A for life, remainder to the heirs of O."

(2) The requirements for applicability of the Doctrine of Worthier Title are:

(a) A must receive an estate less than a fee simple, such as a life estate or a term of years;

(b) O's heirs must receive a remainder (or an executory interest, in the rare case);

(c) both interests must be created by the same instrument; and

(d) both interests must be legal or both must be equitable.

(3) The Doctrine of Worthier Title is a rule of construction, not law. The language leaving a remainder to O's heirs creates a rebuttable presumption that O intended to retain that interest in himself as a reversion. This presumption may be rebutted by clear express evidence that O did intend to create a remainder in his heirs. If the presumption is raised but not rebutted, A gets a life estate and O retains a reversion (and thus O's heirs take nothing on their own).

(4) Under modern law, the Doctrine of Worthier Title applies to *inter vivos* transfers only (the testamentary branch of the doctrine no longer is applied).

c. **Rule of Convenience**

(1) Under the Rule of Convenience, a class closes when a member of the class is entitled to distribution.

(2) The Rule of Convenience applies to the following classes: "children," "grandchildren," "brothers," "sisters," "nephews," "nieces," "cousins," "issue," "descendants," or "family" of a designated person.

(a) If the class is already closed at the time the gift takes effect (i.e., the time of conveyance for an *inter vivos* gift or time of testator's death for a will), all members of the class at that moment will take. However, any individual later conceived or born will not be a member of the class and will not share in the estate.

(b) If, at the time the gift takes effect, the class has members entitled to take immediately but the class has not previously closed, all members of the class conceived at the time the gift is made will be included and may take; however, the class will close to the exclusion of afterborn children, who will not share in it.

(c) If the class has no members at the time the gift is made, all members of the class, whenever born, will be included and may take. The class stays open until all possible members are born.

EXAMPLE: T devises "to the children of A." If A is dead at the time of T's death, the class of A's children will be closed; therefore, all of A's children will be included and will take. If A is alive at the time of T's death and has children at that time, the children born at the time of T's death are entitled to immediate distribution. Therefore, the class will close, and all of those children will be included and may take. However, afterborn children will be excluded. If A is alive at T's death but does not have children at that time, no one is entitled to immediate distribution. Therefore, the class should remain open. All of A's children, whenever born, will be included and should be able to take. Some authorities suggest that the first-born child takes the entire estate on her birth, subject to partial divestment by the birth of later children; however, the case law on this point is sparse.

d. **Postponed Gift to a Class** (**with No Condition Precedent**)

(1) If the class is already closed at the time the postponement ends (e.g., at the end of a present possessory life estate), all members of the class will be included and will take.

(2) If the class has members but is not yet closed at the time the postponement ends, all members of the class conceived at the time the postponement ends will be included and may take. However, the class will close to the exclusion of afterborn children, who may not take.

(3) If the class has no members at the time the postponement ends, all members of the class, whenever born, will be included and may take.

EXAMPLE: T devises "to A for life, remainder to the children of B." If B is dead at the time of T's death, the class of B's children will be closed; therefore, all of B's children will be included and may take. If B dies after T but before A, the class of B's children will also be closed; therefore, all of B's children will be included and may take. If B is alive at the time of A's death and B has children at that time, all children then born are included and are entitled to distribution at A's death. However, the class will close at that time to the exclusion of afterborn children. If B is alive at A's death but does not have children at that time, no child is then entitled to immediate distribution. The class should remain open. Therefore, all of B's children, whenever born, should be included and should be able to take. Again, some authorities suggest that the first-born child takes the entire estate on her birth, subject to partial divestment by the birth of later children.

e. **Immediate Gift to a Class Coupled with a Condition Precedent**

(1) An immediate gift to a class may be coupled with a condition precedent. In such a case, the class closes when the first member of the class satisfies the condition.

(2) All then-born members of the class are included and may take if and when they satisfy the condition.

(3) However, afterborn children will be excluded.

EXAMPLE: O conveys "to B's children who reach 21." If B is dead at the time the conveyance is made, the class of B's children will be closed. Therefore, all of B's children will be included and may take if and when they reach 21. If B is alive at the time the conveyance is made, and B has a child who has reached 21, the class will close because that child is entitled to immediate distribution. All of B's then-born children will be included and may take if and when they reach 21; however, all afterborn children will be excluded. If B is alive at the time the conveyance is made, and B has one child who is, say, 15, the class will remain open. The class will close if and when a child of B reaches 21. All children of B born at the time the first child reaches 21 will be included and may take if and when they reach 21. All children born after the first child reaches 21 are excluded. If B is alive at the time the conveyance is made, and B has no children, the class will remain open. The class will close if and when a child of B reaches 21. All children of B born at the time the first child reaches 21 will be included and may take if and when they reach 21. All children born after the first child reaches 21 are excluded.

f. **Gift to a Class with a Combination of Postponements**

(1) A gift to a class may be made with a combination of postponements combined with a condition precedent. In such a case, the postponement is deemed to end, and the class closes when the last condition is satisfied.

(2) All members of the class born before the class closes are included, and they may take if and when they satisfy the condition.

(3) However, all afterborn persons are excluded.

EXAMPLE: O conveys "to A for life, remainder to B's children who reach 21." If B is dead at the time the conveyance is made, the class of B's children will be closed. Therefore, all of B's children will be included and may take if and when they reach 21. If B is alive when the conveyance is made but dies before A, the class of B's children also will be closed. Therefore, all of B's children will be included and may take if and when they reach 21. If B is alive at the time of A's death and B has a child who is 21, that child is entitled to distribution at A's death. Therefore, the class will close at that time. All children born before A's death will be included and may take if and when they reach 21. However, children born after the class closes will be excluded. If B is alive at A's death and either has no children or has children, none of whom has reached 21, no child is entitled to distribution at A's death (which is the first postponement). Therefore, the class remains open until a child of B reaches 21 (which is the second postponement). When a child of B reaches 21, the class closes. All children conceived at the time a child of B reaches 21 will be included and may take if and when they reach 21. However, children born after the class closes are excluded.

g. **Waste**

(1) The possessor of a life estate or a leasehold interest has the right to possess, use, and enjoy the property during the duration of his estate. However, he may not do anything that adversely affects the future interest that follows the life estate. An act that adversely affects the future interest is called **waste**.

(2) **Voluntary waste** is the voluntary commission of an act that has more than a trivial injurious effect on or change in the property. Despite the prohibition on voluntary waste, natural resources may be consumed:

(a) for the repair and maintenance of the property;

(b) with permission of the grantor; or

(c) under the open mines doctrine, which applies to both life tenants and tenants for years.

1) If the grantor was exploiting the natural resources of the mine, it is presumed that the grantee has the right to continue that exploitation.

(3) **Involuntary** or **permissive waste** occurs if the life tenant or leasehold tenant permits the premises to fall into disrepair. Involuntary waste may also occur if the life tenant fails to pay mortgage interest payments, taxes, or the tenant's share of special assessments.

(4) **Ameliorative waste** occurs if an act of a life tenant increases the value of the premises by permanently altering it. Traditionally, ameliorative waste was prohibited. However, under modern law, a life tenant is allowed to commit ameliorative waste if:

(a) the market value of the remainderman's interest is not impaired; and

(b) either:

1) it is permitted by the remainderman; or

2) a substantial and permanent change in the neighborhood has deprived the property of a reasonable current value.

(c) A holder of a reversion has standing to sue for past or future waste. A vested remainderman also has standing to sue for past or future waste. However, a contingent remainderman has standing to sue to prevent future waste but not for damages for past waste.

C. Cotenancy

1. A concurrent estate exists when two or more persons share concurrently an interest in real property. A concurrent owner is called a co-tenant.
2. **Tenancy in Common**
    a. Tenancy in common is a form of concurrent ownership where each co-tenant owns an undivided interest in the whole of the property with no right of survivorship.
    b. Tenancy in common is now the presumed form of co-tenancy. Therefore, no special words are required to create a tenancy in common.

    EXAMPLE: O conveys "to A and B." A and B hold a fee simple absolute as tenants in common.

    c. Tenancy in common requires unity of possession only. **Unity of possession** means that each tenant in common has the right to possess the whole of the property.
    d. A tenant in common may transfer his interest *inter vivos*:
        (1) voluntarily, through a conveyance, lease, mortgage, or other transfer of a present possessory or future property interest; or
        (2) involuntarily, through a foreclosure on a mortgage of the tenant's interest or an execution of a judgment creditor's lien on the tenant's interest in the property.
    e. A tenant in common may devise her interest, and the interest of a tenant in common may also descend by intestacy.
3. **Joint Tenancy**
    a. Joint tenancy is a form of concurrent ownership where each co-tenant owns an undivided interest in the whole of the property and has a right of survivorship.
    b. Traditionally, the following words are required to create a joint tenancy: "to A and B as joint tenants and not as tenants in common, with full right of survivorship."
    c. A joint tenancy requires the following four unities:
        (1) joint tenants must take at the same time (**unity of time**);
        (2) joint tenants must take by the same instrument (**unity of title**);
        (3) joint tenants must take equal shares of the same type (e.g., each joint tenant takes a legal fee simple) (**unity of interest**); and
        (4) each joint tenant has the right to possess the whole (**unity of possession**).
    d. Under the traditional rule, a sole owner of property cannot create a joint tenancy between himself and another person by conveying a joint interest directly to the other person. Instead, the owner must convey the property to a straw man, who then conveys the property back to the owner and the other person as joint tenants.
        (1) The majority of jurisdictions now do not require the unities of time and title when a sole owner attempts to convey a joint tenancy to

himself and another person. Instead, a sole owner may create a joint tenancy between himself and another person by conveying a joint interest directly to the other person and himself.

e. Each joint tenant has a right of survivorship. At the death of one joint tenant, the interest of the surviving joint tenant "grows" and absorbs the interest of the deceased joint tenant.

EXAMPLE: O conveys Blackacre "to A and B as joint tenants and not as tenants in common, with full right of survivorship." Subsequently, A dies, leaving C as her sole heir. B's right of survivorship takes over, and B becomes the sole owner of Blackacre. C takes no interest.

f. A joint tenant may transfer his interest voluntarily or involuntarily, thereby severing the joint tenancy. However, the right of survivorship prevents a predeceasing joint tenant from devising his interest. In addition, the interest of the predeceasing joint tenant may not descend by intestacy.

g. A joint tenancy is severed if one joint tenant conveys his interest voluntarily or involuntarily. An involuntary conveyance occurs if a creditor forces a sale of a joint tenant's interest to satisfy the debt owed to the creditor by the joint tenant. If a joint tenancy is severed, the unities of time and title are destroyed. Therefore, a tenancy in common is created between the other tenant and the conveyee.

EXAMPLE: O conveys Blackacre "to A and B as joint tenants and not as tenants in common, with full right of survivorship." Subsequently, A conveys her interest in Blackacre to C. The conveyance to C breaks the unities of time and title because C took by a different instrument and time from B. Therefore, B and C hold Blackacre as tenants in common.

h. If both joint tenants join in a mortgage of the subject property, the mortgage will not affect the joint tenancy. However, if only one of the joint tenants mortgages his interest, the effect of the mortgage on the joint tenancy will depend on whether the jurisdiction follows the title theory or the lien theory of mortgages.

(1) In a **title theory** state, the execution of a mortgage by one joint tenant causes the legal interest of that co-tenant to be transferred to the mortgagee. Thus, the mortgage severs the joint tenancy because the unities have been destroyed. Most jurisdictions no longer follow the title theory.

(2) In a **lien theory** state, the mortgagee only receives a lien on the property. Therefore, no severance occurs when the mortgage is made because the unities remain intact. However, in a lien theory state, foreclosure will sever the joint tenancy. Most jurisdictions now follow the lien theory.

NOTE Jurisdictions are split on whether a lease severs a joint tenancy.

4. **Tenancy by the Entirety**
   a. A tenancy by the entirety is a form of concurrent ownership reserved for married couples, which gives each spouse an undivided interest in the whole of the property and a right of survivorship.
   b. Traditionally, to create a tenancy by the entirety, the following words were required: "to H and W as tenants by the entirety and not as joint tenants or tenants in common, with full right of survivorship."
   c. Today, most states have enacted statutes creating a presumption of tenancy by the entirety if a conveyance is made to a married couple, even if they are not identified as a married couple in the deed.
   d. In the states that recognize tenancy by the entirety, an attempted conveyance by either spouse is wholly void.
      (1) One important aspect of a tenancy by the entirety is that an interest in the property can only be conveyed jointly. Any attempt by only one spouse to unilaterally convey or encumber their interest in the property will be considered void.
      (2) Similarly, a judgment creditor may only execute on property held as a tenancy by the entirety to enforce the judgment if both spouses are joint debtors. Otherwise, the entireties property is immune from process, petition, levy, execution, or sale.
5. **Severance**
   a. A tenancy by the entirety cannot be terminated by the unilateral act of either spouse. The tenancy can only be severed:
      (1) by a joint conveyance of both spouses;
      (2) by a conveyance of one spouse to the other of the property; or
      (3) when the spouses divorce.
   b. A joint tenancy may be severed by the unilateral conveyance of the property by one of the joint tenants during the owner's lifetime.
      (1) However, the right of survivorship prevents the joint tenant from devising the property, or from having it pass through intestacy.
   c. A mortgage will not sever a joint tenancy when created except in a title theory jurisdiction.
      (1) In a lien theory jurisdiction, the creation of a mortgage does not cause a severance of the joint tenancy. If the mortgagor dies before the mortgagee forecloses on the interest, the surviving joint tenant(s) will take the property by right of survivorship and free of the mortgage interest.
      (2) If the mortgagee forecloses on the property before the death of the mortgagor, the foreclosure operates to sever the mortgaged interest from the joint tenancy.
6. **Partition**
   a. Each co-tenant has the right to seek partition of the property.
   b. **Voluntary partition** is usually accomplished by an exchange of mutual deeds among co-tenants or by sale of the property and division of the proceeds.

c. **Involuntary** (judicial) **partition** is accomplished by court action, usually at the instance of one, but not all, of the co-tenants. Involuntary partition may be either in-kind (physical division) or by sale.
   (1) Traditionally, physical partition has been preferred, unless a physical partition would be impractical and the interests of the parties would be better served by a sale and division of the proceeds.
   (2) When partition cannot produce equal shares, the party receiving the larger portion must make a cash payment to the other party.

7. **Rights and Duties of Co-Tenants**
   a. Each co-tenant is entitled to possess the whole property.
   b. Wrongful ouster occurs when one co-tenant wrongfully excludes another co-tenant from possession of the whole or any part of the jointly held property.
   c. An out-of-possession co-tenant has the right to share in rents and net profits derived by another co-tenant from third parties, less operating expenses such as taxes, mortgages, interest, and management fees. However, an out-of-possession co-tenant does not have the right to demand rent from a co-tenant who is in actual possession of the premises, unless the co-tenant in possession has effected a wrongful ouster or has exploited the property in a manner resulting in permanent depreciation.
   d. The common law, which is still followed in some states, does not allow a co-tenant to seek contribution from another co-tenant for repairs performed on the property.
   e. However, under the modern trend, contribution may be compelled for necessary repairs if the repairs were requested by the repairing tenant and refused by the other(s).
   f. In a partition suit or an accounting suit, the costs of repairs may be credited in favor of a co-tenant who repairs.
   g. A co-tenant has no right to seek a contribution or setoff for improvements made to the premises, unless the improvements generate increased rents or profits. In that case, costs of improvements are recoverable only in a partition suit.
   h. A co-tenant who pays a mortgage or tax may seek contribution or may recover in an accounting or partition suit. However, there is no separate action to compel contribution. A co-tenant in sole possession will receive reimbursement only to the extent that his payment exceeds the value of the use and occupation of the property (i.e., the rental value).

D. Landlord-Tenant

NOTE **A lease** gives the tenant (lessee) exclusive possession of the premises for a period of time.

1. **Creation**
   a. A lease may be created expressly, either orally or in writing. A writing generally is required by the Statute of Frauds for a term of more than one year.

b. An implied lease may be created by the conduct of the parties when the written lease is an invalid writing. In such a case, the resulting tenancy will be periodic. An implied lease may also be created when a holdover tenant pays rent and the landlord (lessor) accepts the rent.

2. **Types of Leases**

TYPES OF LEASES
Temporarily **P**ick **A**nother **S**ettlement
Term of Years, **P**eriodic, **A**t-Will, Tenancy at **S**ufferance

a. **Term of Years**

(1) A term of years has a definite beginning and end (e.g., until a set date or for a set number of months or years). No notice is required to terminate a lease for a term of years.

EXAMPLE: L leases to T for a period of one year.

b. **Periodic**

(1) A periodic tenancy has a set beginning date and continues from period to period (e.g., from month to month) without a set termination date, until proper notice is given. While under the common law, notice merely has to be sufficient to show intent, some modern statutes require termination notice to be in writing.

(a) The modern rule is that notice can be oral unless the lease specifically states otherwise.

(2) A periodic tenancy may be created expressly or by implication with a holdover tenant.

(3) Under the traditional common law rule, a periodic tenancy could be terminated only on the anniversary date. Improper notice was deemed ineffective, and the notice period was measured by the rent reservation clause.

(4) Under the modern statutory approach, which is the majority rule, termination may take place on any date, and the notice period is measured by the rent payment clause up to a maximum of six months.

c. **At-Will**

(1) An at-will lease has no fixed duration and lasts only as long as the landlord and tenant desire. An at-will tenancy terminates if:

(a) either party dies;

(b) the tenant commits waste;

(c) the tenant attempts to assign her interest;

(d) the landlord transfers his interest; or

(e) the landlord transfers the premises to a third party for a term of years.

(2) If the lease gives the landlord a unilateral right to terminate, most courts find a tenancy at will that may be terminated by either the landlord or the tenant.

(3) If the lease gives the tenant a unilateral right to terminate, some courts find a tenancy at will that may be terminated by either the landlord or the tenant. However, under the modern view, the tenant receives either a life estate or a fee simple, depending on the language used in the lease.

d. **Tenancy at Sufferance / Holdover Tenancy**

(1) A tenancy at sufferance occurs when a tenant remains in possession of the leased premises ("holds over") after the end of the lease term. A tenancy at sufferance is not a true tenancy. In most states, if a residential tenant holds over, the landlord may recover possession and receive the reasonable rental value for the holdover period.

3. **Possession and Rent**

a. **Tenant's Duties**

(1) **Pay Rent**

(a) A tenant has a duty to pay rent. Under the common law estate theory, the tenant's duty to pay rent was not relieved if the premises were destroyed because the tenant would still have possession of the actual land. There was an exception to this common law rule where the tenant leased only a portion of the building. In that instance, if the building was destroyed, the tenant was then excused from paying rent.

(b) Today, there is no distinction between leasing all or part of a building. The tenant leasing all or a portion of a building may be relieved from the duty to pay rent if the premises are destroyed.

1) An exception to this rule exists where the tenant is not relieved from liability for rent when the tenant intentionally or negligently caused the destruction.

(2) **Waste**

(a) The tenant's duties in respect to waste are similar to those owed by life tenants. However, the tenant's duty not to commit permissive waste (primarily in respect to repairs) is not limited to the extent of income derived from or the reasonable rental value of the property when the tenant possesses personally.

(b) At common law, a tenant (except possibly a tenant for a long term) could not commit ameliorative waste, which a life tenant might be permitted to do.

(c) At modern law, a tenant may commit ameliorative waste if:

1) expressly authorized; or

2) there is a change in circumstances that warrants the improvements to be made (provided that the improvement does not depreciate the value of the property).

(3) **Repair**

(a) Under the common law estate theory, the landlord has no duty to repair the premises during the term of the lease. In contrast, the tenant had a duty not to commit waste, which includes a duty to repair the premises (i.e., not commit permissive waste). This duty extended to minor repairs that keep the building's interior safe from water and wind, but absent a covenant to the contrary, the tenant was not required to rebuild the premises if they were destroyed by an act of God. (Under the estate theory, the landlord also had no duty to rebuild.)

(b) Alternatively, landlords and tenants may also agree on how to allocate repair duties. If a tenant assumes a general duty to repair, then absent a covenant to the contrary the tenant would in such a situation be responsible for repairing the premises from casualties, such as damages caused by fire and storms. The tenant would also be responsible for rebuilding or replacing the premises if they are destroyed by such casualties.

(c) Under the modern contract theory, which is the majority rule, the parties are free to covenant for duties that they would not bear under the common law estate theory.

1) Absent any provision in the lease, the common law rule as to the duty to repair still applies.

2) Under a general covenant to repair, the tenant is required to repair the premises. Usually, this covenant excepts ordinary wear and tear. The covenant may also except damages caused "by act of God," such as fire and weather.

3) If the tenant covenants to repair without exception, the tenant must make all repairs, regardless of how the damage is caused.

4) If there is no covenant in place, the landlord is required to repair damages resulting from casualties.

(d) Under the modern trend, in the absence of a contrary agreement, the tenant is not required to rebuild if the destruction was not his fault.

b. **Landlord's Duties**

(1) The landlord has a duty to **deliver possession** of the premises to the tenant at the start of the lease term.

(a) The majority (English) rule requires delivery of actual possession.

(b) The minority (American) rule requires delivery of the legal right to possession only.

EXAMPLE: L and T execute a valid lease giving T a term of one year. On the date on which the lease commences, T discovers that the previous tenant is still on the premises because she has held over after the expiration of her term. Under the American rule, L has properly delivered possession because L gave T the legal right to the leased premises when L and T executed the lease. However, under the English rule, L has not properly delivered possession. The presence of the old tenant on the premises prevents L from delivering actual possession to T on the date on which the lease commences.

(2) Typically, state law creates certain duties for the landlord, such as the provision of running water and heat.

(3) The lease document may also create certain duties for the landlord, such as the duty to repair within the leased premises.

4. **Assignment and Subletting**

a. **Assignment**

(1) **An assignment** occurs when the tenant transfers to a third person (the assignee) all of his rights, title, and interest in the leased premises. An assignee comes into privity of estate with the landlord.

b. **Sublease**

(1) **A sublease** occurs when the tenant transfers to a third person (the subtenant or sublessee) less than all of his rights, title, and interest in the leased premises. A subtenant does not come into privity of estate with the landlord.

c. **Liability of Parties**

(1) A party may be liable to a landlord through either privity of contract or privity of estate.

(a) Privity of contract is the relationship that exists between the original parties to an agreement. Privity of contract will always exist between the original parties and only those original parties, unless there is a novation.

EXAMPLE: L and T enter into a written five-year lease agreement, with rent to be paid monthly. Because L and T are both signatories to the lease agreement, they are in privity of contract with each other.

(b) Privity of estate arises through the succession in rights to the same property by multiple parties.

1) The landlord, by entering into the lease agreement, is conveying a portion of her rights—specifically, the right to presently possess and use the property for the duration of the lease—to the tenant. In doing so, the parties enter into privity of estate.

2) If the tenant then grants anything less than his full rights and interest in the property to another party (i.e., if the tenant subleases the property, rather than assigning

it), that subsequent party does not enter into privity of estate with the landlord, only with the tenant.

a) This is because the subtenant is not acquiring the portion of the property rights that the landlord conveyed to the tenant, and so is not "stepping into the shoes" of the original tenant.

b) Rather, the subtenant is only acquiring a portion of the tenant's rights, while the tenant retains some right or interest to the property.

c) In this situation, the tenant and subtenant enter into privity of estate, but the subtenant does not enter into privity of estate with the landlord, because there is no direct relationship. The landlord and original tenant will instead remain in privity of estate.

EXAMPLE: L and T enter into a written five-year lease agreement, with rent to be paid monthly. L and T are in privity of estate with each other.

EXAMPLE: Two years into the five year lease agreement, T subleases the property to Sub for a period of one year. T and Sub are in privity of estate with each other, but L and Sub are not. L cannot sue Sub directly for unpaid rent or any other breach of the lease agreement. Instead, L must sue T, who can then sue Sub for breaching the sublease agreement between T and Sub.

(2) Absent a novation, the original tenant always remains liable to the landlord even after an assignment or sublease. This is because the original tenant remains in privity of contract with the landlord.

(a) For the original tenant to be discharged from liability, there must be a novation. This is a separate agreement between the landlord, original tenant, and assignee whereby the landlord agrees to discharge the original contracting party (the original tenant) from contractual liability in exchange for the assignee becoming liable as if he had signed the original lease agreement.

(3) Because an assignee comes into privity of estate with the landlord, if the rent is not paid, the landlord may sue the assignee.

(a) However, the landlord may not sue the assignee after the assignee has transferred the premises to another third person, unless the assignee had assumed the duty to pay rent. This is because, by assigning the premises to someone else, the first assignee is no longer in privity of estate with the landlord. The subsequent assignee is now the party in privity of estate.

EXAMPLE: L and T enter into a five-year lease agreement, with rent to be paid monthly. One year later, T assigns the lease to

T2. If T2 fails to pay rent to L, L can sue either T (through privity of contract) or T2 (through privity of estate) for the unpaid rent.

EXAMPLE: Same facts as above, only this time, six months after being assigned the property, T2 assigns the lease to T3. T3 fails to pay rent. L may sue T (through privity of contract) and T3 (through privity of estate). However, L may not sue T2, because T2 is in neither privity of contract nor privity of estate with L.

EXAMPLE: L and T enter into a five-year lease agreement, with rent to be paid monthly. One year later, T assigns the lease to T2. As part of the assignment, L, T, and T2 agree to a novation of T in favor of T2. T2 fails to pay rent. L may only sue T2, because T2 is now in both privity of contract and privity of estate with L. L may not sue T because the novation discharged T from contractual liability, severing T's privity of contract with L.

EXAMPLE: Same facts as above, except that six months after the assignment and novation, T2 assigns the property to T3. T3 fails to pay rent. L may sue T2 (through privity of contract) or T3 (through privity of estate). L may not sue T, because T is not in privity with L as a result of the novation.

d. **Covenants against Assignments and Subleases**

(1) Covenants against assignments and/or subleases are construed strictly against the landlord.

(2) Under the **Rule in Dumpor's Case**, once waived, a covenant against assignment is unenforceable as to the next assignment.

(a) The Rule in Dumpor's Case does not apply to subleases.

(b) The Rule in Dumpor's Case also does not apply where the landlord specifies that the waiver is "one-time only." In this situation, the covenant will remain against subsequent assignments.

(3) Where the prohibition does not give a standard or condition for the giving or withholding of consent, this is commonly known as a "silent consent" clause.

(4) The traditional rule, which is still the majority rule today, is that a silent consent clause gives a landlord the right to withhold consent for any reason or for no reason at all, even if the withholding of consent is arbitrary and unreasonable. However, this rule is subject to statutory housing discrimination laws.

(5) The minority rule is that silent consent clauses require that the landlord be reasonable in withholding consent for an assignment.

5. **Termination**

a. **Landlord's Remedies for Tenant's Breach of Duty**

(1) If the tenant fails to pay rent or commits another material breach of the lease, the landlord may seek:

(a) to evict the tenant; and/or

(b) to recover damages for the tenant's breach.

(2) Traditionally, acceleration of rent was not available to the landlord for anticipatory breach of a lease by the tenant. However, the modern majority rule permits the use of **rent acceleration clauses** in leases.

(a) In an action for rent, the tenant may defend on the grounds of non-compliance by the landlord or on the ground of destruction of the premises.

(3) A tenant **abandons** the premises if she vacates the premises without intent to return and fails to pay rent. If the tenant abandons the premises, the landlord may:

(a) retake the premises;

(b) ignore an abandonment and continue to hold the tenant liable for rent; or

(c) reenter and relet the premises.

1) Under the traditional common law view, if the tenant abandons the premises, the landlord has no duty to mitigate by attempting to relet the premises. However, under the modern majority view, the landlord has a duty to mitigate if the tenant abandons. If mitigation is required, the burden of proof is placed on the landlord to show that he attempted to mitigate his losses.

2) Where the landlord relets the premises on the tenant's behalf, the landlord is entitled to damages from the tenant based on the difference between what the tenant owed for rent and what the landlord collected from reletting.

(4) At common law, a landlord was allowed to use **self-help** to remove a breaching tenant from the premises. However, under the modern approach, self-help is prohibited or carefully constrained. The landlord must seek court action to reenter the premises.

(5) A security deposit may be retained by a landlord only to the extent necessary to cover actual loss that the deposit was intended to secure (e.g., unpaid rent, damage).

(6) **Retaliatory eviction** (e.g., eviction in response to tenant's complaints about landlord) is prohibited in most states.

b. **Tenant's Remedies for Landlord's Breach of Duty**

(1) A tenant may seek money damages for the landlord's breach of the lease.

(a) At common law, a tenant could vacate the premises and terminate the lease if the tenant had been evicted by the landlord, actually or constructively.

(b) Statutes in many jurisdictions provide the tenant with the following statutory remedies:

1) withholding rent; or

2) repairing the premises and deducting the cost of repair from subsequent rent payments.

(2) A landlord is not liable to the tenant or others on the premises with the consent of the tenant for injuries caused by a condition of the premises, except in the following situations:

(a) an undisclosed dangerous condition exists that is known or should have been known to the landlord but is unknown to the tenant;

(b) a condition exists that is dangerous to persons outside of the premises;

(c) the premises are leased for admission to the public;

(d) parts of land are retained in the landlord's control but are available for use by the tenant;

(e) the landlord has contracted to repair; or

(f) the landlord has been negligent in making repairs.

c. **Anticipatory Repudiation**

(1) When a tenant breaches a lease agreement, the common law rule was that the landlord can only sue for rent as it accrues.

(2) However, under modern law, when the lease is for a tenancy for years and the tenant abandons the property, the landlord may treat this as an anticipatory breach of the entire lease, entitling the landlord to sue immediately for all rent due on the entire agreement (subject to the landlord's duty to mitigate damages).

d. **Security Deposits**

(1) There are three types of security deposits:

(a) where the tenant deposits a sum of money against which the landlord may draw to make up any default or to pay for damages;

1) This type of security deposit requires the landlord to account to the tenant for anything the landlord withdraws from the deposit. At the end of the tenancy, any balance goes to the tenant.

(b) a deposit that will be forfeited if the tenant defaults; and

1) This type of deposit is essentially a liquidated damages clause, and should be treated as such.

(c) a deposit that is denominated as advance rent.

1) This last type is not considered a "true" deposit, but rather, an advance payment of rent. The tenant has the right to have that advance payment attributed toward rent due at the end of the lease.

(2) Today, security deposits are heavily regulated by statutes in most jurisdictions, and vary greatly from one state to another.

e. **Death of Either Party**

(1) In general, a lease will not be terminated by the death of either the landlord or the tenant.

(2) In the absence of a contrary provision, the death of a tenant for years will not terminate the tenancy, and the leasehold will pass as personal property through the tenant's estate.

(a) This may not be the case if, for example, the terms of the lease contain a provision that it terminates upon the death of either party, or the nature of the lease and peculiar qualifications of the tenant make the lease personal to the tenant.

(3) A tenancy at will, however, will be terminated by the death of either party.

(4) If the landlord holds a life estate in the leased property, the lease is considered void upon the death of the landlord.

f. **Sale of the Property by the Landlord**

(1) When a landlord sells the property, there is generally no effect on the tenant, unless the lease provides otherwise, except for the tenant paying rent to the new landlord.

(a) If the lease contains such a term, then the buyer may terminate the lease upon the conclusion of the sale. Otherwise, the buyer "steps into the shoes" of the original landlord as to all contract obligations.

(2) If the buyer purchased the property without any notice of the lease, and qualifies under the jurisdiction's applicable recording statute, they would take the property free of the lease.

(a) Leases are considered encumbrances on the property. If the buyer knows about the lease and purchases the property anyway, they have accepted that encumbrance and are bound to the lease.

(b) On the other hand, if the buyer has no actual notice of the lease, it is not recorded (no constructive notice), and the buyer could not have discovered the leasehold by visiting the property (no inquiry notice), then the buyer would not be bound by the lease, and their purchase (free of the lease) would have higher priority to the property than the tenant would have.

6. **Habitability and Suitability**

a. **Implied Warranty of Habitability**

(1) Under the modern trend, the landlord is deemed to have impliedly warranted that the residential premises are fit for habitation. The **implied warranty of habitability** guarantees that the landlord will deliver and maintain premises that are safe, clean, and fit for human habitation.

(a) To prove that the landlord has breached this warranty, the tenant must show a defect in essential residential facilities.

1) In the majority of jurisdictions, the defect may be patent (obvious) or latent (nonobvious).
2) Some jurisdictions exclude patent defects from the scope of the implied warranty of habitability.

(b) To claim a breach of the implied warranty of habitability, the tenant must:
1) provide the landlord with notice of the defect; and
2) allow the landlord reasonable time to make necessary repairs.

NOTE The implied warranty of habitability applies to residential leases. Commercial leases are not covered by the warranty. The following leases may also be excluded from coverage under the implied warranty of habitability: leases for single-family residences, agricultural leases, long-term leases, and casual leases made by non-merchant landlords.

(2) In some jurisdictions, a housing code violation automatically breaches the implied warranty of habitability. In other jurisdictions, the housing code provides the standard; however, substantial compliance with the code is sufficient so long as habitability is not affected. In some jurisdictions, the standard for the implied warranty is found in the common law, even in the absence of a housing code. In those jurisdictions, a breach of the warranty may be found if the premises are uninhabitable in the view of a reasonable person.

(a) If the landlord breaches the implied warranty of habitability:
1) the tenant is excused from further performance under the lease;
2) the tenant may, but need not, vacate the premises;
3) the tenant may treat the lease as canceled, and the rent is abated;
4) the tenant may seek money damages; and
   a) Some courts use the contract measure of damages for breach of warranty, which is the value of the premises as warranted less the value of the premises as received, and agreed rent is evidence of the rental value.
   b) Other jurisdictions measure damages by finding the difference between the agreed rent and the fair rental value of the premises received.
5) the tenant may seek reformation or other traditional contract or tort remedies.

b. **Covenant of Quiet Enjoyment**

(1) Every lease contains a **covenant of quiet enjoyment** (express or implied). In the covenant of quiet enjoyment, the landlord promises that the tenant will not be disturbed by the

landlord (or someone claiming through the landlord) during her possession of the premises. A tenant may treat the lease as terminated and withhold rent if the covenant of quiet enjoyment has been breached by an actual or constructive eviction.

(a) A tenant may treat the lease as terminated and withhold rent if the landlord or someone claiming through him breaches the covenant of quiet enjoyment by **actual eviction** of the tenant.

1) Under the majority rule, if a tenant is actually evicted from part of the premises by the landlord, the tenant is relieved of all liability for rent, even if the tenant continues to occupy the rest of the premises. However, the Second Restatement of Property rejects the majority rule and calls for a rent abatement only.

2) Under the Second Restatement of Property minority rule, when a tenant is partially evicted by an act of the landlord (or his agent), rent abatement attributable to the portion from which the tenant has been evicted is appropriate.

(b) A tenant may treat the lease as terminated and withhold rent if the landlord breaches the covenant of quiet enjoyment by **constructive eviction** of the tenant. For a constructive eviction to exist:

1) the landlord's act must substantially and permanently interfere with the tenant's use and enjoyment of the premises;

2) the tenant must give the landlord notice of the problem and a reasonable amount of time to repair it; and

3) the tenant must move out.

(c) The following acts by the landlord constitute constructive eviction:

1) withholding something essential to the full enjoyment of the property that is included within the terms of the lease, such as heat; or

2) withholding something required by statute, such as hot and cold running water.

(d) A landlord probably constructively evicts the tenant if he breaches one of the following landlord duties created at common law:

1) making and keeping the premises habitable in a short-term lease of a furnished dwelling;

2) disclosing latent defects existing in the premises, known to the landlord, and undiscoverable by the tenant at the time the lease was made;

3) maintaining common areas used by all tenants;

4) using due care in making promised or volunteered repairs;

5) refraining from making fraudulent misrepresentations concerning the condition of the leased premises; or

6) in some jurisdictions, abetting immoral conduct or abetting nuisances on properties owned by the landlord that may affect the leased premises.

(e) Under the majority rule, if a tenant is constructively evicted from part of the premises, the tenant may receive a rent abatement but is not relieved of all liability for rent.

(f) In some states, if a landlord's breach of the covenant of quiet enjoyment does not constitute actual eviction or is not substantial enough to constitute constructive eviction, the tenant who remains on the premises can seek money damages from the landlord.

CONSTRUCTIVE EVICTION AND BREACH OF IMPLIED WARRANTY OF HABITABILITY			
Theory	**Basis for Cause of Action**	**Effects of Breach on the Lease**	**Remedies Available**
Constructive Eviction (Breach of Covenant of Quiet Enjoyment)	The tenant must show an interference with beneficial use and enjoyment of the premises serious enough to amount to an eviction.	The tenant is excused from further performance under the lease. The tenant must vacate the premises within a reasonable time.	The tenant may treat the lease as canceled. Rent is abated.
Breach of Implied Warranty of Habitability	The tenant must show a patent or latent defect in essential residential facilities.	The tenant is excused from further performance under the lease. The tenant may, but need not, vacate the premises.	The tenant may treat the lease as canceled. Rent is abated. The tenant may seek money damages, reformation, or other traditional contract or tort remedies.

E. Special Problems

1. Rule Against Perpetuities

a. The common law Rule Against Perpetuities provides that "[n]o interest is good unless it must vest, if at all, not later than 21 years after some life-in-being at the creation of the interest."

b. To determine whether an interest violates the common law Rule Against Perpetuities, the following analysis should be applied:

(1) Identify the interests subject to the Rule Against Perpetuities.

(a) Interests which are not subject to the Rule Against Perpetuities include:

1) present possessory estates;

2) charitable trusts;

3) resulting trusts; and
4) interests that are fully vested at the time of creation. The following interests are fully vested:
   a) reversionary interests; and
   b) completely vested remainders.

(b) Interests which are subject to the Rule Against Perpetuities include:
1) options to purchase land not incident to a lease;
2) powers of appointment;
3) rights of first refusal; and
4) interests that are not fully vested at the time of creation, including:
   a) remainders that are subject to open;
   b) contingent remainders; and
   c) executory interests.

(2) Identify the life or lives in being, express or implied by the instrument creating interests. There is no limit on the number of lives in being, as long as they may be identified by or through the creating document. A life-in-being may, but need not, receive an interest in the document that creates the interest. However, to serve as a measuring life, a life-in-being must in some way be connected to the vesting of the interest under scrutiny.

(a) An express life-in-being is a person named in the document that creates the interests under scrutiny. In the grant "O conveys to A for life," O and A are express lives in being.

(b) An implied life-in-being is a person who is not named in, but may be implied from, the document that creates the interests under scrutiny. In the devise "to my grandchildren," the testator's children are implied lives in being.

(c) A class cannot be used as measuring lives unless the class is closed at the time the gifts are created.

(3) Determine whether the interest will vest or fail within 21 years of the life or lives. Under the common law Rule Against Perpetuities, interests are analyzed under the "might have been" rule. Under the "might have been" rule, an interest violates the Rule Against Perpetuities if there is any chance, however remote, that the interest might vest more than 21 years after a life-in-being.

(a) Under the might-have-been rule, interests are scrutinized at the time of creation. The time of creation is the date that the creating instrument takes effect. If the interests under scrutiny are created in a deed, the time of creation is the date that the deed is delivered. If the interests under scrutiny are created in a will, the time of creation is the date of the testator's death.

(4) Treat the part of the gift that violated the Rule Against Perpetuities as void, leaving the remainder of the gift intact.

EXAMPLE: O conveys "to A for so long as liquor is not served on the premises, but if liquor is served, then to B." Because the vesting of the future interest is unlimited in time, it is not certain to vest or fail within 21 years of any life-in-being. Therefore, the shifting executory interest in B is void. A is left with a fee simple determinable, and O has a possibility of reverter.

EXAMPLE: O conveys "to A, but if liquor is served, then to B." Again, the shifting executory interest in B is void. However, in this case, A is left with a fee simple. Therefore, O retains nothing, and A is left with a fee simple absolute.

c. **Applications**

(1) **Fertile Octogenarian**

(a) Imagine that O conveys "to A for life, remainder to A's children for life, remainder to A's grandchildren."

(b) A's life estate is presently possessory, and therefore is not subject to the Rule Against Perpetuities. The remainder for life in A's children is either contingent or subject to open because A is conclusively presumed to be capable of having more children, and therefore is subject to the Rule Against Perpetuities. The remainder in A's grandchildren is either contingent or subject to open, and therefore is subject to the Rule Against Perpetuities.

(c) O and A are express lives-in-being. Even if children or grandchildren are already born, these persons are members of an open class and therefore cannot serve as lives-in-being. Therefore, O and A are the only possible measuring lives.

(d) A's children will take (or not take) at A's death; hence, their interest is valid. However, A's grandchildren may well take more than 21 years after O and A die. Thus, their interest violates the Rule Against Perpetuities.

(e) A retains her life estate. A's children will take for life after A dies. Because the interest in A's grandchildren is void, O retains a reversion that will become possessory after A's children die.

(2) **Unborn Widow**

(a) Imagine that O conveys "to A for life, remainder to A's widow for life, remainder to A's children living at the death of A's widow."

(b) A's life estate is presently possessory, and therefore is not subject to the Rule Against Perpetuities. The remainder for life in A's widow is contingent because there cannot be a widow of a living person, and therefore is subject to the Rule Against Perpetuities. The remainder in A's children living at the death of A's widow is contingent because there is a condition precedent to vesting, and therefore is subject to the Rule Against Perpetuities.

(c) O and A are express lives-in-being. A's widow is not a life-in-being because she has not yet been identified. A's children, even if some are already born, may not be lives-in-being because their class is open. Therefore, O and A are the only possible measuring lives.

(d) A's widow will take (or not take) at A's death; hence, her interest is valid. However, A's children may well take more than 21 years after O and A die. Thus, their interest violates the Rule Against Perpetuities.

(e) A retains his life estate. A's widow will take for life after A dies if she survives A. Because the interest in A's children is void, O retains a reversion, which will fall in when A's widow dies.

(3) **Charity-to-Charity Rule**

(a) Imagine that O conveys "to A Charity for so long as liquor is not served on the premises, but if liquor is served on the premises, then to B Charity."

(b) As illustrated above, a shifting executory interest in fee will violate the Rule Against Perpetuities, because an heir of A could violate the condition more than 21 years after the death of O, A, and B, causing the property to shift to B.

1) However, for policy public reasons, if both A and B are charities, the shifting executory interest in B Charity will be deemed to be valid under the Rule Against Perpetuities.

(4) **Rule of Convenience**

(a) Imagine that O conveys "to such of A's children as shall reach the age of 25."

1) Assume A is living at the time of this grant and has two children: B, age 26; and C, age 24. Because she is 26, B is entitled to immediate distribution. As a result, the Rule of Convenience will operate to close the class of A's children immediately. All children born as of the date the class closes (B and C) will be allowed to take upon reaching the age of 25. However, no child born after the date the class closes may take, even if he should eventually reach the age of 25.

(b) Assume that A is alive at the testator's death and has three children: B, age 24; C, age 23; and D, age 19.

1) Because no child of A has reached 25, A's children have a springing executory interest, which is subject to the Rule Against Perpetuities.

2) O and A are express lives-in-being. The class of A's children cannot be measuring lives because the class remains open; A is alive, and no child of A is entitled to immediate distribution because no child of A has reached the age of 25.

3) It is possible that a child of A could reach 25 more than 21 years after the deaths of O and A. Therefore, the springing executory interest in the children of A violates the Rule Against Perpetuities.

4) O is left with a fee simple absolute.

(5) **Uniform Statutory Rule Against Perpetuities**

(a) Some states have adopted uniform statutory revisions of the Rule Against Perpetuities ("USRAP"). Under the USRAP, a nonvested interest in real or personal property is invalid unless:

1) it satisfies the common law Rule Against Perpetuities; or

2) it vests or terminates within 90 years of its creation (this is known as the "**wait and see**" **test**). Under the wait-and-see branch of the USRAP, the court waits until the end of the prescribed period to determine whether the interest actually vested or failed within the prescribed period.

EXAMPLE: In 1990, O conveys "to A for life, remainder to A's children for life, remainder to A's grandchildren." Assume that, at the time the conveyance is made, A is 55 and has one child, B, who is 16. In 1995, B marries. In 2001, C is born to B. A dies in 2004 at the age of 69. B dies in 2040 at the age of 66. C may take the property in 2040. The remainder to A's grandchildren would be void under the common law Rule Against Perpetuities; however, because C actually takes within 90 years of the conveyance, her interest is valid under the USRAP.

2. **Powers of Appointment**

a. A **general power of appointment** gives the holder of the power the right to appoint the property to anyone, including the holder of the power. Thus, a general power of appointment is considered to be equivalent to ownership of the property.

(1) To be valid under the Rule Against Perpetuities, a general power of appointment must be exercisable, but not necessarily exercised, during the period allowed by the Rule Against Perpetuities.

b. A **special power of appointment** gives the holder the right to appoint the property to a limited class of persons.

(1) To be valid under the Rule Against Perpetuities, a special power of appointment must be exercised in a manner that causes the interest in property thereby created to vest within the period of the Rule Against Perpetuities.

3. **Restraints on Alienation**

a. A **restraint on alienation** is a condition placed on the ownership of real property that restricts the free conveyance of that property.

(1) Under a disabling restraint, A may not convey. Disabling restraints are always void.

EXAMPLE: O conveyed Blackacre "to A and his heirs so long as A or his heirs do not sell, mortgage, or otherwise transfer his interest in the property." This is a disabling restraint, and will be considered void. A (or his heirs) may freely sell, mortgage, or convey the property.

(2) Under a forfeiture restraint, A loses his estate if he attempts to convey. Forfeiture restraints are valid for life estates and future interests, but are not enforceable for fee simple estates.

EXAMPLE: O conveys Blackacre "to A and his heirs, but if A or his heirs should ever convey the property to anyone, then to B and her heirs." This is a forfeiture restraint on a fee simple estate, and would not be enforceable.

EXAMPLE: O conveys Blackacre "to A for life, then to B and her heirs, provided, however, that should A ever sell, mortgage, or otherwise transfer the property, then A's estate shall immediately terminate in favor of B and her heirs." This is a forfeiture restraint on a life estate, and would be enforceable.

EXAMPLE: O conveys Blackacre "to A for life, then to A's children, provided, however, that should A's children attempt to sell, mortgage, or otherwise transfer the property, then to B and her heirs." This forfeiture restraint would be valid only while A's children possess a future interest in Blackacre, and would be enforceable if they attempted to convey their future interest in the property. Once their interest becomes possessory as a fee simple estate, however, the restraint would no longer be valid.

(3) Under a promissory restraint, A promises not to convey. Promissory restraints are valid for life estates and future interests, but are not enforceable for fee simple estates. The breach of a promissory restraint does not void the conveyance; it just makes the promisor liable for breach of contract damages.

EXAMPLE: O conveys Blackacre "to A for life, then to B and her heirs. A hereby promises not to convey the property during his lifetime." This is a promissory restraint, and is valid to the same extent that a similar forfeiture restraint would be valid.

(4) Partial restraints may be enforced, with the court weighing the duration and number of persons excluded.

(5) Some courts will uphold a reasonable restraint in a commercial transaction on the theory that it appears in an agreement of the parties, is the product of their bargaining, and presumably serves a useful purpose in facilitating the parties' objectives.

4. **Fair Housing and Discrimination**

a. The Fair Housing Act is Title VIII of the Civil Rights Act of 1968 [42 U.S.C. §§ 3601, et seq.]. Under it, among other prohibitions, a person cannot:

(1) refuse to sell or rent a dwelling, or discriminate in sales or rental terms, to any person based on race, color, religion, sex, handicap, familial status (presence or anticipated presence of children), or national origin;

(2) advertise the sale or rental of a dwelling indicating discrimination based on race, color, religion, sex, handicap, familial status, or national origin; or

(a) The prohibition against discriminatory advertising applies not only to landlords and sellers, but also to the publishers themselves [Ragin v. New York Times Co., 923 F.2d 995 (1991)].

(3) coerce, threaten, intimidate, or interfere with a person's exercise of housing rights for discriminatory reasons or retaliate against anyone who encourages the exercise of housing rights.

b. The anti-discrimination rules (other than the prohibition against discriminatory advertisements) do not apply if the owner occupies one of the units in a multiple-unit dwelling containing no more than four units occupied by persons "living independently of each other" [42 U.S.C. § 3603(b)(2)].

c. Religious organizations providing housing for members of their order are exempt [42 U.S.C. § 3607].

d. Housing specifically for older persons is exempt, subject to certain requirements [Id.].

e. **Enforcement by HUD**

(1) An aggrieved person, within one year after an alleged discriminatory housing practice has occurred, may file a sworn complaint with the Secretary of Housing and Urban Development (HUD) [42 U.S.C. § 3610].

(2) The Secretary may also file complaints [Id.].

(3) Within 10 days after the complaint is filed, the Secretary must notify the complainant and the respondent, after which the respondent has 10 days to file a sworn answer [Id.].

(4) The Secretary must complete the investigation into the complaint within 100 days, unless it is impracticable to do so [Id.].

(5) The Secretary must encourage the complainant and the respondent to create a conciliation agreement [Id.].

(6) The Secretary, based on reasonable cause to believe that a discriminatory housing practice has occurred or is about to occur, must either issue a charge on behalf of the complainant or dismiss the complaint.

(7) If a charge is issued, the complainant may then elect whether to have an administrative hearing or a judicial trial [42 U.S.C. § 3612].

(8) At the conclusion of either an administrative hearing or a trial, where the complainant has prevailed, equitable and legal

remedies may be awarded, including actual damages, statutory monetary penalties, attorneys' fees, and costs [Id.].

(9) The result of either an administrative hearing or a trial may be appealed through the federal court system [Id.].

f. **Enforcement by a Private Person**

(1) An aggrieved person may file suit in a federal or state court no later than two years after an alleged discriminatory housing practice [42 U.S.C. § 3613].

(2) The aggrieved person may file suit without having exhausted administrative remedies by first filing a complaint with the Secretary of Housing and Urban Development [Id.].

(a) However, if a complaint has been filed and is in the hearing stage, no suit may be filed [Id.].

(3) An aggrieved person may also file suit to enforce a conciliation agreement reached through HUD [Id.].

(4) If the aggrieved person prevails in a civil action, the court may award actual damages, punitive damages, and such other legal and equitable relief as the court deems appropriate, including attorneys' fees and costs [Id.].

g. **Enforcement by the United States Attorney General**

(1) Upon reasonable cause to believe that a person or group is engaged in a pattern or practice of housing discrimination, the Attorney General may commence a civil action in federal court enforce the Fair Housing Act [42 U.S.C. § 3614].

(2) The Attorney General may also enforce conciliation agreements [Id.].

h. **Intent Not a Required Element**

(1) The United States Supreme Court has held that no proof of intent to violate the Fair Housing Act is needed in order for a complainant to prevail [Texas Department of Housing and Community Affairs v. The Inclusive Communities Project, Inc., 576 U.S. 519 (2015)].

(a) Thus, disparate impact claims are cognizable under the Act. The complainant, if using such a theory, must show a disparate impact on a protected group caused by the respondent's actions. The burden then shifts to the respondent to prove that the challenged practice is necessary to achieve a substantial nondiscriminatory interest [Id.].

5. **Conflicts of Law Related to Real Property**

a. In property cases, two characterizations must be made.

(1) First, the problem must be characterized as to whether or not it involves a property interest (e.g., an agreement to sell land might be characterized as a contract, rather than a property, problem).

(2) Once it is determined that a property interest is involved, that interest must be characterized as a "movable" or "immovable"

interest [Restatement (Second) of Conflict of Laws § 222, cmt. e].

(a) If an interest is closely connected with or related to land (e.g., a leasehold or the right to rents), it is **immovable**; if it is not, the interest falls into the **movable** category.

1) Characterization of the interest traditionally has been made by the forum using its own internal law. However, the Second Restatement suggests that characterization should be made according to the law of the *situs* of the property [Restatement (Second) of Conflict of Laws § 189, cmt. c].

(b) The law of the *situs* governs all rights in land and other immovables. In applying the law, the forum state refers to the whole law of the *situs,* including its choice-of-law rules [Restatement (Second) of Conflict of Laws §§ 223; 223, cmt. b].

1) Generally, the validity and effect of a conveyance (e.g., the form of the deed or the capacity of the grantor) are governed by the law of the *situs* [Restatement (Second) of Conflict of Laws § 223(1)].

2) Mortgages likewise are deemed so closely related to the land that their creation, validity, and foreclosure are governed by the law of the *situs* [Restatement (Second) of Conflict of Laws § 228].

3) However, the underlying contract or note is usually governed by the law of the place of making [Restatement (Second) of Conflict of Laws § 224, cmt. e].

4) Liens (such as materialmen's or laborers' liens) are also governed by the law of the *situs* [Restatement (Second) of Conflict of Laws § 230].

5) Some courts hold that executory contracts for the sale of land are generally characterized as a contracts problem and governed by the law of the place of making.

a) However, the Second Restatement provides that in the absence of an effective choice of law by the parties, the validity of a contract for the transfer of an interest in land, and the rights created thereby, are to be determined by the local law of the state where the land is located, unless, with respect to the particular issue, some other state has a more significant relationship to the transaction and the parties, in which event the local law of the other state will be applied [Restatement (Second) of Conflict of Laws § 189].

II. RIGHTS IN LAND

A. Covenants at Law and Equity

1. Nature and Type

a. A **covenant that runs with the land** is a promise that attaches to land. In that covenant, the covenantor promises to do or refrain from doing something on his land.

(1) In contrast to easements, most running covenants are negative in nature.

EXAMPLE: Landowner promises that she will not build anything other than a single-family residence on her premises.

(2) Running covenants include promises to pay rent, condominium common charges, or maintenance fees.

b. **Equitable Servitude**

(1) A court may enforce a covenant as an **equitable servitude** if:

(a) the plaintiff can establish at law all of the elements for a covenant that runs with the land, but the plaintiff seeks equitable relief; or

(b) the plaintiff cannot establish at law all of the elements for a covenant that runs with the land, but the plaintiff can demonstrate the relaxed requirements for an equitable servitude. These elements relate closely to the elements required for a covenant to run at law.

c. **Implied Reciprocal Servitude**

(1) If the owner of two or more lots, so situated as to bear the relation, sells one with restrictions of benefit to the land retained, the servitude becomes mutual and the owner of the lot or lots retained may not do anything forbidden to the owner of the lot sold, creating an implied reciprocal servitude.

2. Creation

a. **Covenants**

(1) For a covenant to run with the land, the following elements must be satisfied:

(a) writing;

1) A covenant that runs with the land is a promise that attaches to land. Therefore, a covenant that runs at law must be embodied in a writing that satisfies the Statute of Frauds.

(b) intent;

1) The writing must include language that shows the parties' intent for the covenant to run.

2) Typically, the covenant will state that the covenantor promises on behalf of himself and his heirs, successors, and assigns to do or to refrain from doing something on

his land for the benefit of the covenantee and his heirs, successors, and assigns.

(c) privity;

1) **Horizontal privity** is the relationship that exists between the original covenantor and covenantee.

2) In most jurisdictions in the United States, the horizontal privity requirement is satisfied by a conveyance of land between the covenantee and covenantor, which occurs by the same deed that includes the covenant.

3) Horizontal privity may also exist when the covenant is created in a lease or in the transfer of an easement.

a) Traditionally, horizontal privity was required for both the benefit and the burden to run.

b) Under the modern rule, horizontal privity is not required for the benefit to run.

4) **Vertical privity** is the relationship that exists between an original party to a running covenant and the successor in interest to the original party.

5) To demonstrate vertical privity, the plaintiff must show that the successor "stepped into the shoes of" the original party by taking the entire interest held by the original party.

a) For example, if the original covenantor took a fee simple interest in land and then attempted to make a conveyance to a subsequent party, vertical privity would exist between the original covenantor and the successor only if the successor received a fee simple interest.

b) Traditionally, vertical privity is required for both the benefit and burden to run.

c) For the burden to run, privity of estate will only exist when the holder of the servient estate transfers all of his interest in the servient estate to the new owner.

d) For the benefit to run, privity of estate can exist when the holder of the dominant estate is transferring all or part of his interest.

(d) touch and concern; and

1) To touch and concern, a covenant must exercise direct influence on the occupation, use, or enjoyment of the premises.

2) Traditionally, both the benefit and the burden had to touch for either side to run.

3) The benefit touches if it increases the value of the benefited property.

4) The burden touches if it decreases the value of the burdened property.

(e) notice.

1) Originally, notice was not a requirement for a covenant to run with the land at law. However, the introduction of recording statutes into American law caused a notice requirement to be grafted onto the requirements for a running covenant.

2) The parameters of notice are determined according to the terms of the relevant recording statute.

3) Notice under recording acts is necessary for the burden to run.

b. **Equitable Servitudes**

(1) If the plaintiff cannot show that the covenant was embodied in a writing, the plaintiff may prove the covenant through part performance or estoppel.

(2) If the plaintiff cannot show intent in a writing for the covenant to run, she may nevertheless establish intent by showing a common scheme.

(a) A **common scheme** typically exists in a subdivision. If a sufficient number of lots in the subdivision are burdened by the same covenant, the court may find that a common scheme binds all of the lots in the subdivision, including those that do not have the restriction written into the deed.

(b) The following factors may show a common scheme:

1) a large percentage of lots expressly burdened;

2) oral representations to buyers;

3) statements in written advertisements, sales brochures, or maps given to buyers; or

4) recorded plat maps or declarations.

(c) In the absence of an express restriction in the deed, the burden will not be imposed on a lot conveyed before the conveyance of the first lot with an express restriction.

(d) The burden will be imposed on lots (even in the absence of an express restriction in the deed to those lots) if a common scheme was evident at the time of conveyance of those lots.

(e) The original subdivider may enforce a benefit unless he has sold all of the property.

(f) Traditionally, a benefit could not be enforced by a buyer who purchased his subdivision lot before the conveyance of the burdened lot. In some jurisdictions, the existence of the common scheme is sufficient to show that the subdivider intended to benefit all purchasers, whether they took prior or subsequent to the conveyance that created the burden. In other jurisdictions, a previous grantee may sue as a third-party beneficiary.

(g) If a common scheme is present, suit may be brought by the purchaser of a lot conveyed after the lot with the express restriction (because that restriction was for the benefit of the grantor and his heirs and assigns, and the subsequent purchaser is a successor to the grantor).

(3) Neither horizontal nor vertical privity are required for the enforcement of an equitable servitude.

(4) The intent element must be demonstrated for both the benefit and burden.

(5) The touch and concern element must still be demonstrated for both the benefit and burden.

(6) The parameters of notice for the burden to run are determined according to the terms of the relevant recording statute.

c. **Implied Reciprocal Servitudes**

(1) In most jurisdictions, a negative reciprocal easement may be created by filing a declaration containing the restrictions (the "CC&Rs", which are covenants, conditions, and restrictions) before any lots are sold.

(2) A condominium or subdivision association may enforce a benefit if the covenant is to benefit common land conveyed by the developer to the association.

3. **Termination**

a. As with easements, covenants can be terminated by merger, release, abandonment, or estoppel.

b. Covenants may also be terminated by changed circumstances (also known as the "change of neighborhoods" doctrine). Under this concept, where the neighborhood or circumstances have changed so greatly that it no longer makes sense to enforce the restriction, it will be deemed terminated.

4. **Property Owners' Associations and Common Interest Ownership Communities**

a. A property owners' association generally has standing to enforce a restrictive covenant.

b. When a court is examining whether an association's board has acted properly, the standard applied appears to be similar to the business judgment rule applied to corporations.

(1) Under this rule, there is a rebuttable presumption that an association's board members are honest, well-meaning, and acting through decisions that are informed and rationally undertaken in good faith.

(2) As a result, a board will not have breached any duty of care for making a good-faith error of judgment.

B. Easements, Profits, and Licenses

1. **Nature and Type**

a. **Easements**

(1) An **easement** is an interest in the land of another.

(2) Easements may be either affirmative or negative, and they may be either appurtenant or in gross.

(a) Most easements are affirmative in nature. An **affirmative easement** gives the holder the right to do something on the land of another.

<u>**EXAMPLE**</u>: Alpha has the right to walk across Beta's land.

(b) A **negative easement** gives the holder the right to prevent a landowner from doing something on his land. The common law recognized only the following four types of negative easements: light, air, water, and lateral and subjacent support. A writing is always required to create a negative easement.

<u>**EXAMPLE**</u>: Alpha may prevent Beta from building a house that blocks light to Alpha's land.

(c) An **easement appurtenant** requires a dominant and servient tenement.

<u>**EXAMPLE**</u>: A has the right to cross over B's property from the road to reach A's property. A has the dominant estate because the easement benefits A in the use of her property. B has the servient estate because her land is burdened with the easement. Therefore, A has an easement appurtenant.

(d) An **easement in gross** is personal in nature, resulting in a servient but not a dominant estate.

<u>**EXAMPLE**</u>: A utility company has the right to lay its utility cable across A's land. The cable assists the company in providing its utility services to its customers. A's land is the servient estate because it is burdened by the utility company's right to lay its cable across A's land. However, there is no dominant estate; the benefit of the easement is personal to the utility company because the easement does not benefit the company in the use of its land. Therefore, the utility company has an easement in gross.

b. **Profits**

(1) A **profit à prendre** is a nonpossessory interest in land.

(2) The holder of the profit has the right to take resources from the land of another.

(a) Profits, unlike easements, permit the right to remove something from the land, as opposed to mere use of the land.

(b) Examples of resources include, but are not limited to, soil, timber, and minerals.

<u>**EXAMPLE**</u>: A has the right to take gravel from B's land.

c. **Licenses**

(1) A **license** is a privilege, usually to do something on someone else's property.

2. **Methods of Creation**
   a. An easement may be created expressly through a writing, by implication, or by prescription.
   b. **Express**
      (1) An easement is an interest in land. Therefore, the Statute of Frauds generally requires a writing to create an easement.
   c. **Implied**
      (1) An affirmative easement may be created by implication either by prior (*quasi-*) use or by necessity.
      (2) **Implied by Prior or Quasi-Use**
         (a) An easement **implied by prior use** requires:
            1) severance of title to land held in common ownership;
            2) the use giving rise to the easement was in existence at the time of the severance;
               a) That use alone cannot constitute an easement because an owner cannot have an easement across his own property.
            3) the prior use must have benefited the other portion of the land;
            4) the use was apparent and could be discovered upon a reasonable inspection; and
            5) at the time of the severance, the easement was necessary for the proper and reasonable enjoyment of the dominant tract.
               a) However, some courts may require strict necessity if the implied easement is reserved and not granted.
      (3) **Implied by Necessity**
         (a) An easement **implied by necessity** requires:
            1) severance of title to land held in common ownership; and
            2) strict necessity for the easement at the time of severance.

            <u>**EXAMPLE**</u>: O owns a large parcel of land. The parcel is bordered by a two-lane road on the east and dense forest on the north, south, and west. O lives in a house at the northwest corner of the parcel and regularly drives to and from her house on a gravel road that crosses the northeast portion of the parcel and opens onto the road. O then conveys the west half of the parcel to A. When A attempts to access the road by driving across the northeast portion of the parcel, he finds O has erected a barrier. The question is whether A has an implied easement across the portion of the parcel retained by O. O initially owned the entire tract, thereby satisfying the initial unity of ownership requirement. She then severed that unity when she conveyed the west half of the parcel

to A. A has no direct access to his parcel because it is surrounded by O's parcel on the east and dense forest on the north, south, and west. The landlocked nature of A's estate should satisfy the strict necessity requirement for an implied easement by necessity.

(4) **Implied by Plat**

(a) A purchaser who acquires a lot in a platted subdivision will generally acquire an implied private easement to use any streets or alleys (and possibly even parks) shown on the plat.

d. **Prescription**

(1) An affirmative easement may be created by prescription, which requires proof of the use of property that is:

(a) open and notorious;

(b) actual;

(c) continuous (the traditional period for prescription is 20 years);

(d) hostile; and

(e) exclusive.

1) Most courts require the prescriptive use to be "exclusive." In this context, **exclusive** means that the use is not shared with the whole world. The user may share use of the easement with the owner.

e. **Profits and Licenses**

(1) Profits can only be created expressly or by prescription.

(2) Neither a writing nor consideration is required to create a license.

3. **Scope**

a. If the language creating the easement limits its use, then that language will be enforced.

b. However, when language is not specific as to use, the easement holder can make reasonable use of the easement.

c. If an easement holder overuses the easement (i.e., beyond what is reasonable), this is known as **surcharging the easement**. This does not result in a termination of the easement, but will entitle the owner of the servient estate to sue for damages caused by the surcharging, and/or seek an injunction to stop future surcharging.

4. **Transfer**

a. Both the benefit and the burden of an easement may be transferred according to the following rules:

(1) when the dominant tenement is transferred, the benefit of an easement or a profit appurtenant follows the transferred estate, even if the deed of conveyance does not specifically mention the easement or profit; or

(a) Traditionally, the benefit of an easement in gross could not be transferred. However, the modern rule permits transfer of an easement in gross if the grantor of the easement so intends, and the easement is commercial in nature.

(2) in the case of an express easement, transfer of the servient estate will result in an accompanying transfer of the burden, so long as the holder of the dominant tenement has complied with the provisions of the relevant recording statute.

b. All rules governing the alienation of easements are applicable to profits.

c. Because a license is personal, it is not transferable unless the licensor so intends.

5. **Termination**

a. An easement may be terminated by any of the following methods:

(1) an easement may be created for a specific term, such as 10 years;

(a) When the time period ends, the easement is terminated.

(2) a release occurs when the holder of the dominant estate releases his interest to the holder of the servient estate;

(3) an easement is terminated when the dominant and servient estates come into common ownership;

(4) an easement may be terminated by abandonment;

(a) Abandonment requires proof of:

1) intent to abandon; and

2) an affirmative act in furtherance of the intent.

(5) an easement may be terminated by estoppel;

(a) Estoppel requires proof of:

1) an act or representation in respect to the easement;

2) justifiable reliance on that act or representation; and

3) damages.

(6) an easement may be terminated by prescription (use adverse to the easement for the statutory period);

(7) an easement will be terminated when a governmental body acquires the servient estate through an exercise of the eminent domain power; or

(8) an easement may be terminated by the sale of the servient estate to a *bona fide* purchaser for value without notice.

(a) Easements are interests in land, and so follow the same recording rules as other interests. Thus, a subsequent *bona fide* purchaser for value and without notice who satisfies the requirements of the recording statute will take the servient estate free of the easement.

(b) This applies to express easements. Courts are split as to whether a servient estate subject to an implied easement, such as an easement implied by necessity, would be transferred with or without the easement in such a situation.

b. All rules governing the termination of easements are applicable to profits.

c. A license expires on the death of the licensor or the conveyance of the servient estate.

d. A license is generally revocable at the will of the licensor. However, a license may become irrevocable in two situations:

(1) a **license coupled with an interest** exists when one person owns personal property on the land of another and has a privilege incidental to such personal property to come on the land to use or recover the personalty; and

(2) an **executed license** is based on estoppel and often involves substantial expenditure of funds in reliance on the promisor's promise to allow the promisee to use the land. An executed license is sometimes deemed to be the equivalent of an easement.

C. Fixtures

1. In General

a. A **fixture** is a chattel that has become so connected to real property that a disinterested observer would consider the chattel to be part of the realty.

EXAMPLE: If a homeowner attaches a bookshelf to the wall of her home, it retains its separate identity after the attachment, and thus is not a fixture. However, the same bookshelf built into the wall becomes part of the realty, and thus is a fixture.

b. When one person owns a chattel and the land to which the chattel is to be fixed, the chattel becomes a fixture if:

(1) it is annexed to the real property;

(2) it has been appropriated to the use of the land; and

(3) the annexor intends it to be a fixture.

c. A chattel may be deemed annexed to the land if:

(1) it is permanently attached to real property or to something appurtenant to the real property;

EXAMPLE: A chain-link fence may be deemed annexed to the land if it is erected around a parcel of land by placing posts into holes in the ground.

(2) it would be difficult to move solely based on its own weight; or

EXAMPLE: A large, heavy statue may be deemed annexed to the land if it is placed on the ground in a backyard garden.

(3) it is constructively annexed to the property by being specially designed for the property or a fixture on the property.

EXAMPLE: Hurricane shutters custom designed for a house may be classified as annexed to the house, even if they are removed and stored in the garage during winter months.

d. An annexed chattel may become a fixture if the chattel is so necessary or convenient to the use of the land that it is commonly regarded as part of the land. In determining whether a chattel has been appropriated to the use of the land, the court will consider the nature of the land or structure to which the chattel is affixed.

EXAMPLE: Chairs in a movie theater will be deemed appropriated to the use of the land, while chairs placed in the kitchen of an apartment may not be regarded as such.

e. Intent to annex a chattel is a question of fact that is judged objectively, according to a reasonable person standard. The finder of fact considers the nature of the chattel, the degree of annexation, and the appropriateness of the chattel to the property's use.

2. **Transfers, Severance, and Change of Ownership**

a. When both the chattel and the land are owned by the same person, a deed to the real property will transfer all of the fixtures on the property. However, the buyer and seller may agree that the seller may remove certain fixtures from the property before title is transferred to the buyer.

EXAMPLE: A deed describing a lot of land also transfers the house on the lot and the plumbing fixtures in the house.

b. An owner of a chattel may affix it to land also owned by that person which later becomes encumbered by a mortgage. In that case, the mortgage extends to both the land and the fixture. If the chattel is attached to land already encumbered by a mortgage, the prior mortgage also encompasses the chattel, even though the mortgagee thereby receives a security interest that is greater than the one bargained for by the mortgagee.

c. If a fixture and the land to which it is attached are subject to common ownership, the owner is free to sever the chattel physically and permanently from the premises. In that case, the fixture regains its status as personal property. A constructive severance of a fixture may occur when the owner of the land expressly reserves the fixture in a contract of sale for the land or deed of conveyance of the land.

d. Under Article 2 of the Uniform Commercial Code, a contract for the sale of a structure to be removed from realty is a contract for the sale of goods if the structure is to be severed from the land by the seller. Article 2 also applies to contracts for the sale of other things attached to realty and capable of severance without material harm to the land, regardless of whether the item is to be severed by the buyer or by the seller.

3. **Trade Fixture**

a. A **trade fixture** is a chattel that is annexed to the land by a tenant (i.e., a life tenant, tenant for a term, periodic tenant, or tenant at will) to advance his business or trade during his tenancy.

b. During a tenancy, a tenant is free to remove a trade fixture. If a tenant removes a trade fixture, he is responsible for repairing damages caused by its removal. In some states, the trade fixture exception has been broadened to include domestic and/or ornamental fixtures.

c. At common law, if the tenancy is for a definite term and ends on a certain day, trade fixtures must be removed before the end of the term or they become part of the realty.

(1) Most states refuse to follow the common law rule that a tenant forfeits his trade fixtures by failing to remove them before expiration of the lease term. To encourage trade and industry, a tenant is permitted to remove trade fixtures within a reasonable time after the expiration of a lease.

EXAMPLE: L leases Blackacre to T as a store for three years, with a set termination date. During the term, T firmly affixes shelves to the floor of the store building. These shelves are still standing the day after the lease terminates. Under the common law rule, the shelves remain fixtures on the property and belong to L because T did not remove them before the end of the term. However, under the modern view, T has not yet forfeited her interest in the shelves. Instead, T will be given a reasonable time after the termination date to remove the shelves.

D. Zoning

1. Authority and Scope

a. Authority

(1) The power to zone is granted by statute from a state to a city, county, township, or other appropriate political subdivision. It gives the political subdivision the ability to divide its geographical areas into zones where some uses are permitted and other uses are prohibited.

(2) Ordinances that do not conform to state enabling acts are considered ultra vires, or unauthorized and beyond the scope of power allowed or granted by law.

b. Classifications

(1) Common zoning classifications include residential, commercial, agricultural, industrial, spatial, and mixed-use, as well as subsets of these classifications.

EXAMPLE: A developer wishes to build a high-rise apartment building in a desirable area of the city, but the area is zoned for single-family residential uses only. The developer needs a district that is zoned high-density residential.

EXAMPLE: A small airport is planned for a district that is currently zoned agricultural. The district must be rezoned to add spatial as an additional classification.

c. Purpose

(1) Zoning ordinances must promote the public health, safety, prosperity, morals, and welfare because the ordinances arise from the state's police power [Berman v. Parker, 348 U.S. 26 (1954)].

d. **Uniformity**

(1) Zoning ordinances must be uniform for each class or kind of buildings and uses throughout each district, but the regulations in one district may differ from those in other districts.

e. **Scope**

(1) The regulations in each district may regulate, restrict, permit, prohibit, and/or determine:

(a) the use of land, buildings, and structures;

(b) the size, height, area, location, construction, repair, and removal of structures;

(c) the areas and dimensions of land, water, and air-space to be occupied and open spaces to be left unoccupied; or

(d) the excavation or mining of soil or other natural resources.

EXAMPLE: A homeowner planned to build a garage that was flush with the edge of his street, for ease of entering the garage. However, he learned, upon applying for a building permit, that a 15-foot set-back from the road was required for any structure.

EXAMPLE: The owner of a shopping mall intended to expand in order to build additional stores. Before proceeding too far in the planning process, she reviewed the local zoning code to see how many new parking spaces would be required.

f. **Enforcement**

(1) **Notice of Zoning Violation**

(a) When a property is found to be out of compliance with the zoning code, the political subdivision will issue to the property owner a Notice of Zoning Violation.

(2) **Cease and Desist**

(a) A Notice of Zoning Violation may contain instructions to cease and desist from a certain use, or instructions on how to modify the property to bring it into compliance, or other information that informs the property owner about the violation and how to cure it.

EXAMPLE: The buyer of a house is told by the seller that the house is a "legal triple," by which he means that it is permitted as a three-family home. The buyer sees the three separate entrances and the three separate utility meters. The buyer purchases the house intending to live in one part and rent out the other two parts. As soon as the buyer rents out the other parts of the house, the buyer receives a Notice of Zoning Violation, stating that the area is zoned for single-family houses only, that the house has no Certificate of Occupancy for three families, and that the buyer must cease and desist renting out the other parts of the house.

(b) If the property owner does not protest the notice, and does not bring the property into compliance, the political subdivision may choose to obtain a court-ordered injunction or take other steps to enforce the notice.

(3) **Civil Fines**

(a) A Notice of Zoning Violation usually recites that civil fines will be owed if compliance is not achieved by the deadline set in the notice. It is a common practice for fines to accumulate daily until compliance is achieved.

(4) **Criminal Misdemeanor**

(a) In some jurisdictions, zoning violations can also be prosecuted as criminal misdemeanors, if left uncorrected.

(5) **Recording**

(a) Some state laws provide that zoning violations that are not corrected by the deadline contained in the notice will be recorded, so that potential buyers of the property or lenders are aware of the zoning violation.

(6) **Challenges**

(a) A Notice of Zoning Violation must include information on how to protest the notice by appealing to the local board of zoning appeals. If relief is not granted, an appeal to a court must be provided.

(7) **Tenants and Occupiers**

(a) While the property owner is always liable for civil zoning violations, whether committed by the owner or a tenant or other occupier, in most jurisdictions a tenant or other occupier who is committing the violation is also liable.

(b) An owner, however, cannot be liable for a criminal misdemeanor committed by the tenant or occupier because the element of intent is lacking.

2. **Constitutional Limitations**

a. **In General**

(1) The Due Process Clause of the Fourteenth Amendment provides for both procedural and substantive due process.

(a) **Procedural Due Process**

1) Procedural due process requires notice and a fair hearing, meaning an opportunity to be heard by a neutral decision-maker.

2) When a property owner receives a Notice of Zoning Violation and appeals it to the local board of zoning appeals or other administrative board, there is a public hearing. If the owner does not receive relief, an appeal to the courts must be provided.

3) When a property owner requests a variance from the zoning code, the owner is entitled to a public hearing that has been noticed to all who might take an interest in her request, including nearby property owners. If relief is not granted, an appeal to the courts must be provided.

4) Where appeal to the courts is taken, the court reviews the administrative decision to see if it was illegal, arbitrary or capricious, or unsupported by a preponderance of the evidence.

(b) **Substantive Due Process**

1) A zoning ordinance violates substantive due process if it is arbitrary and capricious, meaning that it is not reasonably related to public health, welfare, or safety.

(2) **Equal Protection**

(a) A zoning ordinance may give rise to an equal protection challenge if similarly situated people are treated differently.

(b) However, where there is no fundamental right impacted, and where there are no suspect classifications, then the rational basis test will be applied. The zoning ordinance, as economic and social legislation, will be upheld if it has a rational relationship to a legitimate government interest, meaning the public health, safety, and welfare [Village of Belle Terre v. Boraas, 416 U.S. 1 (1974)].

(3) **First Amendment**

(a) A zoning ordinance may also be subject to a First Amendment challenge if it regulates billboards or aesthetics.

EXAMPLE: A city ordinance prohibiting the erection of billboards in residential districts was found to be constitutional as not unreasonable, arbitrary, or discriminatory, and as a proper exercise of the police power [Thomas Cusack Co. v. City of Chicago, 242 U.S. 526 (1917)].

b. **Protection of Preexisting Property Rights—Takings**

(1) The Fifth Amendment provides that private property shall not be taken for public use without just compensation. This prohibition applies to the states through the Due Process Clause of the Fourteenth Amendment.

(2) A land-use regulation is a "taking" if it denies an owner all reasonable, economically beneficial uses of his land [Lucas v. South Carolina Coastal Council, 505 U.S. 1003 (1992)].

(3) To analyze regulations that merely decrease economic value, the court uses a balancing test to determine if there is a taking, which happens rarely, considering the following factors [Penn Central Transportation Co. v. New York, 438 U.S. 104 (1978)]:

(a) the economic impact of the regulation on the claimant;

(b) the extent to which the regulation has interfered with distinct investment-backed expectations; and

(c) the character of the governmental action.

3. **Rezoning and Other Zoning Changes**

a. **Rezoning**

(1) If rezoning by the political subdivision is inconsistent with a comprehensive plan for that area, then it must be based on a change of conditions in the land, neighborhood, environment, or public opinion.

(2) Rezoning of a particular piece of land is quasi-judicial and requires procedural due process. A broader rezoning is legislative.

(3) If a property owner wants to use his land in a way that is not allowed under the zoning classification, the owner may petition for a rezoning to change the classification. While this is an option, a use variance or special use permit is much easier to obtain.

b. **Nonconforming Use**

(1) A nonconforming use is a use permitted by zoning statutes or ordinances to continue, notwithstanding the fact that similar uses are not generally permitted in the area.

(2) A nonconforming use may not be expanded or rebuilt after substantial destruction.

(3) Local ordinances often prohibit the enlargement, alteration, or extension of a nonconforming use.

(4) Some local ordinances require certain nonconforming uses to be amortized (reduced) over a specified period, at the end of which they must be terminated.

(5) While a nonconforming use cannot be extended or intensified in ways that constitute a substantial change, insubstantial changes are permitted. Owners are entitled to make reasonable alterations to repair their facilities and render them practicable for their purposes.

c. **Variances**

(1) A variance is the permission by the local zoning authorities to use property in a manner forbidden by the zoning ordinances in order to alleviate conditions peculiar to a particular parcel of property.

(2) If a variance is sought from an area restriction, the petitioner must show that there are practical difficulties in meeting the requirements of the zoning code or that the requirements are unreasonable or create an undue hardship.

EXAMPLE: An accountant buys land in a commercial district to set up a business office, but the zoning code requires 50 square feet of landscaping near the front door. There is no physical space for 50 square feet of landscaping, so the accountant seeks an area variance.

(3) If the variance is sought from a use restriction, the petitioner must show undue hardship, meaning that, without a use variance, there is no viable use of the property.

EXAMPLE: An heir inherits a sawmill that has not been used in decades, and is in a district that has been rezoned to retail. The sawmill is not viable under the current zoning designation, nor is it appropriate for a retail store. The heir seeks a use variance to allow it to be remodeled into a warehouse.

d. **Special Use Permits**

(1) A special use permit is required for uses in an area not zoned for those uses, but which would be beneficial to the public welfare and compatible with the area.

(2) An applicant for a special use permit is entitled to a public hearing that has been noticed to all who might have an interest in the application, including nearby property owners.

EXAMPLE: A hospital is planned to be built in a residential district. A special use permit is needed because a hospital is not a residential use.

EXAMPLE: A temple is planned to be built in a residential district. A special use permit is needed because a temple is not a residential use.

e. **Conditional Use Permits**

(1) A conditional use permit is required for uses in an area not zoned for those uses, but which would be beneficial to the public welfare, and compatible with the area if certain conditions are met.

(2) The use is granted only if the applicant agrees to meet the additional conditions that the political subdivision imposes in order to reduce the potentially objectionable impact of the use.

(3) An applicant for a conditional use permit is entitled to a public hearing that has been noticed to all who might have an interest in the application, including nearby property owners.

EXAMPLE: A group home for the developmentally disabled desires to operate in a residential area. A conditional use permit is granted on the conditions that the group home be fully staffed at all hours and that the staff not park their cars on the street.

EXAMPLE: A lawyer wants to run her practice out of her home in a residential area. A conditional use permit is granted on the conditions that she not have more than two clients with cars visiting at the same time, and that she post no signage.

f. **Spot Zoning**

(1) A parcel or small area may be zoned for a use or structure that is inconsistent with the rationale of the overall plan or ordinance. This is called spot zoning.

(2) Spot zoning is illegal when the zoning ordinance is designed solely to serve the private interests of one or more landowners. It

is permissible if the purpose is to further the welfare of the entire political subdivision.

g. **Exactions**

(1) An exaction is an approval of use in exchange for money or a dedication of land. An exaction is permissible only if the local government can demonstrate that the increased public need is causally related (i.e., has an essential nexus) to the owner's use, and the amount of the exaction is approximately equal to the additional public cost imposed by the use (i.e., has a rough proportionality to the use).

EXAMPLE: The owner of a plumbing and electrical supply store applied for a permit to expand her store and pave the parking lot. The city was not allowed to insist that the owner also dedicate land to a greenway and develop a pedestrian and bicycle pathway by the store [Dolan v. City of Tigard, 512 U.S. 374 (1994)].

E. Support Rights

1. An owner of real property has the exclusive right to use and possess the surface, airspace, and soil of the property.

2. **Lateral Support**

   a. An owner of land has no liability if a subsiding of neighboring land is caused by natural conditions on the owner's land. However, a landowner may be strictly liable if his excavation causes adjacent land to subside (sink). If the adjacent land is improved, strict liability applies only if the adjacent land would have collapsed in its natural state. Even if the adjacent land would not have collapsed in its natural state, the landowner is only liable for damages resulting from negligence. The courts are split on whether money damages may be recovered for injury to the improvements.

3. **Subjacent Support**

   a. The right of support extends to land in its natural state and buildings existing on the date when the subjacent estate is severed from the surface. However, the underground landowner is liable for damages to subsequently erected buildings only if she is negligent.

   b. An underground occupant (e.g. mining company) is liable for negligently damaging springs and wells, but an adjoining landowner is not liable for interfering with underground percolating water.

F. Water Rights

1. **Riparian rights** are rights in water enjoyed by an owner of land that abuts a navigable natural river, stream, or lake. Several different sets of rules have been developed concerning the use of riparian water by adjoining landowners.

   a. Traditionally, a riparian owner was entitled to make only such use of riparian water as would not interrupt the natural flow of the body of water.

Under the **natural flow doctrine**, a landowner may make unlimited use of riparian water for domestic or natural uses such as drinking and bathing. However, a landowner may use riparian water for artificial uses, such as irrigation, only if the use does not substantially diminish the flow of the body of water. Today, very few jurisdictions follow the natural flow doctrine.

b. Under the **reasonable use doctrine**, a riparian owner may make reasonable use of riparian water so long as his use does not interfere unreasonably with the rights of other riparian owners. Such reasonable use is restricted to riparian land, which is defined as land lying within the watershed. Most American jurisdictions currently follow the reasonable use doctrine.

c. The **prior appropriation doctrine** awards the right to use water to the first person to take the water for beneficial purposes. The prior appropriation doctrine was developed and is still followed in western states where water resources are scarce. Prior appropriation rules are usually set by state statute.

2. **Diffuse surface water** is water from rain or melted snow that runs over the surface of land outside of a recognizable body of water. Several different sets of rules have been developed concerning the use of diffuse surface water.

   a. Under the **common enemy rule**, an owner may use any method available to keep diffuse surface water from coming onto her land. Traditionally, the common enemy rule was followed in crowded urban areas, primarily in northeastern states.

   b. Under the **civil law rule**, an owner was not permitted to interfere with the flow of diffuse surface water. Traditionally, the civil law rule was followed in western states with vast open spaces.

   c. Under the **reasonable use rule**, an owner may use reasonable means to alter the flow of diffuse surface water, even if surrounding landowners are harmed.

3. **Underground water** is water that runs beneath the surface of the land.

   a. The use of underground streams—where the water flows in a well-defined, known, and permanent channel—is governed by the rules applied to riparian waters.

   b. **Percolating underground water** is water that percolates through the subsurface of the land. The rules governing the use of percolating underground water vary from state to state.

      (1) Under the English absolute ownership doctrine, a possessor of land may take as much of the water percolating under his land as he desires. This is known as the **rule of capture**.

      (2) Some states apply the reasonable use test to percolating underground water.

      (3) A few states use a **correlative rights test**, which provides that all owners of land situated over a pool of underground water have equal rights to use the water.

      (4) In some states, prior appropriation statutes have been enacted to govern the use of percolating underground water.

III. CONTRACTS

A. Creation and Construction

1. **Statute of Frauds**
    a. The Statute of Frauds requires a writing signed by the party to be charged for a transfer of an interest in real property.
    b. **Exceptions to the Statute of Frauds**
        (1) The **doctrine of part performance** may be used to enforce an otherwise invalid oral contract of sale, provided the acts of part performance unequivocally prove the existence of the contract. To satisfy this doctrine, a showing of at least two of the following three facts must be made:
            (a) payment of all or part of the purchase price;
            (b) taking of possession; and
            (c) making substantial improvements.
        (2) Equitable and, under the modern trend, promissory estoppel may also be used to prove an oral contract for the sale of land.
            (a) **Equitable estoppel** is based on an act or a representation.
            (b) **Promissory estoppel** is based on a promise.
2. **Essential Terms**
    a. The signed writing must include the following essential terms:
        (1) description of the property;
        (2) description of the parties;
        (3) price; and
        (4) any conditions of price or payment if agreed on.
3. **Time for Performance**
    a. As with other contracts, if no time is stated, then performance is to occur within a reasonable time.
    b. A "time is of the essence" clause means that nonperformance at the time specified in the contract (i.e., the closing date) will be considered a material breach. In other words, a late payment or inability to transfer title at that time will be considered a breach of contract, and specific performance will not be awarded to a breaching party after that party fails to perform at the specified time.
        (1) Because this is a harsh result, courts often try to find ways around such a clause. Some courts will consider an acceptance of a late payment as a waiver of a time-is-of-the-essence clause.
    c. Time may be considered essential to the agreement either through express stipulation or where the course of dealings of the parties implies that time is of the essence.
    d. Even where time is considered essential to an agreement, specific performance may be ordered despite a breach if:

(1) the breach was not due to gross negligence or deliberate or bad-faith conduct by the breaching party;

(2) the nonbreaching party could be adequately compensated for the injury caused by the delay; and

(3) the forfeiture that would otherwise result would be harsh and unreasonable.

4. **Remedies for Breach**

a. **Seller's Remedies for Buyer's Breach**

(1) **Remedies at Law**

(a) Traditionally, if the buyer breaches a contract for the sale of real property, the seller is entitled to **expectation damages**, measured by the difference between the contract price and the market price at the time of the breach. To compensate the seller in a falling market, some courts now measure expectation damages based on the difference between the contract price and the resale price.

(b) The seller may also recover **foreseeable consequential damages**, such as mortgage interest payments that the seller is required to make after the buyer's breach.

(c) The seller may recover **reasonable reliance damages**, such as repairs and the cost of inspections.

(d) Traditionally, if the buyer breaches, the seller may elect to retain the entire amount of the down payment, even in the absence of a liquidated damages provision.

1) Most courts now restrict the traditional rule to a down payment that equals 10% or less of the purchase price.

2) The modern approach requires the seller to return to the buyer the amount by which the down payment exceeds the damages caused by the buyer's breach.

(e) A contract for the sale of real property may include a **liquidated damages** clause, which states that the seller may retain the entire amount of the down payment if the buyer breaches. If the contract does contain a liquidated damages clause, most courts permit the seller to retain the down payment if the clause is found to be reasonable. A liquidated damage clause is **reasonable**, and therefore is enforceable, if:

1) the injury caused by the breach is one that is difficult or incapable of accurate estimation (traditionally judged at the time the contract was made); and

2) the liquidated damages are a reasonable forecast of the harm caused by the breach.

NOTE Traditionally, the reasonableness of the forecast was judged at the time of the contract. Under the Second Restatement of Contracts, the reasonableness of the forecast may be judged at the time the contract was made (anticipated harm) or by the loss actually caused (actual harm).

(f) The seller may recover punitive damages if the buyer's breach was willful.

(2) **Remedies in Equity**

(a) If the buyer breaches, the seller may elect to seek rescission of the contract.

(b) Traditionally, mutuality of remedy was required. Under this rule, because the buyer is entitled to specific performance, the seller is also entitled to specific performance. However, as mutuality of remedy has fallen out of favor, some courts have begun to question the general availability of specific performance for sellers.

1) Some courts have now declined to classify a condominium unit as unique realty. Those courts refuse to grant a seller's request for specific performance.

b. **Buyer's Remedies for Seller's Breach of Contract**

(1) **Remedies at Law**

(a) Traditionally, if the seller breaches a contract for the sale of real property, the buyer may recover **expectation damages**, measured by the difference between the market price at the time of the breach and the contract price. To compensate the buyer in a rising market, some courts now measure expectation damages based on the difference between the resale price and the contract price. The buyer may also recover foreseeable consequential damages, such as lost profits.

(b) The buyer may recover reasonable **reliance damages**, such as the cost of inspections.

(c) If the seller breaches a contract for the sale of real property, the buyer may seek **restitution of the down payment**.

1) Under the English rule, if the seller fails to deliver marketable title, the buyer may seek restitution of her down payment, plus interest and reasonable expenses incurred in investigating title. However, under the English rule, the buyer may not receive expectation damages that exceed the down payment amount unless the seller acted in bad faith or assumed the risk of failing to obtain marketable title. A small minority of jurisdictions follow the English rule.

2) Under the American rule, if the seller fails to deliver marketable title, the buyer is not restricted to restitution

of his down payment. Rather, the buyer may recover expectation damages plus reasonably foreseeable consequential damages. A majority of jurisdictions follow the American rule.

(d) The buyer may recover **punitive damages** if the seller's breach is willful.

(2) **Remedies in Equity**

(a) If the seller breaches, the buyer may elect to seek **rescission** of the contract for sale, accompanied by restitution of the down payment.

(b) Traditionally, each piece of land is considered unique. Therefore, if the seller breaches the contract by failing to sell the property to the buyer, the buyer may seek **specific performance** of the contract for sale. If the seller fails to deliver marketable title, the buyer may elect to sue for specific performance, with an abatement in the purchase price that reflects the decrease in value caused by the title defect.

B. Marketability of Title

1. All contracts for the sale of real property include an implied promise to convey marketable title. **Marketable title** is title that is reasonably free from doubt in both fact and law. Title is not reasonably free from doubt if it contains any of the following defects:

a. defects in the chain of title, such as:

(1) adverse possession;

(a) Traditionally, title acquired by adverse possession is unmarketable.

(b) However, recent cases (though still the minority view) suggest that title acquired by adverse possession may be marketable if:

1) the possession has been for a very long time;

2) the risk that the record owner will sue is remote; and

3) the probability of the record owner's success is minimal.

(2) the defective execution of a deed; or

(3) significant variation of the description of land from one deed to the next;

b. encumbrances;

(1) For the purposes of marketable title, an **encumbrance** is a right or interest that another person has in real property that diminishes the value of the property but is consistent with the conveyance of a fee interest in the property.

(2) In this context, encumbrances include:

(a) mortgages;
(b) liens;
(c) easements; and
1) An easement that reduces the value of the property (e.g., the burden of a right-of-way) renders title unmarketable. However, an easement that benefits the burdened estate, such as the installation of utilities, and which is visible or known to the buyer, does not render title unmarketable.
(d) covenants and servitudes.

(3) An encumbrance excepted in the contract may not serve as the basis for a finding that title is unmarketable.
(a) A seller may satisfy a mortgage or lien at closing with the proceeds of the sale. If the purchase price is sufficient and satisfaction occurs simultaneously with the transfer of the land, the buyer may not complain because closing will result in marketable title.

c. encroachments; or
(1) A significant encroachment renders title unmarketable.
(2) In contrast, a slight encumbrance, such as a boundary overlap of several inches only, will not render title unmarketable.
(3) An encroachment does not render title unmarketable if the owner says she will not rely on the encroachment as a basis for suit.

d. zoning restrictions.
(1) The existence of a zoning restriction does not make title unmarketable.
(2) However, a zoning violation may render title unmarketable.

2. Physical defects in the property, such as termites, do not render title unmarketable.

NOTE If title is unmarketable, the purchaser may get: (1) rescission; (2) money damages for breach of contract; or (3) specific performance with an abatement of the purchase price.

C. Equitable Conversion and Risk of Loss

1. A purchaser becomes an equitable owner of title at the time of the execution of a binding contract.
2. Under the common law, the risk of loss is on the buyer on execution of a binding contract for the sale of real property. The common law rule is the majority rule.

   EXAMPLE: A house burns down after the contract is signed but before the deed is signed; the purchaser must pay the purchase price.

3. Under the Uniform Vendor and Purchaser Risk Act, the risk of loss is placed on the seller unless the legal title or possession of the property has passed to the buyer. The rule of the Uniform Vendor and Purchaser Risk Act is the minority rule.

D. Options and Rights of First Refusal

1. Options and rights of first refusal are primarily contracts concepts, and governed as such. They will be upheld if their terms are deemed reasonable.

E. Fitness and Suitability

1. **Duty to Disclose Defects**
   a. A seller of a residential home has a duty to disclose to the buyer material latent defects known to the seller but not readily observable and not known to the buyer.
      (1) Generally, the duty applies only to commercial builders and developers of new residential homes.
         (a) Some states extend the duty to all sellers.
         (b) Real estate agents and brokers may also be included in some jurisdictions.
      (2) The duty to disclose defects applies to new homes. However, some states extend the duty to used homes.
         (a) In no state is the duty extended to commercial property.
   b. **Material** is often limited to defects that affect the health and safety of the occupants. However, some states define material to include defects that affect value as well as health and safety.
      (1) In some states, materiality is judged by an objective standard, which asks whether a reasonable person would attach importance to the defect in determining whether to purchase the home.
      (2) In other states, materiality is judged by a subjective standard, which asks whether the defect actually affected the value or desirability of the property to the buyer.
   c. At a minimum, **defect** means a physical defect on the premises.
      (1) A few jurisdictions extend the duty to physical defects both on and off the premises (e.g., nearby environmental hazards).
      (2) Some states also extend the duty to physical and nonphysical defects (e.g., noise from neighbors).
2. **Implied Warranty of Quality**
   a. Most jurisdictions recognize an **implied warranty of quality**, sometimes called an implied warranty of workmanlike quality, an implied warranty of habitability, an implied warranty of fitness, or an implied warranty of suitability.
   b. The implied warranty of quality generally applies to the sale of new or remodeled homes.
      (1) The implied warranty of quality does not extend to commercial structures.
      (2) The implied warranty is imposed on contractors, developers, and other commercial vendors of real property. The warranty covers significant latent defects caused by the defendant's

poor workmanship. The defects must be discovered within a "reasonable time" of construction or remodeling.

(a) The jurisdictions are split on whether the implied warranty of quality extends to subsequent purchasers, i.e., purchasers who are not in privity of contract with the builder or remodeler. The jurisdictions are also split on whether economic loss may be recovered for breach of the implied warranty of quality.

c. Most jurisdictions permit the enforcement of an unambiguous disclaimer of the implied warranty of quality. However, some jurisdictions do not give effect to a general disclaimer (e.g., "as is") for residential premises.

d. In some jurisdictions, the statute of limitations begins to run when construction is completed. In other jurisdictions, the statute of limitations begins to run when the buyer to whom the warranty was first made takes possession of the premises, even if the buyer does not know of the breach. In other jurisdictions, the statute of limitations does not begin to run until the purchaser discovers or should have discovered the breach.

THEORY	DEFINITION	TYPE OF STRUCTURE	PARTY BOUND	TYPE OF DEFECT
Marketable Title	Title must be reasonably free and clear from doubt at closing.	Residential and commercial property.	Any seller.	Defects in title, including chain-of-title defects, encumbrances, encroachments, and zoning violations.
Duty to Disclose	Seller of residential home must disclose to buyer material latent defects known to seller but not to buyer.	• New homes. • New and used homes.	• Commercial builders and developers. • All sellers. • All brokers.	• Physical defects affecting health and safety. • Physical defects affecting health, safety, and value. • Physical and nonphysical defects.
Implied Warranty of Quality	Homes must be built and remodeled with workmanlike quality.	New and remodeled homes.	Contractors, developers, and other commercial vendors.	Significant latent defects caused by the defendant's poor workmanship.

• Denotes jurisdictional variations

F. Merger

1. Traditionally, covenants in a contract of sale merge into the deed at closing. However, under the modern trend, merger does not apply to matters that are collateral to or not mentioned in the deed.

2. This means that, if the buyer discovers a problem with the title acquired from the seller after closing, the buyer cannot sue the seller for breach of the implied covenant of marketable title, because that covenant was implied into the contract, which has now merged with the deed.
3. Instead, the buyer must now sue on the basis of a breach of any covenant of title contained in the deed.
    a. If the deed does not contain any covenants of title (i.e., a quitclaim deed), then the buyer has no course of action.

IV. MORTGAGES/SECURITY DEVICES

A. Types of Security Devices

1. **Mortgages**

a. **In General**

(1) A **mortgage** is a conveyance of an interest in real property made to secure performance of an obligation. The obligation often arises out of a loan of money made to facilitate the purchase or development of real property. A mortgage is typically evidenced by two documents:

(a) a mortgage deed; and

(b) a promissory note (mortgage note).

(2) A **mortgage deed** is a document that conveys an interest in real property designed to secure performance of a debt. Because a mortgage involves a transfer of an interest in realty, a mortgage must be evidenced by a writing (e.g., a mortgage deed) that is properly executed and delivered to the mortgagee. The mortgage deed must include, at a minimum, the following elements:

(a) the identity of the parties;

1) The **mortgagor** is the owner of the real property, who borrowed money and secured the debt with a mortgage on the property.

2) The **mortgagee** is the lender of the money borrowed, to whom the mortgage is made.

(b) a description of the property; and

1) The property should be described with sufficient detail to put a subsequent *bona fide* purchaser on notice of the mortgage (which may require more detail than is required to satisfy the Statute of Frauds).

(c) the intent to create a security interest.

1) The mortgage deed should contain evidence of an intent to create a security interest in the mortgagee.

2) The mortgage deed is a recordable document, which is generally subject to the terms of the applicable recording statute.

(3) The **mortgage note** represents the mortgage obligation. The note is an "IOU" that creates personal liability in the mortgagor. The note typically includes, *inter alia*, the following provisions:

(a) the loan amount;

(b) the interest rate, which may be fixed (set for the term of the loan) or adjustable (it may vary over the term of the loan);

(c) the loan term (e.g., 15 or 30 years);

(d) a clause permitting prepayment but exacting a penalty for the privilege of prepayment;

(e) a clause that permits the mortgagee to declare the entire amount of the mortgage obligation due and payable if the mortgagor defaults (an **acceleration clause**); and

(f) a "due on sale" clause, which requires the entire balance due on the note to be paid before the property may be transferred by the mortgagor/seller to a buyer.

NOTE When the mortgagor satisfies (pays) the mortgage note, the mortgagee executes a document that releases the mortgage. The release document should be recorded.

b. **Purchase-Money Mortgages**

(1) A purchase-money mortgage (PMM) is a mortgage given to secure a loan that enables the mortgagor to acquire title to the property at issue, or to make improvements on the property, and which is given as part of the same transaction as the buyer's purchase of the property.

(2) A purchase-money mortgage, whether recorded or unrecorded, is entitled to priority over other liens on the property arising through the actions of the buyer-mortgagor, even those recorded earlier than the purchase-money mortgage, but only if they were executed prior to the acquisition of title.

(a) The rationale is that the purchase-money mortgage enabled the mortgagor to acquire title to the property (remember that the purchase-money mortgage must be given as part of the same transaction in which title is acquired). Therefore, the purchase-money mortgage should have the superior right.

NOTE A mortgage given the day after the buyer acquired the property (through the use of a PMM), if recorded before the PMM is recorded, would have priority over the PMM based on recording statute priority.

(3) Where the instruments are silent, a purchase-money mortgage given to the vendor of the property will have priority over one given to a third-party lender.

EXAMPLE: Buyer acquires Blackacre by giving a purchase-money mortgage to Seller and one to Bank, and defaults on both; Seller has priority over Bank.

c. **Future-Advance Mortgages**

(1) Future-advance mortgages include line-of-credit or home-equity loans. Future-advance mortgages are most commonly used to fund ongoing construction.

(2) The most common issue involving future-advance mortgages is the fact that the arrangement is being executed at the present time, but the funds are not being accessed until a date in the future. The question then involves determining at what point the mortgage attached to the property.

(a) If proper notice is given to future creditors, the mortgage interest attaches on the date that the future-advance mortgage arrangement is made, not on the date that the funds are actually accessed.

(3) A future-advance mortgage can be either obligatory or optional. A future-advance mortgage is **obligatory** if the lender has a duty to advance funds, and it is **optional** if the lender has discretion whether to make future advances.

(a) A commitment is obligatory only when the lender commits to making future advances without discretionary conditions.

(b) The general rule is that, if a future advance is obligatory, the mortgage securing that advance takes priority over creditors who file liens after the mortgage is recorded, even if all advances on the loan have not actually been made.

EXAMPLE: A clause based on whether the construction is making satisfactory progress makes a future advance optional, because it is designed to allow a bank or other creditor to withhold funds if any difficulties arise with the project's completion that may threaten the creditor's security.

d. **Mechanic's or Materialmen's Liens**

(1) Many states have enacted statutes allowing for a lien to be created against real property as the result of materials being supplied or labor being performed that improves the property. These liens are most commonly referred to as mechanic's liens or materialmen's liens.

(2) These types of liens are governed by state statutes, and the rules vary by jurisdiction as to who can file them and what their priority would be compared to other mortgages. While the lien will not be filed and recorded until after money is owed to the lienholder, they will often relate back to an earlier time, giving the lienholder priority over an intervening lienholder.

(3) In many states, the mechanic's lien will be considered to have attached to the property (and provide notice to subsequent creditors) at the time that visible construction begins. In some states, the mechanic's lien will relate back to when the contract was signed with the landowner, even before any work begins.

EXAMPLE: A homeowner decided to build a new guesthouse on his property, and hired a contractor to do the work for $50,000. The contractor began the work on June 1. In order to finance the construction, as well as purchase new furniture for the guesthouse once the work was complete, the homeowner took out a $75,000 mortgage with a bank on June 15, secured by a lien on the property. The bank properly recorded its mortgage on the same day. The homeowner paid $20,000 to the contractor over the course of construction, but made no further payments, and made no payments on the mortgage with the bank. The contractor finished building the guesthouse on August 1 and, after receiving no further payments, properly filed for a mechanic's lien against the property for $30,000 on August 15. On

September 1, the bank filed a foreclosure action against the homeowner, joining the contractor in the action. After the foreclosure sale, the contractor will have priority to the proceeds over the bank and be paid first, even though it recorded its interest after the bank.

e. **Mortgage Alternatives**

(1) In a **deed of trust**, the debtor/note-maker is the settlor, who gives a deed of trust to a trustee who is closely connected to the lender. In the event of a default, the trustee is directed to proceed with a foreclosure sale. Deeds of trust are generally treated like mortgages.

2. **Installment Land-Sale Contracts**

a. In an **installment land-sale contract**, the buyer takes possession under a contract of sale and makes payments to the seller. The seller delivers a deed and legal title only when the payments have been completed.

b. If the buyer defaults, an installment land-sale contract usually provides for forfeiture of all installments paid, allowing the lender to retake the property. However, some states require a foreclosure proceeding for an installment land-sale contract.

(1) In some states, if a foreclosure occurs, the seller is required to refund to the buyer all installments already paid, as long as these payments are more than the damages suffered by the seller.

c. In many states, a buyer who defaults under an installment land-sale contract is granted a grace period to pay off the loan. The buyer may keep the land while she is paying under a new payment schedule.

(1) If a seller under an installment land-sale contract has accepted late payments from the buyer, the seller may be deemed to have waived his right to demand timely payment.

(2) If this is the case, when the seller wishes the buyer to begin paying in a timely manner, he must send the buyer written notice and allow the buyer a reasonable amount of time to make back payments owed.

3. **Absolute Deeds as Security**

a. This situation arises when a debtor borrows money and issues a deed to the creditor that appears to be absolute on its face. However, extrinsic evidence shows an agreement between the debtor and creditor that, when the debt is repaid, the creditor will reconvey the property to the debtor.

b. If that extrinsic agreement can be proven to the satisfaction of the court, the arrangement will not be treated as an absolute deed of the property, but rather, as a mortgage interest.

(1) The deed then becomes what is known as a **mortgage deed**.

B. Some Security Relationships

1. **Theories**

a. The jurisdictions are split on the nature of the interests held by mortgagor and mortgagee after the execution of the mortgage deed. The following three mortgage theories are in effect in various jurisdictions of the United States.

b. **Title Theory**

(1) The title theory is the classic common law model for determining the nature of the interests held by the mortgagor and the mortgagee.

(2) Under the traditional title theory, the mortgagee receives legal title to the mortgaged real property and has a right to take possession of and to collect rents and profits from the property.

(a) The mortgagee's title to the property is subject to a condition subsequent that divests title from the mortgagee if the mortgagor repays the loan by the due date.

(b) Until she repays the loan in a timely fashion, the mortgagor retains only an equitable interest in the property.

(3) The traditional title theory is now the minority view.

(a) In addition, a title theory state is likely to recognize that the mortgagee holds title for security purposes only. Under this approach, the mortgagor is viewed as the owner of the land.

(b) Some title theory states have also eliminated or reduced the incidents of legal title by, *inter alia*, giving the mortgagor the right to possession until default.

c. **Lien Theory**

(1) In a lien theory jurisdiction, the mortgagee receives a lien, and the mortgagor retains legal and equitable title and possession to the mortgaged real property, unless and until foreclosure occurs.

(2) Most states now adhere to the lien theory.

d. **Intermediate Theory**

(1) In an intermediate theory jurisdiction, the mortgagor retains legal title until default occurs.

(2) After default, legal title and possession pass to the mortgagee, who may then begin to collect rents and profits.

(3) Only a few states adhere to the intermediate theory. According to the Restatement of Property, the intermediate theory differs very little from the title theory, because title theory mortgagees rarely assert a right to possession prior to default.

2. **Rights and Duties prior to Foreclosure**

a. **Mortgage-Related Waste**

(1) A person holding a remainder in mortgaged property has a duty to pay the principal. A life tenant has a duty to pay the interest on a mortgage. However, the life tenant's duty is capped at:

(a) rents and profits derived from a third person in possession of the property; or

(b) the reasonable rental value of the premises, if the life tenant remains in possession of the property.

(2) The mortgagor or a life tenant of mortgaged property also commits waste if, without the mortgagee's consent, the mortgagor or life tenant:

(a) fails to make timely payments of property taxes or governmental assessments secured by a lien that have priority over the mortgage;

(b) makes physical changes to the real property, negligently or intentionally, that reduce the value of the property;

(c) fails to maintain and repair the property in a reasonable manner, except for repair of casualty damage or acts of third parties not the fault of the mortgagor;

(d) fails to comply materially with mortgage covenants respecting the physical care, maintenance, construction, demolition, or insurance against casualty of the property or improvements on it; or

(e) retains rents to which the mortgagee has a right of possession.

MORTGAGE-RELATED WASTE
My Rubbish Makes The Castle Ruined
Mortgage, Reduce Value, Maintain, Taxes, Covenants, Rents

(3) The mortgagee has the following remedies if the mortgagor or life tenant commits waste:

(a) foreclosure or the exercise of other remedies available under the mortgage for default on the secured obligation, if the waste has impaired the mortgagee's security;

(b) an injunction prohibiting future waste or requiring correction of waste already committed, but only to the extent that the waste has impaired or threatens to impair the mortgagee's security; and

(c) recovery of damages, limited by the amount of the waste, to the extent that the waste has impaired the mortgagee's security.

(4) Absent a leasehold provision to the contrary, a tenant for years or a periodic tenant has no common law duty to make mortgage payments.

3. **Right to Redeem and Clogging the Equity of Redemption**

a. The mortgagor's interest in the mortgaged property is called the "equity," which is short for "equity of redemption."

b. At any time after default but before foreclosure, the mortgagor has the right to redeem the property by paying the debt due.

c. The right to redeem may not be waived ("clogged") at the time the mortgage is created.

C. Transfers by Mortgagor

1. **Assumption and Transfer Subject to the Mortgage**

a. If the mortgagor transfers the property **subject to the mortgage**, and mortgage payments are not made, the mortgagee may foreclose and force the property to be sold. However, the transferee of the property does not have personal liability for the debt.

(1) While the transferor remains personally liable to the mortgagee for the outstanding debt, the transferee agrees to liability to the transferor for the debt.

(2) The seller is ultimately responsible for the mortgage debt (because the seller retains personal liability), but the buyer agrees to make mortgage payments on behalf of the seller. Typically, the buyer makes payments to the seller over the course of the mortgage, and the seller pays off the mortgage to the mortgagor.

b. If the transferee of mortgaged real property **assumes the mortgage**, and mortgage payments are not made, the mortgagee may foreclose and force the property to be sold.

(1) In addition, the transferee of the mortgage has personal liability and can be held liable for any deficiency.

c. In a **novation**, the transferee of real property and the mortgagee agree that the transferee will assume the mortgage and the mortgagor will be released from liability.

2. **Rights and Obligations of Transferor**

a. If, after there has been an assumption, the debt falls into default, the grantor can get an exoneration, which is a court order compelling the grantee to pay the debt.

b. If, following the assumption, the grantor has made any payments on the mortgage, the grantor can sue the grantee for reimbursement.

3. **Application of Subrogation and Suretyship Principles**

a. The grantor can pay off the debt and can then be subrogated to the mortgage and note, allowing the grantor to sue the grantee *in personam* or *in rem*.

4. **Restrictions on Transfer (including Due-on-Sale Clauses)**

a. Due-on-sale clauses and due-on-encumbrance clauses are now routinely upheld. Federal law preempts state laws restricting the enforcement of such clauses.

D. Transfers by Mortgagee

1. The mortgagee may also transfer his interest in the mortgaged property.
2. The mortgage generally follows the transfer of the mortgage note. If the note is negotiable, the transferee may qualify as a holder in due course, who takes free and clear of certain “personal” defenses, such as lack of consideration, duress by nonphysical threat, and fraud in the inducement.

a. However, the transferee will take subject to “real” defenses, such as infancy, duress by physical threat, and fraud in the factum.

E. Discharge

1. **Payment (including Prepayment)**

a. There is no absolute right to prepay a mortgage debt early. Such an option must be spelled out in the mortgage.

b. If the mortgage does allow for early payment, it will generally always include a prepayment fee. Such a fee is valid, because it compensates the creditor for loss of interest income.

2. **Deed in lieu of Foreclosure**
   a. A mortgagee can accept a deed to the property in lieu of foreclosure. However, the mortgagee takes the deed with all mortgages still attached to the land.
   b. In other words, the mortgagee steps into the shoes of the mortgagor in this situation.

F. Foreclosure

1. **Types**
   a. In most jurisdictions, when there is a default on an obligation secured by a mortgage, the mortgagee may:
      (1) obtain a judgment against any person who is personally liable on the obligation and, to the extent that the judgment is not satisfied, foreclose the mortgage on the real estate for the balance; or
      (2) foreclose the mortgage and, to the extent that the proceeds of the foreclosure sale do not satisfy the obligation, obtain a judgment for the deficiency against any person who is personally liable on the obligation.
   b. Today, a mortgagee may foreclose by forcing the sale of property secured by a mortgage after the mortgagor has defaulted on the promissory note.
   c. A foreclosure sale may be accomplished either through a power of sale or by court order.
      (1) A **power-of-sale foreclosure** occurs without judicial action, pursuant to a power-of-sale clause included in the mortgage documents.
      (2) A **judicial foreclosure** sale must:
         (a) be public;
         (b) be properly noticed;
         (c) be conducted in a reasonable manner (usually regulated by statute); and
         (d) result in a "fair" sale price.
            1) A **fair price** is not necessarily the fair market price. Rather, it is arrived at as a result of the mortgagee's due diligence in conducting the foreclosure sale.
            2) A foreclosure sale will not be set aside for inadequacy of the sale price unless the inadequacy is so gross as to shock the conscience.
   d. A foreclosure sale terminates the mortgagor's interest in the mortgaged real estate.

2. **Acceleration**
   a. An acceleration clause operates to make the entire debt become due on the happening of some specified event, such as a default,

encumbrance, or sale.

b. Such clauses are generally upheld.

3. **Parties to the Proceeding**

a. **Junior interests** (i.e., second or later mortgages) in the property are destroyed by a foreclosure sale.

(1) However, a junior mortgage is not extinguished if the junior mortgagee is not made a defendant in the judicial proceeding culminating in a foreclosure sale and does not receive notice of the foreclosure sale.

(2) Senior interests not participating in the foreclosure are not affected by a foreclosure sale.

b. **Modification**

(1) If a senior mortgage is modified, a junior mortgage prevails over the modification to the extent that the modification materially prejudices the holder of the junior mortgage, such as by:

(a) increasing the amount of principal; or

(b) increasing the interest rate (if the rate under the original mortgage was fixed).

EXAMPLE: First Bank has a senior mortgage on Blackacre for $100,000. Second Bank has a junior mortgage for $20,000. First Bank and the homeowner negotiate an increase in the interest rate of the mortgage with First Bank, which will result in First Bank receiving an extra $5,000. This is a modification that materially prejudices Second Bank. If the homeowner defaults and First Bank forecloses on the property, joining Second Bank, First Bank will receive the first $100,000 of the foreclosure sale price. Second Bank will receive the next $20,000. Then, after Second Bank is paid, First Bank would receive the additional $5,000.

(2) Modifications that normally do not materially prejudice the holder of the junior mortgage include:

(a) extension of the mortgage maturity date; and

(b) rescheduling installment payments.

4. **Deficiency and Surplus**

a. The proceeds of a mortgage foreclosure sale will be distributed in the following order:

(1) to the costs of the sale;

(2) to the security interest foreclosed;

(3) to junior lienholders terminated by the sale; and then

(4) to the mortgagor, if any proceeds remain.

b. If the proceeds of a foreclosure sale are not sufficient to cover the lien(s) foreclosed, the mortgagee/creditor(s) may obtain a deficiency judgment against the mortgagor (or a party that has assumed the mortgage) personally, based on the note. Some states limit deficiency judgments by:

(1) prohibiting deficiency judgments when foreclosure is accomplished privately through a power-of-sale clause;

(2) requiring deficiency judgments to be sought at the same time as foreclosure;

(3) scrutinizing the fairness of the foreclosure sale, particularly if the foreclosure is accomplished by a private sale; or

(4) requiring the mortgagee to set a minimum foreclosure sale price ("upset price").

5. **Redemption after Foreclosure**

a. About one-half of the states have a fixed time period (6–12 months) after a foreclosure sale has occurred for the mortgagor to redeem (by matching the foreclosure price).

b. Because this is a right created by statute, the ability of the parties to waive (clog) this right would depend on the wording of the statute in that jurisdiction.

6. **Marshaling Assets**

a. **Marshaling** is an equitable doctrine intended to prevent a senior creditor, who has access to more than one source of funds from the debtor, from prejudicing a junior creditor, who can seek recourse from only one source of funds from the debtor, by foreclosing on the common source of funds first. It compels a creditor with more collateral options at its disposal to exhaust those other assets first, so as not to defeat another creditor.

b. The doctrine of marshaling is often raised by a junior lien creditor as an affirmative defense to a foreclosure action undertaken by a senior lienholder.

c. There are two common techniques to marshal assets: the **two funds doctrine** and the **inverse order of alienation doctrine**.

d. **Two Funds Doctrine**

(1) Marshaling may be applied for the benefit of a junior lien creditor when [In re Southeastern Materials, Inc., 452 B.R. 170 (Bankr. M.D. N.C. 2011)]:

(a) the junior lien creditor and the senior lien creditor are dealing with a common debtor who owns two or more properties;

(b) the senior lien creditor has a lien on two or more of the debtor's properties; and

(c) the junior lien creditor has a junior lien on fewer of the properties than the senior lien creditor.

<u>**EXAMPLE**</u>: Homeowner takes out a purchase-money mortgage with Bank 1 in order to finance his acquisition of Blackacre and Whiteacre, two separate parcels of land located in a city. Later, wanting to renovate Blackacre into a bed and breakfast, Homeowner takes out a mortgage with Bank 2, using Blackacre as collateral. Several years later, tourism to the city plummets, and Homeowner defaults on his loan to Bank 1. Bank 1 initi-

ates a foreclosure action against Blackacre, joining Bank 2 as a junior lienholder. The value of Blackacre at this point is well below the outstanding amount of Bank 1's mortgage. Bank 2 can raise the doctrine of marshaling as an affirmative defense to this action and ask the court to compel Bank 1 to foreclose first on Whiteacre so as to avoid prejudicing Bank 2, whose only source of recovering from Homeowner is Blackacre.

e. **Inverse Order of Alienation**

(1) The inverse order of alienation doctrine provides that, where land subject to a lien has been divided into separate parcels and sold to different grantees successively and without a release from the mortgagee, a mortgagee must first satisfy its lien out of the land remaining in the grantor or original owner's possession if possible [Savings Bank v. Creswell, 100 U.S. 630 (1879)].

(2) If that land is insufficient to satisfy the debt (or the grantor did not retain any property), the mortgagee must resort to the separate parcels in the inverse order of their alienation (in other words, the most recently conveyed parcel first, then working backwards to the first parcel conveyed). The equity resides in an earlier (or the earliest) grantee of a parcel of property.

EXAMPLE: Landowner mortgages Blackacre to Bank for $500,000, which was duly recorded. Several years later, Landowner breaks Blackacre up into 10 equal lots of land. She keeps Lots 1 and 2 for herself, and then conveys Lots 3 through 10 to various friends and buyers, in numerical order, all of whom take subject to the mortgage. A couple of years after that, Landowner defaults on the mortgage to Bank. If the court applies the inverse order of alienation doctrine, Bank would need to foreclose first on Lots 1 and 2, and then on Lot 10, then Lot 9, and so forth, in descending order of alienation, until the mortgage obligation is satisfied.

(a) The doctrine does not apply where it appears from the conveyance or junior encumbrance that the subsequently conveyed parcel was intended to be primarily liable for the payment of the debt.

(3) Where a grantee assumes the mortgage, an opposite, "direct order" of alienation applies. In this situation, as between the mortgagor and the grantee, the mortgagor is the holder of the equity, and the grantee should pay the mortgage and his land be sold first to satisfy the debt, before the mortgagor.

V. TITLES

A. Adverse Possession

1. Adverse possession requires proof of possession that is all of the following:
   a. open, visible, and notorious;
   b. actual;
      (1) An adverse possessor is required to possess the premises for the requisite time period. Actual possession gives notice to the world at large and the property owner in particular that someone is possessing the premises.
      (2) A person **actually possesses** property when she is on the premises physically.
      (3) A person may also possess the premises constructively. **Constructive adverse possession** requires color of title (usually a defective deed) and actual possession of at least a significant part of the premises.
      (4) If those elements are satisfied, the possessor will constructively possess the whole property as described in deed. However, there are certain exceptions to the constructive possession rule:
         (a) if land is divided into two or more distinctive lots, constructive possession will extend only to the lot that the possessor actually occupies; and
         (b) if a third person is in possession of part of the premises, constructive possession will not extend to the portion the third party possesses.

NOTE Many courts require some reasonable relationship between the area actually possessed and the additional area alleged to be constructively possessed.

   c. exclusive;
   d. hostile and under a claim of title or right; and
      (1) To acquire title by adverse possession, a person must possess the premises in a "hostile" manner. In this context, a person possesses **hostilely** if he holds the premises in a manner that is inconsistent with the rights of the owner.
      (2) Under the majority rule, hostility is judged objectively, which means that the possessor's state of mind is irrelevant. The element is satisfied if the possessor intends to be on the premises, regardless of whether the possessor knows that the premises are owned by someone else.
      (3) In a minority of jurisdictions, the possessor must act in good faith, which means that the possessor must believe the land is hers.
      (4) A few courts require bad faith, which means that the possessor must show that he knows that the land is not his but intends to claim it nonetheless.

NOTE ▶ Adverse possession questions often involve mistaken boundaries. A typical example involves a building on one parcel of land that encroaches slightly on the adjoining parcel, often without the knowledge of the owner of the adjoining parcel. Two standards have been developed to judge those cases. Under the **objective majority** ("Maine") view for mistaken boundaries, possession is hostile so long as the possessor intends to claim the land as her own, even if she is unsure as to the location of the boundary. Under the **subjective minority** ("Connecticut") **view** for mistaken boundaries, the possessor must actually know that she has crossed over the boundary.

NOTE ▶ Boundary disputes may also be determined by methods other than adverse possession. An oral agreement to settle a boundary dispute is enforceable if the parties subsequently accept the line for a long period of time. Long acquiescence (perhaps for a period shorter than the statute of limitations) may also be used as evidence of an agreement between the parties to fix the boundary line. In addition, if one party makes a representation through words or acts to the other concerning the location of a common boundary, and the other party changes position in reliance on that representation, the first party may be estopped from denying the validity of his representation.

e. continuous for the statutory period.

(1) To acquire title by adverse possession, the possessor must show that she has possessed the property continuously for the statutory period. In some cases, a possessor may satisfy this element even if she has not been on the premises every day during the statutory period.

(a) Seasonal use may suffice if that use constitutes the best use of the property.

EXAMPLE: The annual summer use of an unheated cabin in the north woods.

(2) The requisite time period for adverse possession is established by statute. In many states, the common law period of 20 years has been supplanted by a shorter statutory period, which is often five, seven, or 10 years.

(3) If an adverse possessor has not been in possession for the full statutory period, he may still meet the time period by **tacking** his possession onto possession by a previous adverse possessor.

(a) Tacking is allowed if the adverse possessor and his predecessor are in privity of estate.

(b) **Privity of estate** requires an intentional transfer of possession from one person to the next.

(c) An adverse possessor may not tack his possession onto that of a previous person if the adverse possessor dispossesses the previous possessor.

(d) If the ownership of the property changes hands during the period of adverse possession, the adverse possession continues to run uninterrupted against the subsequent owner if the two owners are in privity of estate.

EXAMPLE: In 2000, A adversely enters onto Blackacre, which is owned by O. In 2001, O conveys Blackacre to B for life, remainder to C. In 2008, B dies without ever having entered Blackacre. The jurisdiction has a five-year statute of limitations for adverse possession claims. C now seeks to quiet title against A. A entered against O before O devised to B for life, remainder to C. Therefore, the statute of limitations continued to run against both B and C. Under the five-year statute of limitations, the time period ran out in 2005; as a result, A will prevail over C.

(4) The running of a statute of limitations may be tolled in certain circumstances.

(a) **Tolling** means that the statute will not run for a period of time.

(b) For tolling to occur, a disability must be in existence at the time the adverse possessor enters.

1) **Disability** typically includes nonage, legal incompetence, and imprisonment. Most states extend the time to bring an action to a certain period after the disability has been removed (e.g., 10 years).

EXAMPLE: In 1999, O, the owner of Blackacre, is adjudicated legally incompetent. In 2000, A enters adversely on land owned by O. In 2003, O dies without regaining legal competence; however, O leaves a valid will that devises her entire estate to B, who is under no disability at the time. The jurisdiction has a statute of limitations for adverse possession, which provides that, in the case of disability, the statutory period expires seven years after the adverse possessor enters or 10 years after the owner's disability is removed, whichever date is later. B sues to quiet title to Blackacre in 2008. The statute is tolled in this case because O was under a disability at the time that A entered the premises. O's disability was removed in 2003, when O died. The statute gives B, as the successor owner (who is in privity of estate with O through O's will), 10 years after the removal of O's disability, which means the statute would run out against B in 2013. Therefore, B will prevail over A in B's 2008 quiet title suit.

2) When property is acquired by adverse possession, the adverse possessor acquires only what the current possessory estate owner has in terms of title. This means the title acquired is of the same type and subject to the same conditions or encumbrances.

EXAMPLE: An adverse possessor enters into and, after meeting the requirements, acquires title to land held by an absentee landowner in a life estate. The adverse possessor acquires a life estate *pur autre vie*, measured by the life of the original landowner.

EXAMPLE: An adverse possessor enters into and acquires title to property subject to a recorded easement held by the neighboring landowner. The adverse possessor's title is also subject to that easement.

B. Transfer by Deed

1. Requirements for Deed

a. Conveyance of real property by deed requires:

(1) donative intent;

(a) The grantor must intend to transfer an interest immediately to the grantee. If the grantor intends the deed to take effect only on the death of the grantor, will formalities must be observed.

(2) delivery; and

(a) Delivery is usually accomplished through the physical act of handing the deed over to someone. However, it is possible to accomplish delivery by mere words (e.g., by a declaration of intent and relinquishment of control). A presumption of delivery arises if:

1) the deed is later found in the grantee's possession;

2) the deed is properly executed and recorded; or

3) the deed contains an attestation clause that attests to delivery.

(b) Handing the deed to the grantor's agent does not constitute valid delivery. Delivery does not occur until the grantor's agent delivers the deed to the grantee or grantee's agent, which then triggers the relation-back doctrine. However, handing the deed to the grantee's agent does constitute valid delivery.

(c) **Doctrine of Relation Back**

1) Handing the deed to a third party (i.e., an escrow agent) constitutes valid delivery if the grantor relinquishes all control over the deed.

2) If a delivery is accomplished through an escrow agent, delivery will relate back to the date the grantor handed the deed to the escrow agent.

EXAMPLE: If the grantor dies before the escrow agent delivers the deed to the grantee, the delivery will relate back to the date the grantor handed the deed to the agent. Therefore, the deed was delivered during the lifetime of the grantor, and will formality and probate issues are avoided.

(d) When the grantor hands the deed to the third party and places conditions on the delivery, it gives rise to concerns regarding a situation where the grantor transfers the property to someone else before the condition occurs.

EXAMPLE: Grantor gives the deed to X, a third party, and says, "X, give this deed to Grantee if Grantee graduates from law school." A month later, Grantor conveys the property to C. At first glance, it would seem that C would win out. However, once the condition is met, the conveyance will relate back to the date Grantor gave X the deed, which was before the transfer to C.

1) The more conditions the grantor places on the conveyance, the more likely the conditioned conveyance will fail.
2) When a grantor gives the deed to a third party with instructions to deliver the deed at the grantor's death (a death escrow), the grantor is making a present transfer of a life estate with a remainder to the grantee.

EXAMPLE: Grantor gives the deed to X, the third party, and says, "X, give this deed to Grantee when I die."

(e) If the grantor expressly retains the right to reclaim the deed from the third party, transfer of title through the escrow agent will fail.

(3) acceptance.

(a) Acceptance is presumed if the conveyance is beneficial to the grantee.

b. To satisfy the Statute of Frauds, a deed must be in writing and:

(1) sufficiently identify the parties;
(2) contain words indicating an intent to make a present transfer of the property;
(3) sufficiently describe the property; and
(4) be signed by the grantor.

c. Parol evidence is always admissible to show that a deed absolute on its face is intended as a mortgage. Parol evidence may also be used to show that the grantor did not intend the deed to have present effect.

(1) Most courts permit proof of oral conditions on deeds if delivery is to a third party.
(2) Under the majority rule, if delivery has been made to the grantee with an oral condition, the conveyance is valid, but the oral condition may not be proved. Under the minority rule, if delivery has been made to the grantee with an oral condition, the conveyance is void (particularly if the condition is delivery on the grantor's death). In a few jurisdictions, if delivery has been made to the grantee with an oral condition, the conveyance is valid, and the oral condition may be proved.

d. Natural monuments prevail over all other descriptions. Artificial monuments prevail over all descriptions except natural monuments. Courses and angles prevail over distances. All of the descriptions listed above prevail over a general description (e.g., "Blackacre"). Natural monuments, artificial monuments, courses, and distances all refer to a "metes and bounds" description. A description may also be by government survey, name of parcel, or street address.

2. **Types of Deeds**
   a. The following three types of deeds are generally used in conveyances of real property.
      (1) In a **general warranty deed**, the seller warrants that no title defects have occurred during his ownership of the property. The seller also warrants that there are no defects in the chain of title from which he derived title.
      (2) In a **special warranty deed**, the seller warrants that no title defects have occurred during his ownership of the property. However, the seller does not warrant that there are no defects in the chain of title from which she derived title.
      (3) In a **quitclaim deed**, the seller does not make any warranties. Instead, the grantor simply conveys whatever interest he may have.
      (4) A **tax deed** is a legal instrument that transfers absolute title to the purchaser of property sold for non-payment of taxes (in a tax sale), after the expiration of the redemption period. It is also known as a tax sale certificate.
   b. **Covenants of Title**
      (1) A general or special warranty deed contains a series of promises or covenants, which are divided into present and future covenants.
      (2) **Present covenants** are broken, if at all, at the time of conveyance. Present covenants are considered to be personal and do not run with the land. They include the following:
         (a) in the **covenant of seisin**, the covenantor promises that she owns and possesses the estate granted;
            1) The existence of an encumbrance does not breach the covenant of seisin.
         (b) in the **covenant of right to convey**, the grantor promises that he has the right to convey the property; and
            1) The covenant of the right to convey is often co-extensive with the covenant of seisin. However, there are several differences between the two covenants:
               a) a trustee may be seised of the fee but may not have the right to convey if the trust deed prohibits the trustee from conveying; and
               b) an owner of a life estate may be seised but may not have the right to convey if the life estate is subject to a valid restraint on alienation.
         (c) in the **covenant against encumbrances**, the grantor promises that there are no encumbrances on the property.
            1) For the purposes of the covenant against encumbrances, an encumbrance is any right in a third person

that diminishes the value or limits the use of the land granted. In this context, encumbrances include:

a) mortgage and judgment liens;
b) taxes;
c) leases;
d) water rights;
e) easements; and
f) restrictions on use.

NOTE An encumbrance expressly noted in the deed cannot serve as the basis for a breach of the covenant against encumbrances. In most cases, if a defect renders title unmarketable (e.g., a mortgage or an easement), the defect also breaches the covenant against encumbrances. However, in a majority of jurisdictions, a violation of a zoning ordinance renders title unmarketable but does not breach the covenant against encumbrances. The jurisdictions are split on whether a visible or known encumbrance breaches the covenant against encumbrances.

(3) **Future covenants** may be broken after the time of the conveyance, and they run with the land. Future covenants include the following:

(a) in the **covenant of quiet enjoyment**, the grantor covenants that the grantee will not be disturbed by a superior claim;

(b) in the **covenant of warranty**, the grantor guarantees that he will assist in defending title against lawful claims and will compensate the grantee for losses sustained by an assertion of superior title; and

1) The covenant of warranty is virtually identical to the covenant of quiet enjoyment.

(c) in the **covenant of further assurances**, the grantor promises to take whatever steps may be required to perfect defects of title.

1) Under this covenant the grantor may, for example, be called on to defend a lawsuit or to execute a curative deed.

NOTE A future covenant is not breached until the grantee or her successor is evicted from the property, buys up the paramount claim to avoid suit, or is otherwise damaged.

c. **Remedies for Breach of Covenant by the Grantor**

(1) Monetary recovery is generally capped at the amount the grantor/defendant received for the property (plus interest).

(a) For breach of the covenants of seisin, right to convey, general warranty, and quiet enjoyment, the grantee may recover the full purchase price (if the conveyance is voided) or a percentage thereof (if a portion of the conveyance is voided).

(b) For breach of the covenant against encumbrances, damages are measured by the cost of removing the defect, if removal is possible, or the diminution in the value of the property if the defect cannot be removed.

NOTE In some jurisdictions, attorney's fees may also be recovered for breach of future covenants if the grantee loses the property to a lawful superior claim.

(2) Some states permit a grantee to recover damages from a remote grantor to the extent of the consideration received by the remote grantor from his immediate grantee, even if the remote grantee paid his immediate grantor less for the property. However, in some states, if the remote grantee paid less than the remote grantor received from his grantee, the remote grantee's recovery is limited to the amount the remote grantee paid to his immediate grantor.

(3) Specific performance is available for the covenant of further assurances.

d. **Statute of Limitations**

(1) For present covenants, the statute of limitations begins to run when the deed is delivered.

(2) For future covenants, the statute of limitations does not begin to run until a third party asserts a superior title.

3. **Dedication**

a. A **dedication** is a transfer of an interest in land from a private owner to the public generally or to a public agency. A dedication may be accomplished by deed, but may also be done by acts of the owner that would not constitute a valid deed and would not satisfy the Statute of Frauds.

b. For a dedication to be accomplished without a deed, the following requirements must be met:

(1) there must be an offer by the owner to dedicate the property; and

(a) The offer may be evidenced by words or acts of the owner indicating an intent to turn the property over to the public.

(b) A clear oral statement is sufficient. If a writing is used, there are no particular formalities; words on a document used for some other purpose, such as a subdivision map that shows public streets or other public areas, may be used.

(c) An owner who invites or permits the public to use her land for a long period may be held to have impliedly made an offer of dedication.

(2) there must be an acceptance by the public.

(a) Acceptance will not be presumed, as is the case with acceptance of a private deed when the conveyance would be beneficial. Affirmative proof of acceptance is necessary.

(b) Examples of acceptance include:

1) a formal acceptance by the public body;

2) taking over maintenance or construction of improvements;

3) cessation of property taxation; or
4) any other act indicative of government control.

4. **Drafting, Review, and Negotiation of Closing Documents**

a. The contract between the parties to a real estate transaction sets out the important points of agreement of the sale of the land, including time of closing, time of possession, transfer of keys, responsibility for payment of utilities owing and property taxes owing, what items remain with the property, and in what condition the seller will leave the property. These are in addition to the parties, the property description, the price, and the payment terms, if any, which are essential terms.

EXAMPLE: A buyer contracted to purchase a house, but inserted a clause that the contract would be rescinded if the buyer could not obtain financing within 30 days.

b. After the contract has been executed by both parties, and the down payment, if any, has been deposited into escrow, the contract is delivered to the entity that will handle the closing.

(1) In some jurisdictions, this entity is an attorney; in other jurisdictions, the entity is a title company.

(2) The attorney or title company begins the process of performing the title search and writing an Abstract of Title, in order to assure that marketable title will be able to be transferred on the day of the closing. The title company also prepares the title insurance that the buyer will purchase.

(3) The attorney or title company also reviews which liens have been filed against the property, and obtains an accurate pay-off sum from each lender, so that the lender on each lien can be paid in full on the closing date. Each lender must agree to file a Release of Lien after being paid.

(4) The attorney or title company drafts the deed that will transfer title from the grantor to the grantee. In many cases, the buyer has stated in the contract how she would like to take title, whether in her own name, as joint tenants with someone else, as a tenancy by the entirety, as the trustee for a trust, or in some other manner.

(a) It is essential that the buyer know the language of the deed before closing on the property in order to avoid errors in titling the property. The buyer should clearly inform the drafter of the deed of the manner in which she intends to take title. The deed must also be read closely by the buyer on the closing date, before the deed is recorded.

(b) It is essential that the property address and the address to which any property tax bills will be mailed are both correct. The buyer should request to see a draft of the deed before closing, for these reasons.

EXAMPLE: A buyer contracted to purchase a rental house that was situated at 123 Berry Street. The buyer's home address was 789 Elm Street. The buyer did not intend to live at the house, but to rent it out to tenants. Unfortunately, the deed listed the property tax mailing address as 123 Berry Street, when the buyer had specifically asked that his home address be used for this purpose.

(5) In commercial transactions, many additional documents require drafting, review, and negotiation. It is common for issues to arise after contract execution but before closing that need a negotiated resolution.

EXAMPLE: A buyer contracts to purchase a shopping center, contingent on obtaining a building permit to expand it. After the contract is executed, the buyer finds that there is a leaking underground storage tank on the property, left after a previous gas station on the property closed. The buyer insists that the seller perform the expensive environmental removal of the tank and restoration or paving of the surface afterward, while the seller insists that it is the buyer's responsibility. Regardless of their negotiated resolution, the closing cannot occur until the environmental violation is cured. The closing documents are likely to include waivers of liability granted by one party to the other.

(6) A real estate broker who lists a seller's real property for sale is the seller's agent and, as such, owes the seller a fiduciary duty of disclosure. Under this duty, the broker must disclose any information that the broker obtains that would be beneficial to the seller in negotiating the sale of the property.

(7) A real estate broker who contracts with a buyer to assist in the purchase of real property is the buyer's agent and, as such, owes the buyer fiduciary duties of loyalty and obedience. The duty of loyalty requires the broker to give her undivided loyalty to the buyer and to put the buyer's interests before her own, while the duty of obedience requires the broker to follow the buyer's lawful orders.

5. **Persons Authorized to Execute Documents**

   a. Ordinarily at a real estate closing involving individuals, the buyer and the buyer's spouse, if any, execute all documents requiring the buyer's signature. As a practical matter, photo identification is usually requested.

   b. In the same way, at a real estate closing, the seller and the seller's spouse, if any, execute all documents requiring the seller's signature. Again, photo identification is usually requested.

   c. In corporate transactions, the person executing the documents must have corporate authority to engage in the transaction, with documentation to reflect this authority.

   d. If, for some reason, a party cannot attend a real estate closing in person, a Power of Attorney may be granted to a third party to act in his place.

e. A special type of power of attorney that is used frequently is the **"durable" power of attorney**. A durable power of attorney differs from a traditional power of attorney in that it continues the agency relationship beyond the incapacity of the principal. Most often, durable powers of attorney are created to deal with decisions involving either property management or health care.

EXAMPLE: A couple owned a house in State A, which they intended to sell as soon as they could. The couple had already moved to State B. Their realtor in State A informed them of an offer on the house and emailed them the contract. The couple printed out the contract, signed it, scanned it, and emailed it back, finalizing the deal. However, the couple did not intend to return to State A for the closing, so they executed a Power of Attorney to the realtor so that the realtor could sign all the closing documents on their behalf.

C. Transfer by Operation of Law and Will

1. In General

a. If the seller dies after the execution of the contract for sale but before closing, legal title passes to her heirs or devisees. However, they must honor the sales agreement, and the purchase money passes as personalty.

b. If the buyer dies after execution of the contract but before closing, the buyer's estate will be bound to complete the closing and pay the purchase price.

2. Ademption

a. A testamentary gift is **adeemed by extinction**—that is, it fails—when property specifically bequeathed or devised is not in the testator's estate at his death.

b. An **ademption by satisfaction** occurs when a testator makes an *inter vivos* gift of property to a beneficiary of a general or residuary disposition with the intent that the provision of the will be thereby satisfied.

c. Property a testator gave in her lifetime to a person is treated as a satisfaction of a devise only if [UPC § 2-609(a)]:

(1) the will provides for deduction of the gift;

(2) the testator declared in a contemporaneous writing that the gift is in satisfaction of the devise or that its value is to be deducted from the value of the devise; or

(3) the devisee acknowledged in writing that the gift is in satisfaction of the devise or that its value is to be deducted from the value of the devise.

3. Exoneration

a. If the buyer dies after the execution of the contract for sale but before closing, the party that takes the decedent's realty may demand a closing and exoneration of liens from the personal estate of the decedent.

b. The majority rule is that the beneficiary of a devise or bequest under a will takes the property subject to any lien or mortgage outstanding at the testator's death.

(1) In other words, the majority rule is that a beneficiary is not entitled to an exoneration of liens.

(2) A testator can provide, expressly or by necessary implication, that the lien on the property should be paid off. However, a general directive In the will for the payment of debts does not qualify as such a provision.

4. **Lapse**

a. Under the common law, a **lapse** occurs when a disposition fails because the beneficiary predeceases the testator.

b. The common law lapse doctrine applies, except where prevented by an anti-lapse statute [UPC § 2-603, cmt.].

c. Under such a statute, if no alternative disposition of the property in question is made in the will, lapse will nonetheless be prevented in certain circumstances if a devisee fails to survive the testator and is a grandparent, a descendant of a grandparent, or a stepchild of either the testator or the donor of a power of appointment exercised by the testator's will [UPC § 2-603(b)].

D. Title Assurance Systems

1. Recording Acts

a. In General

(1) Recordation of the deed of conveyance is not required to validate the transfer of title. However, recording becomes important when two or more parties claim that the owner has conveyed (or mortgaged) the property to them.

(2) Recording statutes generally apply to conveyances of freehold interests, easements, profits, covenants, servitudes, mortgages, assignments, and liens.

(3) Title based on adverse possession or prescription is not recordable.

(a) Title based on adverse possession provides good title to the property, superior to that of the original landowner.

(b) However, in order to be marketable and recordable, the adverse possessor must first obtain a quiet title judgment in his favor.

(4) Recordation will not cure defects in a deed caused by lack of delivery, forgery, or fraud.

b. Types of Recording Statutes

(1) **Race Statute**

(a) Under a race statute, the person who records first prevails.

(b) Typical race statutes read: "No (i) conveyance of land, or (ii) contract to convey, or (iii) option to convey, or (iv) lease of land for more than three years shall be valid to pass any property interest against lien creditors or purchasers for a valuable consideration from the donor, bargainor, or landlord but from the time of registration thereof in the county where the land lies...."

EXAMPLE: O, the owner of Blackacre, conveys Blackacre to A, who does not record her deed. O then conveys Blackacre to B, who pays value, immediately records his deed, and has actual notice of A's deed. Although B had actual notice of A's deed, B will prevail over A because B recorded before A.

(2) **Notice Statute**

(a) Under a notice statute, an unrecorded conveyance or other instrument is invalid as against a subsequent *bona fide* purchase for value and without notice.

(b) To prevail under a notice statute, a claimant of real property must prove the following three elements:

1) the claimant took subsequent in time to another person claiming ownership of the real property in question;

2) the claimant was a *bona fide* purchaser for value; and

3) the claimant took the property without actual, constructive, or inquiry notice.

(c) A subsequent purchaser must pay value to prevail under a recording statute.

1) Value exists if the purchaser has paid all of the purchase price.

(d) A purchaser under a contract of sale who has not yet paid any money should not be protected under the recording statute. However, if the purchaser has paid some but not all of the purchase price before receiving notice, the courts are split as to whether the purchaser is protected under the recording statute.

1) Some courts state that partial payment is not sufficient to protect the subsequent purchaser.

2) The majority holds that the buyer is protected *pro tanto* (so much as he has paid), which may be accomplished by:

a) giving the land to the holder of the outstanding interest and giving the buyer restitution (the most common method);

b) awarding the buyer a fractional interest in the land proportional to the amount paid prior to notice; or

c) allowing the buyer to complete the purchase but to pay the remaining installments to the holder of the outstanding interest.

(e) Typical notice statutes read: "A conveyance of an interest in land shall not be valid against any subsequent purchaser for value, without notice, unless the conveyance is recorded."

EXAMPLE: O, the owner of Blackacre, conveys Blackacre to A, who does not record her deed. O then conveys Blackacre to B, who pays value, does not have actual or inquiry notice of A's deed, and does not record his deed. Although B did not record his deed, B prevails over A because B paid value and did not have notice of A's deed; B did not have actual or inquiry notice of A's deed and B could not have constructive notice of A's deed because the deed was not recorded.

EXAMPLE: O, the owner of Blackacre, conveys Blackacre to A, who promptly records her deed. O then conveys Blackacre to B, who pays value, does not have actual or inquiry notice of A's deed, and promptly records his deed. A will prevail over B because B had constructive notice of A's deed.

(3) **Race-Notice Statute**

(a) Under a race-notice statute, an unrecorded conveyance or other instrument is invalid against a subsequent *bona fide* purchaser for value, without notice, who records first.

(b) To prevail under a race-notice statute, a claimant of real property must prove the following four elements:

1) the claimant took subsequent in time to another person claiming ownership of the real property in question;
2) the claimant was a *bona fide* purchaser for value;
3) the claimant took the property without actual, constructive, or inquiry notice; and
4) the claimant recorded first.

(c) Typical race-notice statutes read: "Any conveyance of an interest in land shall not be valid against any subsequent purchaser for value, without notice, whose conveyance is first recorded."

EXAMPLE: O, the owner of Blackacre, conveys Blackacre to A, who does not record her deed. O then conveys Blackacre to B, who pays value, does not have actual or inquiry notice of A's deed, and promptly records his deed. A then records her deed. B prevails over A because B paid value, did not have notice of A's deed, and recorded first.

EXAMPLE: O, the owner of Blackacre, conveys Blackacre to A, who does not record her deed. O then conveys Blackacre to B, who pays value, does not have actual or inquiry notice of A's deed, and does not record his deed. A prevails over B because B did not record his deed, and therefore, A prevails under the common law rule of first-in-time, first-in-right.

c. **Indexes**

(1) In **tract index** jurisdictions, the searcher looks at the legal description of the tract of land followed by a chronological listing of all conveyances involving that piece of land.

(a) This type of search always provides constructive notice of a claim to property.

(b) A minority of jurisdictions require tract index searches.

(2) In **grantor and grantee index** jurisdictions, the searcher establishes a chain of title by searching two index books.

(a) First, the searcher looks back in time within the grantee-grantor index.

(b) Then, the searcher looks forward in time within the grantor-grantee index to see if any grantor conveyed an interest to someone outside of the backwards chain.

(c) A majority of jurisdictions require grantor and grantee index searches.

d. **Chain of Title**

(1) The **shelter rule** provides protection for a subsequent taker who does not satisfy the applicable recording statute. Under the shelter rule, a person who is a successor in interest to a person protected by the recording statute is also protected.

(2) The shelter rule applies in race, notice, and race-notice jurisdictions.

EXAMPLE: O, the owner of Blackacre, conveys Blackacre to A, who does not record. O then conveys Blackacre to B, who pays value, records immediately, and takes without notice of A's deed. B then conveys Blackacre to C, who takes by gift. Under either a notice or a race-notice statute, C cannot prevail over A because C did not pay value. However, when B took Blackacre, B would have prevailed over A under the relevant recording statute. C may take shelter under B's protected status. Therefore, C will prevail over A under either a notice or a race-notice statute.

(3) **Exceptions to Shelter Rule**

(a) A subsequent person may not take advantage of the shelter rule if that person:

1) attempts to "wash" his deed by conveying to a third person and then immediately taking a reconveyance of the property; or

2) commits fraud in respect to the deed.

e. **Protected Parties**

(1) Recording statutes only apply to protect subsequent purchasers for value.

(a) For purposes of recording statutes, this includes mortgagees and lien creditors.

(2) A grantee who acquires the property by gift, devise, or adverse possession will not qualify as a subsequent purchaser for recording statute purposes.

(a) However, such a grantee may still record her interest to protect it against subsequent purchasers of the property.

EXAMPLE: O, the owner of Blackacre, conveys Blackacre to A as a gift in 2000. A does not record. In 2002, O sells Blackacre to B, who has no notice of the previous gift to A.

B immediately records. A then records. B will have a superior claim to the property over A in any recording jurisdiction.

EXAMPLE: O, the owner of Blackacre, conveys Blackacre to A for value. A does not record. Five years later, O dies, and bequeaths Blackacre to his son, B. B immediately records. A then records. Under any recording statute, A will prevail. This is because B took title to Blackacre by devise, and as such, is not a subsequent purchaser for value. Therefore, B is unable to obtain priority through a recording statute.

(3) **Judgment and Tax Liens**

(a) A **judgment lien** is a lien filed in the county where a defendant resides after the defendant has lost a lawsuit.

(b) The lien, once recorded, covers all real property that the defendant owns, or may own in the future, in that county.

1) In some states, a judgment lien covers personal property as well.

(c) A **tax lien** is recorded in a similar manner to judgment liens, and it covers all real property and personal property that the taxpayer owns or may own in the future in that county.

(d) Either type of lien can be enforced through a specific levy or foreclosure action on a piece of property, or by waiting until the debtor sells a parcel of real estate, at which time the liens are paid off as part of the closing.

(e) In most jurisdictions, a judgment creditor is deemed not to have paid value for the property, and so will not be entitled to protection under the recording statute.

f. **Priorities**

(1) Under the common law, if two persons claimed title under deeds to one parcel of real property, the property was awarded to the person who took the property first in time.

(a) The common law rule still applies if the person who took later in time fails to qualify under the relevant recording statute.

(2) If two parties claim under a relevant recording statute, the first to satisfy the requirements of the recording statute will have priority.

g. **Notice**

(1) **Actual notice** exists if the claimant actually sees the deed under which the other party is claiming, or otherwise knows of the conveyance.

(2) **Constructive** or **record notice** exists if the other party's deed is recorded in the proper place in the record books.

(a) **Wild deeds** are deeds recorded outside of the chain of title, and which do not impart constructive notice on a subsequent purchaser.

(b) The courts are divided on whether an easement or restriction that appears in a prior deed to one lot made by a common grantor is constructive notice to the grantee of another lot from the common grantor.

(c) The courts are also split on whether a subsequent *bona fide* purchaser has constructive notice of a prior deed from the grantor that is recorded after a subsequent deed from the grantor is recorded.

(3) **Inquiry notice** exists if the appearance of the property is such that the claimant should have asked more questions about the title to the property.

(4) ***Lis pendens* notice** is notice of a pending lawsuit that will affect a particular piece of property; it is not a lien itself, but provides notice that there is or may be a lien against the property as a result of a judgment. When the *lis pendens* notice is properly recorded, it will serve as constructive notice to other lien holders, but does not serve to record the lien itself.

2. **Title Insurance**

a. Title insurance acts like a contract of indemnity. It is an alternative to doing a lengthy and expensive title search.

(1) A buyer can purchase an insurance policy on the title received, such that if there is a flaw in the title, the insurance policy will pay for the loss suffered.

(2) The specifics will be detailed in the insurance policy itself.

b. **Marketable Title Act**

(1) A marketable title act provides a "cut-off" point, which limits the time period during which a subsequent purchaser is required to search the records. The cut-off point is fixed by identifying a deed that has been of record for the required period, which is usually 30 or 40 years. Any interest that is not recorded or refiled within the required period is extinguished.

EXAMPLE: In 1960, O, the record owner of Blackacre, grants a right-of-way easement across Blackacre to A, which was recorded. In 1967, O conveys Blackacre to B in a deed that does not mention A's easement. B promptly records. In 2004, B conveys Blackacre to C. In 2005, A attempts to use the easement, but C prevents A from crossing over Blackacre. The jurisdiction has a 30-year marketable title act. The 1967 deed becomes the "root of title" in 1997, when it had been recorded for 30 years. Under the marketable title act, all competing interests recorded prior to the root of title are extinguished. Therefore, A's easement was extinguished in 1997.

E. Special Problems

1. After-Acquired Title and Estoppel by Deed

a. Under the majority rule, **estoppel by deed** is an equitable remedy that is applied on a case-by-case basis. Pursuant to this rule, when a grantor grants title to property that she does not own, and then subsequently acquires title to that property, she will be estopped from asserting anything in derogation of the deed.

(1) The grantee has to go to court to assert title against the grantor, or to otherwise enforce the deed against the grantor.

b. Under the minority rule, after-acquired title is a legal theory that provides for automatic flow-through of the property.

(1) With the after-acquired title doctrine, title to the property automatically inures to the benefit of the grantee when the grantor subsequently acquires title.

2. Forged Instruments and Undelivered Deeds

a. A forged deed is deemed to be a void deed, and does not operate to transfer title.

(1) This is most likely to arise in the situation with a potential *bona fide* purchaser. One who would otherwise be a *bona fide* purchaser will lose out to the original grantor where the property has been taken away from the original grantor by way of a forged deed.

b. An undelivered deed does not operate to pass title.

3. Judgment and Tax Liens

a. Judgment and tax creditors are not generally considered to have paid value for the property. As such, they will not be considered *bona fide* purchasers for value and will not qualify for protection under recording statutes.

KAPLAN BAR REVIEW

Torts

TABLE OF CONTENTS

I. INTENTIONAL TORTS

Elements of Intentional Torts 630
Battery 631
Assault 631
False Imprisonment 632
Intentional Infliction of Emotional Distress 632
Trespass to Land 633
Trespass to Chattels 635
Conversion 636
Defenses and Privileges to Intentional Torts 638

II. NEGLIGENCE

Duty 647
Standard of Care 664
Breach of Duty 670
Cause-in-Fact (Actual Cause) 671
Proximate (Legal) Cause 674
Damages 677
Defenses to Negligence 678

III. STRICT LIABILITY

In General 684
Categories 684
Defenses 685

IV. PRODUCTS LIABILITY

Strict Products Liability in Tort 687
Products Liability on a Negligence Theory 694
Products Liability on a Warranty Theory 695

V. NUISANCE

Types of Nuisance 698
Defenses 700
Remedies 700

VI. DEFAMATION

In General 704
Defamatory Message 704
Pleading Problems 705
Publication 706

Type of Defamation 707
Damages 708
Common Law Defenses 708
Constitutional Issues 710

VII. INVASION OF PRIVACY

Intrusion into Seclusion 713
Appropriation of Identity or Likeness 713
Public Disclosure of Private Facts 714
Portrayal in a False Light 714
Defenses and Privileges 714
Constitutional Principles 715

VIII. WRONGFUL INSTITUTION OF LEGAL PROCEEDINGS

Malicious Prosecution 716
Wrongful Institution of Civil Proceedings 717
Abuse of Process 718

IX. ECONOMIC TORTS

Intentional Misrepresentation (Fraud) 719
Negligent Misrepresentation 721
Interference with Contractual Relations 721
Interference with Prospective Advantage 722
Injurious Falsehood (Trade Libel) 723

X. MISCELLANEOUS TORT CONCEPTS

Vicarious Liability 725
Joint and Several Liability 729
Survival of Action and Wrongful Death 731
Satisfaction and Release 732

I. INTENTIONAL TORTS

A. Elements of Intentional Torts

1. An intentional tort consists of the following elements:
   a. a **voluntary act**;
      (1) A defendant is not liable in tort for acts that are not voluntary. Acts are not voluntary if they are a product of pure reflex or if the defendant is unconscious when the act is performed.

      EXAMPLE: Dex, during a sudden epileptic seizure, hits Pon. While Dex did not intend the harm, there is also no liability because there was no voluntary act by Dex.

   b. **intent**;
      (1) All intentional torts require the defendant to have a certain mental state when he performs the wrongful act. This mental state is called **intent**. For most intentional torts, intent is established if the defendant either:
         (a) desires that his act will cause the harmful result described by the tort; or
         (b) knows that it is substantially certain that such a result will occur.
      (2) **Incompetency**
         (a) The fact that a defendant is mentally incompetent or a minor does not preclude a finding that she possessed the intent to commit an intentional tort, but incompetency may affect whether such intent actually existed.
      (3) **Transferred Intent**
         (a) If a defendant acts with the necessary intent to inflict certain intentional torts, but for some reason causes injury to a different victim than intended, the defendant's intent is "transferred" to the actual victim. This **transfer of intent** applies only to assault, battery, false imprisonment, and trespass to land or to chattels.

         EXAMPLE: Darryl swung a baseball bat, intending to strike Astrid. However, the person Darryl hit was Plato. Darryl's intent to cause a harmful touching of Astrid will be "transferred" to Plato so that Darryl will be liable for committing a battery against Plato.

   c. **causation**;
      (1) As to intentional torts, the defendant's act or a force set in motion by that act must cause the plaintiff's injury.
   d. **harm**; and
   e. **lack of a privilege or defense**.

B. Battery

1. A **battery** is an intentional act that causes a harmful or offensive contact with the plaintiff or with something closely connected thereto.
2. The defendant must either:
   a. desire to cause an immediate harmful or offensive contact; or
   b. know such contact is substantially certain to occur.

   EXAMPLE: Dagwood intentionally swings his fist into Pickles' face, intending to hit Pickles. Dagwood has committed a battery.
3. The harmful or offensive contact element is satisfied if the contact would inflict pain or impairment of any body function, or if a reasonable person would regard it as offensive.
   a. It is sufficient for a battery if the defendant causes a contact with something close to the plaintiff, as where the defendant snatches a hat from the plaintiff's hand.
   b. Unlike assault, plaintiff need not be aware of the contact.

   EXAMPLE: Ryan intentionally spits on Prudence while she is asleep. Several weeks later, Prudence learns of Ryan's act. Ryan is liable for battery.

C. Assault

1. An **assault** is an intentional act that causes the plaintiff to experience a reasonable apprehension of an imminent harmful or offensive contact.
2. The defendant must act with the desire to cause an imminent harmful or offensive contact or the imminent apprehension of such a contact, or know that such a result is substantially certain to occur.
3. Liability for assault will not be found unless a reasonable person in the same position as a plaintiff would have experienced the same apprehension. However, if the plaintiff's apprehension is reasonable, the fact that the defendant lacked the actual ability to cause the harmful or offensive contact does not defeat liability.

   EXAMPLE: An assault is committed if Delson points an unloaded gun at Paulson, as long as Paulson reasonably thought the gun was loaded.
4. This element is satisfied if the contact threatened would inflict pain or impairment of any body function or if a reasonable person would regard it as offensive.

   EXAMPLE: Donahue holds a knife to Petunia's throat and threatens to hurt her. He is liable for assault and battery.

   EXAMPLE: Delilah, a bank robber, points a gun into a crowded bank and says, "Everyone lie down and keep quiet or else I'll shoot." This conditional threat is an assault.

D. False Imprisonment

1. **False imprisonment** is an intentional act that causes a plaintiff to be confined or restrained to a bounded area against the plaintiff's will, and the plaintiff knows of the confinement or is injured thereby.
   a. The defendant has the requisite intent for false imprisonment if he:
      (1) desires to confine or restrain the plaintiff to a bounded area; or
      (2) knows that such confinement is virtually certain to occur.
   b. The plaintiff may be confined by the use of physical barriers (e.g., locking the plaintiff in a room), by failing to release the plaintiff where the defendant has a legal duty to do so, or by the invalid assertion of legal authority. No duration of confinement is required—a very brief confinement will suffice, though the duration of the confinement may affect the amount of damages.
      (1) The plaintiff is under no duty to resist if the defendant uses or makes a credible threat to use physical force. A plaintiff is not "confined" if there is a reasonable means of escape of which she is actually aware.

      EXAMPLE: Stuart takes all of Susan's clothes and leaves her in the middle of the woods. Because Susan does not have a means of escape, Stuart has falsely imprisoned her.

      (2) In general, the plaintiff must be aware of the confinement or must suffer actual harm as a result of the confinement. Some cases have held that infants or incompetents who are incapable of being aware of their confinement can, nevertheless, recover for false imprisonment.

E. Intentional Infliction of Emotional Distress

1. **Intentional infliction of emotional distress** is an intentional or reckless act amounting to extreme and outrageous conduct that causes the plaintiff severe mental distress.
   a. The defendant must act with intent to cause severe mental distress or be reckless in creating the risk of emotional distress.
      (1) Recovery for infliction of emotional distress is allowed where a defendant acts **recklessly**, meaning that the defendant acts in deliberate disregard of a high degree of probability that the emotional distress will follow. This is contrary to the general notion that reckless conduct is somehow "less wrongful" than intentional conduct, and should be considered an exception limited to this tort.
   b. The element of **extreme and outrageous conduct** is satisfied if the defendant's conduct is beyond the bounds of decency—conduct that a civilized society will not tolerate.
      (1) Offensive or insulting language is generally not considered outrageous, except in cases involving defendants who are common carriers or innkeepers, or plaintiffs with known sensitivity, such as the elderly, children, or pregnant persons.

EXAMPLE: Damien, who does not like children, dresses up like a monster and runs into a kindergarten classroom shouting, "I'm going to eat all of you little children!" Damien's conduct may be extreme and outrageous.

(2) There is a trend toward permitting recovery for offensive insults made by one in a position of authority (e.g., a workplace supervisor).

c. The plaintiff must prove that the distress suffered was **severe**—more than the level of mental distress a reasonable person could be expected to endure. The emotional distress must be substantial, not trivial or transitory. The more outrageous the defendant's conduct, the easier it will be for plaintiff to establish the requisite mental injury.

(1) Most states no longer require the plaintiff to show that actual physical injury accompanied the severe emotional distress.

2. Where the defendant's conduct is directed at a third party, the defendant is subject to liability to a plaintiff, assuming the other elements of the tort are satisfied, if the defendant intentionally or recklessly causes severe emotional distress:

a. to a plaintiff who is an immediate family member or close relative of the third party, where the plaintiff is present at the time and the defendant is aware of the plaintiff's presence; or

(1) Recovery is available whether or not such distress results in bodily harm.

b. to any other plaintiff (regardless of relationship) who is present at the time, if such distress results in bodily harm and the defendant is aware of the plaintiff's presence.

F. Trespass to Land

1. **Trespass to land** is an intentional act that causes a physical invasion of the plaintiff's land.

a. A defendant need only act with intent to cause a physical invasion of a particular piece of land, not the specific intent to invade the plaintiff's land. Intentional entry onto land is a trespass even though the defendant does not realize he has crossed a boundary line, or has a good faith belief that his entry is lawful. In other words, mistake is not a defense as to a trespass action.

EXAMPLE: Don is out for a walk with his dog, Rover. Believing that he is the rightful owner of a grove of pecan trees near his property line, Don allows Rover to wander into the trees to "do his business." The trees are actually on Pam's property. Although Don is mistaken about his ownership of the trees, he may still be liable for trespass.

b. In order to bring an action for trespass, the plaintiff must be in actual possession or have the right to immediate possession of that land. It is important to distinguish "possession" from "ownership"—an adverse possessor or a lessee may maintain a trespass action against a defendant entering wrongfully onto land possessed, but not owned, by her.

However, if the person who holds legal title to the land is not in possession, that person may not maintain a trespass action as to that land.

c. The element of physical invasion is satisfied if the defendant enters or causes a third person or object to enter onto the plaintiff's land, enters onto the plaintiff's land lawfully but then remains when under a legal duty to leave, or fails to remove an object from the plaintiff's land when under a legal duty to do so.

EXAMPLE: Don is hitting baseballs in his backyard. For kicks, he decides to see if he can hit a baseball into his neighbor Paxton's yard, 100 feet away. If he succeeds in hitting a baseball over the fence into Paxton's yard, absent Paxton's consent, Don is liable for trespass.

EXAMPLE: Paxton calls Don and asks him to remove a baseball that Don accidentally hit onto his land. If Don fails to remove the baseball, he may be liable for trespass.

2. Some events that might logically be considered intrusions onto land, such as airborne pesticides that float onto a plaintiff's land from the defendant's crop dusting of adjacent property, were traditionally addressed by tort law under nuisance or strict liability principles. Some jurisdictions have begun treating such invasions as trespasses to land if actual harm was caused.

EXAM TIP Consider nuisance and strict liability, along with trespass to land, whenever there are facts involving something entering the plaintiff's land and causing harm.

3. **Plaintiff's land** includes the area both above and beneath the surface. Traditionally, plaintiff's land was thought to include the airspace and the subsurface to a level that the plaintiff did or could make beneficial use of.

EXAMPLE: Debbie loves to climb trees. She regularly climbs a tall tree in her backyard. One day, she climbs high into the tree and out onto a limb that overhangs onto Peggy's property. Debbie may be liable for trespass.

EXAMPLE: Dirk digs a tunnel to escape from his basement bedroom, where his mother thinks he is sleeping. As he digs, he digs under his own house and under the neighbor's yard. Dirk may be liable for trespass.

a. Aircraft flying at or above normal flight altitude do not "trespass" on the land above which they are flying. An intrusion into a plaintiff's "airspace" may be trespassory if it both enters into the "immediate reaches" of that airspace and interferes substantially with the use and enjoyment of the plaintiff's land.

4. Traditionally, nominal damages are recoverable where the defendant trespasses but causes no real injury, as a way to vindicate the land possessor's rights. If the trespasser causes injury during the trespass, however, he is liable for that harm as well. Further, where the defendant acts willfully or maliciously, he may be liable for punitive damages.

EXAMPLE: Dex drives onto Paula's land, believing wrongly that he has permission to do so. While on the land, driving with all possible care, Dex hits a concealed pothole, loses control of the car, and destroys a rare and expensive bush on Paula's property. Dex is liable for the harm to the bush.

5. **Ejectment**
   a. **Ejectment** is an action at law to recover possession of real property.
   b. The following elements are required for ejectment:
      (1) proof of legal title;
      (2) proof of the plaintiff's right to possession; and
      (3) wrongful possession by the defendant.
   c. A successful plaintiff is entitled to judgment for recovery of the property and for *mesne* damages. ***Mesne* damages** compensate for the loss of use of the land and are measured by the rental value of the property or the benefit gained by the wrongful possessor, whichever is greater.
   d. At common law, where the defendant mistakenly trespasses on or takes possession of the plaintiff's property and makes improvements thereon, the plaintiff is entitled to recover the property and need not compensate the defendant for these improvements. This is true even though the defendant acted in good faith, believing that she had rightful possession of the property.

G. Trespass to Chattels

1. **Trespass to chattels** is an intentional act by the defendant that interferes with the plaintiff's chattel, causing harm.
   a. Intent is satisfied when the defendant intentionally performs the physical act that interferes with the plaintiff's chattel. The defendant is liable even though he did not intend or recognize the legal significance of his act. Mistake is not a defense to trespass to chattels.

      EXAMPLE: Dorothy needs a black evening bag to carry to her sorority formal. Without asking Paula's permission, Dorothy goes into Paula's room in the sorority house, takes Paula's black bag, carries it to the formal, and then returns it to Paula's closet the next morning. Because Dorothy has Paula's bag, Paula does not have a bag to carry to the formal. Dorothy may be liable for trespass to chattels.

   b. **Chattel** means tangible personal property or intangible property that has a physical representation, such as a promissory note, or documents in which title to a chattel are merged, such as warehouse receipts or bills of lading.
   c. Interference with plaintiff's chattel is actionable if it constitutes dispossession or intermeddling. More serious interferences with the plaintiff's chattel may amount to a conversion, discussed below.
      (1) **Dispossession** is a direct interference with the plaintiff's possession, such as where a defendant temporarily takes the plaintiff's chattel or wrongfully refuses to return it.
      (2) **Intermeddling** is an interference with a chattel that does not directly affect the plaintiff's possession.

EXAMPLE: Smearing mud on the plaintiff's truck or kicking the plaintiff's dog.

2. In order to bring a trespass to chattel action, the plaintiff must have been in actual possession or have had the right to immediate possession of the chattel.
3. Unlike other intentional torts, proof of actual damages is an element of the cause of action for trespass to chattels. **Actual damages** would include the value of loss of use (e.g., rental value) of the chattel during a dispossession or the cost to remedy an intermeddling.

H. Conversion

1. **Conversion** is an intentional act by a defendant that causes the destruction of or a serious and substantial interference with the plaintiff's chattel.
   a. As with trespass to chattels, mistake is not a defense to conversion. A defendant is liable even though she did not intend or recognize the legal significance of her act.

   EXAMPLE: Drew sees Peter's 1978 Volkswagen Bug parked by the curb. Drew has always wanted to drive a vintage Bug, so she decides to hotwire it and take it for a spin. Seven hours later, she returns the Bug to the same parking spot where she found it, full of gas and in perfect condition. Drew may be liable for conversion. If, while Drew is driving the car, the Bug is hit and totaled, Drew is liable for conversion, even if the accident is not Drew's fault.

   b. "Destruction" or "serious and substantial interference" with a plaintiff's chattel is alternatively described as "the exercise by defendant of dominion and control" over the chattel. This is an interference with the plaintiff's property interest that is more serious than in a trespass to chattels. In distinguishing between the two torts, the longer the period of interference and the greater the use of the chattel by the defendant, the more likely it will be considered a conversion rather than a trespass to chattels. The following types of acts are likely to be classified as conversions:
      (1) wrongful acquisition (e.g., theft, embezzlement, and receiving stolen property);
      (2) wrongful transfer (e.g., selling, misdelivering, or pledging);
      (3) wrongful detention (withholding from owner);
      (4) loss, destruction, or severe damage;
      (5) material alteration; or
      (6) significant misuse.

   c. In determining the seriousness of the interference and the justice of requiring the defendant to pay the full value, the following factors are important:
      (1) the extent and duration of the defendant's exercise of dominion or control;
      (2) the defendant's intent to assert a right inconsistent with the other's right of control;
      (3) the defendant's good faith;

(4) the extent and duration of the resulting interference with the plaintiff's right of control;
(5) the harm done to the chattel; and
(6) the inconvenience and expense caused to the plaintiff.

2. The plaintiff is generally permitted to elect either recovery of damages, usually fair market value at the time of conversion plus consequential losses, or replevin/detinue/claim and delivery, compelling the defendant to return a converted chattel, with recovery of damages attributable to its wrongful detention.
3. If the defendant offers to return the plaintiff's chattel, this does not alleviate the conversion, and the plaintiff need not accept the return. Such an offer might be considered in mitigation of damages by a defendant who "innocently" converted the plaintiff's chattel (e.g., the defendant unknowingly received property stolen from the plaintiff by a third person).

TRESPASS TO CHATTELS	CONVERSION
Intentional tort.	Intentional tort.
Committed by intentionally dispossessing or intermeddling with a chattel in the possession of another.	Committed by intentionally exercising dominion or control over a chattel and seriously interfering with the rights of the owner.
Defendant is liable for damage or diminished value of chattel.	Defendant is liable for the full value of the chattel at the time of the conversion.

EXAMPLE: On leaving a restaurant, A mistakenly takes B's hat from the rack, believing it to be his own. When he reaches the sidewalk, A puts on the hat, discovers his mistake, and immediately reenters the restaurant and returns the hat to the rack. This is not a conversion. However, if A keeps the hat for six months before discovering his mistake and returning it, this is a conversion. If A reaches the sidewalk, puts on the hat, and a sudden gust of wind blows it off his head and into an open manhole, this is also a conversion. If A takes B's hat from the rack intending to steal it, and he approaches the door, sees a policeman outside, and immediately returns the hat to the rack, this too is a conversion.

4. **Replevin**
   a. **Replevin** is an action at law for the recovery of specific chattels that have been wrongfully taken or detained. It is also called "claim and delivery" in some states.
   b. Replevin is a possessory action that permits the plaintiff to recover immediate possession of the property (at the beginning of the action).
      (1) When the plaintiff seeks to recover the chattel at the beginning of the action, she must post a bond as security against the possibility that judgment will be found for the defendant. Note that the defendant may post bond if he wishes to retain the chattel until the action has concluded.

(2) No seizure of the chattel is allowed until a hearing has taken place to determine the plaintiff's entitlement to the chattel [Fuentes v. Shevin, 407 U.S. 67 (1972)].

c. Any damages suffered from the deprivation may also be recovered.

(1) The measure of damages is either the market value of the chattel at the time of the deprivation minus the market value at the time the action is commenced (if the chattel is held for sale) or the value of lost use (rental value or lost profits).

(2) Where judgment is for plaintiff but the chattel is not returned, the plaintiff recovers the present value of the chattel as established at trial.

d. If the defendant has hidden the chattel or removed it from the jurisdiction, and it cannot be seized, then an injunction for equitable replevin may issue.

e. Replevin may be brought only to recover tangible personal property; it is not available for recovery of real property or intangible personal property.

(1) Under the Uniform Commercial Code, the buyer has a right of replevin for goods identified to the contract if [UCC § 2-716(3)]:

(a) after reasonable effort he is unable to effect cover for such goods;

(b) the circumstances reasonably indicate that such effort will be unavailing; or

(c) if the goods have been shipped under reservation and satisfaction of the security interest in them has been made or tendered.

(2) In the case of goods bought for personal, family, or household purposes, the buyer's right of replevin under Article 2 vests upon acquisition of a special property interest, even if the seller had not then repudiated or failed to deliver.

f. Article 2 of the UCC also provides for restitution of amounts paid in sales of goods. Where the seller justifiably withholds delivery of goods because of the buyer's breach, the buyer is entitled to restitution of any amount by which the sum of his payments exceeds [UCC § 2-718(2)]:

(1) the amount to which the seller is entitled by virtue of terms liquidating the seller's damages; or

(2) in the absence of such terms, 20% of the value of the total performance for which the buyer is obligated under the contract or $500, whichever is smaller.

I. Defenses and Privileges to Intentional Torts

DEFENSES
POPCANS
Privilege, Defense of Others, Defense of Property, Consent, Authority, Necessity, Self-Defense

1. **Privilege**
   a. Under certain circumstances, a defendant may not be liable for conduct that would ordinarily subject her to liability.
   b. A **privilege** may exist where:
      (1) the person affected by the defendant's conduct consents;
      (2) some important personal or public interest will be protected by the defendant's ordinarily prohibited conduct, and this interest justifies the harm caused or threatened by the defendant's conduct; or
      (3) the defendant must act freely in order to perform an essential function.

      EXAMPLE: Delbert looks out his window and see his neighbor's house on fire. He grabs his hose and goes over to the house, putting out the fire. Delbert's entry onto his neighbor's land will be privileged.
   c. The defendant has the burden of proving the existence of a privilege and that the privilege was exercised reasonably under the circumstances.
2. **Consent**
   a. Even though a defendant has otherwise committed an intentional tort, he is not liable if the plaintiff consented to the act which constituted the tort. In order to invoke this defense, the consent must be effective, and the defendant must not exceed the scope of the consent.
   b. A plaintiff can manifest consent expressly, by implication, or as a matter of law.
      (1) **Express consent** exists where the plaintiff affirmatively communicates permission for a defendant to act.
      (2) Consent is **implied** under circumstances where a reasonable person would interpret the plaintiff's conduct as evidencing permission to act.

      EXAMPLE: David, a football player, tackles Pat, a player on the other team. Because the boys are engaged in a football game, it is apparent from Pat's conduct that he consents to the tackle.
      (3) Consent may be found to exist as a matter of law where the plaintiff is unable to consent, and:
         (a) emergency action is necessary to prevent her death or serious injury;
         (b) a reasonable person would be expected to consent under the circumstances; and
         (c) no reason exists to believe that the plaintiff would not consent.

         EXAMPLE: Della falls and hits her head, splitting it open. She is unconscious. A surgeon may operate to repair the damage under the premise that Della would have consented had she been awake.
   c. **Defenses to Consent**
      (1) Even where consent is expressly or impliedly given by the plaintiff, the circumstances may be such that this consent is ineffective

and will not operate as a defense for the defendant. The most frequently tested situations involve mistake, fraud, duress, incapacity, and violation of criminal statutes.

(2) **Mistake**

(a) Consent is not effective if:

1) it is the product of a mistake of fact or law as to the nature or consequences of the defendant's act; and

2) the defendant is aware of the mistake.

(3) **Fraud**

(a) Consent is not effective if it is induced by the defendant's intentional deceit as to the essential nature or consequence of his act. If the fraud relates to a collateral matter, the consent may still be effective, but the fraud itself may be independently tortious as to a plaintiff.

(4) **Duress**

(a) Consent is not effective if it is induced by a threat of imminent harm to the plaintiff or by a false assertion of lawful authority over the plaintiff. The same principle operates if the threat or false assertion of authority is made as to a member of the plaintiff's immediate family.

(5) **Incapacity**

(a) As a matter of law, young children and people whose mental capacities are impaired by mental disease, mental defect, or intoxication are incapable of consenting to tortious conduct. Without particular knowledge, the defendant may interpret a plaintiff's actions as manifesting consent.

(6) **Violation of Criminal Statute**

(a) Most jurisdictions treat consent as ineffective where the defendant's tortious conduct also constitutes a crime. A minority of jurisdictions and the Restatement regard consent to a criminal act as effective for purposes of civil liability for that conduct.

1) Minority rule jurisdictions consider consent to be effective, for tort law purposes, to an act that is also a violation of a criminal statute, so long as the defendant's act does not constitute a breach of the peace. The majority rule is that a person cannot consent to a crime. The minority rule (Restatement rule) is that a person can consent to a crime, provided it is not a crime that is also a breach of the peace (in other words, a person cannot consent for everyone). In addition, a person cannot consent to a violation of a criminal statute that was meant to protect her (e.g., consent is not a defense to statutory rape).

2) All jurisdictions regard consent as ineffective if the plaintiff is a member of the class of persons protected by the

violated criminal statute. This is thus an "exception" to the minority/Restatement approach as well as the "no breach of peace" principle in a majority jurisdiction.

d. While a physician's treatment of a patient without the patient's informed consent is typically treated as a form of negligence liability, there remain situations where there is such a gross deviation on the part of the defendant-doctor that a battery action will lie.

EXAMPLE: Parth gives Dr. Darth permission to remove his tonsils. Parth awakes from surgery to find that Dr. Darth cut off one of his toes instead. This would likely be a battery, as Dr. Darth far exceeded the consent given to her.

e. If the defendant's conduct substantially exceeds, in degree or nature, the scope of the plaintiff's otherwise effective consent, the defendant may still be held liable for his tortious actions.

3. **Self-Defense**

a. A defendant charged with an intentional tort may defend on grounds that she used reasonable force to prevent the plaintiff from engaging in an imminent and unprivileged attack.

(1) A defendant otherwise acting in self-defense may only use the degree of force reasonably necessary to avoid the harm threatened by the plaintiff. A defendant could not successfully assert self-defense if he used deadly force against a plaintiff whose conduct did not threaten death or serious bodily harm to that defendant.

EXAMPLE: Dylan sees Percy approaching him in a bar with a baseball bat poised to hit him. Percy shouts, "I'm going to get you, Dylan!" If necessary, Dylan may tackle Percy to the ground or grab his arms to prevent Percy from hitting him. However, if Dylan sees Percy approaching him with a flyswatter, Dylan may not shoot Percy, as he would be meeting non-deadly force with deadly force.

(2) A defendant cannot successfully assert self-defense when the purported threat represented by the plaintiff's conduct is not about to happen, has been averted, or has ended.

EXAMPLE: Percy says to Dylan, "I'm going to come back here tomorrow and kill you."

(3) Where the plaintiff's conduct, which purportedly threatens an imminent attack, is privileged, a defendant may not invoke self-defense and will be liable for any tortious acts committed toward the plaintiff.

EXAMPLE: A police officer makes a lawful arrest of a defendant.

(4) A defendant cannot successfully assert self-defense if she used force to defend herself when she knew an impending attack was based on a mistake as to her identity, and she would have had time to correct the mistake and prevent the attack.

b. Even where there is actually no harm threatened against the defendant, he may successfully assert self-defense if a reasonable person in the same circumstance would have believed that he was under attack. Thus, so long as the defendant subjectively (i.e., honestly and in good faith) believes that a sufficient threat exists to justify defensive force, and there is an objective basis for that belief (i.e., a reasonable person would believe so under the circumstances), self-defense is available.

c. In a majority of jurisdictions, a defendant acting in self-defense has no duty to retreat; even if a safe retreat is possible, the defendant may choose to use reasonable force against the attacking plaintiff. In a minority of states, a defendant outside her home must retreat before using deadly force if that is safely possible; if inside her own home or where safe retreat is not possible, use of defensive force is permitted.

d. Where a defendant otherwise properly acts in self-defense, he is not liable for an intentional tort if he thereby inadvertently inflicts injuries on innocent third persons. However, that defendant will be liable if he deliberately injures a third party, and may be liable for negligence if he unreasonably inflicts such injuries in the course of defending himself against an attack by the plaintiff.

4. **Defense of Others**

a. A defendant is entitled to defend another person from an attack by the plaintiff to the same extent that the third person would be lawfully entitled to defend herself from that plaintiff.

EXAMPLE: Dora and Terry are walking down the street. Dora sees Terry's ex-girlfriend, Phoebe, coming toward Terry with a knife. Realizing that Terry does not see Phoebe, Dora jumps out and grabs Phoebe's wrist, wrestling the knife from her. Because Terry could have been injured, Dora is privileged to protect him.

b. At common law, a defendant who made a mistake about whether defense of a third person was justified, or as to the degree of force that was reasonable, could not assert the defense and would be liable to the plaintiff for an intentional tort.

c. The modern majority rule applies the **reasonable mistake doctrine**. Under this rule, even if the third person (the victim) would not be permitted to assert self-defense against the plaintiff, the defendant will still be relieved of liability if a reasonable person would have believed that defense of the third person was justified and that the defendant's action was necessary to prevent harm to the third person.

EXAMPLE: Dakota sees Xenobia run out of a doorway pursued by Patton. Patton tackles Xenobia and they struggle. Xenobia cries out, "Help, he's hurting me!" Dakota seizes Patton and forces him to release Xenobia. It is subsequently established that Xenobia had robbed Patton of his wallet and Patton was lawfully seeking to restrain Xenobia. At common law, Dakota was liable to Patton for battery. At modern law, Dakota will not be liable to Patton for battery if a reasonable person in Dakota's position would have believed that Xenobia was entitled to exert force in defense against Patton.

5. **Defense of Property**

a. A defendant is permitted to use reasonable force to prevent a plaintiff from committing a tort against the defendant's property.

(1) The defendant must first demand that the plaintiff desist the conduct that threatens injury to his property before he can use force in defense, unless it would be futile or dangerous to make such a demand.

(2) The amount of force used by the defendant must be no greater than necessary to prevent the threatened harm. In addition, it is never permissible to use deadly force to protect one's property from injury.

(a) A defendant may not indirectly use a greater degree of force than would be justified if she were acting personally against a plaintiff. Thus, use of dogs or mechanical devices to protect property will generally result in liability, even if the plaintiff's conduct is otherwise tortious, because such force inflicted on the plaintiff is almost always considered unreasonable.

b. A defendant may use reasonable force to promptly recover his personal property if tortiously dispossessed of that property by the plaintiff. The defendant may also use reasonable force to recover such property from a guilty third party (one who took possession knowing of the tortious dispossession).

(1) The defendant may apply only such force against the plaintiff as is reasonably necessary to recover the property. A defendant may never use deadly force to recover property.

(2) A defendant must act with reasonable diligence to discover the dispossession and to recover her property. This has often been described by the courts as a requirement that the defendant be "in hot pursuit" of the tortiously dispossessing plaintiff or the guilty third party.

(3) Before being otherwise entitled to use force to recover personal property, the defendant must demand that it be returned by the wrongfully dispossessing plaintiff or guilty third party in wrongful possession.

EXAMPLE: Pam takes Darla's gold bracelet. Pam knows that the bracelet belongs to Darla, but she really likes it, so she takes it. Darla asks Pam to give it back, but Pam refuses. Darla may go up and grab the bracelet away from Pam.

(4) Even if otherwise proper, a defendant may not use force to recover property as to which the plaintiff came into possession under a claim of right.

EXAMPLE: Defendant may not use force to recover property from a withholding bailee or a purchaser on credit who has defaulted on the obligation to pay.

(5) A defendant cannot successfully assert the defense of recovery of property if he is mistaken about the fact that he was tortiously dispossessed of it by the plaintiff. This is so even if the mistake is reasonable.

(6) If otherwise proper for the defendant to use reasonable force to recover property, that defendant may enter upon the land of the plaintiff or guilty third party in order to effectuate the recovery. Such entry must be at a reasonable time and must be accomplished in a reasonable manner. The same rule applies if the property is on the land of an innocent possessor. However, the defendant will be held liable for any actual damage such entry causes.

EXCEPTION: Defendant may not enter upon the land of an innocent party and recover tortiously dispossessed property if that property is so situated as a result of the defendant's fault.

c. **Recovery of Wrongfully Dispossessed Land**

(1) In the majority of jurisdictions, the modern rule is that a defendant may never use force to recover land of which she has been wrongfully dispossessed. Such jurisdictions provide civil statutes that offer prompt judicial remedies and thus avoid any necessity for violent confrontations over possession of land.

(2) A minority of states still apparently follow the traditional rule that permits a defendant to use reasonable, non-deadly force to recover tortiously dispossessed land, so long as she acts promptly after discovering the dispossession.

6. **Necessity**

a. A defendant is permitted to injure a plaintiff's property if this is reasonably necessary to avoid a substantially greater harm to the public, to himself, or to his property.

(1) A defendant may successfully assert this defense if a reasonable person in the same circumstance would believe it necessary to injure the plaintiff's property. This is an objective standard.

(2) If the defendant reasonably but mistakenly believes that her actions are justified under the objective standard set forth, she is privileged to act, even if it subsequently is established that there was no actual necessity.

(3) If the defendant is acting to protect private, individual interests, he is justified in doing so if the threatened harm he is acting to avoid is substantially greater than the harm that will result from the action he actually takes.

(4) If the defendant is acting to protect the public interest, she is justified in doing so only if the threatened harm is severe—essentially, a disaster (e.g., the 1906 San Francisco earthquake and fire).

(5) In most jurisdictions, when a defendant acts out of private necessity, the defendant is still liable for any actual damage to the

plaintiff's property, but is not liable for any technical tort (such as trespass). In some jurisdictions, necessity is a complete defense.

(6) If a defendant acts out of public necessity, he incurs no liability whatsoever for damage to the plaintiff's property.

7. **Authority**

a. **Arrest**

(1) Where the defendant is a police officer acting pursuant to a duly issued warrant, valid on its face, she is not liable in tort for the fact of arrest. This rule applies to both felony and misdemeanor arrests, and applies even if the warrant is subsequently held to be invalid by a court.

(a) This defense is available even though the arrested plaintiff is not the person against whom the warrant was issued, so long as the defendant-police officer's mistake as to the identity of the person to be arrested was reasonable.

(2) Where a police officer or private citizen acts to prevent a felony that is being committed or appears about to be committed in his presence, he is not liable for an intentional tort based upon such an arrest.

(a) The defendant may assert the defense even though he was mistaken in his belief that a felony was being or about to be committed, so long as the mistake is reasonable.

(3) Both police officers and private citizens may assert the defense for arrest of a person who has, in fact, committed a felony. Treatment varies where a mistake is made as to either the fact that a felony has been committed or the identity of the felon, depending upon whether the defendant is a police officer or not.

(a) A police officer is not liable in tort for a warrantless felony arrest, even if he makes a mistake about whether a felony was committed or about the identity of the person who committed the felony, so long as the mistake is reasonable.

(b) Where a private citizen makes a felony arrest but makes a mistake about whether a felony was committed the defense of authority is not available, even if the mistake is reasonable. If a felony was committed but the private citizen makes a mistake about the identity of the person who committed the felony, the defense of authority is available if defendant's mistake as to identity is reasonable.

(4) A police officer or private citizen is not liable for an arrest made without a warrant as to a breach of the peace (e.g., a misdemeanor involving violence) that is committed or appears about to be committed in her presence.

(a) A defendant may assert this defense even though mistaken in his belief that a breach of the peace was being or about to be committed, so long as the mistake is reasonable.

(5) In the majority of jurisdictions, a defendant may not assert the defense of authority if he makes a warrantless arrest for commission of a misdemeanor not involving a breach of the peace.

(a) Statutes in a few jurisdictions give police officers the authority to make warrantless misdemeanor arrests not involving a breach of the peace if the misdemeanor is committed in their presence.

(6) If a defendant is otherwise entitled to make an arrest, the defendant may also enter upon the plaintiff-arrestee's land to effectuate the arrest.

b. **Shopkeeper's Privilege**

(1) A defendant-shopkeeper is not liable for false imprisonment or a related tort if she has a reasonable suspicion that the plaintiff has stolen goods, uses reasonable force to detain the person, and detains the plaintiff for a reasonable period and in a reasonable manner, either on the premises or in the immediate vicinity.

(a) The defendant-shopkeeper may assert the defense, even if the detained plaintiff has not, in fact, stolen any property, so long as the defendant's mistake is reasonable. It is often stated that the shopkeeper must have a **reasonable suspicion** that goods were stolen and that the detained plaintiff was the person who stole them.

c. **Discipline**

(1) If a defendant is charged with maintaining discipline (e.g., a parent or teacher), he may use reasonable force to perform this duty.

(a) Force that is reasonably necessary to maintain discipline varies according to the circumstances. Factors considered include the nature of the misconduct; the age, sex, and physical condition of the disciplined plaintiff; and the motivation under which the defendant acted.

II. NEGLIGENCE

A. Duty

1. The element of **duty** is usually described as an obligation, recognized by law, requiring the defendant to conform to a certain standard of conduct for the protection of others against unreasonable risk. Where the defendant engages in conduct that is claimed to have injured the plaintiff, the issue can be framed as: did the defendant have a duty to the plaintiff to conform to a certain standard of conduct?
2. In some situations the general duty rule will not apply.
3. **Foreseeable Plaintiffs**
   a. In the famous Palsgraf case, Justice Cardozo articulated the rule that a defendant owes a duty only to **foreseeable plaintiffs** [Palsgraf v. Long Island R.R. Co., 162 N.E. 99 (N.Y. 1928)]. (Justice Andrews' dissent in that case argued that "[e]veryone owes to the world at large the duty of refraining from those acts which unreasonably threaten the safety of others.")
      (1) Justice Cardozo's view is the prevailing view.
      (2) If taken literally, the Cardozo view that a duty is owed only to foreseeable plaintiffs could prevent some worthy persons from recovering for negligence. A key example of a worthy plaintiff is a rescuer who is injured due to a person's negligence. Cardozo claimed, and virtually all jurisdictions have agreed, that rescuers are *per se* foreseeable plaintiffs, and thus are owed a duty.

   b. The traditional rule is that there is no affirmative duty to take action to aid or protect a plaintiff who is at risk of injury unless such action is taken. This is based on the distinction between nonfeasance and misfeasance. The law does recognize certain situations, however, in which a duty to take action does arise.

      EXAMPLE: Darren sees Polly injured by the side of the road. Late for an appointment, Darren does not stop to help Polly. Polly bleeds to death. Polly's estate does not have a cause of action against Darren.

      (1) If the defendant's conduct is responsible for placing the plaintiff in a position where she requires aid, the defendant has a duty to take action to aid the plaintiff.
         (a) A **negligent omission** occurs when the defendant fails to do something that a reasonable person would have done, such as stopping at a stop sign. Negligent omissions are treated as misfeasance for which a duty is typically owed.
         (b) The traditional application of this exception recognized a duty to act only when a defendant's conduct that caused a plaintiff to be in peril was itself negligent. The modern approach is to recognize a duty to take action even when a defendant's conduct creating the peril was not tortious.

EXAMPLE: Danielle is on her way to the bar exam. She is worried about being late, so she is speeding. As she turns a corner, she fails to notice Pedro on his bike. Her car strikes Pedro's bike and causes Pedro to fall into the road and become trapped under his bicycle. Pedro sustains a broken ankle. Danielle must stop and help Pedro out of the road so that another car will not hit him.

(2) A defendant has no general duty to take affirmative action to aid a plaintiff where the defendant did not create the risk of harm to the plaintiff (i.e., put the plaintiff in peril) [Restatement (3d) of Torts § 37]. However, there are certain situations that may give rise to an affirmative duty.

(a) **Continuing Risk of Harm**

1) When a defendant's prior conduct, whether tortious or not, creates a continuing risk of harm of a type characteristic to the conduct, the defendant has a duty to exercise reasonable care to prevent or minimize the harm [Restatement (3d) of Torts § 39].

EXAMPLE: The defendant is playing a round of golf. After checking that nobody else was on that particular hole, the defendant swings and drives the ball. Suddenly, the plaintiff emerges from some nearby woods and enters the area where the defendant's ball is heading. The defendant owes the plaintiff a duty of reasonable care with regard to the risk of being hit by the golf ball.

EXAMPLE: A transportation company operates a shuttle from a hotel to a private beach, where hotel guests engage in various activities. While parked at the beach and eating his lunch, the shuttle bus driver notices one of his passengers from that morning riding a jet ski into an area with dangerous sandbars. The driver does not attempt to warn the passenger, who then hits a sandbar and crashes the jet ski, injuring herself in the process. Neither the shuttle bus driver nor the transportation company will be liable to the passenger, because the driver owed no duty to the passenger. While the company was responsible for driving the passenger to the beach, this transportation did not create a characteristic risk of harm from crashing a jet ski.

(b) **Duty Based on Undertaking**

1) When a defendant, gratuitously or for compensation, undertakes to render services to a plaintiff and knows or should know that the services will reduce the risk of physical harm to the plaintiff, the defendant will have a duty of reasonable care to the plaintiff in conducting the

undertaking if [Restatement (3d) of Torts § 42]:

a) the failure to exercise such care increases the risk of harm beyond that which existed without the undertaking; or

b) the person to whom the services are rendered or another relies on the actor's exercising reasonable care in the undertaking.

2) While most often applied in the situation of rescuers, this duty arises whenever a defendant promises to perform services for another and knows that the failure to do so (or to act reasonably in doing so) may increase the risk of physical or emotional harm to the plaintiff.

EXAMPLE: John asks Mary to check in on his cat once a day for a week while he is on vacation, giving the cat food and scooping its litter box. Mary agrees. After checking in on the cat for the first three days, Mary stops doing so. Mary will be liable for any harm caused by her negligent failure to check in on John's cat.

3) At common law, a distinction was made between **malfeasance**, where the defendant acted negligently in the undertaking, and **nonfeasance**, where the defendant failed to act entirely after making a gratuitous promise to do so. As such, jurisdictions varied as to whether or not a promise alone (unaccompanied by an attempt to complete the undertaking) was sufficient to be considered an undertaking and impose a duty on the defendant.

4) The majority of jurisdictions today have largely done away with this distinction due to the recognition and application of promissory estoppel. The Third Restatement of Torts reflects this modern rule by imposing a duty when the plaintiff relies on the promised undertaking [Restatement (3d) of Torts § 42, cmt. e].

EXAMPLE: While driving down a highway, Adam comes upon a recent car accident. Adam pulls the plaintiff from the wrecked car and immediately calls 911. However, rather than carrying the plaintiff to the shoulder, Adam leaves him near the car, in the middle of the lane. While waiting for an ambulance to arrive, Adam notices another car coming toward the accident at high speed. Adam tries to get the attention of the driver, but the driver fails to see the victim lying on the road and hits him, causing additional harm. Adam will likely be liable to the victim for this additional harm, because he failed to exercise due care in his undertaking (the rescue) and, by moving the victim from his car to the ground in the middle of the highway, he increased the risk of harm to the victim beyond that which existed if he hadn't acted at all.

EXAMPLE: While driving down a highway, Adam comes upon a recent car accident. Adam approaches the driver of the car and checks if she is okay. He then gets back in his car and leaves, without ever having talked to the driver. Adam has no liability to the driver, because he did not promise to provide assistance.

EXAMPLE: While driving down a highway, Adam comes upon a recent car accident. Adam approaches the driver of the car and asks if he is okay. The driver says that he's hurt and asks Adam to call for help. Adam promises that he'll do so but, when he gets back into this car, realizes that his cell phone is dead and he forgot a charger. Adam drives off, intending to stop at the next exit, but soon forgets about the accident and continues on to his destination. Several other drivers come upon the accident, but the driver of the wrecked car tells them that help is on the way already. Hours later, another driver finds the accident victim unconscious and calls for help. Because of the delayed response and treatment, the victim suffered significant additional injuries. Adam will be liable to the driver because he promised to provide assistance, and the driver relied upon that promise to his detriment, causing him harm.

5) Many jurisdictions have Good Samaritan statutes, which limit the liability of rescuers who provide emergency aid. For example, some only impose liability for reckless or intentional wrongdoing on the part of the rescuer, while others specifically shield emergency personnel, such as doctors, in rescue or first aid situations.

(c) **Statutory Obligation**

1) Where a statute imposes an obligation to protect another, a court will rely on that statute to determine whether an affirmative duty exists and what the scope of that duty may be [Restatement (3d) of Torts § 38].

(d) **Special Relationships**

1) A person in a **special relationship** with another has an affirmative duty of reasonable care to the other with regard to risks arising within the scope of that relationship [Restatement (3d) of Torts § 40].

2) If the defendant derives or occupies a position of power over the plaintiff (e.g., the plaintiff is particularly

vulnerable and dependent upon the defendant), there is a duty to take action. The following relationships have been generally recognized as triggering the duty to care for the plaintiff:

a) employer-employee during and in the scope of employment;

b) common carrier- and innkeeper-customer;

c) school-pupil;

d) parent-child;

e) landlord-tenant (with respect to common areas under the landlord's control);

f) business-patron; and

g) those in a custodial relationship to each other, whether voluntarily or by law (e.g., jailer-prisoner, daycare-child, or hospital-patient).

(3) **Duty to Control Third Parties**

(a) There is no duty to control the conduct of a third person as to prevent her from causing physical harm to another, unless:

1) a special relationship exists between the defendant and the third party that imposes a duty upon the defendant to control the third party's conduct; or

EXAMPLE: Dean is in a movie theater sitting next to Perry. Dean and Perry do not know one another; they just happen to be sitting in adjacent seats. Perry gets very angry with the usher because the usher tells him to take his feet off the seat in front of him. If Perry decides to slug the usher, Dean has no duty to control him.

2) a special relationship exists between the defendant and the third party that gives the third party a right of protection.

EXAMPLE: Dean is in the movie theater sitting next to his son when Eliza enters. Eliza takes one look at Dean's son, realizes that he is the kid who bit her child on the playground, and lunges at him. Dean has a duty to protect his son from Eliza and to control her conduct.

(b) A parent is under a duty to exercise reasonable care to control his minor child so as to prevent the child from intentionally harming others or creating an unreasonable risk of bodily harm to them, if the parent:

1) knows or has reason to know that he has the ability to control his child; and

2) knows or should know of the necessity and opportunity for exercising such control.

EXAMPLE: Milly and Erica, two 13-year-olds, are building bombs in Milly's garage. Their parents do not supervise their free time and giggle when they find bomb-making manuals in the house, saying, "Kids will be kids!" If Milly and Erica set off a bomb and damage their neighbor's property, their parents may be liable.

(c) A master is under a duty to exercise reasonable care to control her servant while acting outside the scope of the servant's employment in order to prevent the servant from intentionally harming others or creating unreasonable risk of bodily harm to them, if:

1) the servant:
   a) is upon the master's premises or premises upon which the servant is privileged to enter only as her servant; or
   b) is using a chattel of the master; and
2) the master:
   a) knows or has reason to know that she has the ability to control her servant; and
   b) knows or should know of the necessity and opportunity for exercising such control.

EXAMPLE: Darnell owns Silver Skates, an ice-skating rink in Coldville. Ellie is a skating teacher at the rink. Darnell is in the office overlooking the rink one day when he sees Ellie, who is supposed be taking the day off, doing skating lifts with skaters that Darnell knows to be beginners. Darnell knows that beginning skaters are not ready to do lifts and can really hurt themselves if they do. Darnell has a duty to intervene to protect the students if he is able to do so.

(d) The defendant-employer has a duty to a plaintiff to exercise reasonable care in hiring employees, such that a defendant may be liable to a plaintiff if an employee subsequently injures the plaintiff. This is distinguished from the vicarious liability of an employer for her employee's torts—*respondeat superior*, where the negligent conduct is that of the employee and liability is attributed by law to the employer. In negligent hiring, the employer is liable for her own negligence in hiring the employee, in addition to possibly being vicariously liable for the wrongful conduct of the employee.

(e) Where a defendant permits a third person to use his personal property, the defendant has a duty to control such use and to exercise due care in permitting the third person to use the property. The context in which this issue is frequently tested is an auto owner-defendant who permits a member of his family to drive his car.

(f) In some jurisdictions, a defendant who has the requisite special relationship with a third person and who becomes aware that the third person intends to do specific harm to an identified plaintiff has a duty to warn the plaintiff of the harm. The special relationships that have been recognized as triggering this duty include:

1) psychotherapist-patient; and
2) custodian-prisoner.

EXAMPLE: Zazu tells his therapist, Dr. Drew, that he intends to kill his ex-wife, Pru. Dr. Drew takes no action to warn Pru of the threat, which Dr. Drew believes to be credible. Pru is killed. In a negligence action against Dr. Drew, most jurisdictions would find that he had a duty to take reasonable steps to warn Pru of the impending danger based on his relationship with Zazu, his patient.

(4) Based on the distinction between nonfeasance and misfeasance, one generally does not have a duty to protect a person from third-party criminal conduct. In certain circumstances, however, a special relationship (such as a landlord-tenant or business-invitee) will trigger a duty. Jurisdictions vary on the amount of foreseeability that must exist before a court will find a duty to protect.

(a) Some jurisdictions will only find a duty to protect where there were **prior similar incidents**, making the third-party criminal conduct particularly foreseeable. Others use a more flexible **totality of the circumstances test**, while some others balance the degree of foreseeability against the burden that would be placed on the defendant to protect the plaintiff from harm.

c. When the defendant is a governmental entity, the question of whether the defendant owes a duty to the plaintiff will depend on the function the government is fulfilling that gives rise to the cause of action.

(1) If the governmental entity is acting in a **proprietary function**–that is, acting in an area traditionally occupied by private entities–the government will be treated as any other defendant for the purpose of determining duty.

(2) When the governmental entity is engaged in a **discretionary activity**–that is, where the governmental entity is using judgment and allocating resources–the courts will not find a duty.

(3) When the governmental entity is acting in a **ministerial function**, courts will find a duty; once the governmental entity has undertaken to act, it must do so non-negligently.

(a) Under the **public duty doctrine**, when a government agency (e.g., the police or fire department) is sued for failing to provide an adequate response, courts will find no duty unless:

1) there has been reliance on the response of the agency;
2) there is a special relationship between the plaintiff and the agency; or

3) the agency has increased the danger beyond what would otherwise exist.

EXAMPLE: Paul's third-story apartment catches fire, and he calls 911. Paul asks the dispatcher if he should jump out the window, and she tells him that the fire department is only a minute away, and he should wait for the firemen to arrive so that he can climb down the ladder. In reality, the firemen have stopped off to grab a snack before responding, and by the time they arrive the fire has spread, blocking Paul's access to the window to jump.

(b) If the defendant is a utility, courts have refused to impose duty beyond those who are in privity of contract to the utility.

4. **Negligent Infliction of Emotional Distress**

a. If the plaintiff's injury is not personal injury or property damage, duty issues arise.

b. Courts have traditionally been reluctant to allow liability for emotional distress, and apply special rules for claims for pure emotional distress.

NOTE Pain and suffering, though emotional damages, are not subject to the limitations placed on claims for pure emotional distress.

c. **Direct Claims**

(1) In most jurisdictions, to recover for emotional distress the plaintiff must:

(a) have been in the **zone of danger**—that is, the area in which she was at risk of being physically injured; and

EXAMPLE: Paula and Peter are crossing the street when Dexter comes driving down the road at twice the speed limit. Paula manages to get out of the way, but Peter is hit by Dexter. Paula was in the zone of danger and may have a cause of action for emotional distress.

(b) have suffered some accompanying physical manifestation of the emotional distress.

(2) Two exceptions exist to the zone of danger and physical manifestation requirements:

(a) if the defendant negligently communicates the announcement of the death of a loved one; and

(b) if the defendant negligently mishandles a corpse.

(3) In a minority of jurisdictions, if the defendant has a preexisting duty to the plaintiff, the plaintiff may recover for negligent infliction of emotional distress.

(4) Some jurisdictions have eliminated the requirement of physical manifestation of emotional distress and allow plaintiffs to prevail based on a showing of severe emotional distress without accompanying physical symptoms.

d. **Bystander Actions**

(1) In a bystander action, the physical harm occurs to a loved one, and the plaintiff sues for his emotional distress as a result of the injury to another. It is premised upon the defendant's violation of the duty not to negligently cause emotional distress to people who observe the conduct which causes harm to another.

(2) The majority rule is that a plaintiff may recover for negligent infliction of emotional distress under a **bystander theory** if he:

(a) was located near the scene of an accident;

(b) suffered a severe emotional distress ("shock") resulting from the sensory and contemporaneous observance of the accident; and

(c) had a close relationship with the victim.

(3) Before the recognition of bystander liability, American courts permitted a person to recover for negligently caused emotional disturbance only if the person suffered physical impact due to the defendant's negligent conduct or, later, was personally in the **zone of danger** created by the defendant's negligent conduct. Most American courts have now adopted some version of the bystander liability rule.

(4) Bystander emotional distress is a derivative claim in most jurisdictions. As a result, the bystander's recovery may be reduced proportionally if the injured party is found to be comparatively negligent.

EXAM TIP The requirements for negligent infliction of emotional distress ("NIED") are different than the requirements for intentional infliction of emotional distress ("IIED"). IIED is covered in depth earlier in this outline. See the chart below for a recap of the different elements required for both NIED and IIED.

INTENTIONAL INFLICTION OF EMOTIONAL DISTRESS		
Elements Required for Plaintiff Recovery When Conduct Directed at Third-Party		
Theory 1		**Theory 2**
1. Plaintiff must be **present** when conduct occurs to third party/victim; 2. Plaintiff must be a **close relative** of the third party/victim; 3. Defendant is **aware of plaintiff's presence**; and 4. Plaintiff suffers **severe emotional distress** (whether or not it results in bodily harm).	**OR**	1. Plaintiff (no special relation to the third party/victim required) must be **present** when conduct occurs; 2. Plaintiff suffers **actual bodily harm** (a physical manifestation of the emotional distress); and 3. Defendant is **aware of plaintiff's presence**.

NEGLIGENT INFLICTION OF EMOTIONAL DISTRESS		
Elements Required for Recovery		
Theory 1: Direct Claim		**Theory 2: Bystander Action**
1. Plaintiff is within the **"zone of danger"**; and 2. Plaintiff suffers **emotional distress** and some accompanying **physical manifestation** of the emotional distress.	**OR**	1. Plaintiff is **present** at the scene and **witnesses** the event; 2. Plaintiff is a **close relative** of the third party/victim; and 3. Plaintiff suffers **severe emotional distress.**

5. **Wrongful Conception, Wrongful Birth, Wrongful Life**
   a. **Wrongful conception** applies where the injury is the birth of a healthy child.
      (1) Generally, wrongful conception actions arise where the plaintiff has had a negligently performed vasectomy or other negligently administered form of birth control.
      (2) Damages typically involve the cost of the birth and the cost to rectify the ineffective contraceptive measure.
      (3) Courts are very reluctant to award the costs of raising a child through the age of majority.
   b. **Wrongful birth** is the claim of the parents for the birth of an unhealthy child.
      (1) Wrongful birth claims generally stem from a physician's failure to diagnose a disability in the fetus, which the plaintiff claims would have led her to not give birth to the child.
      (2) Many courts will not recognize a claim for wrongful birth.
      (3) Some courts will award the extraordinary costs of having a child with special needs, but the jury may offset this award by the benefit obtained from having the child.
   c. **Wrongful life** is the child's action for having been born unhealthy.
      (1) Most courts will not award damages for wrongful life.
      (2) A small number of courts have awarded damages for the costs of the child's special needs after the age of majority.
6. **Land Possessor Liability**
   a. The standard of care applied to owners and occupiers of land varies according to which of three categories of danger or activity were involved in the injury to the plaintiff. These categories are:
      (1) activities—the injury to the plaintiff derived from the conduct of persons on the land;
      (2) artificial conditions—the injury to the plaintiff derived from circumstances created by persons on the land, such as buildings, excavations, cultivation, etc.; and
      (3) natural conditions—the injury to the plaintiff derived from circumstances not created by persons but existing on the land, such as natural bodies of water, trees occurring naturally, falling boulders, etc.

b. In addition to considering the category of danger or activity that injured the plaintiff, the analysis of the standard of care varies according to the categories of the plaintiffs who claim injury.

c. **Plaintiffs on the Land**

(1) **Invitees**

(a) An **invitee** is a person who enters onto the defendant's land at the defendant's express or implied invitation, and who enters for a purpose relating to the defendant's interests or activities. Invitees are classified as either business invitees or public invitees.

1) A **business invitee** is an invitee who enters onto the defendant's land for a purpose related to the defendant's business activities or interests.

EXAMPLE: Customers and persons accompanying them, delivery persons, salespersons (if reasonable for them to expect that someone on the non-private, non-residential premises may be interested in purchasing), and job applicants (if reasonable for them to expect that employment may be available) are examples of business invitees.

2) A **public invitee** is a member of the public who enters onto the defendant's land for a purpose as to which the land is held open to the public.

EXAMPLE: Visitors to airports and visitors to churches.

a) In a minority of jurisdictions, the classification of public invitee is not recognized. However, courts in such jurisdictions readily find a business purpose in visits by persons who would otherwise be considered public invitees.

(b) A defendant has a duty to exercise reasonable care to prevent injuries to invitees caused by activities conducted on his land.

(c) The defendant also has a duty to exercise reasonable care to discover dangerous artificial conditions that invitees would not reasonably be aware of, and to warn invitees of the existence of such conditions or to make the conditions safe. If it would be insufficient to make the dangerous condition reasonably safe by providing only a warning, the defendant's duty includes a duty of reasonable care to provide other precautions.

(d) The defendant's duty to invitees with regard to dangerous natural conditions is the same as that applicable to artificial conditions.

(e) An invitee may be regarded as a licensee or even as a trespasser if the invitee enters areas of the defendant's property to which her invitation does not extend, or if the invitee stays in a permitted area longer than was contemplated by the invitation.

(2) **Licensees**

(a) A **licensee** is a person who enters onto the defendant's land with the defendant's express or implied permission, and who does not enter for a purpose benefiting the defendant or the defendant's activities.

EXAMPLE: Visiting relatives, social guests, and door-to-door salespersons.

NOTE Invitees who exceed the scope of defendant's invitation are treated as licensees.

(b) As to licensees, a defendant has a duty to exercise reasonable care to protect them from injury arising from activities conducted by the defendant or on the defendant's behalf. It is usually sufficient for the defendant to warn the plaintiff-licensee, but the defendant's duty includes the exercise of reasonable care to discover licensees of whom he is not aware.

(c) A defendant has a duty to exercise reasonable care to warn of any artificial conditions of which she is aware, which present an unreasonable danger, and of which the plaintiff-licensee is unaware and unlikely to discover. The defendant has no duty to inspect her land for such dangerous artificial conditions.

1) The standard of care applicable to licensees requires defendant to protect them from dangerous natural conditions to the same extent required for artificial conditions.

(3) **Trespassers**

(a) If a plaintiff enters onto a defendant's land without the defendant's permission or without a privilege to so enter, the plaintiff is classified as a **trespasser**.

EXAMPLE: Demi wants to see the great view of the Mississippi from the top of Blueberry Hill. Blueberry Hill is entirely on Philip's property. If Demi hikes up Blueberry Hill without Philip's permission, she is a trespasser.

(b) The trespasser category is further broken down into four subcategories, as to which the standard of care may vary.

1) **Unknown**

a) A defendant has no duty of care as to a trespasser whose presence is unknown to him. The defendant also has no duty to inspect his land to attempt to discover unknown trespassers.

2) **Known**

a) If the defendant becomes aware that a particular plaintiff has trespassed on her property or becomes aware of facts from which she should reasonably conclude that a plaintiff has trespassed, the plaintiff is regarded as a **known trespasser**. The applicable standard of care varies according to the category of danger.

b) Most jurisdictions require the defendant to exercise reasonable care to protect a known trespasser from injuries deriving from activities conducted on her land.

c) A defendant will be liable to a known trespasser for failing to exercise reasonable care in warning him of an artificial condition maintained on the premises by the defendant if [Restatement (2d) of Torts § 337]:

i) the possessor knows or has reason to know of their presence in dangerous proximity to the condition; and

ii) the condition is of such a nature that the defendant has reason to believe that the trespasser will not discover it or realize the risk involved.

d) The defendant has no duty to protect a known trespasser from injuries deriving from natural conditions on her land.

3) **Frequent**

a) If the defendant knows or reasonably should know that trespassers frequently enter upon a portion of his land, the standard may be higher than that normally applicable to unknown trespassers. For example, if the defendant observed that a beaten path cuts across his property, he would be alerted to the presence of frequent trespassers. Frequent trespassers are owed the same duty of care owed to known trespassers, even if the defendant is not aware that a particular plaintiff is present on his land or has ever previously trespassed upon his land.

4) **Children**

a) Where activities and natural conditions are involved, the standard of care as to children who trespass is the same as that for the applicable category of adult trespassers. A heightened standard of care may apply as to artificial conditions on the defendant's land.

i) Horses, livestock, pets, and other owned animals are "artificial conditions" for these purposes insomuch as the owner placed them where they are, if they are not naturally occurring in the landscape. However, note that they may not pose a foreseeable, unreasonable risk of danger to children trespassers unless the owner knows or reasonably should know of the danger posted, and so the liability of the owner will depend on the facts of the case.

b) If the heightened standard of care as to children trespassers is invoked, a defendant has a duty to exercise reasonable care to prevent injury to the children, applicable to dangerous artificial conditions. The heightened standard of care set forth above arises if five prerequisites are shown to exist [Restatement (2d) of Torts § 339]:

   i) it is foreseeable that children are likely to trespass where the artificial condition is located;

      a. If a defendant has no reason to anticipate that children are likely to trespass where an artificial condition is located, the heightened standard of care is not triggered. Foreseeability of the likelihood of children trespassers may arise from a defendant's knowledge of past trespasses, proximity to places where children are likely to be, accessibility to the artificial condition, and other relevant factors. Thus, if the artificial condition is located near a park, playground, or street, or is easily climbed, a defendant should reasonably know that children are likely to trespass there. It was from this aspect of foreseeability that the traditional label **attractive nuisance doctrine** was derived.

   ii) the artificial condition is a foreseeable risk of unreasonable danger to trespassing children;

      a. An artificial condition on a defendant's land poses a foreseeable, unreasonable risk of danger to children trespassers if a defendant knows or reasonably should know of the existence and nature of the artificial condition. A defendant has no independent duty to inspect the land to discover such artificial conditions.

      b. It is relevant to whether a condition poses a foreseeably unreasonable danger to children trespassers that the danger is one which a child might ordinarily be expected to recognize. Thus, a child old enough to play without immediate parental supervision can ordinarily be expected to recognize the danger represented by water, fire, and falling.

   iii) the child trespasser is unaware of the risk;

      a. This prerequisite is satisfied if the child trespasser, because of her age or immaturity, did not discover the condition or appreciate the danger it represented. If the child trespasser is aware of the condition, understands the risk of danger it poses, and is able to avoid that risk, the defendant owes no heightened duty to prevent injury to that child (i.e., the child is treated as if she were an adult trespasser).

iv) the risk of danger of the artificial condition outweighs its utility; and

a. It is said that the utility of maintaining the dangerous artificial condition must be "slight" compared to the risk to trespassing children in order for this prerequisite to be satisfied. This is similar to the negligence calculus (cost of precautions balanced against probability and gravity of harm considering social utility).

v) the defendant fails to exercise reasonable care to eliminate the danger or otherwise protect the child.

EXAMPLE: Paloma is a six-year-old girl who frequently trespasses on Donatella's land. Donatella knows that Paloma sometimes trespasses on her land. If there is a dangerous dumpsite on Donatella's land, Donatella must make it safe. If there is an abandoned car that is rusty and dangerous on Donatella's land, Donatella should remove it or cover it to prevent Paloma from injuring herself. However, Donatella does not have to build a fence around her pond, as natural bodies of water are generally not included within the rule.

(4) **Privileged Entrants**

(a) Where there has been no express or implied permission or invitation extended by a defendant, certain persons are nevertheless privileged by law to enter onto the defendant's land. These include police officers or firefighters responding to an emergency, census takers, or private persons exercising a privilege (e.g., where unauthorized entry is necessary to avoid a greater harm). **Privileged entrants** are classified as either licensees or invitees, usually depending on the purpose for which they entered.

(b) If the public purpose for which the privileged entrant was acting has a connection with the defendant's activities conducted on the premises, the privileged entrant is regarded as an invitee for standard of care purposes. Courts readily find that such a connection exists.

(c) Police and firefighters entering onto the premises have traditionally been regarded by the courts as licensees. As set forth above, a defendant has no duty to inspect and discover dangerous conditions as to licensees.

(d) A private person entering onto a defendant's land under some legal privilege is regarded as a licensee.

STATUS	DUTY OWED
Trespasser—Undiscovered	No duty.
Trespasser—Known or Anticipated	Ordinary care—duty to warn of dangerous conditions that are known to possessor (**exception**: no duty to warn of obvious natural conditions of the land (e.g., lake)).
Licensee	Ordinary care—duty to warn of dangerous conditions which are known to possessor.
Invitee	Ordinary care—duty to (1) inspect premises and/or land; and (2) make safe for protection of invitees who enter.

d. **Plaintiffs Not on the Land (But Adjacent to It)**

(1) A defendant must exercise reasonable care to prevent a plaintiff not on his land from an injury deriving from the defendant's activities or the activities of others conducted on his land.

(2) A defendant must exercise reasonable care to prevent a plaintiff not on her land from an injury deriving from unreasonably dangerous artificial conditions that abut or protrude onto adjacent land. A defendant must also exercise reasonable care to protect passersby on a public street from injury deriving from dangerous artificial conditions on his land.

(3) A majority of jurisdictions impose no duty on a defendant to protect a plaintiff not on the defendant's land from dangers deriving from natural conditions on his land. The minority rule is that the defendant must exercise reasonable care to prevent injury to a plaintiff not on his land from dangers deriving from natural conditions on his land.

(4) Many jurisdictions require that in urban areas, a defendant must exercise reasonable care to protect a plaintiff passing by her land on adjacent public streets from injury deriving from native trees on her land.

(5) The defendant to whom the standard of care is applied is the person in possession of the land, which includes the owner, a tenant, a purchaser, or an adverse possessor. The standard of care may also vary if the possessor of land is a landlord or seller of land.

(6) A substantial number of jurisdictions have eliminated the distinctions between the various classes of persons entering the land, and simply hold the landowner to a "reasonable under the circumstances" test. In applying the test, the nature of the entry is simply one factor in determining foreseeability and reasonability.

e. **Landlords and Tenants**

(1) The standard of care applicable to owners and occupiers of land is invoked in connection with possession of land. Thus, the appropriate standard of care (determined as discussed above) applies when a defendant is a tenant in possession of leased premises. Areas retained in the landlord's possession, such as common areas in multiple housing units, remain the landlord's responsibility. Under certain circumstances, however, a landlord may be liable to the tenant or to third persons for injuries they suffer in areas to which the landlord has surrendered possession to the tenant.

(a) The nature and extent of the landlord's duty to protect a tenant in possession from harm arising from a dangerous condition on the premises varies according to whether the defect was patent or latent, or whether it arose after the transfer of possession.

1) Dangerous natural or artificial conditions that are or should be reasonably apparent to the tenant upon transfer of possession are called **patent defects**. The landlord is under no duty to warn of or repair such obvious conditions.

2) Dangerous natural or artificial conditions of which the tenant is unaware and which are not reasonably apparent to him, and of which the landlord is aware, are classified as **latent defects**. The landlord has a duty to warn the tenant of such dangers or repair them. The landlord has no duty to inspect the premises for latent dangers.

3) The landlord has no duty to exercise reasonable care as to dangerous conditions that arise after possession has been transferred to the tenant, unless the landlord actually undertakes to repair such conditions or covenants to repair them. This latter view is a modern minority position, imposing liability where the tenant is injured because the landlord failed to perform a contractual duty to repair a dangerous condition of which the landlord knew or should have known and as to which the landlord had a reasonable opportunity to repair.

(b) Under the traditional view, a landlord had no duty to protect third persons from injuries arising from dangerous conditions or activities on the leased premises. Today, many jurisdictions treat third persons who would otherwise be classified as licensees or invitees of the tenant as though they were tenants themselves in assessing the tort liability of the landlord.

1) Even under the traditional view, if the landlord knew that the tenant intended to open the leased premises to the public, the landlord had a duty to prevent injury to members of the public who came onto the premises. This standard of care required the landlord to exercise reasonable care to discover and repair any dangerous natural or artificial conditions existing at the time of transfer of possession.

f. **Sellers of Land**

(1) Where a defendant transfers both possession and ownership of land to another, there is generally no further duty to protect anyone from injuries arising from the conditions of the land or activities conducted thereon. Under limited circumstances, however, the vendor-seller of land has a continuing duty even after the transfer of possession and title.

(a) A defendant-seller has a duty to disclose to the purchaser of land any hidden dangerous natural or artificial conditions of which the seller knows or reasonably should know and which the seller reasonably could anticipate the purchaser will not discover. The duty to disclose hidden dangers continues until the purchaser has had a reasonable chance to discover and remedy the dangers.

(b) The seller's duty to disclose hidden dangerous conditions applies to the purchaser and the purchaser's invitees and licensees as to injuries occurring on the land, and to persons not on the land if the dangerous conditions create an unreasonable risk to such persons.

(c) Where the defendant-seller actively conceals the existence of a dangerous condition, the duty to disclose continues until the purchaser actually discovers the dangerous condition and remedies it (i.e., the seller may not argue that the purchaser reasonably should have discovered the condition).

(d) In many jurisdictions, the builder of a residence has a tort law duty to exercise reasonable care in construction so that such builder remains liable for defects in its construction.

B. Standard of Care

1. Reasonably Prudent Person under the Same or Similar Circumstances

a. In general, a defendant breaches the duty to a plaintiff if he fails to conduct himself as a reasonable person would in the same circumstances.

(1) **Exceptions**

(a) The reasonable person standard is applied as though the reasonable person possessed the same physical characteristics as the defendant. Thus, the trier of fact assesses what conduct a reasonable person of the same height, weight, ability to see or hear, and disabilities as the defendant would have engaged in under the circumstances.

EXAMPLE: Del, blind since birth, is walking down the street using a cane. He knocks into Pol, injuring him. In Pol's negligence action against Del, Del will be held to the standard of care of a reasonably prudent blind person.

NOTE The reasonable person standard is not altered to account for a defendant's physical disability if the disability is the result of the defendant's voluntary intoxication.

(b) For purposes of analyzing a negligence action, the conduct of defendants whose cognitive abilities are diminished due to mental illness, mental disability, or intoxication is assessed without such diminishment of abilities.

1) However, to the extent that a defendant possessed greater knowledge or expertise than the average person, the "reasonable" person to whom the defendant is compared is thought of as also possessing that greater knowledge or expertise.

EXAMPLE: Dennis has an IQ of 75. Dennis places a large number of rocks in the back of his pickup truck but does not tie them down. When he drives his truck on the highway, a lot of rocks fall out of the back of the truck, causing a pile-up accident behind him. In a negligence analysis, Dennis's actions will be compared with persons of average intelligence, not those of other people with mental challenges.

(c) Where a defendant's conduct occurs in an emergency situation, it is recognized that a reasonable person might accept greater risk or have less opportunity for reflection in determining the reasonable course of action. The defendant must act as a reasonable person would behave in the emergency situation.

1) If a defendant's own negligent conduct is responsible for creating the emergency situation, the above principle is not applied in assessing the reasonableness of the defendant's conduct during the emergency.

(2) In determining whether a defendant's conduct constituted a breach of duty under the "reasonable person" standard, Judge Learned Hand offered the following analysis: if the burden (or cost) to the defendant of taking precautions against the threatened risk was outweighed by the likelihood (or probability) that the plaintiff would be injured by the risk-producing activity, considering also the gravity (or severity) of the injury to the plaintiff if the risk manifests itself, and considering the social utility of the activity in which the defendant is engaged, then the defendant failed to act as a reasonable person would. In short, if the burden of taking precautions is less than the probability of injury "times" the severity of that injury, plus the social utility of the defendant's activity, the defendant breached his duty of care by not taking such precautions. Although legal problems cannot

be reduced to simple mathematical formulae, this is a useful way to remember and to articulate the relevant considerations.

(a) The greater the benefit society derives, viewed in the aggregate, from the activity engaged in by a defendant, the more likely the defendant will not be found to have breached a duty to a plaintiff merely by engaging in such an activity or by not undertaking certain precautions.

EXAMPLE: Driving a car presents a fairly high probability of colliding with others and a relatively severe danger of death or great injury, which might be thought to justify significant precautions, such as driving very slowly or avoiding driving at all when there is great congestion or pedestrian activity. However, the social utility of driving is also very great, so that such precautions are considered to be "outweighed" in the Learned Hand calculus, and a reasonable person would not undertake them. Less burdensome precautions, such as remaining alert and operating the vehicle competently, are regarded as sufficient to fulfill the duty of care.

(b) The determination of whether a person has acted unreasonably is very fact-intensive. Use Hand's formula as a guide in asking whether the probability of harm multiplied by the likely magnitude of that harm outweighs the burden of avoidance.

(c) The reasonable person standard of care is an objective one. In other words, the standard is applied as though the reasonable person possessed the experience, knowledge, and mental capabilities of an average member of the community, even if the defendant did not himself actually possess it.

(d) In determining how a reasonable person would behave under the circumstances, it is relevant how a person engaging in the defendant's activity would customarily behave. However, evidence of custom is not conclusive; the trier of fact may find either that the customary manner of behavior was not reasonable under the circumstances or that a reasonable person would have engaged in behavior other than what is customary.

1) A plaintiff may submit evidence of a defendant's deviation from custom as evidence of the defendant's unreasonable conduct. Conversely, a defendant may put on evidence of compliance with custom to show the reasonableness of his conduct.

EXAMPLE: In trying to show that her landlord, Darv, was negligent for failing to install unbreakable glass in her shower, Penny may put on evidence that most landlords use unbreakable glass. This evidence is persuasive, as it suggests that the burden of using that glass is not too great.

2. **Children**
   a. The reasonable person standard specifically takes account of age when a defendant is a minor.
      (1) In the majority of jurisdictions, a minor defendant's conduct is assessed according to what a reasonable child of the same age, education, intelligence, and experience would have done.
      (2) A minority of states follow the traditional rule, which divided minors into three age levels:
         (a) age six and below, as to which the defendant was conclusively presumed incapable of being negligent;
         (b) ages seven to 13, as to which it was rebuttably presumed that the defendant was not negligent; and
         (c) age 14 and up, as to which it was rebuttably presumed that the defendant was capable of being negligent.

         EXAMPLE: Darlene is seven years old and is very intelligent. One day, she leaves her roller skates on the front walk. Patrick, who is walking down the walk, does not see the skates and slips and falls on them, breaking his leg. If Patrick sues Darlene, her act of leaving the skates on the walk will be compared with that of a seven-year-old with similar experience and intelligence.

   b. Children engaging in adult activities (e.g., operating an automobile, boat, or airplane), however, are required to conform to an adult standard of care.

      EXAMPLE: Nine-year-old Dilbert takes his dad's motorboat out for a spin. While driving the boat across the bay, he hits Patricia, a swimmer, and knocks her unconscious. Patricia drowns. If Patricia's estate sues Dilbert, he will not be compared with other children's standard of care. Instead, he will be held to the objective, adult reasonable person's standard of care.

3. **Statutory**
   a. A statute that provides for civil liability supersedes the common law of torts. A defendant's civil liability will be determined by the specific statutory provisions. Such civil statutes are rare.

      EXAMPLE: A legislature could enact a statute stating that anyone injured in a car accident who was not wearing a seatbelt is barred from pursuing a negligence action.

   b. Where a defendant's conduct also violates a statute that does not provide for civil liability (usually a criminal statute), the statute may establish the standard of conduct for breach of duty purposes. In a majority of jurisdictions, this means that an unexcused violation conclusively establishes that the defendant breached his duty to the plaintiff (often referred to as **negligence *per se***).
      (1) Other (minority) jurisdictions regard a qualifying violation of statute by a defendant as either raising a rebuttable presumption

(so that the plaintiff wins unless the defendant introduces enough evidence to overcome the presumption) or as *prima facie* evidence (so that the plaintiff wins unless the defendant introduces any evidence, but the plaintiff retains the burden of proof if the defendant offers evidence) that the defendant's conduct breached the duty of care owed to the plaintiff.

c. In a jurisdiction that has adopted a negligence *per se* rule, a defendant's violation of a criminal statute has the effect of establishing the standard of care only when all of the following three conditions are present:
   (1) the injury caused by the defendant's conduct is the type that the statute was intended to prevent;
   (2) the plaintiff is a member of the class intended to be protected by the statute; and
   (3) the defendant's violation of the statute is not excused.
d. A defendant's violation of an applicable statute is excused if compliance with the statute:
   (1) would have resulted in a harm greater than the harm produced by the violation; or
   (2) would have been impossible.
e. A few statutes are regarded as so important that their violation cannot be excused as a matter of law (e.g., the statutory obligation to maintain a vehicle's brakes in proper working order).

EXAMPLE: To prevent children from getting poisoned, the legislature passes a law making it a crime to sell toxic substances without a child-proof cap. DunCo fails to put a child-proof cap on its rat poison. Four-year-old Pablum finds the rat poison, drinks it, and suffers harm. Even though the statute is criminal in nature, in most states it would become the standard of care because it was designed to protect children from ingesting poison. Breach would be the violation of that statute—i.e., not putting a child-proof cap on the poison. The plaintiff must still prove the other elements of negligence.

f. Compliance with a statute is regarded as mere evidence on the issue of whether a defendant breached her duty of care, and does not raise any presumption in the defendant's favor.

4. **Professionals**
   a. Historically, defendants who engaged in certain activities were held to a higher standard of care to the public or to their customers.
      (1) Common carriers (e.g., trains, bus lines, etc.) were traditionally said to have a duty to avoid harm to their passengers through exercise of "the highest degree of vigilance, care and precaution," or "the utmost caution characteristic of very careful, prudent persons."
      (2) Some jurisdictions utilize the same standard of care for assessing the conduct of innkeepers toward their customers as that applied to a common carrier regarding its passengers.

(3) The dangerous products or services dispensed by public utilities (e.g., electricity, and gas) caused many jurisdictions to impose a duty of care which required that such utilities "take every reasonable precaution suggested by experience or prudence" to avoid injury to the public.

b. Professionals are treated differently from other defendants in negligence. For most defendants, custom is only evidence related to providing breach of duty. For professionals, such as doctors, lawyers, and accountants, custom is everything. The customary practice of professionals in good standing sets the standard of care. If the defendant deviates from that custom, he has breached his duty; if he has complied with that custom, he cannot be found to have breached his duty.

EXAMPLE: Dr. Dell uses a certain procedure to remove Penn's tonsils, and in so doing causes Penn harm. In Penn's malpractice action against Dr. Dell, if it is established that Dr. Dell performed as other doctors in good standing would have performed, she is free from liability. Conversely, if the evidence is that Dr. Dell deviated from the customary way tonsils are removed, even if she did so in good faith, she will have committed malpractice.

(1) The effect of this rule is that a defendant will be found to have breached the standard of care if she did not conduct herself as would a competent member of the profession with minimally adequate knowledge and expertise. If the defendant is a specialist within a profession, the standard of care is applied according to the standards appropriate to that specialty.

(a) Where there are several accepted ways of acting, the defendant's compliance with any of these accepted schools of thought protects her from liability.

(2) Traditionally, the conduct of a defendant with specialized skill or expertise was assessed for reasonable person/breach of duty purposes with regard to the community in which the defendant practiced his profession. Some jurisdictions apply a more modern, national standard, recognizing that technology permits communication and exchange of knowledge that transcends traditional geographic limitations. Specialists are particularly likely to be held to a national standard.

(3) While expert testimony is almost always needed to establish the requisite standard of care for that professional and to establish breach of that standard, no expert testimony is required when the subject matter is within the common knowledge of untrained persons. This is known as the "common knowledge exception."

(a) This occurs when the failure was so egregious, so obvious, and so flagrant that no one could miss it. The judge determines when no expert testimony would be required.

c. Traditionally, a physician was liable for the intentional tort of battery if he failed to properly inform a plaintiff-patient about the risks and alternatives of a proposed medical procedure or treatment; the plaintiff's consent was said to be negated by the lack of disclosure. This is still the case where there is a gross deviation from consent, such as where a patient agrees to a tonsillectomy, but her leg is amputated instead. Most jurisdictions now treat nondisclosure as a form of malpractice.

(1) In some jurisdictions, malpractice based on the failure to disclose is treated like any other kind of medical malpractice. The physician-defendant must disclose risks that doctors in good standing customarily divulge. The failure to do so is malpractice.

(2) The trend, based on recognition of patient autonomy, has been to require physicians to divulge all material risks—that is, risks that a reasonable patient would want to know in deciding whether to undergo a specific procedure. The failure to divulge a material risk is malpractice provided the patient can show that he would have refused the procedure had the risk been divulged.

C. Breach of Duty

1. *Res Ipsa Loquitur*

a. A plaintiff generally meets her burden of proving breach of duty by establishing that the defendant's conduct fails to conform to the applicable standard of care. This is rendered difficult or impossible where a plaintiff does not know and cannot effectively determine specifically what a defendant's injurious conduct was. The doctrine of *res ipsa loquitur* ("the thing speaks for itself") helps the plaintiff in such situations.

(1) In the majority of jurisdictions, if a plaintiff makes a qualifying showing of *res ipsa loquitur*, she has produced evidence sufficient, if believed by the jury, to support a finding that a defendant breached his duty. *Res ipsa loquitur* is thus merely a means of adducing evidence of breach of duty to satisfy the burdens of producing evidence and persuasion. In most jurisdictions, *res ipsa loquitur* permits the jury to infer the defendant's breach of duty.

(2) A small minority of jurisdictions regard a qualifying showing of *res ipsa loquitur* as shifting the burden of producing evidence to the defendant as to the issue of breach of duty. The defendant must then produce sufficient evidence to support a verdict in his favor, or the court will instruct the jury that breach of duty is established. If the defendant produces qualifying evidence, the burden of persuasion remains on the plaintiff, and the jury may find for the defendant if the plaintiff has not established breach of duty by a preponderance of the evidence.

(3) Some jurisdictions—another small minority—give a qualifying showing of *res ipsa loquitur* the effect of shifting the burden of persuasion to the defendant. If the defendant does not then

persuade the jury, by a preponderance of the evidence, that he did meet the applicable standard of care, breach of duty is established.

b. A plaintiff must establish that three requisites are present in order to invoke the doctrine of *res ipsa loquitur*:

(1) the event that caused the plaintiff's injury was one which would not ordinarily occur in the absence of negligence;

(a) The trier of fact may determine whether an event is one that would not ordinarily occur in the absence of negligence with reference to common experience, or if that is not sufficient, by resort to evidence provided by the plaintiff. Expert testimony may be required to establish that negligence is the likely cause of the injury-causing event. The plaintiff is not required to show that negligence is the only possible cause of the injury-causing event; it is enough if the trier of fact finds that negligence was more likely than not the cause.

(2) it is more likely than not that it was the defendant's negligence that was responsible for the injury-causing event; and

(a) Traditionally, a plaintiff was required to show that the defendant was in exclusive control of the instrumentality that inflicted injury upon the plaintiff. Today, this requirement has become less rigid in many states. In some states, for instance, it is sufficient if a plaintiff shows that it is more likely than not that the defendant is responsible for the negligent event. Control, either exclusive or not, is merely a circumstance relevant to determination of the defendant's responsibility.

(3) the plaintiff was not responsible for the event that caused injury.

(a) A plaintiff must demonstrate that she did not set in motion the forces that resulted in her injury. However, it is immaterial that the plaintiff placed herself in a situation of peril or that she did not take precautions to avoid injury. In light of the current move to comparative fault, this element has become less important.

D. Cause-in-Fact (Actual Cause)

1. The element of cause-in-fact ties the defendant's breach of duty to the plaintiff's injury. Without proof of this element by a preponderance of the evidence, the plaintiff loses his negligence claim.

EXAMPLE: Dorkas fails to use his headlights after dusk, as required by statute, and hits Petunia when she comes running out between two parked cars. Even though Dorkas has breached the duty he owes to Petunia, she would lose her negligence claim if the jury determines that he still would have hit Petunia even if his lights had been on.

2. **"But-For" Test**

a. A defendant's conduct was the cause-in-fact of an event if that event would not have occurred but for the existence of the conduct.

EXAMPLE: City negligently mixes its drinking-water line with its sewage-water line. Pyn, who drinks City-provided water, contracts typhoid. Pyn may recover if he can show that it is more likely than not that "but for" the negligent mixing of the water lines, he would not have contracted typhoid.

3. **"Substantial Factor" Test**
   a. A defendant's conduct is also the cause-in-fact of a plaintiff's injury if that conduct was a substantial factor in bringing about the injury. An actor's negligent conduct under this test will be considered a legal cause of harm to the plaintiff if:
      (1) her conduct is a substantial factor in bringing about the harm; and
      (2) there is no rule of law relieving the actor from liability because of the manner in which her negligence has resulted in the harm.
   b. This accounts for the situation where the conduct of two or more defendants results in injury to the plaintiff, and each individual defendant's conduct, taken alone, would have been sufficient to directly cause the injury. A mechanical application of the "but-for" test would permit each defendant to claim that the plaintiff's injury would have occurred whether he acted or not and thus "but for" causation did not exist.
   c. However, it does not require that an actor's conduct be a possible sole cause of the plaintiff's harm. An actor's conduct under this test will be considered a proximate cause as long as her actions amount to a more than trivial contribution of the plaintiff's injury.

      EXAMPLE: Kramer negligently sets a fire that would have burned down Jerry's house on its own. Separately, Elaine negligently set a fire that also would have destroyed Jerry's house. The fires combine and burn down Jerry's house. Each fire is a substantial factor of the harm and both Kramer and Elaine are the cause-in-fact of the harm. Note that the "but-for" test doesn't work where there are multiple causes, either of which would have brought about the harm.

   d. Where there are multiple negligent parties, each of whom contributes to the plaintiff's indivisible harm, they are jointly and severally liable. That means that the plaintiff may recover fully against any of the defendants, and those defendants can sue each other for contribution.

      EXAMPLE: If Jerry's torched house is worth $1 million, he could sue just Elaine to recover that amount. Elaine could then sue Kramer, a joint tortfeasor, for contribution (partial repayment of that judgment). Note that Jerry cannot recover more than the total amount of his damages—$1 million.

4. **Alternative Liability Theory**
   a. Where a plaintiff's injury arises from the negligent conduct of two or more independently acting defendants, only one of whom can actually be responsible, and the plaintiff is unable to establish which defendant is in fact responsible, each and every defendant's conduct is regarded

as a cause-in-fact of the injury unless a defendant can prove that he did not cause the plaintiff's injury. In effect, the burden of proof as to cause-in-fact is shifted from the plaintiff to the defendant [Summers v. Tice, 199 P.2d 1 (Cal. 1948)].

EXAMPLE: Wyn negligently shoots in the direction of a rustling bush at the same moment that Fahn does. One bullet hits Pantaloon, who cannot identify which gun the bullet came from. Because both Wyn and Fahn breached a duty owed to Pantaloon, and because both are before the court, the court will shift the burden of proof on the element of cause-in-fact. If Wyn and Fahn cannot prove they were not the responsible party, they will be jointly and severally liable.

5. Where a plaintiff demonstrates that the injury resulted from the conduct of several defendants, each acting independently, but cannot identify which particular defendant's conduct actually injured her, each defendant's conduct may be regarded as a cause-in-fact of the plaintiff's injury. Liability is apportioned among the defendants based upon the economic benefit, as measured by percentage or market share, each defendant derived from the risk-producing conduct. Market share liability applies only to generic products such as DES.
6. As a general matter, like the other *prima facie* elements of negligence, the plaintiff must prove cause-in-fact by a preponderance of the evidence (i.e., by more than 50%). This has led to the result that where a doctor commits malpractice on a patient who, due to illness, had a likelihood of death, the doctor escapes liability for his malpractice. A growing number of jurisdictions allow the plaintiff to proceed by recharacterizing the injury as "loss of chance."

   EXAMPLE: Dr. Dyl commits malpractice and fails to diagnose cancer in his patient, Prax. Had Dr. Dyl done so, Prax would have had a 40% chance of survival. By the time the cancer is found, the cancer is incurable. Under the traditional cause-in-fact rule, Prax loses his malpractice case because he cannot show that it is more likely than not that, but for Dr. Dyl's malpractice, he would have survived. However, some jurisdictions would allow the case to proceed, finding that it is more likely than not that, but for Dr. Dyl's malpractice, Prax would not have lost his 40% chance of survival.

   a. Statutes in many jurisdictions reduce the duty of care owed by the driver of an automobile to a **guest** (a non-paying passenger) in that auto. Such statutes frequently provide that the driver of an auto is not liable for injuries suffered by the guest unless the driver's wrongful conduct amounted to gross negligence or recklessness.
   b. **Slip-and-Fall Cases**
      (1) In cases where a person is injured because of a fall on the defendant's premises, the plaintiff must show evidence from which a jury may reasonably infer unreasonable conduct on the part of the defendant. Typically, the plaintiff must put on evidence about the condition of the item on which she fell so that a jury may infer that the object was there long enough that the

defendant was unreasonable in not discovering and remedying the dangerous condition.

EXAMPLE: Pashanda is injured when she slips on a grape on the floor in the produce section of Dexto's market. If this is all the evidence she presents, Pashanda's negligence claim will be thrown out. If she can show, however, that the grape on which she slipped was blackened and gritty, she will proceed to a jury because there is circumstantial evidence that would permit the jury to find that the grape had been on the floor long enough that Dexto's should have discovered it.

E. **Proximate (Legal) Cause**

1. In addition to being a cause-in-fact of a plaintiff's harm, the defendant's conduct must also be a proximate, or legal, cause of the injury.
2. Proximate causation requires both that the plaintiff be foreseeable and that the type of harm is a foreseeable outgrowth of the defendant's actions.
    a. A defendant owes a duty of reasonable care only to **foreseeable plaintiffs** (i.e., those individuals who are within the risk of harm created by the defendant's unreasonable conduct). The majority view holds that a defendant only owes a duty of care to foreseeable plaintiffs who are within the **zone of danger** (i.e., under the circumstances, a reasonable defendant would have foreseen a risk of harm to the plaintiff). The broader minority view allows recovery to any person thereby harmed due to a breach of the defendant's duty of care.
3. Not all injuries "actually" caused by the defendant will be deemed to have been proximately caused by his acts. As such, the doctrine of proximate or legal cause deals with a limitation of liability with respect to persons and consequences that bear some reasonable relationship to a defendant's tortious conduct.
    a. **Unforeseeable Extent of Harm**
        (1) If the defendant's conduct is a substantial factor in bringing about the harm to another, the mere fact that the defendant neither foresaw nor should have foreseen the extent of the harm does not prevent her from being liable.
        (2) Under the so-called **thin-skulled** or **eggshell plaintiff rule**, a defendant is liable for the full consequences of a plaintiff's injury, even though, due to the plaintiff's peculiar susceptibility to harm (of which the defendant was unaware), those consequences were more severe than they would have been in a normal person.

        EXAMPLE: Peyton is a hemophiliac. Derek leaves a bunch of paper and boxes lying around in the hall just outside his cubicle. When Peyton walks by, he falls and hits his head on the side of Derek's desk. He begins to bleed heavily. Eventually, he loses so much blood that he must be hospitalized. Derek will be liable to Peyton for the full extent of Peyton's injuries, even if he did not know about Peyton's inability to clot blood.

b. **Unforeseeable Type or Manner of Harm**

(1) **Superseding Cause**

(a) A **superseding cause** is an unforeseeable, intervening cause that breaks the chain of causation between the initial wrongful act and the ultimate injury, and thus relieves the original tortfeasor of any further liability.

(b) Commonly occurring examples of superseding causes:

1) naturally occurring phenomena;

2) criminal acts of third persons;

3) intentional torts of third persons; or

4) extraordinary forms of negligent conduct.

(c) An **intervening force** is one that actively operates in producing harm to another after the actor has already committed his negligent act or omission.

1) As a general rule, a defendant will be held liable for harm caused by foreseeable intervening forces.

2) Because rescuers are foreseeable, the original tortfeasors will be held liable for the ordinary negligence of the rescuer.

EXAMPLE: Don is throwing balls around at a playground. Don hits Poppy in the head, causing her to lose consciousness. Casey arrives and tries to resuscitate Poppy, breaking Poppy's ribs while doing compressions. Because Casey was merely negligent, Don will be liable for both Poppy's head injury and broken ribs.

3) The original tortfeasor is usually held liable for the ordinary negligence of the plaintiff's treating physician or nurse.

EXAMPLE: When Poppy is hit in the head, Casey does not come to her aid. Instead, an ambulance takes her to the hospital. The triage nurse does not examine Poppy carefully and concludes that she does not need medical attention. The nurse keeps Poppy lying on a gurney in the hallway for eight hours. During that time, Poppy has a cerebral hemorrhage and sustains irreversible brain damage. Don will be liable for Poppy's brain hemorrhage and the strike on the head.

4) The original tortfeasor is usually held liable for diseases contracted or subsequent injuries sustained because of the impairment of the plaintiff's health resulting from the original injury caused by the defendant's tortious conduct.

EXAMPLE: When Don hits Poppy in the head, her sinuses are affected. As a result, Poppy becomes much more susceptible to sinus infections. She must go to the doctor frequently and take expensive medications. Don will be liable for both the head injury and the sinus infections.

5) A defendant will be held liable for negligent efforts on the part of persons to protect life or property interests endangered by his negligence.

6) In situations where the plaintiff suffers a subsequent injury after the original injury, and the original injury was a substantial factor in causing the second accident, the original tortfeasor is held liable for damages.

EXAMPLE: Doug negligently fractures Prudence's left leg. While walking on crutches, Prudence trips and falls, breaking her right leg. Doug will be liable for both leg injuries.

(d) Considerations of importance in determining whether an intervening force is a superseding cause of harm to another include:

1) the fact that its intervention brings about a harm different in kind from that which would otherwise have resulted from the defendant's negligence;

2) the fact that its operation or the consequences thereof appear to be extraordinary and unforeseeable after the event; and

3) the fact that the intervening force is operating independently of any situation created by the defendant's negligence.

4. Another highly tested area of proximate causation deals with rescuers. A negligent defendant owes an independent duty of care to a rescuer. Even where the rescue efforts are done negligently (but provided they are not wanton), the negligent defendant will be liable for both personal injury and property damage, whether the rescuer succeeds in injuring himself, the person rescued, or a stranger.

a. In a minority of jurisdictions, there is an exception to this rule for professional rescuers, known as the "firefighter's rule" (though it includes any emergency personnel). Under this exception, professional rescuers will not be able to recover from the defendant for any harm resulting from the defendant's negligence. The emergency personnel are considered to have assumed the risk of such harm.

EXAMPLE: A defendant negligently left her stove on, causing her house to catch fire. While pulling the defendant out of the burning home, a firefighter was injured by the flames, and another was injured by smoke inhalation. Neither firefighter would be able to recover from the defendant for these injuries.

	FORESEEABLE	UNFORESEEABLE (I.E., SUPERSEDING)
Effect	Chain of proximate causation unbroken—original defendant remains liable.	Chain of proximate causation broken—original defendant's liability cut off for consequences of antecedent conduct.
Typical Examples	• Subsequent medical malpractice, including aggravation of plaintiff's condition. • Subsequent disease or accident, including all illnesses and injuries resulting from plaintiff's weakened condition, but not deadly, rare diseases. • Negligent rescue efforts.	• Criminal acts and intentional torts of third parties, but only where they are unforeseeable under the facts or circumstances. • Highly extraordinary harm arising from defendant's conduct, as viewed by the court, including grossly negligent conduct of third parties. • Unforeseeable, naturally occurring phenomena.

F. Damages

1. A plaintiff must affirmatively prove **actual damages**. Nominal damages are not available, and punitive damages generally are not allowed.
2. Personal injury and property damages are recoverable. Included are general and special damages, past and future pain and suffering, medical expenses, lost wages, and loss of consortium, but not attorney's fees. The plaintiff's duty to mitigate damages applies.
3. Payments made to or benefits conferred on the injured party-plaintiff from other (i.e., collateral) sources are not credited against the tortfeasor's liability, even where they cover all or a part of the harm for which the tortfeasor is liable. This is known as the **collateral source rule**.
   a. The rule that collateral benefits are not subtracted from the plaintiff's recovery applies to the following types of benefits:
      (1) insurance policies, whether maintained by the plaintiff or a third party;
      (2) employment benefits;
      (3) gratuities, including cash gratuities and the rendering of services; and
      (4) social legislative benefits.

      EXAMPLE: Della negligently injures Pasha when she sets off firecrackers incorrectly. Pasha has second-degree burns over most of her body. If Pasha collects disability or health insurance benefits, these will not be subtracted from the amount of damages that Della owes Pasha.

      EXCEPTION: Payments made by a tortfeasor or by a person acting for him (e.g., the defendant's insurance company) to the injured plaintiff are credited against the defendant's tort liability.

4. **Punitive Damages**
   a. **Punitive damages** are an amount over and above the compensation needed to make the plaintiff whole. They are intended to punish the defendant for egregious conduct and to act as a deterrent against future conduct by the defendant or others, and are thus also called "exemplary" damages.
   b. Punitive damages are available in tort cases when there has been willful, wanton, or malicious conduct. They are generally not available in negligence actions or in contract actions.
   c. A plaintiff is never entitled to an award of punitive damages, but a jury may award them at its discretion. Jury rewards may be reversed or overturned if excessive. Due process requires that punitive damage awards not be grossly excessive on three measures [State Farm Mut. Auto. Ins. Co. v. Campbell, 538 U.S. 408 (2003); BMW of No. America v. Gore, 517 U.S. 559 (1996)]:
      (1) the degree of reprehensibility of the defendant's conduct, considering such factors as whether:
         (a) the defendant acted intentionally, maliciously, or with reckless disregard for harm;
         (b) such conduct was repeated or isolated; and
         (c) the harm caused to the plaintiff was economic or noneconomic (e.g., lost profits or personal injury);
      (2) the ratio between the plaintiff's compensatory damages and the amount of the punitive damages (presumptively, punitive damages should not exceed 10 times the compensatory damage award); and
      (3) the difference between the punitive damage award and the civil or criminal sanctions that could be imposed for comparable misconduct.
   d. There may also be specific limitations on entitlement to punitive damages under state law.

G. Defenses to Negligence

1. **Contributory Negligence**
   a. Tort law requires a plaintiff to exercise due care to protect herself from injury by the defendant. Thus, the plaintiff's own negligence—called **contributory negligence** at common law—may bar the plaintiff's recovery. The analysis is similar to that for the defendant's negligence—whether the plaintiff acted as a reasonable person would under the same circumstances. Contributory negligence is conduct on the part of the plaintiff that falls below the standard to which she should conform for her own protection, and which is a legally contributing cause cooperating with the defendant's negligence in bringing about the plaintiff's harm.
   b. To show contributory negligence, the defendant must prove by a preponderance of the evidence that the plaintiff fell below the relevant standard of care and that this failure was the cause-in-fact and proximate cause of the plaintiff's damages.

(1) Traditionally, if a plaintiff is found to have engaged in contributory negligence, he is barred from recovery for a defendant's otherwise negligent conduct, even if the plaintiff is only 1% at fault.

EXAMPLE: Delbert, who is speeding, hits Pol's car one night. Pol will be barred from recovery because he is contributorily negligent *per se* if he was hit because, in violation of the statute, Pol did not have his headlights on.

(2) Contributory negligence does not bar recovery if the plaintiff's theory is intentional tort, recklessness, or strict liability.

c. Risks or dangerous acts undertaken by a plaintiff that might otherwise be regarded as contributory negligence are often viewed as reasonable in an emergency (i.e., the plaintiff is threatened with immediate danger of bodily harm or death because of the defendant's negligence) or if the plaintiff is attempting to rescue someone.

d. The analysis of whether a child plaintiff is contributorily negligent is similar to the negligence analysis for children generally.

(1) A majority of jurisdictions apply the "reasonable child" standard—whether a child of the same age, education, intelligence, and experience, in the same circumstances, would have acted as the plaintiff did.

(2) A minority of states utilize the traditional age categories:

(a) below age six, contributory negligence is precluded as a matter of law;

(b) ages seven to 13, the child-plaintiff is rebuttably presumed incapable of contributory negligence; and

(c) 14 and older, the child-plaintiff is rebuttably presumed capable of contributory negligence.

e. The concept of negligence *per se* is applicable to the plaintiff in a contributory negligence situation.

(1) Contributory negligence is not available, even though the plaintiff's conduct violates a statute, where the defendant's negligent act violates the same statute, the plaintiff is a member of the class of persons the statute was intended to protect, and the harm suffered by the plaintiff is the type the statute was intended to avoid.

EXAMPLE: 15-year-old Pasha, who was hired by DunCo in violation of a statute prohibiting the hiring of children, will not be found to be contributorily negligent.

f. In order to invoke contributory negligence, a defendant must prove that the plaintiff's conduct is the actual and proximate cause of the injuries suffered by the plaintiff.

g. In two limited situations, the contributory negligence of a third person may be imputed to the plaintiff so as to bar recovery against the defendant:

(1) the plaintiff and the contributorily negligent third person are sufficiently related such that the plaintiff would be vicariously liable

for the third person's negligence (e.g., partners and joint enterprisers, employers and employees); and

(2) the plaintiff's claim against the defendant is completely derivative of the third person who was contributorily negligent (e.g., wrongful death, loss of consortium).

(a) A minority of states do not impute one spouse's contributory negligence to another in an action against a defendant for loss of consortium.

h. The **last clear chance doctrine** provides a basis for recovery even where a plaintiff is otherwise contributorily negligent. The focus is on the time period after the plaintiff has engaged in contributory negligence. If injury to the plaintiff could still have been avoided through a subsequent exercise of due care by the defendant, then the defendant is said to have had the last clear chance to avoid harm, and the plaintiff's contributory fault will not bar recovery.

(1) If the defendant is aware that his breach of duty has placed the plaintiff in danger, the last clear chance doctrine is always available to the plaintiff. The majority of jurisdictions deny a plaintiff the benefit of the last clear chance doctrine if the defendant is not aware that the plaintiff is in danger, and the plaintiff is in "inattentive peril" rather than "helpless peril." A plaintiff in helpless peril may take advantage of the last clear chance doctrine if the defendant had either actual or constructive knowledge of the plaintiff's danger.

(a) A plaintiff is in **helpless peril** when her negligence has placed her in a position of danger from which she cannot extricate herself. A plaintiff is in **inattentive peril** when her contributory negligence has placed her in a position of danger from which she could escape if observant enough to recognize her peril.

(b) In a majority of jurisdictions, if a defendant is under a duty to discover danger to the plaintiff (e.g., an owner/occupier of land has duty to exercise due care to discover dangerous conditions and protect invitees from them), no distinction is made between helpless and inattentive danger.

2. **Comparative Negligence**

a. Under a modern comparative negligence regime, where a plaintiff's negligence has contributed to his own injuries, the total damages caused by the defendant may be apportioned based upon a determination of the relative fault of each party. Virtually every state has adopted a comparative negligence system, either by statute or judicial decision. The analysis of comparative fault is identical to the analysis of contributory negligence, though the effect is different.

(1) Some states have adopted a **pure comparative negligence** scheme. In such states, apportionment of damages tracks apportionment of fault perfectly—if a defendant is 25% responsible and

a plaintiff is 75% responsible, plaintiff recovers from the defendant 25% of the total damages she suffered.

(2) Other states have adopted a **partial comparative negligence** system. Here, damages are apportioned only if the defendant's responsibility exceeds the plaintiff's responsibility. The plaintiff is denied any recovery if he is responsible for 50% or more of his own damages.

(3) If there are two or more defendants who are not jointly liable, two different systems of comparative negligence have been developed—the "aggregate" system and the "individual equality" system.

(a) In an **aggregate system**, the plaintiff does not recover anything if her responsibility exceeds the total percentage responsibility of all the defendants combined. Thus, if two defendants each contributed 24% of a plaintiff's damages, totaling 48%, and the plaintiff contributed 52%, she would not recover.

(b) Under an **individual equality system**, a plaintiff does not recover anything if his responsibility exceeds that of any single defendant. Thus, if two defendants each contributed 33% of a plaintiff's damages, and the plaintiff contributed 34%, the plaintiff would be barred from recovery.

EXAM TIP On the MBE®, assume that a pure comparative negligence system applies unless the question states otherwise.

3. **Assumption of Risk**

a. A plaintiff "assumes the risk" of injury from a defendant's negligence if the plaintiff expressly or impliedly consents to undergo the risk created by the defendant's conduct.

(1) A plaintiff may expressly assume the risk of a defendant's negligent or reckless conduct by contract or otherwise. The agreement may be general (relieving the defendant of all obligation) or specific (limited to the risks specified in the agreement). For there to be an express assumption of risk [Restatement (2d) of Torts § 496B]:

(a) the plaintiff must be aware of and understand the terms;

(b) the injury that occurs must be within the risks of which the plaintiff agreed to relieve the defendant; and

1) In order for the assumption to be effective to bar or reduce recovery, it must be apparent that the terms were intended by both parties to apply to the particular conduct that caused the defendant harm.

(c) the agreement must not be contrary to public policy.

1) Examples of situations that are contrary to public policy include:

a) agreements purporting to relieve an employer for any injury to an employee occurring in the course of employment;

b) common carriers and those providing a duty of public service (i.e., innkeepers or public utilities) can limit, but not completely disclaim, liability; and

c) where there is such disparity of bargaining power that the agreement does not represent a free choice on the part of the plaintiff. This disparity may arise through the defendant's position of power or because of the plaintiff's specific subjective needs.

EXAMPLE: A plaintiff drives to a stadium to attend a sold-out sporting event but drives around for some time without being able to find a place to park. The plaintiff finally finds one of the last parking garages with an available space. As she drives in, an attendant hands her a ticket with an industry-standard disclaimer purporting to relieve the garage of all liability for loss or damage, even when due to the garage's negligence. During the game, the parking attendant negligently fails to make routine security checks, and the plaintiff's car is stolen. The plaintiff will not be barred from recovering from the garage for the loss of his car.

(2) A plaintiff may also impliedly assume the risk of a defendant's conduct.

(a) A plaintiff is barred from recovery, or recovery will be reduced, under the assumption of the risk doctrine if the defendant establishes that:

1) the plaintiff had knowledge of and appreciated the nature of the danger involved;

a) This is a subjective standard. Youth, lack of information, or lack of experience may justify a finding that a plaintiff actually failed to comprehend the risk involved. If so, there can be no assumption of the risk, even if a "reasonable plaintiff" would have recognized the danger under similar circumstances.

2) the plaintiff appreciated the specific danger that injured him; and

EXAMPLE: A plaintiff who knowingly agrees to ride in a car where the driver is speeding does not assume the risk that the driver might also be intoxicated.

a) Some risks are regarded as so obvious that any competent adult is expected to be aware of them.

EXAMPLE: The danger of falling through an unguarded opening, slipping on ice, or being struck by a baseball at a baseball game.

3) the plaintiff voluntarily chose to subject himself to that danger.

   a) Voluntariness can be established by express consent (e.g., an exculpatory clause in a contract providing that one party will hold the other party harmless for injuries caused by the first party), or consent may be implied from the fact that the plaintiff continued in the face of a known danger. With regard to implied assumption of the risk, courts closely examine whether behavior is voluntary when there is a lack of alternatives.

(b) In some circumstances, a court will determine that a defendant has no obligation to be non-negligent toward the plaintiff because of the nature of the activity that they are engaged in. The most common context is sports.

(c) Assumption of the risk may not be asserted where a plaintiff is a member of a class intended to be protected by a statute, and the defendant's conduct both violates the statute and threatens the risk the statute was designed to prevent. In some states, any risk-creating violation by a defendant of a public safety statute has the above effect.

EXAMPLE: Petunia and Drucilla are playing basketball. Petunia's eye is severely injured when Drucilla pokes Petunia in the face trying to get a rebound. Even if Drucilla was negligent, many courts would conclude that the harm that befell Petunia was an inherent risk of the game, and thus Drucilla had no duty to avoid such harm. However, if a court found Drucilla's conduct to be more than negligent, Petunia would be permitted to proceed with her tort claim.

III. STRICT LIABILITY

A. In General

1. In strict liability, a defendant is liable for injuring a plaintiff whether or not the defendant exercised due care. As to certain activities, the policy of the law is to impose liability regardless of how carefully a defendant conducted herself.

B. Categories

1. A defendant may be held strictly liable as to two categories of activities:
   a. **possession of animals**; and
      (1) The analysis of strict liability in connection with the possession of animals varies according to the nature of the plaintiff's injury and whether the animal is wild or domestic.
      (2) A defendant can be held strictly liable for personal injuries inflicted by his animal if it has "known dangerous propensities."
         (a) This is, in part, a "scienter-like" element, in that the defendant is subject to strict liability only if he knew or had reason to know of the dangerous quality of the animal.
            1) Wild animals generally have "known dangerous propensities" for this purpose. A **wild animal** is one not customarily devoted to the service of humankind at the time and in the place where it is kept.
            2) Domestic animals have "known dangerous propensities" only if a reasonable owner would realize that the animal presented a danger of death or injury. The classic example of a domestic animal with known dangerous propensities is a dog that has previously bitten a human being (the "one bite" rule—after one bite, the owner is presumed to know that the dog is dangerous).
               a) Strict liability does not apply to possession of domestic animals as to which dangerous propensities are normal, such as bulls, stallions, mules, rams, and bees.

               EXAMPLE: Parker is seriously injured when bitten by Damien's pet tiger. Damien is strictly liable for this injury even if Damien's tiger has been as gentle as a kitten until that moment. If Parker had been bitten by Damien's cat, Damien is only strictly liable once Damien should have known of his cat's dangerous propensity.
         (b) If the plaintiff is an unknown trespasser, most jurisdictions do not impose any liability for injuries inflicted by a defendant's animals while the plaintiff is on the defendant's land, even as to animals with known dangerous propensities. If the plaintiff is any other type of trespasser (known, frequent, or child),

a defendant is liable only for negligence. The plaintiff must establish that the defendant failed to exercise due care to warn of or protect the trespasser from his animal.

(3) A defendant is held strictly liable for any trespass to the land or chattels of a plaintiff by wild animals if of a kind likely to escape, trespass, and do damage, or by "livestock" possessed by the defendant. Domestic pets (e.g., dogs and cats) are not considered livestock.

b. **abnormally dangerous activities**.

(1) A judge determines whether an activity is abnormally dangerous by considering if:

(a) the activity creates a risk of serious injury as to the plaintiff, her land, or her chattels;

(b) this risk cannot be eliminated by the exercise of due care; and

(c) the activity is not usually conducted in that area. Such things as dynamiting, crop-dusting, and exterminating have been found to be abnormally dangerous.

(2) Principles of causation generally applicable to negligence are also applied in a strict liability analysis.

(3) In order for strict liability to apply, the harm to the plaintiff must have resulted from the type of danger that justified classifying the animal or activity as dangerous.

(4) An unforeseeable, intervening force could relieve a strictly liable defendant of liability as well.

C. Defenses

1. Contributory Negligence

a. Where strict liability is applicable, a defendant generally may not raise contributory negligence as a defense.

EXCEPTION: Where a plaintiff knew of the danger that justified imposition of strict liability, and his contributory negligence caused exactly that danger to be manifested, such contributory negligence will bar the plaintiff's recovery, assuming the jurisdiction applies the traditional contributory negligence doctrine.

EXAMPLE: If Pat O'Pheline stands next to a circus tiger's cage knowing that the tiger is dangerous and can reach between the bars of the cage, and despite seeing and understanding warning signs and ropes posted to keep circus patrons at a safe distance, he may be barred from recovery by the doctrine of contributory negligence if the tiger claws him.

NOTE Contributory negligence is not a complete defense to strict liability; it can only reduce recovery.

2. Comparative Negligence

a. Some states that have adopted comparative fault systems reduce the recovery of plaintiffs whose negligence contributes to their own injuries involving strict liability situations.

3. **Assumption of Risk**
    a. A plaintiff may be found to have assumed the risk of injury and be completely barred from recovery in a strict liability situation if the plaintiff knows of and appreciates the danger justifying imposition of strict liability and voluntarily exposes herself to such danger.

IV. PRODUCTS LIABILITY

A. Strict Products Liability in Tort

1. Strict products liability is invoked when a defective product, for which an appropriate defendant is responsible, injures an appropriate plaintiff. To analyze an action for strict products liability, it is necessary to consider certain specific factors.
2. **Proper Plaintiff**
   a. In general, if strict liability is otherwise applicable, any plaintiff injured while using a defective product may recover damages from an appropriate defendant. This includes purchasers and consumers, as well as families, friends, guests, and employees.
   b. There is a modern trend to permit one not using a defective product to invoke strict liability against an appropriate defendant if it was reasonably foreseeable that such a plaintiff might be injured by the defective product. Examples include bystanders (e.g., the plaintiff was a pedestrian injured when an automobile manufactured by the defendant with defective steering went out of control and struck him) and rescuers (e.g., the plaintiff attempted to rescue a third person who was endangered by a defective product manufactured by the defendant).
3. **Proper Defendant**
   a. Commercial suppliers at all levels of the distribution chain (i.e., the manufacturer, distributor, or retailer) as well as commercial lessors, new home developers, and sellers of used goods are all potential defendants. Occasional sellers and those supplying services (i.e., an optometrist) cannot be strictly liable, but may be sued for negligence.
      (1) A person who assembles component parts into a finished product is strictly liable for defects in the components used. The manufacturer of the component part is also strictly liable for defects in the component. If the finished product is defective not because of a defect in a component part but because the assembler put the component to a use for which it was not suited, the component manufacturer is generally not liable unless the component manufacturer knew or should have known that her component was being misused. A person who rebuilds or reconditions used goods is often held to be the equivalent of a manufacturer, and may be subject to strict liability for injuries caused by defects in the rebuilt or reconditioned goods.

      EXAMPLE: Dunlop Tire Co. manufactured a tire that proves to be defective. Ford Motor Company purchases Dunlop tires to put onto its new car model, the Stallion. Ford sells a Stallion to Jen Smyth Ford, a car retailer. While driving a Stallion purchased by Paxtona at Jen Smyth Ford, Penelope is physically injured because of the defect in the tire. Dunlop, Ford, and Jen Smyth are all proper defendants for a strict products liability claim because they are all in the business of dealing with this product and part of the marketing chain. Note that these defendants are liable even though there is likely no fault on their part.

b. Retailers and commercial lessors are subject to strict liability for defects in new goods that they sell or lease. Commercial lessors are subject to strict liability for defective used goods leased, but there is a split in authority as to whether a retailer of used goods is strictly liable for defects in those goods.

c. Most jurisdictions hold sellers of mass-marketed new residences strictly liable for defects in those homes. There is a split in authority as to whether other new home sellers, such as custom builders who construct a few houses at a time or building contractors who construct residences under specific contracts, may be held strictly liable for defects in those constructions. No court has imposed strict liability on a defendant who sold a home he did not construct.

d. Occasional or one-time sellers are not proper defendants for purposes of strict products liability because they are not in the position to further the goals of the tort—safer products and cost-spreading.

EXAMPLE: Pumpkin is injured as a result of a defect in a new widget she bought at Della's garage sale. Della is not a proper defendant for strict products liability. To recover, Pumpkin will have to prove negligence or a breach of warranty.

e. A few states have imposed strict liability on a franchisor, at least where it was found that the franchisor exercised substantial control over the operations of the franchisee.

4. **Proper Context for Strict Products Liability**

a. Generally, providers of services are not held strictly liable for injuries received by their customers. If defective goods are supplied along with services, strict liability is still not applicable so long as the goods supplied were merely "incidental" to rendition of the services. In this regard, restaurants are frequently regarded as sellers of goods (food) subject to strict liability. Doctors, dentists, and blood banks are usually regarded as primarily providing services, so defective products (medicines, blood, etc.) provided are incidental and not subject to strict liability.

5. **Defect**

a. Almost all jurisdictions impose strict liability where a product is "in a defective condition unreasonably dangerous."

b. Formulations of liability occur under three categories of defects.

(1) **Manufacturing Defects**

(a) A product manufactured in a form other than the manufacturer intended contains a **manufacturing defect**. Almost all jurisdictions impose strict liability on the manufacturer and everyone else in the chain of distribution for personal injury or property damage to a plaintiff caused by a manufacturing defect.

EXAMPLE: Pachina cuts her lip on a piece of metal in the tuna fish she was eating. The tuna fish was manufactured by Tuna-of-the-Ocean and purchased from Delmon Grocery. Because Tuna-of-the-Ocean did not intend for there to be a piece of metal in the tuna fish, this is a manufacturing defect. It, along with Delmon as part of the marketing chain, will be strictly liable to Pachina for her personal injury.

(2) **Design Defects**

(a) A product manufactured as the manufacturer intended, but that still presents a danger of personal injury or property damage to a plaintiff, suffers from a **design defect**. The analysis of whether such a defect is sufficient to invoke strict liability is complex.

1) Under the **consumer expectation test** standard, a product is in an unreasonably dangerous defective condition when it is more dangerous than would be contemplated by the ordinary consumer who purchases it, with the ordinary knowledge common to the community as to its characteristics. Thus, a product is dangerously defective if a reasonably foreseeable purchaser would not have expected it to present the danger that resulted in her injury.

a) One interpretation of the consumer expectations test would hold that obvious danger could not be a dangerous defect because it would not be unexpected to a reasonable consumer.

b) Many jurisdictions that apply the consumer expectation test expand "consumer" to include a nonpurchasing user. A product is thus considered defective and unreasonably dangerous if more dangerous than a reasonable user would have expected.

2) Under the **danger-utility test** approach, a product is defective if a jury determines that the danger it threatens (the cost in human injury and property damage) outweighs its utility to society. The danger-utility test balances the likelihood, nature, and potential severity of injuries caused by a product against the usefulness of the product, considering the availability and cost of safer alternative designs. A product's design is usually defective under this test if an alternative design could have reduced the danger at about the same cost.

a) Almost all jurisdictions that utilize the danger-utility test apply it so that the inquiry as to the availability of alternative designs focuses on the time the product was put on the market rather than considering alternatives that were discovered in the period up until trial.

3) Under the **hindsight-negligence test**, a product is defective if a reasonable person, knowing of the danger it presented, would not have placed it in the stream of commerce. This test imposes constructive prior knowledge of the defect on the defendant, in effect presuming that the defendant knew of the risk, whether or not he actually did know or reasonably could have known of it.

EXAMPLE: Dun Motors manufactures a new lightweight, fuel-efficient car, the Stallion, which because of the placement of the gas tank proves to be vulnerable to explosion upon a low-speed rear-end collision. Pafto is injured when the Stallion he is driving is rear-ended and explodes due to the placement of the gas tank. This is a design defect because the product is in the condition intended by the manufacturer. It may be defective if it is more dangerous than an ordinary consumer would expect when using the car in its intended or foreseeable manner. However, a consumer may have no particular expectations about the placement of the gas tank, so many jurisdictions would permit Pafto to show that the car was defective because the risk of the car with the gas tank placed where it was outweighs the benefit of such a design.

(3) **Absence of Warnings**

(a) A product may be considered dangerously defective when it is accompanied by an **inadequate warning**—for example, its message to the user (e.g., a child who cannot read) fails to sufficiently describe the danger, fails to mention all dangers, or is inconsistent with the instructions for use of the product.

(b) A defendant's failure to warn a plaintiff that a product presents a threat of personal injury or property damage may be considered a defect. Where a plaintiff establishes that the manufacturer of a product knew or reasonably should have known of a danger presented by the product and failed to take the precautions a reasonable person would have taken to warn adequately of that danger, the absence of such warning is sufficient to impose strict liability.

1) Certain products are regarded as so obviously dangerous that a warning is considered unnecessary, (e.g., a sharp knife).

2) Whether absence of a warning of allergic or other adverse reactions is a dangerous defect depends upon the severity of the potential reaction and the number of people expected to be affected. A small number of reactions justifies a warning if the adverse reaction threatens death or serious illness. A mild reaction

might require a warning if a substantial number of people likely will experience it.

6. **Cause-in-Fact**
   a. That the injury is attributable to the defendant is usually proven by showing that the defect that injured plaintiff was in existence at the time it left defendant's control. It may be necessary in this regard to establish that intermediate handlers (distributors and suppliers) did not mistreat or alter the product.
   b. Plaintiff shows that the injury was caused by the defect by proving that the defect was a substantial factor in bringing about his injury.
   c. Warning defect claims often pose difficult issues of causation because the plaintiff must prove that she would not have been injured by the product had there been a warning on the product or had the warning been adequate. Some jurisdictions employ a "heeding presumption," which puts the burden of proof on the defendant to prove that a warning or adequate warning would not have made a difference.
7. **Proximate Cause**
   a. Principles of legal or proximate cause relevant to negligence are applied in like fashion to strict products liability, except for where the intervening conduct of third persons occurs.
   b. The negligent handling of a product by a third party after it leaves the defendant's control is regarded as foreseeable and is not a superseding intervening force. This includes negligent handling not directly affecting the defectiveness of product, e.g., where a third party negligently collides with plaintiff's car, which is dangerously defective in a manner attributable to defendant.
   c. A defendant will be relieved of strict products liability where an intervening force is the sole proximate cause of the harm. In other words, the intervening force will sever the defendant's liability where it is such that the injury would not have been suffered but for that superseding or intervening force, independently of the act or omission which constituted the defendant's negligence.
   d. A third party's criminal or intentionally tortious conduct is regarded as an unforeseeable intervening force that supersedes a defendant's wrongdoing, unless the defect somehow increased the risk that a third party would engage in such conduct.
8. **Damages**
   a. General principles of tort damages apply to strict liability, except for the following:
      (1) In a majority of jurisdictions, pure economic losses, such as loss of profits due to the defective product not performing as expected, additional expenses incurred in obtaining replacement equipment or materials, etc., may not be recovered by a plaintiff in strict liability. However, most jurisdictions permit recovery of

economic losses as derivative elements of otherwise appropriate personal injury or property damage claims.

(2) Some jurisdictions look to the nature of the harm threatened by the defect to determine the availability of damages in strict liability, rather than distinguishing between property damage and economic losses. Under this approach, any loss suffered is recoverable if caused by a defect that threatened personal injury, even if the actual loss did not include personal injury. If the defect was not such that it would threaten personal injury, no property damage or economic losses are recoverable in strict liability.

9. **Defenses**

a. **Misuse**

(1) If a plaintiff uses a product in a manner that is neither intended nor foreseeable, she has misused the product and it cannot be defective.

EXAMPLE: Parker stands on a chair manufactured by DrekCo to reach a pot in his kitchen. The chair collapses under him. While sitting is the intended use of a chair, it is foreseeable that a person would stand on a chair, and thus, there is no misuse. If Parker was using the chair as part of an act in which he has an elephant balance on the chair, this would be a misuse because it would be an unforeseeable use of the chair.

b. **Alteration**

(1) A manufacturer or seller may have its liability reduced (or in a contributory negligence jurisdiction, relieved entirely) for a product where the product is altered after leaving its hands.

(a) Alteration or modification includes changes in design, formula, function, or use of a product from that originally designed, tested, or intended by the product seller [Potter v. Chicago Pneumatic Tool Co., 694 A.2d 1319 (Conn. 1997)].

(b) An alteration must be substantial in order to relieve the manufacturer or seller of liability. A substantial change consists of any change which [E.Z. Gas, Inc. v. Hydrocarbon Transp., Inc., 471 N.E.2d 316 (Ind. Ct. App. 1984)]:

1) increases the likelihood of a malfunction;

2) is the proximate cause of the harm; and

3) is independent of the expected and intended use to which the product is put.

(2) Alteration or modification of a product constitutes a defense to claims in strict liability, negligence, and warranty.

(a) In product liability actions based on negligence or breach of warranty, the defense of alteration is raised as an intervening or superseding cause.

(3) In order to preclude liability, an alteration or modification must occur between the time the product leaves the manufacturer's

control and the time of the plaintiff's injury [Banner Welders, Inc. v. Knighton, 425 So. 2d 441 (Ala. 1982)].

(4) For the defense to prevail, the modification or alteration must be independent of the expected and intended use of the product.

(5) The mere fact that the product has been altered or modified does not necessarily relieve the manufacturer or seller of liability. The defendant will remain liable if the alteration or modification:

(a) did not in fact cause the injury; or

(b) was reasonably foreseeable to the manufacturer or seller.

(6) Material alteration is not a defense in a products liability action based on a design defect theory; it is only a defense when the alteration makes it impossible to conclude that a defect at the time of manufacturer was a cause of the injury giving rise to the suit.

c. **Contributory Negligence**

(1) As initially conceived, a plaintiff's unreasonable conduct was not a defense to a strict products liability action unless the plaintiff knew of the defect, comprehended the risks posed by the defect, and voluntarily elected to expose himself to those risks. That is, only an assumption of the risk was a defense to strict products liability.

EXAMPLE: Because of a defect, Parker's television set, manufactured by DuMont, starts to spark. A reasonable person would have noticed this, but Parker, because he is totally engrossed in his favorite sitcom, does not. DuMont has no defense.

(2) At modern law, contributory negligence only applies as a defense to strict products liability if the plaintiff's conduct rises to the level of misuse, abnormal use, or independent negligence (i.e., not where the plaintiff's wrongful conduct is a failure to discover the defect).

(3) A plaintiff's continued use of a product which the plaintiff knows to be defective is not voluntary, and thus not an assumption of the risk, if there are no practicable alternatives to such use.

EXAMPLE: If while in the desert hundreds of miles from a city, Plaintiff discovers that her car has a dangerous steering defect, it would not be an assumption of the risk that Plaintiff continued to use the car to drive back to civilization.

(4) Where a defendant can show that his product was subsequently altered in an unforeseeable manner by someone in the chain of distribution or a third party, courts usually relieve that defendant of liability.

d. **Comparative Negligence**

(1) Some jurisdictions that have adopted a comparative negligence system as to negligence also apply that system to strict liability. A plaintiff's wrongful conduct that contributes, along with the defective product, to her own injury reduces her recovery in

some amount. This is usually limited to misuse, abnormal use, or independent negligence situations (i.e., not where the plaintiff's wrongful conduct is a failure to discover the defect).

(2) In some jurisdictions that permit comparative fault, the plaintiff's unreasonable conduct in failing to discover and guard against the defect is not a defense.

B. Products Liability on a Negligence Theory

1. Proper Defendants

a. If negligence, rather than strict liability, is the theory of recovery in a products liability action, the plaintiff must establish a greater personal degree of fault. Negligent conduct should result in liability for the following:

(1) a defendant selling used goods (i.e., a commercial seller of used goods unreasonably passes on a defective product or negligently fails to discover a dangerous defect);

(2) a defendant repairing used goods (i.e., where the negligent repair of used goods renders or leaves them dangerously defective);

(3) a defendant leasing real property;

(4) a defendant providing services; and

(5) franchisors.

2. Elements

a. The elements of a products liability claim based in negligence are the same elements that are part of the negligence cause of action in general.

b. **Duty**

(1) A duty is owed to any foreseeable plaintiff. No contractual relationship is required.

EXAMPLE: If Tom buys a car negligently manufactured by Ford for his wife, Katie, she may bring a negligence claim against Ford, as she is a foreseeable plaintiff.

c. **Breach of Duty**

(1) The defendant will typically be judged by the reasonable person standard of care, and breach of duty will be unreasonable conduct on the part of the defendant. On a negligence theory, proof that a product is defective does not automatically establish that each defendant in the chain of distribution breached a duty. The plaintiff must therefore establish that each defendant failed to exercise due care.

(2) If a reasonable person would have realized that a product was dangerous in normal use, a defendant's failure to inspect and discover the defect is a breach of duty under negligence principles. It is relevant to consider the nature of the product, the source of the product, and the extent of information available to the defendant.

(3) In general, a failure to inspect packaged goods for defects is not a breach of duty if they come from a reputable manufacturer or distributor. If the goods are manufactured or otherwise supplied by a previously unknown or questionable source, a defendant's unreasonable failure to inspect is a breach of duty. It likely would be a breach of duty not to inspect a particular product as to which a defendant had received or otherwise became aware of complaints from customers.

(4) If the defendant inspects or becomes aware of a defect, his subsequent failure to find the defect or to take reasonable precautions is judged by the reasonable person standard.

d. **Cause-in-Fact and Proximate Cause**

(1) The principles of actual (cause-in-fact) and legal (proximate) causation which govern a negligence analysis generally apply equally to products liability claims where negligence is the theory of recovery.

e. **Damages**

(1) Damages in negligence products liability are assessed according to the same principles applicable to strict liability.

f. **Defenses**

(1) Those defenses generally applicable to negligence are also available in products liability sounding in negligence.

C. Products Liability on a Warranty Theory

1. Today, there is little left of the historical requirement for products liability on a warranty theory that the parties be in privity. Only where a plaintiff seeks recovery for pure economic losses and the theory of recovery is implied warranty is privity a relevant consideration. **Privity** in this context refers to the relationship between the injured plaintiff and the last commercial seller in the chain of distribution of the defective product.
2. UCC Section 2-318 offers three alternatives regarding privity (a legislature could enact any one of the three). Each provides that if the purchaser of goods was the beneficiary of a warranty, privity extends to:
    a. members of the purchaser's family or household, plus guests of the purchaser, if they suffer personal injury;
    b. any natural persons who may reasonably be expected to use, consume, or be affected by the goods, if they suffer personal injury; and
    c. any persons who may reasonably be expected to use, consume, or be affected by the goods, if they suffer injury.
3. On a warranty products liability theory, liability arises from the fact that a product is not as represented (i.e., it breaches a warranty made either expressly or impliedly by the defendant). The plaintiff must establish that a warranty existed as to the product and that the product does not conform to the warranty.
    a. An **express warranty** exists where the defendant made a representation as to the nature or quality of the product. This can occur via advertising, during negotiations for purchase, or as a provision of the contract of sale.

b. The UCC provides that an express warranty may be created by a defendant's promise, by affirmation of fact, by description, or by use of a sample or model [UCC § 2-313].

c. An **implied warranty** may arise under a variety of circumstances.

(1) The UCC is limited by its own terms to the sale of goods. There are two types of warranties that may be implied under the proper circumstances:

(a) where a merchant deals in goods of a particular kind, the sale of such goods constitutes an implied warranty that those goods will be merchantable—that is, they are of average quality for goods of that kind and generally fit for the purpose for which such goods are normally used [UCC § 2-314(1)]; and

(b) where a defendant knows or has reason to know that [UCC § 2-315]:

1) the plaintiff is purchasing the goods for a particular purpose; and

2) the plaintiff is relying upon the defendant's skill or judgment to furnish appropriate goods—sale of the goods will constitute an implied warranty that those goods will actually be fit for the plaintiff's purpose.

(2) Many states recognize judicially created implied warranties of merchantability and fitness for a particular purpose that apply to leased goods.

(3) The decisional law of a small minority of states extends the implied warranties applicable to sales of goods to real property as well.

4. Recovery of damages for breach of warranty is governed by the same principles applicable to strict liability in tort, except that pure economic losses are recoverable (e.g., loss of profits, cost of obtaining replacement equipment or materials, etc.). The plaintiff must also be in privity with the defendant, as discussed above.

5. **Defenses**

a. **Disclaimer**

(1) The UCC enables a defendant to disclaim or limit the applicability of all warranties by a sufficiently conspicuous writing.

(2) The UCC provides that it is *prima facie* unconscionable for a seller to attempt to limit the remedies available for breach of warranty so as to exclude recovery for personal injuries (e.g., by limiting responsibility for breach to repair or replacement) where consumer goods are involved.

(3) Where goods are sold "as is," it is often implied that the seller is disclaiming any warranties, implied or express.

(4) Federal law provides that a seller who gives a written warranty to a consumer may not thereby disclaim any implied warranties.

b. **Failure to Notify Seller**

(1) The UCC provides that a plaintiff-buyer must notify a defendant-seller of the breach of warranty within a reasonable time after the buyer

discovers or should have discovered it. This provision is often not applied where the plaintiff is a bystander who suffers personal injury.

c. **Contributory and Comparative Negligence**

(1) With respect to personal injury or injury to property, contributory negligence and comparative fault defenses are available where warranty is the theory on a similar basis to strict liability in tort.

d. **Assumption of Risk**

(1) As to products liability in warranty, this defense is similar in application to strict products liability in tort. If the plaintiff voluntarily and unreasonably continues to use a product after she discovers that it is not fit for the purpose purchased or not of merchantable quality, the defendant is exonerated from liability for personal injuries or property damage suffered by the plaintiff.

V. NUISANCE

A. Types of Nuisance

1. Public Nuisance

a. A **public nuisance** is an unreasonable interference with a right common to the general public.

b. Circumstances that may sustain a holding that an interference with a public right is unreasonable include the following:

(1) whether the conduct involves a significant interference with the public health, safety, peace, comfort, or convenience;

(2) whether the conduct is proscribed by a statute, ordinance, or administrative regulation; and

(3) whether the conduct is of a continuing nature or has produced a permanent or long-lasting effect, and as the actor knows or has reason to know, has a significant effect upon the public right.

c. To recover damages in an individual action for a public nuisance, a plaintiff must have suffered harm of a kind different from that suffered by other members of the public.

d. To maintain a proceeding to enjoin or abate a public nuisance, a plaintiff must:

(1) have the right to recover damages;

(2) have authority as a public official or public agency to represent the state or a political subdivision in the matter; or

(3) have standing to sue as a representative of the general public, as a citizen in a citizen's action, or as a member of a class in a class action.

2. Private Nuisance

a. A **private nuisance** is a thing or activity that substantially and unreasonably interferes with the plaintiff's use and enjoyment of his land.

b. The interference with the plaintiff's use and enjoyment must be substantial. This means that it must be offensive, inconvenient, or annoying to an average person in the community. A plaintiff cannot, by devoting her land to an unusually sensitive use, complain of a nuisance based on conduct that would otherwise be relatively harmless.

c. The interference must be unreasonable, which means that either:

(1) the gravity of the plaintiff's harm outweighs the utility of the defendant's conduct; or

(2) if intentional, the harm caused by the defendant's conduct is substantial and the financial burden of compensating for this and other harms does not render unfeasible the continuation of the conduct.

d. A trespass is an invasion of a plaintiff's interest in the exclusive possession of land (e.g., an entry of something tangible onto the property). On the other hand, a nuisance is an interference with a plaintiff's interest in the use and enjoyment of the land, which does not necessarily require a physical intrusion.

EXAMPLE: Amanda is a writer. Every day, she tries to get work done in the morning. If her neighbor, Callie, calls her every morning, this will not be a private nuisance. However, if Callie calls her fifteen times a morning after Amanda has asked her not to, this may be a private nuisance.

e. For a private nuisance, there is liability only to those who have property rights and privileges in respect to the use and employment of the land affected, including:
   (1) possessors of the land;
   (2) owners of easements and profits in the land; and
   (3) owners of nonpossessory estates in the land that are detrimentally affected by interferences with its use and enjoyment.

f. A defendant is subject to liability for a private nuisance if, but only if, his conduct is a legal cause of an invasion of another's interest in the private use and enjoyment of land, and the invasion is either:
   (1) intentional and unreasonable; or
   (2) unintentional and otherwise actionable under the rules controlling liability for negligent or reckless conduct.

EXAM TIP Often the key determination on an examination question is to evaluate the reasonableness or unreasonableness of the defendant's conduct. This analysis involves weighing the gravity of the harm done to the plaintiff against the utility of the defendant's activity. Unlike in trespass, the court will balance several factors: compliance with applicable zoning ordinances; priority of occupation; the frequency and extent of the interference, applied objectively to normal persons; and the utility and social value of the defendant's activity.

TRESPASS ON LAND	NUISANCE
A defendant who intentionally, negligently, or recklessly enters the land in the possession of another or causes a thing or a third person to do so is subject to liability.	Substantial and unreasonable interference with the plaintiff's use and enjoyment of the land; basis of nuisance may be intentional, negligent, or absolute.
Consists of intrusions upon, beneath, and above the surface of the earth.	Consists of: (1) interference with the physical condition of the land (such as by vibrations or blasting which damages a house, the destruction of crops, the flooding or pollution of a stream, etc.); or (2) a disturbance of the comfort or convenience of the occupant (such as by unpleasant odors, smoke, dust, loud noise, excessive light, or even repeated telephone calls).

B. Defenses

1. **Contributory Negligence**
    a. When a nuisance results from negligent conduct of the defendant, the **contributory negligence** of the plaintiff is a defense to the same extent as in other actions founded on negligence.
    b. When the harm is intentional or the result of recklessness, contributory negligence is not a defense.
    c. When the nuisance results from an abnormally dangerous condition or activity, contributory negligence is a defense only if the plaintiff has voluntarily and unreasonably subjected herself to the risk of harm.
2. **Assumption of Risk**
    a. In an action for a nuisance, the plaintiff's assumption of risk is a defense to the same extent as in other tort actions.
3. **Coming to the Nuisance**
    a. The fact that the plaintiff has acquired or improved his land after a nuisance will not by itself bar his action, but it is a factor to be considered in determining whether the nuisance is actionable.
4. **Compliance with Statute**
    a. A relevant and persuasive, but not absolute, defense to nuisance arises upon evidence that the defendant's conduct was consistent with applicable administrative regulations (i.e., a zoning ordinance or pollution control regulation).

C. Remedies

1. For a private or public nuisance, the usual remedy is damages.
2. Where the legal remedy (i.e., money damages) is inadequate or unavailable, courts may grant injunctive relief. The legal remedy may be deemed to be inadequate for a number of reasons (e.g., the nuisance is a continuing wrong or the nuisance is of a kind which will cause irreparable harm). In determining whether an injunction will be granted, the court will undertake to balance the equities, namely taking into account:
    a. the relative economic hardship to the parties for granting or denying the injunction; and
    b. the public interest in the defendant's activity continuing.

EXAM TIP Keep in mind that a court may require the defendant to pay damages while denying injunctive relief.

3. A plaintiff has the privilege to enter upon the defendant's land and personally abate the nuisance after notice to the defendant and her refusal to act. The privilege extends to the use of all reasonable action that is necessary to terminate the nuisance, even to the destruction of valuable property, provided the damage done is not greatly disproportionate to the threatened harm, but does not extend to unnecessary or unreasonable damage. There will be liability for any excess.

EXAMPLE: It may not be justifiable, for instance, to destroy a house merely because it is used for prostitution.

4. A plaintiff who has suffered some unique damage has a similar privilege to abate a public nuisance by self-help. However, a public nuisance may be abated by a private individual only when it causes or threatens special damage to himself apart from that to the general public, and then only to the extent necessary to protect his own interests.

5. **Injunctions**

   a. **Nature and Forms**

      (1) The injunction is the most common form of equitable remedy. An **injunction** is a court order directed to a person or entity, usually to refrain from doing a particular act (a **prohibitory injunction**).

      (2) Less commonly, a court may issue an order to do a particular act (a **mandatory injunction**). Requests for mandatory injunctions are subject to heightened scrutiny, requiring a showing that the facts and law clearly favor the moving party [Dahl v. HEM Pharmaceuticals Corp., 7 F.3d 1399 (9th Cir. 1993)].

      EXAMPLE: Plaintiff, a 30-year-old male, brings an action against Health Club, an all-women's health facility, to allow him to take aerobics classes there. If the court requires the health club to admit him, it may do so in the form of a mandatory injunction.

      EXAMPLE: Plaintiff, a women's health clinic, brings an action against Defendant, an anti-abortion group, to enjoin it from harassing patients and passersby on the sidewalk in front of the clinic. If the court enjoins Defendant, it will do so in the form of a prohibitory injunction.

   b. **Availability**

      (1) In accordance with the general rules on the availability of equitable remedies, injunctive relief is generally available when money damages would not afford adequate relief, such as where it would be extremely difficult to ascertain the amount of compensation that would afford adequate relief or where injunctive relief is necessary to prevent a multiplicity of judicial proceedings.

      EXAMPLE: Injunctive relief has been the primary remedy in civil rights litigation because a deprivation of the individual's constitutional rights is not deemed remediable by money damages.

      EXAMPLE: If the defendant repeatedly trespasses on the plaintiff's land, equity may enjoin the trespass rather than force repeated actions at law to redress the injury.

      (2) The plaintiff who seeks an injunction must specifically show that:

         (a) she is about to suffer or will continue to suffer an irreparable injury for which money damages would be inadequate compensation;

(b) the balance of hardships between the plaintiff and defendant supports an equitable remedy; and

(c) the public interest would not be disserved by the grant of an injunction.

(3) Injunctive relief is generally not available to:

(a) stay court proceedings, unless necessary to prevent a multiplicity of proceedings;

(b) enforce the criminal laws other than those that restrain a public nuisance; or

(c) prevent the breach of a contract that is not specifically enforceable, such as where the terms of the agreement are not sufficiently certain to make the precise act which is to be done clearly ascertainable.

c. **Temporary Restraining Orders and Preliminary Injunctions**

(1) **Showing Required**

(a) Courts apply a number of other factors to determine whether preliminary injunctive relief is appropriate. The following criteria are the most commonly applied:

1) the plaintiff is likely to succeed on the merits of the underlying claim;

2) the complaint shows that the plaintiff is entitled to the relief demanded (restraining the commission or continuance of the act complained of) either for a limited period or perpetually;

3) denial of injunctive relief would produce waste, or great or irreparable injury, to the plaintiff, such as where it appears, during litigation, that a party to the action is doing or is about to do some act in violation of the rights of another party to the action that would tend to render the judgment ineffectual; and

4) the public interest as well as the balancing of hardships between the parties favors the grant of an injunction.

(2) **Notice Requirements**

(a) A preliminary injunction may not be granted without notice to the other party. During the time required for notice and hearing on the preliminary injunction, however, the moving party may seek immediate relief through a temporary restraining order ("TRO").

(3) **Duration**

(a) A TRO granted without notice remains in effect for only a specified period of time, generally 10 to 20 days (a TRO issued without notice in a federal court is effective for a maximum of 14 days [Fed. R. Civ. P. 65(b)(2)]).

d. **Permanent Injunctions**

(1) The plaintiff must have prevailed on the substantive claim and shown a need for continuing protection to be eligible for permanent injunctive relief.

EXAMPLE: When a claimant who insisted the famous lawyer Johnnie Cochran owed him money, and picketed Cochran's office with signs containing insults and obscenities, indicated that he would continue to engage in the activity absent a court order, the court permanently enjoined the claimant from making defamatory statements about Cochran and his firm in any public forum [Tory v. Cochran, 544 U.S. 734 (2005)].

(2) Unlike the interlocutory temporary injunction, a permanent injunction is a final judgment and continues in force until dissolved, but the permanent injunction need not be perpetual—it may be set to expire by its own terms.

VI. DEFAMATION

A. In General

1. For a defamation action, a plaintiff must establish that the defendant published defamatory material concerning the plaintiff that caused reputational damage. In analyzing an action for defamation, one must check for:
   a. a defamatory message;
   b. certain pleading problems;
   c. publication of the message;
   d. the type of defamation;
   e. damages;
   f. common law defenses; and
   g. constitutional issues.

B. Defamatory Message

1. A message is **defamatory** if it lowers a plaintiff in the esteem of the community or discourages third persons from associating with him.
   a. A **defamatory message** has been characterized as one that holds a plaintiff up to hatred, ridicule, contempt, or scorn. Whether or not a defendant's statement includes this notion of disgrace, it should be actionable if it causes third persons to avoid contact with the plaintiff. A message is also defamatory to an entity if it causes customers to stop doing business with the entity, causes persons to stop making charitable contributions to it, or causes them to avoid membership.
2. In general, only statements of fact are actionable as defamatory. However, expressions of opinion which imply that the speaker knows certain facts to be true, or which imply that such facts exist, may be sufficient to classify the messages as defamatory. If a reasonable person would interpret a statement as one of fact, considering the context and the nature of the utterance, a jury may find that the message is defamatory.
   a. A statement is more likely to be regarded as a statement of fact rather than opinion to the extent that it is more specific and detailed. It is not sufficient to change what is otherwise a statement of fact to one of opinion by adding qualifiers such as, "I think…" or "It is my opinion…."

   EXAMPLE: The Daily may be subject to defamation liability to Paxton for stating falsely: "In our opinion, Paxton was involved in the planning of the assassination of Robert F. Kennedy." The Daily cannot be liable for publishing: "Paxton was once a very stylish dresser, but this year his clothes seem drab."
3. A message is defamatory if it has the required injurious effect on any substantial minority of reasonable people. If a negligible number of people are affected, or only those whose views are too antisocial, the message is not defamatory.
   a. A message is defamatory *per se* if it is apparent on the face of the message that it will injure the plaintiff's reputation. If the message at issue

does not on its face seem injurious to the plaintiff's reputation, or defamation *per quod*, the plaintiff must plead additional, extrinsic facts that render the message defamatory. The plaintiff must also explain how the message, with the extrinsic facts, injures her reputation. Where a statement is defamatory only upon a showing of extrinsic facts, the plaintiff must:

(1) plead and prove inducement;

(2) establish a defamatory meaning by innuendo; and

(3) show that she herself was the intended plaintiff by colloquium.

EXAMPLE: The Daily prints, "Petunia married Donald yesterday." This does not appear reputation-harming on its face, but it may become so through the inducement that Petunia is already married to someone else.

4. The defamatory message must be understood by the person who receives it. A judge decides whether a communication could be understood as defamatory, and the jury decides whether it was defamatory in the case before it.

   EXAMPLE: The Daily falsely states in an article that Penelope used to be best friends with a drug addict. A judge may determine that a false statement that a person was once friends with a person who was addicted to drugs is not capable of causing reputational harm. If the judge instead determines that it could be harmful, then it would be up to the jury to determine if such a statement harmed Penelope's reputation in the situation before it.

C. Pleading Problems

1. To bring an action for defamation, the party suffering the defamation must have been a living person or an existing organization.

   a. A defamatory message published about a third person is actionable only to the extent that it also defames the plaintiff. A defamatory message concerning only a third person, even one closely related to the plaintiff, cannot defame the plaintiff.

   b. Where a defendant makes an otherwise defamatory statement about a group of persons, his liability to individual plaintiffs varies according to the size of the group and the nature of the defamatory message.

   (1) A defamatory message made concerning all members of a large group does not create a right of action in favor of any particular member of that group. However, if the circumstances would indicate to a reasonable person that a particular plaintiff is the actual subject of the defamatory message, the fact that the message is spoken of the group does not relieve the defendant of liability.

   (2) If the group that is the subject of the defendant's defamatory message is sufficiently small, each member of the group is generally regarded as sufficiently identified so that each could bring an action for defamation.

   EXAMPLE: In a case involving a sportswriter who published an article stating that all 20 members of the University football team had used illegal steroids, each member of that team was permitted to bring an action against the sportswriter for defamation.

(3) Traditionally, no individual member of a small group was permitted to bring an action for defamation where the defendant defamed some but not all of them. Today, whether a particular member was sufficiently identified is examined on a case-by-case basis, considering all the circumstances.

D. Publication

1. A defamatory message is commonly a spoken or written statement. Any form of communication may be defamatory, however, including television and radio broadcasts, films, plays, novels, cartoons, sculpture, etc.

   a. A plaintiff must prove that some reasonable third person who received the defamatory message understood it to refer to the plaintiff. Thus, if the plaintiff is not specifically named in the allegedly defamatory communication, she must allege through colloquium that some people will interpret the communication to be about him.

   EXAMPLE: The Daily states that the longest serving Torts professor at Acme School of Law does not know the difference between battery and assault. Pinnafore may proceed in his action for defamation by alleging and proving that he is the longest serving Torts professor at Acme.

2. It is not actionable to utter a defamatory message to the plaintiff alone. For the defendant's message concerning the plaintiff to constitute defamation, it must be communicated to a third person, who receives and understands it.

   a. In most situations, it is apparent that the defendant desired that third persons receive the defamatory message. However, a message is "published" if the defendant negligently permitted it to be communicated to third persons. If it is reasonably foreseeable that an eavesdropper might overhear a message, for example, and one does so, there is a sufficient publication.

3. In addition to the defendant who originates the defamatory message, other persons who repeat it may be liable to the plaintiff, varying according to their relationship to the original publisher. Such republication may also increase the originator's liability to the plaintiff.

   a. All persons who participate in originating a defamatory message are liable as primary publishers.

   EXAMPLE: The author of a book defamatory to a plaintiff, the editor who selected it for publication and provided editorial services, and the company that employed the editor and printed the book would all be liable as primary publishers.

   b. Any person who repeats the defamatory message is liable as a publisher. This is so even where the repetition is qualified by such terms as "alleged" or is said not to be the opinion of the republisher.

(1) Where the original publisher could reasonably foresee that the defamatory message would be republished, he is liable to the plaintiff for additional damages caused by the republications.

c. A person who distributes the original defamatory message as a commodity (e.g., a bookseller, newspaper vendor, retailer, etc.) is liable only if she knew or should have known that the material distributed contained the defamatory message.

E. Type of Defamation

1. Historically, **libel** was a written form of defamation. Today, a defamatory message embodied in any relatively permanent form is a libel.

 EXAMPLE: A sound recording, video recording, picture, sculpture, etc.

 a. **Libel *per quod*** is a libel as to which it is not apparent on the face of the communication that it is defamatory. A plaintiff must plead and establish extrinsic facts to establish that the libel was defamatory and that it referred to the plaintiff. A large minority of jurisdictions require proof of special damages for libel *per quod*.

2. Historically, **slander** was defamation in spoken, rather than written, form. Today, a defamatory message not preserved in permanent form is classified as slander.

 a. **Slander *per se*** is a type of slander historically regarded as so harmful that it was presumed that the plaintiff suffered damage from the very fact of its utterance. Four types of slander were so classified:

 (1) a slander that imputed to the plaintiff the commission of a crime involving moral turpitude or infamous punishment (imprisonment or death);

 (2) allegations of the plaintiff having a loathsome disease were slander;

 (a) Historically, a loathsome disease was one that was incurable and persisted over time, such as venereal disease or leprosy. Allegations of insanity or tuberculosis have been held not within the slander *per se* category.

 (3) slander which imputed to the plaintiff behavior or characteristics that were incompatible with the proper conduct of his business, profession, or office; and

 (4) it was slander *per se* to falsely impute unchastity to a woman.

 (a) Scholars have concluded that the same conclusion would follow if the target of the defamation were a man, but no case has so held. The Restatement defines this form of slander *per se* in terms of false imputation of "serious sexual misconduct" to any person. A small minority of jurisdictions hold it slander *per se* to falsely impute impotency to a man. In addition, commentators have suggested that false imputation of deviant sexual behavior might fall within this category.

3. Where it is not clear whether a defamatory message is libel or slander, factors to distinguish the two include:

a. the permanence of the form;
b. the area of dissemination; and
c. the extent to which the message was planned rather than spontaneous.
   (1) The more permanent the form, widely disseminated, and planned a defamatory message is, the more likely it is to be considered libel.

F. Damages

1. Three different types of damages are potentially recoverable for defamation. In some situations, the need for actual proof of damages is affected by the type of defamation involved.
   a. **Pecuniary damages** are quantifiable monetary losses suffered by the plaintiff due to the injury to her reputation. Examples include loss of customers, loss of a job, or other diminishment of economic advantage. The plaintiff must present evidence of specific actual monetary losses in order to recover pecuniary damages.
      (1) Proof of pecuniary damages is necessary to establish a *prima facie* case if the form of defamation is slander and, in some states, if it is libel *per quod*. Once pecuniary damages are established, presumed damages are also available.
   b. In certain circumstances, the jury is permitted to presume that plaintiff suffered **general damages** as a result of the defendant's defamatory statement. These include nonpecuniary aspects of the injury to reputation, such as humiliation, loss of friends, etc. The jury is instructed to estimate the amount of presumed damages based upon the extent of injury to the plaintiff's reputation.
      (1) It is "presumed" that the plaintiff suffered general damages, and thus no proof of actual damage need be offered, when the form of defamation is slander *per se* or "ordinary" libel (i.e., not libel *per quod*).
   c. Damages that are assessed against the defendant to punish and deter future wrongful conduct are called **punitive damages**. The plaintiff must make some additional evidentiary showing of vexatiousness or evil intent (i.e., common law malice) to recover punitive damages.

G. Common Law Defenses

1. **Truth**
   a. Historically, falsity was presumed once the plaintiff established the publication of a defamatory communication. In other words, truth was a substantial defense. The defendant had to prove that the communication was "substantially true."
   b. Now, in all defamation cases except possibly those where the plaintiff is a private plaintiff and the matter is of private concern, the plaintiff must prove falsity as part of his *prima facie* case.

2. **Absolute Privilege**
    a. Where an **absolute privilege** applies, the defendant may not be held liable for an otherwise defamatory message as a matter of law.
        (1) A legislator is not liable for a defamatory message uttered while on the floor of the legislature or during hearings or committee proceedings. The nature or content of the defamatory message or its relationship to any matter before the legislature is immaterial to availability of this privilege.
        (2) A participant in judicial proceedings (e.g., a judge, attorney, witness, or juror) is not liable for any defamatory message that is reasonably related to the proceedings.
        (3) The privilege for statements made during judicial proceedings arises upon filing of the complaint and continues until final termination of the action. It includes pleadings, pretrial proceedings, and discovery, and may include settlement negotiations occurring prior to the filing of the litigation. *Quasi*-judicial administrative hearings are considered judicial proceedings for this privilege.
        (4) An absolute privilege from liability for defamation applies to policy-making officials of the executive branches of state and federal governments, so long as the defamatory utterance was made in the course of their duties and was relevant to those duties.
        (5) A defamatory message communicated by one spouse to another is absolutely privileged from defamation liability.
        (6) The U.S. Supreme Court has held that a broadcast media defendant compelled by the fairness doctrine to permit a third person to utilize its facilities is absolutely privileged as to defamatory statements made by the third person. Commentators suggest the same rule might be applied to a newspaper compelled by law to print public notices.
    b. The defendant has the burden of establishing that an absolute privilege applies to her defamatory message.
3. **Qualified Privilege**
    a. If a **qualified privilege** is applicable, a defendant is not held liable for otherwise defamatory messages he utters unless he loses the protection of the privilege.
    b. A defendant is qualifiedly immune from liability for defamatory messages made in a communication that appears reasonably necessary to protect or advance the defendant's own legitimate interests.
    c. A defendant who communicates on a matter of interest to the recipient of the communication or a third person is qualifiedly immune from liability for defamatory messages in the communication.

        EXAMPLE: Duncan was employed for seven years with ABC Company. After being terminated, he sought employment with XYZ Company. XYZ contacted ABC and asked for a recommendation. The president of ABC stated, "If I were you, I wouldn't hire Duncan—he's a thief." As long as the speaker reasonably believed the information to be true, there is a qualified privilege to act in the interest of others. Thus, ABC would not be liable for defamation.

d. A defendant who communicates concerning a matter of public interest to one empowered to protect that interest is qualifiedly privileged as to a defamatory message contained in the communication.

e. A defendant has a qualified privilege as to defamatory messages contained in a criticism of a matter of public interest.

f. A defendant is qualifiedly immune from liability for defamatory messages that are republished in a report of public hearings or meetings, so long as the defendant's report is fair and accurate.

g. The defendant bears the burden of establishing that a qualified privilege is available.

h. The defendant loses an otherwise available qualified privilege if:

(1) she acts out of malice;

(a) **Malice** is present if the defendant's primary motive in publishing the defamatory message was something other than furthering the interest that justified the privilege.

(2) she exceeds the scope of the privilege; or

(a) A qualified privilege may be lost if the defamatory message includes matters not relevant to the interests protected by the privilege or is published in a manner or to persons outside the legitimate scope of the privilege.

(3) she does not believe the truth of the defamatory communication.

(a) A qualified privilege is lost if the defendant does not possess an honest belief in the truth of the defamatory message. Some states also require that the defendant have a reasonable, honest belief.

i. While a defendant bears the burden of establishing that a qualified privilege is applicable, a plaintiff bears the burden of establishing that conditions exist under which the privilege is lost.

4. **Consent**

a. Generally applicable principles relating to the defense of consent apply to defamation.

H. Constitutional Issues

1. Decisions interpreting the Free Speech Clause of the First Amendment have altered the common law of defamation with regard to:

a. the degree of fault required of a defendant;

(1) At common law, defamation was a strict liability offense, in the sense that the plaintiff need only establish that the defamatory statement was made in order to recover (all other elements being present), not that defendant had any particular mental state or degree of fault.

b. the nature of the plaintiff;

(1) Where a plaintiff is a public official or a public figure, the plaintiff must establish that the defendant acted with "malice" before any

recovery may be had [New York Times v. Sullivan, 376 U.S. 254 (1964)].

(a) A **public official** is a government official who has or appears to have substantial responsibility over governmental operations. While this does not include every public employee, courts have, for example, generally included police officers among public officials.

(b) A **public figure** is a person who has either:

1) achieved such pervasive fame or notoriety such that he becomes a public figure for all purposes (e.g., a celebrity); or

2) voluntarily injected himself or allowed himself to be drawn into a particular public controversy such that he becomes a public figure as to the limited issues present in that controversy.

(c) **Malice**, for this purpose, is defined as knowing falsity or recklessness as to truth or falsity. In order for malice to exist, the defendant must have actually known the defamatory message was false or actually entertained serious doubts about its truth (i.e., had reckless disregard) [Id.].

(d) The plaintiff must establish malice with "convincing clarity." Commentators have analogized this language from New York Times v. Sullivan to the "clear and convincing" evidence standard, which requires something more than proof by a preponderance of the evidence, and something less than the "beyond a reasonable doubt" standard used in criminal matters.

c. the subject matter of the defamatory statement;

(1) Where the plaintiff is neither a public official nor public figure, constitutional protection of free speech still precludes application of the common law strict liability scheme if the subject matter of the defamation is a matter of public concern. In such a case, the defendant must be shown to have exhibited some degree of fault higher than strict liability, which presumably means negligence. However, actual malice must be proved for presumed or punitive damages.

(2) Where a private plaintiff sues in defamation and the subject matter is also private (i.e., not a matter of public concern), the U.S. Constitution does not require that the plaintiff prove actual malice to recover presumed or punitive damages.

(3) This can be a blurry line, but the test is to look at the "form, content, and context" of the communication. As a practical matter, if the defendant is a member of the media, or if the communication is widely disseminated, it is probably of public concern. Conversely, if the case involves slander that is shared with only very few people, it might be a matter of private concern.

d. the availability of presumed and punitive damages; and

(1) General damages may be presumed if otherwise available under defamation law, and punitive damages may be awarded upon proper proof in two situations:

(a) in any case where the plaintiff establishes that the defendant acted with malice; and

(b) where the common law still applies—that is, where a private plaintiff sues for defamation as to a matter not of public concern.

(2) Where negligence is the applicable degree of fault required by constitutional principles and the plaintiff does not show malice, the plaintiff may only recover actual damages.

(3) **Actual damages** are broader and more inclusive than the common law pecuniary damages, and include all injuries to the plaintiff's reputation. They need not be supported by evidence of quantifiable monetary losses, but there must be introduction of some evidence as proof.

(4) The U.S. Supreme Court has held that speech such as parodies, cartoons, and other satirical utterances cannot be actionable as an intentional infliction of emotional distress unless they contain false statements of fact made with malice.

e. the media status of the defendant.

VII. INVASION OF PRIVACY

A. Intrusion into Seclusion

1. This form of invasion of privacy is present when a defendant unreasonably intrudes into the plaintiff's seclusion.
   a. The wrongful conduct is an interference with the plaintiff's seclusion, including physical intrusions (placing a webcam in the plaintiff's bathroom) and non-physical intrusions (i.e., photographing the plaintiff in her backyard from off the property).
   b. To be actionable, the defendant's intrusion must be one that would be highly objectionable to a reasonable person.
   c. **Seclusion** refers to a plaintiff's right to physical solitude or to the privacy of personal affairs or concerns. In circumstances where the plaintiff has no reasonable expectation of solitude or privacy, conduct by the defendant that might otherwise be intrusive is not an invasion of seclusion (e.g., eavesdropping on a conversation between the plaintiff and another person as they walk down a public sidewalk).
2. Damages recoverable for invasion of seclusion include compensatory damages (e.g., mental distress unaccompanied by physical injury) and, under appropriate circumstances, punitive damages.

B. Appropriation of Identity or Likeness

1. **Appropriation** is an unauthorized use of the plaintiff's identity or likeness for the defendant's commercial advantage.
   a. The plaintiff bears the burden of proving that he did not consent to the defendant's use of his identity or likeness.
   b. Use of "identity or likeness" is present if the defendant uses any object or characteristic sufficient to identify the plaintiff. Use of an object or characteristic that does not identify the plaintiff is not actionable.
   c. The wrongful use of the plaintiff's identity or likeness must be in connection with the promotion of a product or service. The fact that the defendant derived economic benefit from the use of the plaintiff's identity is not enough alone to constitute a violation (e.g., a biographer paid to write an unauthorized book about a famous plaintiff).
2. Compensatory damages are recoverable, measured by the reasonable value of the use of the plaintiff's identity or likeness. Punitive damages should be recoverable on a proper showing.

   EXAMPLE: Jonathan wishes to advertise a weight-loss product. Without asking her permission, Jonathan puts a celebrity's photo in an ad for the product. The celebrity will have a cause of action against Jonathan.

C. Public Disclosure of Private Facts

1. This form of invasion of privacy is present when a defendant unreasonably discloses private facts about a plaintiff to the public.
   a. Disclosure is actionable if it would be highly offensive to a reasonable person and not of legitimate public concern.
   b. The private facts must be disseminated to the public. Communicating them to a third person is not sufficient to constitute this tort (as distinguished from defamation, where communication to a single third person is a sufficient publication).
   c. The information or material disclosed by the defendant must be an aspect or component of the plaintiff's life not open to public view or inspection and not a matter of public record.
2. The plaintiff can recover compensatory damages, including mental distress unaccompanied by physical injury.
3. Public disclosure of private facts is not actionable where the publication is newsworthy. This broad defense can apply to pictures published in newspapers as well as magazine articles on former celebrities and public figures. Private matters contained in public records are absolutely privileged.

D. Portrayal in a False Light

1. This tort is present when a defendant publishes matters that portray a plaintiff in a false light.
   a. The defendant must communicate the material to a substantial number of people.
   b. **Portraying in a false light** means attributing to the plaintiff views he does not hold or attributing actions to him that he did not take. In addition, the false light in which the plaintiff is placed must be such that a reasonable person would find it highly offensive.
      (1) This is a "lesser" form of offensive falseness than required for defamation.
2. The plaintiff can recover compensatory and, in a proper case, punitive damages.

E. Defenses and Privileges

1. **Truth**
   a. Truth is not a defense to appropriation or intrusion, since truth or falsity is not a relevant issue. However, truth is a complete defense to portrayal in a false light.
2. **Consent**
   a. Consent is a defense to disclosure, intrusion, and false light to the same extent it is to any other intentional tort.
   b. The plaintiff is required to prove lack of her consent as an element of her *prima facie* case for appropriation.

3. **Privilege**

   a. The absolute and conditional privileges applicable to defamation should be available as to public disclosure of private facts and portrayal in a false light.

F. Constitutional Principles

1. Where a plaintiff is portrayed in a false light as to a matter of public interest, the plaintiff must prove that the defendant had acted with malice—knowledge of falsity or reckless disregard for truth or falsity—in order to recover.

VIII. WRONGFUL INSTITUTION OF LEGAL PROCEEDINGS

A. Malicious Prosecution

1. **Malicious prosecution** is the institution of criminal proceedings by a defendant, done for an improper purpose and without probable cause, that terminate favorably for the plaintiff and cause the plaintiff damages.
   a. The wrongful conduct is the taking of action that results in the commencement of the criminal prosecution of the plaintiff. Such actions include persuading a prosecutor to bring charges against a plaintiff, signing an affidavit for a warrant, or giving false information to the authorities with knowledge of its falsity. It does not constitute malicious prosecution to give information to authorities while relying upon their discretion as to whether to prosecute.
   b. The defendant must act for a primary purpose other than to bring a guilty person to justice. That there was no probable cause supporting the initiation of proceedings is evidence that the defendant's purpose was improper.
   c. The defendant lacks probable cause for initiation of criminal proceedings when either:
      (1) a reasonable person possessing the same facts as the defendant would not have believed that the plaintiff was guilty of the charged offense; or
      (2) defendant did not actually believe that the plaintiff was guilty.

      EXAMPLE: Dahlia is still angry with her former boyfriend, Preston. Dahlia contacts the police and has Preston arrested on suspicion of being a terrorist. Preston is not a terrorist, and Dahlia knows this fact. A judge eventually dismisses the case. Preston will have a cause of action against Dahlia for malicious prosecution.

   d. A grand jury indictment returned against a plaintiff after the defendant's action or a magistrate holding the plaintiff to answer after a preliminary hearing are *prima facie* evidence that probable cause existed to believe the plaintiff was guilty. A plaintiff's conviction on criminal charges is conclusive evidence of probable cause, even if the conviction is subsequently reversed on appeal.
   e. An attorney's advice to the defendant to institute criminal proceedings conclusively establishes probable cause in most jurisdictions, at least where the defendant made a full and fair disclosure of all relevant facts, and the attorney is competent and duly admitted to practice in the jurisdiction or otherwise qualified to render an opinion.
   f. The criminal prosecution must have terminated in a fashion indicating that the plaintiff was innocent of the charges. Terminations on the merits (i.e., acquittal after trial or court dismissal for lack of sufficient evidence) are sufficient in this regard; terminations based on procedural or technical defects, prosecutorial discretion, or similar grounds are not.

2. When a plaintiff establishes the essential elements of a cause of action for malicious prosecution, he is entitled to recover damages for:
   a. the harm to his reputation resulting from the accusation brought against him;
   b. the emotional distress resulting from the bringing of the proceedings; and
   c. attorney's fees and costs associated with defending against the malicious prosecution.
3. **Defenses**
   a. **Privilege**
      (1) Judges and prosecutors are absolutely privileged as to malicious prosecution.
      (2) Law enforcement officers have a more limited immunity. A law enforcement officer will not be protected from malicious prosecution if the particular conduct complained of consisted of acts outside the scope of the officer's official duties or authority. If the officers act within the scope of their authority or with probable cause, they will enjoy immunity from malicious prosecution.
   b. A defendant may prevail in a malicious prosecution action by a plaintiff if the defendant can establish by a preponderance of the evidence that the plaintiff was actually guilty of the crime for which the plaintiff was prosecuted.
      (1) A termination of the criminal proceeding in favor of the plaintiff does not preclude this result, having no *res judicata* effect due to the higher standard of proof in criminal proceedings (because the prosecution must prove the defendant's guilt beyond a reasonable doubt).

B. Wrongful Institution of Civil Proceedings

1. A person who takes an active part in the initiation, continuation, or procurement of civil proceedings against another is subject to liability to the other for wrongful civil proceedings, if:
   a. she acts without basis and primarily for a purpose other than that of securing the proper adjudication of the claim on which the proceedings are based; and
   b. except when they are *ex parte*, the proceedings have terminated in favor of the person against whom they are brought.

   EXAMPLE: Deborah dislikes her new neighbor, Parker. To try to get him to move out of the neighborhood, Deborah sues Parker for private nuisance, alleging that his music is too loud. Deborah knows that Parker rarely plays his music so that it can be heard outside of his home and he always turns it down if asked. When the court hears the evidence against Parker, it dismisses the case. Parker has a cause of action against Deborah for the wrongful institution of civil proceedings.

C. Abuse of Process

1. Abuse of process exists where a defendant intentionally misuses a judicial process (whether civil or criminal) for a purpose other than that for which the process is intended. This tort also parallels malicious prosecution.
2. The plaintiff need not show the defendant's lack of probable cause, as proof of the defendant's improper purpose serves the same function.

IX. ECONOMIC TORTS

A. Intentional Misrepresentation (Fraud)

1. An **intentional misrepresentation** by a defendant, made with scienter, which is material and justifiably relied upon by a plaintiff and which causes damages to the plaintiff, is actionable.
2. An actionable **misrepresentation** is an assertion of a false past or present fact. The generally cited principle that a misrepresentation of opinion is not actionable is subject to exceptions, which are discussed in connection with reliance.
3. A misrepresentation can consist of:
   a. a false, affirmative assertion;
   b. active concealment; or
      (1) In a majority of jurisdictions, a defendant cannot be liable for active concealment if his transaction with the plaintiff is stated to be "as is," or the plaintiff is otherwise put on notice as to the concealed facts.
   c. an omission of fact (i.e., a failure to disclose).
      (1) Traditionally, a defendant was not liable for misrepresentation if her only wrongdoing was the omission of facts. Many exceptions have been developed over the years, including:
         (a) where the defendant is a fiduciary for the plaintiff;
         (b) where the defendant makes an assertion believing it to be true, subsequently discovers that it was false or that circumstances have changed, and fails to disclose the truth or changed circumstances;
         (c) where the defendant makes an incomplete or ambiguous assertion, omitting additional facts that render her assertion misleading;
         (d) where the defendant makes a false assertion not intending that anyone rely upon it, subsequently discovers that the plaintiff intends to act in reliance upon the false assertion, and fails to disclose that the assertion was false; and
         (e) where the plaintiff reasonably expects disclosure.
            1) A minority of modern jurisdictions impose liability on a defendant for the omission of facts where, under the circumstances, the plaintiff could reasonably expect disclosure. Factors to consider include:
               a) the relation of the parties;
               b) the nature of the undisclosed facts; and
               c) the nature of the transaction.
4. The defendant must intend that the plaintiff or a class of persons of which the plaintiff is a member will act or fail to act in reliance on his misrepresentation.

   EXCEPTION: Any plaintiff may recover for misrepresentation regardless of defendant's intent if the misrepresentation is characterized as ongoing (e.g., a mislabeled product).

a. Some cases have found liability for misrepresentation in any situation where the defendant could reasonably foresee that someone would rely upon his misrepresentation, regardless of whether the defendant intended that the particular plaintiff rely on it.

5. Scienter is present when the defendant makes a misrepresentation knowing it to be false or recklessly possessing insufficient information as to its truth or falsity.

6. A representation or omission is material if it would influence a reasonable person in determining his course of action in the particular transaction at issue. A fact is also material, even if a reasonable person would not regard it as important, if the defendant knows that the plaintiff actually regards it as important.

7. The plaintiff must rely on the defendant's misrepresentation, and that reliance must be justified. In general, reliance on an assertion is justified if a reasonable person would have relied upon it. Factors considered in this analysis include the nature of the misrepresentation, the parties, and the relationship of the parties.

   a. Reliance on a misrepresentation of fact is generally regarded as justified except where the representation is patently false. A plaintiff has no duty to investigate, even where not burdensome to do so. If the plaintiff actually investigates, she may not rely on representations inconsistent with what she actually or might reasonably have discovered.

   b. In general, reliance on a misrepresentation of opinion is not justified. There are numerous exceptions to this principle, however.

      (1) A plaintiff's reliance on a defendant's assertion of opinion is justified where the defendant owes the plaintiff a fiduciary duty.

      (2) In circumstances not amounting to a fiduciary relation, but where a defendant has the confidence of a plaintiff (e.g., the defendant is the plaintiff's uncle), reliance on the defendant's misrepresentations may be justified.

      (3) Reliance on a defendant's opinion is more likely to be justified if the defendant possesses much greater expertise than the plaintiff as to the subject of the transaction.

      (4) If the defendant has an interest that he fails to disclose to the plaintiff, it is justifiable for the plaintiff to rely on the defendant's expression of opinion on the subject of that interest.

   c. Traditionally, representations of law were regarded as expressions of opinion, and thus a plaintiff's reliance was not justified. Today, courts apply the principles discussed above. In addition, courts are quite willing to find implied statements of fact in legal opinions.

8. The element of causation is met if a defendant's misrepresentation played a substantial part in inducing the plaintiff to act as she did.

9. **Remedies**

   a. Victims of intentional misrepresentation may recover the following remedies:

      (1) avoidance, as a defense against a breach of contract claim brought by the misrepresenting party;

      (2) rescission of the agreement and damages for reliance on the misrepresentation, including consequential damages; or

(3) enforcement of the benefit of the bargain, measured by the difference between the value of the goods or services actually received and the value of the promised goods or services.

b. The plaintiff may also recover punitive damages against the defendant to penalize the defendant on the basis of the fraudulent intention.

B. Negligent Misrepresentation

1. The traditional rule, followed by a majority of jurisdictions, is that **negligent misrepresentations** are not actionable. Many of these jurisdictions nevertheless allow recovery where there is arguably no intentional misrepresentation by resorting to legal fictions that permit their courts to find intent because a defendant's honestly held belief in the truth of his assertion is unreasonable.

   a. Many jurisdictions impose liability for negligent misrepresentation only in certain situations where a special relationship exists between the defendant and the plaintiff, and the nature of the defendant's activity justifies holding the defendant liable for a failure to exercise due care. The most widely recognized circumstance involves a defendant in the business of supplying information to be used by others in making economically significant decisions (e.g., accountants, title abstractors, or lawyers). Such defendants are liable if they fail to exercise due care in determining the truth or falsity of the representations they make. The elements of this cause of action are identical to those for fraud, with the following differences:

      (1) The mental state a defendant must have for liability under negligent misrepresentation is the same for negligence analysis generally. Thus, a defendant's representations, made in good faith, are actionable if they are inaccurate because the defendant failed to exercise due care.

      (2) A defendant is liable for a negligent misrepresentation only to:

         (a) the person to whom the misrepresentation was made; and

         (b) to any other specific persons or identifiable group of persons that the defendant knew would rely upon the misrepresentation.

            1) Note the absence of foreseeability, a common negligence concept; courts expanding the reach of fraud into negligent misrepresentation sought to limit the class of potential plaintiffs.

C. Interference with Contractual Relations

1. The main type of interference with economic relations that has been marked out by the courts and regarded as a separate tort is referred to as **inducing breach of contract** or **interference with contract**.

2. Virtually any type of contract may be the basis for this type of tort action. The contract must:

   a. be in force and effect;

   b. be legal; and

   c. not be opposed to public policy.

3. For reasons that have not been clearly stated, contracts to marry have received special treatment, and almost without exception the courts have refused to hold that it is a tort to induce the parties to break them.
4. To be held liable for interference with a contract, the defendant must be shown to have caused the interference. It is not enough that he merely has reaped the advantages of the broken contract after the contracting party has withdrawn from it.

   EXAMPLE: Dani calls Jeffrey, whom she knows to be involved in a contract with PubCo. Dani promises Jeffrey that she will go on a date with him if he breaks the contract with PubCo. Unbeknownst to Jeffrey, Dani plans to have her company take over Jeffrey's business with PubCo once Jeffrey breaks the contract. If Jeffrey does breach as a result of Dani's bribe, Dani will be liable for interference with a contract.

5. There have also been many decisions in which the action has been allowed where the defendant has merely prevented the performance of a contract or has made the performance more difficult and onerous.

   EXAMPLE: Donald Defendant prevents Peter Promisor from supplying Paul Plaintiff with goods by calling an illegal strike among his workmen. Donald will be liable for interference with a contract.

6. Interference with a contract is almost entirely an intentional tort. Liability has not been extended to the various forms of negligence by which performance of a contract may be prevented or rendered more burdensome.
7. Where the damages suffered can be compensated with money, then an action at law is appropriate.
   a. If substantial loss has occurred, one line of cases tends to adopt the contract measure of damages, limiting recovery to those damages that were within the contemplation of the parties when the original contract was made.
   b. Another line of cases, however, applies a tort measure, but limits the damages to those which are sufficiently "proximate," with some analogy to the rules of negligence.

D. Interference with Prospective Advantage

1. This tort protects the probable "expectancy" interests of the future contractual relations of a party, such as the prospect of obtaining employment or the opportunity to obtain customers.
2. The *prima facie* tort of intentional interference with a prospective economic advantage has the following elements:
   a. the existence of a professional or business relationship;
      (1) Modern courts have expanded this to be satisfied in situations where the plaintiff establishes the existence of a voluntary relationship with another party that would have very likely resulted in a pecuniary benefit for the plaintiff but for the defendant's interference. This protects such noncommercial expectancies as interference with an expected gift or legacy under a will.

(2) In such cases, courts of equity have granted relief by imposing a constructive trust.

(3) It should be noted, however, that all such cases (e.g., suppression of a will or fraudulently inducing a testator to make a will or prospective gift), whether in a tort action or under a constructive trust, have involved tortious conduct such as fraud, duress, or defamation.

b. intentional interference with that relationship;

c. by a third party;

d. accomplished through improper means or for an improper purpose;

e. a causal effect between the interference and damage to the economic relationship; and

f. damages.

3. Although earlier decisions required so-called "malice," modern decisions hold a defendant liable where her conduct is unlawful in itself (e.g., where it involves violence, intimidation, defamation, injurious falsehood, fraud, etc.) or is malevolent, such as evincing a desire to do harm to the plaintiff for its own sake.

a. Proof of the intentional interference and resulting damages establishes what the courts have called a "*prima facie* tort," and cast upon the defendant the burden of avoiding liability by showing that her conduct was privileged.

b. The most common defense centers around the privilege of competition. In sum, it is not a tort to beat a business rival to prospective customers. Thus, in the absence of prohibition by statute, illegitimate means, or other unlawful conduct, a defendant seeking to increase her own business may cut rates or prices, allow discounts, or enter into secret negotiations behind the plaintiff's back; refuse to deal with plaintiff; or threaten to discharge employees who do.

E. Injurious Falsehood (Trade Libel)

1. An **injurious falsehood** is a false statement made to another by the defendant that causes economic injury to the plaintiff.

a. The plaintiff bears the burden of proving the falsity of the challenged statement.

(1) The false statement need not be defamatory, personally relate to the plaintiff, or cause others to shun the plaintiff's company.

b. The false statement must be made to a third person. An otherwise actionable statement made to the plaintiff will not result in liability.

c. The defendant must intend to cause others not to do business with the plaintiff or to otherwise interfere with the plaintiff's relations with others to the plaintiff's economic disadvantage. In many jurisdictions, such motives will be found upon proof that the defendant knowingly made the false statement or was reckless with regard to its truth or falsity.

2. Recovery is only for those pecuniary losses that the plaintiff proves have been realized or liquidated (e.g., specific lost sales). Proof is generally sufficient if equivalent to that which would establish lost profits in a breach of contract case.

   EXAMPLE: On The Day Break Show, Brian Gumdrop insults Milan Hyatt's new line of handbags, calling them "made of pigskin." Sales of the bags noticeably diminish, and Milan is forced to declare bankruptcy. Milan may have a cause of action against Brian for trade libel if they are not made of pigskin.

3. **Defenses**
   a. **Consent**
      (1) A defendant will not be liable for an injurious falsehood if speaking with the consent of the plaintiff.
   b. **Privilege**
      (1) The same absolute and qualified privileges applicable to defamation are available to a defendant in an injurious falsehood action. If the plaintiff establishes that the defendant acted with common law malice, conditional privilege will be lost.

NOTE: If the defendant's speech involves a matter of public concern or affects a plaintiff who is a public official or figure, the constitutional principles applicable to defamation law may also be applicable to injurious falsehood. The commercial nature of this tort suggests that most cases would affect only matters of private concern, and thus not invoke constitutional limitations.

X. MISCELLANEOUS TORT CONCEPTS

A. Vicarious Liability

1. **Vicarious liability** describes liability imposed on a defendant because of his relationship with the actual wrongdoer that directly caused injury to the plaintiff.
2. **Employer-Employee (*Respondeat Superior*)**
   a. An employer is liable for injuries caused by the negligence or strict liability of an employee if the tortious act occurred within the scope of the employment.
      (1) To determine whether the tortious acts occurred within the scope of employment, a distinction is made based on whether the tortious conduct was committed while the employee was on a **frolic** (major deviation; outside of scope) or on a **detour** (small deviation from an employer's directions; within the scope).

EXAM TIP The more minor the deviation is in time and geographic area, the more likely it will be only a detour, and therefore torts committed during that time will be considered within the scope of employment, making the employer vicariously liable.

   b. Acts are within the scope of employment if they are so closely connected with what the employee was hired to do and so fairly and reasonably incidental to it that they may be regarded as methods, even though improper, of carrying out the objectives of the employment.
   c. Intentional torts committed by an employee are generally not given *respondeat superior* effect, even if committed during working hours. However, if an employee uses force, even misguidedly, wholly or partly to further the employer's purpose, such use of force may fall within the scope of employment, resulting in vicarious liability for the employer.
3. **Independent Contractor**
   a. A defendant generally is not liable for torts committed by someone she has engaged as an independent contractor, because the defendant has no right to control the activity of the contractor.
   b. In two situations, contrary to the general rule set forth above, a defendant may be held vicariously liable for the torts of an independent contractor. These are applicable where:
      (1) the contractor undertakes a duty the law does not permit to be delegated to another (a "nondelegable" duty); and

      EXAMPLE: Keeping streets in good repair, maintaining a fence around an excavation, or an owner-occupier's duty to have safe premises for business invitees.

      (2) a contractor engages in inherently dangerous activities, defined as any activity as to which there is a high degree of risk in relation to the particular surroundings, recognizable in advance as requiring special precautions.

EXAMPLE: Fumigating with poisonous gases or using explosives in an urban setting.

c. Traditionally, the employer-independent contractor relationship shielded hospitals from liability for the malpractice of many of the physicians who worked there, because they were hired as independent contractors and were not direct employees of the hospital.

d. However, a majority of courts today have eroded this immunity and hold hospitals liable for a physician's medical malpractice in certain situations through either an apparent agency or agency-by-estoppel relationship. While a majority of the courts that have held hospitals liable apply the apparent agency approach, some jurisdictions have accepted both arguments, and both reach the same result.

(1) In an apparent agency context, the hospital is being held liable because it employs an independent contractor to perform services which are being accepted by another in the reasonable belief that the services were being rendered by the hospital or its servants.

EXAMPLE: One court, applying this doctrine, recognized that hospitals were "corporate entities capable of acting only through human beings whose services the hospital engages" and that the hospital derives financial profits by holding itself out to the public as offering quality health services [Sharsmith v. Hill, 764 P.2d 667 (Wyo. 1988)].

(2) In an agency-by-estoppel context, the hospital is held liable because it represents to the patient that the physician is its employee or agent and cause the patient to justifiably rely on the care and skill of the apparent agent.

(3) Regardless of which approach is used, courts generally focus on two factors to determine whether or not a hospital should be held liable:

(a) the existence of conduct by the hospital that would cause a reasonable person to believe that the physician was an agent of the hospital; and

1) This factor is often met even without express conduct by the hospital, as long as the hospital has not given the patient contrary notice (i.e., through a sign or consent form) [Mejia v. Community Hospital of San Bernardino, 99 Cal. App. 4th 1448 (2002)]. However, many courts have held that even prior notice is insufficient in an emergency room context, where a patient is in need of immediate medical care.

(b) reliance on that apparent agency relationship by the plaintiff.

1) This element is met when the plaintiff establishes that he looked to the hospital, rather than an individual physician, to provide him with medical care and services.

(4) Vicarious liability through an agency relationship is most often found in the context of emergency rooms, where patients have no choice in physician or opportunity to consent to the fact that the physician is an independent contractor of the hospital.

(5) In a non-emergency room setting, the most important factor considered is whether, at the time of admission, the plaintiff patient was looking to the hospital for treatment or if the hospital was merely the site where the patient's physician would treat them. In other words, did the patient go to the hospital for treatment and have a physician assigned to them, or did the patient already have a relationship with the physician outside of the hospital, and the hospital is merely the place where the patient and physician are meeting for treatment?

(6) Other factors considered by courts in finding an apparent agency or agency-by-estoppel relationship include:

(a) whether the hospital has actively advertised its medical services and/or the qualifications, availability, or affiliation of certain physicians with the hospital;

(b) the control that the hospital has over the independent contractor (e.g., setting the schedule, hours, or rotation of the physician);

(c) whether the physician is "on call" with the hospital;

(d) whether the forms signed by the patient are printed on hospital letterhead;

(e) the existence of a prior or ongoing treatment history between the patient and physician;

(f) whether the hospital has attempted to notify the patient of the physician's independent-contractor status through signs, communications, and/or consent forms; and

1) The mere fact that a patient signs a consent form is not dispositive; courts will look to the circumstances surrounding how and when the signature was obtained to determine whether the notice was sufficient or valid.

(g) the plaintiff patient's testimony regarding how she understood and perceived the physician's status with regard to the hospital.

4. **Joint Enterprise (Partners and Joint Venturers)**

a. Partners and joint venturers are vicariously liable for each other's torts if those torts were committed in the course and scope of the partnership or joint venture.

b. A partnership is a legal relationship arising from an agreement between two or more persons to operate a business for profit. A joint venture is like a partnership, except it is of more limited scope and duration. A joint venture is present when two or more people engage in concerted activity for a common business purpose and each person has a mutual right to control the activity—for example, two people on a shared-expense auto trip.

5. **Negligent Entrustment**
   a. Courts generally recognize liability for negligent entrustment, whereby a defendant will be held liable for negligently permitting a third party to use a thing or engage in an activity.
   b. To be liable for negligent entrustment, the plaintiff must generally prove that:
      (1) the entrustee was incompetent, unfit, inexperienced, or reckless;
      (2) the entrustor knew, should have known, or had reason to know of the entrustee's condition or proclivities;
         (a) Some jurisdictions require actual knowledge.
      (3) there was an entrustment of the chattel;
         (a) The entrustment does not need to be express; the entrustment or permission can be implied. The test is whether the owner knew, or had reasonable cause to know, that he was entrusting his property.
         (b) While negligent entrustment is usually applied to motor vehicles or firearms, it has been applied to other chattels which, if placed in the hands of an incompetent or inexperienced person, present a likelihood of unreasonable risk of harm to third persons.
         (c) Some courts refer to entrustment of a "dangerous instrumentality." Other courts, as well as the Restatement (2d) of Torts, simply refer to supplying chattel that is likely to be used in a manner involving risk of physical harm to others.
      (4) the entrustment created an appreciable risk of harm to others; and
      (5) the harm to the injury victim was proximately caused by the negligence of the entrustor and the entrustee.

6. **Owner of Auto or Driver**
   a. At common law, the owner of a motor vehicle was not liable for its negligent operation by another using it with or without her permission, unless:
      (1) the operator was acting as her agent;
      (2) the owner was present in the car and maintained some control over its operation;
      (3) the owner negligently entrusted the vehicle; or
      (4) the owner and driver were engaged in a joint enterprise or partnership activity.
   b. At modern law, the owner of a motor vehicle is liable for its negligent operation by any person granted permission to use or operate it, for whatever reason.
      (1) The owner's liability is generally limited to acts of the driver which the owner would have been primarily liable for if operating the vehicle.

         EXAMPLE: If a third party is driving the vehicle and a gratuitous guest is injured, the owner is generally accorded the benefit of a guest statute limiting his liability to cases of gross negligence, or where there has been willful or wanton misconduct.

c. Under the family-purpose doctrine, adopted in some jurisdictions, the driver of a family car, in pursuit of recreation or pleasure, is considered to be engaged in the owner's business and is viewed as either an agent or servant of the owner. The driver must be a family member for the doctrine to apply.

d. To sustain a claim against a vehicle's owner under the family-purpose doctrine, the plaintiff must show that [Hicks v. Newman, 641 S.E.2d 589 (Ga. Ct. App. 2007)]:

(1) the defendant owned or had an interest in or control over the vehicle;

(2) the defendant made the vehicle available for family use;

(3) the driver was a member of the defendant's immediate household at the time of the collision; and

(4) the driver drove the vehicle with the defendant's permission.

e. While many jurisdictions have expressly rejected the family-purpose doctrine, the practical results of most jurisdictions, including many which rejected the doctrine, reach similar liability results through statutes holding the owner responsible for all injuries negligently inflicted while her motor vehicle is being used by another with the owner's express or implied consent, including members of the owner's family.

7. **Parent-Child**

a. A parent is normally not vicariously liable for a tort committed by his child. A few courts that have imposed vicarious liability on a parent for the tort of a child characterized the relationship as "principal-agent," akin to employer-employee, where the child was running an errand for the parent.

8. **Bailor-Bailee**

a. A bailor is not vicariously liable for the torts of a bailee.

9. **Tavernkeepers**

a. Historically, a tavernkeeper was not vicariously liable for injuries inflicted by an intoxicated patron, whether the person injured was a third person or was the intoxicated patron herself.

b. Some states statutorily impose vicarious liability on tavernkeepers as to injuries to third persons caused by intoxicated patrons.

B. Joint and Several Liability

1. Where two or more defendants acting in concert injure the plaintiff or where two or more defendants acting independently injure the plaintiff, and the resulting damages cannot be allocated to particular defendants, all of the defendants are liable for the entirety of the plaintiff's injury. The plaintiff can execute against each defendant for the total damages suffered, although the plaintiff may only recover from any or all defendants an amount equal to the total damages awarded.

EXAMPLE: Matt was walking down the street one day when he was hit in the head by a flower pot that fell off the roof of a building. It was discovered that the flower pot was knocked off the roof during a drunken brawl by two men, Randall and Perry. Matt sued Randall and Perry in negligence for damages, and a jury found them liable. Matt may recover up to the full amount of damages from either Randall or Perry (though he will only be able to recover a total amount equal to the total damages awarded).

2. In jurisdictions that adopt comparative negligence systems, joint and several liability is still available to a plaintiff. Any defendant compelled to pay damages to a plaintiff greater than the percentage amount for which he was found responsible may usually obtain contribution for the *pro rata* shares of the other defendants.

3. **Contribution**

   a. Most jurisdictions have by statute permitted one of several defendants responsible for negligently injuring a plaintiff to compel the others to contribute an equal share toward any judgment satisfied by the plaintiff against one of them.

      (1) Contribution is not applicable where the defendants have intentionally injured the plaintiff.

      (2) A minority of states retain the traditional common law rule that did not permit contribution among tortfeasors.

   b. Most jurisdictions apportion contribution equally. Thus, the judgment against all defendants is divided into as many equal portions as there are defendants, and a defendant against whom the plaintiff has executed for the full amount of damages may obtain the appropriate amount paid from each of the other defendants.

   c. Other jurisdictions allocate the amount payable by each defendant by reference to the share of the plaintiff's injuries for which that defendant is responsible, as would be determined under a comparative negligence system for example.

      EXAMPLE: Same facts as above, only the jurisdiction is one that has adopted comparative negligence. The jury determined that Randall was 60% liable and Perry was 40% liable for causing Matt's injury, and awarded Matt $100,000 in damages. If Matt recovers the full $100,000 from Randall, Randall can seek contribution from Perry for his share of the damages, or $40,000 (40% of the total $100,000 damage award).

4. **Indemnity**

   a. One of two or more defendants responsible for a plaintiff's injuries may in some situations cause one or more of the other defendants to satisfy the entire amount of the plaintiff's damages.

      (1) Where one defendant is only vicariously liable for the tort of another directly liable defendant, the first defendant may recover the entire amount of any damages paid to the plaintiff from the second defendant, who was actually responsible for the plaintiff's injury.

         EXAMPLE: A fiddler was injured by a truck driver that negligently went through a red light while making a delivery. The fiddler sued the truck driver as well as his employer, through respondeat superior. The court found in favor of the fiddler and awarded her $100,000 in damages. The fiddler recovered this amount from the truck driver's employer. The employer may then sue the truck driver for indemnity.

(2) In some jurisdictions, where a plaintiff has obtained and satisfied a judgment against one defendant who is jointly liable with others, that defendant may recover from the other defendants if their conduct was "more wrongful" than the first defendant's. In general, intentional tortfeasors are viewed as "more wrongful" than negligent tortfeasors.

(a) Courts also make distinctions between "active" wrongdoing (e.g., a manufacturer who makes a defective product) and "passive" wrongdoing (e.g., the retailer who fails to discover the defect), attributing "more wrongfulness" to the former.

(3) A defendant who injures a plaintiff may be liable when another defendant subsequently injures the plaintiff and aggravates the injuries the plaintiff suffered from the first defendant. Courts generally permit the first defendant to obtain indemnity from the second for the portion of additional damages imposed on the first defendant attributable to the aggravating injury.

C. Survival of Action and Wrongful Death

1. Traditionally, the death of either the victim or the tortfeasor abated a tort action between them. Nearly all jurisdictions provide via statute (called **survival statutes**) that the death of the victim or tortfeasor no longer abates the tort action. Statutory treatment varies according to the type of injury suffered and the damages recoverable.
   a. Most jurisdictions provide for survival of actions where a plaintiff suffered personal injuries. A minority permit survival of the action only where the injury suffered is property damage.
   b. Only a few jurisdictions allow survival of the action where the injury suffered is reputational (defamation) or involves privacy interests.
   c. Some jurisdictions do not permit recovery in a survival action for the deceased victim's pain and suffering if the victim died before his case went to judgment.
   d. Most jurisdictions do not permit any recovery of punitive damages against the estate of a tortfeasor who dies before judgment is rendered.
2. All jurisdictions statutorily provide for an action by which either the heirs of a deceased victim or the personal representative of the victim's estate may bring an action against the tortfeasor responsible for the victim's death. Recovery may generally be had for pecuniary losses resulting from the death, such as wages the victim might have earned over her lifetime, and for damages, such as victim's medical expenses or loss of wages.

D. Satisfaction and Release

1. A **satisfaction** occurs when more than one defendant is liable for a plaintiff's injuries, but the plaintiff recovers fully from one defendant. The effect of a satisfaction is that the plaintiff may not seek further recovery from any other defendant. The defendant against whom satisfaction was had may seek contribution or indemnity from the other defendants.
2. At common law, if a plaintiff agreed with one defendant to give up his rights in exchange for a settlement, the plaintiff lost his rights against all other defendants who might be otherwise jointly responsible for the plaintiff's injuries. Most states have modified this doctrine by permitting the plaintiff to release one defendant while expressly retaining his rights against others, or by permitting a plaintiff to make a covenant not to sue with one defendant while proceeding against the others. Other jurisdictions have entirely abolished the doctrine of release.